MARYLAND GENEALOGIES

A Consolidation of Articles from the Maryland Historical Magazine

MARYLAND GENEALOGIES

A Consolidation of Articles from the Maryland Historical Magazine

IN TWO VOLUMES

Volume II

Indexed by Thomas L. Hollowak

Excerpted and reprinted from the
Maryland Historical Magazine
With added Introduction, Contents, and Indexes
Genealogical Publishing Co., Inc.
Baltimore, 1980, 1997
Library of Congress Catalogue Card Number 80-80064
International Standard Book Number: Volume II: 0-8063-0886-9
Set Number: 0-8063-0887-7
Made in the United States of America

CONTENTS

vi

NOTE

P AGE citations in the text and in the footnotes to articles as
they previously appeared in the *Maryland Historical Magazine*
may be worked out by referring to the descriptive table of contents in this volume, which contains the inclusive page numbers
of the original articles.

ROBERT GOLDSBOROUGH OF ASHBY, AND HIS SIX SONS

Notes Collected by the Late ANNE SPOTSWOOD DANDRIDGE

Edited by ROBERTA BOLLING HENRY

The family of Goldsborough is Anglo-Saxon and was seated before the Norman Conquest at Goldsborough Hall or Chase near the town of Knaresborough in Yorkshire. A grant of land was made to the head of the family by William the Conqueror, and for many generations the estate descended from father to son. The last of the Goldsborough name who owned the Hall were two maiden sisters, it is said, the survivor of whom at her death left most of the estate to York Minster and public charities. In 1756 the Hall was bought by the Lascelles, of the family of the Earl of Harewood, after being for nearly eight centuries the home of the elder branch of English Goldsboroughs. The younger branches had spread into different shires of England.

Nicholas Goldsborough, the progenitor of the American Goldsboroughs, was born in 1640 or 1641 in Melcomb Regis, a seaside town which has been for many years incorporated with Weymouth, and of which an old writer says: "Weymouth and Melcomb Regis . . . beinge two haven towns and frontier townes joyninge very neere together directly over against the coast of Normandy in France . . ."

Prior to 1659 Nicholas Goldsborough was living in Blandford, "A faire markett towne pleasantlie situated upon the river [the Stour] and near unto the downes, well inhabited and of good traffique." He was a merchant, and in the list of "Tradesmen's Tokens current in Blandford Forum" is the description of one issued by him in 1663. At that time the Crown issued none but gold and silver money; but, as smaller money was needed for many transactions, permission had been granted to certain cities and towns and also to the considerable merchants to issue what were known as "Tokens." They were made of lead, brass or copper, and were circulated as farthings, half pence and pence. The one issued by Nicholas Goldsborough is described in Hutchins' *History of Dorset* (p. lxxxiv).

In the year 1669 Nicholas Goldsborough left England. The

story of his emigration is briefly told by his son, Robert of
Ashby, who on the 20th of August, 1722, wrote on a blank leaf
of his own large Bible (now owned by Robert Goldsborough
Henry of Myrtle Grove) the following:

A memorial for the use of my children—My father Nicholas Gouldes-
burgh, or Goldsborough was a younger brother, he was born at Melcolm
Regis near Waymouth in the county of Dorset in or about 1640 or 1641.
My Mother was the sole daughter of Abraham Howes, the son of William
Howes of Newberry in the County of Berks (see his last will and testa-
ment [1] in my possession).

My father married my mother in the year 1659 at Blandford [2] in the
county of Dorset where myself was born the beginning of December 1660.

My father went from England to Barbadoes in 1669 from thence he
came to New England and from thence to Maryland in the beginning
of the year 1670 he died on Kent Island and was there buryed on Tobias
Wells plantation. I came into Maryland in the beginning of the year 1678.
I was marryed to Elizabeth Greenberry Sept. 2nd 1697. My mother came
into Maryland in or about the year 1670. She here intermarried with
George Robins.

Nicholas Goldsborough had besides Robert of Ashby a son
Nicholas, the progenitor of the Otwell Goldsboroughs and a
daughter Judith. The latter was brought over by her stepfather,
George Robins, and to him she assigns the right of land due her.
Robert of Ashby transported himself but also assigns his rights
to his step-father, George Robins,[3] who had Dec. 10th, 1672,
been granted letters of administration on the estate of " Nicholas
Goldsborough late of Kent County, merchant, having inter-
marryed with Margaret his widow." [4]

ROBERT OF ASHBY

The entry into Maryland of Robert the eldest son of Nicholas
and Margaret (Howes) Goldsborough is recorded in the " Early
Settlers List," Liber LL, 801, (Land Office, Annapolis) as follows:

---

[1] Now lost.   [2] St. Mary's Church, Blandford.
[3] George Robins, of " Jobs' Content," later known as Peach Blossom and his
wife Margaret had five children, Thomas born 1672, George, William, Lambert,
and Mary. In 1694 the death of George Robins left her again a widow. By his
will she and her son Thomas were appointed executors and guardian to the four
minor children. To Thomas was bequeathed the estate of " Jobs' Content," with
the right reserved to his mother of dwelling thereon. Mrs. Robins survived her
second husband some years, remaining at Jobs' Content where she died and is
buried. The homes of her two sons by her first husband were not far distant from
her own—Robert, the eldest was living at Ashby, and Nicholas near Oxford; of
Judith nothing is now known with certainty.
[4] Test. Proc. Lib. 5, fol. 374.

JUDGE WILLIAM GOLDSBOROUGH
1709–1760

By John Hesselius

Portrait Owned by Mr. and Mrs. Robert Goldsborough
Henry of Myrtle Grove.

These may certify that Robert Goldsborough transported himself into this province to inhabit in the year one thousand six hundred seventy-seven proved before me this eighteenth day of October, one thousand six hundred seventy-eight as witness my hand the day and year above said

Geo. Robins

Know all men by these presents that I Robert Goldsburgh doe assigne over unto George Robins his heirs execrs, admin or assigns forever the right of land due unto me as witness my hand and seal this eighteenth day of October 1678

Robert Goldsburgh, [sealed]

Robert was then a young man of eighteen and as his mother had long been married to Mr. Robins he was free to make a home of his own and soon began to look about for desirable land. A paper discovered in the Land Office at Annapolis establishes the fact that land was bought in Dorchester County by Mr. Robins for his two step-sons, but there arose some defect in the title to the tract, and the young men lost both the land and "the Sloope Charles of Boston" which had been given for it by their step-father. This tract of land consisted of 1,000 arces on the south side of Choptank River and was called Edmundson's Desire. It lay not very far from the estate Horne, afterwards so well known as Horn's Point, the home of William Tilghman Goldsborough.

Their Dorchester plan failing, the two brothers, Robert and Nicholas, settled in Talbot. Nicholas (the younger) lived near Oxford; Robert bought an estate on St. Michael's River, already known as Ashby. By purchase and grant he acquired a large quantity of land in Talbot County, the different tracts being known by different names, but the home of Robert Goldsborough I, the first home of the elder branch of Goldsboroughs in America was Ashby.

This estate, first surveyed for Roger Gross, July 20, 1663, passed successively to his son, Roger Gross, Junior; to William Gross, uncle and heir-at-law of Roger Gross, Jr.; to Anthony Mayle; to the widow of Anthony Mayle; to Robert Smith; and was by Robert Smith deeded to Robert Goldsborough on 16th October, 1690.

Robert Goldsborough was then thirty years of age and for fifty-six years he lived at Ashby; there in September 1697 he brought his bride, Elizabeth Greenberry, from her home on the Severn; there their twelve children were born, and five who died in infancy or childhood were buried; there, in 1719 his wife died and was buried; and finally there "Sitting in his chair, at nine o'clock on Christmas morning 1746" an old man of eighty-six, Robert of Ashby died; and was laid to rest in the same grave-yard which has since received five generations of his descendants. After his death Ashby remained unoccupied, as the son to whom he left it (Robert II) had, previous to inheriting it, established his own home at Myrtle Grove, about two miles distant. The old brick house at Ashby gradually fell into a heap, the lawn was ploughed up and became a field, and in the course of years Myrtle Grove came to be considered "the oldest Goldsborough home," since it was there that the elder branch of the family lived, one by one being taken to Ashby to be buried.

The early years of his life at Ashby were busy ones for Robert Goldsborough. Besides attending to his large estate and giving much thought and care to the proper training and establishment of his six sons, he liberally gave the province of Maryland the benefit of his fine abilities and clearsighted energy. Having studied law, he was admitted to practice in Maryland on the 4th of October, 1687; and, December 3rd, 1696, was "constituted one of his Ma. Councillors at Law"[5] from which office he was discharged at his own request in 1699. Upon his application for dismissal, the Attorney General, George Plater, asks the Council to take into consideration "how faithfully the said Mr. G. had discharged his trust, and accordingly, upon his application he is dismissed."[6]

From 1698 to 1705 he was justice of the peace in Talbot County; from 1705 to 1707 he was Associate Justice, and from 1719 to 1740 Chief Justice of the Provincial Court. From 1704 to 1708 as member of assembly from Talbot he took a prominent part in the lower house. In an old manuscript list of "Civil Officers in Maryland" under the date 1696 is his name: "Robert Goldsborough; Burges, Justice, Deputy Commissary General for Talbot, Register of Wills, and Attorney for King William."

Previously (1685) he is mentioned as "Under Sheriff of Talbot"; and in 1689 he and his brother Nicholas were both hold-ing office, the former attorney for the government, the latter, deputy sheriff of Talbot.[7]

---

[5] *Archives of Maryland*, XX, p. 549.   [6] *Archives of Maryland*, XXV, p. 75.
[7] Samuel A. Harrison's "Memoranda of the Civic Annals of Talbot County," I, p. 8-10, Maryland Historical Society.

During this year (1689) "the loyal and dutiful Subjects, and Antient Protestant Inhabitants of Talbot . . . Doe in prostrate and humble manner testifie to your Majestys that we abhorr and detest the falsehood and unfaithfulness of John Coode . . ." and petition that the Government " may be again restored to the Rt. Hon^bl Lord Baltemore, which will make him and us happy. . . ." To this paper, with the name of other gentlemen, is attached the signature: Ro Gouldesbrough.[8] In 1696 an Address was sent to King William congratulating him on his " Escape from a Horrible Intended Conspiracy; " it is signed by gentlemen of every county, and the list of Talbot County names is headed by " Robert Goldsborough."

On the 2nd of September, 1697, Robert Goldsborough of Ashby was married by the Rev. Peregrine Coney of Annapolis to Elizabeth Greenberry of Greenberry's Point. His own entry in his large Bible is as follows:

Robert Goldsborough was marryed to Elizabeth Greenberry daughter of Nicholas Greenberry Esq. and of Ann his wife, the second day of September 1697 thursday . . .   My dearly beloved wife Elizabeth departed this life thursday March 3rd 1719 about ten at night and was buryed the thursday following being the tenth of the same month, aged 41 years and 6 months being born the 25th of September 1678 in Annarundell County, Wednesday

R. G.

In the Bible known as the Greenberry Bible now at Myrtle Grove her father, Nicholas, has recorded the birth of his three daughters, on a page which he has signed. Of the nine sons born to Robert and Elizabeth Goldsborough, six lived to be men. The three little sons who bore their mother's maiden name all died early. The " Six Brothers," sons of Robert of Ashby for whom he bought land or whom he settled upon parts of his own estate as they grew to manhood were: Robert and Nicholas (twins), Charles, William, John and Howes. The brothers were all married; Robert, Charles, John and Howes, left children, and their descendants are now almost countless in number. They were all men of wealth, position, and influence, good and useful in their generation as their father had been in his own; and as he became an old man he saw them taking up, well and ably, the duties public and private, which he was one by one dropping from his weakening hands.

Robert of Myrtle Grove, Eldest of the Six Sons

Robert Goldsborough gave to his eldest son, Robert, an estate to which the latter gave the name of "Myrtle Grove" and upon which he built in 1734 a small frame house which is still standing, and now forms the wing of the brick house which was completed in 1790 by Robert, third of the name. Although, upon the death of his father in 1746, Robert inherited the older residence Ashby, he continued to live at Myrtle Grove, thus since 1746 the home of the eldest branch of Goldsboroughs. Owners of both Ashby and Myrtle Grove have lived at the latter place.

The entry of his birth is recorded by his father in the family Bible: "Robert and Nicholas born Saturday Feb. 17, 1704." His will [9] leaves

to my son Robert the plantation and lands where I dwell on, namely, Part of the land called Ashby and the land adjoining to the same which I bought of Griffith Jones, and also the land called Fox Harbor, and Newnams Addition all these lands with their appurtinances I do give to my son Robert and his Heirs for ever. . . . I do also give to my said son Robert all the goods and plate in my dwelling house together with the furniture belonging to said house and I do also give my said son all my part of the Goods, debts, bonds, bills and accounts of any sum or sums of tobacco, or money contained in the same or that have become due in Partnership between me and my said son. . . .

Robert and his twin brother Nicholas were named executors. The will was probated 2 Feb., 1746.

The eldest son of Robert of Ashby, Robert Goldsborough II of Myrtle Grove, was thus sketched by a contemporary writer: "A high-minded gentleman, esteemed for probity and intelligence . . . . his house was the home of hospitality, rational, generous, elegant. His mind was richly stored with the best literature of the day, his conversation improving and charming. Fully aware of the value of knowledge, he paid great attention to the education of his children, who amply repaid his care . . ." He was twice married. His first wife was Sarah, daughter of the Rev. Henry Nicols, of St. Michael's Parish, Talbot, to whom he was married the 7 Nov., 1739, by her father. To them a son was born on the 8th of November, 1740, and was named Robert. A week afterwards the young mother died, having been married two days less than a year. On the 8th of July, 1742, Robert

[9] Wills, Talbot Co., 1722-1746, f. 443, dated 28 June, 1744.

Goldsborough was married to Mrs. Mary Ann Turbutt Robins, widow of John Robins and daughter of Foster Turbutt. She died 29 Aug., 1794, leaving three children: Howes, William ("Uncle Billy, of Haylands") and a daughter, Mary Ann Turbutt, known as "Aunt Molly of Haylands." Robert's death is entered in the family Bible by his son, Judge Robert Goldsborough: "My Honoured Father died 30th April anno 1777 in his 74th year, being born in Feb. 1704."

NICHOLAS GOLDSBOROUGH, JR.

Of Nicholas, twin brother of Robert, little is known beyond the main facts of his life. "Robert and Nicholas born, Saturday, Feb. 17, 1704." "Nicholas Dyed the 14 Nov. 1756 with the Small Pox." "My dear Brother Nicholas Departed this life Sunday Nov. 14 about twelve o'clock noon 1756."

These three sentences in the Ashby Bible record the beginning and the end of the life of the second of the Six Brothers but of the half century of earthly existence lying between the two dates it tells nothing.

From county records and other sources it is known that Nicholas Goldsborough, Jr., was at an early age justice and burgess. The commission of the peace issued to Talbot County Feb. 23, 1726, bears the names of Robert and Nicholas Goldsborough as members of the quorum; that of Oct. 29, 1730, is headed by the same names, which for more than ten years afterwards recur in the commissions; but whether the office was held by the twin brothers or by their father Robert and his nephew Nicholas there is now no way of determining with certainty. It is probable that during the latter part of the time the two younger men were indicated.

Nicholas Goldsborough was deputy collector of the Port of Oxford. In the Myrtle Grove library there is a leather-bound volume *English Customs,* by Crouch of the Custom House, giving tables of Duties, etc., on a fly-leaf of which is written: "Nicholas Goldsborough, Deputy Collector, Port of Oxford, Province of Maryland." The date is 1731.

Robert of Ashby gave his second son a liberal share of his estate:

To my son Nicholas I do give and bequeath all my lands lying on Plaindealing creek, namely Part of the land Called Plain Dealing, Wyatt's

Fortune, Grundy's Addition, and part of Hall's Neck, all which said lands I do give to my son Nicholas. . . . . . . I do hereby appoint and nominate my sons Robert and Nicholas my sole Executors.

This will was signed on the 28th of June, 1744, about two years before Nicholas's marriage, which took place on the 7th of April, 1746, when he was forty-two years of age. The lady whom he married is said by a family record at Myrtle Grove to have been "the daughter of one Spencer of the Bay Side." She was then Mrs. Jane Banning, widow of James Banning (who also wrote his name Bandy, his father being William Bandy) and the mother of three sons: Jeremiah, Henry and Anthony Banning. These three boys were adopted by Nicholas Goldsborough, their step-father, and when he died, ten years after his marriage to their mother, it was found that his will gave them all of his property. They were, however, always known by the name of their own father. Being thus provided for, the three Bannings received the bringing-up and education of gentlemen, and in time became quite prominent men in Talbot County. Nicholas Goldsborough's will is in substance as follows: [10]

I Nicholas Goldsborough of Talbot . . . do bequeath unto Jeremiah Banning my land Hall's Neck, Grundys Addition etc. . . . Unto Henry Banning Plain Dealing, Wyatt's Fortune, Grundy's Add'n resurveyed; To Anthony Banning 1000 lbs. of tobacco, to be paid by Jeremiah and Henry . . . My Wife to leave at her decease the thirds of my estate to be equally divided between Jeremiah, Henry and Anthony Banning . . . and as for my personal estate after my wife has her part the remainder to be equally divided between Jeremiah, Henry and Anthony . . . Executors: Jeremiah and Henry Banning. Witness: Thos. Cooper, Mary Cooper, Ann Davis.

The will was probated December 24, 1756.

CHARLES GOLDSBOROUGH I, THE COUNCILLOR

Charles Goldsborough, third son of Robert of Ashby and Elizabeth Greenberry Goldsborough, was (according to his father's entry in the old Bible) "born thursday June 26, 1707"; on the margin opposite is added in the handwriting of his eldest brother, Robert II of Myrtle Grove: "Dyed the 14th July 1759."

Charles was born at Ashby and lived in Talbot during his boyhood and youth, but shortly after coming of age he moved to

[10] Wills, Talbot Co., 1755-1760, f. 263.

Dorchester County, where he spent the rest of his life and where he is buried.[11] In August, 1728, he was admitted to the bar of Talbot, and practiced law in the different courts of the State with distinguished ability. His mental powers were fine; he was a clear writer, and brilliant speaker, and seems to have been regarded as a leader of opinion and action on the Eastern Shore. In 1728 Charles Goldsborough was appointed to the then important office of clerk of the court of Dorchester County; on the 15th Dec. 1761, he took his oath as commissary general,[12] (an office which was abolished in 1777); from 1752 to 1763 he represented Dorset County in the Lower House of Assembly;[13] in 1762 he was removed to the Upper House by his appointment as member of the Lord Proprietor's Council. He took his seat there in July 1762,[14] Horatio Sharpe being then Governor. Prior to this appointment there had been a long correspondence concerning it between the Calverts and Governor Sharpe, who for some years opposed it on the ground that Mr. Goldsborough was " a favourer of popular measures," but after carefully watching his course in the Lower House, the Governor seems to have changed his opinion of Mr. Goldsborough altogether, and in October, 1760, writes to Lord Baltimore strongly advocating his appointment, speaks with approbation of " his unexceptionable conduct in the Lower House," calls His Lordship's attention to the " moderate and respectful behaviour of the Goldsborough Family . . . of

[11] The exact date of Charles Goldsborough's removal from Talbot to Dorset is not now known. He was in 1728 clerk of the court of the latter County, and a practicing attorney there as well as in Talbot. In the year 1734 he bought from the widow and daughter of John Kirke part of the property now known as " The Point " in Cambridge, which continued to be his home until the time of his death. The price was " 1000 lbs. of good merchantable tobacco " (then worth about two shillings a pound). The house at that time consisted of a single room below and above, with a large pantry and kitchen (with gable rooms over them) being the part of the house on the right of the hall. There was a porch the whole length of the north side, the front door of the house was entered from this porch. Tradition (which is sustained by architectural evidence) says that Mr. Goldsborough doubled the width of the porch and turned it into the hall; he also added the two rooms below and above on the left, and built the stairway leading from the hall to the upper story of the mansion. In 1737 Elizabeth Orrell widow of John Orrell conveyed to Joshua Kennerly and he to Charles Goldsborough " one-third interest in the aforesaid Orrell lots, where said Charles Goldsborough now resides," and by deeds from Orrell's children of their respective interests therein, beginning in 1739 and ending in 1760, Mr. Goldsborough finally acquired the title to the entire " Point " property. He devised it to his son Robert. (The house is now, 1941, entirely gone).

[12] *Archives*, XXX, p. 565.

[13] *Archives*, L, pp. 28, 544, 587.   [14] *Archives*, XXXII, p. 38.

considerable Figure and Influence in the Province . . . ." and suggests that it will be "good Policy to take another of that Family into the Upper House since their brother William is dead " . . . ; and further urges the step by saying that the removal of Mr. Charles Goldsborough to the Council (Upper House) will probably result in the election to the Lower House of "his son, a young gentleman of good abilities and character lately returned from the Temple . . . who will hereafter be of service . . .;" thus the "Number of Moderate men" secured to the Government will be not lessened but increased. He admits his former prejudice, but excuses himself by hinting that at that time Mr. Goldsborough had been represented to him "in an unfavourable light . . . by some who I believe had their views in doing so."

The appointment (delayed for ten years by his opposition) soon followed Governor Sharpe's change of opinion; and at a meeting of the Council in Annapolis in July, 1762, Mr. Charles Goldsborough took his seat as Councillor.

At this date there was already a slight stir in the political air: the dissatisfaction was slowly progressing which a few years later culminated in the Revolution. The two Goldsborough brothers (John in the Lower House, and Charles in the Council) stood for the King, with the steadfastness inherited from a long line of loyal English gentlemen and Churchmen faithful to law and order. John slowly and reluctantly, within the next decade, found himself forced to a change of attitude towards the government; but Charles did not live long enough to see this new aspect of affairs, and seems always to have been counted one of the " members favourable to the Crown" during the four years intervening between his appointment as councillor and his death.

Gov. Sharpe's desire that Mr. Goldsborough's place in the Lower House should be taken by his eldest son Robert Goldsborough was not immediately fulfilled. A writ of election was issued, Oct. 25, 1763, to the Sheriff of Dorchester County "to elect a delegate for the said County in the room of Charles Goldsborough Esquire called to the Upper house" but the result was the return of Mr. Henry Steele, who qualified as member for Dorchester on the 16th of November following.[15] At the next election, however, Robert Goldsborough was elected in Mr.

---

[15] L. H. Jour., 1762-1768.

Steele's place; and at the beginning of the session, Sept. 23, 1765, he took his seat in the Lower House,[16] his father being in his seat [17] in the Upper House when the young man appeared before that body to take the usual oath of qualification. The father was then fifty-eight years of age; the son thirty-two.

Charles Goldsborough was married twice, first to Elizabeth Ennalls and secondly to Elizabeth Dickinson. He married Elizabeth Ennalls on the 18th of July, 1730; she was a daughter of Joseph and Mary (Brooke) Ennalls, and a grand-daughter of Bartholomew Ennalls who during his life was a large land owner in Dorchester County, and who left vast estates to his sons and their children. By this marriage Mr. Goldsborough had two children, Betty and Robert. The daughter, Elizabeth Greenberry Goldsborough, was born July 4, 1731, and died Sept. 29, 1820; in 1754 she married her cousin William Ennalls, and is known to later generations as "Aunt Ennalls;" she lived at Shoal Creek and (having no children) devised that estate and all her land in Dorchester to Gov. Charles Goldsborough, eldest son of her half-brother Charles.

Robert Goldsborough, second child of Charles and Elizabeth (Ennalls) Goldsborough, was born December 3rd, 1733, and died Dec. 31, 1787. He studied law in the Temple in London, and after his marriage to Sarah Yerbury remained for several years in England, returning to Maryland in the summer of 1759, from that time until his death being a prominent figure in the Province.

The date of death of Charles Goldsborough's first wife is not known. On the 2nd of August, 1739, he married as his second wife, Elizabeth Dickinson of Crosiadore, Talbot County, daughter of Samuel Dickinson and his first wife, Judith Troth, and half sister of Gen. Philemon and John Dickinson of the Revolution. She had but one child, Charles, born April 2nd, 1740, who died two years after his father when but twenty-nine years of age.

Charles Goldsborough I died in Cambridge on the 14th of July, 1767. The following obituary is from the *Maryland Gazette,* Thursday, July 16, 1767:

Tuefday morning Laft died at his Houfe in Cambridge, after a lingering Indifpofition the Honourable Charles Goldsborough Efq; one of His Lordfhips Council of State and Commiffary General of this Province.

---

[16] *Ibid.*   [17] U. H. Jour., 1762-1773, p. 200.

He was a Gentleman eminent for many Years in the Knowledge and Practice of the Law; and was formerly one of the Reprefentatives for Dorchester County.

He was buried in the churchyard in Cambridge. His tomb is near the church, and many of his descendants (now including great-great grandchildren) are buried around him. The inscription is as follows:

Hic conduntur ossa
Caroli Goldsborough, Armiger
Roberti Goldsborough
Elizabethae, uxoris suis
Filii
Qui post hujus Vitae Taedia Vigilias
Laboresque Perquam assiduos
Tandem Animam exhalavit
July Die decimo quarto
Annos Christi MDCCLXVII
Aetatis suae LX[18]

The voluminous will of Charles Goldsborough, dated 18 February, 1766, is recorded in Wills, Volume 3, f. 429, Hall of Records, Annapolis, and has the usual preamble. An abstract follows:

To daughter Betty, wife of Wm. Ennals and her heirs tracts on Choptank R. where she lately lived, viz Richardson's Folly, Edmondson's Add'n, Sherwins Folly and part of Skipton which lye on the westward side of a branch where Wm. Edmondson, dec'd, formerly had a water mill. Also . . . as much of the Indian land bought of Joseph Fooks and William Benn . . . as will make up one half the sd. Indian lands . . . [metes and courses follow] [19]; personalty and one-half sterling money in England at time of decease.

To son Charles and heirs the land east of Wm. Edmondson's water mill, to the lands of Charles Dickinson lying on Hunting Creek and Choptank R.; personalty and stock at Hunting Creek where he now lives.

To eldest daughter of [niece] Elizabeth Campbell 500 acres at head of this county.

To 3 daughters of son Robert, Rebecca, Sarah and Elizabeth, residue of money in England . . .

To Mary McKeel . . . in consideration and full satisfaction of her services for life or until her marriage . . . six lots in Cambridge and

[18] Here are stored the bones of Charles Goldsborough, armiger, son of Robert and Elizabeth Goldsborough, who after the tiresomeness of this life, the watches and the labors very severe, at length breathed out life, 14th day of July, in the year of Christ 1767, in his 60th year.
[19] Bounded by " Shallow Creek."

dwelling house "where I now live;" personalty, including 6 leather chairs at lodgings in Annapolis.

To grandson John, son Robert's son, half of Marshy Hope; reversion to Charles, son of Robert.

To grandson William, son Robert's son, land on Transquakin River.

To Charles, after Mary McKeel's death or marriage, land devised her.

To grandson Charles all other lands which lie on west side of main road which leads from Cambridge to the plantation bought of Thomas Howell; all the rest of personal estate given to Mary McKeel to be divided at her death or marriage between testator's three children, Robert, Betty and Charles.

Attested by John Dickinson, Henry Murray, John Anderson, Dan'l Maynadier. Admitted to probate July 28, 1767.

William Goldsborough

William Goldsborough was born at Ashby, the seventh child and fourth son of Robert and Elizabeth Greenberry Goldsborough. His father in the Ashby Bible records his birth; the date of his death is added by his brother Robert II:

William born Wednesday July 6, 1709.
Dyed Septem'r 1760.

On another page is written (by Robert):

William July 6th 1709 Dyed Sep'r 21, 1760 about 5 o'clock Morning being Sunday.

As there were at that time no good schools in the country and there is no mention (in the old letters or in the "Expense Books" among the Myrtle Grove papers) of the boys being sent home to England to school, it is probable that the Six Brothers were educated by schoolmasters who, as was then customary, lived in the family. In November, 1733, William Goldsborough was admitted to practise law, but seems to have practised only for a short time.

William Goldsborough was married twice; first to the sister, and then to the widow of George Robins. He was twenty-five years of age when his first marriage took place, his young wife being Elizabeth Robins (daughter of Thomas Robins, his half-uncle) of Peach Blossom. The record on the faded page of the Register of St. Peter's Parish, Talbot Co., is:

[p. 92] William Goldsborough and Elizabeth Robins were married January y'e 23rd Day 1734.

By this marriage he had two sons and two daughters, who all died young, and were buried in the same grave with their mother at Peach Blossom.

In Memory of Elizabeth Goldsborough who died the 2nd Day of Oct'r. 1746 Aged 36 years and of Greenbery, Henrietta Maria, William, and Elizabeth Her Children this is Erected by their Most Affectionate Sorrowful Husband and Father William Goldsborough.[20]

On the 2nd of September, 1747, eleven months after the death of his first wife, Elizabeth, Mr. Goldsborough married her half-brother's widow, Mrs. George Robins, who was then forty years of age and was the mother of six children. Her maiden name was Henrietta Maria Tilghman; she was the fourth child of Richard Tilghman II of The Hermitage and Anna Maria Lloyd of Wye, and was born at The Hermitage, August 18, 1707. On the 2nd of April, 1731, she married George Robins, of Peach Blossom, who died December 5, 1742; five years later she married William Goldsborough, by whom she had no children, and whom she survived eleven years. She died Nov. 7, 1771, and "was buried at Peach Blossom on the following Saturday, with a numerous procession, the Rev. John Bowie officiating."[21] In a letter written during her second widowhood, dated Peach Blossom, June 5, 1768, she says of her family:

Of my six children four daughters only are living, and all are Robins and live near me, the farthest about six miles off. My eldest, Ann Maria, is married to Henry Hollyday [of Ratcliffe Manor] . . . My next, Margaret, is married to Mr. William Hayward, a lawyer. The next, Henrietta Maria, married James Lloyd Chamberlaine whose brother Thomas married my youngest daughter, Susannah. Thanks be to God, we all live far above want, and can spare to our poor neighbors. We possess, and indeed are burthened with, what people falsely call riches. I mean the Negroes . . . I think we have full enough of them. . . .

William Goldsborough was, at the time of his death, a member of the Lord Proprietor's Council, judge of the Provincial Court, and judge of the Court of Admiralty. The estimation in which he was held is expressed in a letter from Governor Sharpe to Secretary Calvert concerning him, written when Mr. Golds-

[20] This stone is now (1941) at Ashby.
[21] John Bozman Kerr, *Genealogical Notes of the Chamberlaine Family of Maryland*, (Baltimore, 1880), p. 40.

borough's failing health seemed to make it probable that a successor must (in a short time) be appointed to the offices held by him:

> 7th July 1760 . . . No person in the Country had a better character than this Gent'n, he had never courted popularity yet was well esteemed by the People of his Co'ty, had better Abilities than most and by his Behaviour on the Provincial Bench where I had placed him soon after my Arrival in the Province gave me the greatest Reason to believe that his Behaviour would be equally satisfactory to his Ldp and myself nor have I been disappointed in my Expectations concerning him.[22]

There is a fine portrait of William Goldsborough now (1941) at Myrtle Grove, of particular interest as being the only portrait of any of the Six Brothers in existence. It represents a man about fifty years of age, large and vigorous, and of stately bearing. He wears a brown velvet coat; his full-bottomed, powdered wig is pushed back from his broad high forehead. The face with its somewhat severe aquiline features and grave dark eyes, is one of quiet power, intellectual and thoughtful, yet with rare sweetness and kindness of expression.

Mr. Goldsborough lived on Island Creek in Talbot, upon an estate known later as Evergreen which he devised to Greenberry Goldsborough, son of his brother John. This estate was not inherited by William Goldsborough from his father, who left him no land. The clause relating to him in the will of Robert of Ashby is as follows:

> . . . Forasmuch as I am not Pofsefsed of any other Lands, and it hath pleased God to Blefs my two Sons Charles and William with Handsome Estates I do therefore give to my said Sons Charles and William in Lieu of Lands all the Money I now Have in the Hands of Mr. Samuel Hyde of London Merchant and in the Hands of Mr. John Hanbury, of the fame Place Merchant to be Equally divided between them. . . .

After his appointment as Provincial Judge (1754) and, later, as councillor, Mr. Goldsborough necessarily spent much time in Annapolis, being punctual in attendance at Court and Council while his health permitted. About 1756 his health began to fail, and in September, 1760, he died. The following notice appeared in the *Maryland Gazette,* September 25, 1760:

> Sunday last Died at his Seat near Talbot Court House, after a very long and lingering Indisposition the Honourable William Goldsborough

---

[22] *Archives,* IX, p. 425.

Esq'r. one of his Lordship's Council, and Judge of the Court of Vice Admiralty in this Province: A Gentleman of a very fair Character.

William Goldsborough was buried at Peach Blossom, near the grave of his first wife, Elizabeth, and their four children. Eleven years afterwards his second wife was laid near him, and beside the grave of her first husband, George Robins. The inscription on William Goldborough's tomb is as follows:

Here is depofited
the Body of
the Hon. Wm. Goldsborough
who died the 21ft of Sep 1760
Aged 51 Years
He was Sometime a Member
of the Lord Proprietarys Council
and one of the Judges
of the Provincial Court
and was Justly Efteemed
a faithful Councellor
an upright Judge
an Honeft Man
and a Good Chriftian
To his Memory
This Stone is Infcribed
by HENRIETTA MARIA his widow.[23]

An abstract of the will of William Goldsborough is as follows:

. . . my late dwelling plantation lying upon Island Creek in Talbot Co. lands houses & appurtenances unto my loving wife, Henrietta Maria Goldsborough for life, without Impeachment of Waste, . . . & after her decease I give & devise said plantation unto my nephew Greenbury Goldsborough the son of my Brother John Goldsborough . . .

. . . unto each of my two nieces Mary Money and Ann Money (the daughters of my late Sister Mary Money) £20 Sterling . . .

. . . unto each of my brothers, Robert, Nicholas, Charles and John one Mourning Ring . . . unto my niece Caroline Goldsborough the daughter of my brother Howes lately deceased £20 sterling. . . . unto said nephew Greenbury . . . negroes Caro, Liverpool, . . . All that Tract of land lying near Choptanck Bridge in Dorchester County lately resurveyed by me Called by the name of Goldsborough's Range containing 671 acres more or less unto my Son in Law Thomas Robins. . . . unto my daughters-in-law Anna Maria Holiday, Margaret Robins, Henrietta Maria Robins, &

---

[23] This stone is now (1941) at Ashby; also those of Elizabeth Robins, his first wife; Robins Chamberlaine, Stanley Robins, and George Robins, the last the first husband of Henrietta Maria Tilghman.

Susannah Robins the sum of ten pounds sterling to be paid by my Executrix
when it shall suit her circumstances to do it.

I give unto my daughter in Law and Goddaughter Elizabeth Robins the
sum of 100£ sterling at age of 21 years . . . All residue of personal
estate unto my said Loving Wife Henrietta Maria, her executors adminis-
trators and assigns for Ever . . .
No appraisement or inventory to be made . . .
Wife Henrietta Maria Goldsborough Sole Executrix.
Witnesses William Thomas, Robert Harwood, Jacob Hindman, Tris'm
Thomas, Edw. Knott (Probated Nov. 5, 1760) [24]

In the autumn of 1897, one hundred and thirty-seven years
after William Goldsborough's death, the great-great-granddaughter of his brother Charles (A. S. Dandridge) was moving
some old books in the office at Myrtle Grove, when a yellow sheet
of paper fell from one of them. On it were the following lines,
in the clear handwriting of Robert, the elder brother of William
Goldsborough:

> Elegy To the Memory of William Goldsborough
>   Esq'r. late of Talbot County deceased.
>
> From Earth removed in ev'ry Virtue warm
> Adieu! bright Seraph in a human Form
> To whom at once indulgent Heav'n Afsign'd
> Whate'er could please or edify Mankind:
>   My much loved Muse Urania, heav'nly Maid,
> With artlefs Grief bewails her fav'rite Dead,
> No more with pleasing Harmony she sings
> Nor airs soft-sounding warbles from her Strings,
> Her once engaging Lyre, relax'd and broke,
> Hangs now neglected on the blasted Oak.
> Not causelefs Anguish this, Illustrious fhade
> Thy great good deeds have thee immortal made.
> Say ye, how knowing in his Country's Laws,
> Who've heard him plead the injured Widow's Cause,
> Who've heard him bold t'afsert the Orphan's Right,
> And clear up Fraud tho hid in darkest Night:
> Who've seen the guilty Felon trembling stand
> As he dealt Justice with impartial Hand.
> But not the Graces Science can impart,
> Vy'd with his Moral Excellence of Heart:
> There unaffected Goodnefs reigned, and thence
> Rush'd the strong Tide of warm Benevolence.
> Easy of Access   In the social Hour [25]

[24] Hall of Records, D.D. 1760-1764, f. 77.
[25] Part of this line illegible.

Censure grew dumb, and Envy ceased to lour,
Surpriz'd to hear his copious Accents flow,
Wise without Art, and learned without the Show.
Just is the Tribute of the silent Tear,
To him whose Friendship ever was sincere,
Who knew to give true Merit its Reward,
Respect the humble, and the meek regard.

R. Goldsborough.

JOHN GOLDSBOROUGH, 5TH OF THE SIX BROTHERS

Of John Goldsborough, his father Robert writes in the Ashby Bible: "John born Fryday, October 12, 1711."

There is no record of John's death, as Robert (its second owner, who recorded there the deaths of all his other brothers), died the year before John. John Goldsborough, the 8th in date of birth of Robert of Ashby's children, outlived all of his brothers and sisters; he died in 1778, just one hundred years from the date of his father's arrival in America. He was married twice, had nine children, and has a larger number of descendants than any of the Six Brothers, among them being the Henrys of Hambrooks near Cambridge, Hammonds of Talbot, Gardners and Quinbys of New York, the families of Admiral Louis Goldsborough, of Judge Henry Hollyday Goldsborough, of Dr. Robert Goldsborough of Centreville.

John Goldsborough lived at Four Square, an estate of 1000 acres in Chapel District, Talbot, which he inherited from his father. The will of Robert of Ashby devised to John as follows:

To my Son John I do give and bequeath the Lands Called Four Square, the Triangle, Woodland Neck, and one Hundred Acres of Land Part of the Land called the Adventure together with the Cattle Sheep Hogs Horses and negroes that are on or do in any Wise belong to the said Lands and Plantations I do hereby Give unto my said Son John the third Part of the Cargo that is now in his Hands or that hath at any time been in the Hands of my said Son not accounted for . . . To my two Grandsons viz. Robert the Son of my Son Robert and to Robert the Son of my Son John, I do hereby give and bequeath five Hundred Acres of Land lying in Queen Annes County Called the Controversy to be equally divided Between them.

By his wife, Ann Turbutt, daughter of Foster Turbutt, John Goldsborough received a large accession to his already large estate, which was still further increased by his second marriage to the widow of Mr. John Loockerman.

The first public office held by John Goldsborough was that of sheriff of Talbot, then an important position. During the thirty years preceding the Revolution he was almost continuously a member of the Lower House of Assembly. The record of his votes shows full and unwavering allegiance to the Crown until such allegiance was no longer possible. He was also a member of the Stamp Act Court which passed the resolution given below, recorded in the Court Records of Talbot County.

November—At a Court of the Rt. Hon. Frederick Lord and Prop'y of the Province of Maryland and Avalon, Lord Baron of Baltimore held for Talbot County, at the Court House, in the same County the first Tuesday in November Anno Dom. 1765, before the same Prop'ry his Justices of the Peace for the County afsd of whom were present the Worshipful Major Risdon Bozman, Mr. John Goldsborough, Mr. Robert Goldsborough, Mr. William Thomas, Mr. Jonathan Nicols, Mr. Tristram Thomas, Mr. Jacob Hindman, Justices. John Bozman, Sheriff; John Leeds, Clerk.

The Justices afsd. taking into consideration an act of Parliament lately made, entitled " An Act for granting and applying certain stamp duties and other stamp duties in the British Colonies and Plantations in America," towards further defraying the expense of defending, protecting, and securing the same, and for amending such parts of the several Acts of Parliament relating to the trade and revenues of the sd. colonies and plantations, as direct the manner of determining, and recovering the penalties and forfeitures therein mentioned, and finding it impossible at this time to comply with the said act, adjourned their court until the 1st Tuesday in March, 1766. At which sd. first Tuesday in March 1766 the Justices above mentioned would not open or hold any Court.

John Goldsborough as chairman of the important " Committee of Instructions " drew up the paper guiding the conduct of the three members sent from Maryland to New York to confer with Committees from other colonies.[26] John did not live to see the outcome of the war but died in the early part of 1778. His will [27] after the usual preamble leaves to his son John his dwelling plantation of 520 acres, The Four Square, a tract called Goldsborough Tryangle, part of Adventure, Kennedy's Hazard and Kennedy's Addition. To his son William part of Chamber's Adventure containing 118 acres, a tract called Benstead's Adventure containing 64 acres, a tract called Crams Delight of 56 acres and part of a tract called Warwick containing 255 acres, should

[26] L. H. Journal, Sept. 26, 1765.   [27] Talbot County, 3, f. 33.

son William die during his minority these tracts to son Greenbury and heirs. To son Robert he gives part of a tract called Summerly containing 202 acres and the adjoining 130 acres of The Four Square, also part of Warwick; should son Robert die during his minority said tracts to grandson John Goldsborough. To his daughter Mary Brice, Henrietta Maria, and "littel daughter" Ann Maria personalty. Sons Greenberry, William and Robert, and daughters Henrietta and Ann Maria to divide residue of personal estate equally. Sons John and Greenbury exs. Dated 24th February, 1778. The witnesses are James Berry [a Quaker] Samuel Thomas, William Porter and Rachel Porter. It was probated with the usual attestations before John Bracco, register of wills, 14 July, 1778.

The inventory of his estate is recorded in Vol. A, fol. 126-129, and is much too long to reproduce. A few of the items are:

Cash £391, 8 day clock walnut case £20, 1 walnut table in the room 35/, 1 ditto square in the Hall 30/, 1 Large Bible 45/, 1 old ditto 20/, 1 Aynsworth's Dictionary 60/, 22 pamphlets 22/, Coles Dictionary 30/, Bacon's abridgment 80/, 2 large Prayer Books 20/, 2 small ditto 3/9, 19 old books 70/, 24 old Lattin Books 60/, 2 old Law books 15/, Laws of Maryland unbound 7/6 34½ oz. plate A. M.)
) @ 16/8 £120.4.2
110 Oz. ditto   )
There is also mentioned Queens ware, Delft, Pewter, a number of trunks, chests, a sea-chest, 27 lights for windows, Pair polished steele andirons, 7 window pullies, 3 old rugs £6 [listed with bedding no other rugs or floor coverings],
2 pair old window curtains,
1 old walnut table with drawer 17/6,
1 Bedstead and cord 20/, some old deposted bedsteads 60/,
4 old Bedsteads 40/, 2 old ditto small 10/,
4 old Bedsteads 3/9, 2 new Bedsteads 60/,
30 slaves, (noted that one hath fitts, value £5.)

The inventory of his personal estate totals £6956-3-4. The house at Four Square has disappeared but to contain all the articles listed in the inventory it must have been quite large.

HOWES GOLDSBOROUGH

The entry in the Ashby Bible relative to Howes, the youngest of the Six Brothers, is written by his father, Robert of Ashby. "Howes born Monday Nov. 14, 1715. Dyed the 30th March

1746." His brother Robert has added in another entry in the same Bible "Howes Nov. 1715, ob. 30 March 1746." In his will Robert of Ashby leaves to

> son Howes . . . the land called Cottingham & the land called Benjamins Lott together with all and singular the negroes (except one Negro man named Joel) Cattle, Hogs, Horses, Mares, Gelding, & sheep in or upon the said lands being or appertaining or shall or may in any way hereafter be on or belong to the land aforesaid to my son Howes & his Heirs forever.

Howes died nine months before his father and the latter added a codicil to this will "All that is given to Howes I give to Caroline his daughter. R. G."

His death is noted in the *Maryland Gazette* for Friday, April 8, 1746. "Last week died in Dorchester County Mr. Howes Goldsborough Clerk of that County. He is succeeded in office by Mr. John Caile."

It is supposed that Howes Goldsborough, when a young man, lived at Cottingham; but he soon moved to Dorset. An old sheet of paper at Myrtle Grove, with a (partial) family record written upon it says: "Howes one of the six brothers lived on Fishing Creek in Dorset County . . . . 'tis thought he marr'd Rosanna Piper."

Rose Anne Piper was the daughter of the Rev. Michael Piper, a clergyman of the Church of England, who was at the time living in Annapolis. Her birth is there recorded:

> December 1723, 22nd. Born Rose Anna Daughter of Mic'l Piper & Rose his wife Godfather Capt. Thos. Larkin, Mrs. Beale & Mrs. Trausum Godmothers, 29th Baptized Rose Anna the Daughter of Mic'l Piper psent Reg'r and Rose his wife God father Capt. Larkin Godmothers Mrs. Elizabeth Beale and Mrs. Trausum.[28]

In 1747, a year after Howes Goldsborough's death, his young widow married James Auld, then living in Dorset Co., but afterwards (1765) of Halifax, North Carolina. By her second marriage she had eight children. These Auld children are not related to the Goldsboroughs of Myrtle Grove, Shoal Creek, or Horn's Point; nor to any of the Four Square line except the descendants of John II, who married their half-sister, Caroline Goldsborough.

[28] Register of St. Ann's Parish, Annapolis, p. 422.

GOUGH–CARROLL BIBLE RECORDS.

Harry Dorsey Gough, son of Thomas and Sophia Gough, was born January 28, 1745, at five minutes after six o'c. p. m.; was married to Prudence Carnan May 2, 1771. He departed this life May 8, 1808.

Prudence Carnan, daughter of John and Achsah Carnan, born January 16, 1755.

Charles Ridgely Carnan, son of John and Achsah, born December 6, 1762; married to Priscilla Dorsey, October 17, 1782.

Priscilla Dorsey, daughter of Caleb and Priscilla Dorsey, born July 12, 1762. Mrs. Priscilla Ridgley departed this life April 30, 1814.

James Maccubbin, son of Nicholas and Mary Clare, was born December, 1762; married to Sophia Gough in December, 1787. James Maccubbin above mentioned was born in the year 1761, December 8. [Last entry interlined and signed James Carroll, January 21, 1827.]

Sophia Gough, daughter of Harry D. Gough and Prudence his wife, was born August 2, 1772.

Mrs. Sophia Carroll departed this life December 11, 1816.

Mrs. Margaret Carroll departed this life March 14, 1817, aged 76 years. [Wife of Charles Carroll, Barrister.]

John Gough Carroll, son of James and Sophia Carroll, died August 2, 1817, half past three o'clock a. m., aged 6 years 11 months and 25 days.

Charles Ridgely Junior of Hampt., died at Epsom Saturday, June 19, 1819, aged 35 years 10 mo. He died at half past nine o'clock p. m.

Mrs. Prudence Gough died at Baltimore 23 June, 1822, 10 o'clock p. m., aged 68 years.

Died at Hampton October 2, 1822, at half past three o'clock p. m., Mrs. Prudence Gough Ridgely. She was born October 15, 1795.

Died at Baltimore April 18, 1828, Mrs. James Howard, aged 27 years.

Died at Baltimore July 17, 1829, General Charles Ridgely of Hampton, in the 69th year of his age.

Departed this life in Balto. Friday 27th January 1832, at 9 o'clock p. m. James Carroll aged 70 years 1 month and 19 days.

Died at Baltimore, April 11, 1834, Eliza Onion aged 79 years 5 months and 10 days.

Died at Balto. August 7, 1841, Mrs. Achsah Carroll aged 49 years.

Harry Dorsey Gough Carroll, son of James and Sophia Carroll, born April 4, 1793.

Eliza Ridgely, daughter of Charles and Priscilla Ridgely, born May 24, 1797.

Harry D. G. Carroll was married to Eliza Ridgely, January 19, 1815. [He died

Priscilla Ridgely Carroll, daughter of Harry D. G. Carroll and Eliza his wife, was born April 5, 1816, at 1 o'clock a. m., in North Gay Street.

Charles Ridgely Carroll, son of Harry D. G. and Eliza Carroll, was born Tuesday May 20, 1817, at 10 minutes before 7 o'clock a. m. in Holliday St.

Harry Dorsey Gough Carroll, son of Harry D. G. Carroll and Eliza his wife, was born on Saturday February 27, 1819, at 20 minutes before 2 o'clock a. m. in Front Street, O. T.

Prudence Gough Carroll, daughter of H. D. G. Carroll and Eliza his wife, was born in South Frederick Street, Baltimore, on Thursday, 21 December 1820, at 10 minutes before 4 o'clock a. m.

James Clare Carroll, son of Harry D. G. and Eliza Carroll, was born in Frederick Street, Baltimore, on Thursday may 1st, 1823, five minutes past 1 o'clock p. m.

Eliza Carroll, daughter of Harry D. G. and Eliza Carroll, was born in Frederick Street, Baltimore, on Wednesday September 7, 1825, fifteen minutes past 7 o'clock p. m.

Harry D. G. Carroll, son of Harry D. G. Carroll and Eliza Ridgely, died July 12, 1882, aged 63, No. 90 W. Monument St., Baltimore.

Priscilla Ridgely Carroll, died Thursday March 22, 1821, aged 4 years 11 months and 17 days.

Charles Ridgely Carroll, died Tuesday May 29, 1821, aged 4 years and 8 days.

Prudence G. Carroll, died on Monday July 18, 1825, aged 4 years, 6 months, and 27 days.

Eliza Carroll, died at Perry Hall, Wednesday August 2, 1826, aged 10 months and 25 days.

My beloved wife Eliza Carroll, departed this life Wednesday 12 of August 1828, at 9 o'clock p. m., aged 31 years 2 months and 19 days.

James C. Carroll, died December 19, 1934, aged 10 years 7 months and 18 days.

(On loose sheets pinned in the Bible are the following records) :

James Carroll, son of James Carroll and Achsah Ridgely, died April 20, 1887, at 3:15 p. m., 70 years old on February 23.

Mary Wethered Ludlow (Carroll), daughter of Robert C. Ludlow and Anne C. Wethered, died 31st August, 1888, 70 years.

Harry D. G. Carroll, died on Friday March 2, 1888, aged 36 years and 4 months.

HALL FAMILY OF CALVERT COUNTY.

CHRISTOPHER JOHNSTON.

1. RICHARD HALL [1] entered rights in the Maryland Land Office, 26 August 1663, for himself, Elizabeth his wife, and other persons (L. O., Lib. 5, fol. 416). He probably arrived in the Province not long before, and may have come from Virginia, but though this is sometimes asserted, there seems to be no positive evidence for or against the statement. He settled in Calvert County and was elected, 12 December 1665, one of the four representatives of his County in the Provincial Assembly (Md. Archives, ii, 8). He sat in the Assembly from 10 April 1666 until 1670 (Archives, ii, 10. 153; Lib. C. D., 401), and again from 1674 until 1685 (Archives, ii, 345; vii, 4.6. 113. 266. 526; xiii, 21). He was Delegate for the assessment of the Public Levy in 1678 (Lib. C. D., 182) and, in November 1683, he was appointed one of the Commissioners for laying out towns and ports in Calvert County (Archives, vii, 611). Richard Hall was a prominent member of the Society of Friends; his name frequently appears on their records; and he was on the Committee of Cliffs Meeting in 1684 (Meeting Minutes, p. 13). He died in 1688. The following is a brief abstract of his will. RICHARD HALL of Calvert County; will dated 17 Sept. 1687, proved 28 August 1688 (Annapolis, Lib. 6, fol. 13):—1°. To my son Elisha Hall, 750 acres, part of Hall's Hills (1000 acres) where my dwelling house and plantation are. 2°. To my son Joseph Hall, 250 acres, being the remainder of Hall's Hills, and 150 acres adjoining called "The Defence"; also two negroes. 3°. To my son Benjamin Hall, 100 acres called Micham, also 100 acres on the South side thereof. 4°. To my son Aaron Hall, 200 acres called Spittle; also Additional Spittle adjoining Thacham, lately given to my son-in-law John Smith. 5°. To my daughter Rachel, now wife of Walter Smith, 300 acres called Aldermason. 6°. To my daughter Elizabeth Hall, 300 acres part of "The Hope,"

in Cecil County. 7°. To my daughter Sarah Hall, 100
acres, being the residue of " The Hope," and 200 acres
adjoining. 8°. Various bequests of real & personal property to testator's children already named, to his wife
Elizabeth, and to his daughter Lucia " now wife to John
Smith." 9°. Testator's wife Elizabeth is constituted executrix, and his friends William Richardson, Edward Talbott, and Samuel Chew are appointed overseers. 10°. Testator's children are to be brought up as Friends, and the
sum of £2 is left " to the stock of my friends (called
Quakers) on the Western shore of Maryland." Richard
Hall and Elizabeth his wife had issue as follows, the dates
of birth being derived from family record:

2.   i.   ELISHA HALL,[2] b. 8 July 1663; d. 6 Feb'y 1716/7.
3.   ii.   JOSEPH HALL, b. 1665; d. 1705.
4.   iii.   BENJAMIN HALL, b. 1667; d. 1721.
    iv.   AARON HALL, b. 1669; mar. Mary . . . .; d. s. p. 1704.
    v.   RACHEL HALL, b. 1671; d. 28 Oct. 1730; mar., 1686, Col.
       Walter Smith (d. 1711) of Calvert County.
    vi.   ELIZABETH HALL, b. 1673; d. 1743; mar. 1°. Richard Evans
       (d. 1702), 2°. Dr. James Kingsbury (d. 1725).
    vii.   LUCIA HALL, b. 1675; mar. John Smith.
    viii.   SARAH HALL, b. 1677; mar. . . . . Bradley and had a son,
       Robert Bradley (b. 1700) of Prince George's Co.

2.   ELISHA HALL [2] (*Richard* [1]) was born 8 July 1663, and died
6 February 1716/7, according to a family Bible in possession of Mr. Wm. Coleman Hall of Hall's, Lycoming County,
Penna. This agrees with a deposition, wherein Elisha
gives his age as 51 years in 1714 (Chancery, P. L., 233),
and with the date of probate of his will, 8 February 1716/7.
Like his father, he represented Calvert County in the Provincial Assembly, serving from 1698 to 1704 (Md. Archives,
xxii, 3. 20. 191. 342; xxiv, 17. 128. 233. 356. 360). He
married, 28 September 1688, Sarah widow of Jonas Wingfield, and daughter and coheir of Richard Hooper (d. 1673),
son of Henry (d. 1676) and Sarah Hooper of Calvert
County. 21 July 1688, administration is granted to Sarah,
widow of Jonas Wingfield, late of Calvert County, deceased,
on the estate of her said husband (Test. Proc. xiv, 84)
and, 6 Oct. 1688, the administration bond of Sarah, administratrix of Jonas Wingfield, in the sum of 4000 lb.
tobacco, is filed, with Elisha Hall and John Holloway as
sureties (*ibid.,* 100). Mrs. Sarah Wingfield is, however,
soon cited in regard to another matter. 5 November 1688,

command was given to the sheriff of Calvert County to
cite and summon Sarah Whinfell and Ellinor Hooper,
daughters and coheirs of Richard Hooper, deceased, and
Richard Ladd executor of Francis Swinfen deceased, to
appear and show cause, if any they have, why the bond of
administration on the estate of William Chaplin deceased
should not be assigned to William Chaplin, &c. Then came
Elisha Hall in person, and by consent of Anthony Underwood, procurator of the complainants, day is given to the
defendants until next January Court (*ibid.,* 118). 26 June
1693, citation to Elisha Hall of Calvert County and Sarah
his wife, administratrix of Jonas Winfield deceased (*ibid.,*
xv, 38). The will of Elisha Hall is dated 7 May 1716,
and was proved 8 February 1716/7 (Annapolis, Lib. 14,
fol. 317). In it he names his wife Sarah, his sons Richard
and Elihu, his daughter Sarah " now wife of Samuel Harrison," and his grand-daughter Mary Hall, daughter of
Richard. A bequest of £5 is " to be put into the stock of
my friends called Quakers," for charitable purposes. Sarah,
wife of Elisha Hall, survived her husband and died in
October 1739. Her will dated 2 October 1739, was proved
26 October 1739 (Annapolis, Lib. 23, fol. 121). She
mentions her son Elihu Hall, her daughter Sarah Harrison,
the five children of her son Richard Hall lately deceased,
and her grandsons John and Jonah Winfield. Her two
children, Elihu Hall and Sarah Harrison are appointed
executors.

    Elisha Hall and Sarah his wife had issue:—

5.   i.   RICHARD HALL,[3] b. 8 July 1690; d. 7 August 1739.
    ii. ELIZABETH HALL, b. 8 Dec. 1691; mar. 1708, Richard Har-
          rison, Jr.
6.   iii. ELIHU HALL, b. 28 February 1692; d. 1753.
    iv. SARAH HALL, b. 28 July 1694; d. 1741; mar., 1711, Samuel
          Harrison of A. A. Co.

3. JOSEPH HALL [2] (*Richard* [1]) of Calvert County was born,
according to family record, in 1665, and died in 1705.
His will, dated 14 September 1705, and proved 7 November
following (Annapolis, Lib. 3, fol. 652), mentions his wife
Ann, his son Joseph Hall, and " the child my wife now
goes with." Testator's wife, Ann, is appointed executrix.
Joseph Hall's widow, Ann, married secondly Rev. Thomas
Cockshutt, Rector of All Saints Parish, Calvert County.
20 Nov. 1710, Calvert County: Thomas Cockshutt, who

married Ann Hall widow and executrix of Joseph Hall,
rendered an additional account (Test. Proc., xxi, 299). 28
July 1731, Thomas Lingan and Martha his wife against
Ann Cockshutt, administratrix of Thomas Cockshutt, late
of Calvert County, Clerk, deceased. The said Thomas
Cockshutt died in 1722 leaving a widow Ann, and children
Thomas, Martha (wife of Thomas Lingan), Elizabeth, and
Ann.

Joseph Hall and Ann his wife had a son:—

    i. Joseph Hall,[3] mar., 1722, Sarah, dau. of John Smith of
        Calvert County, and widow of William Richardson.

4. Benjamin Hall [2] (*Richard* [1]), of Prince George's County,
was born in 1667 (family record) and died in 1721. Although brought up as a Friend, he later became a Roman
Catholic and died in that faith. He married Mary, daughter of Maj. Thomas Brooke and widow of Capt. James
Bowling of St. Mary's County. Capt. Bowling, in his will,
dated 7 May 1692, and proved 10 October 1693 (Annapolis,
Lib. 2, fol. 272) constitutes his wife, Mary, his executrix
and the residuary legatee of his personal estate, and appoints
his " honored father-in-law " Col. Henry Darnall overseer.
Col. Darnall had married Eleanor (Hatton) the widow of
Maj. Thomas Brooke and was thus the stepfather of Mrs.
Mary Bowling (See *Maga.,* i, 71). The will of Benjamin
Hall, to be cited presently, refers to testator's " brother-in-
law " Mr. Henry Darnall, whose father, Col. Henry Darnall,
died some ten years previously. Henry Witham, of Prince
George's County, having " intermarried with the relict and
widow of Mr. Benjamin Hall of the County aforesaid
deceased," they object to deceased's will, and prefer to take
" what the law allows " (Annapolis, Lib. 16, fol. 527). The
will of Benjamin Hall, of Prince George's County, is dated
4 September 1720, and was proved 29 March 1721 (Annapolis, Lib. 16, fol. 354). In it he mentions his wife
Mary Hall, his minor son Francis Hall, his nephews Richard and Elisha Hall, sons of his brother Elisha Hall, and
Joseph Hall, son of his brother Joseph. His brothers-
in-law Mr. Henry Darnall, Mr. Clement Brooke, Mr. William Digges, and Mr. Clement Hill are to manage his son's
estate. A bequest of £5 is left to the priests of the Roman
Catholic Church. Testator's wife, Mary, is appointed executrix.

Benjamin Hall and Mary (Brooke) his wife had a son:—

7.   i. FRANCIS HALL,[3] b. about 1696; d. 1785.

5. RICHARD HALL [3] (*Elisha,*[2] *Richard* [1]) of Calvert County
was born, according to family record, 8 July 1690, and
died 7 August 1739. He married, 4 September 1712, Mary
widow of Aquila Johns and daughter of Henry Hosier
(Friends' Records). The will of Richard Hall, dated the
day of his death, 7 August 1739, was proved 19 December
following (Annapolis, Lib. 22, fol. 113). In it he names
his sons Elisha and Richard (both under 18), his brother
Elihu, his wife Mary, his eldest daughter Mary Hopkins,
his second daughter Mary Hance, and his third daughter
Elizabeth Hopkins. Testator's wife Mary is appointed
executrix. The will of Mary Hall of Calvert County, widow
of Richard Hall, is dated 28 January 1762, and was proved
4 June following (Annapolis, Lib. 31, fol. 1000). She
mentions her son Richard Hall, who is appointed residuary
legatee and executor, her daughter Sarah, widow of John
Hance, her grand-son Gerard Hopkins (son of Philip Hopkins), and her grand-daughter Rebecca Hance (daughter
of John Hance).

Richard Hall and Mary (Hosier) his wife had issue:—

   i. ELISHA HALL.[4]
  ii. RICHARD HALL, living 1762.
 iii. MARY HALL, mar., 1736, Philip Hopkins.
  iv. SARAH HALL, mar., 1735, John Hance (d. Dec. 1761).
   v. ELIZABETH HALL, mar., 1730, Gerard Hopkins.

6. ELIHU HALL [3] (*Elisha,*[2] *Richard* [1]) was born 28 February
1692 (family record) and died in 1753. He married first,
in 1720, Elizabeth daughter of Philip Coale, but she appears to have died soon, leaving no issue (Friends' Records).
His second wife, married in 1722, was Elizabeth widow of
John Chew, and daughter of Richard Harrison of Calvert
County, and Elizabeth his wife (d. 1693) daughter of
Thomas and Alice Smith of Calvert County. Richard Harrison, in his will dated 10 Sept. 1713, and proved 15 Feb'y
1716/7 (Annap's, Lib. 14, fol. 142), mentions, among
others, " my daughter Elizabeth, wife of John Chew." Her
husband, John Chew, died in 1718, and his widow, Elizabeth, filed her bond as his administratrix 4 November of
that year, with Wm. Holland and Samuel Chew as her

sureties, in the sum of £3000 sterling (Test. Proc., xxiii,
287). 14 June 1722, Elihu Hall and Elizabeth Chew declared, in Meeting, their intention of marriage, and doubtless the wedding soon followed (Friends' Records). To
complete the identification we have the following: 16 October
1733, Additional Account of Elihu Hall of Anne Arundel
County, Gent., and Elizabeth his wife administratrix of
John Chew late of Anne Arundel County, merchant, deceased (Accounts, xii, 60). Soon after this, Elihu Hall
removed to Cecil County, as is proved by the following:
27 October 1736, 2nd Additional account of Elihu Hall of
Cecil County, Gent., and Elizabeth his wife administratrix
of John Chew, late of Anne Arundel County, merchant,
deceased (Accounts, xv, 207). The will of Elihu Hall of
Cecil County is dated 13 December 1752, and was proved
13 June 1753 (Annap's, xxviii, 548). He mentions his
daughter Sarah wife of Andrew Bay, his daughter Elizabeth
Hall, and his sons Elisha and Elihu Hall who are constituted executors. The probate clause states that the will was
proved " in the presence of the heir at law Elisha Hall,"
&c. Testator's wife is not mentioned in the will and was
doubtless dead at the time it was made.

Elihu Hall and Elizabeth (Harrison) his (second) wife
had issue:—

8.   i.   DR. ELISHA HALL,[4] b. 1723; d. 1757.
9.   ii.   COL. ELIHU HALL, b. 1724; d. 1790.
    iii.   SARAH HALL, mar. Andrew Bay of So. Carolina.
    iv.   ELIZABETH HALL.

7.   FRANCIS HALL [3] (*Benjamin,*[2] *Richard* [1]), of Prince George's
County, was probably born about 1696, and died in 1785.
He married, in 1718, Dorothy Lowe (b. 1704, and d. 1803
aged 99 years) daughter of Col. Henry Lowe of St. Mary's
County and Susanna Maria his wife, daughter of Richard
Bennett, Jr. (See *Maga.,* i, 74; ii, 181. 281). Col. Henry
Lowe was a nephew of Jane Lowe who married first Henry
Sewall (d. 1665) Secretary of Maryland, and, secondly
Charles, Third Lord Baltimore. The will of Francis Hall,
dated 22 August 1782, was proved 19 Sept. 1785, and is
recorded in Prince George's County. Francis Hall and
Dorothy (Lowe) his wife had issue:—

    i.   BENJAMIN HALL,[4] b. 1719; d. 1803; mar. Eleanor, dau. of
        William and Anne (Addison) Murdock.

ii. RICHARD BENNETT HALL, d. 1805; mar. Margaret Magruder.
iii. FRANCIS HALL of Queen Anne Co., b. 1732; d. 13 Feb'y 1798; m. 1º. Martha Neale, 2º. Anne Hawkins.
iv. SUSANNA HALL, mar. .... Darnall.
v. ELEANOR HALL, mar .... Digges.
vi. HENRIETTA HALL, mar. John Waring.

8. DR. ELISHA HALL [4] (*Elihu,*[3] *Elisha,*[2] *Richard* [1]) was born about 1723 and died in 1757 at his brother's place, Mt. Welcome, while on a visit there. He seems to have been the elder son, since the probate clause of his father's will states that the will was proved " in the presence of the heir-at-law Elisha Hall." It is fair to state, however, that a strong and persistent family tradition, advocated by Mr. Wm. Coleman Hall, asserts that the probate clause contains a clerical error, and that the elder son and heir-at-law was Elihu, and not Elisha. The similarity of the names would favor such confusion. Dr. Elisha Hall lived in Winchester, Virginia, and married Ruth Hall, aunt of Dr. Rush of Philadelphia. Their issue :—

   i. ELIHU HALL,[5] of Winchester, Va., b. 1752; d. 1808. He is said to have married Mary Ball, and to have had two sons and a daughter.
10. ii. DR. ELISHA HALL, of Fredericksburg, Va., b. 1754; d. 1814.
   iii. DR. JOHN HALL, mar Mrs. Eliza Ann Baynard, and had a son, Rev. Baynard Rush Hall, who d. in 1863.
   iv. RICHARD HALL, mar. Sophie Wilmot of Christopher's Camp, Harford Co., Md., and had a) Julia Lee Hall, b) Richard W. Hall, c) William W. Hall.

9. COL. ELIHU HALL [4] (*Elihu,*[3] *Elisha,*[2] *Richard* [1]) of Mt. Welcome, Cecil County, Md., was born in or about 1724 and died, according to family record, in January 1790. He lived at Mt. Welcome, an estate of 2000 acres extending from the Susquehanna to the Octoraro, and there exercised an open-handed hospitality according well with the name of the place. Only four rooms of the original mansion are now standing. It stood on an elevation near the Susquehanna, and was a mansion of such importance as to be located on a map of Pennsylvania, made a few years after the running of Mason and Dixon's Line (Johnston's *Cecil County,* p. 480). Elihu Hall was appointed, 6 June 1776, Major of the Susquehanna Battalion of Militia (ibid., p. 482), and was commissioned Lieutenant-Colonel of the same Battalion, 9 September 1778 (Md. Archives, xxi, 196). He was one of the Justices of Cecil County from 1756 till 1771 (Commission Book), and was appointed, 4 June 1777,

Judge of the Orphans' Court for the same County (Archives, xvi, 274). Col. Hall married, 16 June 1757, Catherine (b. 19 Aug. 1736) daughter of John Orrick and Susanna his wife, daughter of Col. Thomas Hammond of Baltimore County. They had issue:—

11.   i.   MAJ. ELIHU HALL,⁵ b. 9 August 1758.
12.   ii.   JOHN HALL, b. 6 May 1760; d. 1826.
13.   iii.   JAMES HALL, b. 12 March 1762; d. 1793.
14.   iv.   DR. ELISHA JOHN HALL, b. 19 May 1764; d. March 1835.
       v.   SUSAN HALL, b. 4 February 1766; d. July 1852; mar. Maj. Robert Lyon (b. 1754, d. 29 Jan'y 1842) of Baltimore Co., Md.
15.   vi.   CHARLES HALL, b. 2 Nov. 1767; d. 1821.
       vii.   SAMUEL CHEW HALL, b. 28 Jan'y 1769; d. unmarried.
       viii.   GEORGE WHITEFIELD HALL, b. 16 Sept. 1770; d. unmarried.
       ix.   ELIZABETH HARRISON HALL, b. 25 May 1772; mar 1°. .... Ogle, 2°. .... Gordon.
16.   x.   HENRY HALL, b. 1 Oct. 1773; d. 25 May 1808.
       xi.   CATHERINE ORRICK HALL, b. 24 April 1775; mar. .... Churchman.
17.   xii.   WASHINGTON HALL, b. 24 August 1776.
       xiii.   JULIA REED HALL, b. 9 May 1778; d. unmarried.

10. DR. ELISHA HALL ⁵ (*Elisha,*⁴ *Elihu,*³ *Elisha* ²) of Fredericksburg, Virginia, was born in 1754, and died in 1814. He married Caroline Carter and they had issue:

       i.   DR. BENJAMIN HARRISON HALL,⁶ b. 1781; mar. Lucy Fitzhugh; settled in St. Louis and died there.
       ii.   MARIA CARTER HALL, b. 1784; d. 1832; mar. 1°. Dr. Wormley, 2°. Dr. Caldwell.
18.   iii.   JOHN BYRD HALL, b. 1787; d. 1862; mar. Harriet Stringfellow.
       iv.   CHARLES RUSH HALL, mar. Louise Crutchfield.
       v.   SOPHIA HALL, mar. William Gregory of St. Louis.
       vi.   ELIZA A. HALL.

11. MAJ. ELIHU HALL ⁵ (*Elihu,*⁴ *Elihu,*³ *Elisha* ²) of Cecil County, was born 9 August 1758, and was commissioned, 21 April 1778, as " Elihu Hall Jr.", Major of the Susquehanna Battalion of Militia, in which his father was Lieutenant-Colonel (Archives, xxi, 48). At the time he lacked several months of being twenty years of age. The following year he accepted a commission, dated 1 August 1779, as Lieutenant in the Maryland Line, and served until January 1782 (Archives, xviii, 364. 520). According to family tradition, he was captured and held for some time as a prisoner by the British. While serving on Long Island he became acquainted with Gertrude Covenhoven (later Conover), daughter of Niklaus Covenhoven and

Nitje van Peet his wife and they were married. Their issue:

    i. NICHOLAS HALL.[6]
    ii. SUSAN HALL, mar. .... Morgan.
    iii. SARAH HALL, mar. .... Gillesbie.
    iv. ELLEN HALL, mar. .... Wills.
    v. ELIHU HALL.
    vi. CATHERINE HALL, b. 1789; d. 1860; mar. Maj. Wm. Richardson of Belair, and had issue.

12. DR. JOHN HALL [5] (*Elihu,*[4] *Elihu,*[3] *Elisha* [2]) of Harford County, Md., was born 6 May 1760, and died in 1826. He married Sarah Ewing, whose father was Provost of the University of Pennsylvania, and they had issue:—

    i. JAMES HALL,[6] b. 1781; d. 1868; mar. 1o. Mary Harrison Posey, 2o. Mary Alexander.
    ii. JOHN ELIHU HALL, b. 1783; d. 1829; Prof. of Law in Univ. of Md.; mar. Fanny M. Chew.
    iii. HARRISON HALL, b. 1785; d. 1866.
    iv. EDWARD HALL, b. 1791; d. 1814.
    v. CATHERINE HALL, b. 1796; d. 1865.
    vi. ALEXANDER H. HALL, mar. Jane Foulk.
    vii. SARGENT HALL.
    viii. THOMAS MIFFLIN HALL.
    ix. CHARLES HALL.
    x. MARGARET ANN HALL.

13. DR. JAMES HALL [5] (*Elihu,*[4] *Elihu,*[3] *Elisha* [2]) was born 12 March 1762, and settled in Georgia, where he died in 1793. He married Julia Hartley, daughter of Gen. Hartley of York, Penna., and they had issue:—

    i. CATHERINE HALL,[6] b. 15 May 1788; d. unmarried.
19.   ii. THOMAS HARTLEY HALL, b. 1792; d. 1848.
    iii. JULIA HALL, b. 4 April 1790; d. unmarried 1864.

14. DR. ELISHA JOHN HALL [5] (*Elihu,*[4] *Elihu,*[3] *Elisha* [2]) was born 19 May 1764, and died in March 1835. He married Catherine Smythe, and is buried, with his wife, in St. Thomas' Church Yard, Batimore County, Maryland. Their issue:—

    i. ALEXANDER HALL.[6]
    ii. CAROLINE HALL, mar. Matthew Markland.
    iii. CATHERINE VIRGINIA HALL, mar. Otho Wilson.
    iv. EDWARD E. HALL.
    v. ADELAIDE HALL, mar. S. T. Stonestreet.
    vi. W. H. DISSASUA HALL, mar. 1o. .... Hill, 2o. .... Briscoe.
    vii. ELISHA J. HALL, mar. Mary Matthews Brooke, dau. of Roger and Mary Brooke.
    viii. GEORGE D. HALL, m. .... Morgan.
    ix. ELIZABETH S. HALL, b. 5 June 1822, and now living.
    x. JAMES HALL, b. 1825.

15. CHARLES HALL [5] (*Elihu,*[4] *Elihu,*[3] *Elisha* [2]) of Pennsylvania, was born 2 Nov. 1767, and died in 1821. He married Elizabeth Coleman of Cornwall, Penna., and had issue:—

    i. ROBERT COLEMAN HALL,[6] b. 1792; d. 1844; mar. Sarah A. Watts.
    ii. CHARLES H. HALL, b. 1798; d. unmarried, 1847.
    iii. ANN CAROLINE HALL, b. 1800; d. unmarried, 1841.
    iv. CATHERINE ORRICK HALL, b. 1802; d. 1866; mar. H. M. Blodgett, but had no issue.
    v. MARGARET C. HALL, b. 1804; d. 1879; mar. Rev. W. Dickenson, D. D., of New York, and had two daughters.
    vi. WILLIAM COLEMAN HALL, b. 1806; d. unmarried, 1844.
    vii. LOUISA HALL, b. 1808; d. 1884; mar. F. W. Rawle.
    viii. HARRIET HALL, b. 1810; d. 1870; mar. W. B. Norris.
    ix. JAMES HALL, b. 1812; d. 1882; mar. Mary Johns Craig.
    x. SUSAN E. HALL, b. 1814; d. unmarried, 1895.
    xi. SARAH J. HALL, b. 1818; d. 1877; mar. T. F. Potter of Savannah, Ga.

16. HENRY HALL [5] (*Elihu,*[4] *Elihu,*[3] *Elisha* [2]) was born 1 October 1773, and died 25 May 1808. He married, 26 April 1800, at Harrisburg, Penna., Esther Maclay (d. 6 Sept. 1819) of that city, and had issue:—

20.   i. WILLIAM MACLAY HALL,[6] b. 16 Feb'y 1801; d. 28 Aug. 1851.
    ii. MARY ELIZABETH HALL, b. 21 Sept. 1802; d. Jan'y 1884; mar. G. W. Harris.
    iii. CATHERINE JULIA HALL, b. 14 Aug. 1804; d. 17 July 1832; mar. Garrick Mallory.

17. WASHINGTON HALL [5] (*Elihu,*[4] *Elihu,*[3] *Elisha* [2]) was born 24 August 1776. He married Ann Given and had issue:—

    i. EDWARD G. HALL,[6] mar. .... Sands.
    ii. WASHINGTON HALL, mar. Blanche Bujac.
    iii. SAMUEL CHEW HALL.
    iv. CHARLES NORRIS HALL.
    v. RICHARD HALL, mar. Margaret Mitchell and had a son, Washington Hall, who mar. Ann Lee.
    vi. REBECCA HALL, mar. Robert L. Rogers.
    vii. ACHSAH HALL.

18. JOHN BYRD HALL [6] (*Elisha,*[5] *Elisha,*[4] *Elihu* [3]) was born in 1787, and died in 1862. He married Harriet Stringfellow and had issue:—

    i. HORACE BYRD HALL,[7] d. 1896.
    ii. MARIA CARTER HALL.
    iii. CHARLOTTE HALL, mar. Robt. Pleasants Hall of St. Louis.
    iv. JULIA HALL, mar. Wm. D. Henry of So. Carolina.
    v. ALBERT HALL.

     vi. HARRIET HALL, mar. John Tevis of Phila.
    vii. ROBERT CARTER HALL, mar. 1°. Lucy Baskerville, 2°. Maria
          Carter Wormley.
    viii. HARRISON HALL.
     ix. ELIZA HALL.
      x. CHARLES HALL.
     xi. FRANK HALL.
    xii. JOHN HALL.
    xiii. MARIA HALL, mar. .... Watkins of Pittsburg, Penna.

19. THOMAS HARTLEY HALL [6] (*James,*[5] *Elihu,*[4] *Elihu*[3]) was
born 1792, and died in 1848. He and his family lived
in Georgia. He married Harriet E. Harris and had
issue:—

     i. ANN HALL.[7]
    ii. JAMES A. HALL.
    iii. WILLIAM H. HALL of Milledgeville, Ga.
    iv. JULIA ELEANOR HALL.
     v. DR. CHARLES HENRY HALL, b. 1832; d. 1906; mar. Auria Keenan,
         and left issue.
    vi. THOMAS H. HALL.

20. WILLIAM MACLAY HALL [6] (*Henry,*[5] *Elihu,*[4] *Elihu,*[3]) of
Pittsburg, Penna., was born 16 February 1801, and died
28 August 1851. He married, 7 March 1826, Ellen
Campbell Williams and had issue:—

     i. HENRY WILLIAMS HALL,[7] b. 12 Dec. 1826; d. 1833.
    ii. WILLIAM MACLAY HALL, b. 3 Nov. 1828; mar., 8 Sept. 1859,
         Ellen Rowan Cramer and had issue.
    iii. GEORGE DUFFIELD HALL, b. 19 Feb'y 1831; d. 6 Dec. 1883; mar.
         1°. Louisa Augusta Miller, 2°. Lucretia Pope Allen.
    iv. LOUIS WILLIAMS HALL, b. 4 July 1833; mar., 25 Nov. 1867,
         Eliza Cameron Warford.
     v. CATHERINE JULIA HALL, b. 10 Nov. 1835; mar., 22 Oct. 1857,
         Nathaniel Breading Hogg, but had no issue.
    vi. MARY HALL, b. 7 May 1838; mar., 25 Jan'y 1865, Francis
         Jordan; no issue.
    vii. ELLEN WILLIAMS HALL, b. 3 June 1846; mar., 25 April 1872,
         James Heron Crosman.

NOTE. For a considerable part of the foregoing genealogy,
my thanks are due to Mr. William Coleman Hall, who
kindly placed his family papers and his extensive genealogical collections at my disposal. He also read the manuscript of this paper, and made a number of valuable
suggestions and additions. At all times Mr. Hall has
rendered cheerful assistance, and has contributed most
generously the copious material gathered in the course of
many years of study.

HALL FAMILY.

Dr. J. Hall Pleasants has kindly called attention to some slight errors in the article on *The Hall Family of Calvert County,* that appeared in the September number of the *Magazine,* and makes some interesting additions. On page 295, the marriages of Mary and Elizabeth Hall, daughters of 5. Richard Hall[3] and Mary Hosier, are by some accident transposed. The Friends' Records show that it was Gerard Hopkins who married Mary Hall, 7 May 1730, while Philip Hopkins married her sister Elizabeth Hall in 1736. On page 297, 8, Dr. Elisha Hall[4] (Elihu)[3] was not a doctor, nor did he live in Winchester, Va. He married, 27 May 1746, Ruth, daughter of Jacob Hall, and died in 1757, leaving a will proved in Cecil County, Md., 30 Nov. 1757. The Bible record is indistinct, but it would seem that he was born in 1723, which favors the claim of those who hold that he was the elder and his brother Elihu the younger son. His widow Ruth married, secondly, Rev. James Hunt, a Presbyterian minister who kept a school at his place, called Tusculum, near Rockville, Montgomery County, from 1761 until his death 2 June 1793. Elisha Hall[4] and Ruth his wife had issue:

    i. ELIHU HALL, lived in Virginia, though not in Winchester. His wife's name was Mildred, and she is said to have been a Ball.

    ii. DR. JOSEPH HALL, of Locust Grove, Montgomery Co. He was commissioned, 7 Sept. 1776, Surgeon to Col. Griffith's Battalion of the Flying Camp (Md. Archives, xii, 260); was appointed, 4 Sept. 1777, Surgeon to Col. Murdock's Battalion of Marching Militia (ibid. xvi, 362); and was one of the founders of the Md. Med. and Chirurg. Faculty in 1799. He was living in 1804. He married Ann (b. 18 July 1758,

d. 9 May 1802) daughter of Basil Waring and widow of
Jesse Wharton (d. 1796) of St. Mary's Co.

iii. RICHARD HALL, little is known of him, except that he was frequently in money difficulties. His wife's name is unknown,
but he had one daughter, Elizabeth Lee Hall.

iv. ELISHA HALL. The account of him given in the Magazine,
p. 298, is correct.

v. DR. JOHN HALL is said to have been born in 1755. His wife,
Mrs. Eliza Ann Baynard, was of Hilton Head, S. C.

vi. ELIZABETH HARRISON HALL.

In thanking Dr. Pleasants for his interesting account of this
branch of the Hall family, I desire to say that such communications are always welcome. It is usually impossible for the
compiler to verify personally all the details of an extensive
genealogy; he must occasionally depend upon others, and from
this and other causes errors readily creep in. Those who detect
errors or inaccuracies, are cordially invited to write to the
Magazine, with the assurance that their communications will
always receive attention. In fact, one of the chief advantages
of the publication of these genealogies is that it facilitates the
detection and correction of error.

CHRISTOPHER JOHNSTON.

BIBLE RECORDS.

Contributed by Sarah Elizabeth Stuart.

HARRISON FAMILY OF CAROLINE COUNTY

Bible in possession of Mrs. George W. Smith, Chestertown, Md.

BIRTHS

Mary Harrison Daughter of Robert Harrison and Sarah his wife was Born 5th Dec. 1799—Ann Letittah Harrison Daugt of Robert Harrison and Sarah his Wife was Born 24th April 1801—Benjamin Harrison Son of Robt Harrison and Sarah his Wife was born 11th Sept 1804—Edmond T. Harrison son of Robt Harrison and Sarah his wife was Born 26th Feby 1808—Katie K. Harrison was born 21st Day of March 1867 W. S. E. Harrison was born March 8th 1869 Robert Harrison Son of Robt Harrison and Esther his wife was Born 23rd November 1811 William Henry Harrison Son of Robt Harrison and Easther his wife was Born 28th day of February 1814

Mary H. Harrison daughter of Robert Harrison and Easther his wife was Born 7(?) day of october 1815

Turbet K. Slauter Son of Noah Slauter and Easther his wife Born 27 June 1804

William Henry Harreson son of William Henry Harrison and Margaret Ann his wife was born April 29 1840

Robert Harrison and Sarah his Wife was Married 22d day of Febuary in the year of our Lord One Thousand Seven Hunde and ninety-Eight

Robt Harrison and Esther his wife was married 3rd January 1811

Wesley Clements and Mary Hester Harrison was married April 12th A. D. 1836 William Henry Harrison and Margaret Ann Clements was married June 25 1839 Henry B. Slaughter and Margaret Ann Harrison was Married April 6th 1841 W.

H. Harrison and L. A. (Louisa) Williamson ware married June 12th 1866

Mary Harrison daughter of Robert Harrison and Sarah his Wife Departed this life 17th Nove 1800

Aged 11 mo & 12 days

Sarah Harrison Wife of Robert Harrison Dept this life 2d Day March 1808 Agd 27 years & 6 Months.

Edmond T. Harrison Son of Robert Harrison & Sarah his Wife departed this life 4th March 1808 Aged 7 Days old.

Robert Harrison Departed this life 6 Day of november 1815 Aged 41 years.

H. Esther Harrison departed this Life November the 23rd 1831 about nine Ocl P. M. Aged Fifty-one years.

Nathan Keirns, son of Nathan Cenr died 3 July 1829 Aged

— — —

Mary Hester Clements wife of Wesley Clements departed this life December 21st 1836

William Henry Harrison departed this life June 8 1840 age 26 years 3 month 10 days

William Henry Harrison son of William Henry and Margaret Ann his wife died febuary 2" 1877 age 36" 9 months 3 days.

Rachel Rogester departed this life July 14th 1867

CLEMENTS FAMILY OF CAROLINE COUNTY

Bible in possession of Mrs. George W. Smith, Chestertown, Md.

Joel Clements Son of James Clements & Elizabeth his wife was born July 27th 1781—Elizabeth Clements Daughter of Nathan Keirn and Ann his Wife was Born Febury 24 in the year of our Lord 1782

Joel Clements & Margaret Roe was married Nov 7th 1802

Mary Clements daughter of Joel Clements & Margaret his wife was born feb 7th 1804

Reubin Clements Son of Joel Clements & Margaret his wife was born Oct. 24—1805

James Roe Clements Son of Joel Clements & Margaret his wife was born March 8th 1808

Joel Clements Son of Joel Clements & Margaret his wife was born Au^t 20th 1809

Kittemeria Clements daughter of Joel Clements & Margaret his wife was born april 6—1811

Wesley Clements Son of Joel Clements & Margaret his wife was born no^v 19th 1813

David Clements son of Joel Clements & Margaret his wife born october 21st 1817

Margaret Ann Clements daughter of Joel Clements and Margaret his wife was born Sep^t 20 1820

DEATHS

Departed this life oct 5th 1820 Margaret Clements wife of Joel Clements aged thirty nine years one month twenty five days.

Departed this life Augth 6″ 1837 Reubin Clements Son of Joel Clements & Margaret in Florida of Polmonery deseas aged thirty one years nine months & 18 days

Departed this life January 15th 1854 Wesley Clements son of Joel Clements and Margreat his Wife aged 40 years one month and 25 days

Departed this Life octob^r 28 1865 Elizabeth Clements Wife of Joel Clements and Daughter of Nathan and Ann Kiern aged Eighty three years Eight Month and four days.

Joel Clements Departed this life December 11th 1865 age 84 years 4 mo 15 Days

BIRTHS

Joel Clements & Elizabeth Keirn was married June 11th 1822

Joshua —Richard Clements Son of Joel Clements & Elizabeth his wife was born May 8th 1823

John Fleather Clements Son of Joel Clements & Elizabeth his wife was born Sept second in the year 1806

Margaret Ann Baggs Daughter of Sylvester Baggs & Ann his wife was Born September 26 in the year 1829

DEATHS

Departed this Life Augt 27th 1860 Elizabeth Jump Widdow of John Jump Dest Daughter of James Clements and Elizabeth, his wife, aged 59 years ten months and twelve days.

Joshua Richard Clements Departed this life June 3″ 1878 age 55 years 25 days.

Joel Clements departed this life June 3″ 1882 age 72 years 11 months 17 days

James Roe Clements departed this life September 1893

Mary Clements departed this life December 29th 1893

Departed this life Feb 10th 1903 Margaret Ann Slaughter, wife of Henry B. Slaughter and daughter of Joel & Margaret Clements

A True and perfect account of the marage of James Clements & Elizabeth his wife and the Children's ages, James Clements & Elizabeth Baggs his wife was married 18th day of october 1778 our daughter Martha was born Aug^h 7th 1779 our Son Joel was born July 27th 1781 our Son Richard was born march 18th 1783 our Son John was born march 30th 1785 our Son James was born Jany 31st 1787 our Son Thomas was born october 23rd 1788 our Son Isaac was born october 31 1790 our Son Caleb was born June 29th 1792 & our Son Joshua was born August 6th 1795 our daughter Mary was born Sept 19th 1797 our daughter Elizabeth was born october 15th 1801

True Transcript of the original
Joel Clements
Febeury 1st 1848

Reuben Clements red the old Testament through in one day less than three weaks and examined Clark's notes on the most important Texes and red but little after sun down also Red the new Testament through in one weak commencing in January

and finishing the twelfth day of February 1836 it the winter
that one so much indesposed writen by Reuben Clements

Reuben Clements

NOTES ON STEWARTS OF KENT COUNTY

Edward Stewart (or Stuart) came to America from Scotland
and lived near Millington, Kent County, Maryland.

He was born before 1763 and died after 1792. In 1784,
Sept. 9, he leased a parcel of land called Partnership, for a term
of seven years. This was near Millington, Md.

July 17, 1776 he enlisted in the Revolutionary War, under
Capt. Isaac Perkins. (See Archives of Md. Vol. 18, p. 63.)
Later, under acts of 1780 and 1781 he was drafted from Kent
County. (War Department record.)

He married Sarah Evans, daughter of Jonathan Evans, of
Queen Anne's County, and had four sons: 1st, William, wife
unknown; sons were Edward and William Alexander; 2nd son,
Henry, who married —— Buchanan and their children were
Henry Jr., and Rachel and Sarah Ann. Of these two lines
there appear to be no living descendants. 3rd son, Edward Jr.,
born Mar 14, 1790, died Oct. 20, 1854. He lived in Easton,
Md., and is buried there. It is said that Edward Jr. married
three times, the 1st and second wives were sisters, named Davids,
the third Morrison. By the 1st wife there was one child, Ellen,
who married Jas. Wooters of Centreville, Md., and by the 2nd
wife a daughter Sadie, who married Rev. Wm. H. D. Harper, a
Southern Methodist minister who died Jan 23, 1917. Mrs.
Harper was living in 1914 in Roanoke, Va., 528 Church ave.

4th son of Edward and Sarah Stewart was John Evans
Stuart, born 1793, died Jan 1st, 1846. Dec. 3, 1815 he married
Elizabeth Rochester who was born 1796, died 1857. Their
children were,

I b. 1816 John Evans Stuart, Jr. d. 1859. Married 1st
wife 1844. Susan Brown, b.   d. 1858.
2nd wife Emily D. Wright d—

II   b. 1819   Francis Thomas, d. 1845 m. 1844 Sarah Hamilton.

III   b. 1823   Mary Elizabeth, d. 1900. Married Sam'l Blackiston.

IV   b. 1828   Wm. Henry d.   Married Josephine Newnam and they went to Terre Haute, Ind.

V   b. 1831   Horace Montgomery Stuart, d. 1899. Married Martha Ellen Walraven in 1867.

VI   b. 1833   George Washington Stuart, d. 1875.

VII   b. 1836   Martha Ann, d. 1899. Married Thos. Price in 1864.

Of the descendants of Edward Stewart there is no one of the name living east of Ind. except Frances Ellen & Sarah Elisabeth Stuart, daughters of Horace Montgomery & Ellen Walraven Stuart. There are, however, a number of sons and their children, (children and grandchildren, etc.) of Wm. Henry Stuart, and his wife Josephine Newnam. They (Wm. Henry & Josephine) had a large family and they are scattered from Terre Haute to China.

In my father's young manhood the males of the family all changed the spelling of their names from Stewart to Stuart, because one member of the family claimed connection with the Royal Family of Scotland. The proof of this has been lost, but they must have had some good reason for the stand they took, to have made the change at all, as they were very plain and unassuming people. The women of the family refused to make the change, so in the cemetery and in the Bible record, both ways are found, side by side. Mrs. Harper, of Roanoke, Va., tells me, under date of Sept. 1, 1914, that she remembers the family tree and the old Bible, having seen it in her childhood, but no records can now be found, except the Bible of my grandfather's,—John Evans Stuart.

Sarah Elisabeth Stuart.

Apr. 5, 1917.

GENEALOGIES OF FOUR FAMILIES OF DORCHESTER COUNTY: HARRISON, HASKINS, CAILE, LOOCKERMAN.*

JOSEPH S. AMES.

THE HARRISON FAMILY OF DORCHESTER COUNTY

1. CHRISTOPHER HARRISON [1] of Appleby, Co. Westmoreland, England, is the earliest known[†] ancestor of the Dorchester family. His will, dated June 20, 1733 and proved Oct. 1, 1733, is on record in Carlisle. This is witnessed by Thomas Harrison and James Perkins; and in it he mentions his wife Jane, his daughter Sarah, and his son Christopher, "not yet 21."

   According to authentic family records his wife was Jane Gilpin.

   Issue (according to his will):—

   2. i. CHRISTOPHER HARRISON,[2] b. 1717 Nov. 17; d. 1799 Feb. 6; m. 1739 Feb. 7 Mary Caile.
      ii. Sarah Harrison.

2. CHRISTOPHER HARRISON [2] (*Christopher* [1]), son of Christopher and Jane (Gilpin) Harrison, was born Nov. 17, 1717 and died Feb. 6, 1799. He lived and died in Appleby, England, where he was a "grocer," according to a statement in the will of his mother-in-law, Mrs. Margaret Caile. On Feb. 7, 1739, he married Mary Caile (b. 1716, Oct. 7; d. 1782, Aug. 2), daughter of John and Margaret Caile (See Caile Family, this *Magazine* post).

   In St. Lawrence Church, Appleby, there is an extended tombstone record of him and his family.

---

* These genealogies are due to a large extent to the investigations made by Mrs. Clara Earle and Miss Dandridge.

† In Bishop Nicholson's *Episcopal Visitation of the Diocese of Carlisle* in 1703 there is recorded an inscription on a seat, at the Choir entrance of Brough Church: "Mr. Chrisr. Harrison, Parochuset Rectoriæ Firmarius S. S. fieri fecit Deo O. M. etc. 1682." This Christopher Harrison was matriculated at Queen's College, Oxford, June 14, 1649. His history is known. A seal brought to America by the family bears arms identical with those confirmed to William Harrison, of Tower Ward, London, Nov. 24, 1607, whose pedigree is given in the Harleian MSS., *Visitation of London*, 1633-35, p. 355, and who descended from a Cumberland family.

Issue:—

3. i. ROBERT HARRISON,⁸ b. 1740 Nov. 5, d. 1802 May 16; m. 1770
        Oct. 10 Milcah Gale.
    ii. Sarah Harrison, b. 1743 May 14; d. 1745 Nov. 5.
    iii. Margaret Harrison, b. 1745 Dec. 6, d. 1785 July 23; m. Rev.
        Gilpin Gorst (1726-1803) son of William Gorst, Steward
        of Appleby Castle. Issue:
4. iv. JOHN CAILE HARRISON, b. 1747 Sept. 3, d. 1780 Nov. 8, m.
        1773, Nov. 18, Mary Caile.
    v. Christopher Harrison, b. 1749 June 22, d. 1752 Aug 12.
    vi. Thomas Harrison, b. 1751 July 15, d. 1830 Mar. 20; m. Mar-
        garet Birbeck (d. 1833 Jan. 21, aged 79).
        Issue: i. Christopher Harrison, d. 1853 Apr. 27, aged 72.
                ii. Robert Harrison, d. 1795 Feb. 1, aged 3.
    vii. William Harrison, b. 1753 Oct. 14, d. 1835; m. ——. No issue.
    viii. Jane Harrison, b. 1755 Sept. 9; d. 1755.
    ix. Mary Harrison, b. 1758 Dec. 25, d. 1759.

3. ROBERT HARRISON ³ (*Christopher,*² *Christopher* ¹), son of
Christopher and Mary (Caile) Harrison, was born in
Appleby, England, Nov. 5, 1740, and died in Maryland on
May 16, 1802. He came to the colony in Mar., 1755,
bringing letters for Governor Sharpe.‡ In one of these
he is recommended for an office "on account of his
alliance." The Governor was importuned repeatedly by
Pownall, Sir Richard Abdy and others to appoint Mr.
Harrison to a suitable office; but he was unable for various
reasons to do anything for many years. Finally the Governor writes back to England that he has appointed "Mr.
Robert Harrison, merchant of Cambridge" to be Sheriff
of Dorchester County at Martinmas, 1767. This office
he held for two years. In 1770 he was one of the three
Commissioners appointed to build the new Court House
in Cambridge.

As the Revolution approached he took a leading part in
Dorchester. He was a Deputy to the Maryland Convention of June 22, 1774, and also to the Association of the
Freeman of Maryland, July 26, 1775. His name also
appears among the Dorchester Justices in the years 1777,
78, 79, 80, 81 and 83.

He was appointed in 1776 First Major of the Lower
Battalion of Dorchester; on May 20, 1778, he was commissioned Colonel of the battalion; and in Feb., 1781,
he was reappointed.

In 1785 he was one of the Trustees of the Poor; and

‡ Gov. Sharpe's Correspondence, vol. I, p. 185; II, pp. 76, 478; III, p. 347.

in 1791 he was appointed Associate Justice of the Fourth
Judicial District.

His wife was Milcah Gale (b. 1751, June 20, d. 1780),
youngest child of George Gale of Somerset County and
his wife Elizabeth Airey, whom he married Oct. 10, 1770.
He called his home, near Cambridge, Maryland,
" Appleby " after the town of his birth.

Issue:—

    i. Mary Harrison,[4] b. 1774 May 23, d. 1840 Sept. 14, m. 1802 Oct.
        10 Jacob Loockerman, son of John Loockerman, Jr. (See
        Loockerman Family *post*.)

    ii. Christopher Harrison, b. 1775 Aug 29, d. 1862 Apr. 4, unm.
        He was the first Lieutenant Governor of Indiana 1816-
        1818, and helped to lay out the city of Indianapolis.
        He returned East in 1835 and lived there till his death.
        He is buried at " Fair View " Talbot Co.

5. iii. ELIZABETH HARRISON, b. 1777 Aug. 27, d. 1857 Oct., m. 1803
        Apr. 28 Andrew Skinner.

    iv. John Gale Harrison, b. 1779 Dec. 21, d. 1802 Jan. 26 unm.

4. JOHN CAILE HARRISON [3] (*Christopher,*[2] *Christopher* [1]),
son of Christopher and Mary (Caile) Harrison, was born
in Appleby, England, Sept. 3, 1747, and died in Maryland, Nov. 8, 1780. Soon after coming of age he crossed
the ocean to Dorchester County, Maryland, to join his
brother Robert. The first official record of him is as being
Clerk of the Committee of Observation of Dorchester
County in 1776; and in September of that year he was
appointed Ensign of a Company of Militia in the 19th
battalion. He held about this time the office of Register
of Wills, which he resigned in May, 1777; and from then
till 1780 he was Clerk of Court of Dorchester.

On Nov. 18, 1773, he married his first cousin, Mary
Caile (1756-1812), daughter of Hall and Elizabeth (Has-
kins) Caile (after his death, she married Judge Thomas
James Bullitt. See Caile Family this *Magazine,* post).

Issue:—

6. i. HALL HARRISON,[4] b. 1774 Oct. 13, d. 1830 Sept. 3; m. 1800
        Mar. 17 Elizabeth Galt.

    ii. Hannah Harrison, b. 1777 Nov. 20; d. 1799 Nov. 4, unm.
        [According to another record, she d. 1779 Oct. 4.]

    iii. William Harrison, b. 1780 July 7; d. 1827 Nov. 29, unm.

5. ELIZABETH HARRISON [4] (*Robert,*[3] *Christopher,*[2] *Chris-
pher* [1]), daughter of Col. Robert Harrison and Milcah
Gale, was born at " Appleby " near Cambridge, Md., Aug.
27, 1777, and died in Oct., 1857. On April 28, 1803,

she married Andrew Skinner (b. 1763, Sept. 11; d. 1843,
Aug 18), of " Fair View," Talbot County, son of Andrew
and Anna (Sutton) Skinner.
Issue:—

    i. John Gale Skinner,' b. 1804 d. in the West.
    ii. William Skinner, b. 1806, d. 1831.
    iii. Mary Amelia Skinner, b. 1809, d. 1879.
    iv. Louisa Skinner, b. 1811, d. 1831 Nov. 5.
    v. Elizabeth Grant Skinner, b. 1814 Feb. 14, d. 1902 May 25, m.
        1847 May 25 Thomas Poole Williams. No issue.
    vi. Milcah Matilda Skinner, b. 1817 Sept. 4. d. ——, m. 1839
        Nov. 14 Henry Cooke Tilghman (b. 1808 June 28, d.
        1880 Feb. 19) son of Richard Cooke and Elizabeth (Van
        Wick) Tilghman.
        Issue:
            i. Elizabeth Harrison Tilghman, b. 1840 Oct. 26.
            ii. Richard Cooke Tilghman, b. 1843 Oct. 18, d. 1873
                Jan. 14; m. 1871 Dec. 5 Agnes Riddell Owen. Issue.
            iii. Louisa Tilghman b. 1845 Dec. 14, m. 1867 Nov. 26
                William Sterett Carroll. Issue.
            iv. Fannie Tilghman, b. 1848 June 4, m. 1872 Nov. 5
                Robert Hough. Issue.
            v. Anna Sophia Tilghman, b. 1851 Apr. 29, m. 1886
                Mar. 11 Powell Hollyday.
            vi. Sallie Skinner Tilghman, b. 1853 July 12; d. 1865
                July 5.
            vii. Susan Williams Tilghman, b. 1855 May 2.
            viii. Milcah Matilda Tilghman, b. 1857 May 2, m. 1892
                May 3 John Lusby Pascault.
            ix. Nannie Buchanan Tilghman, b. 1860 Sept. 23, d.
                1863 Feb. 15.
    vii. Robert Sutton Skinner, b. 1820, d. in the West.
    viii. Sally Lloyd Skinner, b. 1822 Oct. 27, d. 1894; m. 1847 Henry
        Robert Wilson (b. 1819, d. 1908).
        Issue:
            i. James Andrew Wilson, b. 1848 d. 1849.
            ii. Henry Melville Wilson, b. 1849.
            iii. Elizabeth Skinner Wilson, b. 1852 m. 1882 Wilson
                Presstman Heyward. Issue.
            iv. Mary Wilson, b. 1854 d. 1866.

6. HALL HARRISON [4] (*John Caile,*[3] *Christopher,*[2] *Christopher* [1]), eldest child of John Caile and Mary (Caile)
Harrison, was born at Cambridge, Md., Oct. 13, 1774, and
died in Baltimore, Sept. 3, 1830.

He came to Baltimore when still a youth, was apprenticed to Mr. George Grundy as clerk, and brought up in
the dry goods business. He lived in Mr. Grundy's family
until his majority, when he went to England and visited
his relations in Appleby. A portrait of him is in the
family, on the back of which is written " H. Harrison
sailed from Baltimore on the ship Carrollton, Capt. Martin, May 14, 1797." He came back to Baltimore after a

few years; and on March 17, 1800, he married Elizabeth
Galt, daughter of Robert * and Elizabeth † (Thompson)
Galt of Coleraine, Ireland.   At this time she was on a
visit to her uncle, Hugh Thompson, of Baltimore.

In 1802 or 3 he moved to Easton, Md., and was Cashier
of the Branch of the Farmer's Bank of Maryland until
1810, when he returned to Baltimore and formed a partnership with Govert Haskins in the iron business, on
Bowly's wharf.   In 1811 this partnership was dissolved;
and he formed a new one with Maj. Thomas Yates.   On
the death of the latter after a year, Samuel Sterett joined
him; and the firm became " Harrison and Sterett, Vendue
Merchants."

Issue:—

     i. Elizabeth Harrison,' b. 1800 Dec. 22, d. 1801 Apr. 7.
7. ii. WILLIAM GILPIN HARRISON, b. 1802 Feb. 3, d. 1883 Nov. 17,
       m. 1832 Anne Elizabeth Ross (d. 1833 aged 20).
    iii. Thomas Bullitt Harrison, b. 1804 Jan. 8, d. 1829 Sept. 12
       unm.   He was on the unfortunate U. S. Sloop of War,
       the " Hornet," which foundered at sea.   He was returning
       from Vera Cruz, Mexico, as a guest of the officers of
       the ship.
8. iv. MARY CAILE HARRISON, b. 1805 Dec. 29; d. 1873 July 10, m.
       1826 Aug. 17 Thomas Oliver.
     v. Robert Galt Harrison, b. 1807 Sept. 12, d. 1811 Aug. 23.
9. vi. HUGH THOMPSON HARRISON, b. 1810 Feb. 8, d. 1872 June
       21; m. 1834 June 3 Eliza Catherine Thompson.
10. vii. JOHN CAILE HARRISON, b. 1812 Mar. 3, d. 1859 June 9, m.
       1839 May 20 Sarah Barker.
    viii. Margaret Sprigg Harrison, b. 1813 Mar. 27, d. 1893 Apr. 17
       unm.
11. ix. SAMUEL THOMPSON HARRISON, b. 1815 Jan. 13, d. 1857 Nov.
       5, m. 1846 May 5, Emily Kuhn.
12. x. GEORGE LAW HARRISON, b. 1816 Oct. 1, d. 1885 Aug. 26 m.
       (1) 1845 Jan. 25 Maria Jeanette Bathurst; (2) 1855
       Nov. 20 Helen Troup Davidge.
    xi. Hall Harrison, b. 1818 Jan. 23, d. 1818 July 4.
    xii. Elizabeth Thompson Harrison, b. 1820 July 21, d. young.

7. WILLIAM GILPIN HARRISON [5] (Hall,[4] John Caile,[3] Christopher,[2] Christopher [1]), son of Hall Harrison and Elizabeth Galt, was born Feb. 3, 1802, and died Nov. 17, 1883.
In the year 1832 he married Anne Elizabeth Ross (d. 1833
aged 20), daughter of William and Catherine Worthington (Johnson) Ross, of Frederick, Md.   They had only
one child, who died at birth.

He was one of the leading business men of Baltimore

* Son of William and Elizabeth Galt.
† Daughter of John Thompson, of Muckamore, Ireland.

and one of its most respected citizens. He began his business career by continuing his father's business as "vendue merchant," and he soon was forced by its growth to limit it to the sugar and molasses trade. He was most successful, and became prominent in all the business life of the city. In 1853 he was elected President of the Baltimore and Ohio Railroad, a position he held until 1856. Just before the Civil War he was an unsuccessful candidate for Congress, his opponent being Henry Winter Davis. In 1861 he accepted an election to the Maryland House of Delegates; and, upon the legislature being suppressed by the military forces of the national government, he, with Teackle Wallis, Otho Scott, Charles Pitts, Lawrence Sangston, W. H. Gatchell and others, was arrested and imprisoned, first at Fort McHenry and Fortress Monroe, and finally at Fort Warren, Boston Harbor. Here he was kept for fourteen months. At the close of the War he resumed his business activity, becoming a Director in the Canton Company, President of the Union R. R. Co. in 1870, a Director in the Franklin Bank, and President of the Baltimore Fire Insurance Co.

His home on Eutaw Place was the home of the entire family, many living there and all regarding it as the family centre.

He was for many years a vestryman of St. Luke's Church and was deeply interested in all the religious and charitable work of the city. When he died his executors found that during his life-time he had given away over $1,000,000.

8. MARY CAILE HARRISON [5] (*Hall,*[4] *John Caile,*[3] *Christopher,*[2] *Christopher* [1]), daughter of Hall Harrison and Elizabeth Galt, was born Dec. 29, 1805, and died July 10, 1873. On Aug. 17, 1826, she married Thomas Oliver (b. 1802, June 7; d. 1848, Dec. 29, at Naples), son of Robert and Elizabeth (Craig) Oliver.

Issue:—

i. Mary Oliver,[6] b. 1827 May 18; d. 1840 July 25.
ii. Robert Oliver, b. 1829 July 27; d. 1830 Aug.
iii. Robert Oliver, b. 1831 Mar. 8; d. 1886 May 7 unm.
iv. John Oliver, b. 1832 Aug. 12; d. 1836 Dec. 25.
v. Thomas Harrison Oliver, b. 1834 Aug. 20; m. 1901 Nov. 23, Alicia Lloyd daughter of Col. Edward and Mary Eager (Howard) Lloyd of "Wye." No issue.
vi. Elizabeth Oliver, b. 1836 May 12; d. 1908 Sept. 12 unm.

vii. Margaret Sprigg Oliver, b. 1839 Apr. 26; d. 1902 Apr. 4; m.
1864 June 7 Henry Fenwick Thompson, son of Henry
Anthony and Julie Zelina (de Macklot) Thompson. He
d. 1910 Oct. 11.
Issue:
i. Henry Oliver Thompson.
ii. Charlotte de Macklot Thompson.

9. HUGH THOMPSON HARRISON [5] (*Hall*,[4] *John Caile*,[3] *Christopher*,[2] *Christopher* [1]), son of Hall Harrison and Elizabeth Galt, was born Feb. 8, 1810, and died June 21, 1872.
On June 3, 1834, he married Eliza Catherine Thompson
(b. 1813, Jan. 19; d. 1892, Nov. 20), daughter of Craven
Peyton Thompson, of Alexandria, Va. (see Hayden's
" Genealogies," p. 629).

He graduated from Yale College in 1831 and received
the Master's degree in 1839. He studied for the ministry
of the Episcopal Church, graduated from the Seminary in
Alexandria in 1832, was ordained Deacon on Dec. 2, 1832
and Priest in 1833. He held charges first in Queen Caroline Parish, Va., and later in St. John's Parish, Howard
County, Md.

Issue:—

i. Hall Harrison [*] (Rev.) b. 1837 Nov. 11; d. 1900 Feb. 5; m. 1876
Nov. 4 Agnes Spottiswoode Kennedy (b. 1838 May 10,
d. 1907 June 30) daughter of Hon. Anthony and Sarah
(Dandridge) Kennedy. No issue.
ii. Elizabeth Harrison, b. 1836 Feb. 17, d. 1866 Mar. 12, unm.
iii. Richard Sprigg Steuart Harrison, b. 1840 Mar. 31; d. 1901 Dec.
15; m. 1864 June 9 Sally Dorsey Pue (b. 1836 Jan. 15,
d. 1892 Dec. 26) daughter of Dr. Arthur and Sally (Dorsey) Pue.
Issue:
i. Rebekah Harrison, b. 1865 Sept. 11.
ii. Katherine Harrison, b. 1867 Jan. 18.
iii. Hugh Thompson Harrison, b. 1868 Mar. 8; m. 1898
Sept. 14 Flora Bower (b. 1879 Oct. 23). Issue.
iv. Eleanor Rogers Harrison, b. 1869 July 30.
iv. William Gilpin Harrison (M.D.), b. 1842 Mar. 27, d. 1895
Aug. 30 unm.
v. Mary Caile Harrison, b. 1847 June 25, d. 1905 Aug. 15 unm.

10. JOHN CAILE HARRISON [5] (*Hall*,[4] *John Caile*,[3] *Christopher*,[2] *Christopher* [1]), son of Hall Harrison and Elizabeth
Galt, was born Mar. 3, 1812, and died June 9, 1859. On
May 20, 1839, he married Sarah Barker (b. 1819, July;
d. 1908, July 31), daughter of Jacob and Elizabeth
(Hazard) Barker of New Orleans. (After his death she
married, on Jan. 2, 1866, the Hon. William H. Hunt.)
He was in partnership with his brother William, and was
manager of the business in New Orleans.

Issue:—

i.   John Caile Harrison,* b. 1840 Feb. 16, d. 1893, m. Mary Burger.
     Issue two children, d. in infancy.
ii. Thomas Bullitt Harrison, b. 1841 July 28, d. 1885 Feb. 25;
     m. 1869 Nov. 16 Mary Boykin Williams (b. 1851 May
     18) daughter of David Rogerson and Katherine Boykin
     (Miller) Williams of Society Hill, South Carolina.
     Issue:
       i.   Katherine Williams Harrison, b. 1871 Apr. 4; m.
            (1) 1894 Oct. 17 Gough Winn Thompson (b. 1869
            Aug. 30, d. 1903 Nov. 17); (2) 1904 Dec. 3 Frank
            Gambrill Baldwin (b. 1870 Oct. 25, d. 1905 May 9).
            Issue first husband.
       ii. Thomas Bullitt Harrison, b. 1872 Nov. 24, d. 1915
            June 30, m. 1901 June 5 Marguerite Elton Baker (b.
            1878 Oct. 23). Issue.
       iii. Robert Barker Harrison, b. 1878 May 14, m. 1907
            June 6 Virginia Elizabeth White (b. 1885 Oct. 5).
            Issue.
iii. Jacob Barker Harrison, b. 1844 Nov. 6, d. 1910 July, m. (1)
     1874 June 6 Delia Fragley (d. 1898 Feb. 11); (2) 1904
     Dec. 6 Rebecca Spritz. No issue. He lived and died in
     New Orleans.
iv. William Gilpin Harrison, b. 1846 Nov. 5; d. 1867 Oct. 11 unm.
v.   Hall Harrison, b. 1848 Aug. 14; d. 1851 Dec. 28.

11. SAMUEL THOMPSON HARRISON [5] (*Hall,*[4] *John Caile,*[3] *Christopher,*[2] *Christopher*[1]), son of Hall Harrison and Elizabeth
Galt, was born Jan. 13, 1815, and died Nov. 5, 1857.   On
May 5, 1846, he married Emily Kuhn (b. Mar. 10, 1816;
d. Oct. 22, 1848), daughter of Charles and Elizabeth
Hestia (Yard) Kuhn, of Philadelphia.   He was a planter
in Louisiana.
     Issue: —

i.   Charles Kuhn Harrison, b. 1847 Feb. 26, d. 1908 Apr. 20, m.
     1868 Dec. 30 Louisa Triplett Haxall (b. 1847 Apr. 25,
     d. 1911 Aug. 18), daughter of Bolling Walker and Ann
     (Triplett) Haxall.
     Issue:
       i.   Anne Triplett Harrison, b. 1869 Oct. 10, m. 1898
             Apr. 12 George Somerville Jackson. No issue.
       ii.   William Gilpin Harrison, b. 1871 Sept. 6, d. 1902,
             June 14 unm.
       iii. Emily Kuhn Harrison, b. 1872 Sept. 30, m. 1897
             Nov. 17 W. Stuart Symington, Jr. Issue.
       iv.   Charles Kuhn Harrison, Jr., b. 1874 Aug. 13.
       v.   Bolling Haxall Harrison, b. 1876 Jan. 29, m.
             1904 May, May Stevens.
       vi.   Louisa Haxall Harrison, b. 1878 Mar. 31, d. 1915
             Mar. 20, m. 1903 Apr. 29 George Reily. Issue.
       vii. Samuel Thompson Harrison, b. 1880 Apr. 17, d.
             1894 Dec. 23.
       viii. Hall Harrison, b. 1881 Oct. 29.
       ix.   Hartman Kuhn Harrison, b. 1883 Aug. 31, m.
             1912 Oct. 19, Katharine Barton Jones.

    x. Evelyn Arnold Harrison, b. 1885 Apr. 13.
   xi. John Triplett Harrison, b. 1887, Mar. 20 m. 1911
       June 17 Gertrude Riker Leverich. Issue.
   xii. Philip Haxall Harrison b. 1889 Mar. 19, m. 1913
       Jan. 22 Gladys Perin.
  ii. Emily Kuhn Harrison, b. 1848 Oct., d. 1870 June 27, m. ——.
    Samuel H. Lyon. No issue.

12. GEORGE LAW HARRISON[5] (*Hall,*[4] *John Caile,*[3] *Christopher,*[2] *Christopher* [1]), son of Hall Harrison and Elizabeth Galt, was born Oct. 1, 1816, and died Aug. 26, 1885. He was twice married, first on Jan. 25, 1845, to Maria Jeannette Bathurst (b. ——; d. 1850, June 28), daughter of Matthew and Anne (Dickey) Bathurst; second on Nov. 20, 1855, to Helen Troup Davidge (b. 1829, Mar. 14; d. 1885, Jan. 2), daughter of Dr. John Beale Davidge and Rebecca Troup, his second wife. He was a merchant in Baltimore.

    Issue, first wife:—

    i. Annie Bathurst Harrison,[6] b. 1846 Oct. 20; m. 1885 Apr. 28
       Frank Moss. No issue.
    ii. Bess Harrison, b. 1848 Feb. 26; m. 1874 Nov. 12 Thomas
       Murphy Dobbin, son of George W. and Rebecca (Pue)
       Dobbin.
      Issue:
        i. Jeanette Bathurst Dobbin b. 1876 Jan. 12.
       ii. Rebecca Dobbin, b. 1877 Sept. 27.
      iii. Anne Bathurst Dobbin, b. 1879 Dec. 6.
  iii. Mary Caile Harrison, b. 1850 Feb. 2, d. 1850 Aug. 16.

    Issue, second wife:—

    iv. Helen Troup Harrison, b. 1856 Nov. 10, m. ——, Robert Sale-
       Hill. No issue.
    v. Rebecca Harrison, b. 1857 Oct. 26, d. 1858 Dec. 23.
    vi. Margaret Sprigg Harrison, b. 1859 Mar. 2; m. 1881 Apr. 26
       Mordecai Dawson Tyson (b. 1855 Jan. 16, d. 1901 Jan. 5).
      Issue:
        i. James Wood Tyson, b. 1883 Dec. 2.
   vii. Howard McHenry Harrison, b. 1861 Jan. 31, d. 1861 Nov. 30.
  viii. Henrietta Troup Harrison, b. 1865 Nov. 5, m. 1890 June 4
       Henry Augustus Rowland (b. 1848 Nov. 27, d. 1901
       Apr. 16).
      Issue:
        i. Harriette Heyer Rowland, b. 1891 June 24.
       ii. Henry Augustus Rowland, Jr., b. 1892 July 18.
      iii. Davidge Harrison Rowland, b. 1897 Dec. 25.
   ix. George Law Harrison, b. 1871 Nov. 28, d. 1902 June 5; m.
       1895 Florence Patterson Mordecai, daughter of Randolph
       and Emma (Brown) Mordecai.
      Issue:
        i. George Law Harrison, d.
       ii. Florence Patterson Harrison.

GENEALOGIES OF FOUR FAMILIES OF DORCHESTER COUNTY: HARRISON, HASKINS, CAILE, LOOCKERMAN.

JOSEPH S. AMES.

THE HASKINS FAMILY OF DORCHESTER COUNTY

1. THOMAS HASKINS [1], the first of the family in Maryland, is said to have been born in Ireland. His will, written Sept. 21, 1735, and proved March 5, 1735(6), is on record in Annapolis. His wife was Mary Loockerman, daughter of Govert Loockerman 2d and his wife, Sarah Woolford. They both and their two sons, William and Joseph, are mentioned in the will of Jacob Loockerman, Jr., written June 28, 1730. They were married between 1724 and 1729. (See Loockerman Family.)

After Thomas Haskins' death she married Joseph Ennalls, son of Henry Ennalls and Mary Hooper. Her will was written May 27, 1767 and proved January 20, 1772.

Thomas Haskins in his will appoints his wife his executrix and his brothers-in-law Jacob and Govert Loockerman guardians of his children.

Issue (family records) :—

2.   i.   WILLIAM HASKINS,[2] b. 1729 May 10; d. 1779 May 23, m. 1759 Mar. 11 Sarah Airey.
3.   ii.   JOSEPH HASKINS, b. 1731 Feb. 22, d. 1788; m. 1579 Apr. 15 Sarah Ennalls.
      iii.   Elizabeth Haskins, b. 1733 May 25; d. 1805 Nov. 3, m. 1754 June 2 Hall Caile.
      For their descendants see Caile Family.

2. WILLIAM HASKINS,[2] (Thomas [1]), son of Thomas Haskins and his wife Mary Loockerman, was born May 10, 1729, and died May 23, 1779. On Mar. 11, 1759 he married Sarah Airey (d. 1786 Dec. 13) daughter of the Rev. Thomas Airey and his wife Elizabeth Pitt.

He was a Justice of Dorchester Co. in 1764, 65, 66, 67, 68, 69, and 70. In 1774 he was a member of the Committee of Correspondence from Caroline Co. (*Gaz.* 1774, June 30.)

Issue:—

    i.   Mary Haskins,[3] b. 1760, d. 1818.
4. ii. JOSEPH HASKINS, b. 1762 Feb 28, d. 1826 Mar. 23, m. 1788 Oct.
        23 Sarah Barclay.
  iii. Thomas Haskins, b. 1763, d. 1777.
  iv. William Haskins, b. 1765 d. 1822 Dec. unm. of Easton.
   v. Sarah Haskins, d. before 1780 Sept. 5 (date of mother's will).
5. vi. GOVERT HASKINS, b. 1769, d. 1829, m. 1800 Leah Eccleston.
  vii. Elizabeth Haskins, b. 1767 d. 1806 May, at Easton, unm.

2. JOSEPH HASKINS [2], (Thomas [1]), son of Thomas Haskins
and his wife Mary Loockerman, was born Feb. 22, 1731 and
is said to have died in 1788. On Apr. 15, 1759 he married
Sarah Ennalls (b.   d.   ), daughter of
Thomas Ennalls and his wife Ann Skinner.

He was a sea-captain; and once on a visit to England he
became a Master Mason, 3d degree, of Dundee Arms Lodge,
London (Oct. 9, 1759).

Issue:—

6.   i. THOMAS HASKINS [3] (Rev.) b. 1760 Nov. 7, d. 1816 June 29; m.
       (1) 1785 Aug. 25 Martha Potts (2) 1799 Apr. 4 Elizabeth
       Richards.
   ii. Sarah Haskins, b. 1769, d. 1803.
7. iii. HENRY HASKINS, b. 1772, m. Sarah Austin.
   iv. Joseph Haskins, b. 1775 d. 1806 Oct.-Nov.; m. 1802 Oct. 10 Hen-
       rietta Sulivane, daughter of Maj. James and Mary (Ennalls)
       Sulivane. They had but one child who died at birth and was
       buried Nov. 14, 1804. (St. Paul's Church, Baltimore, Rec-
       ords). In his will he calls himself " Joseph Haskins, Jr.
       Coppersmith of Baltimore."

4. JOSEPH HASKINS [3], (William [2] Thomas [1]) son of William
Haskins and his wife Sarah Airey, was born Feb. 28, 1762
and died Mar. 23, 1826. On Oct. 23, 1788 he married
Sarah Barclay (b. 1771 Aug. 1, d. 1820), daughter of Rev.
John and Rachel (Goldsborough) Barclay.

At the time of his death he was the Cashier of the Branch
Bank at Easton, Md.

Issue (as given in records of St. Peter's Parish, Talbot
Co.) :—

    i. John Barclay Haskins,[4] b. 1789 Oct. 3, d. 1790 Aug.
8. ii. ANNA MARIA BARCLAY HASKINS, b. 1791 Aug. 12, d. 1825 Sept. m.
       —— James Bowie.
  iii. William Haskins, b. 1793 July 31, d. 1795 Oct. 4.
  iv. Elizabeth Haskins,[*] b. 1794 Sept. 28, d. unm.
   v. Robert Barclay Haskins, b. 1796 Oct. 15, d. s. p. m. (1) Eliza-
       beth Robins Hayward (d. 1845) (2) Mary Trippe.
  vi. Louisa Airey Haskins, b. 1798 Oct. 12, d. 1814 Aug 12.
  vii. Joseph Haskins, d. 1823, a student at law.

* She is called " Louisa " in her baptismal record.

5. GOVERT HASKINS [3], (William [2], Thomas [1]), the son of William Haskins and his wife Sarah Airey, was born in 1769 and died in 1829. In the year 1800 he married Leah Eccleston (d. 1803 Sept. 30), daughter of Thomas Firmin Eccleston and his wife Milcah Airey.

For some years he was a merchant in Baltimore, where he was in partnership with his kinsman Hall Harrison.

    i. Leah Haskins.[4]
   ii. Emily Haskins.

6. The Rev. THOMAS HASKINS [3] (Joseph [2], Thomas [1]), son of Capt. Joseph Haskins and his wife Sarah Ennalls, was born in Dorchester Co. Nov. 7, 1760 and died in Philadelphia June 29, 1816. He was twice married, first on Aug. 25, 1785 to Martha Potts of Coventry, Chester Co., Penn. (b. 1764 Jan. 25, d. 1797 July 20), daughter of Thomas and Ann (Nutt) Potts; second, on Apr. 4, 1799 to Elizabeth Richards (b. 1771, Aug. 26, d. 1857, Sept. 24), daughter of William and Mary (Patrick) Richards.

He was educated at William and Mary College; and after graduating studied law with Gustavus Scott, Esq. of Cambridge, Md. and later with the Hon. Richard Bassett of Dover, Del. He was, however, about this time converted to Methodism and became a preacher in this church. A full account of his life is given in " The Dupuy Family."

Issue—first wife:—

    i. Sarah Ennalls Haskins,[4] b. 1788 Dec. 19, d. 1868 Oct. 14, m. 1810 Sept. 20 Jesse Richards.

Second wife:—

   ii. Mary Richards Haskins, b. 1800 June 1, d. 1858 June 3, m. 1820 May 18 John Dupuy.
  iii. Martha Haskins b. 1805 Aug. 30, d. 1871; m. 1829 Dec. 10 John Wurts.
  iv. Elizabeth Haskins, b. 1807 Dec. 1, d. 1828 Oct. 14 unm.

7. HENRY HASKINS [3] (Joseph [2], Thomas [1]), son of Joseph Haskins and Sarah Ennalls, was born in the year 1772 and died   On   he married Sarah Austin.

He was a Justice of Dorchester Co. in the years 1803, 1804, 1805, 1806, 1808, 1809, 1810, 1811 and 1812.

Issue (as given in will of Joseph Haskins, Jr., 1806 Oct. 22):—

i. Mary Ann Haskins.[4]
ii. Eliza Haskins.
iii. Emmala Haskins.

8. ANNA MARIA BARCLAY HASKINS [4], (Joseph [3], William [2],
Thomas [1]), daughter of Joseph Haskins and Sarah Barclay,
was born Aug. 12, 1791 and died in Sept. 1825. She married James Bowie (b. 1779 Mar. 29, d. 1845 Mar. 7), son
of Rev. John and Margaret (Dallas) Bowie. (See " The
Bowies and their Kindred," pp. 100 and 153.)
Issue:—

   i. Joseph Haskins Bowie,[5] b. 1816 Jan. 15, d. 1879 Jan 5 m. (1)
      Catherine Elizabeth Rau (2) Harriet Godfrey. Issue.
  ii. Louisa Emily Haskins Bowie, b. 1817 Dec. 26, d. ——, m. 1837
      Nov. 28 Charles P. Craig. Issue.
 iii. Isabella Dallas Bowie, b. 1820 July 11, d. 1893 Apr. 16, unm.
  iv. Josephine Haskins Bowie, b. 1823 Aug. 17, d. ——, m. 1854 Jan.
      24 Thomas Smythe Hayward. Issue.

UNPLACED HASKINS

1. Thomas Haskins is called " kinsman " in the will of Col.
William Holland (1724); and reference is also made in it
to " my sister Mary Haskins," " each of her children," and
" my nephew Thomas Haskins."
    This Thomas Haskins, then, apparently had married
Mary Holland, and had at least one child, a son Thomas.
    Query: Is this Thomas the father of Thomas, No. 1, in
the genealogy, or is he the same, and was Mary Loockerman
his second wife?

2. There was a Henry Haskins, Capt. of a merchant-ship ply-
ing from Oxford, Md., to Boston, Mass., in 1756, as appears
from a letter dated Dec. 11 of that year from John Walker
of Boston to Henry Callister of Oxford. (Miss D.)

THE CAILE FAMILY OF DORCHESTER COUNTY

1. JOHN CAILE [1], the father of the two brothers who came to
Maryland, lived and died in Westmoreland, England. Of
himself and his family nothing is known beyond what is
told by his will which is on record in Carlisle. In this he
calls himself " John Caile of Howgate Foot, Co. Westmoreland, Gent." It was written Sept. 27, 1746 and was proved
in May, 1747. He mentions his wife Margaret, his sister

Ann Caile, spinster, and a second sister Jane deceased, his
son-in-law Christopher Harrison, and the children whose
names follow. Only one of his daughters, Mary, was married at this time.
Issue—order of birth unknown:—

    i. Mary Caile,² b. 1716 Oct. 7, d. 1782 Aug. 2, m. 1739 Feb. 7 Chris-
       topher Harrison. (See Harrison Family.)
    ii. Ann Caile* m. —— Crompton.
2. iii. JOHN CAILE, b. 1720, d. 1767 Apr. 27, m. Rebecca Ennalls.
    iv. Thomas Caile.
3. v. HALL CAILE, b. 1733 May 28, d. 1761 Jan. 30, m. 1754 June 2
       Elizabeth Haskins.
    vi. Jane Caile,* m. James Harner.
    vii. Margaret Caile.
    viii. Elizabeth Caile.
    ix. Hannah Caile,† m. (Moses?) Allen.

His widow, Mrs. Margaret Caile, survived him only a
short time, as her will was written on Mar. 17, 1746/7 and
was proved on May 27, 1747. She names the same children
as did her husband and also two Harrison grandchildren.
Her maiden name, according to family tradition, supported
by some documentary evidence, was Margaret Hall.

2. JOHN CAILE, JR.,² (John ¹), son of John Caile and Margaret Hall, came to Oxford, Talbot Co., Maryland, in or
before 1741; but about 1744 he moved to Dorchester Co.
    He was a merchant in Cambridge and Clerk of Court
from 1745 till 1766, when he was succeeded by his son-in-
law Richard Sprigg. According to the record on his tombstone he died Apr. 27, 1767, aged 47.
    His wife was Rebecca Ennalls (b. 1717 July 26, d. 1750
Aug. 28), daughter of Henry Ennalls and his wife Mary
Hooper. (See inter al " Baltimore Sun " May 6, 1906.)
Issue:—

4. i. MARGARET CAILE, d. 1796 July 13, m. 1765 Aug. 1 Richard
    Sprigg.

3. HALL CAILE ², (John ¹), son of John and Margaret Caile,
was born May 28, 1733 and died Jan. 30, 1761. On June,
2, 1754 he married Elizabeth Haskins (b. 1733 May 25,

* Named as married in the will of her brother Hall Caile, Jan. 28, 1761.
† Named as Hannah Allen in will of her brother John Caile, Apr. 16,
1767, who gives her a negro slave. Moses Allen was a witness to the will
of Hall Caile, and was appointed Sheriff to complete his unexpired term.
For other Allen references see Loockerman Family 6.

d. 1805 Nov. 3), daughter of Thomas Haskins and Mary Loockerman. He came to Dorchester Co., Md. about 1750 and on Oct. 27, 1758 was appointed to the office of High Sheriff, a position which he held until his death.

His wife survived him for many years; and at her death was buried in White Marsh Church yard, Talbot Co.

Issue:—

5. i. MARY CAILE,[3] b. 1756 Sept. 10, d. 1812 Feb. 24, m. (1) 1773 Nov. 18 John Caile Harrison (2) 1789 Dec. 22 Thomas James Bullitt.
6. ii. MARGARET HALL CAILE, b. 1759 Mar. 15, d. 1826 July 2, m. 1777 Feb. 16 Gustavus Scott.
   iii. John Hall Caile, b. 1761 Aug. 14, d. 1783 Feb. 14.

4. MARGARET CAILE [3], (John [2], John [1]) only child of John Caile and Rebecca Ennalls, died July 13, 1796. She married Aug. 1, 1765 Richard Sprigg (b. 1739 Dec. 16, d. 1798 Nov. 24), of " Cedar Park," Anne Arundel Co., son of Thomas Sprigg of " Longmeadow " and his wife Elizabeth Galloway. (See Baltimore *Sun* Feb. 11, 18, 1906, and *Md. Hist. Mag.,* viii, p. 82.)

Richard Sprigg was Clerk of Dorchester Co. from 1766 to 1777, succeeding his father-in-law.

Issue:—

i. Sophia Sprigg,[4] b. 1766 Apr. 21, d. 1812, m. 1785 Feb. 3 Col. John Francis Mercer (b. 1759 May 17, d. 1821 Aug. 30), Member of Congress from Virginia, Governor of Maryland 1801, etc.
   Issue:
      i. Richard Mercer, b. 1785 Nov. 19, d. young.
      ii. John Mercer, b. 1788 June 24; d. 1848 May 22, m. 1818 June 15 Mary Scott Swann.
      iii. Anna Mercer, b. 1789 Nov. 12, d. 1790 June 2.
      iv. Margaret Mercer, b. 1791 July 1, d. 1846 Sept. 17 unm.
      v. Thomas Mercer, b. 1792 Sept. 4, d. 1810 at sea.
ii. Rebecca Sprigg, b. 1767 d. 1806 m. 1787 Dr. James Steuart, son of Dr. George and Ann (Digges) Steuart.
   Issue:
      i. George Hume Steuart (Gen.), b. 1790 Nov. 1, d. 1867 m. Ann Jane Edmondson.
      ii. Margaret Steuart, b. 1795 d. 1832 m. John H. B. Latrobe.
      iii. Sophia Steuart, b. 1796 d. ——, m. John C. Delprat.
      iv. Richard Sprigg Steuart (Dr.), b. 1797, Nov. 1, d. 1876 July 13, m. 1824 Jan. 27 Maria Louisa de Bernabeu.
      v. James Steuart, b. 1798 d. 1804.
      vi. Henry Steuart, b. 1799 d. 1804.
      vii. Elizabeth Steuart, b. 1801 d. —— m. Augustus Thorndike.
      viii. Elizabeth Steuart, b. 1802 d. —— m. George H. Calvert.
iii. Elizabeth Sprigg, b. 1770, d. 1813, m. 1795 Hugh Thompson. No issue.
iv. Henrietta Sprigg, b. 1775 d. 1791.
v. Margaret Sprigg, b. 1790, d. 1864 unm.

5. MARY CAILE [3], (Hall [2], John [1]), daughter of Hall Caile
and Elizabeth Haskins, was born Sept. 10, 1756 and died
Feb. 24, 1812. She was twice married, first on Nov. 18,
1773 to John Caile Harrison (b. 1747 Sept 3, d. 1780
Nov. 8), son of Christopher Harrison and Mary Caile;
second, on Dec. 22, 1789 to Thomas James Bullitt (b. 1763
July 1, d. 1840 Nov. 25), son of the Hon. Cuthbert Bullitt
and Helen Scott (See Hayden " Virginia Genealogies," pp.
597 et seq.)

For John Caile Harrison and his descendants, see Harrison family.

Thomas James Bullitt was one of the Judges of Talbot
Co., Md.; and of him it was said " he was one of the most
elegant grandees of his day, he always appearing in top-
boots with knee buckles."

Issue—first husband:—

  i. Hall Harrison.[4] See Harrison Family.
 ii. Hannah Harrison d. young.
iii. William Harrison.

Second husband:—

 iv. Elizabeth Haskins Bullitt, b. 1790 Sept. 11, d. 1851 Oct. 10, m.
     1809 Dec. 19, William Hayward, Jr. (b. 1787, d. 1836 Oct. 19)
     son of William and Henrietta Maria (Lloyd) Hayward.)
     Issue:
        i. Mary Bullitt Hayward,[5] b. 1811 Aug. 17, d. 1847 Jan. 5,
           m. 1837 Jan. 31 Joseph Richardson Price. Issue.
       ii. William Hayward, b. 1814 June 8, d. 1889 Oct. 7 unm.
      iii. Henrietta Maria Chamberlaine Hayward, b. 1817 Mar. 5,
           d. 1884 Apr., m. 1838 Nov. 22 Dr. Samuel Wickes Spen-
           cer. Issue.
       iv. Helen Elizabeth Hayward, b. 1819, Dec. 5, d. 1820 July
           27.
        v. Sally Hayward, b. 1822 Feb. 25, d. 1825 Oct. 15.
       vi. Thomas Scott Bullitt Hayward, b. 1825 May 23, d. 1842
           Feb. 3.
      vii. Hall Harrison Hayward, b. 1828 Oct. 24, d. 1858 July
           14 unm.
     viii. Elizabeth Bullitt Hayward, b. 1831 Jan. 14, d. 1861
           Mar. 2, m. 1851 Jan. 14 Dr. Joseph Ennalls Muse
           Chamberlaine. Issue.
       ix. Margaret Robins Hayward, b. 1835 June 15, d. 1849
           Aug. 8.
  v. Cuthbert Bullitt, b. 1793 Feb. 2, d. 1793 Sept. 19.
 vi. Alexander Caile Bullitt, b. 1795 Sept. 10, d. 1847 Mar. 21, m.
     Mary Dennison. No issue.
vii. Thomas Scott Bullitt, b. 1798 Dec. 6, d. s. p. 1821 Oct. 11 unm.

6. MARGARET HALL CAILE [3], (Hall [2], John [1]), daughter of
Hall Caile and Elizabeth Haskins, was born Mar. 15, 1759
and died July 2, 1826. On Feb. 16, 1777 she married Gus-

tavus Scott (b. 1753, d. 1801), son of Rev. James Scott and Sarah Brown. A full account of his distinguished services to Maryland is given in Hayden "Virginia Genealogies" p. 623.

Issue:—

i. Robert Caile Scott,⁴ b. 1778 Mar. 22, d. in infancy.
ii. Elizabeth Scott, b. 1799 July 28, d. 1847 Mar., m. 1810 Dec. 10 Capt. Robert Rankin.
iii. John Caile Scott, b. 1781 Dec. 10, d. 1840 Mar. 14, m. 1802 Nov. 21 Anne Love.
iv. Mary Caile Scott, b. 1784 Mar. 22, d. 1806 Apr. 4.
v. Hall Gustavus Scott, b. 1786 Apr. 2, d. ——, m. 1806 July 1 Elizabeth Douglas Marshall.
vi. Christiana Scott, b. 1788 Sept. 14.
vii. William Bushrod Scott, b. 1791 July 28, d. ——, m. Anne Halton.
viii. Juliana Scott, b. ——, d. ——, m. Captain Robert DeWar Wainwright.
ix. Robert James Scott, b. 1798, d. 1834, m. 1818 Mary Ann Lewis.

GENEALOGIES OF FOUR FAMILIES OF DORCHESTER COUNTY: HARRISON, HASKINS, CAILE, LOOCKERMAN.

JOSEPH S. AMES.

THE LOOCKERMAN FAMILY OF THE EASTERN SHORE OF MARYLAND.

1. GOVERT LOOCKERMAN [1], the ancestor of the Maryland family, was born in Turnhout, a town in the Netherlands, and came to New Amsterdam in April, 1633. Several histories of his adventurous and active life have been published; the best are in "The Dupuy Family," pp. 107 et seq.,* and in

* In this most valuable book the genealogy of the Loockerman family is carried to Govert's grandchildren; but there are several important errors in this and not a few inconsistencies between the text and the family charts.

the New York Historical and Biographical Register, Vol.
VIII. In the latter may be found references to his brothers
and sister. It may be sufficient to note here that he was the
wealthiest merchant of the Province, that he held in succession nearly all the public offices in his adopted city, and
that he rendered conspicuous service in military and naval
positions. He died in the autumn of 1671.

He was twice married; first on Feb. 26, 1641, in Amsterdam, to Ariaentje Jans, who bore him two daughters; and
second, on July 11, 1649, in New Amsterdam, to Marritje
Jans * (d. 1677 Nov.), he being her third husband.

Issue, first wife:

 i. Marritje Loockerman,[2] b. 1641 Nov. 3; bapt. 1641 Dec. 1; d. ——;
  m. 1664 Nov. 12 Balthazar Bayard, son of Samuel Bayard and
  Anna Stuyvesant.
 ii. Jannetie Loockerman, b. 1643 Sept. 23; bapt. 1643 Sept. 27; d.
  ——; m. 1667 Feb. 12 Dr. Hans Kierstede, son of Dr. Hans
  Kierstede and Sara Roelofs.

Second wife:

2. iii. JACOB LOOCKERMAN, bapt. 1652 Mar. 17; d. 1730 Aug. 17; m.
   (1) 1677/8 Jan 29 Helena Ketin, (2) Dorothy ——.

2. JACOB LOOCKERMAN [2] (Govert [1]), only child of Govert
Loockerman and his second wife Marritje Jans, was baptised in New Amsterdam Mar. 17, 1652, and died in Dorchester Co., Md., it is said on Aug. 17, 1730. His will
was dated July 21, 1729, and was proved Oct. 27, 1730.
On Jan. 29, 1677/8 he married Helena Ketin †; after her
death he married again, for at the time of his death his
wife's name was Dorothy. His first wife was dead probably
in 1695, the date of the ratification of his naturalization,
for no mention is made of her; and he was married to
Dorothy in 1720, when her name appears signed to a deed.
She was living in 1751, when she made a gift of slaves to
her grandchildren.

---

* She was the daughter of Tryn Jansen and sister of the famous Anneke
Jans. Her first husband was Thymen Janzsen; and her daughter by this
marriage married for her second husband the distinguished Jacob Leisler.
See *N. Y. Hist. and Biog.*, vol. VII, 123; also *N. Y. Hist. Soc. Collections*,
1892, p. 60, for her will.

† Purple: *Ancient Families of New York*. It is more than probable that
this should be " Ellinor Keiting," only daughter of Nicholas Keiting of St.
Mary's Co., who came to the Province in 1641 and whose will was written
Apr. 20, 1657 and proved Oct. 10, 1661. The name was spelt Keyton,
Keytin, etc. See *Maryland Wills*, vol. I, pp. 20, 113, etc. His wife's name
was Audrey; and her will was proved in 1659.

He was educated as a physician and for a few years practised his profession in New Amsterdam; but, soon after his marriage, and for reasons undoubtedly connected with the political troubles of Jacob Leisler, the husband of his stepsister, he moved to St. Mary's Co., Maryland, where in 1678 he applied to be naturalized. In 1683 we find him acting as a Land Commissioner of Dorchester Co., and from that time till his death he held prominent official positions in that county.* He served as Justice almost continuously from 1685 to 1724; he was Sheriff in 1694; he was Military Officer in 1696, and later rose to the rank of Colonel; from 1698 to 1704 he was a member of the House of Burgesses.

His will is on record in Annapolis (Lib. 20, p. 109); in it he names his son Jacob his executor; and the instrument is witnessed by Roger, John and Elizabeth Woolford.

Issue: first wife, order of birth not known

3.   i.   JACOB LOOCKERMAN,³ Jr., b. 1678; d. 1731; m. 1711 Apr. 26 Mrs. Magdalen (Stevens) Edmondson.
4.   ii.   GOVERT LOOCKERMAN, b. 1681; d. 1728; m. Sarah Woolford.
5.   iii.   JOHN LOOCKERMAN, b. 1686; d. 1760 or 1761; m. (1) Mabel Dawson, (2) Mary ——.
6.   iv.   MARY LOOCKERMAN, m. (1) Rev. James Hindman, (2) before 1729 July 21 Francis Allen.
7.   v.   NICHOLAS LOOCKERMAN, b. 1697 Nov. 10; d. 1771 Mar.; m. 1721 Sally Emerson.
      vi.   Thomas Loockerman, lost at sea in 1714.†

Second wife

8.   vii.   THOMAS LOOCKERMAN, m. (1) Vienna ——, (2) Mary ——.

3.   JACOB LOOCKERMAN, JR. (Jacob,² Govert ¹), was undoubtedly born in Dorchester Co., but at the time of his death was living in Talbot Co. His will, written June 28, 1731 and proved July 27, 1731, is on record in Annapolis (Lib. 20, fol. 210). His executors were his wife and his nephew Jacob son of his brother Govert; and the witnesses were Col. William Holland and his wife Elizabeth Holland, and Thomas Holland. He is said to have been born in 1678.

On April 26, 1711 he married Mrs. Magdalen (Stevens) Edmondson,‡ widow of James Edmondson, and daughter of

* See *Maryland Archives,* vols. v, vii, xvii, xix, xx, xxii, xxiv, xxvi and Jones' *History of Dorchester Co.*

† In 1712 Jacob Loockerman deeds land to his son Thomas; and in 1724 Jacob Jr. (grandson of Col. Jacob) deeds this same land to his son Jacob, saying in the recitation that Thomas went to sea in 1714 in a sloop belonging to Col. Thomas Ennalls and was lost.

‡ St. Peter's Parish, Talbot Co.

John Stevens and Dorothy Preston. Her will was proved
Oct. 30, 1738.

By this marriage there were apparently no children; at
least none are mentioned in the wills referred to.

In the years 1699 and 1700 he was Clerk of certain committees in the House of Deputies; and in 1701 and again
from 1728 to 1739 he was sheriff of Dorchester Co.*

4. GOVERT LOOCKERMAN,[3] (Jacob,[2] Govert [1]) was born about
1681, as appears from a deposition made Mar. 13, 1721, on
record in Cambridge,** in which appears " Govert Loockerman, aged about 40 years, etc." He died in 1728 probably,
because on Aug. 28, of that year the inventory of his estate
was filed by his father and his brother Jacob.

He held many offices in Dorchester Co.† In 1706 he
was Sheriff; from 1710-1727, with the exception of a few
years he was Clerk of Court; in 1712 and 1713 he was a
member of the House of Burgesses; in 1723 he was on the
Board of Visitors of Parish Schools.

His wife ‡ was Sarah Woolford, daughter of Roger Woolford and his wife Mary Denwood. She was born Mar. 8,
1672 § and was dead before August 1730.¶

The only list of his children we have is that given in his
brother Jacob's will, written June 28, 1730.
Issue:

9.   i.   JACOB LOOCKERMAN,[4] m. Rosannah Woolford.
    ii.   Govert Loockerman, under age in 1731, date of his Uncle Jacob's
          will, d. 1753 Dec. 16; m. 1751 Nov. 13 Mrs. Ann (Rider)
          Billings.‖ No issue. He was a sea-captain. The inventory
          of his estate was filed Apr. 12, 1754; and his sister Mary
          Ennalls and her son Wm. Haskins sign it as next of kin; so
          it is probable that his other two sisters were dead at the
          time. The administrator of his estate was William Allen.

---

* *Maryland Archives*, vol. xxvi, p. 414; xxiv, pp. 62 and 111; xxiv, p. 167;
xxv, p. 530; Jones, *History of Dorchester Co.*

** " Old No. 8," fol. 108.

† Jones, *History of Dorchester Co.*

‡ The fact that his wife was Sarah Woolford is proved, first, by several
deeds to Govert and his wife Sarah, second by the will of Mrs. Elizabeth
(Woolford) Holland, daughter of Roger and Mary (Denwood) Woolford,
in which there are several references to Govert's children as her nephews
and nieces.

§ Jones, *loc. cit.*

¶ Date of deed of Jacob Loockerman to his granddaughter Sarah " dau. of
his son Govert and Sarah his wife, both late of Dorchester."

‖ Her will was written June 2, 1755 and proved June 10, 1756. She
was the daughter of Col. John Rider and Ann Hicks and the widow of
James Billings.

iii. Sarah Loockerman,* m. 1740 ± Joseph Cox Gray. No issue.
iv. Elizabeth Loockerman. She is named in the wills of her grandfather (1729) and her uncle Jacob (1730), but not by her
aunt Elizabeth Holland (1738 Nov. 19) in the list of her
nieces.
10. v. MARY LOOCKERMAN, m. (1) Thomas Haskins, (2) Dr. Joseph
Ennalls.

5. JOHN LOOCKERMAN,³ (Jacob,² Govert ¹), was born in 1686
probably, for in a deposition made in 1745 he gives his age
as 59.** His will was written Nov. 12, 1760 and was
proved Mar. 17, 1761. He lived and died in Talbot Co.
where he was a carpenter.

He was married twice, first before 1711,† to Mabel Dawson, daughter of Ralph and Mary (O'Mealey) Dawson,
second, before 1729,‡ to Mary ——.

John Loockerman in his will names his nephew Jacob
Loockerman as his executor, and leaves bequests to the
children of his son John.
Issue: first wife.

11. i. JACOB LOOCKERMAN,§ m. 1737 Nov. Mrs. Elizabeth (Harris)
Millington.

Second wife:

12. ii. JOHN LOOCKERMAN, m. Mary Skinner.
13.? iii. THOMAS LOOCKERMAN,¶ d. 1754; m. Sidney (Wynne?)

6. MARY LOOCKERMAN,³ (Jacob,² Govert ¹) was twice married,
first to the Rev. James Hindman (d. 1713; will dated 1713
Aug 10, proved 1713, Nov. 25), Rector of St. Paul's Par-
ish, Queen Anne Co.; second to Francis Allen || of Talbot
Co. Issue: first husband.

* She was married at the date of writing of her brother Jacob's will,
Apr. 8, 1741 but was unmarried at the date of her aunt Elizabeth Holland's
will, Nov. 19, 1738. Joseph Cox Gray was a member of Assembly in 1754,
1755, 1756, 1757, 1762 and 1763, and Justice of Dorchester from 1756 to
1764. He married a second time, before 1756, Mrs. Rosannah (Woolford)
Loockerman, daughter of James Woolford and widow of Jacob Loockerman
his first wife's brother.
** Land Records, Easton.
† Date of deed.
‡ Date of his father's will, in which this wife is referred to.
§ Named in will of his uncle Jacob and his grandfather.
¶ Col. Loockerman, in his will (1729) in naming the children of his son
John, mentions Jacob and another " the youngest son by this wife." So it
appears that there were at least two sons by this second marriage. There
is only indirect evidence that Thomas was one of these.
|| Named in will of her father, 1729.

    i. Jacob Hindman,[4] * d. 1766; m. 1739 Jan 29 Mary Trippe (d. after 1781).

        i. James Hindman, b. 1741 June 20; d. s. p. 1830 Feb. 18.
       ii. William Hindman (M. C.), b. 1743 April 1; d. 1822 Jan. 19 unm.
     iii. Jacob Henderson Hindman (Rev.), d. s. p.
     iv. Edward Hindman, m. Ann ——; d. s. p.
      v. John Hindman (Col.), m. Esther _Kush._ Issue.
     vi. Mary Hindman, drowned aged 12.
    vii. Elizabeth Hindman, m. William Perry.
   viii. Sarah Hindman, d. unm.

Second husband (all that are known):

     ii. Moses Allen.†
    iii. Mary Allen,‡ m. 1759 Apr. Rev. John Rosse, of Snow Hill. Issue.
    iv. William Allen, living in Worcester Co. in 1774.

7. NICHOLAS LOOCKERMAN,[3] (Jacob,[2] Govert [1]) was born Nov. 10, 1697,¶ and moved to Delaware in 1723, buying " The Range " near Dover, where he died in March 1771. His wife, whom he married in 1721, was Sally Emerson, daughter of Vincent Emerson, of " The Grange," near Dover. She died before her husband.

For the years 1745 to 1755 he held the important office of coroner of Kent Co., Delaware.

According to Scharf " History of Delaware," he was married twice, first to Susan Emerson, daughter of Vincent Emerson, second to Esther Shurmer, daughter of Benjamin Shurmer.

Issue:

14. i. VINCENT LOOCKERMAN,[4] b. 1722; d. 1785 Aug. 26, m. (1) 1741 Mar. 1 Mrs. Susannah Beswicks, (2) 1774 Feb. 1 Elizabeth Pryor.
    ii. Richard Loockerman, named in father's will 1765 Oct. 31. Of him nothing is known.

8. THOMAS LOOCKERMAN,[3] (Jacob,[2] Govert [1]) was born after the year 1714 when his namesake and half-brother was

---

* Called " under eight " in will of father, 1713. His own will was proved Nov. 5, 1766; and the inventory of his estate was filed at Easton in May 1767. He was Sheriff of Dorchester from 1737 to 1739; and a delegate to Assembly from 1741-1744.

† Signs the inventory of Jacob Hindman as " next of kin," with Mary Allen and Mary Hindman. A Dr. Moses Allen died near Easton Apr. 20, 1805, aged 71; and Moses Allen was appointed Sheriff of Dorchester in 1761 to complete the unexpired term of Hall Caile, dec.

‡ These names are found in letters of Rev. John Rosse.

¶ The authority for this date is not known by the compiler. His will was written Oct. 31, 1765; a codicil was added Mar. 5, 1771; and both were proved Mar. 15, 1771. He named his son Vincent and his grandson Vincent, Jr., his executors. His tombstone bears the inscription " died Mar. 6, 1769, aged 73."

drowned. His father refers to him in his will (1729) as a minor; and his brother Jacob speaks of him in his will (1731) as being at school. His will was written Sept. 20, 1762 and was proved Mar. 29, 1769.

He was maried twice, first to Vienna ——, as appears from the records of the Old Choptank Parish, second to Mary ——, who survived him. This second wife was not named in his will, but claimed her " third " at the time of probate of his will; so it is possible that they were married between 1762 and 1769.

Issue:

    i. Nancy Loockerman,[4][*] m. Samuel Abbott, Jr.
    ii. Elizabeth Loockerman, bapt. [†] 1745 Mar. 4.
15. iii. THOMAS LOOCKERMAN, bapt. 1747 Feb. 4, m. Frances.
    iv. John Loockerman, mentioned in deed of gift of grandmother, Mrs. Dorothy Loockerman, May 9, 1751,[‡] and also in father's will.
    v. Mary Loockerman, bapt. 1751 Jan. 15.
    vi. Lilley Loockerman, bapt. 1753 May 1.
    vii. Jacob Loockerman, named in father' will; and living in 1770.

9. JACOB LOOCKERMAN,[4] (Govert,[3] Jacob,[2] Govert [1]) was the executor of his uncle Jacob Loockerman (d. 1731), and was named by his brother-in-law, Thomas Haskins, as one of the guardians of his children. His will was written Apr. 8, 1741; and he died soon after. His wife was Rosanna Woolford,[§] daughter of James Woolford.

Issue:

    i. Jacob Loockerman,[5][¶] d. s. p.
    ii. Elizabeth Loockerman, m. —— Wing.

10. MARY LOOCKERMAN,[4] (Govert,[3] Jacob,[2] Govert [1]) is named in the will of her uncle Jacob Loockerman (1731), and calling herself " Mary Haskins formerly Mary Loockerman " she is one of those proving the will of Col. William Holland in Oct. 1732, which she had witnessed as Mary Loockerman in 1724. Her own will was written May 27, 1767 and proved Jan. 20, 1772.

---

  * She was named as her father's executrix, but renounced her rights. She was married between the dates of writing and probate of his will.
  † Records of Old Choptank Parish.
  ‡ Records at Cambridge.
  § She married, second, Joseph Cox Gray, whose first wife was Sarah Loockerman, sister of Jacob.
  ¶ His estate was administered in Mar. 1765. In the accounts filed May 1, 1767, reference is made to his own sister Elizabeth Wing and to his half-brothers and half-sister.

Her aunt, Elizabeth Woolford, who married in succession Col. Thomas Ennalls and Col. William Holland, in her will, written Nov. 19, 1738, makes many references to her.

She was twice married, first in or before 1728, to Thomas Haskins (See Haskins Family); second, before 1738 to Dr. Joseph Ennalls (b. 1709, d. 1756), son of Henry and Mary (Hooper) Ennalls.

Issue: first husband (for details see Haskins Family).

i. William Haskins,⁵ b. 1729; d. 1779; m. Sarah Airey.
ii. Joseph Haskins, b. 1731; d. 1788; m. Sarah Ennalls.
iii. Elizabeth Haskins, b. 1733; d. 1805; m. Hall Caile.

Second husband (order of birth not known):

iv. Thomas Ennalls (Col.), b. ——; d. ——; m. Mary Sulivane, daughter of Daniel and Sarah (Ennalls) Sulivane.
    Issue: Sarah Ennalls, b. ——; d. ——; m. Henry Waggaman (1748-1809). Issue.
v. Henry Ennalls, b. ——; d. ——; m. Peggy Bayard.
vi. Mary Ennalls, b. 1738 Sept.; d. 1803 July; m. 1765 Oct. 17 James Sulivane, b. 1737, Mar. 30; d. ——; son of Daniel and Sarah (Ennalls) Sulivane. Issue:
    i. Daniel Sulivane, b. 1766 July; m. Mary Richardson.
    ii. Joseph Ennalls Sulivane, b. 1769 May; m. Anne E. Hooper.
    iii. Henrietta Sulivane, b. 1766 Jan. 16; m. 1802 Oct. 10 Joseph Haskins.
    iv. Mary Sulivane, b. 1773 Nov.; m. 1794 Apr. J. H. Eccleston.
vii. Margaret Ennalls, b. ——; d. ——; m. 1770 William Murray Maynadier (b. 1747 Apr. 28; d. ——); son of the Rev. Daniel and Mary (Murray) Maynadier. Issue:
    i. William Maynadier b. 1754 Aug. 1; m. (1) 1800 Oct. 18 Sarah Brown, (2) Catherine Brown.
    ii. Henry Maynadier, m.
    iii. Daniel Maynadier, d. unm.
    iv. Margaret Murray Maynadier, d. 1840 Dec. 14; m. 1810 Jan. 4 Daniel Dulany Fitzhugh.
viii. Rebecca Ennalls, d. between 1756 and 1767.
ix. Henrietta Ennalls.

11. JACOB LOOCKERMAN,⁴ (John,³ Jacob,² Govert ¹) is named in the will of his grandfather (1729) and is referred to in 1748 as " the heir of Ralph Dawson." The date of his death is not known; the last reference to him being in 1764 when his brother John appoints him his executor and the guardian of his sons. In Nov. 1737 he married Mrs. Elizabeth (Harris) Millington,* widow of Allemby

* By her first husband she had three children; Elizabeth, Margaret and Sarah. The second of these, Margaret, married the Rev. John Miller and was the mother of Mary Miller (b. 1762 July 26) who married for her first husband Vincent Loockerman, Jr. See *Penn. Mag. of Hist.*, VII, p. 307.

Millington, an English sea-captain who had settled in Talbot Co. (Marr. Contract, Nov. 10, 1737; Easton.)

It is said that he died leaving no children, but the evidence in favor of this statement is not strong. (There was a Jacob Loockerman who in 1773 was married to Betty, the daughter of Theodore Madkin of Dorchester, and who had at that time a son John.)

12. JOHN LOOKERMAN,[4] (John,[3] Jacob,[2] Govert [1]) lived in what is now Caroline Co., but was then included in Queen Anne. His will was written Mar. 9, 1764 and was proved June 10, 1766. In it he makes no mention of his wife and appoints his brother Jacob and two friends his executors and the guardians of his children. These last refused to serve, and his widow, Mary Loockerman, probated the will and chose her " third." She became the second wife * of John Goldsborough of " Four Square," Talbot Co., son of Robert and Elizabeth (Greenberry) Goldsborough; and, according to records in the Goldsborough family, she was Mary Skinner, daughter of Richard Skinner and Katherine Sherwood.

Issue:

16.   i. RICHARD LOOCKERMAN,[5] d. 1792 Oct; m. (1) 1775 Aug. 9 Mary Darden (2) 1779 Nov. 22 Ann Wood.
17.   ii. JACOB LOOCKERMAN, b. 1759 Jan 22; d. 1839 June 17; m. (1) 1784 July 17 Eleanor Clarke, (2) 1802 Oct. 10 Mary Harrison.
    iii. Elizabeth Loockerman, probably died unm., not named in brother Richard's will, 1792.

13. THOMAS LOOCKERMAN,[4] (John,[3] Jacob,[2] Govert [1]) of Dorchester, died before Aug. 29, 1754 the date of administration of his estate by Sidney Loockerman,† who represented Thomas Wynn Loockerman, " minor, son of Thomas."

It is impossible to prove at this time who was his father; but it was probably John Loockerman sen. The latter in his will (1760) gives no evidence as to his decendants except by naming the three children of his son John; but Col. Jacob Loockerman in his will (1729) when naming certain of children of John L. sen. uses the words " the

---

* By this marriage there were two children, Robert and Anna Maria who married Arthur Emory and is called " sister " by Richard Loockerman in his will.

† It is probable that she was his widow and was descended from Thomas Wynn of Pennsylvania. She was living in 1757.

youngest son by this wife," which certainly means that
John sen. had at least two sons by his second wife, Mary
————. One of these may have been Thomas. (It is
not impossible that Thomas was a son of Govert, for we
know the names of the latter's children by indirect means
only; but the recitation in the will of Jacob, Jr. seems
to be complete.)
Issue:

18. i. THOMAS WYNN LOOCKERMAN,⁵ a minor in 1754, d. after the Revolution; m.

14. VINCENT LOOCKERMAN,⁴ (Nicholas,³ Jacob,² Govert ¹),
was born in 1722 and died Aug. 26 1785 " aged 63." He
was married twice; first, on Mar. 1, 1741 to Mrs. Susannah
Beswicks of Talbot Co. (d. 1773 Nov. 7, aged 63), second,
Feb. 1 1774 * to Elizabeth Pryor † (b. 1757 Feb. 20, d.
1827 May 9) daughter of John Pryor of Dover, Delaware.

He was a prominent Whig during the Revolution. In
1776 he was a delegate to Assembly, and in 1784 was State
Senator from Kent Co., Del. His will was written Mar.
9, 1784 and proved Aug. 30, 1785.
Issue: first wife:—

19. i. VINCENT LOOCKERMAN, JR.,⁵ b. 1747 Jan. 7 ;d. 1790 Apr. 5; m.
(1) 1767 May 3 Anne Goldsborough, (2) 1781 Aug. 1 Mary
Knight, (3) 1787 Nov. Mary Miller.
ii. Nicholas Loockerman,‡ d. s. p. between 1765 and 1774 Mar.

Second wife:—

iii. Elizabeth Loockerman, b. 1779 Dec. 23; d. 1842 Apr. 12; m. (1)
1798 ± Joseph Miller. (2) 1805 May 8 Thomas Bradford the
younger of Philadelphia. For issue see Vincent, *History of
Delaware.*
iv. Nicholas Loockerman,§ b. 1783 Nov. 27; d. 1850 Mar. 20, unm.

* He made marriage agreements Aug. 7, and Aug. 31, 1776 with John
Pryor and his daughter who was then a minor.
† She married second Hon. Charles Nixon and had among other children
a daughter Mary Nixon (b. 1788 Dec. 19; d. 1876 Jan.) who married, first,
Jan. 9, 1810 Dr. Robert Goldsborough; second, Nov. 1, 1825 Gardner Bayley.
By this Goldsborough marriage there were three daughters and a son,
Nicholas Loockerman Goldsborough.
‡ Called "little grand-son" in his grandfather's will 1765 Oct. 31.
§ His will was written June 22, 1829; codicils were added Aug. 23, 1830;
June 22, 1842; and all were proved Apr. 1, 1850.

GENEALOGIES OF FOUR FAMILIES OF DORCHESTER COUNTY: HARRISON, HASKINS, CAILE, LOOCKERMAN.

JOSEPH S. AMES.

THE LOOCKERMAN FAMILY OF THE EASTERN SHORE OF MARYLAND.

15. THOMAS LOOCKERMAN,[4] (Thomas,[3] Jacob,[2] Govert [1]) was baptized in the Old Choptank Parish Feb. 4, 1747, and he died in 1808 or before. His wife's name was Frances; and she died in 1812.

His will is quoted, without date, in a legal procedure undertaken in 1814 to decide upon a tract of land left by Thomas to his son Levin who died intestate and without heirs in 1809. The children named below are mentioned.

He was High Sheriff of Dorchester from 1785 to 1791; and he certainly died later than 1796, the date of a deed to his daughter Leah Bayley.

Issue:

   i. William Loockerman,[5] " having offended and disobliged me and all his friends and relations by his impudent conduct, etc."
   ii. Levin Loockerman, d. 1809 without issue.
   iii. Thomas Loockerman (A Thomas Loockerman died in Cambridge Oct. 26, 1826 and a Thomas Loockerman had a wife Margaret in 1812).
   iv. George W. Loockerman.
   v. Josiah Loockerman.
   vi. Sarah Loockerman.
   vii. Susan Loockerman m. Henry Pattison.
   viii. Lilly Loockerman.
   ix. Mary Anne Loockerman.
   x. Leah Loockerman, d. 1805 Feb. 4; m. 1796 Apr. 23 Josiah Bayley. He was a delegate to Assembly in 1803 and 1804; and was appointed Attorney-General of Maryland, July 22, 1831.

16. RICHARD LOOCKERMAN,[5] (John,[4] John,[3] Jacob,[2] Govert [1]) lived and died in Caroline Co. His will was written Oct. 6, 1792 and proved Oct. 29, 1792. According to the county records he was married twice, first, on Aug. 9, 1775 to Mary Darden, second, on Nov. 22, 1779 to Ann Wood.

In his will he mentions only one son, Richard, who was

probably the son of his second wife, because in a legal paper
dated July 3, 1793, he is called "minor under 14."
Issue second wife:—

20. i. RICHARD LOOCKERMAN,[6] d. 1834 Nov. 11; m. 1803 Oct. 11 Frances
Townley Chase.

17. JACOB LOOCKERMAN,[5] (John,[4] John,[3] Jacob,[2] Govert[1])
was born Jan. 22, 1759 and died June 17, 1839. He is
buried in the White Marsh Churchyard, Easton. For
many years he was Clerk of Court of Talbot Co., living at
"Oak Hill," near Easton.

He was twice married, first, on July 17, 1784 to Eleanor
Clarke, daughter of Joshua and Ann Clarke of Caroline
Co., second, on Oct. 10, 1802 to Mary Harrison (b. 1774
May 23, d. 1840 Sept. 14) daughter of Col. Robert Harri-
son and his wife Milcah Gale.
Issue first wife:—

i. John Loockerman,[6] b. 1789 Dec. 9; d. s. p. 1846 Dec. 24.
21. ii. THEODORE RICHARD LOOCKERMAN, b. 1798; d. 1851 May 26; m.
1829 June 8 Maria Martin.

second wife:

iii. Mary Elizabeth Loockerman, b. 1806 Aug. 14; m. 1839 Nov. 19
Thomas A. Emory, of Queen Anne Co., son of Gen. Thomas
Emory. No issue.

18. THOMAS WYNN LOOCKERMAN,[5] (Thomas,[4] John,[3] Jacob,[2]
Govert[1]) of Caroline was a minor child at the time of the
administration of his father, Thomas' estate in Aug. 1754,
and but little is known of him. He was appointed 1st Lieutenant of the Caroline Co. volunteers, at the outbreak of
the Revolution; and on June 24, 1777 he was commissioned
Captain. The name of his wife is not known; but family
records give the names of two children. In Sept. 1801,
Margaret Walker, administratrix, advertises the sale of his
property.
Issue:—

i. Thomas Wynn Loockerman, Jr.;[6] d. 1827 Mar.; m. 1824 Sept.
23 Susan Caroline Applegarth.*
Issue: i. Thomas G. Loockerman of Washington, D. C.
ii. Richard Loockerman.

19. VINCENT LOOCKERMAN,[5] (Vincent,[4] Nicholas,[3] Jacob,[2]
Govert[1]) was born Jan 7, 1747 and died 1790 Apr. 5
"aged 43." He was married three times: first, on May
3, 1767 to Anne Goldsborough (b. 1751 Jan. 2, d. 1781

---

* She married May 8, 1838 Richard Linthicum of Baltimore.

May 15), daughter of John Goldsborough of "Four Square" and his first wife Ann Turbutt; second, on Aug. 1, 1781 to Mary Knight (d. 1787 Feb. 10); third, in Nov. 1787, to Mary Miller * (b. 1762 July 26) daughter of the Rev. John Miller and Margaret Millington.

Issue first wife:

i. Susannah Loockerman,[6]; b. 1777 Apr. 17; m. James Stoops.

Second wife:

ii. Nicholas Loockerman, b. 1782 July 24; d. 1783 July 30.
iii. Sarah E. Loockerman, b. 1784 Sept. 16; m. Hon. Nicholas G. Williamson. Issue.
iv. Vincent Loockerman, b. 1786 Sept. 13; d. 1787 Aug. 16.

Third wife:

v. Elizabeth M. Loockerman, b. 1788 Aug. 7; m. Thomas Davy of Philadelphia. Issue.
vi. Vincent E. Loockerman, b. 1790 Mar. 7. See Vincent: "History of Delaware."

20. RICHARD LOOCKERMAN,[6] (Richard,[5] John,[4] John,[3] Jacob,[2] Govert [1]) was born about 1780 and died Nov. 11, 1834. On Oct. 11, 1803 he married Frances Townley Chase, daughter of Judge Jeremiah Townley Chase of Annapolis.

He lived in Annapolis a large part of the year, his wife having been given by her father the beautiful house on the corner of Maryland Ave. and King George Street, now known as the "Harwood House."

Issue: as given in a legal paper 1848.

i. Jeremiah Townley Loockerman.[7]
ii. Francis T. Loockerman, "probably dead."
iii. Matilda Chase Loockerman, m. 1834 Jan. 23 Lyde Goodwin McBlair.
iv. Catherine Loockerman.

21. THEODORE RICHARD LOOCKERMAN,[6] (Jacob,[5] John,[4] John,[3] Jacob,[2] Govert [1]) was born in 1798 and died on May 26, 1851. On June 8, 1829 he married Maria Martin (d. Feb. 17, 1886) daughter of Hon. William Bond Martin of Dorchester Co. He was one of the leaders of the bar of Easton; he represented for many years his county in the state legislature; and at the time of his death he was President of the Branch Bank at Easton.

Issue:—

i. Theodore Richard Loockerman, Jr., d. Oct. 5 1866; m. 1857 Magdalen Labagh (b. 1840; d. 1881 Aug. 28). She married (2) James E. Tyler of Richmond. Issue:

* She married Jan. 6, 1795 Major John Patten.

    i. Robert Cherbonnier Loockerman, b. 1860 Nov. 19; m. 1883 Feb. 15 Marion Stuart Wooddy of Fredericksburg. Issue.

    ii. Arthur Griswold Loockerman, b. 1862 May; m. 1895 Feb. 11 Naomi Trillish of N. Y. No issue. Others died unm.

  ii. John Loockerman, d. 1853 Sept. Killed by his gardener, who shot him thinking him to be a ghost.

 iii. William Bond Loockerman, d. 1838 Aug. 15.

  iv. Mary Elizabeth Loockerman, b. 1832 July 17; d. 1880 Sept. 1; m. 1851 Sept. 18, John William Cooke Loud (b. 1822 July 28; d. 1864 Sept. 21) of Florida. Issue.

NOTES.

1. **Stanley Byus Loockerman** was the grandson of William Byus. He died before 1846, and after 1810, in which year he was a Justice of Dorchester Co. He was twice married; first, on Dec. 8, 1796 to Sophia Dickinson, daughter of John and Ann (Trippe) Dickinson; second, on Oct. 22, 1799 to Mrs. Elizabeth (Craig) Sparhawk (d. 1846). All indications point to his being a grandson of Thomas Loockerman of Dorchester. (See 8).
   Issue first wife:

    i. Charles Stanley Loockerman, d. in Florida about 1843.
    ii. Thomas.

   Second wife:

 iii. Edward Loockerman, d. in New Orleans about 1867.
  iv. Washington C. Loockerman, b. 1809 Dec. 27; d. 1857 Mar. 21; m. 1842 Sept. 29 Mary C. Waters, dau. of Francis Waters, President of Washington College. Issue:
    i. Francis S. Loockerman.

2. **Edward Loockerman** of Cambridge, married about 1795-1800 Margaret Bayley.
   All their children moved to Florida about 1830.
   Issue:

    i. Charlotte Loockerman, d. 1844; m. Dr. Stuart (or Stewart).
    ii. Elizabeth Loockerman, d. 1834 Nov. 20; m. Edward Loockerman her cousin.
 iii. Henrietta Loockerman, m.
  iv. Thomas Loockerman, d. unm.
   v. Mary Loockerman, b. 1812; d. 1865; m. (1) Edward Chandler (2) Dr. John Bradford Taylor. Issue.
  vi. James Loockerman, d. 1862 unm.

3. **Mary Loockerman**, widow and administrator of John Loockerman, late of Baltimore town and county makes an indenture with Timothy Kirk for property on the west side of Jones' Falls, Apr. 15, 1778.

4. Mary Loockerman, m. June 4, 1780 John Vitrie, St. Paul's Parish, Baltimore.

5. Thomas Harrison Loockerman leases lots 52 and 53 South Lane, Baltimore, 1775.

6. Sophia G. Loockerman, b. Apr. 10, 1842, d. Aug. 15, 1863. St. Michael's, Christ Church.

7. Fannie E. Loockerman Townsend, wife of W. F. Townsend, b. Dec. 10, 1839, d. Sept. 7, 1871. St. Michael's, Christ Church. She was the wife of the Rev. Wilbur Fiske Townsend, a Methodist minister.

8. Mary Loockerman, m. 1880 Apr. 28, Jacob Moore. Talbot Co.

9. William Loockerman of Annapolis, part owner of the packets between that city and Baltimore, was drowned off the Magothy River Feb. 22, 1792 by the upsetting of one of his boats. (Riley's *Ancient City*, p. 225.)

10. Jacob Loockerman deeds to George William Reed of Caroline Co. "Bartlett's Partnership," left him in will of Baker Thompson, 1828.

11. Richard Loockerman, m. 1820 Mar. 13 Rebecca Andrew, Caroline Co.

12. Thomas Loockerman was elected to the House of Delegate from Caroline Co., Nov. 1791. (Can this be Capt. Thomas Wynne Loockerman?) In 1796 Thomas Loockerman, living in Caroline Co. is agent for the sale of property in that county belonging to Jacob Loockerman of "Miles River Ferry."

13. Hill Loockerman, m. 1793 Feb. 17 Lovey Jones. Dorchester Co.

14. Records, St. Paul's Parish, Baltimore.

   Edward Loockerman, m. 1803 Nov. 19 Fanny Carr.
   Cassandra Lockerman, m. 1810 May 12 James Berry.
   Mrs. Lockerman, buried 1812 Nov. 29.

15. Records 1st Presbyterian Church, Baltimore.

   Eliza Lockerman, m. 1832 July 12 Robert Green.

16. Hester Ann Lockerman, m. Wm. Harwood, son of Richard and —— (Callahan) Harwood.

   Warfield: "Founders of A. A. Co., etc." p. 97.

17. Jacob Loockerman, Rev. soldier from North Carolina. Pension Records.

18. There was a family of the name Lakerman, settling at Gravesend before 1656 and later moving to Staten Island. The dominant names are Abraham, Isaac and Peter. This name was variously spelled: Laacerman, Lokerman, Lockerman, etc.; but there is no reason to think that there is any connection between it and the one traced in this paper. See: "The Coursens of Sussex Co., N. J.," p. 20; Records of Richmond, Co., N. Y.

NOTES ON HAUSIL FAMILY.

(Extracts from letter of Brantz Mayer to Rev. Dr. George Diehl, of Frederick, October 17, 1877.

Rev. Bernhardt Michael Hausil, married at Rotterdam, Holland, Sybilla Margaretha Mayer (born at Ulm, Wurtemberg, Aug. 4, 1733), daughter of Christopher Bartholomew Mayer of Ulm (who married Eva Margaretha Scheiflion, Sept. 1, 1724,—born Nov. 24, 1700 in Ulm. Hausil was married 1751-2).

Christopher Bartholomew Mayer and family (Hausil accompanying) arrived at Annapolis, Md., early in 1752, and went, at once to Fredericktown or Monocacy, where the old gentleman died in the early fall or early winter of that year, and was buried in the Lutheran burial ground. From Dr. Diehl's discourse, it appears that Hausil must have been clergyman of the Ev. Lutheran Church in Frederick from 1752 for six years, viz., until 1758 *at least*. How long after I cannot tell, though the eccentric Hartwig did not come on the scene until 1762, four years after. I think that I found a *trace* of Hausil afterwards at *Reading* but, it is, I believe, unquestionable, from what I heard in Nova Scotia, that he finally got to New York, was a *loyalist,* and so earnest in his allegiance to King George that he would not tarry after the peace, but emigrated to Nova Scotia, and was settled for the rest of his life in Halifax. This exodus occurred, I understand, in 1783. If you will be so kind as to communicate with the clergy in New York, who have charge of the Church records of the Lutherans of that period, you may probably find out exactly his trail in America from your city to the British Dominion.

Mrs. Davis is the only survivor of the descendants of Mr. Hausil.

The late Rev. Bernard Hauzeal came to Halifax at the Loyalist immigration in 1783, and officiated in St. George's Church, New Brunswick street, Halifax, now called the Round Church. *He conformed to the Church of England,* and died at Halifax early in this century—about its beginning. He was buried in the old Dutch burial ground in N. Brunswick street. He left two daughters, one, it was said, married a military man, and left this country. The other married a person named Leggett. Those of her descendants whom I knew were old Mrs. Morris, widow of Guy Morris, whose daughter married Garrett Miller, Jr., and was author of the " Wild Flowers of Nova Scotia." Mr. Morris had a son, but who left Halifax and died. Mr. Morris had a younger sister who married Thos. Gouge, of the Engineer Department, and has lately gone to England. No children. Mrs. Miller left a family in Halifax.

Rev. Mr. Hauzeal was a gentleman and scholar, highly esteemed in Halifax where he ministered to the Germans about twenty years. They who require more information may refer to the Parish book of Saint George's, where they will find much relative to Mr. Hauzeal, and perhaps the entries of his daughter's marriage.

SOME UNPUBLISHED HAWLEY-HALLEY DATA

By H. T. Cory

At least five Hawleys played important rôles in the development of the Maryland and Virginia colonies prior to 1650 and some revisions of heretofore accepted data concerning some of them are necessary in the light of facts which have recently come to the writer's hands.

One James Hawley lived in Boston near Brentford, County Middlesex, England, from 1558 to his death in September, 1622. His ancestral line is given in *The Hawley Record*[1] as John 1; William 2; and John 3 of Auler, County Somerset, the latter being the first of the family to settle in that country. He married Dorothy, sister of William Walnot of Shopwick. His second son, Jeremy 4, of Boston near Brentwood, County Middlesex, who died in 1593, had as his wife Rynburgh, daughter of Valentine Saunders, of Sutton Court, County Middlesex, Rynburgh dying in February, 1575. They had several children, one being James 5.

This James 5 was born at Boston 1558 and died there September 1622. His first wife was Susanna, daughter of Richard Tothill of Amersham. She died in 1610. His second wife was Elizabeth Burnell and she died in 1621. By his first wife, he had five sons and three daughters and by his second wife, three sons. At least five of these children came to America.

Probably the oldest son was Jeremy, more usually called Jerome, who was born in 1580. His first wife was a Miss Hawkins by whom he had at least three children: Robert, Gabriel, and Judith. His second wife was Elinor de Courtney, widow of Thomas and mother of Sir William De Courtney,[2] who long survived him and by whom he apparently had no issue. He evidently was a dashing courtier, lived extravagantly, gambled for high stakes, especially later in life, and was a gentleman in waiting at the Court of Henrietta Maria, daughter of Henry IV of France and who in May, 1625, married Charles I of England. Many things indicate that there was a close friendship between him and George Calvert, Lord Baltimore, and probably also with George's brother, Leonard. He took an eighth interest in Calvert's Maryland project and was one of the three commissioners assisting Leonard Calvert in the "Ark" and

---

[1] Elias S. Hawley, *The Hawley Record*. Buffalo, N. Y., E. H. Hutchinson & Co., 1890, p. ix f.

[2] *Archives of Maryland*, Vol. X, p. 444.

" Dove " expedition and first settlement of Maryland in 1633-4; the other two commissioners being Thomas Cornwallis and John Lewger. On January 10, 1636/7, possibly on George Calvert's recommendation, Jerome was appointed by Charles I as treasurer of Virginia, which post he held until his death about July, 1638.

The second of James's sons was Henry who was for many years governor of Barbadoes, dying there June 8, 1679, as did his wife Jane, May 11, 1678. Apparently he also visited Virginia and Maryland.

The third of James's sons was Capt. William who acted as deputy governor of Barbadoes for several months while his brother Henry was away on a leave of absence. He was in Virginia as early as 1644 and was deputy governor of the Carolinas in 1645. For him was surveyed St. Jerome's Manor of 2100 acres in St. Mary's County, Maryland, January 15, 1648. He signed the Protestant Declaration there in 1650 and died in 1654. His will disappeared shortly after his death and its provisions are yet unknown.

The fourth of James's sons was James who is said to have died without posterity in England in 1667. It is generally understood he never came to America but he supplied much financial backing to his brother Jerome's Maryland venture. Whether because of Jerome's high living or events in the Maryland Colony, James probably was never fully repaid his advances or investments as on July 30, 1649, he wrote his brother William, hereinabove mentioned, a letter dated Brentford, Middlesex County, in which he stated that Jerome's estate owed him, James, substantial sums. He asked William to do all possible to collect from Thomas Cornwallis large amounts which James felt had been withheld from Jerome's estate.[3]

The fifth son of James, by his second wife, Valentine, went to the Barbadoes. A daughter, Susanna, also by James's second wife, who married Sir Richard Pier, also went to the Barbadoes. Lastly, another son, but by James's first wife, Gabriel, possibly came to America also. The uncertainty is due to there having been two contemporary Gabriel Hawleys in the immediate clan under consideration.

Sherwood[4] gives the following:

In the Records of the Draper's Company, London . . . 1616, January 22.

> HAWLEY, Gabriel, son of James of Brainford (Brentford), Middlesex, " generosus," apprenticed to

---

[3] E. D. Neill, *The Founders of Maryland,* Albany, N. Y., Munsell, 1876, pp. 82-5. 82-5.

[4] George F. T. Sherwood, *American Colonists in English Records,* London, 1933, 1st Series, p. 23 and 2ᵈ Series, p. 103.

PAVIER, William, for 9 years.
    Free of the Company 6 July, 1636. On 11 July, 1636,
    takes apprentice
BOROUGHES, John. Note in 1636/42 Book: "in Virginia."

In the Public Record Office, London. Delegates Examination. vol. 2.
Baltimore v. Leonards.

A. D.
1635 HAWLEY, Gabriel, of London, Gent., aged 34, has lived there 5
        years; before that in Virginia 10 months; and before that
        in London 5 years or more. (signs)
      BALTIMORE, Lord, his house at the Upper end of Holborn; his
        brother and partner
      LEONARDS, Leonard, loaded into "The Ark" sailing to Maryland in
        Sept. 1633, divers tonnes of beer to the use of Lord
        BALTIMORE. There were three or four joined as partners
        in the said ship and her pinnace "The Dove."
      HALLY, Mr. Jerome, a partner in "The Ark," had an eighth part.
      HALLEY, Gabriel, did bespeak and provide beer and victuals for the
        ship.
      CALVERT, Captain Leonard, partner in the pinnace.
      CORNWALLYS, Mr. Thomas, ditto.
      SANDES or SAUNDERS, Mr. John, ditto.
      BOULTER, John, citizen & skinner of London, of St. Batolph, Ald-
        gate, aged 40; has lived there 3 years, and before that for
        12 years in the East Indies. Was purser and steward of
        the ship for the said voyage under the Lord BALTIMORE."
        (signs)

Incidentally note the three spellings of Hawley-Hally-Halley in
the last quotation.

These two records in connection with the fact that Gabriel Hawley
was surveyor general of Virginia until that post was filled, probably
on the death of the incumbent, by Robert Evelyn in 1637, clearly
show there were two Gabriel Hawleys contemporaneously playing
parts in the Virginia-Maryland colonial ventures.

One of these, a son of James Hawley and his first wife Susannah
Tothill (Tuttle?) was in London as an apprentice of William Pavier
for nine years prior to July 6, 1936. He probably was born about
1609. Another, born in 1601, spent ten months in Virginia from
1629 to 1630, and had a significant part in the *Ark* and *Dove* expedition. Doubtless it was the latter who for some time prior to and until
1637 was surveyor general of Virginia.

The writer has just ascertained the identity of this second Gabriel
from Mrs. J. Stanford Halley of Corsicana, Texas, who for years
has been compiling genealogical data of the Halleys in America.
About 1915 Mrs. Halley learned from Mr. J. M. Halley of Mc-

Gregor, Texas, of a Halley record in the possession of a Mr. Samuel
Halley then living in a suburb of Macon, Georgia. Accordingly she
had Rev. J. G. Moreton, a retired Baptist minister and indefatigable
worker in genealogical matters, visit Macon to copy the said records.

Mr. Samuel Halley, then 77 years old, absolutely refused the suggestion of Mr. Moreton that the record should be placed in some
historical collection for preservation in a fire-proof building. However, permission was gladly given to copy it in full. This Mr.
Moreton did, and most fortunately, as a year later Mr. Samuel
Halley's house burned and with it the record, while a year later the
old gentleman died.

Mrs. J. Stanford Halley, like many other genealogists, has not yet
completed for publication her record of the Halleys in America, and
just now is deeply occupied with civic work. So she has loaned me
for preparation of this paper, the report made to her in 1916 by the
Rev. J. G. Moreton of the aforesaid record.

I quote it in full:

Item 1— . . . Thms Halley . . . Ludburgh . . . 15 . . . to . . .
  (NOTE—I thought this to be a birth record or marriage. The date
  appeared to be 1530 or 1538 or 1550. The first numerals were
  fairly distinct.)

Item 2—Jeromie Hawley . . . life ye 17th (or 19th) day . . . 16 . . .
  (Evidently a death record. Note that one date was 1500, the
  other 1600. The writing is the same so evidently copied for a
  purpose, probably to be used in the book. " departed this " I think
  were the absent words.)

Item 3—Wm and Thms Hawley declaired of . . . protesting faiths . . .
  and signers . . . thereof . . . ye . . . 16 . . .
  (Please note the different spellings of the name.)

Item 4—Thms Haley and clerk Francis Walford Staffordshire with . . .
  cousin Sara Hawley with . . . to the number of twenty souls . . .
  with familys and indentured servants . . . in province of Maryland
  . . . Enterprise . . .
  (NOTE—The word after Sara Hawley looks more like " wife "
  than " with." This appears that Thomas was transporting colonists.
  There is no date, but the name of the boat or ship, might help you.
  Note the spelling of the cousins' names.)

Item 5—J . . . Haley to E. Bunche (or Burche)
  (NOTE—No date to this record. It seems rather abrupt.)

Item 6—Thomas Halley to Elizabeth Burche (or Bunche?) wid w/2 1728
  (or 23) with . . . children
  (NOTE—Underneath this is the name of John Hally and another
  not distinct enough to read. The writing is different—it seems to
  be a marriage record but could have been a transfer of property. If
  the latter, it seems odd that it was on record in this book.)

There were a number of other names without dates. I do not know why they were recorded. The writing was indistinct but we satisfied ourselves that they were correct. It is not unreasonable to suppose that some were births or deaths copied from memory, from a prayer book or Bible. At the end of the book is a notation that the " Holy Evangels " was " consumed in the flames." It does not record when or where. The names are.1 & 2 Jerry and Omy, twins, 3. James Hawley, 4. Jeromy Hally, 5. Gabriel Hally, 6. Clemmie Hally, 7. Jerimy Halley (Jeremy is spelled with an " i " this time), 8. Daniel Holly, 9. John S. Hally, 10. Henry L (or S) Hally, 11. William Hally, 12. William Hally, 13. Edward Hally. (NOTE—Please note that the spelling seemed to take the form Hally and keep it until the last record which follows, then the E is inserted. In regard to the above, I believe that after the burning of the Bible some member of the family tried to write the records from memory. The dates were forgotten but the names remembered. This book seemed to take the place of the records, because the last pages contain the complete record of later families whose Bible are extant. You have those last records. I shall not send them at this time. They include Nathaniel, Dr. Samuel's and Henry S. Halley and Elizabeth, and names of the slaves and births of each.)

Item 7—John Halley to Elizabeth Price wid'r with two children Jan. 31, (?) 177—   England.

　　　(NOTE—I tried to get the place in England—even used a hot iron on it to bring out the ink more clearly but no lettering appeared before the word " England." The date should be 1770. If this is a marriage record, we may presume that other like records are marriage records.)

Item 1 is evidently the record of the marriage of Jeremy Thomas Hawley to Rudburgh or Rynburgh Saunders about 1550, the grandparents of the brothers and sisters hereinbefore mentioned who came to America. Item 6 is plainly the genealogical line of descent for twelve generations.

The point of general historical as distinct from family interest is that the Jerome Hawley, partner of Lord Baltimore in the Maryland Province project, including the *Ark* and the *Dove* had a son Gabriel and grandson Clement.

Evidently this son Gabriel was the second Gabriel mentioned in the English records quoted, the other being the son of James and Susannah Tothill and brother of Commissioner Jerome Hawley. Also, incidentally, it may be noted that Clement Haly who died at Chaptico, St. Mary's Co. in 1695 was Jerome's grandson.

Finally, we conclude that the Gabriel Hawley who was surveyor general of Virginia for some time prior to 1637 was the son and not the brother of Jerome Hawley, the treasurer of Virginia from January 1637 to his death July, 1638, and probably that this son's death antedated that of the father.

THE HOLLYDAY FAMILY.

By HENRY HOLLYDAY.

THE ARMS.

Hollyday (of London). Sa: three close helmets, arg., garnished or., within a bordure engrailed of the second.

Hollyday (of London and of Bromley in Middlesex). Sa: three helmets, arg., garnished or., within a bordure, two and one.

> *Crest:* " A demi lion, rampant, gardant, or, supporting an anchor all proper, or, resting his paws on an anchor."

> *Motto:* Used by Col. Thomas Hollyday and his descendants: "Nulli virtute secundus." Granted Sir Walter Hollydaye, by Edward IV of England, May 4, 1470. Regranted to his great-great grandson, Sir Leonard Hollyday, on September 23, 1605, when Lord Mayor of London.[1]

The history of the Hollyday family is one of the most noted of the Lowland families of Scotland. (Being of the " Scottish Chiefs ".) For centuries prior to the year A. D. 1500, the chiefs were engaged in warfare with their Highland neighbors

---

[1] Liber L-XVI, 339, College of Arms, London E. C., also Memoranda made by Col. James Hollyday of Readbourne, prior to the American Revolution.

and were also at war with the Saxons. This clan or tribe was known as " The Annandale Clan," and its chief, styled " Laird of Covehead," near Dumfries.

SIR THOMAS HOLLYDAY (HALLADAYE or HOLLYDAYE), the earliest of the name, was a great patriot, and owned considerable estates in Annandale. He was succeeded by his son,

SIR THOMAS HOLLYDAY, who married the daughter of Sir Malcolm Wallace (son of the noted Sir William Wallace, Kt.), in the year 1297. His descendant, Robert Hollyday, settled in Northumberland County, England, about the year 1391. Another descendant, Thomas Hollyday, commanded two hundred archers at the battle of Agincourt in France, A. D. 1415; and his grandson Walter Hollyday, settled in Gloucester County, England.

1. SIR WALTER HOLLYDAY was the youngest son of the last " Laird of Covehead," Chieftain of Annandale, and chief of all who bore the name. Having settled at Minchin Hampton, Gloucestershire, England, he acquired vast estates, became prominent, especially during the reign of King Edward IV, who made him a Knight and granted him arms as above described, for valor and bravery, etc., at the battle of Tewkesbury (at the junction of the Severn and Avon Rivers), on May 4th, 1470. He died in the year A. D. 1500, and was succeeded by his son,

2. HENRY HOLLYDAY, of Minchin Hampton, married Miss Payne of " Payne's Court," near Frome, and had four sons, viz:
3.   I. Henry, of Minchin Hampton,
      II. Edward, of Rodboro,' (of whom hereafter).
      III. William, of Stroud, and
      IV. John, of Frome Hall.

3. EDWARD HOLLYDAY (Henry,[2] Walter [1]) of Rodborough, near Gloucester, England, where he lived and built the " Hollyday Mansion " on Dowell Hill. This house was standing in the year 1700 and owned by a descendant, William Hollyday. " The Ancient and Present State of Gloucester," published about that year, says: " Mr. Hollyday has a good home and

estate. Sir Leonard Hollyday, Lord-mayor and Alderman of London, was born here." Edward Hollyday was succeeded by by his son,

4. SIR WILLIAM HOLLYDAY, (Edward[3], Henry[2], Walter[1],) who succeeded to the estates of his father, was a man of great prominence, was knighted, but died young. He married in 1548 Sarah Bridges, aunt of Lord Chandas, and they had issue, as follows:

ISSUE [2]

5.   I.   Sir Leonard Hollyday, of whom hereafter,
      II. Edward Hollyday, married Margaret Townsend,
      III. Henry Hollyday, died young in 1583.

5. SIR LEONARD HOLLYDAY (William[4], Edward[3], Henry[2], Walter[1],) went to London, and made great success. In July, 1594, he was elected Alderman of Portsoken, of Broad Street; of Bassishaw in 1600. On April 18th, 1610, was elected Sheriff of London. He was knighted by King James II on September 23rd, 1605; was made Lord Mayor of London in 1605, and served during the year 1606. In 1605/6 he was President of Bridewell and Bethlem Hospitals, and also a member of the Levant Court.

During his Mayoralty occurred the "Gunpowder Plot," (15, Nov. 1605) for which Sir Edward Digby and three others were executed.

When, during a visit in July, 1606, Christian IV, King of Denmark (brother of the Queen Consort) rode through London, accompanied by the King of England in great style, he was preceded by Sir Leonard Hollyday, the Lord-Mayor, bearing a golden sceptre. His pageant, performed at the cost of his company, was written up by Anthony Munday and entitled " The Triumphs of the Re-united Brittanium.[3]

Sir Leonard married on May 21st, 1578, Anne Wincoll, of St. Edmund, Lombard Street, London, who was the daughter

---

[2] *Burke's General Armoury, Berkes History of the Commoners,* under "Halladay—Berke's Landed Gentry. Holliday or Halladay."

[3] From *Lord Mayors and Sheriffs of London, 1601-1625* (by Cokayne).

of Sir William Wincoll of Langham, County Suffolk, England.
He died on January 9th, 1612, and was buried February 7th,
1612, at St. Michaels, Crooked Lane, London. Funeral certificate in College of Arms, London.[4]

Will Of Sir Leonard Hollydaye:

(From Prerogative Courts of Canterbury. Fenner 4.)

" The following is the Abstract of the Will of Sir Leonard
Hollydaye, Knight, Alderman of London, Dated 5, January,
1612."

" To be buried in the Church of St. Michaels, Bassishaw, in
the vault where my son lies buried."

" I give to my wife Anne, one half of all my goods and 2000
pounds."

" To John Hollydaye, my grandchild, 1000 pounds at 21, on
condition that his mother Alice Hollydaye and his other friends
permit my wife to have the education and bringing up of the
said John."

" To my grandchild Elizabeth Hollydaye, a 1,000 pounds on
like condition."

" To the said Alice, 100 pounds; and I remit her of 50 Lbs.,
which she has already received, and which is in difference
between her and me; and I give her half of all the plate that
was given her and my son John on their marriage. All the
rest of my goods I give to my wife, whom I make my Executrix
and Robert Ducy, Citizen and merchant-tailor, John Burton,
Citizen and Grocer, and my friends Sir James Lancaster and
Sir Henry Lillows of London, Knights, overseers."

By me: Leonard Hollydaye

Witnesses:

James Lancaster,	Ric. Wheeler,
Ro. Ducie,	John Burton,
Jno. Howard,	Jo. Dowse.

----

[4] Liber L-XVI, 339, Heraldic Office, London, E. C. See " Berkes Landed
Gentry."

As to the descendants of Sir Leonard Hollyday, the following is from the College of Arms, London:

"HOLLYDAYE, HOLLIDAY, HALLIDAY

Arms: Granted 23 Sept, 1605 by Clarenclure, King of Arms (Camden)
Sa. three helmets, arg. garnished or. within a bordure engrailed of the second.

Sir Leonard Holliday (Halliday or Hollyday) Lord Mayor of London 1605/6-M, 21, May, 1578, (Lic. Lond) d. 9 " Jan, 1611/12) & was buried 7 " Feb, 1611/12 at St.Michaels, Crooked Lane, Funeral Cert. Coll of Arms (L XVL, 339) Will dated 5th & Probated granted 11 " Jan. 1611/12 & again 18 " March 1615/16 (4 Fenner).

Anne, dau. of William Wincoll of Langham, Co. Suff., by dau of —— Vaughan.

Sir Edward Montagu, Recorder of London (1603-15) afterwards Earl of Manchester. 2nd Husband, 2nd wife.

John Hollyday or Holliday only son b. 1580 M. Nov. 27, 1607 (lon. Lic) d. 1609/10, buried at St.Michaels, Crooked Lane.

Alice or Anne, dau. of William Ferrers, mercer of All Hallows, Lombard Street & St. Leonard's, Bromley, Middlesex.

John Holliday (1½ yrs old in 1611) of Bromley, Co. Middlesex. Ped recorded in the Visitation of London, 1664.

Mary, dau. of Henry Rolt, of Davent Co. Kent

Elizabeth—Sir John Jacob, (3 yrs old) bart. 1st wife. (in 1611.)

John Holliday, only son living aged 23, 1664

Elizabeth, only dau. age 2-1664.

(Signed) JOHN HOLLYDAY.

HOLLYDAYS IN EARLY VIRGINIA.

The question who Colonel Thomas Hollyday, the founder of the Maryland family, was and where he came from leads us to survey the Hollydays of Virginia, whence he would be most likely to come. This is what we find:

Thomas Hollyday appears in James City County, Va., in

1651.[5] In 1656 he acquired 350 acres of land on James River, near Jamestown Island, in James City County, Va., said tract being called " Darcy Oatly," originally patented to a certain Samuel Matthews. In 1661 a Patent was granted for the same tract to Thomas Hollyday by Coll. Fra. Moryson, Esq., Governor. Thomas Hollyday signs his name on the Original Record " Thomas Hollyday." (note the spelling).[6]

There was a will at Williamsburg, dated 1660/1, in which the testator, viz: Thomas Hollyday, mentions a son Thomas Hollyday, but as the records were burned during the War between the States, this cannot be verified.[7]

In Hayden's *History of Virginia* it is stated that " Thomas Hollyday who went to Maryland, was the son of Thomas Hollyday of Va. 1660." This was furnished by a Mr. Holliday, of Portsmouth, Va. This statement is also verified in a letter from his daughter (Miss Holliday) to a Mrs. Bernis Brien, of Dayton, Ohio (descendant of the Virginia Holliday family). This, Mrs. Brien wrote the author under date of Sept. 5th, 1925.

George Billingsley, who owned Billingsley Point in Prince George's County, Maryland, was from James City County, Va. Also was Barnaby Kearne, afterwards of Maryland. In the will of George Billingsley (Upper Norfolk, Va.) dated Dec. 21, 1681, he devises to " Barnaby Kearne and hrs. 200 A. residue of Billingsleys Point.[8] William Mills, of James City Co., Va., also owned at one time Darcy Oatly, tract. He came to Maryland.

Of the Early Settlers, who came into Maryland, were:

1. April 16th, 1677, John Holliday was brought in to St. Mary's County, by Richard Taylor.[9]

---

[5] *Early Settlers.*

[6] See Patent Book No. 5, Original, page 168, Land Office at Richmond, Va.

[7] Letter from Miss Hattie Gilliam to author, April 26, 1907.

[8] Liber 4, 118, Md. Wills.

[9] Book No. 15, fol. 401.

This may have been the brother of Col. Thomas Hollyday, 1st. of Maryland.

2. January 27, 1675, Thomas Kempe, of Calvert County, brought into the Providence Henry Hollyday and Margery Kemp.[10]

3. Robert Hollyday, came in December, 1665.[11]

4. William Hollyday, wife, four children, and servants, came into the Province, in 1681. Col. Hollyday, had brothers " William and Robert." [12]

A Silver waiter, now in possession of author, said by Tiffany of New York, to be genuine, and entered about the year 1697, which waiter has been owned continuously and in the possession of the descendants of Col. Thomas Hollyday, shows the Arms, being the same as granted Sir. Leonard Hollyday, in 1605.

The Tombstone of Col. Thomas Hollyday, who died in 1703, and was buried at Billingsley's Point, bore a Coat of Arms, as did also that of his son Col. Leonard Hollyday, who died in 1742 and was buried near Nottingham in Prince George's County, Md. Col. James Hollyday, of Readbourne (of whom hereafter), died in 1747, and his Tombstone, recently removed from Readbourne to the Cemetery at Easton, Maryland, is in a perfect state of preservation, with inscription and the Hollyday Arms, the same as grant—the Lord-Mayor, Sir Leonard. Letters from James Hollyday (his son) to William Anderson, Merchant of London, in 1750 and again in 1751, in reference to procuring of said Tombstone in possession of the author, gives instruction as to engraving " His Arms " thereon, etc.

Family tradition has been that Col. Thomas Hollyday, the founder of the family in Maryland, was the son of Capt. Thos. Hollyday, of Virginia, and a descendant of Sir Leonard Hollyday, the Lord-Mayor of London, 1605. The naming of his son " Leonard " and only daughter " Margery ", strongly supports

[10] No. 15, folio 332.
[11] No. 9, folio 55.
[12] See Vol. XXV, page 6, *Md. Arch.*, and Will of Col. Hollyday, Vol. 3, page 1, *Md. Calendar of Wills.*

the above. Dr. Christopher Johnston, one of the most distin-
guished of American genealogists, and George Norbury
Mackenzie, editor of " Colonial Families of the United States,"
had the same view. In a letter under date of Sept. 2, 1913, Dr.
Johnston wrote the author. " These arms were borne by the
Hollydays of Wiltshire & Somersetshire, but *especially* by the
Hollydays of Rodborough, Co. Gloucester, to which branch Sir.
Leonard Hollyday, Lord-Mayor of London in 1605, belonged.
From the occurrence of the name " Leonard ", I should judge
that the family in Maryland considered themselves rather
closely related to Sir Leonard Hollyday."

Many new facts have been discovered but none that contradict
this assumption of descent from Sir. Leonard. To sum up the
final conclusions which this author has drawn from all the
data here presented, it is the author's opinion that Colonel
Thomas Hollyday, who came to Maryland in 1679 and bought
Billingsleys Point in 1684, was the son of Captain Thomas
Hollyday, of James City County, Va., and the later was the
son of John Hollyday and Mary Roult, of Bromley Kent,
England, who was the only grand-son of Sir Leonard Hollyday,
Lord-Mayor of London in 1605/6.

COL. THOMAS HOLLYDAY, son of Capt. Thomas Hollyday
of Virginia, settled in Calvert County, Maryland, in the year
1679/80, when he brought into the Province eighteen persons,
among whom was *John Rolt* or *Roult* for which he received
certain grants. In 1682, he was granted a Patent for a tract
of land on the West side of the Patuxent River called " Upper
Guitting ".[13]

On August 8, 1687, he purchased from the heirs of George
Billingsley (late of the Colony of Virginia), " Billingsleys
Point " lying in the fork of the Patuxent (then Calvert) in
Prince George's County, containing 1069 acres, which was con-
firmed in his son Col. James Hollyday by Act of Assembly
1724.[14] On this point he built the first Hollyday Mansion, still

[13] See Land Grants N. S. Folio 11, Land Office at Annapolis.
[14] *Md. Arch.*, Vol. XXXVIII, page 339.

standing in 1930. The front of the grounds around the house slopes down in several terraces. The stairways at "Readbourne" and "Ratcliffe Manor" resemble in many respects.

The house, at the time of its being built about the year 1690, was evidently one of art and the place in general of great beauty and dignity.

Col. Hollyday, married (the exact date is not certain) about the year 1690, Mary Trueman, who was related to many of the Southern Maryland Families. She was the daughter of Dr. Trueman (then deceased) and Anne, his wife, formerly Anne Storer of England. Dr. Trueman died in October 1672, and in his will dated July 29th, 1672, he mentions his wife Anne, and his three daughters Martha (afterwards the wife of Thomas Greenfield), Mary (afterwards Mary Hollyday, wife of Colonel Thomas Hollyday) and Elizabeth (afterwards the wife of —— Green, of Lynn, England). He does not mention a son, but brothers Nathaniel and Thomas Trueman.[15]

Mrs. Anne (Storer) Trueman, afterwards married Robert Skinner, whom she also survived, and by her will, she devised certain estate and property to daughter Greenfield and daughter Elizabeth Green (her daughter Mary Hollyday, being deceased), and each grandchild, 4.[16] A grand daughter, —— Green, married Sir William Brown, an eminent surgeon of "Queen's Square", London, who kept up quite a correspondence with his cousin Colonel James Hollyday (grandson of Colonel Thomas Hollyday) during the years 1750-67. Colonel Thomas Hollyday at once came into prominence, was influential and through relatives, closely identified with the Calverts, received numerous appointments. In 1690, he was commissioned by the Lord Proprietary, as a judge of the Calvert County Court and Captain of the Calvert Militia.[17]

When Prince George's County was formed in 1694, he was made, on March 3, 1694, Chief Judge of the County Court and Lieutenant Colonel. He was also one of the first Vestrymen of

---

[15] See Liber I, folio 509, Will Records at Annapolis.
[16] See Vol. IV, page 14, *Md. Calendar of Wills.*
[17] See Vol. XX, folio 78, *Md. Arch.*

Saint Paul's Parish, at Upper Mount Calvert, 1692-1703. The Court minutes at Upper Marlboro, show that he sat as Presiding Judge of the Court from 1695 to 1703 (the year of his death) with great regularity.[18]

Colonel Hollyday was on more than one occasion called into the Military service of the Province, both while Captain of Calvert County and later as Lieutenant Colonel of Prince George's County. And it is not improbable that he had seen military service and training in Virginia as a young man. " Colonel Washington of Virginia and Captain Thomas Trueman of Calvert County, Maryland, had orders to join their forces with those of Colonel Thomas Hollyday, of Prince George's County, Maryland, to pursue Indian Marauders, in the year 1697." [19]

Mrs. Mary (Trueman) Hollyday, died before her husband, and it is believed she died on the birth of her only daughter, Margery in 1699. Colonel Hollyday died in January, 1703, and was buried in the family cemetery at " Billingsley's Point ".

ISSUE:

  I. Colonel James Hollyday, born June 18, 1696 in England, of whom hereafter.
 II. Colonel Leonard Hollyday, born May 4, 1698, and
III. Margery Hollyday, born —————, 1699.

James was named for his maternal grandfather James Trueman; Leonard for his paternal great-great-great grandfather Sir Leonard Hollyday, and Margery for Margery Kempe or possibly Margery Hollyday who died in England in 1682 and buried in Christ Church, Newgate Street, London.

Col. James Hollyday, eldest son of Col. Thomas and Mary Trueman Hollyday, was born in England on June 18, 1696, was educated at the Middle Temple, London, and was a lawyer. He settled in Talbot County in the year 1721, and on May 3rd, 1721, married Sarah (Covington) Lloyd, widow of Major Gen'l. Edward Lloyd, Governor of Maryland 1709-13, of " Wye House ", where he resided until about the year 1731, on com-

---

[18] See Council Book H. D. No. 2, folio 286, Volume XX, 79, 108, and 212, of the *Md. Arch.* Also Minutes of the Prerogative Court at Annapolis.

[19] Volume II, *Md. Arch.*, Proceedings of the Assembly, 475-483.

pletion of the "Readbourne" Mansion House he removed to Queen Anne's County to this beautiful home on the Chester River. The Readbourne estate contained over 2000 acres of land, acquired by various Patents from the heirs of George Read and others. He inherited a large estate in Prince George's County, by his father's will; and upon his marriage with Mrs. Lloyd, was in control of large tracts of land, consisting over 20,000 acres in Talbot County. In 1724 he purchased "Readbourne" in Queen Anne's County. He at once became prominent in State affairs, being Private Attorney to Lord Baltimore. He was elected a Member of the House of Burgesses from Talbot County in 1728.[20] Served until 1732. Appointed Judge of Talbot County Court and one of the Quorum. Commission dated Feb. 26, 1726, and served until 1731.[21] Appointed Justice of the Provincial Court of Maryland, 1732 and served until 1735, when he was nominated Colonel of Militia and Justice of Queen Anne's County Court. Named a member of Lord Baltimore's Council on July 15, 1735, and served until his death in 1747.[22]

In Volumes XX and XXI of the *Maryland Archives*, " Proceedings of the Assembly, Col. Hollyday's name appears on most of the Important Committees of the Upper House, i. e. " Committee to prepare Acts of Assembly "—" To examine Accounts ", etc. The record also shows that he was a most regular attendant upon the meetings of the Council. He died on the 8th day of October, A. D. 1747. The *Annapolis Gazette* of October 14th 1747, gives the following account of his death:

"Last Thursday morning (8, Oct., 1747) died in Queen Anne's County, after a long and lingering indisposition, which he bore with great patience and resignation, The Honorable James Hollyday, Naval Officer of the Port of Oxford, Treasurer of the Eastern Shore, and one of his Lordships Honorable Council. He left the character of a worthy Gentleman and good christian."

[20] Land Commission Record of Talbot County, 1728-30.
[21] See Judgment Records of Talbot County, 1726-27, folio 3, etc.
[22] See *Upper House Journals* and *Archives of Maryland*.

On his Tombstone which has been recently removed from "Readbourne" to the Hollyday lot in Spring Hill Cemetary at Easton, Maryland, is the following inscription, surmounted by the family arms:

TO THE MEMORY OF

JAMES HOLLYDAY, ESQUIRE,

Who departed this life on the 8th day of October, 1747. He was many years one of His Lordships Council, and in Public and private life, always supported the Character of a worthy Gentlemen and good Christian.

ISSUE:

I. Col. James Hollyday, born Nov. 30, 1722, d. s. p.[23]

II. Henry Hollyday, born March 9, 1725, m. Dec. 9, 1749, Anna Maria Robins, built "Ratcliffe Manor" and from this marriage the Hollydays of Maryland descend.

III. Sarah Covington Hollyday, born in 1727, died an infant, 2 years.

Mrs. Hollyday,[24] was a very beautiful woman, and dearly beloved by both her Lloyd and Hollyday children, and survived both husbands. While on a visit to her only daughter Mrs. Rebecca Harriett Anderson, wife of William Anderson, Merchant of London, in 1754-55, she died on the 9th day of April, 1755, and was buried in West Ham Churchyard, in the County of Essex, England, and tombstone bears the following inscription:

"Beneath this Stone lieth buried the body of Mrs. Sarah Hollyday, late of the Province of Maryland, in America, from whence she came to London in the year 1754, and died the Ninth day of April, MDCCLV. Though a stranger here, she was known, esteemed and respected in her native Country. She had been the wife of Edward Lloyd, formerly of the aforesaid Province, Esquire, and after his death of James Hollyday, late of same place, Gent, whom she also survived."

[23] Studied law at Middle Temple. I have Portrait of this eminent lawyer in his Temple Robes. Member, Council of Safety 1774-76.

[24] I have a Portrait of this lady over 200 years old.

HENRY HOLLYDAY (son of Col. James Hollyday) and Anna Maria Robins Hollyday (dau. of Geo. Robins of Peach Blossom, whose wife was Henrietta Maria Tilghman of the Hermitage), had two sons, viz:

    I. James Hollyday, who married Susan Steuart Tilghman, and
    II. Henry Hollyday, who married Ann Carmichael.

For descendants of above sons, see " Old Kent ", " The Chamberlaine Family " (by John Bozman Kerr) and " Colonial Families of the United States ", by Mackenzie, Vol. II, pages 333-342; in the latter a full account is published.

HUNGERFORD FAMILY.

CHRISTOPHER JOHNSTON.

1. WILLIAM HUNGERFORD [1] came to Maryland in 1646 and settled in Charles County. 7 April 1648, William White demands 100 acres of land for transporting himself in 1646, 100 more for William Hungerford, and 100 more for John Ward for transporting themselves in the same year, and receives a warrant for 300 acres on the south side of Hierom's Creek, "commonly known as Poplar Neck " &c. (Land Office, Lib. ABH, fol. 6). 30 May 1648, William Hungerford demands 100 acres for transporting himself in 1647, and receives a warrant for that amount of land to be laid out on Wiccocomico River (Land Office, Lib. ABH, vol. 14). It is probable that William Hungerford had removed to Virginia, and returned to Maryland in 1647, therefore making a new entry of rights. Such cases were of

frequent occurrence. 2 January 1646/7, William Hunger-
ford was among those who swore fealty to the Proprietary
(*Md. Archives*, iii, 174), and 1 May 1647 he gave his note
to James Lindsay for 300 lbs. of tobacco (*ibid.*, iv, 312).
He seems to have been a soldier, for 29 Feb. 1647/8,
William Hungerford and others petitioned "for themselves
and severall soldiers" against the estate of Mrs. Margaret
Brent "for their wages" (*ibid.*, i, 226). 3 Oct. 1648,
William Hungerford was one of a special jury in the case of
Cuthbert Fenwick vs. Mrs. Margaret Brent his Lordship's
attorney (*Md. Archives*, iv, 413), and 5 Dec. 1648 he was
a member of the Provincial Grand Jury (*ibid.*, 447). 15
March 1649, he again appears as member of a trial jury
(*ibid.*, 481), and 3 June 1650 he entered his mark for cattle
and hogs as required by law (*ibid.*, x, 13). 19 Oct. 1650,
he witnesses a bill of sale of a cow by William Evans to
Thomas Thomas (*ibid.*, 190). He died before 1662 as shown
by the following extract: 1 Oct. 1662, "William Barton
Junior delivereth up this ensuing Patent of land and
Assigneth all his Right title and interest of and to the same
unto his brother-in-law Thomas Smoote for the use of
William Hungerford Junior son to William Hungerford
deceased." Subjoined is a patent, dated 20 March 1658, to
William Smoot for 240 acres in Charles County, and
assigned by said William Smoot to William Barton Jr.,
(Charles Co., Lib. A, fol. 243). William Hungerford was
father of

2.   i.   WILLIAM HUNGERFORD,[2] d. 1704.

2.   WILLIAM HUNGERFORD[2] of Charles County, son of William
Hungerford[1] the immigrant, died in 1704. His will, dated
22 January 1704, was proved 14 March following. He
appears to have been a minor in 1662 (see above), and 22
Dec. 1687 a tract of 28 acres called Hungerford's Choice
was surveyed for him (Charles Co. Rent Roll). He married
Margaret daughter of Capt. William Barton of Charles
County, probably about 1686 as their eldest son Barton
Hungerford was born in 1687. In consideration of this
marriage Capt. William Barton deeded, 13 June 1688, to
his son-in-law William Hungerford and his daughter Margaret wife of the latter, two tracts, called Barton's Woodyard
or Capell, aggregating 200 acres. Mrs. Margaret (Barton)
Hungerford married secondly Jacob Miller of Charles

County who died in 1720, but seems to have had no issue by him. She was living in 1733 when she executed a deed of gift to her son Barton. William Hungerford and Margaret (Barton) his wife had issue :—

3.   i.   BARTON HUNGERFORD,[3] b. 1687 ; d. 25 Jan'y 1758.
    ii. WILLIAM HUNGERFORD, b. 12 June 1694 ; living 1756, when he deeds land in Charles County.
    iii. THOMAS HUNGERFORD, d. 1724 ; mar. Mary .... (who mar. secondly Wm. Goodrick) but seems to have had no issue.
    iv. JOHN HUNGERFORD.
    v. CHARLES HUNGERFORD, living 1728.
    vi. ANNE HUNGERFORD, mar. Thomas Lucas of Pr. Geo. Co.
    vii. ELIZABETH HUNGERFORD, b. 14 Feb. 1691 ; mar. John Neale.
    viii. MARY HUNGERFORD.

3. BARTON HUNGERFORD[3] of Charles County, son of William[2] and Margaret, was born in 1687. His age is given in depositions as 44 years in 1731 (Charles Co., Lib. 36, fol. 516); 51 in 1737 (ibid., Lib. 38, fol. 430); 55 in 1742 (ibid., Lib. 39, fol. 425); and 56 in 1742 (ibid., Lib. 39, fol. 464). He died 25 January 1758 leaving a nuncupative will proved the following day by the oaths of witnesses who testify that " last night a little before he died " he made certain dispositions. He married Elizabeth daughter of John and Ann Gwinn of Charles County. She is mentioned in her mother's will and joined her husband in deeds in 1729 and 1743, but evidently died before him. Barton Hungerford executed deeds, in his life time, to his sons Thomas, Charles, and William, and to his daughter Elizabeth, and the names of his other children are derived from the probate records.
Barton Hungerford and Elizabeth (Gwinn) his wife had issue :—

4.   i.   THOMAS HUNGERFORD,[4] d. 4 April 1772.
5.   ii. BARTON HUNGERFORD, d. 1765.
    iii. WILLIAM HUNGERFORD, d. 1761.
    iv. CHARLES HUNGERFORD, living 1764.
    v. JOHN HUNGERFORD, d. 1766.
    vi. ELIZABETH HUNGERFORD, d. unmarried 1764.
    vii. JANE HUNGERFORD, mar. William Vincent.

4. THOMAS HUNGERFORD,[4] son of Barton[3] and Elizabeth, died 4 April 1772 (Family Bible). In 1753 he was living on a tract called Bachelor's Delight in Charles County, Maryland, and in that year had a deed for this land from his father, but prior to 1764 he removed to King George Co.,

Virginia. This is shown by deeds in 1764 and 1765 wherein he disposes of his Charles County lands, styling himself "Thomas Hungerford of King George County, Virginia, Gent." He was High Sheriff of Charles County from 8 Oct. 1746 to 22 Oct. 1748 (Commission Book). He died, according to family record, in Westmoreland Co., Va., where his descendants continued to reside. Thomas Hungerford married in 1738, Ann daughter of John Pratt of Westmoreland Co., Va., and Margaret Birkett his wife. She was born 26 Oct. 1718, and died 8 May 1800.

Thomas Hungerford and Ann (Pratt) his wife, had issue :—

6. i. LIEUT. THOMAS HUNGERFORD,[5] d. May 1803.
 ii. GEN. JOHN PRATT HUNGERFORD, b. 1760 ; d. 21 Dec. 1833.

5. BARTON HUNGERFORD[4] of Charles County, son of Barton[3] and Elizabeth, died in 1765. He married Jane sister of Barton Warren, and in his will appoints his wife and his brother-in-law his executors. Mrs. Jane Hungerford died in 1795.

Barton Hungerford and Jane (Warren) his wife had issue :—

7. i. THOMAS HUNGERFORD,[5] d. 1799.
 ii. MARY HUNGERFORD, mar. .... Thomas.
 iii. JANE HUNGERFORD.
 iv. SUSANNA HUNGERFORD, d. unmarried, Dec. 1796.
 v. ELIZABETH HUNGERFORD, mar. 8 June 1779, Philip Jenkins.
 vi. SARAH HUNGERFORD, mar. William Vincent.

6. LIEUT. THOMAS HUNGERFORD,[5] son of Thomas[4] and Ann, was an officer in the Continental Line in the Revolution, and died, according to family record in May 1803. He was commissioned, 15 Jan'y 1777, Second Lieut. in the 3rd Virginia Regiment, and served until 14 Sept. 1778 (Heitman's Register). He married Anne Washington, sister of Dr. William Washington (b. 1779 ; d. 1853) of Alexandria, Va. Lieut. Thomas Hungerford and Anne (Washington) his wife had issue :—

8. i. THOMAS HUNGERFORD.[6]
9. ii. COL. JOHN WASHINGTON HUNGERFORD.
10. iii. HENRY HUNGERFORD.
 iv. WILLIAM HUNGERFORD, U. S. N. ; b. 1795 ; d. June 1814 ; buried in St. Paul's Churchyard, Norfolk, Va.

7. THOMAS HUNGERFORD[5] of Charles County, son of Barton[4] and Jane, died in 1799 intestate and his estate was adminis-

tered by his widow Violetta. He married, 17 Nov. 1778, Violetta Gwinn of Charles County and had issue :—

11. i. JOHN B. HUNGERFORD,[6] d. 1822.
    ii. ELEANOR ANN HUNGERFORD, mar. her cousin Col. John Washington Hungerford of Westmoreland Co., Va.

8. THOMAS HUNGERFORD,[6] son of Lieut. Thomas[5] and Anne, married Helen Stith and had issue :—

    i. WM. HENRY HUNGERFORD, has descendants in Alabama.
    ii. JOHN H. HUNGERFORD, U. S. N., lost at sea.
    iii. ROSALIE HUNGERFORD.
    iv. HELEN HUNGERFORD.

9. COL. JOHN WASHINGTON HUNGERFORD,[6] son of Lieut. Thomas,[5] married his cousin Eleanor Ann Hungerford daughter of Thomas and Violetta. They had issue :—

    i. THOS. JEFFERSON HUNGERFORD, d. unmarried 24 Dec. 1843.
    ii. VIRGINIA HUNGERFORD, d. 1879 ; mar. Rev. D. M. Wharton.
    iii. LETITIA GWINN HUNGERFORD.
    iv. JOHN WASHINGTON HUNGERFORD, killed in battle 1863.
    v. ELEANOR ANN HUNGERFORD, mar. Dr. F. D. Wheelwright.
    vi. JULIA R. HUNGERFORD, mar. Colville Griffith.

10. HENRY HUNGERFORD,[6] son of Lieut. Thomas[5] and Anne, married Amelia Spence and had issue :—

    i. WILLIAM HUNGERFORD, d. an infant.
    ii. CATHERINE HUNGERFORD.
    iii. AMELIA HUNGERFORD.
    iv. HENRY HUNGERFORD.
    v. HENRIETTA VIRGINIA HUNGERFORD, mar. W. H. Minnix.
    vi. PHILIP CONTEE HUNGERFORD, mar. Amelia F. Spence.
    vii. AMANDA F. HUNGERFORD, mar. Col. J. Warren Hutt.

11. JOHN B. HUNGERFORD[6] of Charles County, son of Thomas[5] and Violetta, died in 1822 intestate and his estate was administered by his widow Juliet. Her will was proved in Charles County in 1837, and in it she appointed her brother-in-law Col. John Washington Hungerford her executor and trustee for her children.
John B. Hungerford and Juliet his wife had issue :—

    i. VIOLETTA G. HUNGERFORD, mar. .... Turner.
    ii. GERARD WOOD HUNGERFORD.
    iii. WINIFRED HUNGERFORD.

HYNSON AND SMITH FAMILIES

CHRISTOPHER JOHNSTON

1. THOMAS HYNSON was born in 1620. In two depositions both made in 1655, he gives his age as 35 years (*Old Kent*, pp. 108, 211). He arrived in Maryland in the year 1651, bringing his family with him. 23 June 1651 he demands 800 acres of land for transplanting in the Province himself, his wife, John, Grace, and Ann Hynson his children, and three servants " this present year. A warrant issued accordingly to lay out for him 600 acres on the Eastern Shore opposite Love Point " (Land Office, Lib. A B H, fol. 164). In this entry the name of his wife is not given, but 21 December 1662, he made a further claim for the transportation of " his wife Grace in 1651," and a number of other persons whose rights he had probably acquired by purchase (*ibid.*, Lib. 5, fol. 488). Thomas Hynson was clerk of Kent County 1652-53 (*Old Kent,* pp. 22, 69, *Md. Arch.,* x, 291), was one of the Justices of the County 1652, 1654, 1656 (*Old Kent,* pp. 28, 78, 214) and was High Sheriff 1655-56 (*ibid.,* pp. 107, 108, 202, 212). He was a member of the General Assembly of Maryland in 1654 (*Md. Arch.,* I, 339) and represented Kent County in the House of Burgesses in 1659-60 (*ibid.,* I, 382). He died in the year 1667, intestate. 20 January 1667, administration on the estate of Thomas Hynson late of Talbot County deceased was

committed to his sons Thomas and John Hynson (*Testamentary Proc.*, Lib. 2, fol. 289). He is here styled "of Talbot County" since that county, erected in 1661 at the expense of Kent County, included the lands he had acquired and upon which he resided.

Thomas Hynson and Grace his wife had issue:

1. THOMAS HYNSON of Talbot County, d. 1679; m. 1663 Ann Gaine who m. secondly in 1680 Robert Smith of Talbot County.
2. ii. Col. JOHN HYNSON of Kent County, d. 1705; of whom further.
   iii. Charles Hynson of Kent Co., d. 1711; m. Margaret dau. of Wm. Harris Esq.
   iv. Grace Hynson, m. Thomas South of Talbot Co.
   v. Ann Hynson m. 1° Maj. Joseph Wickes, 2° Col. St. Leger Codd.

2. COL. JOHN HYNSON of Kent Co., son of Thomas, came to Maryland with his parents in 1651 at which time he was doubtless under age. In addition to the evidence of his parentage given elsewhere, the two following deeds may be cited: 20 June 1665, Mr Thomas Hynson Senr conveys to John Singleton and Richard Jones 200 acres part of a grant of 400 acres whereof 200 acres were formerly given by the said Thomas Hynson to his two sons Thomas and John Hynson (*Talbot Co.*, Lib. A, No. 1, fol. 5). 21 June 1670 John Hynson of Chester River, Talbot County, conveys to his brother Thomas Hynson of the same county, tracts called Hynson Town Creek, and Next Addition (*ibid.*, fol. 109). Subsequently John Hynson was identified with Kent County, and took a prominent part in public affairs. He was commissioned one of the Justices of Kent Co. 2 July 1674 (*Md. Arch.*, xv, 42) and was successively commissioned until 1689 (*ibid.*, xv, 67, 93, 136, 328; xvii, 379; viii, 23; xiii, 241). He was commissioned one of the Quorum 10 April 1688 (*ibid.*, viii, 23) and again 4 September 1689 under the provisional government (*ibid.*, xiii, 241). He was also commissioned Justice of the County 16 October 1694 (*ibid.*, xx, 138), was of the Quorum in 1696 (*ibid.*, xx, 466), and attests a document as Justice in 1701 (*Kent Co. Rec.*, Lib. N, fol. 14). He was High Sheriff of Kent County in 1683 (*Lib.* C D, fol. 369). He represented Kent Co. in the House of Burgesses 1681-1683 (*Md. Arch.*, vii, 166, 288, 299), 1694-1697 (*ibid.*, xix, 30, 127, 242, 350, 376, 555) and 1701-1702 (*Ms. House Journals*). He also served in a military

capacity. 28 February 1681 he was commissioned Lieutenant in the Kent County Militia (*Md. Arch.*, xvii, 78)
and was commissioned Captain 4 Sept. 1689 (*ibid.*, xviii,
241) and Colonel 9 October 1694 (*ibid.*, xx, 152). In the
rearrangement of the militia of the province, 17 August
1695, he was continued as Colonel Commanding the military forces of Kent County (*ibid.*, xx, 281). Although he
held both a civil and military commission in the provisional
government, he signed the address of the Protestant inhabitants of Kent in 1689 (*Md. Arch.*, viii, 129) and the
petition against Cood in 1690 (*ibid.*, 213). Col. Nicholas
Greenberry in a letter dated 25 July 1692, calls him one of
" the grand leaders of the Jacobite Party " (*ibid.*, 343).
He signed the address of congratulation to King William
12 December 1696, as a civil and military officer of Kent
County (*ibid.*, xx, 540-541).

By Rachel, his first wife, he had issue:

 Col. John Hynson was twice married. His first wife
Rachel joins him in a deed executed in 1670 (see above)
and in another dated 14 February 1677 (*Kent Co. Rec.*,
Lib. A, fol. 393). About 1693 he married his second wife
Ann widow of Jonathan Grafton of Kent County (see
appended notes) by whom he appears to have had no issue.
Col. John Hynson was buried 10 May 1705 (*Register of
St. Paul's Par. Kent Co.*).

 By Rachel, his first wife, he had issue:

> i. John Hynson of Cecil Co., m. 1 June 1693, Mary, dau. of
>   John Stoops and left issue; his will, dated 20 Oct., 1705,
>   was proved in Cecil Co., 9 Oct., 1708.
> ii. Col. Nathaniel Hynson of Kent Co., m. 1° Hannah . . .
>   (d. 24 Nov. 1713), 2° 6 Aug. 1714 Mary Kelly; had issue
>   by both marriages; his will dated 4 May 1721, was
>   proved in Kent Co. 26 Jan'y 1721/2.
> iii. Mary Hynson, m. William Glanville.
> iv. Elizabeth Hynson, m. . . . . Rogers.
> v. Anne Hynson, m. 14 Oct. 1702 Rev. Stephen Bordley,
>   Rector of St. Paul's Parish.
> vi. Jane Hynson, m. Philip Holeger.
> 3. vii. SARAH HYNSON, m. 21 Jan'y 1705/6 James Smith.

3. SARAH HYNSON, daughter of Col. John and Rachel his wife,
was married, 21 January 1705/6, to James Smith Esq. of
Kent County. In her father's will she is mentioned as
" my daughter Sarah Hynson " being at that time unmarried. The register of St. Paul's Parish records the marriage
of James Smith and Sarah Hynson on the date given above,
and the will of her brother Col. Nathaniel Hynson mentions

her daughter Hannah as "my niece Hannah Smith" (see appended notes). Her husband, James Smith was born in 1683 and died in March 1750. His age is given in depositions about land boundaries as 48 years in 1731 (*Chancery*, Lib. I R, No. 2, fol. 606), and 60 years in 1743 (*Kent Co. Rec.*, J. S. no. 25, fol. 33.) In the latter deposition he states that he was formerly Deputy Surveyor for Kent County. He represented Kent County in the House of Burgesses from 1719 to 1721 (*Ms. House Jour.*) and was Clerk of the County for fifty-two years. He first appears as clerk in 1708 (*Kent Co. Rec.*, Lib. G. L., No. 1, fol. 151) and the county records bear his official signature from that date until his death.

The *Maryland Gazette* of 20 March 1760 has the following obituary notice: "Last week Died at Chester-Town, in Kent County in a good old Age, Mr James Smith, who had been for a great number of years Clerk of that County. He is succeeded in his office by Mr. Dennis Dulany late of this City" (Annapolis).

James Smith and Sarah (Hynson) his wife had issue:

    i. John Smith, bapt. 15 Oct. 1706; d. Nov. 1732.
    ii. Hannah Smith, b. 14 March 1708; m. 1° 7 Oct. 1725 Edward Scott, d. 1729; 2° Joseph Nicholson (b. 1709, d. 1787).
    iii. Sarah Smith, b. 23 Sept. 1711, m. 11 Augt. 1730, Josias Ringgold.
    iv. James Smith, b. 2 April 1714.
    v. Mary Smith, m. 1° 29 Oct. 1735 her cousin Nathaniel Hynson, Jr. (d. 1752); 2° Samuel Wickes (d. 1767).
    vi. Ann Smith, b. 7 Dec. 1720, d. 18 Aug. 1807; m. 22 Jan'y 1740 Dr. William Murray of Chester Town (see Murray Family).
    vii. William Smith.

NOTE.—The above dates of birth, etc. are derived from the register of St. Paul's Parish, Kent County.

NOTES AND EVIDENCES.

20 January 1667/8. Administration on the estate of Thomas Hynson late of Talbot Co. deceased committed to his sons Thomas and John Hynson (*Test. Proc.*, Lib. 2, fol. 289).

24 July 1673. Estate of Thomas Hynson late of Kent Co. dec'd settled and allowed by the two brothers-in-law of the administrators as follows:

To Joseph Wickes for his wife's portion   10,446 lb tobacco
To Thos Smith for his wife's portion   10,705 " "

To Charles Hynson (minor) one of the
    brothers, his portion   11,000 lb. tobacco
To Thomas & John Hynson the adminis-
    trators   20,800 "   "
            (*Inv. & Accts.*, 1673, fol. 524.)

THOMAS HYNSON " son & heir " of Thomas Hynson senr,
deceased, had a warrant, 15 June 1669, for 300 acres due
to the said Thomas Hynson Senr (*Land Office*, Lib. 12,
fol. 393). He was High Sheriff of Talbot Co. in 1666
(*Md. Arch.*, III, 541) and was Justice of the County in
1662, 1670, 76, 74, 75, &c. (*Md. Arch.*, III, 448; II, 251;
XV, 71). He married in 1663 Anne Gaine (*Talbot Co.
Rec.*, Lib. 2, fol. 16 back) who married secondly in 1680
Robert Smith (*Inv. & Accts.*, Lib. 7 A, fol. 327). The
will of Thomas Hynson of Talbot dated 14 Dec. 1678,
proved 29 July 1679 (*Annapolis*, Lib. 9, fol. 107) mentions his wife Anne, his brother Charles, his sons Thomas,
William, and Richard, and other children (not named).

CHARLES HYNSON, son of Thomas Senr, was born in 1662,
being, according to a deposition 45 years of age in 1708
(*Kent Co.*, Lib. N, fol. 84). He was Clerk of Kent Co.
1692, 1694 (*Md. Arch.*, VIII, 371; XX, 107) and Justice in
1694 (*Md. Arch.*, XX, 138), 1701-1702 &c. (*Kent. Co.*,
Lib. N, fol. 48). He married 25 March 1687 (*St. Paul's
Reg^r*) Margaret daughter of Wm. Harris Esq. He was
buried 24 May 1711 (*St. Paul's*). His will, dated 10 Jany
1703, proved 6 Nov. 1711 (*Kent Co.*, Lib. 1, fol. 144)
mentions his children, Thomas, Charles, Dorcas, Margaret,
and Joan, and his " honored father " Wm. Harris. Another
son, William, born after the date of the will, is named in
the will of his grandfather Harris.

ANNE HYNSON, daughter of Thomas Senr, married 1° Maj.
Joseph Wickes (d. 1692); 2° Col. St. Leger Codd (*Test.
Proc.* Lib. 14b, fol. 6, 11, 12; (*Inventories & Accounts*, Lib.
15, fol. 218).

GRACE HYNSON, daughter of Thomas Hynson Senr, married
Thomas Smith of Talbot Co. before 10 Feby 1663, on which
date " Mr Thomas Smith & Grace his wife " deed 400 acres
called Trumpington to John Hynson and Anthony Piers
(*Talbot Co. Rec.*, Lib. 1, fol. 3). Her husband in his will,
dated 13 Oct. 1673, proved 26 Oct. 1674, mentions his

wife Grace and his sisters Sarah and Anne, but no children (*Annapolis,* Lib. 2, fol. 19).

2 Oct. 1693. Inventory of Jonathan Grafton late of Kent Co. deceased, and bond by John Hynson.

(*Test. Proc.,* Lib. 15 C, fol. 2.)

8 May 1694 Came John Hynson of Kent Co. who inter-married with Anne the relict & administratrix of Jonathan Grafton late of said County deceased, & exhibited Acct &c.

(*ibid.,* fol. 63½.)

26 March 1695 John Hynson of Kent County & Anne his wife to "our son & daughter" William Glanville & Mary his wife, gift of Lords Gift, 300 acres, for life with remainder in general tail to the issue of said Mary, failing which to the issue of the said William.

(*Kent Co. Rec.,* Lib. M, fol. 13.)

7 July 1702 Col. John Hynson records gift of a heifer apiece to his grandchildren, John, Elizabeth, Edward, Rachel, Mary and Nathaniel Rogers.

(*Ibid.,* Lib. G L, No. 1, fol. 9.)

8 March 1702/3 John Hynson of Kent Co. Gent. to his "well beloved sons & daughters" Stephen Bordley of said county, Clerk, and Ann his wife, and William Glanville of said County, Gent, and Mary his wife: gift of Bounty, 200 acres.

(*Ibid.,* Lib. N, fol. 64.)

JOHN HYNSON of Kent County, will dated 29 Dec. 1704, proved 5 June 1705 (*Kent Co.,* Lib. 1, fol. 16) To my son John Hynson, for life, the plantation whereon I now dwell and all the land I have in Eastern Neck; after his death to my grandson John Hynson, and to the male line of my said son John.—My just debts to be paid out of my crop of corn and tobacco, and the remainder of said crop to be equally divided between my wife and my daughter Sarah.— To my loving wife Ann Hynson all the estate that was hers at our marriage, and also a horse, household effects, &c.— Bequest of personalty to wife, to daughter Sarah Hynson, to grandson John Hynson, to daughter Elizabeth Rogers, to Mr Stephen Bordley, to daughter Jane Holeger, & to daughter Mary Glanville, and to son Nathaniel Hynson.

Hannah wife of Nathaniel Hynson died 24 Nov. 1713.

Nathaniel Hynson & Mary Kelly married 6 August 1714.

(*Reg. St. Paul's Parish.*)

NATHANIEL HYNSON of Kent Co.—will dated 4 May 1721, proved 26 Jany 1721/2 (*Kent Co.,* Lib. 1, fol. 213) mentions son Nathaniel—daughter Hannah Hynson (minor)—nephew Thomas Bordley—nephew Thomas Hynson and his sisters Hannah & Elizabeth Hynson—To my wife Mary (who is pregnant) 1000 acres in Kent Co. near head of Chester River called Partnership—Rev. Alex^r Williamson and Mr James Smith guardians to my children and executors, & my daughter co-executor but not to act till she is 17 years old. Bequest to my niece Hannah Smith.

JAMES SMITH of Kent Co.—will dated 2 Feb'y 1760, codicil 5 March 1760 (*Kent Co.,* Lib. 4, fol. 90) mentions granddaughter Mary Sterling wife of Rev. James Sterling—son James Smith—son William Smith—my children Hannah Nicholson, Sarah Ringgold, James Smith, Mary Wickes, Ann Murray, and William Smith—my daughter Hannah and her husband—my son in law William Murray, executor.

JONES BIBLE RECORDS

A small leather-bound book among the papers of the late Edmund Law Rogers has the following memorandum on the cover, written by him:

" The following is written by Rachel Jones, daughter of Philip Jones Junior, who must have copied it from her Great-Grandfather George Saughier's Bible."

My Dear and loving Father George Saughier, born in New port in ye Isle of Wight A^o Domⁿ 1600 in March.

And arrived in Virginia in Decemb^r 1620

106

And Departed this life ye 24 Dec. 1684 and was buried ye day following being ye Christmas Day.

Margaret Saughier was born in Virginia at the trimbell Spring in the new ye 11th 1646 about 6 o'clock in ye morning—baptized by Mr. Grimes, minister ph^r Garlington and Mordecai Cook Godfather's—Mrs Fox and Mrs Dedham, Godmothers.

And married March ye 5th Thomas Beson Jun. in South River, Maryland.

Thomas Besson Jun son of Thomas and Margaret Besson was born y^e of December A^o Dom. 1667 upon a Monday Night about two hours within Night.

Baptized ye 22nd day of February 1673/4 by Rich. Atkinson minister. Departed this life A^o Dom. 1702 ult. Dec. about 1 hour within night and buried Jan ye 3^d 1702/3

Ann Besson Daughter of Thomas and Margaret Besson was born ye 26th of Dec 1670 about 4 or 5 of ye clock in ye morning—baptized ye 22 of Feb 1673/4 by Richard Atkinson, Minister.

Married ye 26 of October 1697 to Mr. Richard Cromwell of Baltimore county and was delivered of a son ye 15 August about one of ye clock in ye morning 1698 and departed this life the 29th August 1698.

Margaret Besson daughter of Thomas and Margaret Besson was born ye 31st of Jan 1673/4 between 12 and 1 of ye night— baptized ye 22^d Feb 1673/4 by Rich. Atkinson, Minister.

Married ye 30th Dec. 1701 to Mr. Jno. Rattenbury and delivered of a still child ye 26th day of Dec. 1702

Hannah Rattenbury daughter of John and Margaret Rattenbury was born the 30th of October Anno Dom^n. 1704 about eleven o'clock in the morning.

Ann Rattenbury daughter of John and Margaret Rattenbury was Born October 20th 1706 about two o'clock in the morning.

Nicholas Besson son of Thomas and Margaret Besson was born ye 22^d of Dec 1677.

My Dear and Loving Mother Margaret Rattenbury departed

this life 22nd Jany 1740 and being on a Thursday night about 12 o'clock and was buried ye third day of February at Mr Philip Jones in Patapsco Neck.

John Rattenbury son of John and Margaret Rattenbury departed this life March ye 30 1745.

Elizabeth Besson Daughter of Thomas and Margaret Beson was born ye last of   1683.

Nicholas Crumwell, son of Rich Crumwell and Anne his wife was born ye 15th of August 1698 about one of ye clock in ye morning and dyed the 10th of July 1715.

John Rattenbury son of John and Margarett Rattenbury was born Sept. 12 1708 about 4 of ye clock in ye afternoon.

Hannah Rattenbury was married to John Cromwell ye 23 day of August 1723.

Margaret Cromwell Daughter of John and Hannah Cromwell was born ye 21 day of August 1724 and departed this life 6 day of November, 1740, it being on a friday night and was buried 10 day of ye month at Curtis Creek.

John Cromwell son of John and Hannah Cromwell was born February 11th day about 1 o'clock in ye morning in ye year of our Lord 1726.

Hannah Cromwell daughter of ye above John and Hannah was born ye first day of April in the year of our Lord 1729.

Ann Cromwell daughter of ye above was born ye fifth day of November in the year of our Lord 1733.

Philip Jones and Anne Rattenbury was married the 2nd day of October 1727.

Henrietta Jones, daughter of the above was born the 19 day of August 1728   died in Baltimore.

Philip Jones son of the above was born 2^d day of March 1729.

Rattenbury Jones 2^d son of the above was Born the 3^d of March 1735

Rachel Jones, 2^d daughter of the above was Born 22nd of April 1731—died in Burlington N. Jersey.

Thomas Jones 3^d son of the above was born the 12 of March 1735.

Nichs. Jones 4th son of the above was born the 12th May 1737 (died)

Hannah Jones Daughter to Philip and Anne Jones was born 4th March 1740 (died)

Anne Jones Daughter to the above was born on the 4th of August 1746

John Jones Last son and child of the above was born the 12th of Aug. 1748 (died)

Philip Jones son of the above Philip and Anne Jones, died the 4 of Oct. 1749 (died in Baltimore.)

Rattenbury Jones 2nd son of the above Philip and Anne Jones died in Antigua the 11 of Sep. 1754 new stile.

My Dear and loving Father Philip Jones, Departed this life the 22 of Dec 1761 between the hours of eight and nine in the morn—aged 60 years 2 months, 6 days.

My Dear and loving Mother Anne Jones departed this life the fifth Day of March 1763 betwixt the hours of 8 and 9 at night aged 56 years, five months wanting one day.

Rachel Jones.

John Jones last son of the above named Philip and Anne Jones died in Christopher, in the West Indies on his return from Grenada to Antigua where he had been to sell a cargo consigned to him, aged about 35 years.

John Worthington, son of William Worthington and Hannah his wife, was born November the   1735.

Thos. Worthington son of the above William and Hannah was Born the 25th of October 1740

William Worthington, son of the above William and Hannah was born in September 1737.

Hellen Worthington Daughter of the above William and Hannah was Born April ye 7th 1743.

AMONG THE "MEETERS AT THE BAYSIDE"

By EMERSON B. ROBERTS

The site of the first Quaker Meeting in Talbot is near the present villages of McDaniel and Wittman. The land was given for the purpose about 1667 by Robert Kemp, a young Quaker recently come to Bayside, as this locality was then called. Today the remains of the burying ground is at the left of the road as one goes from McDaniel to Wittman and on the other side, not far away, are two brown frame houses built in part from lumber thought to have been taken from the old Bayside Meeting House. The land is adjacent to " Boulton," more frequently called " The Quaker Kemp Farm."

Betty's Cove Meeting, visited by George Fox in 1672 and again in 1673, is located on the farm known as " North Bend " owned by James Dixon. The Meeting House was finished or remodeled about 1676 and continued in regular use until about 1693, when the Meeting there was removed to " ye great Meeting House " at Third Haven. Betty's Cove Meeting House, however, was kept in repair, and fences and graveyard kept up for some time.

Long after the death of John Kemp IV, great-great-grandson of Robert, his widow, Sarah, more than a century after the abandonment of these Bayside Meeting Houses, except by the encircling dead, with her children frequently would *sit meeting* alone. From first to last, the Kemps were among the " meeters at the Bayside," to use the phrase current two centuries ago.

It is of those early Kemps, six generations of whom lie in the graveyard, and of the families of Bayside, with whom they were so repeatedly related by ties of blood and of spirit, that we write.

Anciently the name Kemp is of county Norfolk, and from Golfred Kemp of Gissing, who lived in Norwich, 1272. Robert

Kemp is in the Assize Rolls of 1306. The Norfolk family furnished John Kemp, LL. D., Archbishop of Canterbury, and Thomas Kemp, nephew of His Grace, the Archbishop, who was consecrated Bishop of London in 1449. Oddly enough, the name of this Quaker family in Saxon means " combat," and in parts of England to this day a football match is a " kemping," and a " kemper " a contestant, a *combatant*, a *champion*.

The Maryland Kemps begin with Robert, who gave the land. He was born in Yorkshire 1650, or earlier, and died in Maryland 1702. As a youth, he was in Talbot by 1664, and perhaps before that for some time in Calvert. He declared his intentions toward Elizabeth Webb in 1678, but was admonished to wait until the General Meeting. (Third Haven Records, Vol. I.) This, he did, and in due time married Elizabeth, daughter of Edmund and Elizabeth Webb, the immigrant ancestors of the Webb family.

Robert Kemp died in Talbot in November, 1702. His will (Will Book, Hall of Records, Annapolis, Vol. II, f. 394. Baldwin, *Calendar of Maryland Wills*, III, f. 11. Accounts, Land Office, 1704, Vol. III, f. 370) drawn November 6, was probated November 24 in that year. By it he left the Society of Friends certain personalty. To his son, John, he left a tract of land, " Woolf's Harbour " and lands bought from William Fuller and Robert Clark, and also " Boulton " and " Boulton Addition," situated on the bay shore opposite Poplar Island, " given his mother by her father, Edmund Webb." (Chancery Proceedings, P. C. f. 371, the deposition of George Collison of Talbot, 1696. Also see Kemp pedigree in *Society of Colonial Wars in . . . Maryland, Genealogies of the Members* (1905), p. 75.) In later years " Boulton " became known as " The Quaker Kemp Farm." Yet remembered is the old windmill for the grinding of meal and coffee that stood at the end of the long lane.

The widow, Elizabeth, outlived her husband by about nine years. She died between the 29th of the 6th month and the first of the 9th month, 1711. (Third Haven Records, Vol. II, p. 69.) The children of Robert and Elizabeth Kemp were:

John Kemp, later known as John Kemp I. He was the first of a name that has continued to the present. He was born in 1681 (Chancery Depositions, P. C., 757), and died intestate, 1751. He married November 15, 1705, Mary

Ball, daughter of Lieutenant Thomas Ball and his wife, Susannah.

Edmund received under his father's will, equally with William, " Mable " and " Mable's Addition."

William, "joyner, of St. Michael's Parish," married July 5, 1717, Martha Eubank. His will (Baldwin, *Calendar*, VI, 138), probated November 14, 1729, mentions a son, William, who is to have 223 acres, " Mable Enlarged." Then he mentions his daughters Elizabeth, the eldest, and Rachel, Martha, Jane and Constant. The widow survived.

Elizabeth, born May 20, 1683, baptized September 19, 1702 (St. Michael's Parish), married, " outside the good order," George Collison. The ceremony was performed by the Rev. Mr. Lillington of St. John's Parish, then in Talbot. Elizabeth's father spoke of the reverend gentleman wrathfully as a " priest " for failing to heed the warnings of the Quakers not to perform the ceremony. For her disobedience, Elizabeth, then not eighteen years of age, was disowned by the meeting, though her mother had no part in the action. Her father, unforgiving to the last, cut her off with one shilling under his will, and "bade her be content with her own disobedience in lieu of worldly goods."

Jane, married, first, Robert Clothier, and second, after November, 1702, Thomas Eubank. She, too, was cut off by her father with a shilling.

Rachel and Sarah.

From John Kemp I and his wife, Mary Ball, descends the Kemp family of prominence in Talbot and throughout the State. The administration of his estate, May 20, 1752, by his widow, Mary, and son, John, yields much information of the family in this generation. (Hall of Records, Accounts, 32, f. 329.)

John Kemp II, died 1773, married 1734, Magdaline Stevens, daughter of John and Elizabeth Stevens. John and Magdaline Kemp are distinguished in Talbot and in Maryland in that, voluntarily, and long before it became somewhat common practice even among Quakers, they freed their slaves.

Thomas, mentioned in his grandfather Ball's will as inheriting the lower part of "Long Neck" at his mother's death, and the upper part of the same tract at his father's death.

James, married at Tuckahoe Meeting, June 24, 1749, Elizabeth Harwood, daughter of Peter Harwood, Jr., and widow of William Williams. James and Elizabeth Kemp, "late Elizabeth Williams" rendered accounting on the estate of William Williams of Talbot June 14, 1751. (Accounts 30, f. 132). The representatives of the deceased were "James and Elizabeth Kemp, his wife, Quakers, and children of the deceased, Mary, Rachel, Ennion, and Elizabeth Williams." On the 31st of the 1st month, 1788, James Kemp asked the Meeting to receive his own children, James, Samuel, Robert and Elizabeth. (Third Haven Records.)

Benjamin

Joseph

Elizabeth, married her cousin, James Ball.

Susannah, married, first, John Stewart, and second, September 7, 1744, Peter Harwood, Jr. (*Maryland Historical Magazine*, XXXVII, p. 320-326.)

Rachel

The family of John Kemp II and Magdaline Stevens, his wife, were:

Mary, born 31st of the 7th month, 1735, died in infancy.

John Kemp III, born 30th of the 5th month, 1737 at "Boulton," died April 7, 1790, married April 7, 1763, Mary Wrightson, daughter of Francis Wrightson and his wife, Elinor Blake, daughter of Peter Blake, the immigrant. John Kemp was a sea captain, active in the Revolution, in transporting troops and supplies. (*S. A. R. Magazine*, April, 1933, p. 347.)

Elizabeth, born 6th of the 7th month, 1739, married John Dixon, Quaker. In the declaration of their intention, 31st of the 1st month, 1757, she is called "Elizabeth Kemp, the younger." Then on the 28th of the 2nd month, 1757, "John Dixon and Elizabeth Kemp the youngest" appeared in Meeting and declared their intentions of marriage, this being the second time of their so appearing, and they appearing clear of all others, are left to their liberty to accomplish their said intentions as the Truth Directs, making the same public and James Ratcliffe and William Troth are appointed to see the marriage accomplished in Good Order, and to make a report thereon at the next Monthly Meeting . . . 28th of the 3rd month, 1757, the Friends appointed to see the marriage of John Dixon and Elizabeth Kemp accomplished, report that it was accomplished in Good Order. (Third Haven Records and *Maryland Historical Magazine*, XXXVII, 317).

Thomas, born October 4, 1741, married, 1771, Rachel Denny, and had, with eight other children, a daughter, Rebecca who married William Wrightson and had issue.

Mary, born January 13, 1743, married Thomas Norris of West River, Anne Arundel County.

Benjamin, born December 18, 1745.

Sarah, twin with Benjamin, married July 5, 1764, Thomas Cokayne.

James, born August 30, 1749.

Joseph, born December 15, 1750, died young.

Ann, born July 10, 1752, married, first, William Wilson, second, Samuel Register, and third, Howell Powell.

John Kemp III and his wife, Mary Wrightson, were the parents of:

John Kemp IV, always known as " Quaker John Kemp," born January 27, 1764, married October 29, 1790, died March 28, 1829. His wife, Sarah Paschall Troth was born February 13, 1768, died May 27, 1848. These are they spoken of in the first paragraph of this paper. It was she and her daughters who kept the inner light bright at Betty's Cove after it had been abandoned by all others.

Robert, married Sarah Powell and had ten children.

Eleanor, married William Wilson.

Joseph and Thomas, both died young.

John Kemp IV by his wife, Sarah, had these children:

John Kemp V, married (1) 1816, Maria Lambdin, (2) 1842, Susan Lambdin, sister of Maria.

KEMP

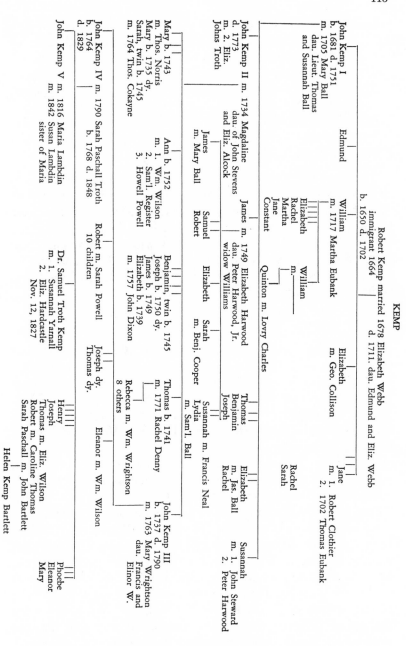

Dr. Samuel Troth married (1) 1819, Susannah Yarnall, (2) Nov. 12, 1827, Elizabeth Hardcastle, and had issue by both marriages.

Thomas, married, 1832, Elizabeth Wilson.

Robert, married Caroline Thomas. (See *S. A. R. Magazine*, April, 1933, p. 347.)

Sarah Paschall, born March 3, 1806, married, 1831, John Bartlett.

Phoebe, Eleanor, Mary, Henry and Joseph.

The names of most of the families into which the Kemps married are among the oldest Quaker families of the State. Charts of some further descents have been transcribed by the author from his collection and copies of these have been deposited for those who are interested in examining them with the Maryland Historical Society. The Kemp family is large in Maryland and its representatives have taken high places in the affairs of the State, politically, socially, and financially.

WEBB

The earliest Talbot patent for Edmund Webb, immigrant of about 1654, is "Webley," 400 acres in Talbot, December 12, 1672. Then on March 3, 1668/9, he acquired by deed from John Cock, 200 acres on the south side of the Sassafras River, " None soe good fin land" (*Maryland Historical Magazine*, XXV, 258 ff). Before coming to Talbot, Edmund Webb had been in Calvert and in Anne Arundel, and had also taken up some land in Dorchester. (*Archives*, XLI, 295.) His will, 1685, however, is a Talbot document. (Baldwin, *Calendar*, I, 166.) By it he devises to his daughter, Elizabeth Ceamp, fifty acres called "Bowlton." So came to the Kemps, "Boulton," long their home place with its long lane. From "Boulton" John Kemp IV and his family saw the British ascend the Bay in 1814. The spy glass used on the occasion was kept in a special niche built in the old home to receive it, but when the British sacked the place on their return, the glass had been removed to safe quarters and so is still in the possession of the Kemps. "Boulton" has passed from the Kemps in recent years, but ultimately it may pass into the sands of the Bay through the constant encroachment of the relentless tides.

In addition to Elizabeth, Edmund and Elizabeth Webb left other children, two sons, Edmund and William, and a daughter, Mary. This William Webb had, with a son William, a daughter Sarah.

STEVENS

William Stevens, the immigrant, settled first at Patuxent in 1650 or 1651, in the Quaker settlement of Calvert County where his first land grant was near the mouth of the Patuxent River. (Land Office, Liber ABH, f. 141, and *Maryland Historical Magazine*, IX, p. 45.) Later he removed to Dorchester where he was appointed a Justice of the Peace. (Liber AM, Proceedings of the Council.) Again as William Stevens of Great Choptank, he was paid by order of the Council £0 24 03 " for his charge in the Indian war." The early records are replete with references to him. One relates to the establishment of the Town of Oxford. There is a Deed of Gift from William Stevens to the Lord Proprietary conveying thirty acres " for the settling and the building of the towne in Tread-Aven Creeke in Great Choptank."

William Stevens married Magdaline Gary (though some authority calls her Magdaline Hodges), eldest daughter of Stephen Gary. William Stevens died December 23, 1687, and his will was probated November 11th of that year. He and his wife are buried on land long held by subsequent members of the family, but now transferred to the family of Huffington. The children were:

> John Stevens married Dorothy Preston, daughter of Richard Preston, " The Great Quaker." The relationship of John and William Stevens, questioned by some, is embraced in the registry of their cattle marks (*Archives*, X, 370), May 23, 1654. John Stevens' will was probated November 7, 1692. Baldwin, *Calendar*, II, 70.)

> William removed to Talbot, married (1) 1670, Mary, the daughter of Dr. Peter and Judith Sharp, and (2) Sarah ——————. (Liber JJ Provincial Court, f. 51 and *Maryland Historical Magazine* X, 284.) He also, in the days of his father, was a justice of the peace for Dorchester. (*Archives*, XVII, 380.) This fact has rendered difficult the separation of the records of the two. His will dated

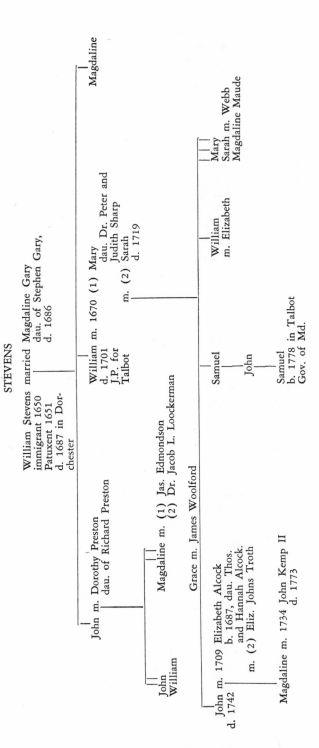

STEVENS

William Stevens married Magdaline Gary
immigrant 1650   dau. of Stephen Gary,
Patuxent 1651   d. 1686
d. 1687 in Dor-
chester

John m. Dorothy Preston
dau. of Richard Preston

Magdaline m. (1) Jas. Edmondson
           (2) Dr. Jacob L. Loockerman

Grace m. James Woolford

John
William

John m. 1709 Elizabeth Alcock
d. 1742   b. 1687, dau. Thos.
              and Hannah Alcock.
       m. (2) Eliz. Johns Troth

Magdaline m. 1734 John Kemp II
                  d. 1773

William m. 1670 (1) Mary
d. 1701   dau. Dr. Peter and
J.P. for   Judith Sharp
Talbot   Sarah
        m. (2) Sarah
               d. 1719

Samuel

John

Samuel
b. 1778 in Talbot
Gov. of Md.

William
m. Elizabeth

Mary
Sarah m. Webb
Magdaline Maude

Magdaline

October 10, 1700, was probated April 17, 1701. (Will Book II, f. 97.) To his sons jointly he left all his lands at the Port of Williamstadt with the provision that if they die without issue the lands were to pass to the three daughters. To his widow, Sarah, he left interest in his son's Samuel's lands as also life interest in " Fowling Creek," to which he refers as bought from Thomas Taylor, and devised to his son, John. The widow, Sarah, died in 1719. The children were:

John Stevens, married first Elizabeth Alcock, daughter of Thomas and Hannah Alcock, May 6, 1704 (or 1709), second, Elizabeth Johns Troth, a widow. He received by his father's will " Dawson's Fortune," " Buckroe," and a part of " Catling's Plaine," which is near Oxford. He died about 1742.

William received the remainder of " Catling's Plaine," married Elizabeth ―――――. He died before 1719.

Samuel received " Compton " and " Edmondson's Lower Cove." From him is descended Governor Samuel Stevens, born July 13, 1778.

Mary, Sarah and Magdaline Maud.

The widow, Sarah, survived until 1719. In her will (Baldwin, *Calendar*, IV, 215) she mentions her daughters, Magdaline Maud and Sarah Webb, her son John, Elizabeth, widow of William Stevens, her granddaughter Sarah Webb, and her grandson Thomas Stevens.

John Stevens and his wife, Elizabeth, were the parents of several children including Magdaline Stevens, who married, 1734, John Kemp II.

―――――

STEVENS GENEALOGY

The recent publication in the *Maryland Historical Magazine* (XXXIX, 4, Dec. 1944) of " Among the Meeters at the Bayside " has brought forth a suggestion that the Stevens chart, accompanying the article (p.

343) is in error in showing the wife of William Stevens as Magdaline Gary, daughter of Stephen Gary. The author has reexamined his evidences for the statement with the conclusion, which he is very glad to acknowledge, that the wife of William Stevens, while certainly Magdaline, in every probability was not Magdaline Gary, but in some probability was Magdaline Hodges, stated in the text (p. 342) to be the opinion of some. There is evidence that William Stevens when he came into the province brought with him his wife, Magdaline. (Early Settlers' List.) Also, examination of the will of Stephen Gary (Baldwin, *Calendar of Maryland Wills*, III, 2), reflects that Stephen Gary had a daughter Magdaline and had close ties with the Stevens family. The daughter, Magdaline, married into the family of Warren, as has been said by those who have called attention to the error in the preceding article. (Jones, *Revised History of Dorchester County*, p. 288.)

Before leaving the Stevens family let it be recorded that several intimate glimpses of the early generations are to be found in Col. Oswald Tilghman's *History of Talbot County*—how the first William Stevens had land both in Dorchester and in Talbot, how William Stevens, Jr., crossed the Choptank and settled on the Stevens land in Talbot almost if not quite within the town of Oxford, and later acquired this land, how in Talbot by 1685, with William Sharp and Ralph Fishbourne, he became one of the three Quakers among the ten Justices of the County, and how, on the lighter side, Henry Callister, the bon-vivant of musical talent or inclinations, referred to him or to his father in a letter to Mr. Tear of Douglas:

" I have had the pleasure of playing a tune with Billy Stevens. He has lost a great deal of his musical capacity. However, his performance was found sufficient to ravish and surprise some of our top men . . . we abound in fiddlers, but most wretched ones they are . . . as to other English tunes they murther them here ten times worse than the county fiddlers in the Island. It is, however, diverting to hear how they do it. . . . "

We learn also that William Stevens, Sr., was a Manxman, as perhaps also was his wife, Magdaline, who had come with him to Maryland.

EMERSON B. ROBERTS.

KEY FAMILY.

CHRISTOPHER JOHNSTON.

1. PHILIP KEY,[1] the first American ancestor of this family, thus begins his will:—" I Philip Key of St. Mary's County in Maryland, son of Richard and Mary Key, born in the Parish of St. Paul, Covent Garden, in London, y⁰ 21st March 1696, O. S." In the Register of St. Paul's, Covent Garden, published by the Harleian Society, this date is entered as that of the baptism, not the birth, of " Philip son of Richard Key and Mary his wife," but the entry confirms the fact of his parentage, in spite of the slight discrepancy as to the date. Philip Key, who is said to have been educated in the Temple, came to Maryland about 1720, and settled near Chaptico in St. Mary's County. In 1723 he witnessed the will of Mrs. Martha Dansey of St. Mary's County (Annapolis, Lib. 18, fol. 256), and in 1725 Charles Ashcom of the same county left a bequest to him and to Richard Ward Key, his young son (Annapolis, Lib. 19, fol. 127). It appears therefore that in 1725 he had been married for some years and had at least one child. Philip Key practiced law in the Courts of Maryland with marked success, his name frequently appearing upon the records, and he soon became prominent in the affairs of the Province. He was one of the Representatives of St. Mary's County in the Maryland Assembly, 1728–32, 1735–38, and 1746–54 (*House Journals*). From 6 June, 1744, to 5 November, 1745, he was High Sheriff of the County (*Commission Book*), and from 1754 until 1764 he was its Presiding Justice (*ibid.*). In 1763 he was appointed a member of the Council of Maryland. Governor Sharpe, who had repeatedly urged Philip Key's

appointment to that position (*Maryland Archives*, xiv, 25, 45, 70, 77, &c.), thus alludes to him in a letter dated 21 August, 1763 : " In consequence of His Lordship's pleasure signified to me, I have advised old Mr. Key of his being appointed a Member of the Council & shall, when he comes hither next month to the Provincial Court, introduce him to the Board to be qualified" (*Md. Archives*, xiv, 110). The following year Governor Sharpe writes (18 Sept., 1764) : " I am likewise to inform you that we have lately lost Mr. Key one of the Members of His Ldp's Council" (*Md. Archives*, xiv, 177). He died in the preceding month. The Annapolis *Maryland Gazette* of 30 August, 1764, has this obituary notice : " On Monday the 20th of this Instant, Died, at his Seat in St. Mary's County, in the 68th Year of his Age, the Hon'ble Philip Key Esq; one of the Council of this Province. He was a truly pious and devout Christian, an affectionate and tender Husband, an indulgent and fond Parent, a humane Master, a warm Friend, a friendly Neighbour, and a most agreeable and chearful Companion. His Death is sincerely lamented by his Family, and all his numerous Friends and Acquaintance." In his will he disposes of a very large landed and personal estate. Philip Key was twice married. His first wife was Susanna, daughter of John Gardiner of St. Mary's County, and Mary his wife, daughter of Major William Boarman. Her father in his will (dated October, 1717, proved in December following) mentions her as " my daughter Susanna Gardiner," so that she was then unmarried. Her brother, John Gardiner, in his will (dated 9 December, 1742, proved 4 August, 1743) appoints " my brother Philip Key " residuary legatee and executor, and leaves a bequest to "my cousin (*i. e.*, nephew) John Key." The second wife of Philip Key was Theodosia, widow of Rev. John Humphreys, who was rector of St. Ann's Parish, Annapolis, from 1725 to 1739, and died 8 July, 1739, aged 53 years (Rev. Ethan Allen, *History of St. Ann's Parish*, p. 60). Her maiden name was apparently Lawrence. She had no issue, and died in April, 1772. The *Maryland Gazette*, 16 April, 1772, has this notice in regard to her : " From St. Mary's we hear that Mrs. Key, relict of the late Philip Key Esq., died there a few days ago." Philip Key and Susanna (Gardiner) his first wife had issue :—

   i. CAPT. RICHARD WARD KEY,[2] Clerk of St. Mary's Co.; d. 10 April, 1765 ; mar. 1°. Rebecca Hammond, 2°. Hannah Clarke, and had 2 daughters.

    ii. EDMUND KEY, Attorney General of Maryland 1763; Mem. of Assembly 1765; d. 4 May, 1766.
    iii. JOHN KEY, M. D., d. August, 1755; mar. Cecilia, dau. of Dr. Gustavus Brown of Charles Co., and left issue. She mar. 2°. Major Thomas Bond.
2. iv. FRANCIS KEY, d. November, 1770, of whom further.
    v. THOMAS KEY, d. March, 1772; Mem. Assembly 1766, &c.; mar. ...... Llewellyn. His son, Hon. Edmund Key (b. 1771; d. 19 February, 1857) was for many years Judge of the Circuit Court of Maryland.
    vi. PHILIP BARTON KEY, High Sheriff of St. Mary's Co. 1754–55; d. at Chestertown, Md., November, 1756.
    vii. SUSANNA GARDINER KEY, b. 17 May, 1742; d. 11 April, 1811; mar. 19 November, 1761, Norman Bruce, High Sheriff of St. Mary's Co. 1761–64, and of Frederick Co. 1768–71.

2. FRANCIS KEY[2] (Philip[1]) was born about 1731–2. He was appointed clerk of Cecil County in 1757 and held the office until his death. He died in November, 1770. The Annapolis *Maryland Gazette* of 22 November, 1770, thus notices his death : " A few days ago died at Charles Town, of an inflammatory fever, Mr. Francis Key, Clerk of Cecil County." Francis Key was a vestryman of the Parish of St. Mary Ann, Cecil County, from 16 April, 1759, to 12 April, 1762, and again from 20 April, 1767, to 16 April, 1770 (*Vestry Book*). He was married 12 December, 1752, and the *Maryland Gazette* two days later had this notice: "Tuesday last Mr. Francis Key, of St. Mary's County, was married to Miss Arnold Ross, eldest daughter of John Ross, Esq., of this City, a well accomplish'd and deserving young Lady, with a pretty Fortune." Her father, John Ross, was Lord Baltimore's Deputy Agent for the Province, and her mother, Alicia Arnold, was maternally descended from the Wolseleys of Staffordshire, and the Zouches and Lowes of Derbyshire. Francis Key and Anne Arnold (Ross) his wife had issue :—

    i. JOHN ROSS KEY, b. 19 September, 1754; d. 13 October, 1821; an officer in the Revolution. He married 19 October, 1775, Anne Phoebe Penn Dagworthy Charlton, daughter of Arthur Charlton of Frederick Co., and their son, Francis Scott Key (b. 1779, d. 1843), was the author of the Star Spangled Banner.
3. ii. PHILIP BARTON KEY, b. 12 April, 1757; d. 28 July, 1815; of whom further.
    iii. ELIZABETH SCOTT KEY, b. 10 August, 1759; d. 1832; mar. 26 July, 1781, Henry Maynadier (b. 31 March, 1759; d. 1849).

3. HON. PHILIP BARTON KEY[3] (Francis,[2] Philip[1]) was born 12 April, 1757. He was educated in England, and after the Declaration of Independence, entered the British Army. In 1778 he held a commission in Lieut.-Col. Chalmer's

Maryland Loyalist Regiment, and in 1782, then holding the
rank of Captain, he went to Jamaica with his troops. He
served in Florida, where he was taken prisoner, and upon his
release on parole went to England. After peace was declared
he retired on half pay, and in 1785 returned to Maryland.
In 1787 he was practicing law at Leonardtown, but in 1790
he removed to Annapolis, where he soon became prominent
in his profession. In 1794 he was elected a Delegate to the
Maryland Legislature and held his seat until 1799. He
removed to Georgetown, D. C., in 1801, and in 1807 he
made a formal resignation of his claims to the British Government in a letter to the British Minister at Washington. In
1806 he was elected to Congress as a Federalist, and his seat
was contested on the ground that he was not a citizen of
Maryland. On this occasion he said in a speech : " I had
returned to my country like a prodigal to his father, had felt
as an American should feel, was received and forgiven, of
which the most convincing proof is—my election." He sat
in Congress from 1807 to 1813, and died at Georgetown 28
July, 1815. He married 4 July, 1790, Anne, daughter of
Hon. George Plater of St. Mary's County, Governor of
Maryland 1791–92, and Elizabeth Rousby his wife. The
Plater family record gives her birth as 23 September, 1772,
but her tombstone in Oak Hill Cemetery, Georgetown, states
that she died 18 December, 1834, " in the sixtieth year of
her age," which would place her birth in 1774. Her husband is buried beside her (*Md. Historical Mag.*, ii, 372; iii,
188–9). Philip Barton Key and Anne (Plater) his wife had
issue:—

      i. GEORGE BARTON KEY, b. 1793; d. in infancy.
      ii. ELIZABETH ROUSBY KEY, b. March, 1796; d. 21 November,
            1860 ; mar. 1 October, 1829, Hon. Henry Johnson, Governor
            of Louisiana.
      iii. MARY LLOYD KEY, b. August, 1801 ; d. 8 November, 1834;
            mar. 13 November, 1822, Rev. William Nevins (b. 17 October,
            1797 ; d. 14 September, 1835) of Baltimore.
4.   iv. PHILIP BARTON KEY, b. 2 September, 1804; d. 4 May, 1854 ;
            of whom further.
      v. REBECCA ANN KEY, b. 2 June, 1809; mar. 1°. 14 May, 1828,
            Dr. William Howard of Baltimore ; 2°. 28 September, 1837,
            Alex. H. Tyson of Baltimore.
      vi. LOUISE EMILY KEY, b. 22 December, 1811 ; d. in Louisiana
            7 March, 1830.
Twins vii. EMILY LOUISE KEY, b. 22 December, 1811 ; d. in New York
            10 January, 1891 ; mar. 19 January, 1835, Dr. Philip Rogers
            Hoffman of Baltimore.
      viii. ANNE ARNOLD KEY, b. 28 December, 1814 ; d. 18 August, 1895 ;
            mar. 21 October, 1835, William E. Thompson of Louisiana.

4   PHILIP BARTON KEY [4] (Philip Barton,[3] Francis,[2] Philip [1])
    was born at "Woodley," Georgetown, D. C., 2 September,
    1804, and died at his plantation, "Acadie," near Thibodeaux,
    Louisiana, 4 May, 1854. He was graduated at Hamilton,
    N. Y., in 1823, and studied law under his cousin Francis
    Scott Key, writer of the Star Spangled Banner. He prac-
    ticed his profession for a time at Annapolis, and in 1835 went
    to Louisiana where he engaged in planting. He was a mem-
    ber of the Louisiana Legislature, and of the State Constitu-
    tional Convention of 1850. He was twice married. His
    first wife, married 4 December, 1828, was Mary Brent,
    youngest daughter of Robert Sewall of Poplar Hill, Prince
    George's County, Md. She had no issue, and died at Poplar
    Hill 1 January, 1831, aged twenty-two years. Philip Barton
    Key married secondly, 25 April, 1833, Maria Laura, youngest
    daughter of Nicholas Sewall of Cedar Point, St. Mary's
    County, cousin german of his first wife. She was born 7
    June, 1812, and died in Baltimore, Md., 10 December, 1897.
    Philip Barton Key and Maria Laura (Sewall) his second wife
    had issue :—

    i.   FRANCES EUGENIA KEY, b. 11 February, 1834 ; mar. 1854 Melchior
         George Klingender of Liverpool, England.
    ii. PHILIP BARTON KEY, b. 10 March, 1836 ; mar. 1861 Anna Thornton.
    iii. NICHOLAS SEWALL KEY, b. 21 May, 1838 ; d. unmar. 1863. A sol-
         dier in the Confederate States Army.
    iv. HENRY JOHNSON KEY, M. D., b. 27 February, 1840 ; surgeon in the
         Confederate States Army.
    v.   WILLIAM THOMPSON KEY, b. 27 November, 1841 ; mar. Josephine
         Baltzell of Frederick, Md.
    vi. MARY CATHERINE KEY, mar. 17 November, 1868, George Carrell
         Jenkins.
    vii. FRANCIS SCOTT KEY, b. 21 September, 1846 ; killed 1858, by acci-
         dental discharge of his own gun.
    viii. ELIZABETH ROUSBY KEY, b. 29 August, 1848 ; d. in infancy.
    ix. EDWARD KEY, b. 28 March, 1850 ; mar. Florence Gross Horwitz of
         Baltimore, Md.
    x.   VIRGINIA PEYTON KEY, b. 2 May, 1853; mar. 1873 Henry Dainger-
         field of Alexandria, Va.

KEY ARMS.

Philip Key, in his will, leaves to his son Richard Ward
Key "my steel seal with my coat of arms." An impression
of this seal on a letter from Philip Key to his son, then in
England, is in the possession of McHenry Howard, Esq., and the
crest, which is partly obliterated on this impression, is found on
old silver belonging to the family. According to these sources
the arms and crest used by the Keys of Maryland were :—

Arms.—Argent, two bendlets.
Crest.—A griffin's head erased argent, holding in its beak a key or.

The bendlets in the arms are generally given as sable, but this is not quite certain. In 1899, Mr. Howard Payn, a retired English Barrister, undertook some researches in regard to the Key arms with the following result:—

John Key of Milcombe, in Oxfordshire, had two sons, Richard and Josiah. The latter, Josiah, applied in 1688 for a grant of arms, and his petition was supported by Lord Clarendon in whose service he was, and by John Thornicroft who married Josiah's daughter and heir, Elizabeth Key. Josiah is described as a man of good repute and ample fortune, well able to support the charges and position of a gentleman. The petition was granted, the coat conferred being: argent, two bendlets humetty purpure. Josiah Key died in 1695, leaving a sum of money to his brother Richard, and his estate to his son-in-law John Thornicroft. In 1701, the latter petitioned to have the bendlets in the arms granted to his late father-in-law changed from purpure to sable, and his petition was granted. But Sir Arthur Kay of Yorkshire, who bore two bendlets sable, opposed the grant as the new arms resembled his own too closely. Accordingly in 1704, the Earl Marshall granted to the Keys: argent two bendlets pean (black and gold fur), the bendlets being no longer humetty. Mr. Payn is inclined to identify Richard Key, brother of Josiah, as the father of Philip Key, and he is probably right, though the proof is not altogether conclusive. Richard Key seems to have been living in Covent Garden until 1710, when, according to Mr. Payn, he gave up his house there.

Burke's General Armory gives the arms of Keys of Milcomb, Co. Oxford, granted 1688, as: Argent two bendlets hummetty purpure, and adds the crest: A griffin's head couped at the breast, wings addorsed argent, holding in the beak a key or. The similarity of the crest supports Mr. Payn's contention that the Keys of Maryland are a branch of the Keys of Milcomb.

APPENDIX.

Baptized—21 March, 1696/7, Philip, son of Richard Key and Mary his wife.
Buried—2 August, 1693, Richard Key.
Buried—15 December, 1694, Isaac, son of Richard Key.
Buried—27 December, 1706, Mary, wife of Richard Key.
    Register of St. Paul's, Covent Garden (Harleian Society).
7

Key, Francis, son of Richard, of London, pleb. Queen College, matric. 11 December, 1696, aged 16 ; B. A. 1700, M. A. 1703.

Foster, Alumni Oxonienses.

Genealogies of the Key Family are to be found in Hayden's "Virginia Genealogies," pp. 167–69, and in Mackenzie's "Colonial Families."

Major Samuel Lane (1628-81): His Ancestry and Some American Descendants

A. RUSSELL SLAGLE

SAMUEL LANE WAS BORN IN 1628, PROBABLY IN LONDON.[1] LATER WE WILL SEE THAT HIS father was Richard Lane, and his mother Alice Carter. First, however, let us look to his background. We shall also see that Samuel had a double first cousin, John Lane, who in 1670 left "several pieces of plate engraven with his name and arms" to Bread Street Ward Church in London.[2] I have seen this plate and made several sketches of the arms. It is obvious that these are the Lane arms described as follows: "per pale azure, and gules three saltires couped argent: issuant from a crescent or two Eagles' Heads the dexter gules the sinister-azure." In a letter dated August 19, 1970, Mr. J. P. Brooke-Little Esqre., M. A., F. S. A. Richmond Herald of Arms, College of Arms, London, states that the first mention of these arms "is in the 1564 Visitation of Northampton (HH. folio 46 r). The pedigree recorded here begins with William Lane of Orlybere, County Northampton. He had four sons, Raufe (Ralph), William, John and George." After further informative data Mr. Brooke-Little ends his letter by saying: "The conclusions I am inclined to draw from this miscellaneous evidence is that the arms were probably of greater antiquity than the crest and may well have been used since the early 15th century by a family of Lane of Northampton or environs."[3] Turning to *Burke's Landed Gentry* under Lane of Badgemore, which family bore the above arms, we find: "This branch of the Lane family is of some antiquity in Co. Northampton. In 1469 (9 Edward IV) William Lane was possessed of Orlingbury Manor or Lordship, and died 1546, leaving it to his eldest son Sir Ralph Lane."[4] Surely the most important genealogical tie in this branch of the Lane family is the marriage of this last named Sir Ralph Lane to Maud Parr, first cousin of Katherine Parr, King Henry VIII's sixth and last wife. Their son, another Sir Ralph Lane, sailed up our Chesapeake Bay in 1585-86, and it is said he was the first white man to do this.[5]

Many branches of the Lane family bore the above coat of arms. From Burke's *General Armour* we find: "Lane (Wycombe, Co. Bucks; Allhallow-Gussing, Co. Dorset; *Herefordshire;* Lord Mayor of London, 1695; Courteen Hall, Hanler Twinden, Horton and Walgrave, Co. Northampton; Somersetshire and Yorkshire). Per pale, az. gu. three saltires ar. Crest-Two eagles' heads issuant out of a crescent or, the dexter gu. the sinister az."[6] Note we italicized *Herefordshire,* for it is here we can document "our" Samuel Lane's

---

A. Russell Slagle is a Baltimore genealogist.
1. John Camden Hotten, *The Original Lists of Persons of Quality . . . Who Went From Great Britain to the American Colonies 1600-1700* (New York, 1874), pp. 67, 68.
2. Robert Seymour [John Mottley], *A Survey of the Cities of London and Westminister,* 2 vols. (London, 1733-35), 1: 708.
3. Letter dated August 19, 1970, to A. Russell Slagle.
4. Sir Bernard Burke, *A Genealogical and Heraldic History of the Landed Gentry of Great Britain and Ireland,* 2 vols. (London, 1882), 2: 926.
5. *Dictionary of American Biography,* s.v. "Lane, Ralph"; *Dictionary of National Biography,* s.v. "Lane, Ralph."
6. Sir Bernard Burke, *The General Armory of England, Scotland, Ireland, and Wales* (London, 1884), p. 581.

The Coat of Arms of John Lane (d. 1670), of Bread
Street Ward Church, London.

earlist Lane ancestor. Muriel Tarkin of Hereford and Hector Carter of Guildford, Surrey,
have sent us records from Saint Peters Church in Hereford, and from these we find Roger
Lane, apothecary, and his wife Beatrix baptizing their ten children between January 29,
1590, and January 10, 1602.[7] However, the records also state that Roger Lane, the father,
was buried April 30, 1603, leaving the mother, Beatrix, with eight living children ranging
from the ages of twelve to one — not a particularly happy outlook for a young mother. It is
their son Richard Lane, baptized August 27, 1596, who is of particular interest to us. He
was six years old at the time of his father's death.

We can only guess that the son, Richard, grew up in the city of Hereford, and how the
mother, Beatrix, managed is another guess. We find no record of her remarrying.[8] But
before leaving Hereford we should note that the Lanes who remained in County Hereford
are known as the Lanes of Ryelands, and under the "Lineage" of this family we find:
"This branch of the family of Lane has been settled for many generations in county
Hereford and represents the very ancient house of Rodd of the Rodd."[9] However, the
Lanes did not marry into the Rodd family until about 1737, when Theophilus Lane of
Hereford married Julian Rodd (born in 1717), daughter of Bramfylde Rodd,[10] so by that
time "our" Samuel, subject of this sketch, had been dead and buried many years in Anne
Arundel County, Maryland.

Richard Lane must have left Hereford and come to London as a very young man, for on
December 14, 1613, we find him apprenticed to Nathaniel Thornhull of Birchin Lane,
London, for seven years.[11] Nathaniel Thornhull was a "merchant taylor" (tailor) and on

---

7. From records of St. Peters Church at Hereford, England: "baptized 27 Aug. 1596 Richard son of
Roger and Beatrix wife, poticary [apothecary]."
8. *Ibid.*: "Beatrix, daughter of Beatrix Lane, widow married 4 May 1609 Jonas Meredith, apothicarie"; since the bride's father, Roger Lane, had been an "apothicarie," we can guess that Meredith
might have been an apprentice to Roger, who married "the boss's daughter" and carried on the
business.
9. Burke, *Landed Gentry*, 2: 927.
10. *Ibid.*
11. "Letter from Mr. Evan James, clerk of the Merchant Taylor's Company: 'Richard Lane, son of

February 26, 1620, Richard Lane was admitted as a freeman of The Merchant Taylors Co.[12] He was twenty-four years old.

The young merchant tailor apparently prospered, because we find in the Bishop of London's Registry, in the records of Saint Mildred Poultry, London, for October 7, 1623, that Richard Lane married[13] Alice Carter (baptized August 24, 1603[14]). She was the daughter of Humfry Carter, citizen and Iremonger of London, and mentioned in his will (dated April 11, 1621; proved London June 1, 1621) as "under 21 and unmarried."[15] Shortly after this we begin to see the unorthodox-nonconformist-Puritan restlessness stirring in this Lane family, and this restlessness can be readily followed. Apparently Richard was not secretive about his opinions, and obviously said what he thought, for in October 1631 we find "Examination of Richard Lane, taylor" recorded in the book *Antinomianism in English History* by Gertrude Huehns.[16] Richard did not like the examination. He began looking around—what should he do, where could he go?. Children were coming along— Samuel, born 1628; Jo, born 1631; Oziell, born 1632—so he must have felt a responsibility at home. Nevertheless, Richard Lane wanted to go where he could be himself. Consequently he took a trip to the West Indies, doubtless with the "incorporation." *The Calendar of State Papers*[17] is our best source of information for that period, so let us have them speak for themselves.

August 31, 1632 (vol. 1, p. 155): a letter from Thomas Wiggin to Master Downing. Complains of the carriage of an unworthy person, Sir Christopher Gardiner, who has lately returned from New England, where he went more than two years ago. Isaac Allerton informed against him to the Governor. Would push some means to stop his mouth, having most scandalously and basely abused "that worthy Governor, Mr. Winthrop." Hopes *Lane, a merchant tailor, who has been in the West Indies,* will talk with Mr. Humphreys concerning a certain staple commodity, which he desired to plant in New England. "Staple commodities are the things they want there." "Need not declare the happy proceedings and welfare of New England. It is a wonder to see what they have done in so small a time."

February 15, 1633 (p. 159): Minutes of a Court for Providence Island—Agreement with *Mr. Lane* to ship himself in the Company's pinnace for Fonseca, if that island be not discovered to Providence, to plant his madder (a small plant, the root of which was used to make a red dye), teach his skill to the inhabitants, and be an agent for the Company in other parts of the Indies. A pattern of drugs and commodities likely to be procured in the Indies to be "sent along with the Indian" for their better discovery.

February 18, 1633 (p. 159): Minutes, etc. . . . Eight more servants assigned to *Mr. Lane* to be sent to Fonseca. . . .

March 26, 1633 (p. 161): Minutes, etc. . . . After debate the intended voyage to Fonseca is respited; the pinnace to be forthwith dispatched to Providence and

---

Roger Lane of the city of Hereford, Apothecary, deceased, was apprenticed to Nathaniel Thornhull of Birchin Lane (London) for 7 (seven) years from the 14th Dec. 1613, and was admitted to the Freedom of the company on the 26th Feb. 1620' " (quoted from Hector Carter to the author, October 21, 1961).

12. *Ibid.*

13. See also Reginald M. Glencross, ed., *A Calendar of the Marriage License Allegations in the Registry of the Bishop of London, vol. 1, 1597-1648,* vol. 62 of *The Index Library* (London, 1937), p. 56.

14. Church records of the Parish of Saint Mildred Poultry in the County of London, now in the Guildhall, London.

15. Will of Humfrey Carter (P.C.C. 60 Dale).

16. P. 62n.

17. Great Britain, *Calendar of State Papers, Colonial Series . . . 1574 to 1660* (London, n.d.), vol. 1.

touching at Association to take in Cpt. Hilton and such persons as he may appoint tor discovery of trade in the Bay of Darien. Mr. Hook to have his full member of servants, Mr. Lane but six, with an addition by the next ship. . . .

April 10, 1633 (p. 162): Letter from the Company of Providence Island to Captain Bell, Governor. . . . Twenty passengers now sent over. Desire he will assign portions of land in the most convenient places to Mr. Hook, Mr. Bradley, and Mr. Lane. Request that Mr. Lane may be afforded every facility for planting his madder. Direct him to entertain Capt. Hilton with all fitting courtesy should he go in the pinnace to Providence, and to allow Lane and Roger Floud to accompany Hilton.

April 15, 1633 (p. 164): Instructions from the Company of Providence Island to Richard Lane, bound in the Elizabeth to the West Indies. On his arrival at Association, if Capt. Hilton resolve not to accompany him, to receive from him and Capt. Bell directions for "our intended trade." If Capt. Hilton goes, to accompany him to Providence, and after planting his madder to depart with Capt. Hilton for managing the trade, an account of which is to be kept. Preservation, making inventories, and sending home the commodities procured; if of value, to be kept with all possible secrecy. To receive instructions from Capt. Hilton and the Governor and Council of Providence and to accompany the goods home if he see cause.

April 15, 1633 (p. 164): London—Instructions from the Company of Providence Island for Rich. Lane, in case Capt. Hilton does not go with him from Association to Providence. After having planted his madder, to take on board Roger Floud and other persons not to exceed eight, as the Governor and Council or Providence think fit. To go to the Bay of Darien, with goods for trade. To provide against fear of discovery by the Spaniards, and foul weather. To use means to ingratiate himself and company with the Indians. . . .

November 23, 1633 (p. 172): Minutes, etc. . . . Mrs. Lane to receive 10£ for a half a years wages due her husband. . . .

November 17, 1634 (p. 193): Minutes, etc. . . . Fifteen pounds to be paid to Rich. Lane for a half a year's service at the Bay of Darien. Recompence to those employed with him in that voyage to be considered.

December 2, 1634 (p. 193): Minutes, etc. . . . Propositions by Mr. Hart concerning goods delivered to Mr. Lane at Association. Statement of Mr. Treasurer's accounts allowed, and Mr. Treasurer fully discharged. . . .

February 5, 1635 (p. 196): Minutes, etc. . . . Mr. Lane agrees to return to Providence by the next ship, at the request of the Company; if any plantation is settled upon the main, he is to have liberty to remove there. Accounts ordered to be made out, of money disbursed by Company for him. He is requested to put in writing his information of some miscarriages in the government there, "that they [the Company] might reprove reform, and order things as shall be fit. . . ."

February 9, 1635 (p. 196): Minutes, etc. . . . Mr. Woodcock's offer to lend his ship of 150 tons for 110£ monthly, including victuals and mariners' wages, after her unlading at Saint Christophers, accepted, an opportunity having presented itself to take over a minister, Mr. Lane, Mr. Sherhard's wife, and some servants, whereby Mr. Sherhard's stay in Providence will be confirmed, and the planters much encouraged. . . .

February 20, 1635 (p. 197): Minutes, etc. . . . As an encouragement to Mr. Lane it is agreed to recommend to the General Court to admit him a Councillor in Providence, and that 20£ be lent to him.

February 22, 1635 (p. 197): Minutes, etc. . . . The proposition for Mr. Lane to be of the Council of Providence is debated, and several considerations submitted by the Treasurer (John Pym) answered, but the Treasurer refused to give his opinion. . . .

March 9, 1635 (p. 199): Minutes etc. . . . Concerning the proposition to appoint *Mr. Lane* of the Council in Providence; Mr. Treasurer states his objections, but *Mr. Lane* is declared to be legally elected by the major part of the Committee. Mr. Treasurer's reasons for consenting to *Mr. Lane's* election. . . .

Here we leave *The Calendar of State Papers* a moment, and quote another source:[18]

16 Aprilis 1635 – Theis p'ties hereafter expressed are to be transported to the Island of Providence imbarqued in ye Expectation Corneilius Billing Mr, having taken the Oaths of Allegiance and Supremacie; As likewise being conformable to the Church of England; whereof they brought testimonie from the Ministers and justices of peace, of their Abodes:

Richard Lane	38 (his age)
Alice Lane	30
Samuel Lane	7
Jo: Lane	4
Oziell Lane	3

And now we return to *The Calendar of State Papers*.

April 20, 1635 (p. 202): Letter from the Company of Providence Island to Capt. Bell, Governor. . . . Received his letter of 10 March 1634 in August last, with a full account by *Mr. Lane* of the success of their intended trade at Darien. Have ordered rewards to those eight persons who accompanied *Mr. Lane*. . . . *Mr. Lane* returns, and has liberty to choose ground in the island not already possessed, for planting madder, indigo, or other commodities . . . *Mr. Lane* to be admitted of the Council, and Lieut. Price to have liberty to come home. . . .

April 20, 1635 (p. 204): Instructions from the Company of Providence Island to Cornelius Billinger, Master of the Expectation, of London. To sail from Saint Christophers direct to Association, "otherwise called Tortuga," and ascertain whether it be in possession of the English. If so to attend *Mr. Lane* 14 days, and from thence proceed to Providence. . . .

February 26, 1636 (p. 222): Minutes, etc. . . . Inquiry into complaints against Capt. Riskinner for taking goods from *Mr. Lane* by force; striking, offering to pistol and threatening to hang him. . . .

March 29, 1637 (p. 249): Minutes, etc. . . . Assistance to be given to *Mr. Lane*, Lord Brooke's agent, in disposing of certain goods. . . .

April 16, 1638 (p. 269): Commission from the Company of Providence Island, appointing Capt. Nath. Butler, Hen. Halhead, Sam Rishworth, and Elisha Gladman to examine *Rich. Lane* concerning the enployment of a magazine of goods of large value committed to him by Lord Brooke, of which no account has been given, with authority to seize his goods, servants, plantations, and debts in case he has been negligent or unfaithful. . . .

July 3, 1638 (p. 278): Letter from Company of Providence Island to the Governor and Council – . . . . *Rich. Lane's* services not thought worthy of much recompense. . . .

January 4, 1641 (p. 317): Minutes, etc. . . . Edw. Thompson, master of the Hopewell, is authorized to permit Messrs. Sherhard, Leverton, Halhead, and *Lane*, sent

---

18. Hotten, *Original Lists of Persons of Quality*, pp. 67–68.

prisoners by the Deputy Governor and Council of Providence Island, to come to London to answer the objections against them. . . .

February 13, 1641 (p. 317): Minutes, etc. . . . The proceedings against Messrs. Sherhard, Leverton, *Lane,* and Halhead, sent prisoners from thence, for opposing Captain Carter in the execution of his place of Deputy Governor, to which he was appointed by Capt. Butler, who supposed himself authorized to do so, considered, and the censure and restraint declared unmerited; they are discharged from all further attendance. . . .

March 25, 1641 (p. 319): Minutes, etc. . . . *Mr. Lane* to go over and to be one of the Council. . . . Transportation of Messrs. Sherhard, Leverton, *Lane,* and Halhead, sent over as prisoners, but since discharged, to be borne by the Company. . . .

March 29, 1641 (p. 319): Letter from Company of Providence Island to the Governor and Council. . . . *Rich. Lane* . . . a standing Council for the affairs of the Plantation, Admiralty, and Council of War. . . .

August 7, 1657 (p. 457): Petition of *Alice Lane* to (the Lord Protector). Sets forth her great sufferings in the West Indies, her husband and son having been drowned in Eleuthera, and that arrears for service in England of £702. 13.6 are certified. Prays relief. Minutes: "report offered to the council that she might have a pension of 10 s. per week. The opinion and directions of the Council desired in similar cases."

Arthur Percival Newton writes that "Leverton's story goes on to tell us that 'at length the Governor [Nathaniel Butler] leaving the Island [Providence], a difference arose in the colony. He names his successor [Capt. Andrew Carter], but the people pleaded a right by charter to choose their Governor and fixed upon a person of their own nomination, one *Captain Lane.* But the other [i.e. Carter] privately arming some of the under sort, siezed *Lane* [a protegé of Lord Brooke] and both the ministers [Leverton, Sherrard and Henry Halhead] and sent them prisoners to England, with an information against them to Archbishop Laud, that they were disaffected to the liturgy and ceremonies of England. When they arrived here, the state of things was changed and Laud was in custody of the Black Rod. They were kindly received by the Lords Patentees or proprietors of the island and encouraged to return'."[19] Still further information about *Richard Lane* is contained in the diary of Nathaniel Butler, Governor of the Isle of Providence: "March 5 [1639]—The new come in dutch captain dined with me this day, Mr. Sherrard, *Mr. Lane,* and Mr. Francis were also with me this day at diner [sic]; as likewise Capt. Axe who came to take his leave of me." Also from this diary we quote: "March 15 [1639]—I dined att *Mr. Lane's* with most of the counsell for ye Islands."[20] Special notice should be taken of this close relationship between Capt. Nathaniel Butler and Capt. *Richard Lane,* because later in Maryland we are to find these Lanes living "next door" to these Butlers and the Lanes selling their property to them.

We probably could find more about Richard Lane in Providence, but we know that he and a son (probably Oziell) were drowned in Eleuthera before August 7, 1657,[21] and it is his son Samuel, the subject of our sketch, who claims our attention now.

Samuel Lane was seven years old when he sailed from London in "ye Expectation" April 16, 1635, with his father Richard, his mother Alice, and two brothers Jo (John) and Oziell. He may have been eight when he arrived in Providence, because "the Expectation . . . did not get away from her first port of call at St. Christophers before July 1635."[22] We

19. Arthur Percival Newton, *The Colonizing Activities of the English Puritans* (New Haven, 1914), pp. 257, 137.
20. Sloane ms. 758, pp. 143–73, British Museum.
21. *Calendar of State Papers . . . 1574–1660,* 1: 457.
22. Newton, *English Puritans,* pp. 195–96.

do not know when Samuel left Providence, but he surely was there from 1635 until Governor Nathaniel Butler left in 1640–41, when his (Samuel's) father, Richard, was nominated for Governor of the island.[23] In 1635 Samuel was 7 years old, and in 1641 he was 13 – surely impressionable years for a growing boy. If Samuel's father, Richard, was close enough to Governor Nathaniel Butler to have him dine at his home,[24] surely young Samuel was not too far away, and must have heard the dangerous, thrilling, adventurous experiences Governor Butler had had on the Chesapeake Bay before coming to Providence. Butler had been governor of Virginia, and his experiences with the Indians, the freezing days and nights on the Chesapeake, and some experiences too scandalous to mention here, must have been an eyeopener for young Samuel. Governor Nathaniel Butler's half niece, Elizabeth Butler, had married William Claiborne, whose life and experiences on Kent Island in our Chesapeake Bay are too well known to describe here, but he too (William Claiborne) had been granted the Island of Roatan off the coast of Honduras by the Providence Company. It is almost a foregone conclusion Governor Butler must have told of his half niece's experiences on Kent Island, Maryland. In addition to this, Governor Butler had two half-nephews, John and Thomas Butler, who had followed their half-uncle (Gov. Nathaniel Butler), to Kent Island in the Chesapeake. We will hear more of this Butler family in Maryland.

We do not know when Samuel left the Isle of Providence, but he was probably back in England by August 7, 1657, when his mother, Alice Lane, petitioned Oliver Cromwell, the Lord Protector, for payment of £702 arrears for the services in England of her husband, Richard. She was doubtless grateful for the grant of the small pension of 10 shillings a week.[25]

We are on firm ground when on September 8, 1670, John Lane, citizen and grocer of All Hallows, Bread Street, London, draws his will (proved October 4, 1670), and leaves "to cozen Samuel Lane, clerk, 120£."[26] By this time Samuel Lane has become a "clerk" (minister), as we will see later. This is the John Lane mentioned earlier, who gave the silver plate with the Lane coat of arms to Bread Street Ward Church, London. John Lane, the testator, and Samuel Lane, the legatee, were double first cousins, their fathers John Lane (1594–1654)[27] and Richard Lane of the Isle of Providence (born 1596)[28] being brothers; their mothers were sisters: Anna (Hanna) Carter[29] and Alice Carter,[30] both daughters of Humphry Carter (will proved June 1, 1621).[31] In addition to the legacy to his double first cousin, Samuel, John Lane (will proved October 4, 1670) left "to Benjamin Lane, my brother 3000£ at 21 or marriage. If he die first his legacy to Captain John Lane my cozen and his sister, Mary Denn wife of William Denn."[32] This last named "Captain

---

23. *Ibid.*, p. 257.
24. Same as footnote 20.
25. Same as footnote 21.
26. Will of John Lane, citizen and grocer of London, P.C.C., 136 Penn, (8 September 1670–4 October 1670).
27. Born "John Lane, son of Roger Lane and Beatrix his wife bapt. 18 Oct. 1594" (Records of St. Peter's Church, Hereford, England).
28. Born "Richard Lane, son of Roger Lane and Beatrix his wife bapt. 27 Aug. 1596" (*ibid.*).
29. "Hanna (Anna) wife of John Lane, buried 2 Sept. 1642" at Parish of All Hallows, Bread Streat, London (tombstone inscription).
30. Baptized "1603 August the xxiii Ales (Alice) daughter of Humfrey Carter Borne the xxth of the same" (Records of the Parish of Saint Mildred Poultry in the County of London).
31. Will of Humphry Carter, drawn April 11, 1621; proved June 1, 1621, a "citizen and Iremonger" of London (P.C.C. 60 Dale): "daughters, Anna, Alice, Mary (all under 21 and unmarried)." Also see the will of Thomas Carter of St. Mildred the Virgin in Poultry, London, a "citizen and Iremonger," dated December 13, 1639; proved December 13, 1639/40 (P.C.C. Coventry): "gold ring to my cousin Anna Lane wife of John Lane."
32. Same as footnote 26.

John Lane my cozen" was the Jo[hn] Lane who at the age of four sailed for the Isle of Providence in "ye Expectation" on April 16, 1635, with his family. Mary Denn, his sister, was born about 1642[33] after arriving in Providence. They were, of course, brother and sister of "our" Samuel Lane, and also double first cousins of the testator (John Lane, will proved October 4, 1670). The testator left William Denn £1,000, and "to my said cozen Captain John Lane 1000£ if he returnes to England alive . . . to Alice Lane widow [mother of the said "Captain John Lane my cousin"] 5100 [sic]." To other cousins he leaves various properties in Hereford, confirming his origin from that city. Some of the other bequests are in the thousands of pounds, so this John Lane must have been a London grocer of some means. In addition to the above wills we have four other Lane (and Denn) wills, which throw considerable light on "our" Samuel, subject of our sketch.

The above John Lane, the testator, was the son of another John Lane, the elder of the parish of All Hallows, Bread Street, a citizen and grocer of London (will drawn October 10, 1654; proved December 20, 1654).[34] In addition to many bequests he left "to John and Mary, children of my brother Richard Lane, deceased 10£ each . . . to Alice Lane, late wife of my brother Richard Lane, deceased, all my lands in the parish of Kingston, Co. Hereford."

We also have the will of Alice Lane, widow (drawn August 22, 1678; proved October 22, 1678).[35] This of course is Alice Lane, widow of Richard Lane of Isle of Providence, and mother of "our" Samuel. She leaves "to my grandson Thomas Denne 50£ at twenty one. To my two granddaughters Elizabeth Denne and Alice Denne 50£ at twenty one or marriage. . . . To my son [son-in-law] William Denne 25£ for mourning for himself his wife and children, if they come to my funeral." William Denn's wife at this time was a second wife named Mary, his first wife, Mary Lane, having been buried on July 28, 1674, at All Hallows, Bread Street.[36] Another church record of All Hallows reads "4 Sept. 1678 was buried Mrs. Alice Lain, Mr. Denn's former wife's mother; she was buried upon her daughter, Mr. Denn's former wife." In the same record we also find "Burried 29 Aug. 1694 William Den, grocer by tread." In addition we have the will of William Denn, "citizen and grocer of London," (will drawn August 11, 1694).[37] Among others he mentions his wife Mary, son Thomas, mother-in-law Mrs. Anne Yate of Bristol, and brother Robert Yate.

Lastly the will of this immediate Lane family is that of John Lane, a mariner of the city of Bristol, (will drawn March 7, 1673; proved October 23, 1674): "To all other chattels, real and personal to my said wife Elizabeth. My brother-in-law, William Denn of London, grocer. To my honoured mother Mrs. Alice Lane and to my wife's mother Mrs. Alice Howell and to my said brother-in-law William Denn and to my sister his wife 10£ each for mourning, and to their children 5£ apiece. My wife to have the use of my silver tankard, silver tumbler and twelve silver spoons during her life, thereafter my tumbler six spoons to her dear son *Charles Saltonstall* and the tankard and six spoons to her dear daughter *Elizabeth Saltonstall*. [my italics]"[38] Of course, the testator is the Jo (John) Lane who sailed for the Isle of Providence and was the brother of "our" Samuel. However, of interest here is information about the prominent *Saltonstall* family of London and Boston, Massachusetts, which I do not think has come to light before. From the Vicar General of London we find the "Marriage license 5 Apr. 1671 to John Lane of All Hallows,

---

33. Marriage license, June 8, 1667: "William Denne of St. Bartholomew the Great London grocer, bachlor about 30 and Mary Lane of Hammersmith, spinster, about 25. License granted by the Vicar-General 8 June 1667 for the marriage of William Denne of St. Bartholomew the Great, . . . and Mary Lane. . . . To marry at Battersey, Surrey, Hammersmith, or Chiswick, Middlesex."
34. Will of John Lane (P.C.C. 31 Alchin).
35. Will of Alice Lane of London (P.C.C. 112 Reeve).
36. Tombstone inscription.
37. Will of William Denn (P.C.C. Box 168).
38. Will of John Lane of Bristol (P.C.C. 115 Bunce).

Bread Street, London Bachelor, about 41 and Elizabeth Saltingstall [note spelling] of St. Botolph's, Aldgate, London, widow, about 34 to marry at White Chapel, Stepney or St. Paul's, Shadwell, Middlesex." Who was this widow Elizabeth *Saltingstall*'s former husband? Note her children's names were Charles Saltonstall and Elizabeth Saltonstall. Now from St. Botolph-without Algate burial register we find: "Buried 1665 Oct. 6 Charles Saltingstone, Towerhill, Precinct." Furthermore, from *The Records of The Virginia Company of London*, we find: "1617, March 4 A Bill of Advanture granted to S'S. Saltingston."[39] This Sir Samuel is undoubtedly Sir Samuel Saltonstall, Knight, son of Richard.[40] Sir Samuel married Elizabeth, the daughter of William Wye. Sir Samuel died June 30, 1640, and one of his sons was Charles Saltonstall. Sir Samuel "was named executor under the will of Captain John Smith, who was concerned in the settlement of Virginia."[41] If Charles Saltingstone was the first husband of the above Elizabeth Lane, he was surely much older than she; however, it looks as if both of Elizabeth's husbands were adventurous mariners. John Lane, the testator, in his will (proved October 4, 1670) wrote "to cozen Capt. John Lane £1000 *if he returns to England alive.*" We quote from the article in the *Dictionary of National Biography* on Charles Saltonstall: "He describes himself as a stranger to the land and his kinsfolk many long voyages having banished him from remembrance of both." This does not sound like an early marriage with children, but how about a marriage late in life? It looks as if Elizabeth Howell, wife of John Lane of Bristol (will proved October 23, 1674) had been previously married to Charles Saltonstall, son of Sir Samuel. We must consult the Boston Saltonstalls about this.

However, Samuel Lane, son of Richard Lane of the Isle of Providence and his wife Alice Carter, is the subject of our sketch. The will of John Lane (proved October 4, 1670) reads: "To cozen Samuel Lane, clerk £20." A clergyman in those days was known as a clerk. Our next reference to Samuel Lane is where he appears as minister of Long Houghton, Northumberland, married to Barbara Roddam, whose date of birth we do not know, but she was "under age in 1632." Barbara was the daughter of Edmund Roddam, who had an uncle, Matthew Roddam, living 1553.[42] We are going to find later a Matthew Roddam on Kent Island in the Chesapeake Bay who was intimately associated with the brothers John and Thomas Butler, also of Kent Island, and half-nephews of Capt. Nathaniel Butler. We will see other intimate ties between Samuel Lane and Matthew Roddam in the Chesapeake Bay area.[43]

These two Matthew Roddams (because of dates) can not be one and the same person, but the name Matthew Roddam in England, great uncle of Barbara Roddam who married Samuel Lane, is too suggestive not to be considered with the Matthew Roddam on the Chesapeake Bay and his connections with Samuel Lane of Anne Arundel, Maryland. Apparently life did not run too smoothly for Samuel Lane in Long Houghton, Northumberland. We must remember that his father, Richard, had had an "examination" for unorthodox, nonconformist, i.e. Puritan religious opinions before sailing for the Isle of Providence. Also we must remember that he still had his own ideas on the Isle of Providence, sided with the Puritan ministers in the religious disputes; and consequently was sent to England as prisoner with the Puritan ministers Leverton, Sherrard, and

39. Ed. Susan Myra Kingsbury, 4 vols. (Washington, 1906), 3: 59.
40. Richard M. Saltonstall, *Ancestry and Descendants of Sir Richard Saltonstall First Associate of the Massachusetts Bay Colony and Patentee of Connecticut* (Boston, 1897), p. 11.
41. *Ibid.*
42. Madeleine Hope Dodds, ed., *A History of Northumberland* (London, 1935), 14: 46.
43. William Hand Browne et al., *Archives of Maryland*, 68 vols. (Baltimore, 1883-), 1: 143, 169; *ibid.*, 4: 69 and 307. Matthew Rodam was transported to Maryland by Leonard Calvert (*Maryland Historical Magazine* 5 (September 1910): 262.

Halhead. He was later kindly "received by the Lords Patentees" . . . and was "encouraged to return" to the island.[44] With this in Samuel's background we are not surprised to hear that a difference of opinion appeared in the church at Long Houghton, Northumberland, and Samuel Lane was "ejected in 1662,"[45] although Calamy said he was "A man of great sincerity and of an unblamable exemplarly conversation."[46] If we are correct in assuming "our" Samuel married Barbara Roddam, she apparently died before 1664, because on that date Samuel Lane emigrated to Maryland.[47] No wife appears.

We now have a Samuel Lane appearing in Maryland in 1664.[48] It is true we do not find a record which says: "Samuel Lane, who sailed in Ye Expectation to the Isle of Providence in 1635 is identical with the Samuel Lane who appeared in Maryland in 1664." Such records are not readily found. However, there are many "coincidencies" which suggest very strongly that the two above mentioned Samuel Lanes are one and the same.

Lest we confuse our two Samuel Lanes, suppose we designate as Samuel Lane (#1) he who sailed for the Isle of Providence in Ye Expectation on April 16, 1635, with his father Richard, mother Alice, and two brothers Jo and Oziel. Let us refer to the Samuel Lane who appeared in Maryland in 1664 as Samuel Lane (#2). We hope to show the two Samuel Lanes are one and the same person.

Samuel Lane (#1) spent his youth on The Isle of *Providence*. Samuel Lane (#2) first appears in Maryland 1664 in what was then known as *Providence*.[49] Samuel Lane (#2) married the widow, Margaret Maulden Burrage, daughter of Francis Maulden and his wife Grace,[50] who married as her third husband Edward Lloyd,[51] progenitor of the Lloyds of Wye House. She (Margaret Maulden Burrage) the widow of John Burrage, bore Samuel Lane (#2) a son, Dutton Lane, to whom he left (in 1681) part of Browsley Hall.[52] On July 19, 1703, Dutton Lane sold 376 acres of Browsley Hall to *James Butler* (then of Prince Georges County).[53] Samuel Lane's (#2) widow, Margaret, married as her third husband Job Evans, and on April 18, 1696, Job Evans sold "Job's Addition" (225 acres) to *James Butler* (then to Anne Arundel County).[54] The *James Butler* of the above two deeds is a direct descendent of *Thomas Butler* of Kent Island in the Chesapeake Bay, mentioned earlier as the half-nephew of *Capt. Nathaniel Butler,* Governor of the Isle of Providence, who dined several times with Richard Lane, father of Samuel Lane (#1) on The Isle of Providence.[55]

Although Samuel Lane (#2) in his will dated January 18, 1681, (Anne Arundel County) appointed his wife, Margaret, executrix,[56] nevertheless his "next door neighbor," Col. Thomas Taylor, acted as executor.[57] Col. Thomas Taylor was the son of Philip Taylor,[58]

44. Newton, *English Puritans,* p. 258.
45. See footnote 42.
46. Edward Calamy, *An Abridgement of Mr. Baxter's History of His Life and Times,* 2 vols. (London, 1713), 1: 511.
47. Gust Skordas, ed., *The Early Settlers of Maryland* (Baltimore, 1968), p. 280.
48. *Ibid.* He was transported to Maryland by one Thomas Vaughan. See also *ibid.,* p. 477.
49. Harry Wright Newman, *Anne Arundel Gentry* (Baltimore, 1963), p. xiii.
50. Will of Grace Lloyd, drawn May 10, 1698; proved Feb. 17, 1700 (P.C.C., 93 Pye); also *MHM,* 43: 231–32.
51. Will of Edward Lloyd, drawn May 11, 1695; proved July 14, 1696 (P.C.C., Bond 121); also *MHM,* 7: 421.
52. Will of Samuel Lane, Anne Arundel County, Jan. 18, 1681. Lib. 2, fol. 185.
53. Anne Arundel County Land Records, Lib. W.T. #2, fol. 59.
54. Patent Lib. C #3, fol 415, 416.
55. See the Appendix for the Butler-Lane Chart. Documentation for this chart is in the library at the Maryland Historical Society.
56. See footnote 52.
57. T.B. 12B, fols. 67, 75, 263.
58. *Archives of Maryland,* 4: 507.

who during the Kent Island controversy was chief Lieutenant of William Claiborne,[59] whose wife was none other than *Elizabeth Butler*, half niece of Capt. *Nathaniel Butler*.[60] ("A conference [was] held between the right Honor[ble] the Lord Baltimore Proprietor of Maryland and William Penn, esq[re] Proprietary of Pennsilvania at the house of colonel Thomas Tailler [Taylor] on the ridge in Anne Arrundel County Wednesday the 13th of December 1682" [*Archives of Maryland*, 5: 382], where "the two . . . discussed the boundaries of Maryland and Pennsylvania" [J. Reany Kelly, *Quakers in the Founding of Anne Arundel County Maryland.*)

As mentioned before, Samuel Lane (#2) married Margaret Maulden Burrage, widow of John Burrage, whose father William Burrage (Burridge) lived on Kent Island[61] and owned property adjoining Fort Crayford (Crafford), the home of William and Elizabeth Butler Claiborne.[62]

Samuel Lane (#1) who sailed April 16, 1635, in *Ye Expectation* with his family had a sister, Mary Lane, born while the family was living on The Isle of Providence. On June 8, 1667, she married William Denn of St. Bartholomew The Great, London, grocer,[63] great nephew of John Denn whose wife, Lucy Ayleworth, was sister-in-law of Thomas Stockett,[64] whose four sons Francis, Thomas, Henry, and Lewis Stockett all came to America. The three brothers, Thomas, Henry, and Francis Stockett, all removed to Anne Arundel County, and owned and lived on "Dodon" and "Obligation," properties adjoining "Browsley Hall"[65] owned by Samuel Lane (#2).

Samuel Lane (#1) married Barbara Roddam, great nephew of Matthew Roddam of Shawdon, Northumberland, England.[66] Matthew Roddam of Kent Island, Maryland, in July 1642 swore "oath"[67] to the will of John Bulter of Kent Island, half nephew of Capt. *Nathaniel Butler*.[68] Thomas Butler, brother of John, also lived on Kent Island with Matthew Roddam.[69]

In 1664 the Maryland Matthew Roddam bought 100 acres ("Come Away") from Col. Thomas Taylor of Anne Arundel County,[70] executor of the 1681 will of Major Samuel Lane (#2). As mentioned earlier, Matthew Roddam of England and the Matthew Roddam of Kent Island (because of dates) cannot be one and the same person. Matthew Roddam in England was involved in the settlement of 1553 in Cuthbert, Proctor of Shawdon, Northumberland, and Matthew Roddam of Kent Island immigrated to Maryland in 1643, "and demandeth 50 acres more as servent to Governor Calvert."[71]

But enough of these "coincidences." I have worked on the Lane genealogy for thirty years, and could bring forth still more. It has been said that Samuel Lane was "a man of parts," and it appears to be a fact. Although a clergyman in England, he appears in Maryland in 1664 as plain "Samuel Lane."[72] However, he seems to have risen rapidly,

59. Susie M. Ames, ed., *County Court Records of Accomack-Northampton Virginia 1640-1645* (Charlottesville, 1973), p. xv.
60. See the Appendix.
61. Skordas, *Early Settlers*, p. 71.
62. *Archives of Maryland*, 54: 235.
63. See footnote 33.
64. *The Publication of the Harleian Society* (London), vol. 54, p. 48; vol. 42, fol. 150. Also John Burke, *A Genealogical and Heraldic History of The Commoners of Great Britain and Ireland*, 4 vols. (London, 1838), 3; 21.
65. "Warrants," vol. 12, fol. 298, 299, Hall of Records.
66. Dodds, ed., *History of Northumberland*, 14: 284, 285, 286.
67. *Archives of Maryland*, 4: 69.
68. See the Appendix.
69. *Archives of Maryland*, 1: 168, 169.
70. St. Marys County Rent Roll (MHS), p. 75. See also *Archives of Maryland*, 4: 507.
71. Skordas, *Early Settlers*, p. 386.
72. *Ibid.*, p. 280.

because between his arrival in 1664 and his death in 1681 we find him mentioned in the *Archives of Maryland* as: gent, chirurgeon, doctor, doctor of physick, commr. of Anne Arundel County, justice of Anne Arundel County, gentleman of the quorum, and major.[73] In addition we find him witness or administrator of the wills of nine of his neighbors, unusual for that time.[74] The fact that he is referred to as "gent" would appear to indicate simply that he was of gentle birth. We do not find in England any reference to a Samuel Lane having any medical training or experience; nor is there any hint of this when Samuel Lane (#2) arrives in Maryland. However, upon further study it would appear that he probably received his medical training and experience after arriving in America, as we find him closely associated with Dr. Francis Stockett, Dr. William Jones, Dr. George Wells,[75] and possibly others. They appear to have informally constituted what today we would refer to as a "medical center." All of these men lived near one another and near Samuel Lane (#2),[76] and it is possible that he obtained his medical training and experience from them.[77] Samuel (#2) was apparently elected to his civic offices, and on September 13, 1681, we find him as a major fighting the Indians, and writing the following letter to the Lord Baltimore: "The country of Anne Arrunall at this time is in great danger. Our men marched all Monday night, the greatest part of South River had been most cut off. We want ammunition exceedingly, and have not where- with-all to furnish half our men. I hope your Ldpp. Will dispatch away Coll. Burgess with what ammunition may be thought convenient. I shall take all the care that lyeth in me, but there comes daily and hourly complaints to me that I am wholly imployed in the Countrys Service."[78] As Samuel (#2) was dead by 1681,[79] we can guess he probably died in these Indian skirmishes.

Major Samuel Lane (#2) lived on Burrage, Burrage Blossom, and Burrages End, properties inherited by his wife, Margaret, from her former husband, John Burrage.[80] We quote an abstract of Samuel Lane's (#2) will: "to son Samuel at 18 years of age and hrs. part of Browsley Hall; to son Dutton at 18 years of age and residue of Browsley Hall; to daughter Sarah personalty and above-mentioned property in event of death of sons withou't issue; to nephew Thomas Lane, in Ireland, property afsd. in event of death of sd. child. without issue; to daughter Grace Burridge, personalty; wife Margaret, execx.; overseers: sons-in-law Saml. Smith and Francis Hutchins; test: Arthur Browne, Jno. Davis, Jno. Hall, Thos. Meridal. 2. 185."[81] His wife, Margaret, had three daughters by her first husband, John Burridge. These were Grace Burridge, who married Benjamin Scrivener; Elizabeth Burridge, who married Francis Hutchins; and Margaret Burridge, who married first Nathan Smith and secondly Thomas Tench, governor of Maryland, 1702-1704, who drew the will and was administrator[82] of the will of Lionel Copley, the first acting Royal Governor of Maryland.[83] Interestingly enough, Governor Lionel Copley was the son of another Lionel Copley, first cousin of Robert Greville, Lord Brooke, whose

---

73. See various issues of the *Archives of Maryland* for the years between 1664 and 1681.

74. Jane Baldwin, *The Maryland Calendar of Wills* (Baltimore, 1904), 1: 39, 47, 61, 62, 63, 68, 74, 183, 209, 215.

75. George B. Scriven, "Doctors, Drugs, and Apothecaries of Seventeenth Century Maryland," *Bulletin of the History of Medicine* 37 (November–December 1963): 516–22.

76. See footnote 65.

77. For evidence of Samuel Lane's medical activities, see the will of Richard Wells, proved June 9, 1671, Anne Arundel County Will Book (1.439).

78. Quoted in J.D. Warfield, *Founders of Anne Arundel and Howard Counties, Maryland* (Baltimore, 1905), p. 51.

79. Will drawn Jan. 18, 1681; see Anne Arundel County Will Book 2, fol. 185.

80. Anne Arundel County deeds, WT #2, fol. 72.

81. See footnote 79.

82. *MHM*, 17: 171.

83. Inventory and Accounts, MHR, Lib. 19½, fol. 60.

protege was none other than Richard Lane of the Isle of Providence,[84] and father of Samuel Lane (#1). Can this again be mere *coincidence?*

As I worked on this Lane genealogy for thirty years with Kenyon Stevenson of Cleveland, Ohio (now deceased), it seems superfluous to repeat what we have already done. Mr. Stevenson was searching for his ancestor Lambert Lane, and I was searching for my ancestor Rachel Lane, who married Alexander Russell about 1798. As I was living in Maryland I searched the records here and sent them to Mr. Stevenson who correlated them. Our work on the American Lanes can be seen in the Maryland Historical Society under Genealogy and History, Washington D.C. May 15, 1944 (call no. CS42.G5). The Dutton Lane family moved first to Towson, Maryland, then northwest of Reisterstown, and later to Ohio. His brother Samuel remained in Anne Arundel County.

It seems appropriate to note that Samuel Lane (#2) left "Hampton Court"[85] to his daughter Margaret, who with her husband William Merryman sold the property in 1746 to Charles Ridgely.[86] On this property Charles Ridgely built the handsome mansion near Towson known today as "Hampton."

---

84. "Mr. Lane, Lord Brooke's agent," *Calendar of State Papers . . . 1574 to 1660,* 1: 249.
85. Baldwin, *Maryland Calendar of Wills,* 5: 231.
86. Baltimore County Land Records, Lib. T.B., no. E. fol. 166.

APPENDIX

Butler-Lane Chart

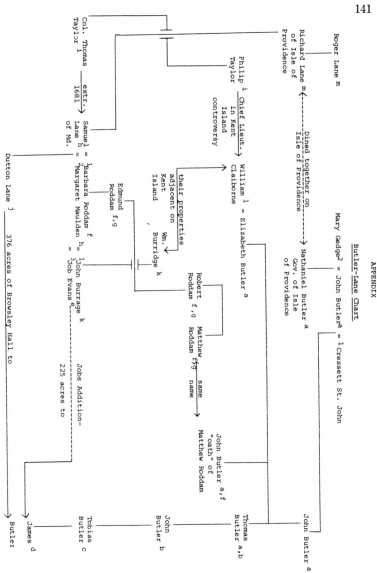

LECOMPTE FAMILY.

FRANCIS B. CULVER.

1. ANTHONY LECOMPTE [1] was born in Picardy, France, and died during the autumn of 1673, in Dorchester County, Maryland. In 1655-6, he appears in the province of Maryland, as the following entry among the land records attests: "I Antoine LeCompte do give all my right and title to Ishmael Wright and my man's Henry Mites right and title which is the 200 acres due to me. As witness my hand, 7th February, 1655."

(Signed) ANTHOINE LE COMPT.

(L. O., Q. 440.441).

In 1658-9, Anthony LeCompte appears as patentee of a free-hold in Calvert County, known as "Compton," and containing 75 acres, originally surveyed 8 August, 1651, for Ishmael Wright, on the North side of the Patuxent River (Calvert County Rent Rolls). Ishmael Wright acquired title to "Compton" in consideration of the transporting of himself and Anne his wife, into the Province, and assigned the same to Antoine LeCompte, 11 February, 1658 (L. O., Q. 401).

Under an entry of 12 March 1658, one Arthur Wright demands land for transporting Katharine his wife, William Squire, Thomas Middleton, Elizabeth Holston: and Thomas Raymond, Barbara Crouch, Thomas Jones, transported by Antoine LeCompte. Warrant then issued to lay out for Arthur Wright and Anthoine Le Compt 700 acres upon "the Eastern Shore" (L. O., Q. 440. 441).

"Whereas, on the 12 March 1658, warrant issued for 700 acres of land upon the Eastern Shore to Anth⁰. Lecompte and Arthur Wright, ret. 29 September foll.— which said warrant being given up, the said Anthony LeCompte hath taken new warrant in his own name. Warrant *inde* for 700 acres on the Eastern Shore, return 25 December next, to the said Anthony LeCompt." (*ib.* IV. 61).

On 13 August 1659, there was laid out for Anthony Le

Compte of this Province, planter, a parcel of land called
" St. Anthoine " (or " Antonine "), lying on the East side
of the Chesapeake Bay, and on the South side of the Choptank River, in Horne's Bay, containing 800 acres (L. O.,
IV. 244: Dorchester County Rent Rolls).

The aforesaid tract was acquired by Anthony LeCompte,
17 January 1659, " in consideration that Anthony Le
Compte hath transported Thomas Raymond, Barbara
Crouch, and Thomas Jones into this Province: and hath
further due to him by assignment of Mary Guilford the
land (200 acres) due to her for transporting herself and
Barnes Johnson; and also, by the assignment of Emperour
Smith, the land due to him for transporting himself, Robert Bailey and William Major. Granted unto said Anthony Le Compte the land called " St. Anthony," on the
East side of Chesapeake Bay, and the South side of the
Choptank River, in Horne Bay, 800 acres." (L. O., IV,
181-378).

Shortly after this, Anthony LeCompte returned to
France, where he met his future wife, took her over to
London to be married, and then returned to Maryland. On
2 March, 1662/3, " came Antonio LeCompte and enters
four rights, vizt., for his wife Easter, John Goteer, Andrew
Gundry and Ambrose, for which he demands warrant,"
which was accordingly issued for 200 acres, of date 21 Feb-
ruary, 1662 (L. O., v. 243). On 22 Feby. 1664, a
" Patent of Denization " was granted to Antoine Le
Compte, his wife and children (Md. Arch. III, 513).

On 18 March 1662, we find the following entry: " I
Andrew Skinner of this Province, do alienate, etc. unto
Mounsier Anthony Compt, land called " Compton," in
Dividing Creek, on the north side of the Choptank River."
This tract consisted of 100 acres, in Talbot county, and was
originally laid out for Andrew Skinner (by assignment
from James Smith). On 26 April 1663, Anthony Le
Compte assigned his rights to John Edmondson, who
assigned the same to James Elvard, merchant (L. O., VII,
120, 125).

In the Proceedings of the Maryland Assembly held at
Patuxent, 24 September, 1657, among the " severall
charges to be Satisfied by way of Levie out of the County
of Patuxent," we find a bill allowed to Anthony LeCompte

for killing three wolves, amounting to 300 lbs. of tobacco
(Md. Arch. I, 365).

In the Proceedings of April-May, 1669, out of the assess-
ments of the Province charged to the several counties, there
were due to Anthony LeCompte, as of Talbot county, 2022
lbs. of tobacco (*ib.* II, 231).

On 6 May, 1669, Anthony LeCompte was appointed a
Justice of Dorchester County, which office he held until
1671 (Md. Arch. v, 52-53: Liber C-D, 431).

The will of Anthony LeCompte, of Dorchester County,
Maryland, was made 9 September 1673, and filed 25
October 1673 (Annapolis, Wills I, 562). He leaves to his
eldest son, John Le Compte, all his " land on the other side
of the creek, south from my house, with 50 acres I bought
of Wm. Willoughby ": all the remainder of his lands,
equally, to his sons Moses, Philip and Anthony LeCompte:
to his eldest daughter Hester Le Compte, 8 cows: to Nicholas Trippe, one cow: and appoints his wife Hester Le
Compte sole executrix. The will was witnessed by Jacob
Seth, Jno. Snookes and Margaret Bryant.

Anthony Le Compte married 11 July 1661, in London,
England, Esther Dottando (or, Dotlando). She was a
native of Dieppe, in Normandy, France. The marriage
record is given in the register of St. Helen's, Bishopsgate,
London, as follows: " Anthony LeCompte of the „parishe
of Macke neere Callis in France & Esther Dottando of
Deepe in France weare mar'ed," 11 July, 1661.

A few months after Anthony LeCompte's decease, his
widow Esther, married (1674), " Monsieur " Mark Cordea, formerly of St. John's, in St. Mary's County, an inn-
holder and merchant, and owner of " St. Elizabeth's
Manor," which he purchased from John Nuthall, Jr., of
St. Mary's County, gentleman (Annapolis, Chancery
Records C D, I, 273).

In Bacon's Laws of Maryland (1674), chapter XII,
(original Libers: C & W H, 240: W H, 123: W H & L,
86), appears the petition for naturalization on the part of
Hester Cordea, *et al.,* as follows: " Petition of . . .
Hester Cordea [born] at Deepe in Normandy, John Le
Count, Mosses Lecount, Phillip Lacount, Anthony Lacount,
all the sonns of Anthony Lacount borne at Picardie in the
Kingdom of France; Hester Lacount, Katherine Lacount,
daughters to the said Anthony Lacount, and both sonns and

daughters borne within Your Lordships Province of Maryland . . . for divers years therein Inhabitants being invited to come and dwell within this Province by and upon
confidence of Your Lordships declaration of the second of
July 1649," etc. They were naturalized under the Act
passed 6 June 1674.

On 17 July 1680, there was issued a subpoena to Mark
Cordea and Hester his wife, executrix of the last will and
testament of Anthony LeCompte, deceased, to answer the
bill of complaint of Henry Fox and Hester his wife, one of
the daughters of the said Anthony (Annapolis, Chancery
Records CD. 273). Committees from the Upper and
Lower Houses of Assembly met occasionally at Mark Cordea's house (Md. Arch. vii: xiii).

Anthony and Hester LeCompte had issue: *

2.   i. JOHN,[2] b. 1662: d. *circa* 1705.
3. ii. MOSES, d. 1720.
    iii. Philip, d. unmarried (a minor).
4. iv. ANTHONY, d. *circa* 1705.
     v. Esther, m. (1) Henry Fox, of Talbot Co.: (2) Wm. Skinner, Jr.
    vi. Katharine, m. (1) James Cullins: (2) Thomas Bruff.

2. JOHN LECOMPTE [2] (Anthony [1]) was born in 1662, in
Maryland, and died 1704/5, in Dorchester county. His
will was made 4 November 1704, and proved 6 June 1705
(Annapolis Wills iii. 455).

He bequeathed to his son William, " Linkwoods " (250
acres), at the head of Transquaking, formerly belonging to
Dr. Robert Winsmore: to son Philemon, " LeCompte's
Adventure," at the head of Ingram's Creek: to sons Anthony and John (equally), part of 200 acres (unnamed)
on the south side of Ingram's Creek, it having been jointly
taken up with John Brannock: to sons James and Robert
Winsmore LeCompte, residue of the tract last referred to,
and lying on the north side of Ingram's Creek: to daughter
Ann, all land taken up by testator jointly with John Bran-
nock and Andrew Skinner, between the branch of Cabin
Creek and the northwest fork of Nanticoke River: to son
John (aforesaid) also " John's Good Luck " (50 acres),
" LeCompte's Delight " (50 acres) and " Indian Ridge "

* The source of a good deal of the following data relating to the LeCompte
family of Maryland is an old manuscript record, said to have been compiled in 1819, but the writer of this sketch can not vouch for its accuracy,
except in so far as he has been able to verify the same from authoritative
sources (F. B. C.).

(87 acres): to wife Ann (executrix), the dwelling plantation during life, the same to revert to son Anthony. All
the children to be of age at 18 years. The witnesses under
the will were Jane Kemp: Margaret Nowell and John
Rawlings.

In the Annapolis Chancery Records there is an entry of
the suit of one Thomas McKeele, lessee of William Warner,
against John LeCompte, which suit was entered by the
Court, 22 February, 1704/5, as " abated by the defendant's death " (Lib. PC. 516).

John LeCompte married Ann Winsmore, daughter of
Dr. Robert Winsmore, and had issue:

5.   i.   JOHN,[3] b. 1686: d. 1754.
6.   ii.   WILLIAM, d. 1749.
7.   iii.   PHILEMON, b. 1690.
8.   iv.   JAMES.
     v.   Robert Winsmore.
    vi.   Anne.
   vii.   Anthony.

3.   MOSES LECOMPTE [2] (Anthony [1]) was born in Maryland
and died in 1720, in Dorchester County. According to a
family record compiled in 1819, Moses LeCompte became
partially blind at 18 or 19 years of age, and altogether so
at 22 or 23, although he was sent to England for treatment
of his affliction. Blindness appeared in several later generations of this branch of the family.

The will of Moses LeCompte was made 1 January 1717,
and proved 15 March 1720/1. He bequeathed to his sons
Philip, Thomas and Samuel LeCompte, " all my lands I
now live on, but if it please God any more of my children
should lose their sight except my sons Moses LeCompte
and Peter LeCompte, that my said children so losing their
sight should be equal partners in my said lands with my
aforesaid three sons ": he gave to " my said children one
small tract called " Padan-Aram," except my sons Moses
LeCompte and Peter LeCompte," and to the last named
" the said land lying in Little Choptank ": he mentions his
three daughters Esther LeCompte, Mary LeCompte and
Elizabeth LeCompte. The witnesses under the will were
John LeCompte, Joseph LeCompte, Elizabeth Bonner
and Rachel Bonner (Annapolis Wills, XVI. 365). The
administration accounts of the estate mention the wife
Mary, with three sons Philip, Samuel and Joseph, as the
executors (Annapolis Accounts IV. 70: v. 18. 286).

Moses LeCompte married Mary Skinner (b. 1667) daughter of " old " (Thomas?) " Skinner of England," (according to family record of 1819). A deposition of Mary LeCompte in 1741 gives her age as " about 74 years " (Dor. Court Records xiv. 200).

Moses and Mary (Skinner) LeCompte had issue:

<table>
<tr><td></td><td>i.</td><td>Philip,³ died 1734 unmarried: said to have been " blind."</td></tr>
<tr><td>9.</td><td>ii.</td><td>Moses, said to have been " blind."</td></tr>
<tr><td></td><td>iii.</td><td>Thomas, died unmarried: said to have been " blind."</td></tr>
<tr><td>10.</td><td>iv.</td><td>Peter.</td></tr>
<tr><td></td><td>v.</td><td>Samuel, died 1775 unmarried: said to have been " blind."</td></tr>
<tr><td>11.</td><td>vi.</td><td>Joseph, said to have been " blind."</td></tr>
<tr><td>12.</td><td>vii.</td><td>Anthony.</td></tr>
<tr><td>13.</td><td>viii.</td><td>William, said to have been " blind."</td></tr>
<tr><td></td><td>ix.</td><td>Esther, died unmarried: said to have been " blind."</td></tr>
<tr><td></td><td>x.</td><td>Mary (" blind ") m. Arthur Rigby, of Talbot County, Md.</td></tr>
<tr><td></td><td>xi.</td><td>Elizabeth (" blind ") m. James Sewers, of Philadelphia, Pa.</td></tr>
</table>

4. ANTHONY LECOMPTE ² (Anthony ¹) was born in Maryland and died in 1705, in Dorchester County. The will of Anthony LeCompte was made 20 January 1704 and proved 6 June 1705 (Annapolis Wills, iii. 456).

He left to his sons Nehemiah and Anthony Le Compte, jointly, the tract called " St. Anthony's," which was bequeathed to the testator by his father: to his eldest son Nehemiah, 25 acres of land " at the Island ": to his son Anthony, " Bluestone Branch " on the western shore, called the " Halfway House." The sons to be of age at 18 years. To his wife Margaret (executrix) he bequeathed all personalty. The witnesses under the will were Henry Beckwith, Magdalen Wardner and Mary Wardner (Baldwin's Cal. of Md. Wills, iii. 51).

Anthony LeCompte married Margaret Beckwith, and had issue:

14. i. Nehemiah,³ b. 1698.
    ii. Anthony (no issue).
    iii. Margaret.

5. John LeCompte ³ (John,² Anthony ¹) was born in 1686 and died in 1754, in Dorchester County, Maryland. In a deposition dated 15 December, 1741, his age is given as 55 years (Dor. Co. Court Records, xiv. 200).

The will of John LeCompte was made 17 Jan'y. 1754, and proved 15 March 1754 (Annapolis Wills, xxix. 76). To his wife Blanche Le Compte he bequeathed " St. Anthony," " Purkerdy " (Picardy), " Chance," " Roxall "

and "LeCompte's Pasture"; and one shilling to each of
his following eight children—John, Charles, Anthony and
Philemon LeCompte, Blanche LeCompte, Mary Woolford,
Esther Cullens, and Clare Fowler (the last mentioned also
received four negroes). His sons were named as the
executors.

John LeCompte married Blanche Powell (d. 1769) and
had issue:

15.   i.   JOHN.[4]
      ii. Charles, m. Sarah Hirth (?), of Talbot County.
15ᵃ. iii. ANTHONY, m. Mary Sewell.
      iv. Philemon, m. —— Hatfield.
16.   v.   WILLIAM.
      vi. Sarah.
      vii. Mary, m. —— Woolford (?).
      viii. Clare, m. —— Fowler.
      ix. Esther, m. —— Cullins.
      x.   Blanche, m. Anthony LeCompte[3] (Moses,[2] Anthony[1]).
      xi. Elizabeth, m. —— Vickers.

6. WILLIAM LECOMPTE[3] (John,[2] Anthony[1]) died in 1749
in Dorchester county, Maryland. His will was made 18
May 1749, and proved 8 July 1749 (Annapolis Wills,
XXVII. 8).

He bequeathed to his sons Philemon and John Le-
Compte, the dwelling plantation and an equal division of
the "land I have at the head of Transquaking"; to son
William LeCompte land in the northwest fork of Nanticoke River, called "Poole's Outlet" (130 acres): he makes
a bequest to his daughter Sarah, "in case she should come
back," and mentions his daughter Anne Baynam and his
son Levin LeCompte.

William LeCompte married —— Smoot, and had
issue:

      i.   Philemon.[4]
      ii. John.
      iii. William.
      iv. Sarah.
      v.   Anne, m. —— Bayman.
      vi. Levin.

7. PHILEMON LECOMPTE[3] (John,[2] Anthony[1]) was born in
1690, according to a deposition made in 1730, when his age
is given as 40 years (Chancery Records I R, No. 1, 314),
and died in 1769. His will was proved 28 August, 1769
(Annapolis Wills, XXXVII. 401).

Philemon Le Compte married Mary Seward (d. 1769)
and had issue:

    i. William.[4]
   ii. James.
  iii. John, d. 1768: m. Mary ——, and had one daughter, Elizabeth.
  iv. Abner, d. 1771.
   v. Esther, m. (cousin) William LeCompte[4] (John,[3] John,[2] Anthony[1]).
  vi. Charles (of "Oyster Shell Point"), d. 26 March 1809, aged 64 years: his wife's name was Drusilla.
 vii. Mary, married —— Dawson.
viii. Ann, married (1) —— Phillips: m. (2) Owens: m. (3) —— Cook.

8. JAMES LECOMPTE[3] (John,[2] Anthony[1]) was the ancestor of the Le Comptes of Caroline County, Md. He married —————— Mallet, and had issue:

    i. James.[4]
   ii. Philemon.
  iii. Anthony.
  iv. Charles.
   v. Nathan.

9. MOSES LECOMPTE[3] (Moses,[2] Anthony[1] joins in a deed, dated 11 Aug. 1731, with Levinia his wife, conveying to " our loving son Matthew Driver," one half of the "Grove," on James Island (Dorch. Co. Deeds, VIII. 429). He also made a deed of gift, bearing date 8 March 1768, for " natural love and affection which I have and do bear to my three grandsons Levin Cator, William Geoghegan and Moses Geoghegan," as follows: " unto my grandson Levin Cator, one half of the whole survey of " Le Compte's Addition " (34½ acres) on James Island, in Dorchester County: unto my two grandsons William and Moses Geoghegan the easternmost half of " Le Compte's Addition," equally, and my part of " Grove," (75 acres) lying on James Island, in Dorchester County." He also refers to his daughter Levinia Geoghegan (Dorch. Co. Land Records, XXII. 222). He married Levinia Pattison, daughter of Thomas Pattison (and widow of Matthew Driver, of James Island), and had issue:

17.   i. MOSES.[4]
   ii. Levinia, m. William Geoghegan, of Dublin.
  iii. Esther, m. Matthew Skinner.
  iv. Mary, m. (1) *ante* 1744 Edward Cator: (2) Marmaduke Dove: (3) —— Davey.

10. PETER LECOMPTE[3] (Moses,[2] Anthony[1]) married —————— Brannock, and had issue:

    i. Thomas, prob. died at sea.
   ii. Samuel, prob. died at sea.
  iii. Peter.

iv. Joseph, m. Elizabeth Sewers: from whom among others were Samuel LeCompte, of Tuckahoe Neck; Joseph LeCompte, of Castle Haven, who married Delilah Thomas (née Barnett) and had Esther Ann, who married Robert Taylor, of Balto.

11. JOSEPH LECOMPTE [3] (Moses,[2] Anthony [1]) d. 1776; he married the widow Shannon, and had issue:

  18.   i. SAMUEL.[4]
         ii. Nicholas, unmarried.
        iii. Joseph.
        iv. A daughter, married John Parker.

12. ANTHONY LECOMPTE [3] (Moses,[2] Anthony [1]) married (1) *ante* Nov. 1744, Catharine, widow of William Bennett, of Talbot county: m. (2) Blanche Le Compte [4] (John,[3] John,[2] Anthony [1]) and had issue:

By first wife:

     i. Elizabeth.[4]
    ii. Catharine.
   iii. Mary.
   iv. Esther.

By second wife:

     v. Sarah.
   vi. Dolly.

13. WILLIAM LECOMPTE [3] (Moses,[2] Anthony [1]) married the widow Martin, of Talbot county, and had issue:

         i. Philip,[4] unmarried: d. *circa* 1846, in New Castle County, Delaware.
  19.   ii. MOSES.
        iii. Thomas, unmarried.
        iv. Daniel, unmarried.
  20.   v. ISAIAH.
        vi. Mary, married Thomas Wingate.
       vii. Nancy, married Levin Wingate.

14. NEHEMIAH LECOMPTE [3] (Anthony,[2] Anthony [1]) was born in 1698, according to a deposition made in 1720, which gives his age as 22 years (Chancery Records, PC. 602).

Nehemiah LeCompte married Clare Poole, and had issue:

         i. Anthony,[4] married Sarah Skinner.
        ii. Nehemiah.
       iii. John.
       iv. Margaret.
        v. Mary.
       vi. Elizabeth.
      vii. Esther.

15. JOHN LECOMPTE [4] (John,[3] John,[2] Anthony [1]) married Sarah Peterkin, and had issue:

    i. John.[5]
   ii. Charles.
  iii. James.

15ª. ANTHONY LECOMPTE [4] (John,[3] John,[2] Anthony [1]) married
Mary Sewell and had issue:

    i. Fannie,[5] m. (1) —— Griffin (s. p.): (2) John Radcliffe
        (issue): (3) —— Leonard (s. p.).
   ii. Katharine, d. 10 Oct. 1803, unmarried.

16. WILLIAM LECOMPTE [4] (John,[3] John,[2] Anthony [1]) married (1) Linah Byus: m. (2) Esther LeCompte [4] (Philemon,[3] John,[2] Anthony [1]), and had issue:
  By first wife:

    i. William.[5]
   ii. Philemon.
  iii. John.
   iv. Sarah, m. Stephen LeCompte, of Chicacomico.
    v. Rebecca, m. Levin LeCompte, of Chicacomico.

  By second wife:
   vi. Charles.
  vii. Caleb.

17. MOSES LECOMPTE [4] (Moses,[3] Moses,[2] Anthony [1]) died in
1776, in Dorchester County, Maryland. The administration bond for the estate of Moses LeCompte, deceased, was
filed 20 February 1776, by Moses LeCompte, Jr., administrator, with Joseph Robson and Henry Keene, as sureties
(Annapolis, Testa. Proc. XLVII. 31). The inventory was
appraised 29 April 1776 by Thomas Creaton (Creighton)
and Henry Travers, in the sum of £710.4.2 (Annapolis,
Inventories, CXXV. 116).
    Moses LeCompte married Nancy Pattison, and had
issue:

21.   i. MOSES,[5] b. 1748 (or 1752).
   ii. Nancy, m. 1759, Jeremiah Pattison.
  iii. Esther.
   iv. Rosamond.
    v. Elizabeth, b. 1761: d. 1803.

18. SAMUEL LECOMPTE [4] (Joseph,[3] Moses,[2] Anthony [1]) married Rachel Watts and had issue:

    i. Edmond.[5]
   ii. Samuel.

19. MOSES LECOMPTE [4] (William,[3] Moses,[2] Anthony [1]) married —— Wheeler and had issue:

    i.   Moses.[5]
   ii.   Hugh.
  iii.   Mary.
   iv. Mahala.

20. ISAIAH LeCOMPTE [4] (William,[3] Moses,[2] Anthony [1]) married Sarah Geoghegan (of John) and had issue:

  22.   i.   WILLIAM G.[5]
  23.   ii. SAMUEL.
       iii. Isaiah ("never married—poor soul"!)

21. MOSES LeCOMPTE [5] (Moses,[4] Moses,[3] Moses,[2] Anthony [1]) was born in 1748, or 1752 (the authorities differ), and died 23 October 1801, on Taylor's Island, Dorchester county.

On 12 February 1776, a commission was issued to Moses LeCompte, Jr., as First Lieutenant of Captain Joseph Robson's Company of Minute-men, in Dorchester county. He succeeded Henry Keene, who had resigned (Md. Arch. XI. 153). On 24 May 1776, he was First Lieutenant in Captain Denwood Hick's Company of Dorchester County militia, but was recommissioned as First Lieutenant of Captain Joseph Robson's Company (ib. 441). He later became Lieutenant Colonel Commandant of the Dorchester county militia in the re-organization of the State forces following the Revolutionary War.

Moses LeCompte married twice. His first wife was Nancy Edmondson, who died prior to 1787. His second wife was Elizabeth Woodward (1763-1803).

There is on record in the Dorchester County Court, a bill of sale deed, bearing date 15 September 1787, from Moses LeCompte and Elizabeth his wife, of Dorchester County, to Benjamin Keene, Jr.; William Geoghegan; Thomas Hooper; John Aschcom Travers; Peter Harrington; John Aaron; John Geoghegan; John Robson and Isaac Creighton, trustees appointed " to take care and management of a chapel lately built on Taylor's Island for the use of ministers of the M. E. Church " (Lib. NH No. 9, 411).

Issue by first wife:

    i.   Nancy,[6] m. Colonel Moses Keene.

Issue by second wife:

  24.   ii. BENJAMIN WOODWARD, b. 1787.
       iii. Samuel W., d. 1861/2: midshipman, War of 1812: Lieut. Com.

U. S. N.: m. Mary Eccleston, daughter of Washington
  Eccleston.
  iv. Elizabeth, m. James Pattison.
  v. Emily W., m. James Bryan, son of Charles Bryan, of Cambridge.
  vi. Margaret.

22. WILLIAM G. LeCOMPTE [5] (Isaiah,[4] William,[3] Moses,[2] Anthony [1]) married Mary A. Eaton, of Talbot County, Md.,
and had issue:

    25. i.   THOMAS.[6]
    26. ii. WILLIAM G.
         iii. Mamie, m. Henry Hooper.
         iv. Sarah, m. Thomas Hubbard.
         v.   Mary Matilda, m. Samuel Brattan.
         vi. Annie Maria, m. John A. Applegarthe.
         vii. Rebecca, m. Stephen LeCompte.
         viii. Araminta, m. William Mitchell.

23. SAMUEL LeCOMPTE [5] (Isaiah,[4] William,[3] Moses,[2] Anthony [1]) married Mary Simmons and had issue:

    27. i.   PHILIP ISAIAH.[6]

24. BENJAMIN WOODWARD LeCOMPTE [6] (Moses,[5] Moses,[4]
Moses,[3] Moses,[2] Anthony [1]) was born in 1787, and died 20
November 1821. He married Mary E. Hooper (1786-
1822), and had issue:

    i.   Mary E. LeCompte,[7] m. John P. Hooper.
    ii. James Laird, d. 1853: m. Ann Werkmiller, of Norfolk, Va.
    iii. Gaston Cleves, b. 1815: d. 1878: m. Mary Hartshorn, daughter
         of Sylvanna Hartshorn, of Norfolk, Va.
    iv. Emily Ann.
    v.   Benjamin Hooper.

25. THOMAS LeCOMPTE [6] (William G.,[5] Isaiah,[4] William,[3]
Moses,[2] Anthony [1]) married Margaret Cook, and had issue:

    i.   Thomas.[7]
    ii. Daniel H.
    iii. Samuel.
    iv. Mary.
    v.   Margaret.

26. WILLIAM G. LeCOMPTE [6] (William G.,[5] Isaiah,[4] William,[3]
Moses,[2] Anthony [1]) married Nannie Stewart, and had
issue:

    i.   William.[7]
    ii. George.
    iii. Mamie.
    iv. Annie.

27. PHILIP ISAIAH LECOMPTE [6] (Samuel,[5] Isaiah,[4] William,[3]
Moses,[2] Anthony [1]) married Susan Hubbard, and had
issue:

    i. John.[7]
   ii. Samuel.
  iii. Philip.
   iv. Mary.
    v. Blanche.
   vi. Eva.
  vii. Lena.
 viii. Susan.
   ix. Daisy.
    x. Lulu.

LECOMPTE NOTES

Samuel LeCompte, called " the surveyor," said to have been
a grandson of James [3] (John,[2] Anthony [1]) married (1) ———
Price, and had issue *Edward P. LeCompte* (d. 1843) who married 1829 Emily White, of Cambridge, and had issue *Edward
W. LeCompte* who married 1853 Elizabeth Wall.

Samuel LeCompte, called " the Surveyor," married (2) Ara-
minta Smoot (née Frazier) and had issue *Samuel Dexter Le-
Compte, Henrietta Maria LeCompte, Araminta Sarah Le-
Compte,* and *Margaret Elizabeth LeCompte.*

Samuel Dexter LeCompte (Samuel) removed to the territory
of Kansas, was appointed Chief Justice in 1854, and there died.
He married Camilla Anderson, of Todd's Point, Dorchester
County, and had issue: *Samuel Edward LeCompte, Eugene
Dexter LeCompte, Edward Palmer LeCompte, Alice Emily Le-
Compte, Camilla A. LeCompte,* and *James Trippe LeCompte.*
Henrietta Maria LeCompte (Samuel) married 1837 Joseph R.
Eccleston. They removed to Keokuk, Iowa, in 1852, and both
died in 1853, leaving issue.

THE LINTHICUM FAMILY OF ANNE ARUNDEL CO. MARYLAND, AND BRANCHES

THOMAS LINTHICUM, the emigrant (probably from Wales, as the name represents a section in Wales, called the Valley of the Lindens), came over with Captain Edward Selby, at the same time as William Warren, Robert Bennett, Eleanor Mathews, in 1658. Eleanor Mathews married Captain Edward Selby. Thomas settled on West River in Anne Arundel County. Captain Selby received warrants for 300 acres of land for transporting these emigrants to Maryland. Thomas Linthicum joined the Friends' Church at West River, and was a member of the men's monthly meeting. At one of these meetings at Thomas Hooker's house, in 1682, he compared these meetings "like a jury meeting," was tried and censured. He and his wife had given 1,000 pounds of tobacco to the yearly meeting. He demanded the return of the tobacco, which was paid December 4, 1784 from William Richardson's tobacco house. He was granted in 1677, Lincecomb Stopp of 50 acres. In 1679, was granted Lincecomb Lott of 75 acres.

Thomas was born in 1640 and died November 12, 1701. Married Jane who survived him.

Issue:

Hezekiah, who married Milcah Francis.
Mary, who married Richard Snowden.
Jane, who married Thomas Rutland.
Thomas (2), who married Deborah Wayman.
Each of above issues to follow.

HEZEKIAH LINTHICUM, son of Thomas (1) and wife Jane, was born ——, will February 4, 1721-2. He married October 5, 1699 Milcah Francis, born November 14, 1666, buried December 22, 1721, daughter of Thomas Francis of Rhoda River 1657, and wife Ruth. Hezekiah is mentioned in his father's will of 1701.

Issue:

(1) Mary Linthicum, born January 20, 1700, died ——, married November 13, 1716.
Edmond Wayman, born May 22, 1699, baptized November 1, 1703, son of Leonard.
Wayman, who died 1721, and wife Dorcus Abbot.
Issue to follow.
(2) Francis Linthicum (1), son of Hezekiah and Milcah, was born September 29, 1709, will August 7, 1765. Married October 5, 1732, Eleanor Williams, baptized June 9, 1717, daughter of Richard Williams who married February 14, 1709, Eleanor Stockett, born December 8, 1693. Eleanor was the daughter of Thomas Stockett and wife Mary.
(3) Thomas Francis Linthicum, son of Hezekiah and Milcah, born February 13, 1716, baptized May 22, 1722, will August 12, 1790. Married Elizabeth Williams, born May 1, 1724.

Issue:
Richard Linthicum, born February 2, 1745, died 1759.
(4) Hezekiah (2), born September 12, 1722.
No record.

MARY LINTHICUM, daughter of Hezekiah and wife Milcah Francis, born January 20, 1700. Married November 13, 1716, Edmond Wayman, son of Leonard and Dorcas, mentioned in his father's will of March 16, 1720-21. He owned Orgenwood Thicket, 200 acres, on Patuxent River. Surveyed January 26, 1688. Transferred to son Edmond and wife September 15, 1718.

Issue:

(1) Hezekiah Wayman, born ——, died January 13, 1747.

(2) Ann Wayman, died October 26, 1750.

(3) Mary Wayman, died 1756.

(4) Edmond Wayman, born December 1, 1721.

(5) John Wayman, died July 9, 1765.

FRANCIS LINTHICUM, son of Hezekiah and Milcah, and wife Eleanor Williams.

ISSUE:

(1) Francis Linthicum, born May 8, 1734, died 1765. Married January 28, 1755, Mary Mayo, born July 20, 1740, daughter of Joseph Mayo and wife Sarah. Joseph Mayo was the son of Joshua of South River, who married, 1707, Hannah Learson.

Issue: Eight children. The youngest, Joshua, married Elizabeth Beard.

(2) Micah Linthicum, daughter of Francis and Eleanor Williams. Born November 21, 1735, married Thomas Wayman.

Issue:

Eleanor, born August 6, 1752.

Francis, born February 11, 1753.

Edmond, born March 3, 1757.

(3) Eleanor Linthicum, daughter of Francis and wife Eleanor, born February 23, 1737-8, married —— Clark.

(4) Thomas Linthicum, son of Francis and Eleanor, born August 29, 1743, married 1764, Cassandra of Dorchester.

(5) Mary Linthicum, daughter of Francis and Eleanor, born July 15, 1746. Mentioned in her father's will of 1765.

(6) Francis Linthicum, daughter of Francis and Eleanor, born November 20, 1749. Mentioned in her father's will of 1765.

(7) Richard Linthicum, son of Francis and Eleanor, born April 12, 1752. Married November 25, 1778, to Mary Lee of Dorchester Co.

(8) Jane Linthicum, daughter of Francis and Eleanor, born April 22, 1755. Not mentioned in her father's will.

MARY LINTHICUM, eldest daughter of Thomas (1) and wife Jane, born 1670, died after 1717, married before 1690, Richard Snowden (3), born 1666, died 1720-3, son of Richard Snowden (2), born 1640, buried May 20, 1711, married Elizabeth (Gross). Richard was the son of the emigrant Captain Richard Snowden (1), of Wales, here in 1679.

CAPTAIN RICHARD SNOWDEN of South River, born in Birmingham, England, was known as Lord of Snowden Manor, as he appears in Lord Baltimore Rent Roll, May 20, 1711. Married first, Deborah Abbot, daughter of William and Magdella Abbot. Second wife, Elizabeth Green, daughter of Roger Green.

CAPTAIN RICHARD SNOWDEN (3), born 1666, died 1723, was Captain in provincial troops. Married Mary Linthicum.

ISSUE: Mary Linthicum and Richard Snowden (3).

(1) Thomas Snowden, buried July 2, 1704.
(2) Richard Snowden, born December 28, 1698, died 1763. Married 1st, May 19, 1707, Elizabeth Coale, born December 5, 1692, died 1713, daughter of William Coale, born October 20, 1667, died 1715, married widow Elizabeth Sparrow Coale July 30, 1689. Richard's 2nd wife, December 19, 1717, Elizabeth Thomas, born December 28, 1698, died August 1775, daughter of Samuel Thomas and wife Mary (Hutchinson).

   Issue: by first wife (Elizabeth Coale).
   Deborah Snowden, married James Brooks.
   Eliza Snowden, married John Thomas.
   Mary Snowden, married Samuel Thomas.
   All moved to Sandy Springs, Montgomery County.

   Issue: by second wife (Elizabeth Thomas).
   Richard Snowden, born 1719-20, died 1753, married October 13, 1748, Elizabeth Crawley, born 1728.

JANE LINTHICUM, 2nd daughter of Thomas (1) and Jane, his wife, was born ——, died ——, married Thomas Rutland January 13, 1695, born 1664, buried December 14, 1731. He lived at South River.

ISSUE:

(1) Elizabeth Rutland, born January 22, 1696, died March 15, 1707.
(2) Jane Rutland, born 1698, married December 18, 1715, Joseph Brewer.
(3) Mary Rutland, born 1699, buried January 19, 1721-22, married January 30, 1717, Thomas Sappington, born ——, died February 18, 1721-22.

   Issue: Mary Rutland and husband Thomas Sappington.
   Thomas Sappington, baptized January 9, 1721, married Frances Brown.

(4) Ann Rutland, born 1701, married March 1, 1719, Leonard Wayman, born April 22, 1699, baptized April 11, 1707, son of Leonard Wayman and Dorcus, baptized November 1, 1703. Leonard was the son of Leonard Sr., died October 16, 1697.

   Issue: Leonard and Ann Rutland.
   Leonard, baptized March 12, 1726.
   Jane, baptized March 12, 1726.

(5) Thomas Rutland(2), son of Thomas (1) and wife Jane Linthicum, was born 1703, died October 4, 1773-4, married Anne Dorsey, born ———, will August 25, 1773.

Issue:

Thomas Rutland (3), born September 29, 1765, will of 1790, married Anne Beale, daughter of John Beale and Elizabeth Norwood. His wife, Elizabeth Norwood was a daughter of Captain John Norwood and Elizabeth Howard. Elizabeth Howard was the daughter of Cornelius Howard and wife Elizabeth, executrix, will of April 15, 1680.

Issue: Thomas Rutland (3) and Anne Beale.

Margaret.

Elizabeth.

Thomas.

(6) Elizabeth Rutland, born ———, died ———, married January 12, 1730, Stephen Stewart, born December 28, 1699, died January 28, 1742. Stephen was the son of Robert Stewart, will March 8, 1738-39, married January 26, 1699, Susan Watts, buried November 16, 1733. Robert Stewart was the son of David Stewart, born 1616, died October 20, 1696 and married Margaret Bevies, who died November 8, 1700.

THOMAS LINTHICUM (2), son of Thomas (1) and wife Jane, was born October 31, 1674, died May 29, 1741, married Deborah Wayman June 22, 1698, daughter of Leonard Wayman and Dorcus Abbott. He owned Morley Gray of 150 acres and Davis Rest of 200 acres. Deborah is mentioned in her father's will of 1721. Thomas (2) had grants of Town Hall, 400 acres, and Linthicum Walk, in 1716.

ISSUE:

(1) Dorcas Linthicum, born August 15, 1700, died ———, license to marry Francis Hardesty, February 4, 1717.

(2) Thomas Linthicum (3), born September 28, 1701, died ———, married Sarah Burton, September 28, 1724. Sarah was born November 17, 1706.

Issue: Thomas and Sarah Burton.

Thomas Linthicum, born June 11, 1725.

Joseph Linthicum, born April 30, 1727.

Burton Linthicum, 173-, will January 4, 1762.

Hezekiah Linthicum.

Asual Linthicum, married Lydia Andrews.

Deborah Linthicum.

(3) Mary Linthicum, daughter of Thomas and Deborah, born August 29, 1703, died ———, married October 6, 1724 John Fowler.

(4) Leonard Linthicum, son of Thomas and Deborah, born August 5, 1705, buried March 6, 1731, married ———.

(5) Deborah Linthicum, daughter of Thomas and Deborah, born September 11, 1707, married January 2, 1726-7, John Jones.

(6) Gideon Linthicum, son of Thomas and Deborah, born February 15, 1709, died ———, married 1737, widow Jane Ford, died 1770.

(7) Ann Linthicum, daughter of Thomas and Deborah, born May 11, 1711, died ———.

(8) Elizabeth Linthicum, daughter of Thomas and Deborah, born August 30, 1714, died ———.

(9) Ruth Linthicum, daughter of Thomas and Deborah, born February 5, 1718, died ———.

(10) Edmond Linthicum, son of Thomas and Deborah, born March 30, 1720, will April 11, 1764, married Elizabeth.

Issue:

Thomas Linthicum, died 1778.

Edmond Linthicum, will April 11, 1764.

(11) Hezekiah Linthicum, schoolmaster, son of Thomas and Deborah, born November 7, 1723, died ———, married Sarah Bateman, born May 11, 1713, died 1778. Sarah was the daughter of Henry Bateman who married December 22, 1707 Sarah Powell.

(Most of the eleven children of Thomas and Deborah were living in 1741.)

Issue: Hezekiah and wife Sarah Bateman:

1. Rachel Linthicum, born ———, died 1767.

2. Elizabeth Linthicum, born ———, died ———, married William Bateman.

3. John Linthicum, born ———, died ———.

4. Archibald Linthicum, born ———, died infancy.

5. Slingsby Linthicum, born ———, died June 28, 1848, first wife Mary Griffith. second wife Mrs. Dorsey.

6. Abner Linthicum, born July 7, 1763, died February 19, 1847, married Baltimore County license, January 3, 1791, first Rachel Jacobs, second wife, December 2, 1828, widow Elizabeth Pitcher, died 1839, whose only child Eugene, died at 4 years of age. Issue to follow: first wife, Rachel Jacobs.

7. Margaret Linthicum, born ———, died ———.

8. Amasa Linthicum, born ———, died ———, married October 13, 1790, Sarah Johnson.

ABNER LINTHICUM, 6th child of Hezekiah and wife Sarah Bateman, was a member of Maryland Legislature during 1812-1826, was Captain in 22nd Regiment, 1809, war of 1812. Married January 3, 1791, Rachel Jacobs 17—, died 1821, daughter of Richard Jacobs, born August 22, 1730, died 1805, will 1802, married Hannah ——— who died August 8, 1806.

He was the son of Richard Jacobs, Sr., born January 30, 1697-8, will November 8, 1777, married January 1, 1718 Hannah Howard, born 1707, died May 1, 1730. Richard Jacobs (1) was the son of John Jacobs, born in Dover, England 1629, buried October 29, 1726, married March 1, 1675 Anne Cheney, baptized 1666, buried 1720. She was the daughter of Richard Cheney and wife Eleanor, Patentee 1663, living 1685, will 1686.

Captain John Jacobs, emigrant, of Anne Arundel County, born Dover, England 1629, came to America 1665, died 1705. In addition to grants in Anne Arundel County, given him by the King of England, he bought large tracts, and became a tobacco planter. He was the son of John Jacobs, gent., of Dover, Kent, born 1560, died 1627, married in Canterbury in 1587, Joan Lucas, daughter of the Mayor of Canterbury, 1574.

Hannah Howard was the daughter of Joseph Howard who died 1736. Joseph Howard was the son of Captain Cornelius Howard, born in Great Britain, 1635, died 1680. Cornelius came to Severn River from Norfolk, Va., with the Puritan Exodus, 1650-58, commissioned Ensign under Captain Benson, Burgess 1671-1676, Justice Peace 1679.

Reference: Maryland Archives, Vol. 3, p. 444, Vol. 2, p. 239.

ISSUE: Abner Linthicum and Rachel Jacobs.

(1) Amasa Linthicum, born November 11, 1791, died October 9, 1810.
(2) Richard Linthicum, born July 22, 1793, died October 15, 1842, blown up in ship Medora. Married first wife February 29, 1816 Anne Robinson, born January 9, 1797, died September 3, 1837; second wife Susan C. Lockerman, in May 8, 1838.
(3) Abner Linthicum, Jr., born May 18, 1796, died September 13 or October 14, 1845, married first January 3, 1820 Rachel Stewart, born April 4, 1800, died May 28, 1839; second wife, married March 20, 1842 Mary Bryan.
(4) William Linthicum, born March 21, 1798, died August 27, 1866, married November 20, 1823, Elizabeth Sweetser, born August 23, 1800, died December 22, 1875. Issue following.
(5) Hezekiah Linthicum, born June 15, 1801, died June 11, 1891, married April 20, 1825 Matilda Phillips.
(6) Thomas Linthicum, born October 12, 1804, died October 4, 1822.
(7) Sarah Linthicum, born December 5, 1809, died December 5, 1882, married January 4, 1829 William Shipley.
Had 11 children.

WILLIAM LINTHICUM (son of Abner and Rachel), married Elizabeth Sweetser, daughter of Seth Sweetser, born June 5, 1762, died 1828, and Ann Valient of Anne Arundel Co., January 9, 1790. Seth Sweetser built the bridge at Annapolis across the River Patapsco, called Sweetser Bridge. Seth was the son of Phineaus, born September 10, 1718, died September 24, 1764, of Stoneham, Mass., who married Mary Rhodes, born March 4, 1727, died 1780, of Lynn, Mass. She was the granddaughter of Rofer William the great Preacher and Leader.

Charts showing these two families for several generations preceding are in the possession of Dr. G. Milton Linthicum of Baltimore.

ISSUE: William Linthicum and Elizabeth Sweetser.

(1) Sweetser Linthicum, born September 10, 1824, died March 29, 1905, married March 4, 1847 Laura E. Smith, born January 18, 1829, died August 13, 1910, daughter of James Hawkins Smith, born December 17, 1778, died December 30, 1836, married Nancy Smith, born October 2, 1800, died June 2, 1881.

(2) Anne Linthicum, born July 20, 1826, died ———, married first, Thomas C. Pitcher, died October 10, 1819; second Phinpenny.

(3) William Abner Linthicum, born April 13, 1828, died 1916, married February 8, 1853, Elizabeth Mulliken.

(4) Dr. Asa Shinn Linthicum, born February 4, 1831, died ———, married first, June 30, 1857, Ella Conoway; second, August 1, 1866, Nettie Crane.

(5) Samuel S. Linthicum, born February 19, 1833, died ———, married Mary Walker.

(6) Eleanor Linthicum, born February 22, 1835, died January 20, 1911, married first Henry Thomas, second Mordica Smith.

(7) Mary Elizabeth, born April 23, 1837, married William Brian.

(8) Victoria Linthicum, born December 23, 1840, died age 18, August 11, 1857.

Sweetser Linthicum, wife Laura E. Smith, was the son of William and Elizabeth Sweetser Linthicum. Laura Ellen Smith was the daughter of James Hawkins Smith, born December 17, 1708, died December 30, 1836, and wife Nancy Smith, born October 2, 1800, died June 2, 1881. James Hawkins Smith was the son of Sebritt Smith and Mary Hawkᵢ Nancy Smith was the daughter of Patrick Smith, born December 23, 1760, died August 30, 1823 and Nancy Bishop, born January 16, 1773, died July 16, 1860. Sebritt Smith was Private, 22nd. Regiment, in Captain Linthicum's Company, War 1812.

In the list of recruits raised in Montgomery County to make good her quota in Continental Army 1780, among the first 30 members is Patrick Smith, number 23 on the list.

Ref.: Vol. 18, *Maryland Archives*, pp. 342-627.

Issue: Sweetser Linthicum and wife Laura Smith Linthicum.

(1) Elizabeth V. Linthicum, born December 17, 1847, married March 9, 1869, Joseph K. Benson.

(2) James S. Linthicum, born September 19, 1850, died June 12, 1912, married June 2, 1874 Sarah McClellan.

(3) Annie S. Linthicum, born December 17, 1853, married September 24, 1874 Luther Shipley, died February 11, 1923.

(4) William Linthicum, born October 16, 1856, married October 26, 1881 Adele Knight.

(5) Dr. Asa Shinn Linthicum, born November 28, 1859, died January 4, 1897, married Iola Benson.

(6) Sweetser Linthicum, Jr., born July 4, 1862, married November 20, 1888, Sarah Crisp.

(7) Victoria Linthicum, born April 17, 1865, died April 11, 1867.

(8) J. Charles Linthicum, born November 26, 1867, married March 9, 1898 Mrs. Helen Clark. Many years a distinguished member of Congress.

(9) Dr. G. Milton Linthicum, born August 17, 1870, married April 12 1898 Lillian N. Howland. A prominent Surgeon, Professor of College 1895-1907; Vice-President, Medical and Chirurgical Faculty 1908-09, President 1909-10; National Guard, Mexican War; Medical Corps of World War, Lieut.-Col. 1917-19.

(10) Seth N. Linthicum, born July 26, 1873, married November 22, 1910 Mary Perkins.

(11) Wade Hampton Linthicum, born February 14, 1876, married Delmar Brown.

Sweetser Linthicum and wife, Laura Smith Linthicum celebrated their fifty-fifth anniversary at the home of their son, Dr. G. Milton Linthicum, in 1902.

LINTHICUMS WHO MOVED TO MONTGOMERY COUNTY.

1798 Sally, daughter of Thomas and Ann.
1799 Ann (Magruder), daughter of John and Priscilla.
1800 Ruth, daughter of Thomas and Ann.
1800 Ann, wife of Zachariah.
1802 Sarah, daughter of John and Priscilla.
1802 Phil McElfresh, son of Frederick and Rachel.
1803 Priscilla, daughter of Thomas and Ann.
1803 Lydia Griffith, daughter of Frederick and Rachel.
1805 Sarah Pitcher.

REFERENCES.

Marriages, births, deaths, records of early churches in Anne Arundel County.
Marriage records, rent rolls, wills, and grants at Annapolis.
Research and manuscripts of Mr. Miles Cary at Maryland Historical Society.

Founders of Anne Arundel County, by Warfield.
Thomas Family, by L. B. Thomas.
Maryland Archives.
Family Bible records of the Linthicum and Sweetser families.
Colonial Families of America, Vol. 3, pp. 291, for Snowden family.
The British Invasion of Maryland, by Marine.

THE LINTHICUM FAMILY.

CORRECTIONS.

[The sketch of the Linthicum family printed in the September issue of the *Magazine,* was not submitted to its compiler, Mr. Ferdinand B. Focke, nor did it carry his name. He therefore had no opportunity to correct typographical and other errors that had slipped in. As there seems to be widespread interest in this family two letters of correction are here inserted. Another correspondent calls attention to another error on page 282, line 19, where Elizabeth Mullikin appears as Mulliken—an entirely different family.

———   —ED.]

As the pages of the *Maryland Historical Magazine* constitute a valuable collection of genealogical information concerning Maryland families and are often quoted as authoritative dicta in such matters, it is gratifying to note that the September (1930) issue has given an appreciable amount of space to the records of several old families of the State. In my opinion, the publication of such records deserves to be encouraged. Of course, we desire that these compilations shall be accurate. Whenever errors are detected, it should be the duty of the reader to correct them if he is in position to do so.

In the present instance, I may, perhaps, be pardoned for submitting a few corrections and introducing some additional data relative to an article on "The Linthicum Family," as it appears in the September issue of the *Maryland Historical Magazine,* Vol. XXV, No. 3, pages 275-283.

Thomas Linthicum, the immigrant, evidently was an intransigeant and troublesome member of the Society of Friends. According to the "Third Haven Meeting" (Talbot County) records, it appears that at a Quarterly Meeting held at John Edmondson's on the 24th day of the fourth month, 1681 (old style), it was determined to discipline Thomas Linthicum, following the receipt of "a full and certain account from the Men's Meeting at the Western Shore concerning the unworthy and disorderly carriage and behavior of Thos. Lincicomb to Thos. Everdon in particular and Friends in general", notwithstanding the previous efforts of Friends to compose the matter at issue. I shall now direct the reader's attention to certain historical and genealogical errors in the Linthicum article aforesaid.

Page 275, fifth line from bottom: "The return of the tobacco" was made in *1684* (not 1784). Same page, second line from bottom: Thomas Linthicum was born about *1640-1645*. We do not know the year of his birth precisely.

Page 276, ninth line from top: "Rhoda" should be *Rhode* River.

Page 277, bottom line: The date given is that of the *burial* of Richard Snowden.

Page 278, second line from top: Richard Snowden's "second wife" is usually given as Elizabeth, daughter of Roger *Grosse*.

Page 278, seventh line from top (*et seq.*): Richard Snowden was born in *1688* (not 1698); he died January 26, 1763, in the 76th year of his age. He married (1) Elizabeth Coale on May 19, *1709* (not 1707). His second wife was Elizabeth Thomas, daughter of Samuel Thomas and his wife Mary *Hutchins* (not Hutchinson). Another daughter (probably by his first wife) was *Ann Snowden* who married Henry Wright Crabbe. By his second wife, he had Richard Snowden, Jr., who died March 18, 1753, and whose wife was Elizabeth *Crowley* (not Crawley). By the second wife he had also other children (dates of birth approximated) as follows: Thomas Snowden (1721-1770), married Mary Wright; Margaret Snowden (1724), married John Contee; Eliza Snowden (1726), married Joseph Cowman; Samuel Snowden (1728-1801), married Eliza Thomas; John Snowden (1730), married Rachel Hopkins.

Page 278, sixteenth line from bottom: Elizabeth Rutland, *buried* March 15, 1707. Page 278, twelfth line from bottom: Thomas Sappington, *buried* February 18, 1721-22.

Page 280, sixth line from top: Gideon Linthicum died *May 11, 1770*. Page 280, nineteenth line from top: Hezekiah Linthicum died in 1767. I am not aware that the maiden surname of his wife has been ascertained.

Page 281, fourth line from top (*et seq.*): John Jacobs was born *1631* (not 1629), and married Anne Cheney who was *born 1660,* or thereabouts, and died April 29, *1730* (not 1720). Page 281, tenth line from top (*et seq.*): John Jacobs was born

1631 (not 1629), and died *1726* (not 1705). If John Jacobs, " of Dover, England·", died in 1627 he could not have been the father of John Jacobs (1631-1726).

Page 282, fifth line from top (*et seq.*): Mary Rhodes was the *great-great-granddaughter* (not " granddaughter ") of *Roger Williams* (not " Rofer William ").

There occur several mistakes in the spelling of baptismal names, such as " Dorcus " for " *Dorcas* ", " Francis " for the feminine *Frances,* " Phineaus " for " *Phinehas* ", Mordeca for *Mordecai,* etc. The foregoing comments are submitted after a rather incomplete examination and analysis of the Linthicum article, and I feel assured that they will be received in the spirit in which they are made.

FRANCIS B. CULVER,

Sept. 27, 1930.   1227 16th St., N. W.,

Washington, D. C.

To the Author of " The Linthicum Family ",

Dear Sir:

Having been set right on one point by your Linthicum family article, may I repay the kindness by sending you a correction.

Page 279. Thomas Rutland, 2nd, b. 1703, married Anne Beale, b. 1709 (not Anne Dorsey). She was the daughter of John Beale who married, 1708, Elizabeth Norwood.

Elizabeth Norwood was daughter of *Andrew* Norwood (not Capt. John Norwood). (Capt. John Norwood died abt. 1673, according to the Colonial Dame Register.) Andrew Norwood married Elizabeth Howard, who I think was the *sister* of Cornelius Howard—although he had a daughter Elizabeth, too. As I have some Norwood ancestry I am interested in following up any reference I see to the family. I also have Dorsey ancestors.

The chart which I enclose will make my references plainer.

Very sincerely yours,

(Miss) FLORENCE WHITTLESEY THOMPSON.

September 25, 1930.   5 Orchard St., Portland, Maine.

Andrew Norwood, A. A. Co. 1701-2. Cal. 2: 232.
To bros. Samuel and Philip, personalty.
To son Andrew, at 17, dwell., plantation.
Wife (unnamed) and bro. Samuel afsd. joint executors.
Testator desires " Strawberry Plain " to be sold.
Test. Cornelius Howard, Philip Howard, Jr., Geo. Slucom.
(C. H., *Sr.,* d. 1680).

————

Andrew Wellplay, A. A. Co., 2 May 1708. 14 July 1708.
To son-in-law Andrew Norwood and hrs., 500 a. at head of
Bush R.
To dau.-in-law Elizabeth Norwood, pers.
To wife Elizabeth, exec. and resid. leg.
Test. Cornelius Howard, Jos. Howard, Samuel Dorsey, Samuel
Leatherwood.

————

Capt. John Norwood.
d. circ. 1673
|
Andrew Norwood m. Elizabeth Howard.
He d. 1702. Md. Cal. Wills, 2: 232.
She m. (2) Andrew Wellplay.
He d. 1708. Md. Cal. Wills, 3: 106.
|

NORWOOD

Andrew	Elizabeth	Anne	Hannah
Only child named in his father's will. He and his sister Eliz. both named by Andrew Wellplay, 1708, but that year Andrew died and the property left him by stepfather went to his sisters, Eliz. Beale, Anne and Hannah Norwood. Land Office, Liber P. L. No. 5, folio 558.	m. 1708 John Beale		

Anne	Elizabeth
b. 1709 m. Thos. Rutland, 2nd, b. 1703. Her will, 1773, names her aunt Hannah Norwood.	

LLOYD FAMILY.

CHRISTOPHER JOHNSTON.

ARMS. Azure, a lion rampant or.
CREST. A demi-lion rampant guardant or, supporting in the paws an arrow in pale argent.

1. COL. CORNELIUS LLOYD,[1] had a patent, 2 July 1635, for 800 acres of land on Elizabeth River and Merchant's Creek, Lower Norfolk County, Virginia, due for the transportation of sixteen persons. In a patent, dated 1636, he is styled " of London, Merchant " (Stanard, *Some Emigrants to Virginia*, p. 41). He was appointed a Justice of Lower Norfolk County in November 1646, and was a Burgess for the County in March 1642/3, October 1644, November 1645, March 1645/6, November 1647, April 1652, and July 1653. He was Lieutenant-Colonel of the County militia in 1652. In July 1641, he made a deposition in Lower Norfolk County, in which he stated that he was then 33 years of age. He died before September 1654, at which time a suit was brought, in Lower Norfolk, by Elizabeth widow of Lieut. Col. Cornelius Lloyd. The inventory of Col. Lloyd contains a suit of armor, and a case of pistols, both together valued at 120 pounds of tobacco. In 1655, Elizabeth, widow of Cornelius Lloyd, from love and affection to Philemon, son and heir of Edward Lloyd of Maryland, conveyed to him certain claims and personal estate. Mrs. Elizabeth Lloyd was the sister of Thomas Evans of the City of Kilkenny, Ireland. (*Va. Mag.*, iii, 187; v, 212-213).

2. COL. EDWARD LLOYD,[1] brother of the above Cornelius Lloyd who executes a deed, recorded in Lower Norfolk, and dated 24 April 1651 as " Cornelius Lloyd Gent. assignee of his brother Edward Lloyd " (*Va. Mag.*, v, 213), had a patent, 30 March 1636, for 400 acres of land on the Westernmost branch of Elizabeth River, adjoining the land of Cornelius Lloyd and John Sibsey, due for the transportation of four

persons into Virginia. He was a Justice of Lower Norfolk
in 1645, and a Burgess for that County in February 1644/5,
and October 1646 (*Va. Mag.,* v, 212-213). Both Edward
Lloyd and his brother Cornelius sympathized with the dis-
senters, and when, in May 1648, the Sheriff of Lower
Norfolk County attempted to disperse the meeting at Elizabeth River Church and to arrest the minister, Rev. William
Durand, the two Lloyd brothers not only refused to aid in
making the arrest, but interfered and released Mr. Durand
(*Va. Mag.,* v, 228). In August 1649, Edward and Cornelius Lloyd with a number of others, were presented for
not attending the parish Church, and for refusing the
Common Prayer (*ibid.,* p. 229). On the 1st of October
1649, they were ordered to give bond to appear on the 8th
inst. before the General Court, composed of the Governor
and Council. Of the Puritan emigration to Maryland,
which followed these religious disturbances in Virginia,
Edward Lloyd was one of the leaders. He was commissioned,
30 July 1650, Commander of the new County of Anne
Arundel, and held the office until 18 December 1652, when
the commission was rescinded (*Md. Arch.,* iii, 257. 290).
He was appointed, 28 June 1652, a commissioner to treat
with the Susquehannah Indians and, in that capacity, signed
a treaty, with them on the 5th of July following (*Md.
Arch.,* iii, 276-278). In 1654, he was a member of the
General Assembly of Maryland and, in the same year, 22
July, was appointed one of the High Commissioners for
regulating affairs in Maryland, a position which he held
until the government was delivered over to Fendall, 22
February 1657/8 (*Md. Arch.,* i, 339; iii, 312. 335). 27
April 1658, he was returned a Burgess for Anne Arundel
County (*Prov. Court,* Lib. S., fol. 26). He was sworn a
member of the Council of Maryland 23 July 1658 (*Md.
Arch.,* iii, 352) and held his seat until 1666 (*Md. Arch.,*
i, 382. 395. 396. 426. 460. 509; iii, 539. 558, etc.). 9 May
1663, he was appointed a commissioner to confer with
commissioners from Virginia with regard to a cessation of
planting tobacco (*Md. Arch.,* iii, 479-480). About the
year 1668 he returned to England, and resided there until
his death which occurred in London, in the year 1696.
In his will, dated 11 May 1695, and proved 14 July 1696
(P. C. C. Bond, 121), he styles himself " Edward Lloyd of

the Parish of St. Mary, Whitechapel, in the County of Middlesex, Merchant, and late a planter in Maryland," and devises Wye, in Talbot County to his grandson Edward, eldest son of Philemon Lloyd and Henrietta Maria (Neale) his wife. Edward Lloyd was at least thrice married. His first wife, according to family tradition, was named Alice Crouch, and the epitaph of his son Col. Philemon Lloyd, at Wye, states that he was " the son of E. Lloyd & Alice his wife." There is a certificate, dated 15 Sept. 1658, recorded in Lower Norfolk County, Virginia, to Mr. Edward Lloyd for the transportation of 30 persons—among them Edward Lloyd and Alice Lloyd (*New Eng'd H. & G. Reg.,* xlvii, 197). The Lower Norfolk records also contain a certificate, dated 5 July 1642, to William Crouch for the transportation of himself, Mary his wife, and John Freeman his servant, in 1641 (*ibid.,* p. 63). The second wife of Edward Lloyd was Mrs. Frances Watkins, widow of John Watkins. There is recorded in Lower Norfolk a deed, dated 6 August 1655, from Frances Lloyd, late wife of John Watkins of Virginia, and now wife of Edward Lloyd of Maryland, resigning her dower in certain lands. Edward Lloyd was to pay a certain sum to her son John Watkins (*Va. Mag.,* v, 213). This is supplemented by the Maryland records: 22 July 1658, Mr. Edward Lloyd assigns 100 acres of land to his son-in-law (*i. e.,* stepson) John Watkins, who also demands 100 acres in his own right (*Land Office,* Lib. Q, fol. 70). This last mentioned John Watkins was the ancestor of the well-known family of Anne Arundel County, one of his descendants being the distinguished Revolutionary officer Col. Gassaway Watkins. The Talbot County records contain a deed, dated 11 June 1668, whereby Edward Lloyd of Wye, " for divers good reasons and for relations sake," conveys to John Watkins, eldest son of John Watkins, William eldest son of William Leeds, Samuel eldest son of William Taylor, and William eldest son of William Hambleton, certain lands in Bayside. The third wife of Edward Lloyd was Mrs. Grace Parker, widow of William Parker Senr. of Stepney. 18 October 1680, Edward Lloyd of the Parish of Whitechapel, Middlesex, and Grace his wife, and Elizabeth Parker of the same place, spinster, give to Samuel Lane of Anne Arundel Co., Md., and Francis Mauldin, also of Maryland, a power

of attorney to receive what is due them from the estate of
William Parker late of the Cliffs deceased (*Prov. Court,* Lib.
W. R. C. No. 1, fol. 207). 11 August 1681, Edward Lloyd
late of the Parish of Stepney, but now of the Parish of
St. Mary, Whitechapel, in the county of Middlesex, and
Grace his wife, late widow and sole executrix of William
Parker Senr. late of Stepney, and Henry Buckerfield of
London, woodmonger, and Elizabeth his wife, only daughter
of the said William Parker Senr., and sister and heir at
law of William Parker, Junr., late of the Cliffs in Maryland, casually (*i. e.,* through accident) deceased, who was
the only son and heir at law of the said William Parker
Senr., give a power of attorney to Samuel Lane, Chirurgeon,
and Francis Mauldin, planter, both of the Province of
Maryland (*ibid.,* fol. 209). Mrs. Grace Lloyd survived
her husband. 14 October 1697, Grace Lloyd of London
widow, relict and executrix of Edward Lloyd, formerly
of the Province of Maryland, planter, but since of the
Parish of St. Mary Whitechapel, in the County of Middlesex, Merchant, assigns to her kinsman Richard Bennett of
Maryland, all debts due her in Maryland, for the consideration of 5 shillings and love and affection (*ibid.,* fol. 838).
So far as is known Edward Lloyd had issue only by his
first wife Alice Crouch. By her he had an only son:—

3.   i. Col. PHILEMON LLOYD,[2] b. 1646; d. 22 June, 1685.

3. COL. PHILEMON LLOYD,[2] (*Edward* [1]) of Wye was born in
    Virginia in 1646, and died at Wye 22 June 1685, in his
    39th year (Epitaph at Wye). 2 June 1667, being then
    barely 21 years of age, he was commissioned Captain com-
    manding the horse in Chester and Wye Rivers, and took
    part, the same year, in an expedition against the Indians
    of the Eastern Shore (*Md. Arch.,* v, 11. 35). In 1681,
    he was Colonel commanding the horse of Talbot, Kent,
    and Cecil Counties (*Md. Arch.,* v, 310) and in this capacity
    was ordered, 20 February 1681/2, to fit out his troops for
    active service (*Md. Arch.,* xv, 73. 76). In 1682, he was
    appointed, together with the officers and men of his com-
    mand, to escort William Penn on his return from Maryland
    to Pennsylvania (*Md. Arch.,* v, 381). He was a member
    of the Quorum of Talbot County 1675-1681 (*Md. Arch.,*
    xv, 70. 227. 327. 346), and doubtless other years as well.

He represented Talbot County in the House of Burgesses from 1671 until his death in 1685 (*Md. Arch.*, ii, 239. 345. 422 etc.), and was Speaker of the House from October 1678 until 1685 (*Md. Arch.* vii, 3; iii, 335, 526; xiii, 58.— See Prorogations of the House from 1676 to 1678, *Md. Arch.*, ii, 109). 15 May 1682, he was appointed, with Henry Coursey, Commissioner to treat with the Northern Indians at Fort Albany, New York (*Md. Arch.*, xvii, 96). For their good services upon this occasion the two Commissioners received, by vote of Assembly, a grant of 12 pounds of tobacco per poll upon the taxable inhabitants of the Province (*Md. Arch.*, vii, 409). Col. Philemon Lloyd married, in 1668 or 1669, Henrietta Maria, widow of Richard Bennett, Jr., and daughter of Capt. James and Anne (Gill) Neale (see *Mag.*, i, 74). They had issue:

4.   i.   Maj. Gen. EDWARD LLOYD,[3] b. February, 1670; d. 20 March, 1718/9.
5.   ii.   PHILEMON LLOYD, b. 1672; d. 19 March, 1732; Mem. of Council, and Sec'y of Md.; mar. Mrs. Freeman of Annapolis.
6.   iii.   JAMES LLOYD, b. 7 March, 1680; d. 27 Sept., 1723.
       iv.   HENRIETTA MARIA LLOYD, mar. Charles Blake.
       v.   ANNA MARIA LLOYD, b. 1677; d. December, 1748; mar., 1700, Richard Tilghman of the Hermitage (b. 23 Feb'y, 1672; d. 23 Jan'y, 1738).
       vi.   ELIZABETH LLOYD, d. unmarried.
       vii.   ALICE LLOYD, b. 1681; d. unmarried, 1744.
       viii.   MARGARET LLOYD, b. 1683; d. s. p. 12 Sept., 1747; mar. Hon. Matthew Tilghman Ward, President of the Council of Maryland.
       ix.   MARY LLOYD, d. unmarried.
       x.   JANE LLOYD, d. unmarried.

4. MAJ. GEN. EDWARD LLOYD [3] (*Philemon,*[2] *Edward*[1]) of Wye, was born in February 1670, and died 20 March 1718/9 (Epitaph at Wye). He was one of the Justices of Talbot County 1694-1697 (*Arch.*, xx, 138. 386; xxiii, 129), and was Colonel of the County militia the following year, if not earlier. 9 August 1698, a number of articles of military equipment are ordered to be delivered to " Col. Edward Lloyd of Talbot County " (*Arch.*, xxiii, 461), and he is thereafter regularly styled " Colonel " in the records. He qualified as a member of Assembly from Talbot County 11 March 1697/8, and continued to represent the County in the Lower House until 1701 (*Arch.*, xxii, 8. 191. 326; xxiv, 45. 159). 29 November 1701, he was appointed and sworn a member of Council and held the position until his death (*Arch.*, xxv, 114. 353). In 1707, he was promoted

to a very unusual rank in the Provincial Militia. 17 July 1707, Col. John Hammond and Col. Edward Lloyd were commissioned Major Generals to command the militia of the Western and Eastern Shores respectively (*Arch.,* xxv, 215). Gov. John Seymour died 30 July 1709, and his place was filled by Maj. Gen. Lloyd, President of the Council, who was thus Acting Governor of Maryland until the arrival of Gov. John Hart in 1714 (*Arch.,* xxv, Preface, p. x). Unfortunately the Council records of Edward Lloyd's administration are lost. He married, 1 February 1703, Sarah Covington (b. 1683) daughter of Nehemiah Covington of Somerset County who mentions in his will (dated 14 Feb'y 1710/1, proved 5 Aug. 1713) his " son-in-law Maj. Gen. Edward Lloyd." Mrs. Sarah Covington married secondly, 3 May 1721, James Hollyday, Esq. of Readbourne, Queen Anne County. She died in England 4 April 1755, aged 71 years, and is buried at West Ham, Essex. A copy of her epitaph is published in *Genealogical Notes of the Chamberlain Family,* p. 29. Maj. Gen. Edward Lloyd and Sarah (Covington) his wife had issue:

    i. EDWARD LLOYD,[4] b. 11 Sept., 1705; d. 14 Feb'y, 1707.
    ii. PHILEMON LLOYD, b. 26 March, 1709; d. 5 March, 1729.
7.   iii. EDWARD LLOYD, b. 8 May, 1711; d. 27 Jan'y, 1770.
    iv. REBECCA COVINGTON LLOYD, b. 11 June, 1713; mar. William Anderson, merchant of London.
    v. JAMES LLOYD, b. 14 Aug., 1715; d. s. p. 14 Sept., 1738.
8.   vi. Col. RICHARD LLOYD, b. 19 March, 1717.

5. PHILEMON LLOYD [3] (*Philemon,*[2] *Edward* [1]) was born 1672, and died 19 March 1732. He qualified, 29 April 1700, as a member of Assembly from Talbot County and sat in the subsequent sessions until 1704 (*Arch.,* xxiv, 13. 129. 306. 356). From 1706 to 1710 he was Deputy Secretary of Maryland (*Arch.,* xxv, 207; xxvii, 178. 374. 430. 511. 579), and was a Justice of the Provincial Court from 1707 to 1709 or later (*Arch.,* xxv, 226; xxvii, 471). In 1711 he was a member of Council and he served in this capacity until his death (*Arch.* xxix, 20. 83 etc.; xxv, 296 etc.; xxviii, 3). He seems to have lived partly in Talbot County, and partly at Annapolis where he had a house in 1709 (*Arch.,* xxvii, 390). Philemon Lloyd married a Mrs. Freeman of Annapolis and had a daughter:

    i. HENRIETTA MARIA LLOYD,[4] d. 10 Dec., 1765; mar. 1°. Samuel Chew (d. 15 Jan'y, 1736), 2°. Daniel Dulany Sen'r. (b. 1686; d. 5 Dec., 1753).

6. JAMES LLOYD [3] (*Philemon,*[2] *Edward* [1]) was born 7 March 1680, and died 27 Sept. 1723. He was one of the representatives of Talbot County in the Maryland Assembly 1712-1714, and 1716-1722 (Ms. House Journals). In the latter year he was called to the Council and qualified as a member 4 Nov. 1722 (Council Journals), holding the seat until his death. He was present at a meeting held 24 May 1723, and at the same meeting, Mr. Thomas Bozman qualified as Burgess for Talbot County, being elected in place of Mr. James Lloyd removed to the Council (Council, Lib. P, fol. 2). James Lloyd married, 12 January 1709, Anne (b. 25 April 1690) daughter of Robert Grundy, Esq. of Talbot County and Deborah his wife, sister of John Shrigley of Anne Arundel County. She married first Thomas Impey of Talbot County, who died in 1687, and, secondly, John Boyden, who died in 1688. Robert Grundy was her third husband, and their marriage contract is dated 2 February 1689. Ann Grundy, wife of James Lloyd, married secondly Edward Fottrell. James Lloyd and Ann (Grundy) his wife had issue:

    i. HENRIETTA MARIA LLOYD,[4] b. 20 Jan'y, 1710; d. 29 March, 1748; mar. Samuel Chamberlaine.
9. ii. ROBERT LLOYD, b. 19 Feb'y, 1712; d. 16 July, 1770.
    iii. MARGARET LLOYD, b. 16 Feb'y, 1714; mar., 2 Aug., 1736, William Tilghman of Grosses.
10. iv. JAMES LLOYD, b. 16 March, 1716/7; mar. Elizabeth Frisby.
    v. DEBORAH LLOYD, b. 19 May, 1719; mar. Jeremiah Nicols (d. 7 Oct., 1753).
    vi. PHILEMON LLOYD, b. 4 November, 1721.
    vii. ANNE LLOYD, b. 13 Feb'y, 1723; d. 15 March, 1794; mar., 6 April, 1741, Matthew Tilghman.

7. COL. EDWARD LLOYD [4] (*Edward,*[3] *Philemon,*[2] *Edward* [1]) was born 8 May 1711, and died 27 Jan'y 1770. He represented Talbot County in the Lower House of Assembly from 1738 to 1741, and is styled " Colonel " in 1741 and continuously thereafter (House Journals). He qualified as a member of Council 1 February 1743 (*Arch.,* xxviii, 307) and served in this capacity until 1767 (*ibid.,* 314. 420. 490. 581 etc.; Ms. Journals). In 1760, he was one of the Commissioners appointed to run the boundary between Maryland and Pennsylvania (*Arch.,* ix, 450). The *Maryland Gazette,* of 8 February 1770, has this notice in regard to him: " Lately died at his seat on Wye River, in Talbot County, Col. Edward Lloyd, Esq., formerly one

of his Lordship's Council of State, and Agent and Receiver General for this Province." Col. Lloyd married, 26 March 1739, Anne Rousby (b. 1721, d. 1 May 1769) daughter of John Rousby, Esq., of Calvert County, member of Council. Col. Edward Lloyd and Anne (Rousby) his wife had issue:

    i. ELIZABETH LLOYD,[5] b. 10 Jan'y, 1742; mar., October, 1768, Gen. John Cadwallader of Philadelphia.

11. ii. Col. EDWARD LLOYD, b. 15 Dec., 1744; d. 8 July, 1796.

    iii. HENRIETTA MARIA LLOYD, b. 28 Jan'y, 1746/7.

12. iv. RICHARD BENNETT LLOYD, b. 13 August, 1750.

8. COL. RICHARD LLOYD [4] (*Edward,*[3] *Philemon,*[2] *Edward* [1]) was born 19 March 1717, and, in 1738, was one of the residuary legatees of his brother James, who also devised to him two tracts of land in Kent County. He was one of the Justices of Kent County 1744-1754, and a Justice of the Provincial Court 1754-1756 (Commission Book). He represented Kent County in the Assembly 1749-1750 and 1762-1766 (House Journals), being styled " Colonel " in the records in 1762 and regularly thereafter. In 1774 he was again commissioned a Justice (Commission Book). He was a member of the Maryland Convention of 1775 (*Arch.,* xi, 3), and also a member of the Council of Safety (*ibid.,* 84). In 1778 he was appointed Judge of the Court of Appeals (*Arch.,* xxi, 265). · Col. Richard Lloyd married Anne Crouch and had issue:

    i. ANNA MARIA LLOYD,[5] mar. Jeremiah Nicols, Jr.

13. ii. Gen. JAMES LLOYD, mar. Elizabeth Tilghman.

9. COL. ROBERT LLOYD [4] (*James,*[3] *Philemon,*[2] *Edward* [1]) of Hope, Queen Anne County, was born 19 February 1712, and died 16 July 1770. He was one of the Justices of Queen Anne County, 1740-1745, 1747-1751, and 1754-1755, and was Presiding Justice from 1749 (Commission Book). He sat for Talbot County in the Maryland Assembly 1738-1751, represented Queen Anne County in the same body 1754-1760, 1762-1770, and was Speaker of the House 1765-1770 (Ms. House Journals). Col. Lloyd married Anna Maria, widow of William Hemsley, and daughter of Hon. Richard Tilghman of the Hermitage (see *Mag.,* i, 282). She was born 15 Nov. 1709, and died 30 Aug. 1763. The *Maryland Gazette* of 8 Sept. 1763 has this obituary notice: " On Tuesday the 30th of last Month,

Died, to the great Grief of her numerous Relations and Acquaintance, Mrs. Anna Maria Lloyd, the virtuous and amiable Consort of Robert Lloyd, Esq.; and one of the daughters of the late Honourable Richard Tilghman, Esq." Col. Robert Lloyd and Anna Maria (Tilghman) his wife had issue:

    i. RICHARD LLOYD.[5]
    ii. DEBORAH LLOYD, mar. Col. Peregrine Tilghman (b. 24 Jan'y, 1741, d. 1807); see *Mag.*, I, 371.
    iii. ANNA MARIA LLOYD, second wife of William Tilghman (b. 11 March, 1745, d. Dec., 1800). See *Mag.*, I, 372.

10. JAMES LLOYD [4] (*James,*[3] *Philemon,*[2] *Edward* [1]) was born 16 March 1716/7, and lived at Parsons Landing, Talbot County. He was a Justice of Talbot County 1751-1769 (Commission Book), and was commissioned, 16 May 1776, Captain of a company in the 4th Battalion of Talbot County (*Arch.,* xi, 428). He married Elizabeth (b. 5 February 1729/30) daughter of Peregrine Frisby (b. 1688, d. 1738) of Cecil County and Elizabeth (d. 1752) his wife, daughter of Maj. Nicholas Sewall of St. Mary's County. James Lloyd and Elizabeth Frisby, his wife had issue:

14.   i. THOMAS LLOYD.[5]
    ii. SARAH LLOYD, mar. John Dickinson.
    iii. DEBORAH LLOYD, third wife of Edward Martin of Easton.
15.   iv. ROBERT GRUNDY LLOYD of Trappe; mar. Mary Ruth.

11. COL. EDWARD LLOYD [5] (*Edward,*[4] *Edward,*[3] *Philemon,*[2] *Edward* [1]) of Wye, was born 15 Dec. 1744, and died 8 July 1796. He represented Talbot County in the Lower House of Assembly 1771-1774 (House Journals), was a member of the Provincial Convention held at Annapolis in 1775 (*Arch.,* xi, 3), and qualified, 29 August 1775, as a member of the Council of Safety of Maryland (*Arch.,* xi, 74). He was a member, from 1777 to 1779, of the first three Executive Councils under the new State government (*Arch.,* xvi, 187; xxi, 549), was Delegate to Legislature 1780, and was elected to the State Senate in 1781, 1786, and 1791 (House and Senate Journals). He was a Delegate from Maryland to the Continental Congress, and was, in 1788, a member of the State Convention for the ratification of the Federal Constitution (Harrison Papers, Md. Hist. Soc'y). Col. Lloyd married, 19 Nov.

1767, Elizabeth Tayloe (b. 6 March 1750, d. 17 Feb'y
1825), eldest daughter of Hon. John Tayloe of Mount
Airy, Richmond County, Va. Their issue:

   i. ANNE LLOYD,[6] b. 30 Jan'y, 1769; d. 20 Feb'y, 1840; mar.
      Richard Tasker Lowndes of Bostock House, Pr. George's Co.
   ii. REBECCA LLOYD, b. 16 Oct., 1771; d. 26 Oct., 1848; mar., 1793,
      Hon. Joseph Hopper Nicholson.
   iii. ELIZABETH LLOYD, b. 5 Sept., 1774; d. 6 March, 1849; mar.,
      14 Feb'y, 1805, Henry Hall Harwood of Annapolis.
   iv. ELEANOR LLOYD, b. 22 Sept., 1776; d. 18 Aug., 1805; mar.,
      1794, Charles Lowndes.
16.   v. EDWARD LLOYD, b. 22 July, 1779; d. 2 June, 1834; mar.,
      30 Nov., 1797, Sally Scott Murray.
   vi. MARIA LLOYD, b. 11 March, 1782; d. 15 Jan'y, 1868; mar.,
      Richard Williams West of the Woodyard, Pr. George's Co.
   vii. MARY TAYLOE LLOYD, b. 26 May, 1784; d. 18 May, 1859; mar.,
      19 Jan'y, 1802, Francis Scott Key, author of " The Star
      Spangled Banner."

12. RICHARD BENNETT LLOYD,[5] (*Edward,*[4] *Edward,*[3] *Phile-*
mon [2]) was born 13 August 1750, and died 12 Sept. 1787.
He went to England in 1770, and became a captain in
the King's Life Guard. He married in England, Joanna
Leigh, a lady of a distinguished family of the Isle of
Wight and a great beauty. After the death of Capt.
Lloyd, she married Francis Love Beckford a first cousin
of Wiliam Beckford of Font Hill. Capt. R. B. Lloyd and
Joanna (Leigh) his wife had issue:

   i. EDWARD LLOYD,[6] settled near Alexandria, Va., and left de-
      scendants.
   ii. RICHARD BENNETT LLOYD.
   iii. HENRY LLOYD.
   iv. EMILY LLOYD, b. 1783; d. 1867; mar., 1816, Rev. Geo. Gifford
      Ward, Dean of Lincoln, and had six children, one of whom
      was the late H. L. D. Ward of the British Museum.

13. GEN. JAMES LLOYD [5] (*Richard,*[4] *Edward,*[3] *Philemon* [2])
was commissioned, 11 Sept. 1776, Second Lieutenant in
Capt. Frisby's Company, Kent County militia (*Arch.,*
xii, 265). He is usually styled major and probably attained that rank either towards the close of, or after, the
Revolution. In the War of 1812 he was promoted to the
rank of General. He married Elizabeth Tilghman (see
Mag., i, 369) daughter of James Tilghman of Chestertown,
and sister of Col. Tench and of Judge William Tilghman.
Their issue:

Twins
   i. MARIA LLOYD,[6] mar. William Hemsley.
   ii. ELIZABETH LLOYD, mar. Philemon Hemsley.

14. THOMAS LLOYD [5] (*James,*[4] *James,*[3] *Philemon* [2]) married
—— —— and had:

    i. JAMES LLOYD,[6].
    ii. EDWARD LLOYD.
    iii. HENRY LLOYD, mar. ——, who mar. 2°. Hanson Smith.

15. ROBERT GRUNDY LLOYD [5] (*James,*[4] *James,*[3] *Philemon* [2])
of Trappe, Talbot Co., married Mary Ruth and had issue:

    i. ROBERT N. LLOYD.[6]
    ii. JAMES P. LLOYD.
    iii. THOMAS E. LLOYD.
    v. SARAH JANE LLOYD.
    vi. PHILEMON LLOYD.
    vii. FRISBY LLOYD.
    viii. MONTGOMERY LLOYD.
    ix. FRANCIS LLOYD.
    x. CHRISTOPHER COLUMBUS LLOYD.

16. EDWARD LLOYD [6] (*Edward,*[5] *Edward,*[4] *Edward* [3]) of Wye,
was born 22 July 1779, and died 2 June 1834. He was
Governor of Maryland 1809-1811, and United States Senator 1819-1826. He married, 30 November 1797, Sally
Scott Murray, daughter of Dr. James Murray of Annapolis, and had issue:

    i. EDWARD LLOYD,[7] b. 27 Dec., 1798; d. 11 Aug., 1861; mar.,
        30 Nov., 1827, Alicia McBlair.
    ii. ELIZABETH TAYLOE LLOYD, mar., 1 June, 1820, Edward S.
        Winder.
    iii. JAMES MURRAY LLOYD, b. 10 Jan'y, 1803; d. 22 July, 1847;
        mar. Elizabeth McBlair.
    iv. SALLY SCOTT LLOYD, mar., 4 June, 1826, Commodore Charles
        Lowndes, U. S. N.
    v. ANNE CATHERINE LLOYD, mar., 19 Feb'y, 1835, Capt. Franklin
        Buchanan, U. S. N., Admiral, C. S. N.
    vi. DANIEL LLOYD, mar. 1°., 22 Nov., 1832, Virginia Upshur, 2°.
        Catherine Henry.
    vii. MARY ELEANOR LLOYD, mar., 26 Oct., 1837, William Tilghman
        Goldsborough.

NOTE. Quite a full account of the later generations of the
Lloyd family is to be found in Hanson's *Old Kent,* pp.
30-40.

LLOYD FAMILY.

The following genealogy of the branch of the Lloyd family residing in Trappe District, Talbot County, has been sent to the *Magazine* by Col. Oswald Tilghman of Easton. It will serve to correct an error in the article on the Lloyds published in the December number, and Col. Tilghman's well-known genealogical skill will vouch for its accuracy.

The Lloyds of Trappe District, Talbot County, Maryland.

1. EDWARD LLOYD of Wye House, died 1695. Puritan Commander of Ann Arundel Co. 1650. Provincial Councillor of Md. Married first a widow, Alice (Crouch) Hawkins, and secondly Frances, widow of John Watkins. After her death he returned to England and died in London. He was appointed Commander of Ann Arundel Co. by Gov. Stone, 1650. He lived to be about 90 years old. He married again in England, Grace, widow of William Parker, who survived him. His only son by first wife:

2. PHILEMON LLOYD, born 1647, died 1685. Member of the Provincial Assembly of Md. 1671-74. Died ten years before his father. He married Henrietta Maria Neale Bennett, widow of Richard Bennett of Bennett's Point, Queen Anne's Co., who was the richest man in the province of Maryland. She was the daughter of Capt. James Neale and Anne Gill. She died May 4, 1697. Issue:
    1. EDWARD II of Wye House.
    2. PHILEMON (married Widow Freeman).
    3. JAMES.
    4. ANNA MARIA, wife of Col. Richard Tilghman II.
    5. MARGARET, wife of Matthew Tilghman Ward.
    6. HENRIETTA M., wife of Henry Blake of Queen Anne Co. Their dau. was mother of Charles Carroll, barrister.
    7. ALICE, unmar.

3. JAMES LLOYD I, born Mar. 7, 1680, died Sept. 27, 1723. Member Provincial Assembly of Md. 1712-14 and 1716-22.

Member of Council 1722-23 under Gov. Charles Calvert.
Married the beautiful Ann Grundy, Jan'y 12, 1709, born
Apl. 25, 1680, died Nov. 18, 1731. She and her husband
James Lloyd lie buried at Hope. She married secondly
Rev. Edward Fottrell by whom she had no children. Issue:

1. ROBERT LLOYD of Hope, who mar. Anna Maria Hemsley, dau. of
Col. Richard Tilghman II.
2. MARGARET, wife of William Tilghman of Grosses, son of Col.
Richard Tilghman II.
3. DEBORAH, wife of Jeremiah Nicols, son of Rev. Henry Nicols of
St. Michael's.
4. HENRIETTA MARIA,wife of Samuel Chamberlaine of Plaindealing.
5. JAMES of Parson's Landing.
7. ANN, wife of Hon. Matthew Tilghman of Rich Neck.

4. JAMES LLOYD II, of Parson's Landing, born Mar. 16, 1716,
d. Mar. 1768. Married Elizabeth Frisby dau. of Peregrine
Frisby of Cecil Co., Md., whose other dau. Susanna Frisby
married Col. Richard Tilghman 3rd, father of Col. Peregrine Tilghman who married Deborah Lloyd dau. of Robert
Lloyd of Hope. Genl. Tench Tilghman's grandfather,
Peregrine Frisby, was a member of the Provincial Assembly
of Md. 1713. Issue:

1. JAMES III.
2. PEREGRINE.
3. ROBERT.
4. PHILEMON.
5. FRISBY.
6. NICHOLAS.
7. ANNA.
8. ELIZABETH.
9. HENRIETTA MARIA.
10. DEBORAH.

5. CAPT. JAMES LLOYD III, died 1815. Married Sarah Martin, dau. of Thomas Martin. Captain 4th Battalion Md.
Militia in the American Revolution. Issue:

1. ROBERT GRUNDY.
2. THOMAS, mar. Elizabeth, dau. of Henry Martin, died 1801. He
mentions in his will sons James, Henry, and Edward.
3. ROBERT (again).
4. PEREGRINE, died 1808 unmarried.
5. DEBORAH, wife of Edward Martin.
6. SARAH.

6. ROBERT GRUNDY LLOYD, died 1839. Married Mary Ruth,
Feb. 5th, 1812. Issue:

1. SARAH JANE.
2. ROBERT NICOLS.

   3. JAMES P.
   4. PHILEMON.
   5. THOMAS E. (married Jane Bradley, Jan. 12, 1846).
   6. FRISBY.
   7. MONTGOMERY.
   8. CHRISTOPHER COLUMBUS.
   9. DR. FRANCIS MARION.

7. DR. FRANCIS M. LLOYD, died 1885.   Married Sarah Miranda Bowdle Jan. 12, 1857.   Issue:

   1. CHARLES BOWDLE.

8. CHARLES B. LLOYD, married Eliza Chaplain Robinson. Issue:

   1. FRANCIS MARION.
   2. HELEN.

9. FRANCIS MARION LLOYD.

OSWALD TILGHMAN.

NOTES.

LLOYD FAMILY. Mrs. Edward Shippen kindly sends the following interesting details, in reference to the article on the Lloyd family, which appeared in the *Magazine*, VII, 420-430. On the authority of his grandson, the late Mr. H. L. D. Ward of the British Museum, Richard Bennett Lloyd (cf. p. 429) was Captain in the Coldstream Guards, and married Joanna, daughter of Sir John Leigh, of North Court, Isle of Wight, and Amelie, his wife. In 1784, Capt. Lloyd and his wife visited America, and in the same year their daughter Amelie was born at Annapolis. The family returned to England in 1787 and, in 1817, the daughter married Rev. John Gifford Ward, Rector of Chelmsford, Essex, later (1825-1845) of St. James', Westminster, and Dean of Lincoln, 1845-1860.

Mrs. Shippen also calls attention to a possible misprint on p. 421. The will of the first Edward Lloyd was dated, in her copy, 11 March, not 11 May. She further points out that, according to their epitaphs in the old graveyard at Wye House, Elizabeth and Mary Lloyd, daughters of Col. Philemon, were twins, born in November, 1678. Elizabeth died 18 May, 1694, and Mary died 20 September, 1690.

LOCKERMAN FAMILY NOTES: THE FLORIDA LINE

By JAMES LOOCKERMAN TAYLOR, JR.

Descendants of the Florida branch of the Lockerman (Loockerman) family of Maryland, wishing to trace their ancestry back to the founder of that family, Dr. Jacob Lockerman (c. 1652-1750), son of the immigrant, Govert Loockermans (1603-1670), are confronted with a statement in the late Dr. Joseph S. Ames' genealogy of the Lockerman family according to which an unidentified Edward Lockerman, of Cambridge, Maryland, married, c. 1795-1800, Margaret Bayley, by whom he had issue a number of children (all named), all of whom, about 1830, settled in Florida.[1] Among these children Dr. Ames mentions a daughter, Mary Lockerman, who married (1) Edward Chandler; (2) Dr. John Bradford Taylor.[2]

---

[1] Loockerman Genealogy, by Dr. Joseph S. Ames, in *Maryland Historical Magazine*, II, 298, note 2.

[2] According to *The Norris Family in Maryland*, by Thomas M. Myers 1916), p. 31, John Norris married Susannah Bradford, by whom he had a daughter, Susannah, born May 10, 1753, who married George Taylor and had issue: Susan Taylor, Mary Taylor, Ann Louisa Taylor (m. H. W. Gray), and Bradford Taylor, who married a Miss Hemp. According to a letter written in 1905 by the late James Loockerman Taylor, Sr., father of James Loockerman Taylor, Jr. and son of Dr. John Bradford Taylor, his (the writer's) paternal grandmother was a Miss Norris, of Baltimore County. According to the same authority, Dr. John Bradford Taylor had a sister, Susan Taylor, who always called him "Bradford." James Loockerman Taylor, Sr., had a younger sisted named Annie *Grey* Taylor. It seems very likely, therefore, that John Bradford Taylor, was the son of George and Susannah (Norris) Taylor. He studied medicine in Philadelphia, 1810-1811, saw service in the War of 1812 as Surgeon's Mate, Fifth Maryland Militia, was in the battle of Bladensburg, at North Point and the storming of Fort McHenry. He resided for a time in Baltimore, where he married, 2 December, 1812, Sarah Camp, his first wife. ("Hemp" of the Norris genealogy is porbably an error for "Camp.")

183

This statement concerning Mrs. Taylor and the other children whom Dr. Ames attributes to Edward Lockerman, is undoubtedly an error in that, according to a Lockerman family Bible, now in the possession of Miss Winifred Lockerman Turville, of Detroit, Michigan, these same children were the offspring of Thomas Lockerman and his wife, Peggy Bayly, of Cambridge, Maryland. Contributory evidence is to be found in the register of Dorchester Parish, Dorchester County, where the births of James Lockerman, Charlotte Haynie Lockerman, Henrietta Haynie Lockerman, Mary Lockerman, and Thomas B. Lockerman, children of Thomas and Peggy (or Margaret) Lockerman, are recorded.

Mr. James Loockerman Taylor, Jr., who contributes the following notes and records, is the grandson of Dr. John Bradford Taylor and Mary (Lockerman) Taylor, his wife. The objects of this contribution are: (1) to correct the error above mentioned; (2) to give to the public an interesting old Bible record not heretofore published; (3) to show that Thomas Lockerman, of Cambridge, Maryland, was the son of Thomas Lockerman, senior, of Dorchester County, Maryland (1747-post 1806), whose place in the Lockerman line is established in Dr. Ames' genealogy.[3]

WILLIAM B. MARYE

The Lockerman Bible, giving family of Thomas Lockerman, is now in Detroit, Michigan, being a valued heirloom. Statement by present owner, as to history of this Bible and with photostats of pages on which records had been written by hand, is now with the Maryland Historical Society. The Bible was printed in 1809. The written records commence with Thomas Lockerman and Peggy Bayly, and list issue as:

THOMAS LOCKERMAN, born 31 October, 1771: died 26 October, 1826, Cambridge, Md. Married 3 May, 1804, PEGGY BAYLY, born 10 January, 1780: died 10 June, 1823, Cambridge, Md.

Issue:

ELIZABETH LEAH LOCKERMAN, born 12 November 1805; died 29 November, 1834, Tallahassee, Fla. Married Edward Lockerman 26 October, 1831, Cambridge, Md.

CHARLOTTE HAYNIE LOCKERMAN, born 18 October, 1807; died 14 June, 1838, lost on Steamer *Pulaski* on passage to Balimore. Married James

---

Prior to 1836 he emigrated to Tallahassee, Florida, with his wife and children, his brothers and sisters. There he resided and practiced medicine, until his death, which occurred in 1864. On July 16th, 1846, he married Mary (Lockerman) Chandler, widow of Edward M. Chandler, and daughter of Thomas and Peggy (or Margaret) (Bayly) Lockerman, both deceased, late of Cambridge, Maryland.

[3] Thomas Lockerman, Sr., whose death appears to have occurred between 1806 and 1809, married not less than twice. Thomas Lockerman, Jr., seems to have been the only surviving child of a wife whose family name and Christian name are both unknown. At the time when he made his will, Thomas Lockerman, Sr., had a wife named Francis (maiden name unknown to this writer), who was the mother of all the rest of his children. (See petition of Henry and Susan Pattison, 21 March, 1814, recorded at Cambridge, Maryland, in Liber E. R. No. 3, f. 176 *et seq.* A copy of Thomas Lockerman's will is included with this petition.)

Edwin Stewart 16 May, 1832, Cambridge, Md., who died 18 June, 1838, on wreck of *Pulaski*. Children:

Samuel Hodson Stewart, born 6 April, 1834; died 21 July, 1835, Tallahassee, Fla.

Samuel Hodson Stewart, born 30 July, 1836; died 14 June, 1838, with his mother.

HENRIETTA HAYNIE LOCKERMAN, born 9 November 1809; died 7 November, 1862, New Orleans, La. Married Joseph B. Brown, of Scotland, 9 August, 1840, Tallahassee, Fla., who died 13 October, 1863, London, Ontario. Children:

Thomas Lockerman Brown, born 19 June, 1841: died 23 March, 1861, Tallahassee, Fla.

Jane Murdoch Brown, born 30 September, 1844, Jefferson County, Fla.: died 25 May, 1932, Wallacetown, Ontario. Married George Turville, of London, Ontario, 30 September, 1869, who died 19 January, 1938. Children:

Sydney Stewart Turville, born 13 August, 1870; died 3 February, 1936.

Ettie Lockerman Turville, born 15 August, 1872; married.

Jessie Turville, born 27 November, 1874; died 1 November, 1934.

Winifred Lockerman Turville, born 21 December, 1877.

Hampden Haynie Brown, born 14 December 1846; died 23 June, 1847.

MARY LOCKERMAN, b. 30 January, 1812. Married Edward M. Chandler, 12 January, 1834, Tallahassee, Fla., who died 25 May, 1836. Children: Elizabeth Leah Lockerman Chandler, born 18 January, 1835.

Note: Not recorded in this Bible, but Mary Lockerman married (second) Doctor John Bradford Taylor, 16 July, 1846, at Tallahassee, Fla., where she died during 1865. Children:

James Loockerman Taylor, born 25 July, 1847; died 15 July, 1925.

Adele Gertrude Taylor.

Annie Gray Taylor, born 12 July, 1854; died 1917.

JAMES BAYLY LOCKERMAN, born 12 December 1813; died 14 October, 1814.

THOMAS BAYLY LOCKERMAN, born 20 September, 1815; died 17 August, 1839, Tallahassee, Fla.

JAMES FISHER LOCKERMAN, born 26 September, 1818.

Examination of grantor deeds recorded at Cambridge, Md., for period 29 March, 1774, to 22 July, 1805, shows 16 deeds by " Thomas Lockerman," of which 9 were undoubtedly by the Senior, as indicated by 3 with release of dower by Fannie, one of very early date, and 5 being qualified by Senior or Elder after the name. Four of these 16 deeds are clearly by Thomas, the son or a younger man, by use of Junior or Younger. Remaining 3 are not readily determined. The first deed conveying specifically from Senior to Junior is dated 27 July, 1796, and includes " for natural love and affection " as well as a monetary consideration. The first grantor deed by Thomas Junior is dated 4 December, 1796. The last deed identified by Senior was dated 22 July, 1805, and conveyed to Thomas Lockerman Junior. Records of these 16 deeds contain Senior 5 times, Elder once, Junior 4 times, and Younger twice.

No deeds with Thomas Lockerman as grantor were observed from July, 1805, to 11 January, 1812, from which date to end of 1826 " Thomas

Lockerman " conveyed by 31 deeds, of which 10 were released for dower by Peggy or Margaret. None of these ten released deeds has been identified as covering land previously conveyed by deed " from father to son." One deed, in 1818, undoubtedly conveys land received by will of his father, but no release by wife is on the record. It is significant that last deed released by Margaret is dated February, 1823, and death of Peggy Bayly Lockerman is given as 10 June, 1823, by the Bible record quoted above. A joint deed was made with John H. Hooper, dated 19 March, 1824, some 9 months after recorded death of Peggy Bayly Lockerman, which deed was released by wife of Hooper only, indicating widowhood of Thomas Lockerman at that time. Total 20 deeds by Thomas Lockerman, all without dower release but included in the total 31 made after February, 1823, and prior to end of year 1826. No wording was found in any of the deeds examined, to indicate that there was more than one " younger " individual in Dorchester County bearing name of Thomas Lockerman.

Thomas Lockerman (1771-1826) died intestate, leaving his affairs seriously involved. Suit was brought in July Term, 1828, as evidenced by Chancery Record, Volume 137, folio 537, at Land Office, Annapolis, Md., against Robert Wallace, Administrator, and the children, for payment of debts. Records of the suit list many parcels of land for sale, but none has been readily and positively identified as a parcel previously conveyed by Thomas Lockerman Senior to Thomas Lockerman Junior. Thomas Lockerman the Elder executed only two deeds to Thomas Lockerman his son, both conveying lots in Cambridge. One of these lots was sold by Thomas Lockerman the Younger during lifetime of his father. No record of alienation of the other lot has been found bearing date within life-time of Thomas Lockerman (1771-1826), and this lot is believed to be identical with a certain lot on High Street, Cambridge, sold by Henry Page, Trustee for sale of the real estate of Thomas Lockerman after death in 1826. The Chancery records do state that Thomas Lockerman left children, naming them as Elizabeth L., Charlotte H., Henrietta H., Mary, Thomas B., and James, and that all are infants under the age of 21 except Elizabeth L. Also, that all are residents of Dorchester County except Henrietta H. This Court record agrees with entries in the Bible, and indicates conclusively that the six children were offspring of Thomas Lockerman, and not of Edward Lockerman as shown by the genealogy published in Vol 2 of this Magazine, page 298.

Other records in the Bible show: Jane Murdoch Brown, daughter of Joseph and Henrietta H. Brown, born at Leguan, Jefferson Co., Florida, 30 September, 1844, baptized at Tallahassee, Fla., by the Rev. F. P. Lee, 1846, married at Medway, London, Ontario, by the Rev. G. M. Innes, 30 September 1869, to George Turville of London, Ontario, died 25 May, 1932, at Wallacetown, Ontario. Turville died 19 June 1938, aged 94 yrs.

Winifred L. Turville, owner of the Bible, is the daughter of George and Jane M. Turville. She writes: " This bible is one of my earliest recollections, and family history is that it came, in 1862, into possession of my mother." She adds that the handwriting from 1841 down is by Joseph B. Brown and George Turville.

LOWNDES FAMILY.

CHRISTOPHER JOHNSTON.

A very full pedigree of the English ancestors of this family, tracing the line back to the year 1582, is given in Earwaker's *History of Sandbach*, pp. 122-123. The arms of the family are as follows :—

Arms.—Arg., fretty az., on a canton gu., a lion's head erased or.
Crest.—A lion's head erased or.

1. CHRISTOPHER LOWNDES,[1] fifth son of Richard Lowndes of Bostock House, in Hassall, Cheshire, England, and Margaret (Poole) his wife, was baptized at Sandbach, 19 June 1713, and is mentioned, 1743, in his father's will. As early as 1738 he was living in Prince George's County, Maryland. 20 July 1738, William Beall Sen., of Prince George's Co., conveys to Christopher Lowndes, who acts in behalf of himself and of Henry and Edward Trafford of Liverpool, merchants, one acre of land called "The 22d Lot," on the Eastern Branch of Potomac (Pr. Geo. Co., Lib. T, fol. 633). 25 May 1741, "Capt." Christopher Lowndes conveys his interest in this lot to Messrs. Henry and Edward Trafford of Liverpool (Pr. Geo. Co., Lib. Y, fol. 293). Further evidence of his residence in Maryland at this time is found in a bill of sale, dated 26 Sept. 1739, wherein James Freeman sells two negroes to "Christopher Lowndes of Prince George's County, in the Province of Maryland, merchant" (*ibid.*, fol. 94). In 1748 he was the senior partner in the firm of Christopher Lowndes and Company, operating both in Maryland and in England. 22 August 1761, Francis Hatfield, attorney in fact for the executors of John Hardman, late of Liverpool, deceased, William Whalley and Edward Lowndes of Liverpool, merchants, convey to Christopher Lowndes of Prince George's Co., Md., merchant, the tract "Simon and Jane," 107 acres, in Prince George's Co., condemned at June Court, 1748, for 5992 lb. tobacco, for the use of Christopher Lowndes and Company, which said company consisted of John Hardman, William Whalley, and Edward Lowndes in Liverpool, and Christopher Lowndes,

merchant, of Maryland (Pr. Geo. Co., Lib. RR, fol. 154). The Edward Lowndes here mentioned as one of the Liverpool partners of the firm was doubtless the younger brother of Christopher (see Earwaker's *Sandbach*, p. 123). Christopher Lowndes was one of the Justices of Prince George's County from 1753 to 1775, and was of the Quorum from 1769 (Commission Book). 4 June 1777, he was commissioned, under the new State government, one of the Justices of the county and Judge of the Orphans' Court (Md. Archives, xvi, 273, 274). He died at Bladensburg, 8 January 1785. *The Maryland Journal and Commercial Advertiser*, Baltimore, 18 Jan'y 1785, has the following obituary notice :—" Died. A few days ago, in advanced age, at Bladensburg, Christopher Lowndes, Esq., for many years an eminent merchant of that place." He died intestate and his sons Benjamin and Francis Lowndes gave bond, 28 Jan'y 1785, in the sum of £5000 current for the administration of his estate, their sureties being Levi Gantt and Richard Contee (Pr. Geo. Co. Admin. Bonds). Christopher Lowndes married 14 May 1747 (Register of St. Ann's, Annapolis), Elizabeth Tasker (b. 4 Feb. 1726; d. 19 Sept. 1789) daughter of Hon. Benjamin Tasker, President of the Council of Maryland. They had issue as follows, the births of the first five children being recorded in Piscataway Parish, Prince George's County :—

  i. ANNE MARGARET LOWNDES,[2] b. 15 June 1748 ; d. unmar. 16. Jan. 1822.
2. ii. BENJAMIN LOWNDES, b. 30 Dec. 1749 ; d. 6 Jan. 1802.
3. iii. FRANCIS LOWNDES, b. 19 Oct. 1751 ; d. April 1815.
  iv. SAMUEL LOWNDES, b. 20 July 1753.
  v. ELIZABETH LOWNDES, b. 7 April 1755.
  vi. REBECCA LOWNDES, b. 1757 ; d. 10 Feb. 1802 ; mar. 17 June 1781, Hon. Benj. Stoddert (b. 1751 ; d. 1813), first Secretary of the Navy of the United States.
  vii. HARRIOT LOWNDES, mar. about 1781, Levi Gantt, Esq., of Pr. Geo. Co.
4. viii. RICHARD TASKER LOWNDES, b. 25 Dec. 1763.
5. ix. CHARLES LOWNDES, b. 1765 ; d. April 1846.

2. BENJAMIN LOWNDES [2] (*Christopher*[1]), was born 30 Dec. 1749, and died 6 Jan. 1802. He married Dorothy Buchanan (b. 18 Feb. 1762) daughter of Gen. Andrew Buchanan of Baltimore County, and had issue :—

  i. ELIZABETH LOWNDES.[3]
  ii. ANDREW LOWNDES.
  iii. BENJAMIN LOWNDES.
  iv. SUSAN LOWNDES, d. 22 Sept. 1822.
  v. ELEANOR LOWNDES.
  vi. CHRISTOPHER LOWNDES, b. 28 May 1799 (Piscataway Par. Rec.).

3. FRANCIS LOWNDES [2] (*Christopher* [1]) was born 19 Oct. 1751, and died in April 1815. He married Jane Maddox (d. 6 July 1829) of Yorkshire, England, and had an only son,

    i. FRANCIS LOWNDES,[3] b. in Yorkshire, England, 1784; d. in Georgetown, D. C., 2 Dec. 1867, without issue. He married Angeletta Craighill, b. in Jefferson Co., Va., 1793, d. in Georgetown, D. C., 7 Sept. 1858.

4. RICHARD TASKER LOWNDES [2] (*Christopher* [1]) of Blenheim, Bladensburg, Md., and of Bostock House, Prince George's Co., was born 25 Dec. 1763. He married Anne Lloyd (b. 30 Jan. 1769 ; d. 20 Feb. 1840) daughter of Col. Edward Lloyd of Wye and Elizabeth (Tayloe) his wife. They had issue :—

    i. ELIZABETH TAYLOE LOWNDES,[3] d. April 1878 ; mar. Right Rev. William Pinkney, D. D., Bishop of Maryland.
    ii. ANNE LLOYD LOWNDES, d. unmar. 1 May 1850.
    iii. EDWARD LLOYD LOWNDES, d. young.
    iv. RICHARD TASKER LOWNDES, b. 1804; d. 19 Sept. 1815.
    v. EDWARD LLOYD LOWNDES, b. 1807 ; d. unmar. 7 Jan. 1832.
    vi. BENJAMIN OGLE LOWNDES, b. 1810 ; d. unmar. 12 July 1897.

5. CHARLES LOWNDES [2] (*Christopher* [1]) was born in 1765, and died in April 1846. He was a merchant in Georgetown, D. C., but settled later in Jefferson County, Virginia. He married first, in 1794, Eleanor Lloyd (b. 22 Sept. 1776 ; d. 18 Aug. 1805) daughter of Col. Edward Lloyd of Wye and sister of his brother Richard Tasker Lowndes' wife; and secondly Francis Whiting (d. 2 Sept. 1841) of Virginia. Charles Lowndes and Eleanor (Lloyd) his first wife had issue :—

    i. HARRIOT LOWNDES,[3] b. 1795 ; d. 15 Aug. 1835 ; married Dr. Samuel Scollay of Jefferson Co., Va.
    ii. EDWARD LLOYD LOWNDES, b. 5 June 1797 ; d. 21 Oct. 1797.
6. iii. CHARLES LOWNDES, b. 19 July 1798 ; d. 14 Dec. 1885.
7. iv. LLOYD LOWNDES, b. 9 July 1800 ; d. 14 March 1879.
8. v. RICHARD TASKER LOWNDES, b. 29 March 1803 ; d. 24 April 1844.
    vi. ELIZABETH ANN LOWNDES, b. 13 April 1805 ; mar. Horace Leeds Edmondson.

Charles Lowndes and Frances (Whiting) his second wife had issue :—

    i. FRANCES PERRIN LOWNDES, d. young.
    ii. BEVERLY BLADEN LOWNDES, b. 1813 ; drowned 14 June 1835, while bathing in the Shenandoah River.
    iii. FRANCES WHITING LOWNDES, b. March 1814 ; d. June 1815.
    iv. FRANCES PERRIN LOWNDES, mar. John James Frame of Charlestown, W. Va.

6. CHARLES LOWNDES[3] (*Charles*[2], *Christopher*[1]) Commodore U. S. N., was born 19 July 1798, and died 14 Dec. 1885. He married, 4 June 1826, his first cousin, Sally Scott Lloyd. daughter of Gov. Edward Lloyd of Wye and Sally Scott (Murray) his wife. They had issue :—

    i. SALLY LLOYD LOWNDES,[4] b. 2 April 1827 ; mar. John W. Bennett, U. S. N.
    ii. ELLEN LLOYD LOWNDES, b. 15 Sept. 1831 ; d. 23 July 1845.
    iii. DR. CHARLES LOWNDES, b. 21 Oct. 1832; mar. Catherine M. Tilghman, daughter of Wm. Gibson Tilghman of Grosses.
    iv. EDWARD LLOYD LOWNDES, b. 11 Oct. 1836 ; d. 20 June 1837.
    v. LLOYD LOWNDES, b. 21 March 1838.
    vi. RICHARD TASKER LOWNDES, b. 14 Feb. 1843 ; d. 6 Aug. 1845.
    vii. ELIZABETH TAYLOE LOWNDES, b. 15 Nov. 1844 ; mar. Dr. Julius A. Johnson of Easton, Talbot Co.

7. LLOYD LOWNDES[3] (*Charles*[2], *Christopher*[1]) was born in Georgetown, D. C., 9 July 1800. In 1824 he settled in Cumberland, Md., but removed in 1831 to Clarksburg, W. Va., where he died, 14 March 1877. He married, in 1840, Elizabeth Moore, daughter of Thomas Moore of Clarksburg, and had issue :—

    i. DR. CHARLES T. LOWNDES,[4] Surgeon U. S. A., d. Feb. 1865.
    ii. RICHARD TASKER LOWNDES, mar. 5 Feb. 1896 Mary Goff.
    iii. HON. LLOYD LOWNDES, b. 21 March 1845; d. 8 Jan. 1905 ; Governor of Maryland, 1896–1900 ; mar. his first cousin Elizabeth Tasker Lowndes, daughter of Richard Tasker Lowndes.
    iv. CLARENCE MOORE LOWNDES, b. 1847 ; d. young.

8. RICHARD TASKER LOWNDES[3] (*Charles*[2], *Christopher*[1]) was born 29 March 1803, settled in Cumberland, Md., in 1824, and died 24 April 1844. He married Louisa Black, daughter of James Black of Cumberland, and had issue :—

    i. ELOISE LOWNDES,[4] mar. Philip Roman of Cumberland, Md.
    ii. ELIZABETH TASKER LOWNDES. mar. her cousin, Hon. Lloyd Lowndes, Governor of Maryland.

This genealogy, except where other authorities are cited, is compiled chiefly from the manuscript family records of Mrs. Edward Shippen of Baltimore, Md., and Mrs. Murray Addison of Washington, D. C., the latter being a great-granddaughter of Levi Gantt and Harriot Lowndes his wife, daughter of Christopher Lowndes. I desire to acknowledge my indebtedness to both these ladies.

THE MAC KEELES OF DORCHESTER

By MARIE DIXON CULLEN

JOHN of the bonny clan MacKeele (MacKeill-McKeel) came to Dorchester County in 1673.[1] Whether he left an ailing wife or a newly turned grave, we do not know. But we do know that in 1680 his son Charles was brought to Dorchester by Henry Aldred who acknowledged receiving from John MacKeele a satisfactory compensation for transporting him.[2] From this new dependency there was now additional land due John which was called " Charles Delight " and " Charles Desires." John MacKeele left the land to his son Charles in his will dated March 13, 1695.[3] John had also been granted a warrant for one hundred acres October 30, 1673, but it was not until almost two years after his arrival in Maryland that he acquired this land, granted under patent May 9, 1675, " John's Desire " and on May 20, 1675, " John's Adventure," on the south side of Little Choptank River " to be holden . . . of our Manor of Nanticoke " with manorial rights.[4]

In possession of his lands, united with his son Charles, gifted with qualities of leadership, John MacKeele prospered and soon became one of the most active and influential men in Dorchester County, contributing to its development and safety. In 1678 he held the rank of Lieutenant in the Dorchester County Militia, and on the occasion of his service against the Nanticoke Indians was paid with 700 lbs. of tobacco, legal tender of the day.[5] By 1690 he had become Captain,[6] and on October 19, 1694, Governor Francis Nicholson appointed him Field Officer of Dorchester

[1] Early Settlers, Liber 17, f. 567, Land Office, Annapolis.
[2] Liber W C 2, f. 233, 312, 366, Land Office.
[3] Liber 7, f. 209, Land Office.
[4] Liber 18, f. 368, Land Office.
[5] Elias Jones, *Revised History of Dorchester County Maryland* (Baltimore, 1925), p. 41.
[6] *Ibid.*, p. 51.

County with rank of Lieutenant Colonel.[7] " At the Ridge " in Anne Arundel during the Assembly of Maryland held October and November 1683, he was appointed Land Commissioner to purchase land and lay out towns, providing plans for churches, chapels, market houses and other public buildings. He was appointed Court Commissioner at the same time.[8] On August 1, 1690, he, with the Hon. Thomas Ennalls and others, were Gentleman Justices of the first court under the reign of William and Mary organized at Cambridge.[9]

The MacKeeles supplemented their prominence and natural abilities by marriage alliances with important and influential families. John MacKeele's son Thomas married Clare, the daughter of Stephen Gary and widow of Charles Powell,[10] who was a member of the first Bar Association organized in Cambridge in 1692.[11]

Steven Gary, Gentleman, who immigrated from Cornwall, England, in 1650, was commissioned to survey 1500 acres on the Eastern Shore.[12] His wife Clare immigrated in 1653.[13] In 1655 Steven Gary demanded land on the Eastern Shore in return for the transportation of himself in 1650, Clare his wife in 1655, John and Nicholas de la Valey, and Mary Bull in 1657. A warrant to lay out to Steven Gary 500 acres was returned July 11, next,[14] and he received in 1662 by patent " Spocot " which he called his home plantation. Gary was another of the outstanding settlers. He and Henry Hooper were appointed as the first Gentlemen Justices or Commissioners of the County in 1699 when Dorchester County was erected.[15] He was also Peace Commissioner in 1675, 1676, 1677-1678,[16] and High Sheriff of Dorchester 1678-1681.[17] The Hon. George L. Radcliffe, direct descendant of Steven Gary through his daughter Clare and her first husband Charles Powell, now owns " Spocot " which he uses for his summer home.

[7] *Ibid.*, p. 475.   [8] *Ibid.*, pp. 56-57.   [9] *Ibid.*, p. 51.
[10] Maryland Genealogical Records Committee Reports, V (1932), 51-52, Daughters of the American Revolution Library, Washington, D. C.
[11] Jones, *op. cit.*, p. 176.
[12] Liber Q, f. 204, Liber 7, f. 581, Land Office.
[13] Jones, *op. cit.*, p. 31.
[14] Liber Q, f. 204, Liber 7, f. 581, Land Office.
[15] Jones, *op. cit.*, p. 31.
[16] *Archives of Maryland*, XV, 69, 131.
[17] *Ibid.*, p. 232.

Steven Gary and John MacKeele were close neighbors on the Little Choptank River and men of similar interests and abilities, having served together often as officers of the court and as commissioners, so it is not surprising that Steven Gary's daughter Clare should take for her second husband Thomas, the son of Col. MacKeele. Thomas died in 1725, dividing his lands between his two sons, John and Thomas.[18]

Thomas, the son of Thomas and Clare MacKeele, following the MacKeele military tradition, was commissioned in 1748 Captain of Troops of Horse and Company of Horse belonging to Dorchester County.[19] He was commissioned one of the Coroners of Dorchester County June 18, 1741.[20] Captain MacKeele married Mary Stevens the daughter of John Stevens[21] and his wife Priscilla, who was the daughter of Henry Hooper II, sole surviving son of Henry Hooper I. The elder Hooper had been a Justice of Calvert County and Captain of the Calvert Militia in 1658.[22] He later removed to Dorchester County where he had taken up land in 1668.[23]

Captain Thomas MacKeele, soldier and churchman, was a large land owner and a man of great influence and prominence on the Eastern Shore. In his will dated September 26, 1760, and probated January 28, 1762,[24] he left to his wife and children large legacies of land (some of the same lands as mentioned in the wills of his grandfathers, John MacKeele and Steven Gary). He specified certain revenues to be used for the education of his children John, Thomas and Mary. He bequeathed to his wife and children (later to go to his elder son John) his pew in the Great Choptank Parish Church in Cambridge, as well as his pew in the Church at Fishing Creek. To his Cousin Mary Ann MacKeele he left a " Sorroll Horse " and " a home with his wife for as long as she thinks fit or until she may be otherwise provided for." He also left to his wife his riding chair (chaise or carriage) and horse, and to each child a riding horse, saddle and furniture. What a gala sight it must have been to see the MacKeeles

---

[18] Jane Baldwin, ed., *The Maryland Calendar of Wills*, VI, 77.
[19] *Maryland Historical Magazine*, VI (1911), 55.
[20] Dielman Biographical File, Maryland Historical Society.
[21] Annie W. Burns, *Maryland Will Book*, XXVII, 83.
[22] Liber S, f. 139, Land Office, *Archives of Maryland*, III, 344-347.
[23] Rent Roll, Dorchester County, Calvert Paper 885, Maryland Historical Society.
[24] Wills, Liber 31, f. 561, Hall of Records, Annapolis, Md.

" en famille " driving from their plantation to church in Cambridge; Captain and Mrs. MacKeele in their riding chair flanked by their children as out-riders, each child on his own mount equipped with handsome harness!

Captain MacKeele's widow Mary married Benjamin Keene as is shown by the will of her mother Priscilla Hooper Stevens Howe, dated March 23, 1769. Mrs. Howe had married Robert Howe after the death in 1750 of John Stevens, her first husband.[25]

The days of comfort and security were soon overtaken by the Revolutionary War and eldest son John, a fitting descendant of Col. John MacKeele, Captain Henry Hooper and the Hon. Steven Gary, when the liberty and independence of his beloved country was threatened, was granted in November, 1776, letters of marque with the rank of Captain. He sailed " The Sturdy Beggar," a small brig, ill-equipped with only fourteen guns and a small, hastily gathered crew, to the mouth of the Chesapeake Bay to harass the Royal British Navy and gain time for defenses to be assembled against invasion.[26] Captain MacKeele lived to see his country win its independence, finally passing away August 6, 1798. His wife Mary had died January 15 of the same year.[27] While John was fighting courageously for liberty at sea, brother Thomas, in keeping with the family military tradition, played his part in the war. He fought with Maryland's "Four Hundred " in the Battle of Long Island, August 27, 1776, under Major Mordecai Gist,[28] whose Independent Cadets laid the cornerstone of Maryland's Dandy Fifth.

Among the other children of Captain John MacKeele one daughter Sarah married Samuel Hooper and moved to Baltimore, where their only daughter Elizabeth Ann Hooper is buried in Old St. Paul's Grave Yard. Another daughter Mary married on March 4, 1788, Richard Pattison, whose mother Sarah was a grand-daughter of Henry Hooper II.[29]

Richard Pattison played his part in the Revolution, serving under Captain Charles Staplefort in the lower Battalion of Dorchester County Select Militia.[30] Richard also was churchman as

[25] Wills, Liber 34, f. 114, Liber 37, f. 147, Hall of Records.
[26] Jones, op. cit., p. 223.
[27] Md. Gen. Rec. Comm. Reports, op. cit.
[28] Md. Hist. Mag., XIV (1919), 118.
[29] Md. Gen. Rec. Comm. Reports, op. cit.
[30] Jones, op. cit., p. 245.

well as soldier, conducting services in the " Old Church " during
the period that church was without a rector, 1794-1806. The
Old Church was reconsecrated by the Right Reverend Bishop
Whitehouse after its restoration from great dilapidation and long
vacancy in the middle of the nineteenth century when it was named
Trinity.[31] " Old Trinity " is now undergoing an authentic restoration through the interest and generosity of Colonel and Mrs.
Edgar Garbisch and the Honorable George L. Radcliffe. Tradition
has it that it is the second oldest Protestant church in America.

After a full life as soldier, churchman and statesman Richard
Pattison rests with his wife Mary MacKeele Pattison in Christ
Church Grave Yard, Cambridge, Maryland. Among Richard and
Mary's children was a son James MacKeele Pattison whose
daughter Aurelia married Dr. James L. Bryan, from which union
there are many living descendants. A daughter Anne Maria
married James Dixon of Cambridge November 29, 1825. Their
youngest son Richard Hooper Dixon, M. D., lived in Cambridge
until the time of his death, April 15, 1912.[32] Dr. Dixon with his
wife Helen Victoria Johnson are buried alongside James and Ann
Maria Dixon, not far from Mary MacKeele and Richard Pattison,
in Christ Church Grave Yard.

The MacKeele family,[33] like a number of other Dorchester
County families, some of whom it had intermarried with, stemmed
from seventeenth century pioneers who struck firm roots in Maryland soil. While the tide of population swept westward in
America, these families remained attached to the cultured and
refined society in Maryland, to which they had contributed its
distinctive qualities, while serving their country as soldiers and
statesmen.

[31] *Ibid.*, p. 116.
[32] Dixon Family Bible.
[33] The MacKeill coats of arms may be found in Burke's *General Armory* (1851).

FOUR GENTLEMEN OF THE NAME—THOMAS MARSH

By EMERSON B. ROBERTS

Capt. Thomas Marsh, of Kent Island, with a residence also at Chestertown, and the fourth in a direct line from the Honorable Thomas Marsh, died at an advanced age during the early stage of the American Revolution. Each generation was represented by one Gentleman only, and they all bore the name of Thomas. The Captain was the last of the male line, the first held a seat in Council—Davis: *Day Star of American Freedom.*

The first Thomas Marsh, of Maryland, was an immigrant from Virginia, with his wife, Margaret, in 1649. He had come to Virginia in 1637, or earlier—one of those brought in by Thomas Holt.[1] First he settled in New Norfolk County, where there are a number of court references to him. More than thirty years ago, these were collected by the late Samuel Troth, of Philadelphia, and since they have never been published, they are recorded here. Thomas Marsh is mentioned several times as "alias Thomas Rivers," but the Virginia records yield no reason for this usage, and it is presumed, if the reason is ever found, it will be uncovered in the English records. The references are:

Thomas Rivers, alias Marsh, deposition at Linhaven, Lower County of Norfolk, July 7, 1637, aged twenty-one years.

Court, April 2, 1638, Thomas Marsh and George Lowe, as to the division of certain land.

Court, April 8, 1639, Thomas Marsh, "being about to go for England."

Court, November 16, 1641, deposition of Thomas Marsh, aged twenty-six years.

Court, December 15, 1642, Thomas Marsh, juryman.

Court at Thomas Meares', June 16, 1643, Thomas Marsh to pay an old bill.

Court, September 6, 1641, Thomas Marsh, constable, applies for one hundred fifty acres for transportation of self and wife, and also William Smith whom he bought of Mr. Flood.

Court, June 15, 1646, Thomas Marsh, the settlement of a debt.

The foregoing records are taken from the unpublished manuscript copy of the Court Record, now in the Virginia Historical Society, Richmond. Further Court Records, from another manuscript volume, follow:

Lower Norfolk County Court, April 2, 1638: "Whereas it doth

---

[1] Greer, *Virginia Immigrants.*

appear that Richard Loe, planter, hath bought of Thomas Marsh, planter, all his estate whatsoever here resident in Virginia . . . but Richard Loe not giving security, it remains in Thomas Marsh."

Court, October 4, 1641, "Thomas Marsh hath made appear to this Court that he hath due him 150 acres of land for the transportation of himself and his wife unto this colony as also one William Smith."

And in the Land Grant Records (Virginia Historical Society, Richmond), these items:

"January 6, 1638, Thomas Marsh, alias Rivers, one hundred fifty acres, Upper County of New Norfolk, northerly upon Elizabeth River. Assigned by Peter Montague, and payment to be made seven years after August 22, 1637, for transportation of William Jones, Thomas Redby, Margaret Harford." This land was originally patented to Peter Montague (Volume I, folio 463), and officially confirmed to Thomas Marsh, alias Thomas Rivers.

And the record of land grant to Thomas Holt, before mentioned, is as follows:

"To Thomas Holt, 22nd of May, 1637, 500 acres in the Upper County of New Norfolk, on the north side of the eastern branch of Elizabeth River, upon a creek adjoining lands of Thomas Renshaw, fifty acres for transporting himself, and four hundred and fifty for nine persons, viz. Thomas Marsh, James Arundell, Yoeman Gibson, John Drabe, William Smith, Toby Smith, Samuel Taylor, George Taylor, and Natl Corder." [2]

From these records, it appears that Thomas Marsh first came to Virginia not later than 1637, at the age of twenty-two, and that he returned to England for a brief visit in 1639, returning with a number of persons, among them Margaret Harford, whom he subsequently married, and that as early as 1638 he was endeavoring to liquidate his Virginia affairs. On his English origin no very serious study has yet been put. Mr. Troth, whose investigations have been mentioned, points to the Registers of St. Dunstan's—Stepney, in which there is record, September 10, 1610, of the marriage of Thomas Marsh, of Ratcliffe, shipwright, to Elizabeth Mayne, of Lymehouse, and asks if he may not be of the same family. Similarity of given names of the children of the two Thomas Marshes leads to this suggestion.

Thomas Marsh was a Puritan, and in Virginia he resided in the Puritan settlement. Surrounded by Royalists who were vastly in the majority and completely in control of the affairs of the colony, the Virginia Puritans were subjected to a persecution which, while it may not have gone further than to be distinctly annoying, was sufficiently stringent to result in their seeking new homes in Maryland, where there was no persecution on account of religion. As a result, Maryland gained immigrants whose descendants have shed luster on her history.

The records of Lower Norfolk County, Virginia, for 1649, contain this entry:

> Whereas, Mr. Edward Lloyd and Mr. Thomas Meeres, Commissioners, with Edward Selby, Richard Day, Richard Owens, Thomas Marsh, George Kemp, and George Norwood were presented to ye board by ye Sheriff for seditious sectuaries for not repairing to their Church, and for refusing to hear Common Prayer, liberty is granted till Occtober next to inform their judgments and to conform themselves to the established law. . . .

However, before the expiration of the time allotted, Thomas Marsh and several of the others mentioned had removed to Maryland, and had established themselves in Calvert and in Anne Arundel Counties.

Of the migration of Thomas Marsh from Virginia to Maryland, there is evidence in the Maryland records. In the index of early settlers in the Land Office in Annapolis, 1648/9 [3] there is record of the coming of Thomas Marsh and his wife as among the " headrights " of William Durand. Neill, in his history of Maryland of this period, asserts that they were brought in as indentured servants of the said Durand, but there is nothing to substantiate this in the record, nor in the subsequent history of Thomas Marsh. It was quite common for those who arranged the coming of new colonists to claim " headrights of land," etc., and indeed, the use of this term itself indicates this limitation to the exclusion of the usual terms of service of indentured persons. It is not infrequent in the Maryland records to find two or more persons claiming " headrights " for the transportation of the same individual. Doubtless some of the early settlers moved about frequently, some returning to England, later coming back to Maryland at the expense of another who consequently claimed new " headrights." There may indeed have existed in some sections a sort of " headright land racket."

Thomas Marsh quickly attained established position in the Province of Maryland, and especially in Anne Arundel County on the Severn in the Puritan community. He took up lands in Herring

---

[3] Liber ABH, folio 35; also *Maryland Historical Magazine*, VIII, 60.

Creek Hundred totaling more than a thousand acres. Among his neighbors were Richard Bennett, John Norwood and Edward Selby. In the Rent Rolls of Lord Baltimore, there is recorded the survey for him, October 24, 1651, of one hundred fifty acres, " Marsh's Seat." Early he is mentioned not only as a planter, but as a merchant of Severn. Then he appears as Justice of the Peace for Anne Arundel County.[4] His tact as a judicial officer is reflected in the report of one of the cases he tried. After effecting an arbitration between the two parties, and giving his award, he added, as his own donation, " a hogshead of sack, to be drunk between the parties."[5] Of sack we remember what Falstaff says,

If I had a thousand sons, the first human principle I would teach them should be, to forswear thin potations, and to addict themselves to sack.

On July 30, 1650, Thomas Marsh was appointed by Governor Stone and the Council one of the commissioners of Anne Arundel County organized at that time.[6] In 1651 " ague " was upon Kent Island, and Thomas Marsh, at least once in the record, is called a " chirurgeon."[7] His standing on Kent Island is reflected in the following minute from the Proceedings: " June 28, 1652, in the case of Captain Robert Vaughan. It is petitioned that Thomas Marsh or some other fitting and able person [be appointed] to the Office of Commander of the Isle of Kent."[8] On January 22, 1651, " Thomas Marsh, Gent., of Kent, his mark of hoggs and Cattle: Both ears swallowtailed, and no other mark."[9]

The religious difficulties, too, that Thomas Marsh had met in Virginia seemed to follow him to Maryland, at least in a slight degree. In 1649, he was presented as a " seditious sectary,"[10] but the matter seems to have had little attention from the Proprietor, who was uniformly liberal in his attitudes on matters of religion and conscience. The staunchness of Marsh's Puritanism, and his prestige during the ascendancy of the Protectorate, may be gleaned from Court Proceedings of Kent County, 1652:[11]

Whereas, the reducing, settling, and governing of Virginia, and all English plantations within the Bay of Chesapeake, was referred to certain Commissioners, by Order from the Council of State for the Commonwealth of England:

[4] Maryland *Archives*, III, 257.
[5] Davis, *Daystar of American Freedom*, 120.
[6] Maryland *Archives*, XXXI, 257; *Maryland Historical Magazine*, XIV, 167.
[7] Liber A #1, folio 11 and 36.
[8] *Archives* III, 277.
[9] Liber A #1, f. 7. See also Hanson, *Old Kent*, p. 20.
[10] *Archives*, II, 83.
[11] Liber A, f. 66, and *Old Kent*, p. 28.

and Whereas, the Governor and Council for the Province of Maryland, in obedience and conformity of said order and power have authorized and deputed the persons whose names are hereunder subscribed for settling the Isle of Kent . . . [then come the names of those who are to constitute the Court] . . . to have power to hear and determine all differences, and to call Courts for that purpose as often as they see cause, to make choice of a Sheriff and a clerk for keeping Records, and execution of writs, and all other purposes, and to act in all things for the peace, safety, and welfare of the said Island, and the inhabitants thereof, as they or the former Commissioners did, or might do, by virtue of their commissions from the Lord Baltimore, and the Governor and Council of the Province under him.

Requiring all the inhabitants of the said Island to take notice of this Order, and to conform themselves accordingly, as they will answer the contrary at their peril.

Given under our Hands at the Island of Kent, the 31st day of July, 1652.

Ri Bennett   Thomas Marsh
Ead. Lloyd   Leo. Strong

In June, 1655, Thomas Marsh was Commissioner of the Provincial Court and a member of the Council, which office he held until his death.[12] The archives of Maryland for this year, 1655, and the year following, are replete with references to his official and public acts.

In 1653, Richard Bennett, Esq., Mr. Edward Lloyd, Capt. William Fuller, Mr. Leonard Strong, and Thomas Marsh were constituted by the regime of the Parliamentary Commission under the leadership of William Claiborne, then in ascendancy in Maryland affairs, a Commission to negotiate with the Susquehannock Indians. The instrument that resulted was decidedly in the interest of the Puritan settlers of the vicinity of Providence, located in the newly erected County of Anne Arundel. Seven days from the appointment of the Commission, the whole affair was concluded " at the River of Severn," and by the terms of it, the Indians gave up a great territory extending " from the Patuxent River unto Palmer's Island on the western side of the Bay of Chesapeake, and from the Choptank River to the northeast branch which lies to the northward of Elk River," in effect, giving the white man the whole of the head lands of the Chesapeake Bay country, and without any western boundaries mentioned. Solemn provisions for friendship, diplomatic relations, etc., were entered into, but apparently the Indians received nothing in return. Record of this treaty is to be found in Maryland *Archives*, Vol. III, page 276, and in Proceedings of the Council, Liber HH, folio 62.[13]

On Kent Island, Thomas Marsh's land by patent was " Poplar Neck," three hundred acres surveyed for him, August 20, 1652.[14]

---

[12] *Archives*, III, 316.
[13] See also Bozman; History of Maryland, II, 452 and 683.
[14] Rent rolls, Queen Anne's County.

Thomas Marsh's older children were by his first wife, Margaret Harford, whom he married in Virginia and brought with him into Maryland. These children were the son Thomas Marsh II, Margaret, and Elizabeth.

Margaret married, first, Richard Preston, Jr., son of "The Great Quaker," the first Richard Preston, who had settled, first in Virginia, then on the Patuxent, and during the Puritan regime, was the most powerful man in Maryland. Later, the Prestons removed to the region of the Choptank and the eastern shore. Richard Preston, Jr., died in 1669, and his widow, Margaret, married, second, in 1670, William Berry, of "Poplar Neck," of another distinguished Puritan family that had come from Virginia with the migration.[15]

Elizabeth, known as Elizabeth Marsh, of Severn, married, April 1, 1669, "at the house of John Webb of Potoxon," Thomas Taylor, of Kent County. Her descendants have been treated in a previous article by the author, "Capt. Phillip Taylor and some of His Descendants" (*Maryland Historical Magazine*, XXXIII, 280).

After the death of his first wife, Thomas Marsh I married a second time, Sarah, very possibly Sarah Pitt, and by her had at least one daughter, Sarah. The second wife, Sarah, seems to have been endowed with considerable energy and initiative. She administered on her husband's estate, March 20, 1656.[16] Because of his activity in the Puritan revolution, the proprietary government in 1658 refused to recognize some of her husband's land titles. As late as 1663, she was taking up additional land. "Heir's Purchase," a ninety-acre tract in Anne Arundel County, "at ye ferry Place" was then taken up for "the use of her [step] son." In the same year, November 18, on the eastern shore, on the north side of the Choptank River in St. Michael's Creek, "Marshland," five hundred acres, was surveyed for her. The last record found of Sarah Marsh, relict of Thomas Marsh, is dated 1664.[17]

Sarah, the daughter, appears to have died unmarried. She is surmised to be that Sarah Marsh, spoken of in the will of Dr. Jacob Neale, as "one of ye friends of ye Ministry." She died, probably in 1688, and her will appoints as administrators, "her loving friend, John Warren" [Warner?] and her uncle, John Pitt.[18] Third Haven Registers record her death: "Sarah Marsh departed this life at night, 1st month, 12th day, 1688, about ye tenth or eleventh hour." It is

[15] Liber X, folio 85-6, Annapolis.
[16] *Archives*, X, 486-7 and 553; Liber BB, f. 72, Land Office, Annapolis.
[17] *Archives*, III, 494.
[18] Test. Proceedings, Liber XIV, f. 108.

this mention of John Pitt, coupled with the fact that the name of this daughter was Sarah, that leads to the conclusion that she was the only child of the second marriage of Thomas Marsh, Sr. It may be added on this score that the fact of her fervency in the Meeting and great activity in its affairs strengthens this view, for the Pitts were more ardent as Quakers than the Marshes.

Thomas Marsh, I, died intestate in 1656.[19] On January 1, 1657, he is mentioned in the records as "Thomas Marsh deceased, late of Severn." [20] The record of his children is confirmed by Liber X, folio 82, Land Office.

Thomas Marsh, II, son of Thomas and Margaret Marsh, was born about 1643. He was first of Anne Arundel, then of Calvert, and later of Kent and Kent Island. The proof of this descent is ample, and is unfolded in the following paragraph, included not alone because of the descent it establishes, but because of its splendid exemplification of a method that frequently must be used in Maryland genealogy.

Thomas Marsh of Anne Arundel County executed a release to Thomas Manning, August 20, 1664, of lands in the Cliff in Calvert County, which lands belonged to his father. On February 1, 1663, Phillip Calvert gave a certificate that while Secretary of Maryland, he had in his custody a deed of a certain tract in the Cliffs of Calvert County from Thomas Marsh, late of Elizabeth River in Virginia, to Thomas Manning of Nansemond; which writing was delivered to Phillip Calvert by Thomas Manning, and acknowledged by Sarah, widow of Thomas Marsh.[21] The identity of the second Thomas Marsh with Thomas Marsh of Kent is developed, as follows: Dr. Jacob Neale, "chirurgeon" of Anne Arundel County, previously referred to, in his will, 1672, left one-third of his estate to Sarah, daughter of Thomas Marsh of Anne Arundel County, and the residue to Thomas Marsh and Margaret, his wife. The will of Thomas Marsh (the second Thomas Marsh, of Kent County) 1679, mentions his wife, Jane, his daughters, Sarah and Mary, and his sisters, Margaret Berry and Elizabeth Taylor. In the will, he mentions certain property for Sarah, "left her by her mother," so she was the child of a former marriage, and with the mention of Margaret Berry and Elizabeth Taylor as sisters, the chain of evidence is nearly complete. The records of Third Haven Meeting show that Thomas Taylor of Kent County married, in 1669, Elizabeth Marsh, of Severn, completing the rigid proof of the descent.

The first official activity of Thomas Marsh, II, was in Anne Arun-

---

[19] *Archives*, X, 486.   [20] *Archives*, XLI, 19.   [21] Liber BB, f. 172.

del County, where he was sworn as Justice of the Peace, May 4, 1667,[22] and Commissioner, May 4, 1668.[23] Within a few years he became powerful in the affairs of Kent County, and resided there. In 1675, Thomas Marsh is spoken of as " one of the Gentlemen of the Quorum, Commission of the Peace in Kent County." [24] Thomas Marsh, I, had taken up land on Kent Island in 1652, and Thomas, II, had another grant there in 1664. In May, 1668, he was commissioned Justice of the Peace for Anne Arundel County.[25]

Further of Thomas Marsh, II, there is his patent for land in Calvert, " Major's Choice," five hundred acres, surveyed for him, June 24, 1664. This tract he sold to Thomas Sterling, May 1, 1676.[26] This tract later became prominent in the litigation over the Calvert-Anne Arundel boundary. In May, 1669, there was an order by the Assembly for him to be paid 104 pounds of tobacco " out of the levy of Talbot County." [27] On June 6, 1676, he was commissioned Justice of the Peace and Sheriff of Kent County.[28] In 1678, he was Burgess of Kent.[29] Later he is called " Captain Thomas Marsh of Kent." [30] The terms in which his land on Kent Island are referred to are significant, and confirm the conclusions already drawn. In the Queen Anne's Rent Rolls, there is recorded the survey of " Marsh's Forebearance," one hundred fifty acres, surveyed March 22, 1664, on Kent Island, " at ye outward bounds of a parcel formerly laid out for him." The reference, doubtless, is to " Poplar Neck," surveyed, as mentioned, in 1652, for Thomas Marsh, his father. This seems to indicate a confusion of father and son on the part of the surveyor or clerk, for the second Thomas Marsh was not old enough to have had land laid out for him in 1652.

Thomas Marsh, II, like his father, married twice. His first wife was Margaret ————, and by her he had a son, Thomas Marsh, III, of Kent Island, and a daughter, Mary. Thomas Marsh married, second, before 1677, Jane Clements, daughter of John Clements, of Kent County, a recent immigrant from England, and by her he had a daughter, Sarah, born 24th of 10th month, 1677.[31]

Thomas Marsh, II, died in 1679. His will is dated August 12 of

[22] *Archives*, V, 30.
[23] *Archives*, X, 230.
[24] *Archives*, XV, 93 and 136.
[25] *Archives*, V, 30.
[26] Land Office, Liber WRC 1, f. 92.
[27] *Archives*, II, 30.
[28] *Archives*, XV, 93-136, and Liber CD, f. 87-11-149.
[29] *Archives*, VII, 4, etc.
[30] *Archives*, XVII, 79.
[31] Third Haven Records, and Annapolis Liber X, f. 85-6.

that year, and the probate was on October 29. In it, he refers to his wife, Jane, as the daughter of John Clements. His daughters, Sarah and Mary, are mentioned, as well as his son, Thomas Marsh, who is under eighteen years of age. The most significant item, however, from the standpoint of this study, is the mention of his sisters, Margaret Berry and Elizabeth Taylor, eliminating any doubt of the descents of the Marsh family in this generation. In September, 1681, a writ was isued for the election of another Burgess in place of Thomas Marsh, of Kent County, deceased. At the same time, there is a commission to Capt. William Lawrence to command the company of foot, formerly commanded by Capt. Thomas Marsh.[32] The inventory of the estate is by John Edmondson, William Berry, and Thomas Taylor.[33]

The son, Thomas Marsh, III, married Elizabeth, daughter of Major John Hawkins, of Queen Anne's County, and had, with two daughters (Mary, who married William Dudley; and Sarah, who married John—or Gideon—Emory), a son, Thomas Marsh, IV.

The extent of the Marsh landed estate is reflected in the assessment of Thomas Marsh, III, on the Rent Rolls of Lord Baltimore, 1709:

Queen Anne's County—"Little Thickett," two hundred acres, surveyed December 9, 1640, for Giles Basha, on Kent Island, in the possession of Mr. Thomas Marsh. "Catlin Neck," three hundred fifty acres, surveyed August 15, 1650, for Francis Lambert, on Kent Island, in the possession of Mr. Thomas Marsh. "Marsh's Forebearance," one hundred fifty acres, surveyed March 22, 1664, on Kent Island, possessed by Mr. Thomas Marsh. "Warner's Discovery," two hundred acres, surveyed, July 24, 1689, for William Warner, possessed by Mr. Thomas Marsh in right of his wife. "Sarah's Portion," five hundred acres, surveyed, September 1, 1681, for Isaac Winchester, possessed by Thomas Marsh. "Cabbin Neck," on Kent Island, three hundred acres, possessed by Thomas Marsh.

"Marshland" appears to have passed out of the family by 1709, for on the rolls of that year, it appears as follows: "Marshland," five hundred acres, surveyed November 18, 1663, for Sarah Marsh, possessed two hundred sixty-five acres, by Mr. Robert Grundy, and one hundred sixty-five acres, John Sherwood, for the heir of James Berry, seventy acres by James Anderson.

Elizabeth, widow of the third Thomas Marsh, married George

[32] *Archives*, XVII, 78.
[33] Test. Proc., Liber XII, f. 61. May 21, 1681.

Connerford, who administered on the estate of Thomas Marsh. It is the record of the settlement of this estate that establishes the Marsh genealogy in the third and fourth generations.[34]

Thomas Marsh, IV, of Kent Island, married before 1738, Mary, the daughter of Augustine Thompson of Queen Anne's County. It is he whom Davis calls " Capt. Thomas Marsh of Kent Island with a residence also at Chestertown." He died during the early days of the Revolution. With him passes the name of a distinguished line of gentlemen, but the blood and tradition of the Marshes is preserved in the descendants of the daughters, most of whom married and had families.

MARSH

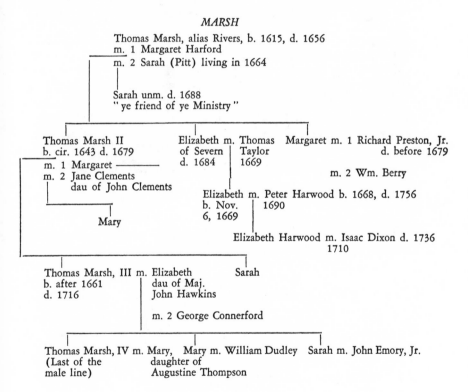

Thomas Marsh, alias Rivers, b. 1615, d. 1656
m. 1 Margaret Harford
m. 2 Sarah (Pitt) living in 1664

Sarah unm. d. 1688
" ye friend of ye Ministry "

Thomas Marsh II
b. cir. 1643 d. 1679
m. 1 Margaret ———
m. 2 Jane Clements
    dau of John Clements

Mary

Elizabeth m. Thomas
of Severn | Taylor
d. 1684 | 1669

Margaret m. 1 Richard Preston, Jr.
        d. before 1679

        m. 2 Wm. Berry

Elizabeth m. Peter Harwood b. 1668, d. 1756
b. Nov. | 1690
6, 1669

Elizabeth Harwood m. Isaac Dixon d. 1736
                1710

Thomas Marsh, III m. Elizabeth   Sarah
b. after 1661   dau of Maj.
d. 1716   John Hawkins

                    m. 2 George Connerford

Thomas Marsh, IV m. Mary, Mary m. William Dudley Sarah m. John Emory, Jr.
(Last of the   daughter of
male line)   Augustine Thompson

[34] Adm. Acts, Vol. II, f. 496; Accts., Liber IX, f. 296; Inventory Liber I, 145.

MARSH, BERRY, PRESTON ET AL.

Since its publication in the *Magazine*, June 1940, the author of " Four Gentlemen of the Name—Thomas Marsh " has received several letters which contribute significantly to the subject. For the permanent record that publication in the *Magazine* affords, the following are gratefully recognized.

Caroline Kemper Bulkley (Mrs. Louis C.) of Shreveport, Louisiana, writes that Mrs. Nugent's transcripts supply the original location of the particular Puritan group with which Thomas Marsh is identified in Virginia, and enable the following of a number of the families to other Virginia locations and to Maryland. She also gives a Virginia record variant of the name Margaret Harford as Margarett Starford.

Reverend Samuel M. Shoemaker, of New York, writes of the descent of the Formans (of Rose Hill), the Chambers, the Houstons and the Ecclestons from the early Maryland Marshes.

Mrs. Frederick Schoenfeld (Virginia Berkley Bowie), of Wynnewood, Penn., contributes the date of the death of Margaret Marsh, daughter of the first Thomas Marsh, she who married first Richard Preston, Jr. and secondly William Berry. The date is February 16, 1688. Mrs. Schoenfeld also reports that William Berry was born in Virginia, 1635, and died in Talbot April 30, 1691. The marriage date is 1670 and the Berry children by this marriage were Benjamin, born October 23, 1670; Joseph, born February 24, 1673, and Richard and Thomas, twins, born November 19, 1678. Also she calls attention to Hulbert Footner's remark in *Charles'* *Gift* that William Berry married first a daughter of Richard Preston, and second, the widow of Preston's only son. Mrs. Schoenfeld asks if anyone can document the dates of the Berry children.

Mrs. Anne Middleton Holmes, of Norfolk, Conn., suggests that the first wife of William Berry was R(h)oder Preston and she points to the will of Richard Preston, 1669, in which a portion is left to James and William Berry, his grandchildren—all of which is consistent with the contribution by Mrs. Schoenfeld.

Then Mrs. Palmer Cushman (Ruth V.), of Wichita, Kansas, adds materially by contributing an extract from an unpublished manuscript by the late Judge Alexander Athey of Prairie du Chien, Wisconsin. This manuscript develops the date of birth of Sarah, daughter of Thomas Marsh II by his first wife, Margaret, and shows her marriage to George Athey and indicates some of their descendants. To quote—

The records of Prince George's County, Md., show that on September 15, 1707, Elizabeth Marsh gave a deed of gift to her nephew, George Athey, Jr., "ye soun of George Athey Sr." (C. 192 P. G. Co.), March 7, 1708/10 (*sic*) Luke Gardner qualified as administrator of the estate of Captain George Athey, late of Prince George's County (Adm. Bonds I, 47), and on December 21, 1709/10 Sarah Athey, wife, and John Athey, son, attest the correctness of the inventory (B. B. I 154 P. G.). On February 17, 1723/24 George Athey made a deposition in Prince George's wherein he swore that he was the son of Captain George Athey and that he was then twenty-three years of age. Sarah Athey, his mother, in her deposition swore that she was then (1723) fifty-seven years of age (I, 542) showing that she was born in 1666. So we have George Athey, born in Galway, Ireland, in 1642, came to America in 1664, married Sarah Marsh . . .

Mrs. Cushman also suggests the interesting probability that Margaret, first wife of Thomas Marsh II, was born Sarah Neale, daughter of Dr. Jacob Neale by whose will, 1672, she and her husband are to have two-thirds of the estate.

Several correspondents call attention to the inconsistency between the text and the chart as to Sarah, daughter of Thomas Marsh II. The chart is correct, the text, next to last line, page 197, quoting Third Haven Records, should read "Mary (not Sarah) born 24th of the 10th month 1677."

There is another inconsistency between a date in the text and on the chart. The date of death of Richard Preston, Jr., correct in the text as 1669, is in error on the chart.

Of Sarah "ye friend of ye ministry," I still can only surmise. Mrs.

Cushman suggests that Sarah of Dr. Neale's will is Sarah, daughter of Thomas Marsh II. With her birth date now shown to be 1666, she was, of course, "under 16" in 1672, just as Dr. Neale says. But there is still the puzzle of Sarah Marsh who died in 1688, aged 10 years, 2 months and 18 days. (Md. Hist. Soc. T. H. Vol. 4, p. 166.)

Needless to say, I very greatly appreciate the response my article has aroused. It was written in 1932, but published in 1940. The review of it in the light of the comments received has renewed my own joy in working it out in the first place.

EMERSON B. ROBERTS

_____

MERRYMAN FAMILY.

FRANCIS B. CULVER.

_____

In the history of Baltimore County, the Merryman family deserves honorable mention. One branch of this family, in the early part of the Eighteenth Century, was seated to the northward of Baltimore Town upon the estate known as "Clover Hill." The entrance to this property was the old "Merryman's Lane," but recently changed to the more fashionable "University Parkway."

Another branch of the Merryman family, a generation later, settled near the village of Hereford, in Baltimore County, and became known as the Merrymans of "Hereford Farm," while a century later, the Merrymans of "Hayfields" established themselves near Cockeysville, in the same county. All of these branches are derived from one common ancestor, who came up from Lancaster County, Virginia, and purchased land in the northern part of Patapsco Hundred, in Baltimore County. There were Merrymans in Virginia as early as 1635. James Merriman patented 150 acres, in the county of Charles City, adjoining Weyanoke: " due 50 acres for his own personal adventure, 50 for the personal adventure of his wife Sarah, and 50 for one servant, William Bird," 6 November, 1635 (*Va. Hist. Mag.,* IV, 77). In a list of passengers to be transported to Virginia, in the ship " George," John Severne, Master, sailing from Gravesend, 21 August, 1635, we find the name of Sara Merriman, aged 20 years (*Hotten,* page 125). We are informed that the 150 acres aforesaid, patented to James Merryman in 1635, adjoined the land of one Pierce Lennon (*Wm. and Mary Qtly.,* IX, 228).

On 20 Dec., 1643, a patent was issued to James Merryman for 100 acres, in Charles City County, called by the name of Martin Brandon, " Opposite against Weyanoake " (*ibid.,* 233). And on 30 April, 1647, there is a reference to an assignment of 100 acres of land in Deep Creek, Warwick County, " part of 1000 acres patented by James Merryman and assigned by Mr. Merryman " (*Va. Hist. Mag.,* XIV, 424).

The county of Anne Arundell, in the Province of Maryland, was erected in 1650, and among the " associate judges " of the County Court, presided over by Commander the Hon. Edward Lloyd, appears the name of James Merryman, commissioned 30 July, 1650. The other Associate Judges were George Puddington, Matthew Hawkins and Henry Catlin (*Wm. and Mary Qtly.,* v, 49).

" James Merryman in 1662 assigned his certificate for 500 acres to John Browne of New England. He left no will or other records " (Warfield's *Founders of A. A. County*).

Contemporaneously with James Merryman in Virginia, appears the name of John Merryman, who, on 10 May, 1638, patented 150 acres of land in Charles City County, " adjoining to Weyanoke and also adjoining to land of Perce Lennon " *Wm. and Mary Qtly.,* IX, 230). What relationship the latter bore to James Merryman we do not know certainly, but it is probable that they were brothers. What relationship (if any) he bore to the John Merryman of whom we shall next speak, we are unable to determine.

JOHN MERRYMAN, the immediate ancestor of the Merrymans of Baltimore County, came to Virginia prior to 1650. In the year 1649, the arrival of his wife, Audrey, is recorded thus: " Audrey Merryman 1649, by John Merriman, ――

county " (Greer's *Early Va. Immigrants,* p. 225). In the Lancaster County, Va., Land Grants (Lib. 3, fol. 46), there is recorded in 1653 a grant to John Merryman and Morgan Heynes for 700 acres of land in said county (Crozier's *Va. County Records,* VI, 85).

Prior to this date a patent had been issued to John Merryman on 14 November, 1649, for certain land in Lancaster County. In the Tax Levy for 1654 in Lancaster, the name of John Merryman appears for " 2 persons " (*Va. Hist. Mag.,* V, 159). One of the earliest divorce trials on record in the county was conducted at his house " at a co'rt held for the Countie of Lancaster, the 6th of August, 1656, at the house of John Merryman: p'sent—Lt. Coll. Moore Fauntleroy, Mr. Tho. Bries, L't Major Toby Smith, Mr. Will'm Underwood, Capt. Hen. Fleet, Mr. Rowland Lawson, Mr. Raleigh Travers.

" This Co'rt doth declare that the marriage between John Smith and Mary his supposed wife is voide & of noe effect, and doe order that the saide John Smith shall have nothing to doe with the estate of the saide Mary in whose hands soever it bee " (*Va. Hist Mag.,* VIII, 175). John Merryman, the settler, died in Virginia prior to 1680, and his widow, Audrey, married Edward Carter of Lancaster County.

There is on record in Lancaster a deed dated 10 Nov., 1680, from William Merriman, of Lancaster, planter, eldest son of John Merryman of the same county, deceased: Charles Merriman, of same, wheelwright, youngest son of said John Merriman: and Edward Carter, of same, planter, and Audrie, his wife, late the widow of said John Merriman: conveying to Lt. Col⁰ Jno. Carter, gent., and Capt. David Fox, of same, gent., for the use of the county, to establish a town, 50 acres, part of a patent dated 14 November, 1649, to said John Merriman, deceased (*Va. Hist. Mag.,* V, 430).

John Merryman had issue:

    i. William Merryman.[2]
2. ii. CHARLES MERRYMAN, d. 22 Dec. 1725.

2. CHARLES MERRYMAN [2] (*John* [1]), " of Currotoman river, in Lancaster County, Virginia, wheelwright," is referred to in the Baltimore County Land Records for the first time, in a deed dated 30 March, 1682, when he purchased from Thomas and Hannah (Ball) Everest, of Patapsco river in Baltimore County, Md., a tract of 300 acres of land, called " East Humphreys," lying in Baltimore County, north of Patapsco river (Lib. IR-AM, 176).

In the lists of Baltimore County taxables for 1692 and 1694, Charles Merryman appears as resident on the north side of Patapsco Hundred, on the south side of Back river (*Records of County Court,* Lib. F., No. 1, 226: G., No. 1., 274). He served on the Grand Jury of the County at the March court term, 1693/4 (Lib. G, No. 1., 171). In August, 1695, there appear the names of Charles Merryman, Sr., and Charles Merryman, Jr., among the taxables residing in the aforesaid locality (*ibid.,* 524).

Charles Merryman, Sr., was identified with St. Paul's parish, in Baltimore County, and also figures in the military affairs of the county, being a Captain of Militia in 1696, when his name appears, among other gentlemen, as one of the military officers of Baltimore County, in an address presented to the King of England, setting forth the loyal sentiments and felicitations of his Majesty's colonial subjects in Maryland (*Md. Arch.,* xx, 544).

In March, 1698/9, Capt. John Ferry of Back river, in Baltimore County, by his will designated his friend, Charles Merryman, Sr., as his trustee, and " to bring up the orphan children " of one John Boring, with whose widow Ferry had intermarried (*Balt. Wills,* Lib. 1, folios 38, 85, 86).

Besides the East Humphreys tract (originally surveyed in 1679 for Mary Humphreys), Charles Merryman, Sr., held other lands in the county, on the north side of the Patapsco, to wit: " Merryman's Lot," 210 acres, in 1688; " Merryman's Addition," 120 acres, in 1694; " Merryman's Beginning," 246 acres, in 1703; and " Merryman's Pasture," 200 acres, in 1704. He deeded in 1714 Merryman's Addition and a moiety of Merryman's Lot to his " second son, John Merryman," and Merryman's Pasture to his " young son, Samuel Merryman " (*Balt. Land Rec.,* Lib. TR-A, 320).

Capt. Charles Merryman, Sr., died 22 Dec., 1725 (St. Paul's). His will, dated 16 Jany., 1724; probated 4 Jany., 1725/6, names his wife Mary (extx.): his eldest (surviving) son, John: his youngest son, Samuel: a daughter, Elizabeth Cox, and a grandson, Merryman Cox (*Balt. Wills,* Lib. 1, fol. 221). His estate was administered 8 Nov., 1726.

Charles Merryman, Sr., had issue:

3.   i.   CHARLES MERRYMAN,[3] JR., d. 17 May, 1722.
4.   ii. JOHN MERRYMAN, d. 1749.
5.   iii. SAMUEL MERRYMAN, d. 1754
     iv. Elizabeth Merryman, m. 25 Sept. 1722, Jacob Cox.

3. CHARLES MERRYMAN, JR.³ (Charles,² John¹), died 17 May, 1722 (St. Paul's). He was a planter and owned " Merryman's Beginning," 246 acres, surveyed 25 February, 1703, lying " on the north side of the Falls of Patapsco," and " Brotherly Fellowship," lying on the Gunpowder river, near Middle Run, in Baltimore County.

By his will, dated 25 Dec., 1720, probated 23 June, 1722, his sons, William and Charles Merryman, received each a half interest in the tracts above mentioned, while the widow, Jane Merryman, was given the choice of either plantation " to live on," and was appointed sole executrix. The remainder of the estate was to be distributed among " all my children." The widow renounced the will and craved her "one-thirds" of the estate (*Balt. Wills,* Lib. 1, fol. 189).

Jane Merryman married (2), 6 August, 1723, Benjamin Knight (St. Paul's register: Balt. Admin. Accts., Liber 2, folios 272-3, 375-6: Balt. County Court proceedings, Liber IS-TW, 230). In the admin. accts. (Lib. 2, fol. 275), reference is made to John Charles Merryman and William Merryman, sons of Charles Merryman, Jr., deceased.

On 3 Aug., 1739, the final account of Benjamin Knight was filed wherein reference is made to the prior account of Aug., 1729, filed by Benjamin Knight and Jane, his wife, and the following children are mentioned, to wit: Mary, who married William Hall; a daughter (unnamed), who married Benjamin Richards; a daughter (unnamed), who married Joseph Cross; daughters Jemima and " Ketdemee " Merryman, and a son, Charles Merryman. Charles Merryman, Jr., had issue:

6.   i.   WILLIAM MERRYMAN.⁴
7.   ii.   JOHN CHARLES MERRYMAN.
     iii.   [Ann?] Merryman, m. Benjamin Richards.
     iv.   Elizabeth Merryman, m. 13 Sept. 1730, Joseph Cross.
     v.   Jemima Merryman, m. 19 June 1735, Henry Stevenson.
     vi.   Kedemoth Merryman, b. 23 March 1717.
     vii.   Mary Merryman, b. 27 March 1719; m. 17 Dec. 1734, William Hall.

4. JOHN MERRYMAN³ (Charles,² John¹) of " Clover Hill," second son of Capt. Charles Merryman, Sr., of Patapsco, died about 1749. In addition to land which he received from his father in 1714, John Merryman purchased, in 1724, from Thomas Broad, 102 acres called " Merryman's Purchase," being a part of " Broad's Improvement," lying near Herring Run, in Baltimore County (Lib. IS-H, 159).

This tract he reconveyed in 1738 to Thomas Broad, who, on the same date, transfers the same to John Merryman, Jr., (Lib. HWS-IA, 199 et seq.).

In 1742, he deeded to his son, Moses Merryman, 150 acres of land called "Merryman's Delight," situated near the site of the Warren factory in Baltimore County (Lib. TB-C, 32). John Merryman lived on his estate known as the "Clover Hill" property, the entrance to which was formerly called "Merryman's Lane," now University Parkway.

His will is dated 13 Jany., 1745, and was probated 6 June, 1749 (*Balt. Wills,* Lib. 1, fol. 458). The will was witnessed by William Carter, Thomas Spicer and Edward Talbott, and it mentions his wife, Martha; sons John and Moses Merryman; a daughter, Mary Edwards, and refers to his "five daughters" (unnamed).

John Merryman married, 30 Dec., 1702, Martha, a daughter of Jonas Bowen (d. 1699), by Martha, his wife (died 1704), of Patapsco river, in Baltimore County (*Wills,* Lib. 1, folios 39, 89). They had issue:

8. i. JOHN MERRYMAN, b. 1703: d. 15 Aug. 1777.
9. ii. MOSES MERRYMAN.
    iii. Joanna Merryman, d. 27 Oct. 1790: m. John Clossey.
    iv. Rebecca Merryman, d. 4 Feby. 1792: m. 1 Jany. 1735, Thos. Spicer.
    v. Mary Merryman, d. 16 Apl. 1791; m. 23 Jany 1727, John Edwards.
    vi. Temperance Merryman, b. 13 Sept. 1720; d. 5 Jany 1813; m. 28 May 1745, Edward Talbott.
    vii. A daughter (died inf.).
    viii. Charles Merryman, b. 28 Sept. 1723; d. 13 Dec. 1729.
10. ix. JOSEPH MERRYMAN, b. 14 Apl. 1726; d. Feby 1799.

5. SAMUEL MERRYMAN [3] (Charles,[2] John [1]), youngest son of Capt. Charles Merryman, Sr., received in 1714, by "deed of gift" from his father, "Merryman's Pasture," 200 acres. He purchased later a tract of 308 acres, called "Drunkard's Hall," which he conveyed to his son, Samuel, Jr., in 1744. Samuel Merryman, Sr., died in 1754, and his will, dated 16 Jany., 1754, probated 23 March, 1754, mentions his eldest son, Samuel, who inherits "Drunkard's Hall;" his son, Nicholas, who is bequeathed "Merryman's Pasture," and names daughters, Rebecca Price and Keturah Parrish (*Balt. Wills,* Lib. 2, fol. 55). He married Mary Eager, the widow of Thomas Eager (d. s. p., 1708), of Baltimore County. She died 26 March, 1728 (St. Paul's).

Mary, the wife of Samuel Merryman and widow of Thomas Eager, was probably the daughter of Humphrey Boone (d. Nov., 1709), of Anne Arundel and Baltimore Counties. Samuel and Mary Merryman had issue:

     i. Keturah Merryman,[4] b. 1717; d. 22 Feby 1789—m. (1), 1 July 1732, Thomas Price (d. 1741); m. (2), 25 Feby 1743, William Parrish, Jr. (d. 1788).
11. ii. SAMUEL MERRYMAN, JR., b. 12 Nov. 1721; d. 25 Sept. 1809.
   iii. Rebecca Merryman, married John Price (d. 1790)
12. iv. NICHOLAS MERRYMAN, b. 8 Feby 1727; d. 1770.

6. WILLIAM MERRYMAN [4] (Charles,[3] Charles,[2] John [1]) received by will of his father, Charles Merryman, Jr., probated 23 June, 1722, a half interest in the tracts called " Merryman's Beginning" and " Brotherly Fellowship," lying in Baltimore County. William Merryman and his brother, Charles, join in a deed conveying to Charles Ridgely, 11 July, 1746, " Merryman's Beginning," 240 acres (*Balt. Land Rec.,* Lib .TB-E, 161). On the same date, William Merryman and Margaret, his wife, convey to Charles Ridgely part of a tract called " Hampton Court," lying in Baltimore County (*ibid.,* fol. 166). By his wife, Margaret ——, William Merryman had issue:

     i. Jemima Merryman,[5] b. 24 Nov. 1726; d. 13 Aug. 1736.
    ii. Margaret Merryman, b. 24 Feby 1727/8; d. 5 Aug. 1736.
   iii. William Merryman, b. 11 April 1729.
   iv. George Merryman, b. 25 Oct. 1734.
    v. Joanna Merryman, b. 15 Oct. 1736.
   iv. Chloe Merryman, b. 28 Feby 1741.

7. JOHN CHARLES MERRYMAN [4] (Charles,[3] Charles,[2] John [1]), otherwise known as Charles Merryman, received by the will of his father, Charles Merryman, Jr., probated 23 June, 1722, a half interest in the tracts called " Merryman's Beginning " and " Brotherly Fellowship." Charles Merryman and Milicent, his wife, and William Merryman, his brother, join in a deed to Charles Ridgely, 11 July, 1746, conveying " Merryman's Beginning," 240 acres (*Balt. Land Rec.,* Lib. TB-E, 161). On 28 Aug., 1742, Charles and Milicent Merryman deed to John Boring, Jr., 100 acres, called " Haile's Folly " (Lib. TB-C, 18).

Charles Merryman married Milicent Haile, 20 Feby., 1730, and had issue (St. Paul's):

     i. Charles Merryman,[5] b. 22 May 1733.
    ii. Mary Merryman, b. 28 Jany 1734/5.
   iii. Milicent Merryman, b. 7 Dec. 1736.

8. JOHN MERRYMAN [4] (John,[3] Charles,[2] John [1]), of "Hereford Farm," was born 1703, and died 13 Aug., 1777, "in the 74th year of his age" (Epitaph), at Piney Hill, Baltimore County (See *Chancery Depositions, Annapolis*, Lib. DD 2, fol. 184). He lived upon and finally owned the estate which was purchased by his father from Thomas Broad, and passed the greater part of his life near Hereford, Baltimore County, where he possessed considerable property.

John Merryman married in St. Paul's parish, 30 Dec., 1725, Sarah Rogers, a daughter of Nicholas Rogers, son of Nicholas the immigrant. She was born in 1708 and died, near Hereford, 3 March, 1775, "in the 67th year of her age" (Epitaph). John Merryman's will, dated 4 Feby., 1774, and probated 11 Nov., 1777, mentions his wife, Sarah; six children, Nicholas, John, Benjamin, Sarah Willmott, Mary Ensor, Elizabeth Gorsuch; and grandchildren, William Ensor (son of Abraham), and Ann Ensor (*Balt. Wills*, Lib. WB 3, fol. 341).

John and Sarah (Rogers) Merryman had issue:

13.   i.   NICHOLAS MERRYMAN,[5] b. 11 Dec. 1726; d. 1801.
      ii. Sarah Merryman, b. 12 May 1729; m. 15 Dec. 1748, Robert Wilmott.
      iii. Mary Merryman, b. circa 1732; m. 30 Jany 1750, Abraham Ensor.
      iv. Elizabeth Merryman, b. 13 June 1734; d. 2 Sept. 1795; m. 11 Mch. 1755, John Gorsuch.
14.   v.   JOHN MERRYMAN, b. 16 Feby 1736/7; d. 14 Feby 1814.
15.   iv. BENJAMIN MERRYMAN, b. 1739; d. 30 May 1814.

9. MOSES MERRYMAN [4] (John,[3] Charles,[2] John [1]), received in 1742, from his father, the tract called "Merryman's Delight" upon which he settled. He married, about 1750, Sarah Glenn (b. 1720), who survived her husband and married (2) on 31 Jany., 1764, George Harryman, in St. John's parish, Baltimore County. She died in Nov., 1799 (Epitaph). Moses and Sarah (Glenn) Merryman had issue:

16.   i.   Micajah Merryman,[5] b. 1750; d. 7 June 1842.

10. JOSEPH MERRYMAN [4] (John,[3] Charles,[2] John [1]), was born 14 April, 1726 (St. Paul's), and died 1799. He lived on the old property on Charles Street Avenue, the entrance to which was known as Merryman's Lane. It is evident that he married twice: (1) Elizabeth ——, of whom was born John, recorded (St. Paul's); and (2) Mary

——, of whom were born Moses and Joseph, recorded (St. Paul's).

His will is dated 19 March, 1797, and was probated 13 Feby., 1799. Six children are mentioned therein: namely, Joseph, Job, Rebecca Demmitt, Jemima Bowen, Elizabeth Bowen, and Mary Baxley (*Balt. Wills,* Lib. 3, fol. 159). Joseph Merryman had issue:

By 1st wife:

    i. John Merryman,[5] b. 6 March 1749.

By 2nd wife:

       ii. Moses Merryman, b. 13 Jany 1758.
17.   iii. JOSEPH MERRYMAN, b. 15 March 1760; d. 17 Aug. 1829.
      iv. Rebecca Merryman, m. 9 Dec. 1783, Richard Demmitt.
       v. Jemima Merryman, m. 20 June 1786, Solomon Bowen.
      vi. Elizabeth Merryman, m. 12 April 1792, Benjamin Bowen.
     vii. Mary Merryman, m. 4 Sept. 1793, George Baxley.
18. viii. JOB MERRYMAN, b. 1770; d. 27 June 1830.

11. SAMUEL MERRYMAN [4] (Samuel,[3] Charles,[2] John [1]), was born 12 Nov., 1721 (St. Paul's), and died 25 Sept., 1809. He married Jane Price, who died 28 April, 1771. His will, dated 8 June, 1799 and probated 13 Jany., 1810, mentions his sons, John, Caleb, Nicholas, Samuel and " Mortico " (Mordecai); and daughters, Rachael Stewart, " Molly " Wells and " Action " (Achsah) Stinchcomb. (*Balt. Wills,* Lib. 8, fol. 468). Samuel and Jane (Price) Merryman had issue:

    i. Rachel Merryman,[5] b. 11 Dec. 1742; m. 17 Oct. 1778, Charles Stewart.
19.   ii. SAMUEL MERRYMAN, b. 17 June 1745; d. 1805.
    iii. Mary Merryman, b. 13 June 1749; m. Benjamin Wells.
    iv. Achsah ("Nackey"), b. 26 Dec. 1751; m. 13 May 1778, McLain Stinchcomb.
     v. Mordecai Merryman, b. 29 March 1754; d. 1807, s. p. (will).
20.   vi. CALEB MERRYMAN, b. 12 March 1758; d. 21 Nov. 1824.
21.   vii. JOHN MERRYMAN, b. Jany 1763; d. 18 Aug. 1849.
   viii. Nicholas Merryman.
    ix. A daughter, m. —— Parks.

12. NICHOLAS MERRYMAN [4] (Samuel,[3] Charles,[2] John [1]) was born 8 Feby., 1727 (St. Paul's), and died in 1770. In November, 1754, Nicholas Merryman, of Samuel, was appointed " overseer of the Roads from Baltimore Town by Benj. Bowen's 'till it intersects the Court Road from said Town by Samuel Hopkins; until it intersects the Court road from said Town by Joseph Taylor's; until it

intersects the Court road & from Hitchcock's old field toward William Parrish's, until it intersects the Court Road " (*Balt. County Court Proc.,* Lib. BB-A, 443). He married 1 May, 1755, in St. John's parish, Avarilla, daughter of Luke Raven.

His will, dated 7 Nov., 1768, and probated 18 July, 1770, mentions his wife, Avarilla; sons, Luke, Samuel and Nicholas; and daughters, Keturah Merryman, Sarah Merryman and Mary Merryman. His son Luke was bequeathed 200 acres of land which was bought of his uncle, Luke Raven. Samuel and Nicholas (minors in 1768) were to have equal shares in the dwelling plantations called "Merryman's Pasture" and "Merryman's Discovery" (*Balt. Wills,* Lib. 3, fol. 152).

Avarilla Merryman, widow of Nicholas, died in 1785. Her will, dated 13 Nov., 1784, and probated 26 Feby., 1785, mentions the afsd. three sons, Samuel being appointed executor of her estate; daughters, Sarah and Mary Merryman, and grandchildren Sarah and Nicholas Hooper (*Balt. Wills,* Lib. 4, fol. 60.)

Nicholas and Avarilla (Raven) Merryman had issue:

    i. Samuel Merryman,[5] d. 1787, s. p. (will).
    ii. Nicholas Merryman, d. 1787. s. p. (will).
    iii. Sarah Merryman, m. 29 Dec. 1787, William Scott.
    iv. Mary Merryman, b. 9 Mch. 1765; d. 23 Apl. 1809; m. 16 Aug. 1787, Caleb Merryman (1st cousin).
    v. Keturah Merryman, m. —— Hooper.
22. vi. LUKE MERRYMAN, d. 12 Feby 1813.

(*To be continued.*)

MERRYMAN FAMILY.

FRANCIS B. CULVER.

13. NICHOLAS MERRYMAN [5], (John [4], John [3], Charles [2], John [1]), was born 11 Dec. 1726, and died 1801 (will). He married (1) *circa* 1750, Elizabeth Ensor, and (2) Jane ————, who survived him but a short while. His will, dated 10 Aug. 1799, and probated 7 Oct. 1801, mentions his wife Jane; a son Elijah (deceased): a son, Nicholas: daughters, Jane Merryman, Mary Bond, Elizabeth Bosley and Sarah Orrick: grandchildren, John and Nicholas Merryman (sons of Elijah Merryman, deceased), Eleanor Merryman (daughter of Nicholas, Jr.), and the children of his daughter, Sarah Orrick. (*Balto. Wills*, Lib. 6, folio 443). The first account of Nicholas Merryman, Jr., administrator of the estate of the widow, Jane Merryman, was filed 10 September, 1803. (*Balt. Admin. Accts*, Lib. 15, folio 357).

Nicholas Merryman had issue, but the order of the births of the children is not determined.

     i. Elizabeth Merryman[6] b. 28 Aug. 1750; m. 29 June 1769, Elisha Bosley.
23.   ii. NICHOLAS MERRYMAN, JR., b. 1751; d. 1832.
24.   iii. ELIJAH MERRYMAN, d. 3 July 1799.
    iv. Micajah Merryman, married and had issue.
    v. Jane Merryman, d. 1819, unmarried (will probated 5 Dec. 1819).
    vi. Mary Merryman, m. 1787, Dennis Bond.
   vii. Sarah Merryman, married John Orrick.
  viii. Ann Merryman, married [Elijah Bosley?].

14. JOHN MERRYMAN [5] (John [4], John [3], Charles [2], John [1]), was born 16 February, 1736/7, and died 14 Feby., 1814 (Epitaph). He removed from near Hereford, Baltimore county, to Baltimore Town about 1763 (*Land Rec. B—L*, 24), and resided on Calvert street, just south of Baltimore street. His name appears in a list of the leading citizens of Baltimore Town, 22 April, 1767 (*Md. Arch.*, xxxii, 204). He was chosen a member of the "Baltimore Town Committee of Observation" 12 November,

1774, and was serving as such in 1776. On 28 Nov. 1778, he was commissioned one of the Justices for Baltimore county, residing in Baltimore Town (*Md. Arch.* xxi, 242), and was a Judge of the Orphans' Court of Baltimore County in 1784. His estate which he owned in Baltimore county, called "Hereford Farm," comprised over 1000 acres in 1788. (*Laws of Md.,* 1788, chap. xxxvii.)

He married in St. Paul's parish 9 December, 1777, Sarah (Rogers) Smith, widow of John Addison Smith. She died 21 August, 1816, aged 74 years, and was buried 23 August, 1816 (St. Paul's), in Loudon Park Cemetery. The will of John Merryman, Sr., of Baltimore Town and "Hereford Farm," dated 19 January, 1813, and probated 23 February, 1814, mentions his wife, Sarah: four children, John, Jr., and Nicholas Rogers Merryman, Sarah Rogers Merryman, and Elizabeth Merryman: and a married step-daughter, Eleanor Addison Bosley. (*Balt. Wills,* Lib. 9, folio 417). The will of the widow, Sarah Merryman, dated 24 February, 1814, and probated 14 September, 1816, mentions her own children by a former husband, namely, Eleanor Addison (Smith) Bosley, William R. Smith; and four children by her husband, John Merryman, who are enumerated above. (*Balt. Wills,* Lib. 10, fol. 216).

John and Sarah (Rogers)-Smith Merryman had issue.

    i.   John Merryman,[6] b. 3 Nov. 1778; d. 24 June 1854.
    ii.   Benjamin Rogers Merryman, b. 27 Oct. 1780; d. inf.
    iii.   Anne Merryman, b. 8 Nov. 1782; d. 8 Mch. 1785.
    iv.   Sarah Rogers Merryman, b. 22 Mch. 1784; m. 1 May 1828, Dr. Ashton Alexander; d. 1856.
    v.   Elizabeth Merryman, b. 4 Mch. 1786; d. 1860, unmarried.
25.   vi.   NICHOLAS ROGERS MERRYMAN, b. 26 Apl. 1788; d. 21 Jan'y 1864.

15. BENJAMIN MERRYMAN [5] (John [4], John [3], Charles [2], John [1]), was born in 1739, and died 30 May, 1814, aged 75 years. He lived near Monkton, Baltimore county, upon the tract known as "My Lady's Manor." He was a staunch patriot in a veritable hot-bed of Toryism: in fact, My Lady's Manor was confiscated during the Revolutionary War as "British property," and was later divided into several lots, or smaller tracts, and sold. The following, from the "Journal and Correspondence of the Council of Safety" of Maryland in the year 1777, indicates

the sentiment which existed in that section in those times. In a letter, dated at " Monecton Mills, 3d January, 1777," from one Samuel Baxter to the Council, reference is made to the existence of an unusually large number of Tories in his section of the county. Baxter continues: " I was sorey to see a set of toreys trampel the good law of the Country under foot as I am shure thare is not a man in this setelment [Monkton] but Mr. Bengeman meriman and myself that would doe anything to suport Government, as they all are glad to heer of hour conquests [defeats] and will say they knew the English would conker," etc. (*Md. Arch.* xvi, 12).

On 4th December, 1778, a commission was issued to Benjamin Merryman, appointed captain of a company belonging to the " Upper Battalion " of militia in Baltimore county (*Md. Arch.,* xxi, 257).

He married in St. John's parish, 2 February, 1762, Mary Bell. His will, dated 6 April, 1812, and probated 18 June, 1814, mentions his wife, Mary, who is bequeathed 200 acres of land, in lieu of her dower, to be laid out upon the east side of " Merryman's Inclosure Rectified." The latter tract he distributes among his children, Nicholas, Philemon, Rebecca, Eleanor and Ann Merryman, and leaves other landed property and money to the remaining children, John and William Merryman, Milcah Carr and Mary Talbott. He mentions his son-in-law, Nicholas Merryman of Nicholas. (*Balt. Wills,* Lib. 9, fol. 465).

Benjamin and Mary (Bell) Merryman had issue.

	i.	Benjamin Merryman,⁶ d. 1796, s. p. (will).
26.	ii.	JOHN MERRYMAN, d. Nov. 1749.
	iii.	Joshua Merryman, d. 1801, s. p. (will).
27.	iv.	NICHOLAS MERRYMAN, d. 1816.
28.	v.	WILLIAM MERRYMAN.
29.	vi.	PHILEMON MERRYMAN.
	vii.	Sarah Merryman.
	viii.	Catharine Merryman, m. 19 Nov. 1793, John Buck.
	ix.	Mary Merryman, m. 29 Jany. 1804, Thomas Talbott.
	x.	Elizabeth Merryman, died unmarried.
	xi.	Eleanor Merryman, m. (lic.) 19 July 1821, Thos. Henry Harland, s. p.
	xii.	Martha Merryman, died unmarried, 1801 (will).
	xiii.	Ann (" Nancy ") Merryman, m. (2d wife) her cousin Nicholas Merryman, Jr.
	xiv.	Milcah Merryman, m. 27 Feby. 1806, Thomas Carr.
	xv.	Rebecca Merryman, bpt. 24 Oct. 1787; m. Lee Tipton.

16. MICAJAH MERRYMAN [5] (Moses [4] John [3], Charles [2], John [1]), b. 4 July, 1750, and died 7 June, 1842, aged 92 years (Epitaph). He was commissioned 12 October, 1776, 1st Major of Col[o]. Edward Cockey's "Gunpowder Upper Battalion" of Baltimore County militia (*Md. Arch.,* xii, 337). The original commission is still in the possession of his grandson, George H. Merryman, of Baltimore county. Micajah Merryman married in 1780 Mary Ensor (daughter of Eleanor Ensor, who died in 1801). Mary (Ensor) Merryman, wife of Micajah, died in June, 1788, aged 35 years (Epitaph), or 30 years (Bible record). The will of Micajah Merryman, dated 31 March, 1838, and probated 18 June 1842, mentions his son, Micajah, Jr.; grandsons, George W., Merryman D. and Joshua F. Todd; and granddaughters, Sarah M. Taylor, of Missouri (wife of Thomas Taylor), and Mary Ann Bucknell (*Balt. Wills,* Lib. 19, fol. 89).

Micajah, Sr., and Mary (Ensor) Merryman had issue.

	i.	Sarah Merryman,[6] b. 1st Oct. 1781; d. Aug. 1806.
30.	ii.	MOSES MERRYMAN, b. 24 Mch. 1783; d. 19 Nov. 1819.
	iii.	Eleanor Merryman, b. 17 June 1785; d. 26 Sept. 1832.
	iv.	Mary Merryman, b. 23 Aug. 1786; d. 2 Jany. 1829; m. 29 Sept. 1803, Geo. W. Todd (d. 1818); (2) Benj. Bucknell.
31.	v.	MICAJAH MERRYMAN, b. 16 May 1788; d. 29 Apl. 1854.

17. JOSEPH MERRYMAN [5] (Joseph [4], John [3], Charles [2], John [1]), was born 15 March, 1760 (St. Paul's), and died intestate 17 August, 1829. He married (lic.) 25 April, 1793, Eleanor Gorsuch. She was born 30 January, 1774, and died 27 July, 1858. The first administration account on his estate was filed 12 November, 1829, by Eleanor, the widow, and Nelson Merryman, and distribution was made to the children enumerated below. (*Balto. Admin. Accts;* Lib. 28, folio 303).

On 16 June 1836, Eleanor Merryman, widow, Nelson Merryman and Sarah, his wife, Charles Merryman and Mary Ann, his wife; Lewis Merryman, Eleanor Merryman, Joseph Merryman, George Merryman and Oliver P. Merryman executed a mortgage to Samuel Brady of all that farm called "Clover Hill," etc., 200 acres, on which Joseph Merryman, deceased, formerly resided, etc. (*Lib. T. K.* 280, fol. 186).

Joseph and Eleanor (Gorsuch) Merryman had issue.

    i.   Nelson Merryman,⁶ married Sarah ——.
    ii.   Mary Merryman, b. 1795; d. 22 Oct. 1815; m. 20 April 1815, Lemuel G. Taylor.
    iii.   Elizabeth Merryman, b. 1797; d. 29 Oct. 1836; m. W. Chalmers.
    iv.   Lewis Merryman, s. p.
    v.   Charles Merryman, m. Mary Ann Davis.
    vi.   Joseph Merryman.
    vii.   George Merryman.
    viii.   Oliver P. Merryman.
    ix.   Eleanor Merryman, d. 8 Sept. 1870, unmarried.
    x.   Deborah I. Merryman, b. 1810; d. 21 Jany. 1838; m. —— Rutter.

18.   JOB MERRYMAN ⁵ (Joseph ⁴, John ³, Charles ², John ¹), was born in 1770, and died 27 June, 1830, aged 60 years. He was, perhaps, thrice married—(1) Ann Neale (lic.) 4 August 1791: (2) (lic.) 1 April 1819, Margaret Lavely, who died in Baltimore 28 January, 1820, aged 40 years (*Balt. Patriot,* 1 Feb., 1820): (3) Keturah C. ——, who administered on his estate 31 December, 1833 (*Balt. Admin. Accts.* Lib. 31, fol. 99).

     Job Merryman had issue.

    i.   John B. Merryman,⁶ d. abt. 1827; m. (lic.) 23 Nov. 1819, Mary Ann Short.

19.   SAMUEL MERRYMAN ⁵ (Samuel ⁴, Samuel ³, Charles ², John ¹), was born 17 June, 1745 (St. Paul's), and died 1805. He married Ruth [Price ?]. His will, dated 16 September, 1805, and probated 26 October, 1805, mentions his wife, Ruth; sons, Mordecai and George Price Merryman; daughters, Rachel Chapman and Rebecca Blizzard, and grandchildren, Samuel and Mordecai Merryman Welsh.

     Samuel and Ruth Merryman had issue.

    i.   Mordecai Merryman,⁶ m. (lic.) 27 Mch. 1811, Margaret May.
    ii.   George Price Merryman, d. abt. 1834.
    iii.   Rachel Merryman, m. —— Chapman.
    iv.   Rebecca Merryman, m. (lic.) 9 April 1804, John Blizzard.
    v.   Mary Merryman, m. (lic.) 17 Oct. 1795, Laban Welsh.

20.   CALEB MERRYMAN ⁵ (Samuel ⁴, Samuel ³, Charles ², John ¹), was born 12 March, 1758, and died 21 November, 1824. He married (lic.) 2 January, 1781, Ann Wells, and (2), 16 August, 1787, Mary Merryman, his first cousin, a daughter of Nicholas and Avarilla (Raven) Merryman. His will, dated 29 May, 1824, and probated

17 January, 1825, mentions his son, John, who receives
certain lands in Virginia: and refers to daughters (unnamed). Appended to the will is a list of "children and
heirs "; namely, John Merryman of C., Avarilla Merryman, William H. Chapman, Rebecca Chapman, Mary
Merryman and Eleanor Merryman. (*Balt. Wills,* Lib.
12, fol. 85).

Mrs. Mary Merryman, second wife of Caleb, died 23
April, 1809, in the 44th year of her age. Caleb and
Mary (Merryman) Merryman had issue.

  i. Avarilla Merryman,[6] b. 25 June 1788; d. unmarried.
32. ii. JOHN MERRYMAN, b. 28 Jany. 1793.
  iii. Ann Merryman, b. 1 June 1796; m. 20 June 1818, Basil Burgess.
  iv. Rebecca Merryman, b. 25 Feby. 1799; d. 16 Sept. 1863; m. 2
   Nov. 1824, Rev. Wm. H. Chapman.
  v. Mary Merryman, b. 7 Feby. 1801; m. Henry D. Carleton.
  vi. Eleanor Merryman, b. 16 May 1804; d. April 1845; m. in 1839,
   Isaac Chapman.

21. JOHN MERRYMAN [5] (Samuel [4], Samuel [3], Charles [2],
John [1]), was born in January 1763, and died 18 August,
1849. He is mentioned in the will of his brother, Mordecai, dated 24 September, 1804, and probated 17 October, 1807, wherein his (John's) two children, Charles and
Elizabeth Merryman, are named (*Balt. Wills,* Lib. 8, fol.
262). The name of John Merryman's wife is supposed
to have been Eleanor.

John Merryman had issue.

  i. Samuel Merryman.[6]
  ii. Henry Merryman.
  iii. John Merryman.
  iv. Charles Merryman.
  v. Elizabeth Merryman (m. lic. 30 July 1817 Joseph Gorsuch?).
  vi. Achsah Merryman, married Luther Wilson.

22. LUKE MERRYMAN [5] (Nicholas [4], Samuel [3], Charles [2],
John [1]), died 12 February, 1813. He married (lic.) 29
January, 1794, Elizabeth Gorsuch, and had issue.

  i. Nicholas Merryman,[6] (?), b. 5 Aug. 1795.
  ii. Caleb Merryman, b. 5 Aug. 1798.
  iii. Ann Merryman, b. 11 Jany. 1813.

23. NICHOLAS MERRYMAN [6] (Nicholas [5], John [4], John [3],
Charles [2], John [1]), called "White-headed Nickey" of
Bacon Hall, was born in 1751, and died in 1832, intes-
tate. (Inventory, 7 April, 1832). He was commissioned

4 February, 1777, 1st Lieutenant of Captain Thomas
Moore's company, in Col. Thomas Gist, Jr.'s battalion
of Baltimore county militia (*Md. Archives,* xvi, 113) and
on 30 August, 1777, captain in the Upper Battalion of
militia in Baltimore county (*ibid.,* 350), He married
twice—(1) (lic.) 5 February, 1778, Deborah Ensor
(daughter of Eleanor Ensor, who died in 1801), and (2)
Nancy Merryman (1st cousin), daughter of Benjamin
Merryman, Sr. (d. 1814).

The first administration account of his estate was passed
31 May, 1832, with John Merryman, of Benjamin, and
Elijah Merryman as administrators (*Admin. Accts.,* Lib.
30, folio 464). Elijah Merryman, one of the administrators, died before the estate was finally settled and the
third account filed by the surviving administrator, 2 September, 1840 (*Lib.* 39, folio 206), mentions the widow,
Ann Merryman, and the following children of Nicholas
Merryman, deceased:

By first wife:

33. i.   JOHN ENSOR MERRYMAN,[7] b. 20 Feby. 1781.
34. ii. ELIJAH MERRYMAN.
35. iii. MICAJAH MERRYMAN.
     iv. Eleanor Merryman, bpt. 16 Aug. 1790; m. James Edwards
          Frisby.
36. v.   NICHOLAS MERRYMAN, b. 20 June 1793; d. June 1823.

By second wife:

     vi. Benjamin Merryman, d. inf.
     vii. Philemon Merryman, d. before his father.

24. ELIJAH MERRYMAN [6] (Nicholas [5], John [4], John [3],
Charles [2], John [1]), died 3 July, 1799. He married twice
(1) Frances Ensor (daughter of Eleanor Ensor, who died
in 1801), and (2) (lic.) 14 November, 1785, Elizabeth
Cromwell, who died in 1833. His will, dated 8 Decem-
ber, 1798, and probated 17 July, 1799, mentions his wife,
Elizabeth: his father, Nicholas Merryman; four children,
John, Nicholas, Thomas and Frances Merryman; a
brother, Nicholas, and a sister, Jane Merryman (*Balt.
Wills,* Lib. 6, folio 192). Elijah Merryman had issue.

By first wife:

     i.   John Merryman,[7] d. s. p. 1801, in Cuba.
37. ii. NICHOLAS MERRYMAN, d. 30 May, 1823.
     iii. Eleanor Merryman, d. young.

By second wife:

iv. Thomas Merryman, b. 1786; d. 6 Dec. 1819; m. (lic.) 17 Sept. 1812, Priscilla Britton, s. p.
v. Frances Merryman, bpt. 2 May 1788; m. (lic.) 24 May 1807, Jacob Bond.

25. NICHOLAS ROGERS MERRYMAN [6] (John [5], John [4], John [3], Charles [2], John [1]), was born 26 April, 1788 (St. Paul's), and died 21 January, 1864, at Piney Hill, Baltimore county. He married (1) 15 September, 1823, Ann Maria Gott (d. 25 January, 1829, aet. 31): (2) 19 June, 1832, Clarissa Philpot (First Presbyterian Church, Balto.). She died 5 November, 1877, aet. 71, and was buried at Piney Hill. Nicholas Rogers Merryman had issue.

By first wife:

38. i. JOHN MERRYMAN,[7] (of "Hayfields"), b. 9 Aug. 1824; d. 15 Nov. 1881.
ii. Sarah Rogers Merryman, b. 17 Sept. 1827; d. 5 Aug. 1828.

By second wife:

39. iii. HENRY NICOLS MERRYMAN.
iv. Richard Smith Merryman, m. Mary Louise Brown.

26. JOHN MERRYMAN [6] (Benjamin [5], John [4], John [3], Charles [2] John [1]), lived at Monkton, Md., and died in November, 1849. He married, 14 December, 1790, Sarah Johnson (St. James). His will is dated 15 April, 1848, and was probated November, 1849 (*Balto. Wills,* Lib. 23, folio 291). John and Sarah (Johnson) Merryman had issue.

i. Catharine Merryman,[7] bpt. 14 Feby. 1792; m. Feby. 1813, Thomas Streett.
ii. Elizabeth Johnson Merryman, bpt. 11 Oct. 1793; m. —— Stansbury.
40. iii. LEVI MERRYMAN, b. Dec. 1795; d. aet. 73.
iv. Ann Maria Merryman, bpt. 17 Dec. 1797; m. Dec. 1834, Nicholas Gatch.
v. Sarah Rogers Merryman, d. July 1867; m. Jany. 1831, Edwd. Philpot, s. p.
vi. Joshua Merryman, b. July 1807.
vii. John Johnson Merryman.

27. NICHOLAS MERRYMAN [6] (Benjamin [5], John [4], John [3], Charles [2], John [1]), died in 1816. His will, dated 4 Jan'y, 1816, was probated 10 February, 1816 (*Balt. Wills,* Lib. 10, folio 118). His brother, Philemon Merryman, was guardian for his two younger children, Ann and Sarah.

(*Admin. Accts.,* Lib. 21, fol. 54: *Gdn. Bonds,* Lib. 3, fol.
343). He married, 26 June, 1798 Sarah Anderson (St.
James), and had issue:

   i. Mary Merryman,[7] b. 11 June 1799; m. (lic.) 6 Mch. 1818, Wm.
      Tipton.
   ii. Benjamin Merryman, bpt. 16 July 1800.
   iii. Martha Merryman, bpt. 9 Apl. 1802; m. (lic.) 21 July 1821,
      John R. Gwynn.
   iv. Gerard Merryman, b. 24 Dec. 1803.
   v. Ann Merryman, b. 21 July 1805; m. (lic.) 29 Aug. 1822,
      John R. Gwynn.
   vi. Sarah Merryman, (m. 21 Aug. 1823, Aquila Sparks?).

28. WILLIAM MERRYMAN [6] (Benjamin [5], John [4], John [3],
Charles [2], John [1]), was elected sheriff of Baltimore Town
and County in October, 1809. He married (lic.) 6 January, 1800, Ann Presbury (1780-1828), daughter of
George G. Presbury. She died 22 November, 1828, in
the 48th year of her age. (*Balt. American,* 26 November, 1828), leaving five children.
They had issue:

   i. Eleanor Merryman.[7]
   ii. Ann Merryman.
   iii. George Merryman, b. Dec. 1805; d. young.
   iv. William Merryman, b. Oct. 1808; d. 1823, unm. (will).
   v. Gerard Merryman, b. 1809.
   vi. Benjamin Merryman, d. inf.
   vii. Martha Merryman.
   viii. Elizabeth B. Merryman.
   ix. Adam C. Merryman.

29. PHILEMON MERRYMAN [6] (Benjamin,[5] John,[4] John,[3]
Charles,[2] John [1]), married (lic.) 4 March 1812, Elizabeth
Norwood, and had issue.

   i. Benjamin Bell Merryman,[7] b. 4 April 1813.

30. MOSES MERRYMAN [6] (Micajah,[5] Moses,[4] John,[3] Charles,[2]
John [1]), was born 24 March, 1783, and died 19 November,
1819. He was a physician and served as a Surgeon's mate
in the 7th Regiment of Baltimore County, Md., militia during the War of 1812-14, being commissioned 9 February,
1814. He married (lic.) 13 June, 1805, Mary Cockey
(1781-1809), daughter of Captain John Cockey. She died
24 February, 1809 (*Balt. Federal Gazette,* 25 February,
1809). They had issue:

   i. Edwin Merryman,[7] b. 13 June 1806; d. 2 April 1809.

31. MICAJAH MERRYMAN [6] (Micajah,[5] Moses,[4] John,[3] Charles,[2] John [1]), was born 16 May, 1788, and died 29 April, 1854. He married 10 April, 1826, Clarissa Harryman, daughter of George and Rachel Harryman. She died 15 April, 1879, aet. 80 years and 6 months. They had issue:

    i. Moses Washington Merryman,[7] M. D., b. 15 Feby. 1827, d. 25 Jany. 1904.
    ii. George Harryman Merryman, b. 27 Jany. 1829; d. 10 Aug. 1829.
    iii. Mary Merryman, b. 9 July 1830; d. 26 Sept. 1830.
41. iv. GEORGE HARRYMAN MERRYMAN, b. 8 Sept. 1831 (living, in his 84th year). . . .
    v. Eleanor Cole Merryman, b. 20 Dec. 1834; d. 16 July 1905.
    vi. Rachel Harryman Merryman, b. 4 Dec. 1836.
    vii. Henry Clay Merryman, b. 27 Dec. 1838.
    viii. Laura Virginia Merryman, b. 9 July 1841; d. 3 Oct. 1870.
    ix. Clara Merryman, b. 2 Sept. 1844; m. Henry R. Crane.

32. JOHN MERRYMAN [6] (Caleb,[5] Samuel,[4] Samuel,[3] Charles,[2] John [1]), married, 24 June, 1824, Catharine Hammond. They had issue:

    i. Ellen Merryman,[7] m. James H. Lloyd.
    ii. Mary Merryman, m. Alex. Finley.
    iii. John Merryman, m. Sarah J. Wotherspoon.
    iv. Henry M. Merryman, m. Christiana Wolbert.
    v. Elizabeth Merryman, m. David Gardner.
    vi. Rebecca Merryman, m. Wm. C. Barclay.
    vii. William Merryman, m. Eliza Roberts.
    viii. Howard Merryman, m. Kate Weats.

33. JOHN ENSOR MERRYMAN [7] (Nicholas,[6] Nicholas,[5] John,[4] John,[3] Charles,[2] John [1]), was born 20 February, 1781 (St. Paul's) and died about 1815 (see *Balt. Wills,* Liber 10, folio 55). Letters of administration on his estate were granted to William Jones 21 July, 1815. He married, 2 April, 1812, Augusta Matilda Deye Harvey, a daughter of Captain William Harvey, and had issue:

    i. Harvey Merryman,[8] b. 19 Aug. 1813; d. 10 Sept. 1876.

34. ELIJAH MERRYMAN [7] (Nicholas,[6] Nicholas,[5] John,[4] John,[3] Charles,[2] John [1]), died in 1840. His will is dated 25 March, 1840, and was probated 4 June, 1840. (*Balt. Wills,* Liber 18, folios 34). He married 20 Sept., 1804, Cassandra Harvey, a daughter of Captain William Harvey, and had issue:

    i. Ann Merryman,[8] m. Samuel W. Merryman (cousin).
    ii. Eleanor Merryman, m. Salathiel Cole.

   iii. Nicholas H. Merryman.
   iv. John H. Merryman.
    v. Thomas Merryman.
   vi. Penelope Merryman, m. Joshua M. Bosley.
  vii. Sarah Harvey Merryman, m. Jacob Gilbert.

35. MICAJAH MERRYMAN [7] (Nicholas,[6] Nicholas,[5] John,[4]
John,[3] Charles,[2] John [1]), was born in 1784 and died prior
to 1828. He married (lic.) 8 April, 1807, Deborah Ensor,
and had issue:

    i. Nicholas Merryman.[8]
   ii. Ellen Merryman, m. Darby Ensor.
  iii. John E. Merryman, b. 1 July 1813.
   iv. George Merryman, b. 28 Dec. 1814.
    v. Elizabeth Merryman, m. Eli Stevenson.
   vi. Abner Merryman.

36. NICHOLAS MERRYMAN [7] (Nicholas,[6] Nicholas,[5] John,[4]
John,[3] Charles,[2] John [1]), was born 20 June, 1793 (St.
James) and died in June, 1823. He married (license)
19 January, 1814, Dorcas Buck.

    i. John B. Merryman,[8] m. Sarah B. Ensor.
   ii. Charles D. Merryman.
  iii. Catharine Rogers Merryman (d. 1904); m. James Andrews, of
       Annapolis.
   iv. Grafton Merryman.
    v. Nicholas B. Merryman.

37. NICHOLAS MERRYMAN [7] (Elijah,[6] Nicholas,[5] John,[4] John,[3]
Charles,[2] John [1]), nick-named "monkey face," died 30
May, 1823. He married 16 December, 1802, Charlotte
Worthington (1780-1859), and the marriage is recorded
in both St. James' and St. Thomas' parish registers.
Issue:

    i. John Merryman,[8] d. s. p. 1841 (will).
   ii. James O. Merryman, d. 27 July 1843.
  iii. Frances Merryman, m. Eli Curtis.
   iv. Catharine J. Merryman, m. Levi Curtis.
    v. Samuel W. Merryman, married thrice.
   vi. Elijah Merryman, b. 3 July 1810; d. 18 Nov. 1835; m. 6
       June 1832, Rebecca Cockey.
  vii. Susan W. Merryman.
 viii. Elizabeth E. Merryman.

38. JOHN MERRYMAN [7] (Nicholas Rogers,[6] John,[5] John,[4]
John,[3] Charles,[2] John [1]), the first of the "Hayfields"
Merrymans, was born 9 August, 1824, near Hereford, Bal-
timore County, Md., died 15 November, 1881, and is bur-

ied near Cockeysville (Sherwood Cemetery). He married in 1844, Ann Louisa Gittings (1825-1897), daughter of Elijah Bosley Gittings and Ann Lux Cockey. "Hayfields" came into the possession of the Merryman family through Nicholas Merryman Bosley, uncle of Elijah Bosley Gittings, the father of John Merryman's wife, Ann Louisa Gittings. Nicholas Merryman Bosley owned the estate in 1808, having acquired it by means of the purchase at sundry times, of certain tracts of land from various parties, until the farm comprised 560 acres. He put all the buildings on the place, and the mansion was finished in 1833. He then moved from the comfortable stone house, which he had previously built and occupied, to the more commodious structure. The first Merryman to occupy the estate was John, of Hayfields, (1824-1881.) Upon the demise of the latter's wife, Ann Gittings Merryman, in February, 1897, the property passed to their eldest son, in whom it was entailed.

In 1847, John Merryman, of Hayfields, was 3d Lieutenant of Baltimore County troops, and in 1861, 1st Lieutenant of the "Baltimore County Horse Guards." On 25 May, 1861, he was arrested and conveyed to Fort McHenry by the Federal authorities, and indicted for treason, but was discharged and never brought to trial. In 1870 he was elected State Treasurer of Maryland, and in 1874 was a member of the Maryland House of Delegates. John and Ann Louisa (Gittings) Merryman had issue:

    i. Ann Gott Merryman,[8] b. 3 Aug. 1845.
    ii. Elizabeth Merryman, b. 24 July 1849; d. 16 Mch. 1895; m. Lt. Com. Charles H. Black, U. S. N.
    iii. Nicholas Bosley Merryman, b. 19 Feb. 1852; m. Willie McCloskey.
    iv. John Merryman, b. 5 Sept. 1854; d. 3 Nov. 1885.
    v. David Buchanan Merryman, b. 9 May 1856; d. 11 Mch. 1900; m. 23 July 1894, Bessie L. Montague.
    vi. Elijah Gittings Merryman, b. 10 Feby. 1858; d. 8 Apl. 1913; m. Emily McLane.
    vii. William Duvall Merryman, b. 29 Nov. 1859; d. 14 Apl. 1915.
    viii. Louisa G. Merryman, b. 19 Sept. 1862: m. 25 Feby. 1913, James S. Nussear, Jr.
    ix. Roger B. Taney Merryman, b. 5 Dec. 1864; d. 5 July 1865.
    x. James McK. Merryman, b. 21 Oct. 1869; m. 4 Dec. 1891, Isabel Brown.
    xi. Laura F. Merryman, b. 21 Oct. 1870; m. Philip A. S. Franklin.

39. HENRY N. MERRYMAN [7] (Nicholas Rogers,[6] John,[5] John,[4] John,[3] Charles,[2] John [1]), is mentioned in the will of his

aunt, Elizabeth Merryman, who died in 1860 (*Balt. Wills,* Lib. 29, fol. 252). He married Mary Griffith, (1836-1891) and had issue:

    i. Harry G. Merryman,⁸ b. 9 Nov. 1861; m. 18 Dec. 1881.

40. LEVI MERRYMAN ⁷ (John,⁶ Benjamin,⁵ John,⁴ John,³ Charles,² John ¹), was born in December, 1795 (St. James), and died in 1868, aged 73 years. He married (1) 31 December, 1822, Mary Jessop (1805-1854), and (2) Mary Carr. He had issue. By 1st wife:

    i. Rosalbert Merryman,⁸ m. Peter Bosley.
    ii. Georgianna Merryman, m. William Murray.
    iii. Charles Merryman, b. 1827; d. 4 June 1829.
    iv. Sarah Rogers Merryman, m. 29 May 1857, James A. Richardson.
    v. Clara A. Merryman, b. 1832; died 4 Aug. 1853.
    vi. Cornelia Merryman, m. Isaac Price.
    vii. George Merryman, m. Fannie Powell.
    viii. Joseph R. Merryman, b. 1844; d. 16 Jany. 1866 (unm.).
    ix. Gussie V. Merryman, b. 14 Feby. 1845; d. 5 Mch. 1871 (unm.).

41. GEORGE H. MERRYMAN ⁷ (Micajah,⁶ Micajah,⁵ Moses,⁴ John,³ Charles,² John ¹), was born 8 September, 1831. He married, 27 October, 1858, Mary Ann Gorsuch, and had issue:

    i. Rev. Charles Gorsuch Merryman,⁸ b. 31 Dec. 1860; d. 3 July 1894.
    ii. Micajah Merryman, b. 31 Dec. 1860; d. 5 Jany 1861.
    iii. George Micajah Merryman, b. 9 Feb. 1863; d. 12 Dec. 1899.
    iv. Andrew Lowndes Merryman, b. 11 Dec. 1864; d. 19 Jany. 1868.
    v. Harry Lee Merryman, b. 9 Feby. 1867.
    vi. Samuel Howard Merryman, b. 10 Dec. 1868.
    vii. Laura V. Merryman, b. 20 Oct. 1870.

(*Concluded*)

NOTE.—The compiler of this Merryman family genealogy will welcome any additions or corrections from readers of the *Maryland Historical Magazine.*

MERRYMAN FAMILY

Wanted—Any information tending to the identification of the following persons bearing the name of Merryman:

Births (Balt. County)

1 February, 1846—Mary Louisa, daughter of Nicholas and Catherine Merryman.

18 March, 1848—Wesley Martin, son of Nicholas and Catherine Merryman.

Marriages (Balt. County)

29 January, 1761—Elizabeth Merryman and Jethro Lynch Wilkinson.

16 February, 1764—Temperance Merryman and Nathaniel Harrington.

14 December, 1837—Elizabeth E. Merryman and Charles R. Powell.

Marriage Licenses (Balt. County)

14 April, 1781—Nicholas Merryman and Mary Ogg.

29 April, 1786—Benj. Merryman, of Wm., and Cynthia Doyle.

16 February, 1796—Nicholas Merryman and Mary Cornley.

10 November, 1804—Rachel Merryman and Jacob Crouse.

3 June, 1816—Juliet Ann Merryman and Stephen Johnson.

13 July, 1818—George Merryman and Eleanor Coleman.

8 May, 1821—Elizabeth Merryman and Joseph Laurence.

14 May, 1822—Thos. Merryman and Margaret Martin.

14 August, 1822—Elias Merryman and Susan Lavely.

27 February, 1823—Philemon Merryman and Maria Wilson.

18 April, 1823—Caleb Merryman, Jr., and Louisa Andrews.

19 November, 1813—Sam'l Merryman and Eliz. Shannaman.

18 March, 1813—Jane Merryman and George Lee.

CORRECTION.

MERRYMAN FAMILY.

Md. Hist. Mag., vol. x, no. 3 (September, 1915), page 297:
Nicholas Bosley Merryman married Willie McCleskey (not McCloskey).
Elijah Gitting Merryman, b. 19 Feby. 1858.

Merryman Family.—Maryland Historical Magazine, x, pp. 291-292. From additional data just discovered in an old Frisby family Bible: Nicholas Merryman (1751-1832), married (2) Nancy Merryman, who died 5 March, 1832, aged 76 years. They had a daughter, Eleanor Merryman: b. 1813; d. 7 June, 1838; married 11 March, 1834, James Edwards Frisby (1813-1838). (Eleanor Merryman, daughter of Nicholas Merryman by his first wife, Deborah Ensor, was baptized 16 August, 1790, and died *unmarried.*) F. B. C.

THE MARYLAND ANCESTRY OF JAMES MONROE.

By MONROE JOHNSON

Students of Maryland history and genealogy will be interested to learn that the Monroe family of Westmoreland County, Virginia, from which James Monroe was descended, had its origin in Maryland. So, if Maryland cannot, like her sister State of Virginia, boast of the honor of being the mother of the fifth President, she can at least claim to be the great-grandmother of that distinguished statesman.

President Daniel C. Gilman of Johns Hopkins University, who wrote the first comprehensive biography of President Monroe, frankly admitted that he had not been successful in tracing the pedigree of his subject. President Gilman did, however, refer to an old statement, which has since been found to be erroneous, that the first of the family in America was one Andrew Monroe, who came to Virginia after the defeat of the Royalist army in England, in which he held the rank of major. Based on this statement, the author of the Monroe Doctrine was, until recent years, thought to have come of Cavalier ancestry—the origin commonly, but mistakenly, attributed to the leading Virginia families. While Doctor Gilman was making his fruitless search among the Virginia archives for a description of the Monroe immigrant, a fairly complete account of him, strange to relate, lay hidden in the old Maryland records, directly under the eyes of the searcher.

More recent researches have disclosed that Andrew Monroe, the great-great-grandfather of President Monroe, arrived in Maryland about 1637, settling on Kent Island, where the turbulent William Claiborne had established a trading post several years before the Ark and the Dove, bearing Lord Baltimore's colonists, dropped anchor off Saint Mary's. The records are silent regarding the immigrant's European antecedents, but, since the name Monroe is a variant of the Scottish clan name Munro, he must have come from Scotland, or perhaps from Ulster in Ireland. Like many another Scottish Highlander of that day, he was unable to write and made his mark, when his signature was required.

The colonial records of Maryland show that Monroe commanded a pinnace, a small vessel, under Cuthbert Fenwick, general agent for Lord Baltimore. But when Richard Ingle, who has been variously described as a " pirate " and a "patriot," according to the political views of the historian, declared for Parliament and attempted to overthrow the Proprietary, Captain Monroe, a Protestant, joined Ingle in the Maryland rebellion, which was a miniature counterpart of the struggle then raging in England between Cavalier and Roundhead.

After the suppression of Ingle's revolt against the authority of the Calverts, Andrew Monroe took refuge across the Potomac in Westmoreland County, Virginia, where a land patent was issued to him in 1650. On this land President James Monroe was born in 1758—over a century after it had been granted to his first American ancestor.

It is interesting to note that Charles Tyler, the ancestor of President John Tyler, also left Maryland for Virginia, probably at the same time and under the same circumstances as Captain Monroe.

The descendants of Andrew Monroe and Elizabeth, his wife, became substantial citizens of the Northern Neck of Virginia, owning respectable estates and many slaves. Although the Monroes were prominent locally, being for several generations justices of the peace and officers in the militia, they did not occupy the same position in society as their wealthier neighbors, the Lees, Washingtons, Alstons and others, whose larger holdings entitled them to greater consideration both socially and politically.

In connection with the discarding of the tradition that the Monroes were of Cavalier stock, it is interesting to note that Thomas J. Wertenbaker in his " Patrician and Plebeian in Virginia " offers convincing evidence that the " first families of Virginia," so many of which are related by blood or marriage to prominent Maryland families, are, with only a few exceptions, derived from ancestors of the English merchant and, in some instances, yeoman classes. Despite the long-cherished belief in the Cavalier origin of these capable and cultured families, which have played such a prominent part in national affairs, Mr. Wertenbaker shows conclusively that the Virginia aristocracy was gradually developed on American soil instead of being transplanted, full-grown, from England, as so many historians have assumed.[1]

MORGAN FAMILY.

1. HENRY MORGAN[1] came to Maryland in 1637 and settled on
Kent Island (Land Office, Lib. ABH, fol. 131). He appears
on the tax list of Kent County in 1642 (*Md. Arch.*, iii, 121)
and, 2 Nov. 1648, was commissioned High Sheriff and commander of the militia of the County (*ibid.*, 197). He was one
of the Justices of Kent County from 1650 to 1659 (*Md. Arch.*,
iii, 363, Kent Co. Records), and represented the County in
the Assembly 1659–60 (*Md. Arch.*, i, 382). In a deposition
made in 1648 he gives his age as 30 years or thereabouts
(*Md. Arch.*, iv, 452), while in another deposition made in
1648/9 his age is stated as 33 years (*ibid.*, 478). The latter
statement is doubtless more exact, so that he was probably
born in 1615 or 1616. His wife, Mrs. Frances Morgan, was
30 years old in 1655 (*Old Kent*, p. 205). Henry Morgan died
in or about 1663. His widow Frances married Jonathan
Sybrey of Talbot County, and died in 1672. A petition,
filed 8 Jan'y 1673/4, by William Coursey and Peter Sayer,
Gent., on behalf of Frances one of the daughters and coheirs
of Henry Morgan late of Kent County deceased, recites that
the said Henry Morgan died about the year 1663. No will
was proved, nor administration committed to any one. Not
long after his decease his widow Frances married Jonathan
Sybrey, who possessed himself of the estate, never taking out
letters during the life of the said Frances, relict of the said

Henry, nor since her death which is now near two years since. Petitioner craves letters on her father's estate in her own behalf, and in behalf of her sister Barbara Morgan now absent in England. Administration was granted as prayed, and bond was given in 40,000 lb. tobacco, with William Coursey and Peter Sayer as sureties (Test. Proc., Lib. 6, fol. 62).

Henry Morgan and Frances his wife, had issue as follows, the dates of birth being derived from the Kent County records :—

    i. HENRY MORGAN,[2] born 28 Jan'y 1651 ; d. young.
    ii. BARBARA MORGAN, b. 28 July 1654 ; buried 5 Sept. 1658.
2. iii. FRANCES MORGAN, b. 1 Oct. 1656 ; d. 1698.
    iv. MARGARET MORGAN, b. 29 March 1659 ; buried 5 Sept. 1659.
3. v. BARBARA MORGAN, b. 5 Nov. 1660.

2. FRANCES MORGAN,[2] daughter of Henry and Frances, was born 1 Oct. 1656 and died in 1698. She married Col. Peter Sayer of Talbot County, but had no issue. The will of Col. Peter Sayer (dated 29 Aug. 1697 ; proved 2 Nov. 1697) bequeaths one third of his estate to his wife Frances ; one third equally between his nephew Charles Blake and his godson John Blake ; and one third in three equal parts to the English Benedictine Nuns at Paris, the English Benedictine Monks at Paris, and the English Friars respectively. The testator also provides for his " old Aunt Varvey," and makes some special bequests, including £5 to " every priest in the Province " (Annapolis, Lib. 7, fol. 334). The will of Mrs. Frances Sayer, dated 26 May 1698, was proved 27 Sept. 1698 (Annapolis, Lib. 6, fol. 166). She leaves to her sister Barbara's children John Rousby, and Walter, Frances, Susanna, and Barbara Smith, £20 apiece. To Mrs. Jenny Sewall, daughter of Major Sewall, a diamond ring. Her niece Elizabeth Rously is constituted residuary legatee, with the proviso that in case of the death of said niece without issue, her real estate is to pass to the heirs of testatrix's father Henry Morgan. Abstracts of both wills are to be found in *Baldwin's Calendar* (ii, 131, 158.)

3. BARBARA MORGAN,[2] daughter of Henry and Frances, was born 5 Nov. 1660, and married, before 29 Sept. 1676, John Rousby of Calvert County. 29 Sept. 1676, John Rousby and Barbara his wife, one of the daughters of Henry Morgan and Francis his wife, deceased, exhibit a complaint against Peter Sayer and Frances his wife, the other daughter of the aforesaid Henry and Frances (Test. Proc., Lib. 8, fol. 217). In

October 1677, John Rousby and Barbara his wife, daughter
and coheir of Henry Morgan deceased, file a petition in the
Land Office in regard to certain lands of said Henry Morgan
on Choptank River (Lib. 19, fol. 603). John Rousby died 1
Feb'y 1685/6 (Epitaph) leaving a will dated 8 May 1685 and
proved 8 Feb'y 1685/6 (Annapolis, Lib. 4, fol. 164; abstract
in *Baldwin's Calendar*, i, 159), in which he mentions his wife
Barbara, his son John, and his daughters Gertrude and Elizabeth. His widow Barbara was married secondly, 13 July
1686, by the Rev. P. Bertrand, to Capt. Richard Smith of
St. Leonards, Calvert County, son of Attorney General Richard
Smith. The certificate of this marriage is entered in the records
of the Provincial Court, Liber WRC., No. 1, fol. 415. Capt.
Richard Smith was thrice married, 1°. to Elizabeth daughter
of Robert Brooke (*Mag.*, i, 69), 2°. to Mrs. Barbara Rousby,
and 3° in 1697 to Maria Johanna widow of Col. Lowther and
daughter of Charles Somerset Esq. of Acton Manor, Middlesex, and Ross, in Hertfordshire, grandson of the first Marquis
of Worcester. He had issue by all three marriages and died
in 1714. His will, dated 31 July 1710, was proved 17 Feb.,
1714 (Lib. 14, fol. 83). During the Revolution of 1689,
when her husband was imprisoned for refusing to take part
with the insurgents, Mrs. Barbara Smith displayed marked
energy and ability, going to England in behalf of Capt.
Smith and laying his case before the authorities there. Her
very interesting narrative of the troubles in Maryland at that
period is published in the *Maryland Archives*, vol. viii, p. 153.
By her first husband, John Rousby, she had issue :—

   i. JOHN ROUSBY,[3] d. 1744 ; twice married, and left issue.
   ii. GERTRUDE ROUSBY.
   iii. ELIZABETH ROUSBY, b. 1682 ; d. 3 April 1740 ; mar. Richard Bennett
       of Bennett's Point, but had no issue.

By her second husband, Capt. Richard Smith, Barbara Morgan
had issue :—

   i. WALTER SMITH[3] of St. Leonards, d. 1748 ; mar. Alethia, dau. of
       Nathaniel Dare of Calvert Co., and left issue.
   ii. FRANCES SMITH.
   iii. SUSANNA SMITH.
   iv. BARBARA SMITH, b. 1693 ; d. 1764 ; mar. 1°. 1 Jan'y 1712, Thomas
       Holdsworth ; 2°. about 1720, Benjamin Mackall.

THE MURDOCK FAMILY OF MARYLAND AND VIRGINIA.

BY WILLIAM B. MARYE,
Chairman, Committee on Genealogy and Heraldry.

Among the genealogical papers of the late Wilson Miles Cary is a chart of the Murdock family of Maryland and Virginia (folder 68) and a bundle of notes representing chiefly researches which Mr. Cary made in England with a view to ascertaining the English origin of the family (researches which, by the way, were unfortunately unsuccessful). Mr. Cary's letters to his clients, several copies of which are contained in the bundle of notes, reveal the fact that he had not had an opportunity, or perhaps had not been authorized, to make extensive researches in Maryland. To this fact may be attributed certain errors which I have been able to correct by extending my researches beyond the point which Mr. Cary reached.

The family history in America, so far as records have been found to prove it, begins with two brothers, John and Jeremiah Murdock. These brothers may possibly have been related to Alexander " Murdough," whose burial, on August 29, 1703, is recorded in the register of All Hallows, Anne Arundel County, Maryland.

There is on record in Prince George's County, Md., a deed bearing date November 13, 1714, by which John Murdock, of Prince George's County, Merchant, conveyed, as a gift, to his brother Jeremiah Murdock a certain piece of land on the west side of Patuxent River being part of a tract called " Padworth Farme." (Prince George's County, Md., Deeds, Liber E, folio 407.)

Part I. Murdock of Virginia

JEREMIAH MURDOCK witnessed the marriage certificate of Joseph Coleman and Mary Thomas, 1712. (Marriage Certificates, West River, Herring Creek and Indian Spring Monthly Meetings, p. 15.) At what time he settled in Virginia is not definitely known. He was a resident of Hanover Parish, King George County, in or before 1726. He was a Justice of the Peace of that county from 1728 until 1741. As he was styled " Major " in King George County records, it is likely that he held a commission in the county Militia. In 1739 " Josiah " Murdock was appointed High Sheriff of King George County. (Virginia Historical Magazine, XIV, 341.) No person of that name is known to have been a resident of King George County at that time, and it is almost certain that the recipient of this honor was Jeremiah Murdock, unless it was his son, Joseph Murdock, who received it. I have the impression that Major Jeremiah Murdock, who was a merchant, as well as an extensive planter, was interested in the Bristol Iron Works of King

George County. In this connection I note the fact that some of his lands lay on Iron Works Creek, others adjacent or near to the Bristol Furnace. His will reveals the fact that he was intimately acquainted with a family of Bristol merchants. It is worthy of note that there were Murdocks in Bristol. Mr. Cary discovered the fact, which seems highly significant, that in a prominent and wealthy family of Coventry merchants named Murdock, of the seventeenth century, the christian name of " Jeremiah " occurs. It is suggested, however, that search for the immediate English ancestor of the Maryland and Virginia Murdocks might be made in Bristol, after which, if successful, connections with Coventry might be found. It would appear probable that the will of the grandfather of Jeremiah Murdock is on record somewhere and that the " silver caudle cup " is mentioned in it as a bequest to the grandson.

JEREMIAH MURDOCK married Jane (or Jean), widow of one Chapman. In her will dated January 23, 1770, and proved in King George County the same year, Mrs. Murdock appointed her grandson, William Chapman, her executor, and mentioned also her granddaughter, Jean Chapman. A Thomas Chapman, of Stafford County is mentioned in 1706. (Stafford County, Va., Will Book 2, 1699-1709, p. 364.) On May 9, 1758, Joseph Murdock and Richard Hooe, gentlemen, gave bond to deliver certain goods to William Chapman, orphan of Taylor Chapman, deceased. (Stafford County, Va., Liber O, p. 345.) It would appear likely that Taylor Chapman, who died circa 1750 was the son of Mrs. Murdock by her former marriage.[1]

JEREMIAH MURDOCK had issue (probably by wife Jane) :

1. JOHN MURDOCK, probably eldest son. No particulars regarding him are available. Did he die s. p.?

---

[1] Among the Cary papers (Bundle 16) I find an abstract of the will of Taylor Chapman, of Overwharton Parish, Stafford County, Virginia, recorded on folio 80 of Liber —, 1748-1763, Stafford County Records. This will bears date 8 Nov., 1749, and was proved 13 February, 1750. The deceased left a widow, Margaret Chapman, two sons, William and Joseph Chapman, and a daughter, Jane Chapman.

2. JOSEPH MURDOCK, of whom presently.
3. "Peggy" (Margaret) Murdock. She married Colonel William
   Fauntleroy, of Richmond County (1713-1793).

The will of Major JEREMIAH MURDOCK of King George
County, Virginia, bears date December 12, 1750, and was probated October 5, 1752. The testator bequeathed certain negroes
to his wife, Jane Murdock. To his daughter, Peggy Fauntleroy,
he bequeathed £100 and a negro. To his son, John Murdock,
he left 527 acres on Occoquon, in Prince William County,
bought of Thomas Stribling, a plantation of 200 acres in Orange
County bought of Anthony Head, and a tract of 500 acres on
Aquia Run in Stafford County bought of Captain Maximilian
Robinson, also ⅓ of his, the testator's negroes. In case the
said John Murdock should die s. p. these lands, etc., were to
go to the testator's son, Joseph Murdock, if certain conditions
were complied with. To his son, Joseph Murdock, conditionally,
the testator left the land he lived on and the land adjoining " in
this neck " bought of Conway Wormley Kendall, also the land
joining Joshua Farquharson's land and the Bristol Furnace
purchased of one Conway (after decease of testator's wife),
also 362 acres on Rappahannock River in Prince William
County, also a plantation in Westmoreland County with land
adjoining in King George County containing 600 acres, being
the land purchased of Kendall, Hews, et al. The testator bequeathed to his " cousin " (nephew) William Murdock land in
Maryland formerly sold to him for £70 and not yet paid for.
To his son, Joseph Murdock, the testator left his " Silver spurs
and the silver caudle cup that are now in the house *ye caudle
cup being a piece of antiquity of my grandfathers and given
me being the youngest child to keep in the family.* I am willing
to perform the will and heartily desire particular care may be
taken if possible to reserve it in ye family to succeeding generations." To Mr. John Scandrett, son of Mr. Charles Scandrett, Merchant in Bristol, England, the testator bequeathed
£150 " as an acknowledgement many favors received from that
family," and to Mrs. Sarah Scandrett, daughter of Mr. John

Scandrett, he left £75. He appointed his friend, Mr. Thomas Turner, executor.

JOSEPH MURDOCK (JEREMIAH) was commissioned captain of the lower company of foot soldiers, King George County, Va., Sept. 14, 1752 (Cary Papers, folder 68). He was a Justice of the Peace of King George County, Virginia, 1759, 1762, 1766, probably continuously. His will bears date 11 October, 1769, and was proved in King George County March 1, 1770. The testator appointed Captain Edward Dixon, John Skinker and George Tankersley, gentlemen, his executors. He mentioned his children John, William, Sally (Sarah), Nelly and Jeany (Jean or Jane) Murdock. No abstract of this will is available to the present writer. The above information regarding it is taken from the Cary papers. Joseph Murdock married Mary Tankersley, who survived him and died in 1784. Her will bears date 5 October, 1783. It was proved (Cary Papers, folders 68) in King George County June 3, 1784. The testatrix mentions her sons, John and William, and her daughters, Sarah Riding and Jane Spencer. According to the tax list of 1782, Mary Murdock had 800 acres in King George County in that year. No other Murdock is listed as a landowner in the county. The family lands seem to have dwindled considerably.

JOSEPH and MARY (TANKERSLEY) MURDOCK had issue:

1. JOHN MURDOCK. He probably died s. p.
2. WILLIAM MURDOCK. Living in 1824. Issue, if any, unknown to the present writer.
3. SARAH MURDOCK. She married —— Riding and probably died s. p.
4. JANE MURDOCK. She married Lieut. William Spencer.
5. JOANNA MURDOCK. Mr. Cary's notes contain no mention of her. She married, in 1792 (Marriage Bond, King George County, Va.) William Storke Jett, Esq. (1763-1844), of "Walnut Hill," near Leedstown, Westmoreland County, Virginia. By him, she had issue a son, William Storke Jett, Jr., Captain, U. S. A., in the War of 1812, whose portrait, in uniform, formerly hung at "Walnut Hill," but was subsequently lost. I believe that he died s. p. He had a sister, I believe, of full blood, Elizabeth Jett, who married (in 1809) George Ashton by whom she had a daughter, Joanna Ashton, living in 1843. William Storke Jett married (2nd) Jane

Turner (d. May, 1819) a cousin of his first wife and daughter of Colonel Thomas Turner of "Smith's Mount," Westmoreland County, Va., and "Walsingham," King George County, and Jane his first wife, daughter of Colonel William and Peggy (Murdock) Fauntleroy.

The following record, while I quote from Burgess's "Virginia Soldiers of 1776 " (Vol. 1, p. 319) establishes the identity of Joanna Murdock, who married William Storke Jett:

" William Murdock who was joint heir at law with his sister Joanna Jett, of his sister, Jane Spencer, who was the relict and heir at law of Lieutenant William Spencer, who died intestate. The said Jane Spencer having also died intestate, Warrant No. 6628 was issued to the above named heirs at law, 1333 ⅓ acres to William Murdock as his moiety of 2660 ⅔ due to the representatives of William Spencer in part consideration of the said Spencer's services as Lieut. in the Continental Line. Issued July 26, 1824."

The " Silver Caudle Cup."

This heirloom, as noted above, was mentioned in the will of Major Jeremiah Murdock as a " piece of antiquity," which had belonged to his grandfather. If still in existance it would be a very valuable family relic indeed. It probably bore the family arms. We are informed that it was given to Jeremiah Murdock " being the youngest child." He bequeathed it to his son, Joseph Murdock, and it was his desire that it should be handed down in the family, probably from youngest child to youngest child. It is not improbable that Joanna Murdock was a posthumous daughter and therefore the youngest child of her parents. In the will of Colonel John Skinker, of King George County, who was one of Joseph Murdock's executors, the testator bequeathed to Miss Joanna Murdock the " gold watch and *silver cup* " he " bought of her father's estate." This will bears date January 19, 1784. In the will of William Storke Jett, dated March 1, 1843, the testator bequeathed to his granddaughter, Joanna Ashton, (who seems to have been the only living descendant of his first wife) " my silver ladle that was her grandmother's," but no mention seems to have been made of a silver cup. It is possible, however, that it may still be in the possession of descendants of the Murdock family.

Part II. Murdock of Maryland

Captain JOHN MURDOCK, brother of Major Jeremiah Murdock of Virginia, settled in Maryland, in Prince George's County, either in the last years of the seventeenth or the first years of the eighteenth century. "Murdock's Addition," adjoining "Essenton," was surveyed for him 26 March, 1703. At a date not ascertained he acquired 233 acres of a tract on Patuxent River called "Padworth Farm," out of which, on November 13, 1714, as heretofore noted, he made a deed of gift to his aforesaid brother, who in his will left it back to his nephew, William Murdock. On April 5, 1721, John Murdock acquired from Richard Taylor the residue of "Padworth Farm," 267 acres. He also owned parts of "Londee" and "Darby," also 479 acres part of "Essenton" purchased at various times. Captain Murdock styled himself a "Merchant." He died intestate at a date not ascertained.

JOHN MURDOCK married Katherine Barton, daughter of Colonel William Barton, Jr., (1662-1705) and Sarah his wife (married 3rd Colonel James Haddock) widow of Basil Waring and daughter of Richard Marsham (d. 1713) by Katherine ———— his first wife.

JOHN MURDOCK had issue, probably by Katherine Barton,[2]

[2] The author has mislaid his notes relative to the marriage of John Murdock and Katherine Barton. On the chart of Miss Rosa Steele, a member of Chapter I, Colonial Dames of America, I have made it appear that William Murdock was the son of Katherine Barton, and it is not improbable that when the chart was made I had more evidence for this belief than I have at present; but Richard Marsham in his will proved in 1713, refers to William Murdock, son of John Murdock, as his "kinsman," a rather singular way of designating a great grandson. On the other hand William Murdock signed the inventory of the estate of Marshall Waring (1732) as one of the "next of kin," and there is a recorded tradition in the Murdock family that a direct ancestor married a Barton.

William Murdock, his heir at law (only son?). William Murdock was born in Prince George's County, Md., in 1710 or thereabouts. In a deposition taken in 1744 he gave his age as forty-four. (Chancery Record, I. R. No. 4, p. 564) He died October 17, 1769, at his seat near Queen Anne's, Prince George's County. Obituaries appeared in the *Annapolis Gazette* and in the *Gentleman's Magazine,* London. According to a " debt-book " of Price George's County, bearing date 1753, Mr. Murdock was then in possession of 2662 acres of land in the county, including the whole of " Padworth Farm." William Murdock was High Sheriff of Prince George's County in 1740. He served as a burgess for that county from 1749 until his death in 1769.

WILLIAM MURDOCK married (1st) Anne Addison, daughter of Colonel John Addison of " Oxon Hill," Prince George's County. Mrs. Murdock died October 25, 1753. William Murdock married (2nd) January 1, 1757, Margaret Dulany, widow of Dr. Alexander Hamilton, of Annapolis, and daughter of Daniel Dulany the younger (Cary Papers, folder 68).

By his first wife, Anne Addison, WILLIAM MURDOCK had issue (Cary Papers, folder 68):

1. JOHN MURDOCK, born 10 February, 1729 (died in infancy).
2. ADDISON MURDOCK, born 31 July, 1731 (s. p.).
3. JOHN MURDOCK (Colonel JOHN MURDOCK) born 10 May, 1733.
4. ANNE MURDOCK. She married Rev. Clement Brooke.
5. CATHERINE MURDOCK. She married Major Patrick Sim and died Nov. 29, 1771.
6. ELEANOR MURDOCK. She married Benjamin Hall.
7. MARY MURDOCK. Died unmarried.

By his second wife, Margaret Dulany, WILLIAM MURDOCK had issue:
1. REBECCA MURDOCK, who married Anthony Addison.

It would appear that all descendants of William Murdock who bear the name of Murdock are descended from his son, Colonel John Murdock.

The Reverend George Murdock

Tradition seems to be positive in asserting that the Reverend GEORGE MURDOCK and Captain John Murdock were very closely related. Mr. Cary was of the opinion that the former was the son of the latter. If this be true, George Murdock was not the child of Katherine Barton, but of an earlier wife. Mr. Cary records the tradition that George Murdock was ninety years old when he died.. This tradition is probably erroneous, because, if true, Mr. Murdock was over fifty years old when he was ordained. Another argument against the theory that he was the son of John Murdock is that William Murdock, because he fell heir to his father's land, must have been his father's eldest son, but George could not have been younger than William.

GEORGE MURDOCK was ordained a deacon in London on February 20, 1724. His first parish in America was Saint James Northam, Goochand County, Virginia. On December 26, 1726, he was appointed Rector of Prince George's Parish. Prince George's County, Md. (Rock Creek.) His will bears date 14 May, 1760, and was proved 14 March, 1761. In it he mentions his son, William Murdock, and his grandsons George, William, George Beale Murdock and Elisha Murdock. (Cary Papers, folder 68.) Mr. Cary was of the opinion that, in addition to his son William, he had a son Benjamin Murdock. According to Mr. Cary, the Reverend George Murdock married, circa 1728-9, Eleanor Sprigg, daughter of Thomas Sprigg (d. 1705) and widow of (1) John Nuthall and (2) Thomas Hillary. It does not appear possible that she was the mother of his children, but the identity of former or of later wives, if there were any, is unknown.

The author of this article desires again to call attention to the fact that Mr. Cary, whose ability and accuracy need no praise, did not have the opportunity to make extensive searches on the Murdock family in Maryland and Virginia records. To this fact maybe attributed any errors which he may have made. Full credit should be given to him for what he did accomplish.

NEALE FAMILY OF CHARLES COUNTY.

BY CHRISTOPHER JOHNSTON.

A pedigree published in the *Visitations of Bedfordshire* (Harl. Soc., xix, 43, 125, 185.) begins with

1. JOHN NEALE [1] of the County of Stafford, father of

2. THOMAS NEALE [2] of Ellesborough, in the county of Bucks. He married Emlyn daughter of —— Cheshire of Willington, in Shropshire, and had issue:—

> i. RICHARD NEALE [3] of Deane Co., Bedford; mar. Alice dau. and h. of Thos. Moore of Burton, in the County of Bucks.
> 3. ii. THOMAS NEALE of Yelden, Co. Bedford, second son.

3. THOMAS NEALE [3] of Yelden, Co. Bedford, second son of Thomas Neale of Ellesborough, married Goditha daughter of Richard Throckmorton Esq. of Higham Park, Co. Northampton, whose pedigree is given in the *William and Mary Quarterly* (Vol. iii, p. 46), and had issue:—

> 4. i. JOHN NEALE,[4] son and heir, of Yelden, Co. Bedford, and Wollaston, Co. Northants.
> ii. RAPHAEL NEALE.
> iii. JANE NEALE, mar. Henry St. John of Keyso, Co. Bedford.
> iv. MARGARET NEALE, mar. Nicholas Franklin of Thurslie, Co. Bedford.
> v. ALICE NEALE, mar. Robert FitzJeffrey of Mylton, Co. Bedford.

4. JOHN NEALE [4] of Yelden, Co. Bedford and of Wollaston, Co. Northampton, eldest son of Thomas Neale, was twice married. His first wife was Jane, daughter of Marlyon Ryve of Lysse, Co. Southampton. His second wife was Grace daughter of John Butler of Cotkenles (or Coytkenles), Co. Pembroke. By his first wife Jane, John Neale had issue:—

> i. GEORGE NEALE [5] son and heir.
> ii. KATHERINE NEALE.

John Neale had issue by his second wife Grace as follows:—

> i. JOHN NEALE [5] of Wollaston, Co. Northampton; mar. 1° Elizabeth dau. of George FitzGeoffrey, 2° Elizabeth dau. of Richard Conquest; had issue by both marriages.

ii. HENRY NEALE of Houghton, Co. Northampton, 1618; mar.
    Elizabeth dau. of Edward Lacon of Willey, in Shropshire.
5. iii. RAPHAEL NEALE of Drury Lane, London.
   iv. ELIZABETH NEALE.
    v. THOMAS NEALE.
   vi. EDMUND NEALE.
  vii. HENRY NEALE.
 viii. JANE NEALE.
   ix. GRACE NEALE.
    x. ELLEN NEALE mar. Stephen Dryden, of Bulwike, Co. North-
       ampton, brother to Erasmus Dryden.
   xi. FRANCES NEALE mar. Robert Freeman of Whitton and Hough-
       ton, Co. Huntingdon.
  xii. MARGARET NEALE, mar. . . . . Cromer.

5. RAPHAEL NEALE [5] " of Drury Lane in London " married,
according to the Visitation pedigree, " Jane widow of ——
Forman Docter of physsick " and the *Genealogist* (New
Series, vol. vii, p. 31) has the entry: " 9 July 1612, mar-
ried with License, Raphael Neale and Jane Forman." In
another reference to this Raphael Neale, he is styled " of
Wollaston." " 13 April 17 James I. (1618), William Rowe
Gent. enters recognizance to appear and answer for his part
in an affray recently fought with drawn swords between
him and a certain Raphell Neale of Wolleston, Co.
Northampton, gentleman " (*Middlesex Records* II, 145).
Raphael Neale and Jane his wife had a son:—

6. i. JAMES NEALE [6]; b. 1615; d. 1684.

6. JAMES NEALE,[6] son of Raphael and Jane Neale, was, according to the Visitation pedigree, " 3 yere old 1618," and
was therefore born in 1615. He came to Maryland about
1636 or 1637. 19 June 1641, James Neale, Gent., demands 1000 acres of land due him for transporting himself
and five servants into the Province " since the year 1635 "
(Land Office, Lib. ABH, fol. 95; *Md. Hist. Mag.*, vi, 200),
and he appears upon record as living in Maryland in 1638
(*Md. Archives*, iii, 78), so that he must have arrived in
the Province between 1635 and 1638. In accordance with
his entry of rights, mentioned above, he received a warrant
for 1000 acres which he assigned to Thomas Hebden. But
he had received a special warrant from Lord Baltimore,
dated at London 25 July 1641, and by the terms of this
warrant he received a patent, dated 31 October 1642, for
a manor of 2000 acres " to be called Wolleston Mannor,
with Court Leet and Court Baron " etc. (*Md. Hist. Mag.* vi,
201-202). This manor, situated in what was later Charles

County, was long the principal residence of the Neale Family. The fact that James Neale called his Maryland manor "Wollaston," is a strong indication of his descent from the Northamptonshire family, and it may be pretty safely assumed that he was the son of Raphael Neale of Drury Lane, London, and of Wollaston, Co. Northampton, mentioned in the Visitation pedigree. In 1684, James Neale leaves by will "to the poor of St. Giles' Parish, near London, £5—to be sent to Mr. Henry Varrin." This undoubtedly refers to the Parish of St. Giles-in-the-Fields, then and for some time thereafter on the outskirts of London, and it was evidently James Neale's former residence. Drury Lane passes directly through this parish, and it can thus be shown that both Raphael Neale and James Neale were residents of the same London parish. Taken in connection with other points, this bit of evidence would seem to leave little doubt of the identity of James Neale of Maryland with James Neale "3 yere old 1618," the son of Raphael Neale of Drury Lane, London, and Wollaston, Co. Northampton. It should be noted that James Neale of Maryland had a grandson Raphael Neale, and that the name occurs in later generations. In 1642, James Neale was sent to Boston with two pinnaces, commissioned by Gov. Calvert to buy mares and sheep. He arrived in Boston September 1st, but failed in his object, having his money in drafts on Lord Baltimore, not then negotiable on account of the war in England. One of the pinnaces was so rotten and worm-eaten that it had to be abandoned (Neill's *Terra Mariae,* pp. 73-74). James Neale was commissioned, 15 April 1643, a member of the Council of Maryland (*Md. Archives,* iii, 131). In January 1643/4, he was indicted for aiding in the escape of Richard Ingle and his ship, the Reformation (*Md. Archives,* iv, 232) and, 11 February following, he was suspended from the Council for not filing an answer to the indictment (ibid. 250). He filed his answer, however, four days later (15 February), and the suspension was vacated and all proceedings against him stopped on the 12th of March (*Md. Archives,* iv, 252, 258). 18 November 1643, he was appointed one of the Commissioners of the Treasury for the Province of Maryland (*Md. Archives,* iii, 140) and 18 September 1644, he was again commissioned Councillor (ibid. 159). Between this last date and the year 1647 he returned to Europe, leaving his father-in-law Benjamin Gill, as his attorney and representative (*Md. Archives,* iv, 332, 365, 500). During his absence from the Province he resided in Spain and Portugal, where he was engaged in commerce, and was also employed in various affairs by the King and the Duke of York (*Md.Archives,* ii, 90). In 1660 he was the agent of Lord Baltimore at Amsterdam to protest against the settlement of the Dutch upon the Delaware (*Md. Archives,* v, 414-415). 9 January 1659/60, .Lord Baltimore issued a special order, reciting that whereas Capt. James Neale, formerly an inhabitant of Maryland, has been absent from the province for some years, and now desires to return with his family, there to reside and inhabit, he is to have full liberty so to do, as also to possess such lands as he has a right to, and to enter and trade freely in any port in Maryland (*Md. Archives,* iii, 386). He returned to Maryland in 1660 and, 20 July of the same year, was appointed commander in chief of an expedition to expel the Dutch from Delaware Bay, but the expedition was not considered advisable by the Council, and was therefore deferred until further orders from Lord Baltimore (*Md. Archives,* iii, 427-428). James Neale qualified as a member of Council 12 October 1661 (*Md. Archives,* iii, 434), and sat during the ensuing year, the last Council meeting he attended being 9 April 1662 (ibid. 448). He is not included in the writ issued 20 July 1663 (*Md. Archives,* i, 460). He represented Charles county in the Assembly 1665-1666 (*Md. Archives,* ii, 8, 10). In 1683, he was appointed one of the Commissioners for laying out towns and ports in Charles County (*Md. Archives,* vii, 611). In 1666, he petitioned for and obtained the naturalization of his children Henrietta Maria, James, Dorothy, and Anthony Neale, born of Anne his wife during the time of his abode in foreign parts (*Md. Archives,* ii, 90). His wife Anne was the daughter of Benjamin Gill of Charles County. Capt. James Neale of Charles County died in 1684, leaving a will dated 27 November 1683, proved 29 March 1684 (Annapolis, Lib. 4, fol. 40). In it he leaves " to my sons James and Anthony Neale," all those tracts of land, negroes &c. which I have formerly given them. To my grandson Raphael Neale, all that 100 acres of land I bought of Arthur Turner in Charles County. To my grand-children Roger, James, and Dorothy Brooke, personal estate, and I appoint my son-in-law William Boarman to oversee it. To my grand-daughter Jane Boarman, personal estate, and I appoint her father William Boarman to oversee it. To my grandson James Lloyd, 5000 lb. tobacco. To Mr. Michael Foster, Mr. Massey, and Mr. Hobart, 3000 lb. Tobacco. To the poor of St. Giles' Parish, near London, £5. to be sent to Mr. Henry Varrin. To my daughter Henrietta Maria Lloyd, personal estate, &c."

The will of Anne Neale of Charles County, widow of James, is dated 28 June 1697, and was proved 3 June 1698 (Charles Co., Lib. A. no. 2, fol. 175). Bequests to grandson Henry Neale; grand-daughter Mary Neale; granddaughter Elizabeth Neale; sons Anthony and James Neale; my grand-children, the children of Mr. William Boarman. Capt. James Neale and Anne (Gill) his wife had issue:—

 i. HENRIETTA MARIA NEALE,⁷ b. 27 March, 1647; d. 21 May, 1697 (epitaph at Wye); mar. 1° Richard Bennett, Jr. (d. 1667), son of Gov. Richard Bennett of Va., 2° Col. Philemon Lloyd (d. 1685); see *Magazine*, i, 73-75.

7. ii. JAMES NEALE of Wollaston Manor, Charles Co.—d. 1727.

 iii. DOROTHY NEALE, mar. Roger Brooke (b. 20 Sept., 1637; d. 8 April, 1700) of Calvert Co.

8. iv. ANTHONY NEALE, of Charles Co., b. 1659; d. 1723.

 v. JANE NEALE, mar. William Boarman (b. 1654; d. 1720) of Charles Co.

7. JAMES NEALE ⁷ of Wollaston Manor, Charles County, was the eldest son of Captain James Neale and Anne (Gill) his wife. He was born during the sojourn of his parents in Europe—perhaps about 1650—and was naturalized by his father in 1666 (Md. Archives, ii, 90). James Neale was twice married. His first wife to whom he was married in 1681, was Elizabeth daughter of Col. William Calvert, Secretary of Maryland and grand-daughter of Gov. Leonard Calvert. 20 December 1681, is the date of the marriage settlement of James Neale, son of James Neale and Ann his wife (daughter and heir of Benjamin Gill deceased), and Elizabeth daughter of Hon. William Calvert and Elizabeth his wife (Prov. Court, Lib. P. L., fol. 884). In 1687, James Neale married his second wife, Elizabeth daughter of Capt. John Lord, of Westmoreland Co., Va. 28 November 1687, John Lord of Washington Parish, Westmoreland Co., Va., conveys land to James Neale of Wollaston, Charles

Co., Md., in consideration of a marriage to be shortly celebrated between the said James Neale and Elizabeth daughter of the said John Lord (Westmoreland Co., Va., Records). 27 May 1696, James Neale of Charles Co. Md., Gent., conveys to John Minor of Westmoreland Co., Va.:— 772 acres of land in the last named County, part of 1544 acres patented, 17 April 1667, to Capt. John Lord and William Horton, and which the said John Lord gave to the said James Neale in marriage with his daughter (Westmoreland Co., Va., Records). In 1702, James Neale conveyed to Mary his daughter by his first wife all the land received with Elizabeth Calvert as her marriage portion, showing that Mary was her mother's only child. 10 April 1702, James Neale of Charles Co., Gent., and Elizabeth his wife, convey to Charles Egerton of St. Mary's Co., Gent., who hath lately married Mary daughter of the said James Neale:—600 acres, part of a tract of 3000 acres, formerly in Charles, but now in Prince George's County, patented to William Calvert Esq. and the aforesaid 600 acres thereof given in marriage with his daughter Elizabeth, to the said James Neale (Pr. Geo. Co., Lib. A, 449).

The will of James Neale Senior of Wollaston Manor, Charles County, is dated 1 April 1725, and was proved 11 October 1727 (Annapolis, Lib. 19, fol. 246). It mentions testator's eldest son James Neale; second son Henry Neale; son Benjamin Neale; son William Neale (minor); wife Elizabeth Neale; daughter Mary Deacon, formerly Van Swearingen; daughter Mary Tawney; daughter Ann now wife of Edward Cole; daughter Margaret Neale; daughter Mildred Neale; wife Elizabeth, and sons Benjamin and William executors; daughter Elizabeth Neale (apparently deceased). Mrs. Elizabeth Neale died in 1734, surviving her husband some seven years. The will of Elizabeth Neale of Charles Co., widow, dated 7 January 1733, and proved 22 April 1734, is recorded in Charles Co. (Lib. AC no. 4, fol. 11). She mentions her son William and daughter Mildred Neale, who are constituted executors, with Mr. Edward Cole of St. Mary's Co., Gent., trustee; son Henry Neale; daughter Ann Cole; son Benjamin Neale; daughter Mary Tawney; daughter Margaret Egglin. Mrs. Neale was born in 1667. In a deposition made in 1733, "Madame Elizabeth Neale, widow of James Neale" gives

her age as 66 years (Charles Co., Lib. 37, fol. 335).
James Neale of Wollaston Manor and Elizabeth (Calvert)
his first wife had issue:—

    i. MARY NEALE, mar. 1º 1702, Charles Egerton, 2º Jeremiah
        Adderton (d. 1713), 3º Joseph Van Swearingen, 4º
        William Deacon.

By his second wife Elizabeth (Lord), James Neale of
Wollaston had issue:—

  9.   i. JAMES NEALE [8] of Wollaston, d. 1730.
10.   ii. HENRY NEALE, b. 1691; d. 1742.
11.   iii. BENJAMIN NEALE, b. 1702; d. 1745.
12.   iv. WILLIAM NEALE,—d. 1766.
      v. ANN NEALE, mar. 1715 Edward Cole, Jr. (d. 1761) of St.
         Mary's Co.; she d. 1768.
     vi. MARY NEALE mar. . . . . . Taney.
   vii. MARGARET NEALE, mar. . . . . . . Egglin (? Edelin?).
  viii. MILDRED NEALE.
    ix. ELIZABETH NEALE.

8. ANTHONY NEALE [7] of Charles County, son of Capt. James
Neale and Anne (Gill) his wife, was born in 1659, the year
before his parents returned to Maryland. His age is given
in depositions as 20 years in 1679 (Charles Co., Lib. 7, fol.
205); 53 years in 1712 (Lib. P. C., fol. 854); and 55 in
1714 (Lib. P. L., fol. 98). 7 March 1686/7, he was commissioned Lieutenant in the Charles County Militia (*Md.
Archives,* v, 539). Anthony Neale was twice married.
His first wife was Elizabeth daughter of William Roswell.
10 October 1681, articles of agreement were signed between
James Neale of Charles Co., Gent., and William Roswell
of said Co., Gent., in contemplation of a marriage between
Anthony Neale, son of the said James, and Elizabeth
Roswell daughter of the said William (Charles Co., Lib. 8,
fol. 132). The second wife of Anthony Neale was Elizabeth daughter of Col. William Digges. Her mother, Mrs.
Elizabeth Digges, widow of Col. William Digges, in her
will dated 13 September 1708, and proved 17 June 1710,
mentions " my daughter Elizabeth Neale," and appoints
" my sons Charles Digges and Anthony Neale " her executors (Annapolis, Lib. 13, fol. 96). Also Edward Digges,
son of Col. William, whose will, dated 10 April 1714, was
proved five days later, mentions in it his nephews Henry
and Edward Neale, his niece Mary Neale, and his brother
Anthony Neale (ibid. fol. 673). 13 November 1716, Anthony Neale of Charles Co. and his son Raphael Neale

convey to James Neale son of said Anthony and brother of
said Raphael, a tract of 400 acres called Neale's Gift
(Charles Co., Lib. 28, fol. 34).

The will of this James, styling himself "James Neale
Jr. of Charles County," is dated 28 February 1718/9, and
was proved 30 March 1719 (Charles Co., Lib. A. B. no. 3,
fol. 138). He mentions only his two brothers Roswell and
Raphael Neale, the latter being appointed executor. The
will of his father Anthony Neale is dated 12 November
1722, and was proved 12 July 1723 (ibid. fol. 166). It
mentions testator's son Raphael Neale; son Henry Neale
(minor) intending to be a priest; my four younger children,
viz: Edward, Charles, Bennett, and Mary; and my son
Roswell Neale.

Anthony Neale and Elizabeth (Roswell) his first wife
had issue:—

13.   i. RAPHAEL NEALE,[8] b. 1683; d. 1743.
14.   ii. ROSWELL NEALE, b. 1685; d. 1751.
      iii. ANTHONY NEALE, mentioned in will of Wm. Roswell, 1694-5;
           d. young.
      iv. THOMAS NEALE, mentioned in will of Wm. Roswell, 1694-5;
           d. young.
      v. JAMES NEALE, d. unmarried 1719.

By his second wife, Elizabeth Digges, Anthony Neale had
issue:—

15.   i. EDWARD NEALE, b. 1704; d. 28 Dec., 1760.
16.   ii. CHARLES NEALE, b. 1705.
17.   iii. HENRY NEALE, d. 1767.
      iv. REV. BENNETT NEALE, a priest, b. 3 Aug. 1709; d. 20 March,
          1787.
      v. MARY NEALE.

9. JAMES NEALE,[8] of Wollaston Manor, son of James Neale
and Elizabeth (Lord) his wife, was born about 1689, since
his parents were married in 1687, and his next younger
brother, Henry, was born in 1691. He was twice married,
but the name of his first wife does not appear. His second
wife was Jane daughter of William Boarman, and they
were married not long after 1720. In the latter year,
William Boarman made his will (Annapolis, Lib. 16, fol.
67) in which he mentions his daughter Jane Boarman, so
that she was not married at that time. The will of Mary,
widow of William Boarman, dated 20 February 1732/3,
proved 29 November 1733 (Annapolis, Lib. 20, fol. 842)
mentions "my daughter Jane Neale." The will of James

Neale dated 7 January, proved 8 March, 1730/1 (Charles
Co., Lib. AB no. 3, fol. 241) leaves Wollaston Manor to
his son James, who is under age; there are bequests to
testator's wife Jane and his daughters Jane and Mary Ann;
to his daughter Elizabeth he leaves "my land in St.
Mary's County which I had with my former wife her
mother"; all testator's daughters are under 16.

By his first wife James Neale had:—

    i. ELIZABETH NEALE.[9]

By his second wife Jane (Boarman), he had:—

    i. JAMES NEALE [9] of Wollaston, a minor in 1730.
   ii. JANE NEALE.
  iii. MARY ANN NEALE.

10. HENRY NEALE,[8] second son of James and Elizabeth
(Lord) Neale, was born in 1691. In a deposition made
in 1737, "Mr. Henry Neale of Charles County" gives
his age as 46 years (Charles Co., Lib. 38, fol. 427). He
married Mary daughter of John Gardiner of St. Mary's
County, and she married secondly John Lancaster who
died in 1760. In her father's will (1717) she is referred
to as "my daughter Mary Gardiner," showing that she was
not then married. Her brother Wilfred Gardiner mentions her in his will (dated 9 Sept. 1743, proved 6 June
1744) as "my sister Mary Lancaster"; and her mother
Mrs. Mary Slye—for she had married Gerard Slye in
1718 (Accounts, Lib. 1, fol. 311) — mentions "my
daughter Mary Lancaster" and "my granddaughter Mary
Neale Junior" in her will made in 1744 (Annapolis, Lib.
24, fol. 163). John Lancaster, who died in 1760, mentions "my present wife Mary Lancaster" in his will (Lib.
31, fol. 45), and his widow Mary Lancaster names in
her will, dated 16 September, proved 8 October, 1765
(Annapolis, Lib. 33, fol. 419) her children James, Gerard,
Richard, Teresa, Mary, and Henrietta Neale; her grandchildren William and Henry Gardiner; and her grand-
daughter Ann (no surname given). Henry Neale of
Charles Co. made his will 3 December 1742, and it was
proved 8 March 1742/3 (Annapolis, Lib. 23, fol. 50).
He mentions his wife Mary, and his children Richard
(to whom he bequeaths "Gill's Land"), Henry, James,
Garrett, Sarah, Mary, Teresa, and Henrietta Neale.

Henry Neale and Mary (Gardiner) his wife had issue:—

   i. RICHARD NEALE,[9] died 1772 leaving a will wherein he names his two children Henry and Mary Neale.

   ii. HENRY NEALE.

   iii. JAMES NEALE, died unmarried 1772, leaving will dated 1766, wherein he mentions his brothers Richard and Gerard Neale; sister Teresa Lancaster; brother-in-law Richard Brooke; and godson James Brooke.

   iv. GERARD NEALE, mar. circa 1768, Elizabeth widow of James Neale of Charles Co.

   v. SARAH NEALE.

   vi. MARY NEALE.

   vii. TERESA NEALE, mar. . . . . . Lancaster.

   viii. HENRIETTA NEALE.

11. BENJAMIN NEALE [8] of Charles County, son of James and Elizabeth (Lord) Neale, was born in 1702 and died in 1745. In a deposition made in 1737, " Mr. Benjamin Neale of Charles County " gives his age as 35 years (Charles Co., Lib. 38, fol. 427). His will dated 15 December, proved 28 January, 1745 (Annapolis, Lib. 24, fol. 307), mentions his son Bennett; son James; daughter Elizabeth Corry; daughter Mary Neale, half the tract given me by Mr. Richard Edelen; daughter Ann Neale; wife Mary executrix, with brother William Neale and brother-in-law Edward Edelen trustees. The wife of Benjamin Neale was Mary daughter of Richard Edelen (b. 1671; d. 1761) of Charles County who mentions in his will (proved 17 Dec. 1761) his grand-daughters Elizabeth Corry and Mary Lancaster, and his granddaughter Ann Neale daughter of Benjamin Neale. The will of Mary Neale of Charles Co., widow of Benjamin, is dated 24 February 1752 and was proved 14 March following (Annapolis, Lib. 28, fol. 293). She mentions her sons James and Bennett Neale; her daughters Ann and Mary Neale, and Elizabeth Corry; and her grand-child Mary Corry. Benjamin Neale and Mary (Edelen) his wife had issue:—

   i. BENNETT NEALE.[9]

   ii. JAMES NEALE.

   iii. ELIZABETH NEALE, d. 1798; mar. John Corry who d. 1772.

   iv. MARY NEALE, mar. . . . . . Lancaster.

   v. ANN NEALE.

12. WILLIAM NEALE [8] of Charles County, son of James and Elizabeth (Lord) Neale, died in 1766. His will, dated 29 October, 1765, was proved 10 June, 1766 and is re-

corded at Annapolis (Lib. 34, fol. 124). In it he names
his eldest son John Neale, who is appointed executor; his
second son Joseph Neale; his third son William Francis
Neale; his daughters Elizabeth, Mary, Ann, Mildred,
Catherine, and Sally; and " my sister Cole." The name
of his wife does not appear.

    i. JOHN NEALE.⁹
    ii. JOSEPH NEALE.
    iii. WILLIAM FRANCIS NEALE.
    iv. ELIZABETH NEALE, mar. Henry McAtee.
    v. MARY NEALE.
    vi. ANN NEALE.
    vii. MILDRED NEALE.
    viii. CATHERINE NEALE.
    ix. SALLY NEALE.

13. RAPHAEL NEALE [8] of Charles County, son of Anthony
and Elizabeth (Roswell) Neale, was doubtless named
for his great-grandfather, Raphael Neale of Drury
Lane, London. He was born in 1683, and died in
1743. His age is given in depositions as 49 in 1732
(Charles Co., Lib. 37, fol. 155), 59 in 1742 (ibid.
Lib. 39, fol. 425, 464), and 60 in 1743 (ibid. Lib.
39, fol. 663). He married Mary daughter of Baker
Brooke of St. Mary's Co., and Ann his wife daughter of
Gov. Leonard Calvert (see *Magazine,* i, 69-70, 184). She
survived him some twenty years, and died in 1763. The
will of Raphael Neale of Charles County, dated 20 July
1743, was proved 10 December of the same year (Charles
Co., AC no. 4, fol. 178). In it he bequeaths to John Lancaster the land he lives on for life, and after his death it is
to go to the heirs of my daughter Elizabeth Lancaster; testator makes bequests to his daughters Mary Taney, Henrietta Neale, Monica Digges, and Ann Thompson: " I desire
that what appears to be due to my grand-children the Hos-
kinses be fully paid, including what Mary Hoskins, now
Mary Boarman, hath already had " etc.; my grand-children
Ann Hoskins, Mary Boarman, Raphael Taney, John and
Joseph Lancaster; my wife executrix. The accounts etc.
show that his wife's name was Mary. The following document from the Charles Co. Records (A. I., part 2, fol.
359) throws much light on Raphael Neale's family. 26
June, 1755, Partition of Wollaston Manor. John Lancaster, Jr., son and heir of Elizabeth Lancaster deceased,

eldest daughter of Raphael Neale deceased; Thomas Taney
who married Mary a daughter of Raphael Neale; Basil
Brooke who married Henrietta another daughter; Ann
Thompson, widow, another daughter; Edward Digges
married Monica, another daughter; Richard Bennett Boar-
man married Mary daughter of Bennett Hoskins and
Eleanor his wife, which Eleanor was also daughter of
Raphael Neale. The will of Mary (Brooke) Neale
widow of Raphael is dated 29 September 1760, and was
proved 24 May, 1763. She mentions her daughters Ann
Thompson, Mary Taney, and Henrietta Brooke; her grand-
children Eleanor Thompson, Raphael Thompson, Mary
Eleanor Combs, John Francis Taney, Raphael Brooke,
John Digges, and Eleanor Digges; and her sons-in-law
John Lancaster, Edward Digges, Thomas Taney, and Basil
Brooke.

Raphael Neale and Mary (Brooke) his wife had issue:—

    i. ELIZABETH NEALE,[9] dead in 1743; mar. John Lancaster.
    ii. MARY NEALE, mar. Thomas Taney, who d. 1762.
    iii. HENRIETTA NEALE, d. 1774; mar. Basil Brooke (b. 16 Nov.
        1717; d. 1761).
    iv. ANN NEALE, mar. James Thompson.
    v. MONICA NEALE, mar. Edward Digges.
    vi. ELEANOR NEALE, mar. Bennett Hoskins (d. 1734).

14. ROSWELL NEALE,[8] of St. Mary's County, second son of
Anthony and Elizabeth (Roswell) Neale, was born in 1685
and died 24 March 1751. His age is given as 59 years
in a deposition made in 1744 (Charles Co., Lib. 40, fol.
222), and his will was proved in 1751. He was twice
married. His first wife was Mary (d. 1716) daughter of
Capt. George Brent of Woodstock, Stafford Co., Va., and
Mary his second wife (mar. 27 March 1687; d. 20 March
1693/4) widow of Col. William Chandler (d. 1685)) and
daughter of Henry Sewall Esq. (*Va. Mag. of H. and B.,*
xii, 443). Her sister Martha Brent in her will dated 7
April, proved 12 May 1715 (Annapolis, Lib. 14, fol. 63),
mentions " my sister Mary Neale," and " my brother
Oswald (*i. e.* Roswell) Neale "; and her half brother
William Chandler of Charles Co., whose will, dated
19 August 1725, was proved 17 Sept. 1730 (Annapolis,
Lib. 20, fol. 75), names in it " William Neale (under 18)
son and heir of my deceased sister Mary Neale," and
" my nephew Henry Neale second son of my said sister."

He also mentions " my two nephews Mr. Edward Neale, and Mr. Charles Neale." The last two persons mentioned cause a certain difficulty. William Neale, a boy under 18, is expressly stated by William Chandler to have been the " son and heir " (*i. e.* the eldest son) of his deceased sister Mary, and Henry Neale was her second son. If now Edward and Charles were also her sons they could hardly have been much over 9 or 10 years old, and it seems strange that they should be styled " Mr." Besides they are not mentioned in the will of Roswell Neale or, indeed, anywhere else. One is inclined to suspect that William Chandler refers here to Edward and Charles sons of Anthony Neale, who may have been his nephews through some marriage or in some way not now apparent. They were certainly the sons of his first cousin Elizabeth Digges. The second wife of Roswell Neale was Elizabeth daughter of John Blakistone of St. Mary's County. Her brother Thomas Blakistone in his will, dated 10 November 1742, and proved 8 December following (Annapolis, Lib. 23, fol. 15) mentions his " sister Elizabeth Neale," his " brother Roswell Neale," and James, Bennett, and Raphael Neale sons of Roswell Neale. The will of Roswell Neale, of St. Mary's County, is dated 24 March, 1751 and was proved 7 May following (Annapolis, Lib. 28, fol. 61). He mentions his wife Elizabeth; his three daughters Anne wife of William Gibson, Mary Wheeler, and Elizabeth Neale. To my two sons William and Henry Neale each one shilling, and I confirm what I have already given them; my present wife; my four sons James, Raphael, Bennett, and Jeremiah Neale executors.

Roswell Neale had issue by his first wife Mary (Brent):—

18.   i. WILLIAM NEALE,[9] d. 1763.
    ii. HENRY NEALE, b. 1713; d. 23 Nov. 1766.

By his second wife Elizabeth (Blakistone), Roswell Neale had issue:—

    i. JAMES NEALE, d. 14 January, 1753.
    ii. RAPHAEL NEALE, b. 1724; d. 6 April, 1787; mar., 9 July, 1749, Elizabeth dau. of John and Eleanor Digges.
19.   iii. BENNETT NEALE of St. Mary's Co., d. 1771.
    iv. JEREMIAH NEALE, d. 19 Oct., 1808; mar. Jane —— and had issue.

v. ANN NEALE, d. 29 Nov., 1789; mar. William Gibson.
vi. MARY NEALE, mar. . . . . Wheeler.
vii. ELIZABETH NEALE.

15. EDWARD NEALE,[8] of Queen Anne's County, son of Anthony and Elizabeth (Digges) Neale, was born in 1704
and died 28 December, 1760. His epitaph at Bolingly,
near Queenstown, Queen Anne Co., states that he was
aged 60 years at his death, but this is probably erroneous
since, in a deposition made in 1742, he states his age as
38 years (Charles Co., Lib. 39, fol. 379) and this would
place his birth in 1704. Edward Neale was twice married.
His first wife was Mary daughter of Col. Henry Lowe of
St. Mary's County, and proof of the marriage will be found
in the *Md. Historical Magazine,* ii, 181, 281. There is also
a deed, recorded in Baltimore County (Lib. IS. no. K, fol.
91), and dated 27 August, 1729, conveying certain property
to John Digges, the grantors being:—Charles Digges of
Prince George's Co., Gent., and Susanna his wife, Henry
Darnall of Portland Manor, Anne Arundel Co., Gent.,
and Elizabeth his wife, Francis Hall of Pr. George's Co.
and Dorothy his wife—three of the heirs of Nicholas
Lowe Esq. late of St. Mary's Co. deceased—and Edward
Neale of Charles Co., Gent., who intermarried with Mary
(since deceased) another sister of the said Nicholas. It
will be observed that Mary wife of Edward Neale was
dead in 1729. His second wife was named Mary, but
her parentage is unknown. According to a notice in the
Md. Gazette of 1 Jan'y 1761, she died the day after her
husband—29 Dec. 1760. The enumeration of the heirs
of Richard Bennett shows that Edward Neale and his
first wife, Mary Lowe, had two daughters viz:—Eleanor
wife of Henry Rozer, and Mary (dead in 1749) wife of
Nicholas Digges (Test. Proc. xxxiv, 276 ff.). Edward
Neale's daughter Mrs. Martha Hall died, according to her
epitaph at Bolingly, 31 May, 1789 aged 50 years and 5
months so that she was born 31 December, 1737, and could
not possibly have been the daughter of the first wife, Mary
Lowe. The will of Edward Neale of Queen Anne Co.,
dated 22 Dec., 1760 and proved 6 Feb'y (Qu. Anne Co.
WHN. no. 1, fol. 243) mentions daughter Martha wife of
Francis Hall; daughter Eleanor wife of Henry Rosier;
grand-daughter Miss Eleanor Digges; sons-in-law Henry
Rosier and Francis Hall executors; a sum of money to Mr.

John Lewis of Cecil Co., to buy a piece of land to live on near the Congregation of the Catholics in Queen Anne County. By his first wife, Mary Lowe, Edward Neale had issue:—

    i. MARY NEALE,[8] dead in 1749, mar. Nicholas Digges (d. 1750).
    ii. ELEANOR NEALE, mar. Henry Rozer of Notley Hall, Pr. Geo. Co.

Edward Neale had issue by his second wife Mary —— :—

    i. MARTHA NEALE, b. 31 Dec., 1737; d. 31 May, 1789; mar. Francis Hall.

16. CHARLES NEALE,[8] son of Anthony and Elizabeth (Digges) Neale, was born in 1705. In a deposition made in 1744 he gives his age as 39 years (Charles Co., Lib. 40, fol. 223). Charles Neale married Mary widow of Clement Brooke, Jr. who died in 1732 (*Magazine* i, 286), and after 1744 removed to Frederick County. 6 October, 1769, Charles Neale of Frederick Co. and Mary, his wife, convey to George Fraser Hawkins of Prince George's Co., all the lands devised to said Mary by her former husband Clement Brooke, Jr., in trust for the use of Rachel Darnall, daughter of the said Mary, and not subject to the control of the husband of said Rachel Darnall, (Pr. Geo. Co., Lib. A. A., fol. 67).

Charles Neale and Mary his wife are said to have had issue:—

    i. ELIZABETH NEALE,[9] mar., before 1754, Leonard Smith of Frederick Co.
    ii. MARY NEALE, d. before 1786; mar. Benjamin Smith.
    iii. HENRIETTA NEALE, mar. Lawrence O'Neal of Montgomery Co.

17. HENRY NEALE [8] of St. Mary's County, son of Anthony and Elizabeth (Digges) Neale, is said in his father's will (dated 12 Nov., 1722) to be a minor, and he died in 1767. He married, in 1744, Ann daughter of Gerard Slye and widow of Francis Ignatius Boarman (b. 1701; d. 1743). Her father's will (1733) refers to her as " my daughter Ann Boarman; " in the will of Mrs. Mary Slye, widow of Gerard, (1744-45) she is called " my daughter Ann Neale; " and the will of her brother George Slye mentions " my nephews Mr. Wilfred Neale, and Mr. Henry Neale " (1773). The will of Henry Neale of St. Mary's County, dated 20 Nov., 1766 and proved 9 Feb'y, 1767 (Annapolis, Lib. 35, fol. 116) mentions testator's son Wilfred Neale;

my two daughters Mary Roach and Henrietta Ford; my
son Henry Neale.

Henry Neale and Ann (Slye) his wife had issue:—

   i. WILFRED NEALE.[9]
   ii. HENRY NEALE.
   iii. MARY NEALE, mar. . . . . Roach.
   iv. HENRIETTA NEALE, mar. . . . . Ford.

18. WILLIAM NEALE,[9] son of Roswell and Mary (Brent)
Neale, was under 18 years of age in 1725, the date of
his uncle William Chandler's will, so that he could not
have been born before 1707, and he could not have been
born after 1716, since his mother died in that year. He
was probably born about 1710, and he died in 1763. He
married Ann daughter of Leonard Brooke (d. 1718) and
Ann his wife daughter of Maj. William Boarman (*Magazine*, i, 184-185). The will of William Neale of Charles
County, dated 3 February 1763 and proved five days
later (8 Feb'y), is recorded at Annapolis (Lib. 31, fol.
1027). Testator desires to be buried near a tombstone
beside my two children at the Chapel Point; mentions
my son Raphael (minor); my youngest son Francis Ignatius Neale; my wife Ann Neale; my son Charles Neale;
my son Leonard Neale; my daughter Clare Neale; my
daughter Mary Matthews; my son-in-law William Matthews; my son William Chandler Neale.

William Neale and Ann (Brooke) his wife had issue:—

   i. REV. WILLIAM CHANDLER NEALE,[10] a priest, b. 1743; d. in
      England, 1799.
   ii. MOST REV. LEONARD NEALE, b. 15 Oct., 1746; d. 15 June, 1817;
      Archbishop of Baltimore, 1815-1817.
   iii. RAPHAEL NEALE, mar., in England, Sarah Howard, and left
      issue.
   iv. REV. CHARLES NEALE, a priest, b. 10 Feb., 1751; d. 1823.
   v. REV. FRANCIS IGNATIUS NEALE, b. June, 1756; d. 1838; a
      priest.
   vi. CLARE NEALE, mar. 1° Henry Brent, 2° George Slye.
   vii. MARY NEALE, mar. William Matthews.

19. BENNETT NEALE [9] of St. Mary's County, son of Roswell
and Elizabeth (Blakistone) Neale, died 27 Feb. 1771. His
wife Mary survived him over twenty years and died in
1792. The will of Bennett Neale, dated 23 February,
1771, and proved 23 May following, is recorded at Annapolis (Lib. 38, fol. 453). He mentions his eldest son
Benoni Neale; second son Charles Neale; daughter Eliza-

beth wife of Kenelm Cheseldyne; wife Mary; my five children, Sarah, Ann, Eleanor, Benoni, and Charles. The will of his widow, Mary Neale of St. Mary's Co., dated 6 Dec., 1790, proved 23 Jan'y, 1792, is recorded in St. Mary's County (Lib. JJ. no. 2, fol. 13). She mentions her daughter Susanna Greenfield; daughters Sarah, Ann, and Eleanor Neale; to my two sons Benoni (executor) and Charles Neale, equally between them, all my part of my grand-daughter Mary Cheseldyne's personal estate given me by her will. Witnesses: Edward Neale, Joseph Neale. The will of Mrs. Neale's grand-daughter, to which she refers, is as follows:—Mary Neale Cheseldyne of St. Mary's County, will dated 16 Oct. 1790, proved 7 March, 1791 (St. Mary's Co., Lib. JJ. no. 1, fol. 529). My grandmother Mary Neale, and my aunts Sarah, Ann, and Eleanor Neale; my uncle Benoni Neale executor. The "daughter Susanna Greenfield" named by Mrs. Neale, was the wife of Truman Greenfield who died in 1775. She is not mentioned in the will of Bennett Neale, so it is possible that she was the daughter of Mrs. Mary Neale by a former marriage.

Bennett Neale and Mary his wife had issue:—

   i. BENONI NEALE.[10]
   ii. CHARLES NEALE.
   iii. ELIZABETH NEALE, mar. Kenelm Cheseldyne, and had a dau., Mary Neale Cheseldyne, who d. in 1791.
   iv. SARAH NEALE.
   v. ANN NEALE.
   vi. ELEANOR NEALE.

APPENDIX.

ARMS. Two shields:—

1. Per pale sa. and gu., a lion passant guardant arg., a crescent for difference. *Neale.*

2. Quarterly 1 and 4, Az., 3 covered cups or, for *Butler;* 2. Gu., fretty arg., a fess az.; 3. Arg. 3 cocks in fess sa., armed gu.

CREST. A demi-lion arg., collared and chained sa.

Visitations of Beds., Harl. Soc. xix, 43, 125, 185.

BENJAMIN GILL, father-in-law of Capt. James Neale, came to Maryland in 1642. Cecilius Calvert, Lord Baltimore, in a letter of introduction to his brother Gov. Leonard Calvert, dated 16 Nov., 1642, directs that whereas this year John Pile and Benjamin Gill intend to transport themselves and others into Maryland, acting in partnership, they are to have 100 acres apiece for themselves, and land in proportion for others transported, according to the conditions of plantation bearing date 10 Nov., 1641 (Land Office, Lib. 4, fol. 543). 29 October, 1649, Benjamin Gill demands 1000 acres for transporting himself and others into the Province in the year 1642, and a warrant issued to lay out the land next to the land of Mr. James Neale (Land Office, Lib. A. B. H., fol. 27). 20 July, 1660, Lord Baltimore, in a letter to Philip Calvert directs that whereas Capt. James Neale married the daughter and heiress of Benjamin Gill, the said Capt. Neale is to have the land due said Benjamin Gill by warrant dated 1 Nov. 1642 (Land Office, Lib. 4, fol. 543). Benjamin Gill died, 22 November, 1655, at the house of Nicholas Causin at Port Tobacco, Charles Co., having made a verbal will whereby he left (among other bequests) a legacy of 500 pounds of tobacco to his cousin Robert Cole of St. Mary's Co., and directed that, in case his son-in-law James Neale did not return to Maryland, his estate should be divided by his executors (Prov. Court, Lib. S., fol. 126-130).

OWENS BIBLE RECORDS.

BIRTHS

Isaac Owens was born the 9th day of May 1729.

Priscilla Norman Owens was born the 7th day of April, 1736.

Joseph Owens was born the 4th day of February, 1780.

Anne Rutter Owens was born the 17th day of April, 1788.

Edward Thomas Owens was born the 24th day of August, 1809.

Isaac Burneston Owens was born the 26th day of December, 1811.

Priscilla Owens was born the 4th day of June, 1819.

Joseph Rutter Owens, son of I. B. and Priscilla Owens, was born the 20th day of February, 1839.

Ann Elizabeth, daughter of I. B. and Priscilla Owens, was born the 5th day of March, 1844.

Virginia Burneston Owens, daughter of I. B. and Priscilla Owens, was born the 23rd day of February, 1847.

Mary Burneston Owens, daughter of I. B. and Priscilla Owens, was born the 14th day of October, 1854.

Bessie Maynard, daughter of J. R. and Gertrude Owens, was born October 22nd, 1869.

Edward Thomas Owens, son of Jos. R. and Gertrude E. Owens, was born March 8th, 1871.

Alice Councilman, daughter of Jos. R. and Gertrude E. Owens, was born March 14th, 1872.

Maggie, daughter of J. R. and Gertrude E. Owens, was born September 3rd, 1873.

Isaac Burneston, son of J. R. and Gertrude E. Owens, was born on the 22nd of December, 1875.

Charles C. Owens, son of J. R. and Gertrude E. Owens, was born December 31st, 1877.

Christiana D. Owens, daughter of J. R. and Gertrude E. Owens, was born September 19th, 1879.

Arthur Burneston, son of Arthur and Mary B. Owens, was born December 25th, 1877.

Rodolphe, son of Arthur and Mary B. Owens, was born April 10th, 1880.

Edward Thomas, son of Arthur and Mary B. Owens, was born May 25th, 1883.

Gertrude Councilman, infant daughter of Arthur and Mary B. Owens, born October 5th, 1881; died October 6th, 1881.

MARRIAGES

Isaac Burneston Owens and Priscilla Owens, were married on the 14th of December, A. D., 1837, by the Rev. T. E. Bond.

Joseph Rutter Owens and Roberta V. Zimmerman, were married on the 24th day of November, 1863, by the Rev. Dr. R. Fuller.

Joseph R. Owens and Gertrude E. Councilman, were married on the 25th day of November, 1868, by the Rev. Dr. Lockwood.

Joseph Owens and Ann Rutter, were married on the 17th day of April, 1805, by the Rev. Mr. Hagerty.

Edward T. Owens and Susan G. Buck, were married on the 15th day of December, 1840, by the Rev. Sam'l Kepler.

Edward T. Owens and Maggie Muller, were married on the 11th day of November, 1858, by the Rev. R. L. Dashiell.

Arthur Owens and Mary B. Owens, were married on the 31st day of October, 1876, by the Rev. T. C. Gambrall.

Arthur Burneston Owens (son of Arthur and Mary Burneston Owens) and Emilie Ethel Bent, were married on the 6th day of November, 1909, at " Fernside " Alameda, California.

DEATHS

Isaac Owens, departed this life on the 21st day of September, 1805. Aged 76 yrs. 4 mos. 12 days.

Priscilla Norman Owens, wife of Isaac Owens, departed this life on April 28th, 1812. Aged 76 yrs. 21 days.

Ann Rutter Owens, wife of Joseph Owens, departed this life

on the morning of the 24th of January, 1844. Aged 55 yrs. 9 mos. 7 days. She was a devoted and affectionate Mother, wife and friend. She lived a Christian and died in the assured hope of a blessed immortality.

Joseph Owens, senior, departed this life on the 15th day of January, 1849. Aged 69 yrs. 11 mos. 11 days.

Annie E. Owens, daughter of I. B. and Priscilla Owens, departed this life on the 18th of April, 1891. Aged 47 yrs.

Isaac Burneston Owens, departed this life on the 23rd day of February, 1854. Aged 42 yrs. 1 mo. 28 days.

Virginia Burneston Owens, daughter of I. Burneston Owens and Priscilla his wife, departed this life on the 9th day of April, 1847. Aged 6 weeks.

Roberta, beloved wife of Joseph R. Owens, departed this life on the evening of the 7th of September, 1864. Aged 22 yrs. 3 mos. 7 days. She needs no tribute to her memory, as she will always live in the hearts of those who knew her.

Bessie Maynard Owens, departed this life the 28th of January, 1870. Aged 3 mos. Daughter of J. R. and Gertrude E. Owens.

Edward Thomas Owens, departed this life the 15th of April, 1871. Aged 5 weeks. Son of J. R. and Gertrude E. Owens.

Annie E. Owens, daughter of I. B. and Priscilla Owens, departed this life April 18th, 1891. Aged 47 yrs.

Mary B. Owens, daughter of I. B. and Priscilla Owens, departed this life June 16th, 1904. Aged 49 yrs.

Joseph Rutter Owens, son of Isaac Burneston Owens and Priscilla his wife, departed this life March 15th, 1909. Aged 70 yrs. 24 days. He needs no tribute to his memory, as he will always live in the hearts of those who knew him.

Edward Thomas Owens, son of Arthur Owens and the late Mary Burneston Owens, departed this life on the 16th day of December, 1921, in the 39th year of his age. May his soul rest in peace.

Arthur Owens, son of Nicholas and Mary D. Owens, departed this life on the 28th of July, 1927, in his 77th year.

Arthur Burneston Owens, son of Arthur and Mary Burneston Owens, departed this life on the 8th day of September, 1932.

Joseph Rutter Owens was baptized (by sprinkling) on the 15th day of December, 1840; by Rev. T. E. Bond.

Anne Elizabeth Owens was baptized (by sprinkling) 26th December, 1844, by Rev. Wm. Hamilton.

Virginia Burneston Owens was baptized (by sprinkling) on the 9th day of April, 1847, by Rev. Robert Cadden.

Mary Burneston Owens was baptized (by sprinkling) by the Rev. M. Morgan (date missing on entry).

Bible published by Joseph N. Lewis, owned by Mrs. Arthur Burneston Owens, Baltimore.

Copied by Ferdinand B. Focke.

OLD MARYLAND BIBLES.

These Bibles were inherited by Mrs. Maria Talbot Selby, 2066 Woodberry Avenue, Baltimore, Md., the grand-daughter of James Winchester Owings. Samuel Owings left the Bible to his grandson, James Winchester Owings. The book has been rebound, so there is no date of publication.

One of the family pages was of Urath Randall Owings, January 22, 1707. Mrs. Selby has a small picture in ink of Samuel Owings and Ruth Cockey; a large photograph of James Winchester Owings; a miniature of Urath Owings, daughter of Samuel, sister of James (who married 1st. Edward A. Cockey, son of Charles Cockey, 2nd. David Carlisle); a gold watch of Martha (wife of James W. Owings, given to her by Talbot Jones, her father, then to Elizabeth Owings, her daughter); three silver table spoons (wedding gift to James W. Owings), with initials on handles. Also a postal card dated Oct. 5, 1903, from Mrs. Mary E. Lattimer, requesting her to call at Towsontown to receive these above old bibles.

Copied Oct. 3, rechecked Oct. 12, 1934, by Ferdinand B. Focke.

URATH RANDALL OWINGS BIBLE.

Jany. 22, 1707.

Samuel Owings, son of Richard Owings, was born first of April, 1702, and married Jany. 1, 1729, to Urath Randall, daughter of Thomas Randall & wife.

Beale Owings, son of Samuel Owings and Urath Owings,

was born ninth day of August, eight o'clock at night on Sunday, 1731.

Samuel Owings, son of Samuel Owings and Urath Owings, was born 17 day of August at 12 o'clock Friday, 1733.

Rachel Owings, daughter of Samuel Owings and Urath Owings, was born the second day of May at about 12 o'clock at night on Sunday, 1736.

Urath Owings, daughter of Samuel Owings and Urath Owings, was born the 26 day June at 3 o'clock in the afternoon of Monday, 1738.

Thomas Owings, son of Samuel Owings and Urath Owings, was born on Saturday about 8 o'clock in the morning, Oct. 18, 1740.

Hannah Owings, daughter of Samuel Owings and Urath Owings, was born on Sunday about 8 o'clock in the afternoon, April 17, 1743, and died Jany. 26, 1745, about 3 o'clock in the afternoon on Friday.

Richard Owings, son of Samuel Owings and Urath Owings, was born 16 day of July, 1749, on Saturday about 8 o'clock in the morning.

Hannah Owings, 2nd. daughter of Samuel Owings and Urath, was born the 27 day of January, 1750, on Sunday about 12 o'clock at night.

Christopher Owings, son of Samuel Owings and Urath Owings, was born 16 day February, 1744, about 9 o'clock on Saturday morning.

Richard Owings, son of Samuel Owings and Urath Owings, was born on the 20 day of August, 1746, on Tuesday about 7 o'clock in the afternoon and died Sept. 28 on Monday about 11 o'clock at night, 1747.

Samuel Owings departed this life in the year 1775 in his 73 year of his life.

Urath Owings departed this life in the year 1792 in the 80 year of her age, 15 Day of December, 1793.

Rebecca Owings, daughter of Samuel Owings and Urath Owings, was born 21st. of October, 1756, on Tuesday about 4 o'clock in the afternoon.

RECORDS FROM AN OLD BIBLE.

Samuel Owings and Ruth Cockey, were married March 22, 1791.

Deborah Owings, born January 6, 1792.

Hannah Owings, born January 5th, 1794.

Urath Cromwell Owings, born July 3, 1796, married Edward A. Cockey; son of Charles.

A daughter still born, 1797.

William Lynch Owings was born Aug. 7, 1799.

A son still born.

Charles Ridgely Owings, born November 14, 1802.

A daughter still born.

James Winchester Owings, born September 5, 1806.

A daughter still born, January, 1808.

A daughter still born, March, 1809.

A son still born, May 7, 1811.

Mary Ann Owings, born April 6, 1814, married 3 September, sick on the 10th, died 2nd October.

Hannah Owings, born January 5, 1794.

Urath Cromwell Owings, born January 8, 1796, died June 1, 1886, in her 90th year.

William *Linch* Owings, was born August 7, 1799.

Charles Ridgely Owings, was born November 14, 1802; died in his 70th year.

James Winchester Owings, was born September 5, 1806; died in his 80th year.

Mary Ann Owings, was born April 6, 1814; died October 2nd; married 3rd September, was taken sick 10th, and died 2 October.

Ruth Owings, consort of Samuel Owings, died in 1834; aged 62.

James Winchester Owings, married Maria Jones, daughter of Talbot Jones, on the 3rd April, 1833.

Elizabeth Jones Owings, was born August 28th, 1834, daughter of J. W. Owings and wife Maria.

William Ballard, was married to *Hanah* Owings, by the Rev. Joshua Weles, 25 May, 1813.

James W. Owings and Maria Jones, were married on the 3rd April, 1833.

Samuel Owings, son of Richard Owings and Rachel, was born 1st day of April, 1702.

Samuel Owings, was marryed to Urath Randall, daughter of Thomas and Hannah Randall, the first day of January, 1730.

Bale Owings, son of Samuel and Urath, was born 9th May, 1731.

Samuel Owings, son of Samuel and Urath, was born 17 August, 1733.

Rachel Owings, daughter of Samuel and Urath, was born 2 May, 1736.

Urath Owings, daughter of Samuel and Urath, was born 26 June, 1738.

Thomas Owings, son of Samuel and Urath, was born 18 October, 1740.

Hannah Owings, daughter of Samuel and Urath, was born 17 April, 1743.

Samuel Owings, departed this life April 6, about 2 o'clock in the morning, 1775; aged 73 years.

William Cockey and Hannah Owings, were married June 30, 1771, by Rev. William Edmonson.

Ruth Cockey, was born 21 of June, 1772.

William Cockey, was born the first April, 1774, and departed this life 18 February, 1783, being the 90th year of his age.

Samuel Owings, son of Samuel and Deborah, was born 3rd April, 1770, and departed this life 26 day of July; aged 59 yrs in 1828.

James W. Owings, was born the fifth day of September, in the year of our Lord one thousand eight hundred and six.

Maria Jones, was born the 15 day of August, in the year of our Lord one thousand eight hundred and seven.

Married on the 3 April, 1833, James Winchester Owings and Maria Jones.

Elizabeth Owings, was born August 28th, in the year of our Lord one thousand eight hundred and 34; married on the 5th day of September, 1855, to Joseph Rutter Disney.

Samuel J. Owings, son of James W. and Maria Owings, died October 22, 1855, in his 19th year.

James W. Owings and Mary E. Leeson, were married 5 Sept., 1855; went to live at Townsontown, September, 1857.

James Winchester Owings, died on 30 day March, 1887, in the 81st year of his age.

JAMES WINCHESTER OWINGS BIBLE.

Mary Winchester Owings, was born on the 12 October, 1851; adopted by James W. Owings on the 21 day of April, 1858; died on 13 day of January, 1861, of Scarlet Fever.

Elizabeth Owings Disney, died 21 February, 1889, in the 55 year of her age.

Mrs. Maria Owings, consort of James W. Owings, died 9 April, 1837.

William Ballard, departed this life 24 December, 1818.

Edward A. Cockey, son of Charles Cockey, born 7/19/1791; died 8/21/1834; married Urath Cromwell Owings, his second cousin; married by Rev. Charles Austin.

Urath Cromwell Owings, married second David Carlisle.

William Owings and Sofia North Moale, married June 5, 1832.

Note: April 10, 1880, the remains of the following persons were removed by James W. Owings, Valley Farm, to the St. Thomas Church graveyard:

Samuel O. Winchester, son of George and Ann Winchester.

Sarah Winchester, daughter of George and Ann Winchester, 10 day January, 1825; aged 39.

Rebecca Owings, born on the 20 October, 1758.

Married on September 5, 1855, in Baltimore, by Rev. John G. Morris, Mary Elizabeth Leeson to James W. Owings, of Baltimore City.

Mary Winchester Owings, was born on the 12 October, 1851; adopted by James W. Owings on the 21 of April, 1858; died on the 13 January, 1861, of Scarlet Fever.

James W. Owings, 2nd wife, was the last one to be buried in the Owings Vault at St. Thomas Church. Charles T. Cockey had the key to the Vault and it was then sealed.

The Baptism certificate of Mary Elizabeth Owings, 19 Aug., 1860. James Winchester Owings, Jr., 19 Aug., 1860. By Rev. Bishop W. R. Whittingham.

Bible owned by

JAMES WINCHESTER OWINGS, of Govanstown, Maryland.

Printed, American Bible Society, N. Y., 1859.

Samuel Owings, departed this life in the year 1775, in the 73rd year of his age.

Urath Owings, departed this life in the year 1792, in the 80th year of her age.

Samuel Owings, son of Richard Owings and Rachel Owings, was born the 1st day of April, 1702; and married the first day of January, 1729, to Ruth Randall, daughter of Thomas Randall and Hannah Randall his wife.

Samuel Owings, was born the 31 April, 1770, and died on 26th day of July, 1828, aged 59 years; was married to Ruth Cockey on the 22nd day of March, 1791.

Deborah Owings, was born January 16, 1792; and died December 11, 1864.

Hannah Owings, was born January 5, 1794.

Urath Cromwell Owings, was born July 8, 1796; died June 1, 1886, in her 90th year.

William Linch Owings, was born August 7, 1799.

Charles Ridgely Owings, was born November 14, 1802; died in his 70th year.

James Winchester Owings, was born September 5, 1806; died in his 80th year.

Mary Ann Owings, was born April 6, 1814; died October 2, 1814.

Ruth Owings, consort of Samuel Owings, died in 1834; age 62 yrs.

James W. Owings, was married to Maria Jones, on the 3 April, 1833; died 9 April, 1837.

Elizabeth Jones Owings, was born August 28, 1834, daughter of J. W. and Maria Owings.

Samuel Owings, son of James W. and Maria Owings, was born February 28, 1837; died at age of 19 yrs. The school teacher whipped him or beat him so he never got over it.

James Winchester Owings, died on 30th day of March, 1887, in his 81st year.

Died in Townsontown, the 2nd of January, 1881, at the residence of James W. Owings, *Mary C. Bain*, daughter of the late Robert Bain, age 12 years.

Died in Townsontown, on the 30th day of June, 1875, at the residence of James W. Owings, *Isabella Mosheir*; was buried at Greenmount Cemetery, July 1, at 6 o'clock p. m.

Married in Baltimore, September 5, 1855, by Rev. John G. Morris, *Mary Elizabeth Leeson* of Baltimore, to *James W. Owings* of Baltimore County.

James Winchetser Owings, was Justice of the Peace, 1855; Assessor Taxes in Bulto. Co., 1876; appointed by Gov. Carroll; Vestryman Trinity Church, Towson.

James W. Owings, married Maria Jones, daughter of Talbot Jones, President of the Eutaw Savings Bank. They went to Evansville, Indiana, on their wedding trip, to live, where he lost his wife by death, also his fortune. He brought his two children back and gave them to his sister, Deborah Stevenson, to raise. Elizabeth J. Owings, Samuel J. Owings.

Newspaper cuts: Died 9th January, 1884, *James L. Wisner*, formerly of Townsontown, of consumption; 38 years of age, kept store at Stevenson, Greenspring Valley. Widow and child survive. He was a nephew of James W. Owings.

Samuel J. Owings, son of J. A. and Maria Owings, was born February 28, 1837.

Maria Owings, consort of James W. Owings, departed this life in Evansville, Indiana, April 9, 1837.

Samuel Winchester Owings, son of J. W. and Maria Owings, died October 2, 1855.

James W. Owings, younger son of Samuel and Ruth Owings, died at his home at Townsontown, on the 30 day of March, 1887, in his 80th year.

Samuel Owings, was born 31st April, 1770.

Samuel Owings, died 26 July in year 1828; aged 59 years.

Departed this life, *Ruth Owings*, wife of Samuel Owings, in the year of our Lord, one thousand eight hundred and 34.

Samuel I. Owings, son of J. W. Owings & Elizabeth, was born February 28, 1837.

THE DISNEY BIBLE.

Josiah Rutter Disney, married Elizabeth J. Owings, daughter of James W. and Maria Owings, December 7, 1854.

Josiah, was born December 30, 1831; died October 10, 1876.

Elizabeth J. Disney, was born August 28, 1834; died Feb. 21, 1889. Issue:

Maria Talbot Disney, born April 27, 1856; married ——— Lawson Selby, born 1852, 1/6.

Mary Ellen Disney, born May 11, 1860.

Charles Watkins Disney, born June 28, 1862; married ——— Georgie Ann Kelley; had three sons.

Lucy Owings Disney, born January 20, 1865; married ——— George M. Timanus; has sons Wilbur, Boyd; live in Florida.

Luther W. Disney, born June 8, 1867; died July 28, 1868.

James Winchester Owings Disney, born March 27, 1870.

Joseph O. Disney, born February 9, 1873; married ——— Minnie Thies; live in Laurel.

THE SELBY BIBLE.

Lawson L. Selby, was born January 6, 1852.

Maria Talbot Disney, was born April 27, 1856; married at Woodberry M. E. Church, October 4, 1877.

Bessie Selby, born July 8, 1878; died Nov. 3, 1879.

George Sherwood, born November 14, 1880; married Katharine Wagner.

Josiah Edward Selby, born September 18, 1882; married Carrie Hubbs.

Mary E. Selby, born August 1, 1885; died April 4, 1887.

Florence Selby, born December 21, 1888; died June 14, 1889.

Josiah's daughter, Ruth Selby, married Harry Rudasill.

Elizabeth Selby, married Henry Davis.

This typewritten copy was made November, 1934, from a manuscript copy made from the original by Mr. Ferdinand B. Focke.

PEARCE-LEVY BIBLE RECORDS.

These extracts are taken from two old family Bibles which formerly belonged to Judge Moses Levy (1756-1826) the distinguished Philadelphia jurist, and which are now owned by his descendant, Mr. J. J. Milligan, of Baltimore. Judge Levy married, June 21st, 1791, Mary Pearce of Poplar Neck, Cecil County, Maryland, to whom the " Tilghman Letters " now appearing in the *Magazine* were written.

One of these Bibles which contains only a few Levy entries, has wafered in it on a separate sheet, a number of Pearce entries relating to his own immediate family, made by Henry Ward Pearce, Sr. (1736-1828 ?). The other book is an interesting old Hebrew Bible the entries in which were evidently begun by Judge Levy's grandfather, Moses Levy (died 1728) of New York, and are a full record of this family for several generations. Owing to the great prominence of both the Pearces and Levys in the eighteenth and nineteenth centuries, the records seem worth publishing in full. As a number of the entries in the Pearce Bible are defective or incomplete, where possible the corrections or additions have been added in brackets from the register of Shrewsbury Parish, Cecil County, in which the Pearces lived.

MEMORANDA FROM PEARCE–LEVY BIBLES.

Benj. Pearce married to Margaret Ward, daughter of Henry ward, 1732. [July 31, 1734]

Elizabeth Pearce, first daughter of Benj. Pearce and Margaret
Pearce, his wife, born Sept. 29, 17— [Sept. 29, 1735]
Henry Ward Pearce, first son of the sd. Benj. and Margaret
Pearce, born 1736. [Dec. 6, 1736]
Benj. Pearce, second son of Benj. Pearce and Margaret, born
1739 [Apr. 13, 1739] and departed this life November
30 following.
Benjamin Ward Pearce, third son of the sd Benj. and Mar-
garet, born Sept. 15, 1740, died September 29, 1743.
William Pearce, fourth son of the sd Benj. and Margaret,
born April 8, 17[42] and departed this life Sept. 16, 1743.
Andrew Pearce, fifth son of the sd Benj. and Margaret, born
October 10, 1744, and was lost at sea in the year —
William Pearce, sixth son of the said Benj. and Margaret,
born Jany 14, 1748.
Mary Pearce, second daughter of the said Benj. and Margaret,
born 28th ———, 1750. [Aug. 28, 1751]
Margaret Pearce, wife of the above Benj. departed this life
June 30, 1755.
Benjamin Pearce, departed this life at Philadelphia, April 9,
1756. [Apr. 10, 1756 in his 45th year]

I, Henry Ward Pearce, son of the above Benjamin Pearce
and Margaret Pearce, his wife, was married to Anna Statia
Carrol, youngest daughter of Dominic Carrol and Mary his
wife, on the — January 16, 1759.
Henry Ward Pearce, first son of the sd. Henry and Anna Statia
his wife born June 23, 1760.
Mary Pearce, first daughter of the sd. Henry and Anna Statia,
born October 22, 1762.
Matthew Pearce, second son of the sd. Henry and Anna Statia,
born August 21, 1764.
Margaret Pearce, second daughter of the sd. Henry and Anna
Statia, born Aug. 21, 1764.
Benj. Pearce, third son of the sd. Henry and Anna Statia,
born April 12, 1770, and departed this life August 4,
1771.

Anna Statia Pearce departed this life April 20, 1770.

I, Henry Ward Pearce, was married to Rachel Relfe, youngest daughter of Tench Frencis and Elizabeth his wife, and Relict of John Relfe of Philadelphia, March 6, 1776.

Maria Pearce, daughter of the said Henry and Rachel, born ———— and departed this life November 22, following.

Benjamin Francis Pearce, son of Henry Ward Pearce and Rachel, his wife, was born Sept. 20, 1780.

The alteration in the birth of the above Benjamin Francis Pearce, was made on the discovery of the mistake by me, H. W. Pearce, and departed this life on the 12th of September, *1782* [1802], at Sea in latitude 43.2 N. Long. 48.24. No vices lurked beneath the mask of candour and sincerity, no meanness ever obscured the lustre of his generosity and benevolence. His thoughts and actions were alike regulated by Honor, truth and Liberality. His heart was a stranger to deceit and his tongue disdained to utter what his judgment disproved and the graces of his person but faintly reflected the innate Beauty of a heart replete with every endearing Quality. This tribute to his memory by his father Henry W^d. Pearce.

Henry Ward Pearce, son of Henry W. Pearce and Anna Statia, his wife, departed this life on the 26th of March 1805 at Col. Richd. Tilghman's in Queen Annes Co. and was there interred. He was an affectionate husband, a dutiful son and an honest man. Henry W^d. Pearce. Rachel Pearce departed this life on the 25th day of Jany, 1808, and was deposited in the family vault of her father.

21 June 1791. I Moses Levy of the city of Philadelphia, son of Sampson Levy, merchant, deceased, and Martha his wife, was married to Mary Pearce, daughter of Henry Ward Pearce, of Cecil County, in the state of Maryland Gentleman and Annastasia, his wife.

1 April, 1793. My daughter, Henrietta Maria was born, she was soon after Christened by Bishop White. In the

winter following she was innoculated for the smallpox and took it.

13 July 1798. My daughter Martha Mary-Anne Levy was born. She was soon after baptized by the Rev. James Abercrombie. She has also taken the smallpox by inoculation.

I was born on the 9th August 1756.

My wife Mary on the 23 O'ct^r 1762.

I am the son of Sampson Levy who died on the 23d March 1781.

My mother, Martha Levy died on the 24th March, 1807, aged 76 years.

My Father-in-law, Henry Ward Pearce was born on Sassafras Neck, in Caecil County, Maryland. He is the son of Benjamin Pearce and Margaret, his wife. His father Benjamin died in the city of Philadelphia, in 1756, as he informs me. His grandfather was also named Benjamin.

Margaret, the grandmother of my wife was the daughter of Capt. Henry Ward, who married an immediate descendent of Augustine Herman. Margaret died in 1765 Jan.

Annastasia Pearce, the mother of my wife was the daughter of Dominic Carrol. She died in the year   aged

Levy Family Hebrew Bible Records.

(Leaf from an older Bible wafered in.)

My Dear Childrin—or to whichsoever of your hands this may fall into.—

This Book is an Extraordinary Hebrew Bible with annotations or Commentaries on the Text—

It was a favourite Book belonging to My Dear Father & Contained the hand writing of him & My Dear Mother for whom I retain the Greatest Affection notwithstanding the long time they have been Dead—the former I knew little of but the Latter I well remember—in this Book is by them set down or wrote the names and Birth of all their Childrin, & the Death of Some of them by My Self—I therefore recommend this Book to your Most particular Care as an old family Bible with which I hope you will never part but to your latest posterity—as I regard it for My Parents Sake as well as its being an Extraordinary Book of itself—So I hope you will Show the Same regard & affection to My request that I do to My Parents memmorary—I am My Dear Child y^r Affectionate Father

Samson Levy

New Castle June 4, 1779.

Turn over

My Father Lived in the City of New York in wch place both him & my Mother Died the former in the year 1728—and the Latter in the year 1740—

My fondness for my Parents made me fond of what they Esteemed. I hope my childrin will have no less affection for me—

Samson Levy

Moses Levy had children by his first wife—Grace was his Second. Grace Levy's children 7.

Rachel born February ye 6, 1719. In London.
Miriem born February ye 5, 1720. In New York.
Hester born February ye 28, 1721. In New York.
Samson born August 19, 1722. In New York.
Hana born August   1723. In New York.
Binjamen born August   1726. In New York.
Joseph born June ye 1, 1728. In New York.

Miriam Levy Died in New York on Saturday Morning ye 4th February 1748/9.

Hannah Isaacs Died in New York Wednesday April 3^d 1751 or ye 5th day of Omer.

Nathan Levy Died in Philad^a. on fryday December 21st 1753 at 7 in ye morning.

Abigal Franks Died in New York Sunday May 16th 1756 in ye afternoon.

Isaac Levy Died in Philadelphia March 1777.

Joseph Levy Died in South Carolina.

This Departed this Life in her 46 year of age Mrs. Grace Hays ye 14th Octo^r 1740.

This day Departed her life Miriam Levy in New York aged 28 years February 4th 1748/9.

Wednesday April 3^d 1751 Hannah Levy or Hannah Isaacs Died in New York.

Fryday December 21st 1753 this Day at 7 o'clock in ye morning My Brother Nathan Levy Died in Philadelphia.

Samson Levy's Son Nathan Levy was born in Philad^a on thursday August 15th 1754 at 45 minutes after ten in the Evening which answers with ye 28th   or :5514 by our Acco^t & was Circumcised on ye fryday 8 days after by Jacob Moses of New York—

Samson Levy's Son Moses Levy was born in Philadelphia on Monday August 9th 1756 at aboute half An Hour After Two in the After noon which answers with ye

Samson Levy's Son Joseph Levy Was born in Philadelphia on Sunday December 10th 1758 at half an hour after Eleven in the forenoon it being the 10th Day of the Moon's age—and Died on Fryday March 28th 1760 at half an hour after three in the afternoon.

This day departed this life in her 46 year of her age Mrs. Grace Hays Thursday ye 14th October 1740.

My mother Grace Levy was Marrid to Mr. David Hays of New York who's wife She was at the time of her Death.

PLATER FAMILY.

1. GEORGE PLATER [1] of St. Mary's County, the immigrant ancestor of this family, was born about 1664 and came to Maryland before 1689. In a deposition made in 1694 he states his age as upwards of thirty years (*Md. Arch.*, xx, 179) and, 28 Nov. 1689, he signed the address of the Protestant inhabitants of St. Mary's County (*ibid.*, viii, 146). He was commissioned, 8 Jan'y 1691, Receiver of the Revenues for Patuxent River (Lib. WRC. no. 1, fol. 588). In 1691 he was Attorney General of Maryland (*Md. Arch.*, viii, 247–248) and held the position until 21 Oct. 1698 when he resigned and was succeeded by William Dent (*ibid.*, xxv, 13). On the following day he was commissioned Naval Officer of Patuxent (*ibid.*, xx, 528). He died in 1707 intestate, and letters of administration on his estate were issued 22 October in that year (Test. Proc., Lib. 19, fol. 257). He married, about 1694, Anne daughter of Attorney General Thomas Burford and widow of Robert Doyne. She subsequently married, in October 1708, John Rousby of Calvert County. George Plater and Anne (Burford) his wife had issue :—

2.   i. GEORGE PLATER,[2] b. 1695; d. 17 May 1755.
    ii. ANNE PLATER, living at Annapolis in 1738 (Chancery, Liber IR., no. 3, fol. 33 ff.).

2. GEORGE PLATER [2] of St. Mary's County was born in 1695 and died 17 May 1755. He was Clerk of the Upper House of Assembly 1725–1729 (*U. H. Journals*), Justice of the Provincial Court 1729–1732 (Commission Book), and Member of the Council of Maryland from 18 April 1732 until his death (*U. H. Journals*). The Annapolis *Maryland Gazette* announces, 20 March 1755, that "the Hon. George Plater Esq. is appointed Secretary of the Province in the room of the Hon. Edmund Jennings Esq. (now in England) who has resigned." The same newspaper, in its issue, of 22 May 1755, has the following obituary notice : "Saturday last died, at his Seat in St. Mary's County, aged upwards of Sixty, the Honourable George Plater Esq ; who was for many Years one of his Lordship's Council of State, Naval Officer of Patuxent, and Lately

285

appointed Secretary of this Province; a Gentleman eminent
for every social Virtue, which could render him truly valuable; He was as Horace says, ad unguem factus Homo. As
his Life was a Pleasure, so was his Death a Greif, to every
one that knew him." In the *Gazette* of 17 June 1729 we read:
" On Tuesday last (10 June) George Plater Esq ; was married
to Mrs. Rebecca Bowles, the Relict of James Bowles Esq; a
Gentlewoman of considerable Fortune." She was the daughter
of Col. Thomas Addison, in whose will she is mentioned as
"my daughter Rebecca Bowles," and she died between 1742
and 1749. The second wife of George Plater was also a
widow. " Last Monday (25 June), the Honourable George
Plater Esq ; of St. Mary's County was married to Mrs. Elizabeth Carpenter, Widow of Capt. John Carpenter, late of this
place deceased." (*Md. Gazette*, 28 June 1749). She died the
following year. Under date of 14 Nov. 1750, the *Gazette*
states : " We hear from St. Mary's County, of the death of
Madam Plater, the virtuous Consort of the Hon. Col. George
Plater, on the Thirtieth of October past; a Gentlewoman
much esteem'd when living, and whose Death is greatly lamented." By his second marriage George Plater had no issue.
By his first wife, Mrs. Rebecca (Addison) Bowles, he had issue
as follows, the dates of birth being derived from entries in his
own handwriting in a prayer book :—

 i. REBECCA PLATER,[3] b. 8 Aug. 1731; d. 22 Jan'y 1787; mar. 11 July
  1747, Col. John Tayloe of Mt. Airy, Member of the Council of Virginia.
 ii. ANNE PLATER, b. 31 Oct. 1732.
3. iii. GEORGE PLATER, b. 8 Nov. 1735 ; d. 10 Feb. 1792.
 iv. THOMAS ADDISON PLATER, b. 27 Oct. 1738 ; d. young.
 v. ELIZABETH PLATER, b. 7 Aug. 1742.

3. GEORGE PLATER[3] was born 8 Nov. 1735, and died at
Annapolis 10 Feb. 1792, being at the time of his death
Governor of Maryland (*Md. Gazette*, 16 Feb. 1792). He was
one of the Justices of St. Mary's County 1757–1771 (Commission Book) and represented the County in the Assembly
1757–1759 and 1762–1768 (*L. H. Journals*). He was a Member of the Council of Maryland 1771–1774 (*U. H. Journals*),
and was Governor of the State from 1791 until his death. He
married first, 5 Dec. 1762, Hannah, daughter of Hon. Richard
Lee (*Md. Gazette*, 16 Dec. 1762), and she died 20 Sept. 1763
leaving no issue (*ibid.*, 29 Sept. 1763). He married secondly,
19 July 1764, Elizabeth, only child of John Rousby of Calvert County and Anne his wife, daughter of Peregrine Frisby.

Mrs. Elizabeth Plater died 23 Nov. 1789 ; the dates of her marriage and death and of the births of her children are derived from the Plater prayer book record. George Plater and Elizabeth (Rousby) his wife had issue :—

  i. REBECCA PLATER,[4] b. 18 Sept. 1765 ; mar. Philip Barton Key.
 ii. GEORGE PLATER, b. 21 Sept. 1766 ; mar. 1°. 9 March 1795, Cecilia Brown Bond, who d. 23 Dec. 1796 ; 2°. 29 March 1798, Elizabeth Somervell.
iii. JOHN ROUSBY PLATER, b. 15 Oct. 1767 ; mar. Elizabeth Tootell.
 iv. THOMAS PLATER, b. 9 May 1769 ; was mar. 1°. —— —— ; 2°. Evelina Buchanan.
  v. ANNE PLATER, b. 23 Sept. 1772 ; mar. Uriah Forrest.
 vi. WILLIAM PLATER.

POE CHART

By FRANCIS BARNUM CULVER

John Poe
1698-1756
from Ireland to

1741
=

Janet McBride
1706-1802
America ca. 1743

Catharine Dawson
1742-1806

David Poe
1742-1816
Asst. Q. M. Gen'l
Rev. War

=

Elizabeth Cairns

William Clemm
1755-1809
Lieut. Md. Troops
Rev. War

1778
=

Catharina Schultz
1759-1835
of York Co., Pa.

George Poe
ca. 1743-1823
Capt. Md. Militia
Rev. War

1775
=

Bridget Amelia Fitzgerald Kennedy
1775-1844

David Poe, Jr.
. . . . —1811

=

Eliz. (——) Hopkins
. . . . —1811

Maria Poe (2)

=

William Clemm, Jr.
1779-1826

1804
= (1)

Harriet Poe
1785-1816

Jacob Poe
1775-1860

1803
=

Neilson Poe
1809-1884

Edgar Allan Poe
1809-1849

=

Virginia Clemm
. . . . —1847

Josephine Emily Clemm
1810-1889

1831
=

LINEAGE OF EDGAR ALLAN POE

AND

THE COMPLEX PATTERN OF THE FAMILY GENEALOGY

By FRANCIS BARNUM CULVER

The name Poe is a nickname. It came from the Anglo-Saxon *pawa*, old Norse *pa*, Latin *pavo*, "peacock." Middle English forms include *paw, pay, po,* etc. "As proud as a po" is preserved in an old English political song.

The Poe family of Maryland had an Irish provenance. Edgar Allan Poe, great-grandson of John Poe who came to America about 1743, was born in Boston, Mass., in 1809 and died in Baltimore, Md., at the age of forty years. During his nonage, he lived in Virginia. At the age of twenty-one his benefactor, Mr. John Allan of Richmond, procured for him a cadetship at the West Point, N. Y., Military Academy where he remained for a very brief period. He resided for a time in New York City and in Philadelphia, subsequently removing to Fordham, N. Y. His young cousin-wife Virginia (née Clemm) died in 1847. Edgar Allan Poe spent the summer of 1849 at Richmond, Va. He died, during a visit to Baltimore, on 7 Oct. 1849 and his remains are interred in the burial grounds of Westminster Presbyterian Church, an old cemetery belonging to the First Presbyterian Church of Baltimore.

Neilson Poe, a second cousin to Edgar Allan Poe, was born in Maryland, in the same year as the poet. He occupied a prominent place at the Maryland Bar. He, likewise, was devoted to literature and his life was characterized by "public spirit, courage, intellectual vigor, force and skill as a writer, and strength and fervor as a speaker." He befriended his unfortunate relative, the poet, in the latter's fatal illness and was with him to the end. Neilson Poe was the father of the illustrious John Prentiss Poe, Esq., of Baltimore. The latter had six sons, each of whom in turn entered Princeton University, where they became famous as outstanding members of the "Varsity" football teams. It was remarked that as soon as one of the brothers was graduated, another arrived to take his place on the Princeton team; which gave a foundation to the story that their father "was under contract to supply Poes for Princeton."

Edgar Allan Poe married his first cousin, Virginia Clemm. His second cousin, Neilson Poe, married Josephine Emily Clemm who was a half-sister of Virginia Clemm. The father of these two sisters, William Clemm, Jr., married (1) Harriet Poe, mother of Josephine Clemm and aunt of Neilson Poe. William Clemm, Jr., married (2) Maria Poe, mother of Virginia Clemm, step-mother of Josephine Clemm and aunt of the poet. The father of Edgar Allan Poe, David Poe, Jr., was cousin-germane to Jacob Poe, father of Neilson Poe. This is all very perplexing, of course, and only a diagram will serve to clarify the puzzle (see chart on page 420).

Price and Emory Families.

Contributed by Mrs. Charles H. Jones,
South Orange, New Jersey.

James Price and wife Margaret Tatnall (widow of Isaac
Starr), b. 1776, m. June 12, 1802, d. June 10, 1840.

Issue: (1) Joseph Tatnall, born May 27, 1805, died June 2, 1867, married
Matilda Louise Sanderson.
(2) John Hyland.
(3) James Edward.
(4) Mary Thomas.

Joseph Tatnall Price was born May 27, 1805. He married
Matilda Louise Sanderson, b. 1809, d. 14 Feb. 1894.

Issue: John Sanderson, born 1829, died Nov. 17, 1899, and 12 other
children.

John Sanderson Price, married Mary Emory, Oct. 13, 1859,
b. Oct. 24, 1831, d. Dec. 19, 1899.

Issue: (1) Thomas Emory, Dec. 22, 1860.
(2) Eliza Grant, Aug. 28, 1864.
(3) Matilda, unmarried March 24, 1866.
(4) John Sanderson, died in infancy.
(5) Isabel Emory, June 19, 1869—Joseph Woodley Richardson,
no issue.

Thomas Emory Price married Juliet Hammond, Dec. 22, 1886.

ISSUE: (1) Rosalie Emory, born May 7, 1888.
(2) Thomas Emory, born Sept. 29, 1889.
(3) Marie Adele, born March 29, 1891.

Rosalie Emory Price married Ernest Adams Gill, June 25, 1914.

ISSUE: (1) Ernest, born April 10, 1915.
(2) Rosalie Emory, born Sept. 4, 1917.

Marie Adele Price married Gray Hamilton Creager, Oct. 23, 1915.

ISSUE: Gray Hamilton, Oct. 31, 1916.

Eliza Grant Price married Charles Hyland Jones, Junior, Feb. 20, 1884.

ISSUE: (1) Charles Hyland (III), born Dec. 4, 1885.
(2) Isabel Emory, born Aug. 1888, died in infancy.

Charles Hyland Jones, III, Capt. A. E. F. Trans. Corps World War, b. 22 Feb. 1897, married Annis Amy Freemeyer, Dec. 17, 1910.

ISSUE: (1) Esther Annis, born Nov. 4, 1914.
(2) Ruth Grant, born March 3, 1918.
(3) Mary Evelyn, born January 19, 1922.

1. Arthur Emory,[1] immigrated to Maryland in 1666, d. circa 1699. His second wife was Anne Smith, d. circa 1692.

ISSUE: i. *Arthur*[2] the Elder, b. circa 1671, d. 1747.
ii. John, b. circa 1673.
iii. William, b. circa 1674.
iv. Anne, b. circa 1676.

2. Arthur Emory,[2] the elder married Anne Thomas, Nov. 20, 1721.

ISSUE: i. John, b. 1698, d. 11 Jan. 1761.
ii. Arthur, d. 1765.
iii. *Thomas*,[3] d. 1765.
iv. Anne.
v. Sarah.
vi. Juliana.
vii. Letitia.
viii. Gideon.
ix. James.

3. Thomas Emory married Sarah Lane. He died 1765.

ISSUE: 4. i. *Thomas Lane*, b. 1751.

4. Thomas Lane Emory,[4] 1st. Lieut. 4th Md. Battalion of The Flying Camp, b. 1751, d. 2 May, 1828, in Balto. Co., Age 77. Married Elizabeth Hopewell.

ISSUE: 5. i. *Thomas Lane, Jr.*,[5] b. 1789, d. Feb. 5, 1835.
   ii. Richard.
   iii. Mary.

Thomas Lane Emory Jr., United Volunteers of Baltimore War, 1812, married 13 June, 1815, Eliza Harwood Grant, b. 14 Aug. 1795, d. 15 June 1852.

ISSUE: i. Eliza Lindenberger, b. 15 Nov. 1816, d. 22 Nov. 1863.
   ii. George Lindenberger, b. 7 Dec. 1820.
   iii. Isabella Rebecca, b. 22 Mar. 1822.
   iv. Thomas Lane, b. 25 Nov. 1825, d. 28 Oct. 1863.
   v. Daniel Grant, b. 14 Feb. 1828.
   vi. *Mary*,[6] b. 24 Oct. 1831, d. Dec. 19, 1899, m. John Sanderson Price, Oct. 13, 1859.
      ISSUE: see Price Family.

Daniel Grant Emory borne 14 Feb. 1828, died Feb. 14 1885. Married 2nd wife Mary Virginia Fulton.

ISSUE: i. Edith Grant.
   ii. Lucretia Van Bibber mar. Fred. Sampson.
   iii. Mary.
   iv. Thomas Lane.
   v. Isabel Neilson.

Edith Grant Emory married William Brown Hanson.

ISSUE: i. William Brown.
   ii. Elizabeth.
   iii. Daniel Grant.
   iv. Summerfield Tilghman.

Mary Emory married Julien L. Eysman.

ISSUE: i. Julien L.
   ii. Emory.

Thomas Lane Emory, III, married Mary Campbell of Portland Ore.

ISSUE: i. Thomas Lane.
   ii. Jerry.
   iii. Elizabeth.

Isabel Neilson Emory married Floyd Keeler.

ISSUE: i. Mary mar. Charles Warwick.
  ii. Isabel.
  iv. Ruth.
  v. Edith.
  iii. Fenelon.

PRITCHETT FAMILY.

HENRY DOWNES CRANOR.

The Pritchett or Prichard family appears to have been of considerable antiquity in Wales, having an unbroken male descent from the Princes between Wye and Severn, a dynasty that lasted from Caradoc Vraich Vrais, A. D. 520 to the death of Bleddyn the last Prince, in 1190 (Cambrian Journal). *The Genealogist,* *N. S.,* Vol. 8.

JOHN PRITCHETT[1] (Chemist), the progenitor of the Dorchester county branch, was in Maryland in 1669 as is shown by the following records of land grants, rent rolls and wills. He was probably the son of John Pritchett who was a witness to a receipt given by Margaret Brent, January 21, 1647 (*Md. Arch.*, 4, 449), but as yet positive proof is lacking. John Pritchett the witness, died intestate in 1657. (*Ibid.*, 10, 552.)

In 1669 John Pritchett[1] bought land called "Apes Hill" at mouth of Hunger river, Dorchester county, containing 50 acres for 3000 pounds of tobacco. (Land Records Dorchester county. Old Book No. 3, p. 156.)

In 1697 John Pritchett (Chymist) purchased land from William Hopper, 50 acres more or less by patent, and another tract called *Longacre* and *Bettys Chance*, containing 110 acres on Charles Creek, another from Ferguson, Ship Carpenter, all that part called *Edinborough* containing 100 acres. (ibid.)

"This indenture made Eight day of June 1710, John Pritchett with Abigail his wife of the County of Dorchester in the province of Maryland of the one part and Henry Lake, Blacksmith of the other part, in same county. Witnesseth that the said John and Abigail Pritchett for and in consideration of the sum of six thousand pounds of Tobacco to them paid in hand for parcel of Land being partly belonging to a tract of Land called *Longacre* and partly to a tract of land called *Bettys Chance*. Beginning at a marked white oak standing near the head of Charles Creek being the bounded tree of the land of Richard Kendall and running from thence south west eight perches to a marked oak standing by Hunger River running from thence up the river bounded therewith Two hundred and eighty seven perches to the head of a small creek running up by a point commonly called Long Point and from thence north east to Charles Creek and from thence running up the Creek bounded therewith two hundred and Eighty seven perches to the first marked post containing one hundred and ten acres (110)."

Signed   John Pritchett
Abigail X Pritchett

(Ibid., Old Book, No. 6.)

The following entries may be found in the Rent Roll book of Dorchester and Somerset Counties, in the possession of Maryland Historical Society.

"50 Acres. Rent 0-2-0. Apes Hill surveyed 10 March 1672 for Richard Mockins the upper side of the Straights of Hunger River. Possest by John Pritchett A 16 by seven Downward.

"70 Acres. Rent 0-2-9. The Hope surveyed 17 Nov. 1677 for Timothy MacNamara on the east side Hungor River by the upper straights in possession of John Pritchett.

"150 Acres. Rent 0–4–5. Longacre surveyed 13 Aug. 1678 for Andrew Jusloy on the east side of Hungor river the west side of Charles Creek sold to John Pritchett by Henry Lack but not yet made over.

"50 Acres. Rent 0–6–0. Horseley down surveyed 28th Dec. 1679 for George Hopper on the south side of North East branch of Charles Creek in possession of John Pritchett.

"50 Acres. Rent 0–2–0. Ringwood surveyed 20th Feby. 1680 for John Pritchard on the north side of a small Bay called Rohoby Bay.

"100 Acres 0–4–0 qt. rent Ebenborough surveyed 29th April 1682 for George Ferguson on the West side in fox Creek in Ash Comos Marsh in possession of John Pritchett."

The date of John Pritchett's death is uncertain. His will made in 1711 and probated in 1723, bears the following note : "The above will was found in August 1723 among some papers and ordered to be recorded by the Court at Annapolis, A. A. Co., Md." The will mentions the following nine children by name and devises "Apes Hill," "Horsey Doron" [Horseley Down?], "Edinborough," and "Hope." To his wife Abigail he left her thirds only.

John Pritchett[1] and Abigail, his wife, had issue :—

    i. ZEBULON PRITCHETT.
    ii. EDWARD PRITCHETT, died 1760 or 1761.
    iii. JOHN PRITCHETT.
    iv. FURBECK or PLUMBECK PRITCHETT.
2.   v. LOTT PRITCHETT,[2] married Ann ——, died 1777.
    vi. PHILLIS PRITCHETT.
    vii. MARY PRITCHETT, married Henry Fisher.
    viii. JANE PRITCHETT, married —— Leake.
    ix. MARGERY PRITCHETT.

Zebulon, the oldest son, having received the home plantation "Apes Hill," the other sons divided the real property as required by the will, the division being recorded in Old Book No. 9, at Cambridge, Md. Lott Pritchett's part included two tracts "Donbar" and "Holydown" [Horseley Down?].

Edward Pritchett's will, made October 21st, 1760, probated February 6, 1761, is as follows :

To brother Lot Pritchett 8 pistoles and 1 English Guinea to Edward the son of Lot; to Edward, son of Plumback, 8 pistoles; to Evans Pritchet, 1 five pistole piece; to Henry Fisher, son of Henry Fisher, 1 four pistole piece; to William Prichet, son of

Zebulon, 3 English Guineas and one Buckaneer Gunn ; to Jates Pritchet, son of Plumback, one pistole ; to Thomas Prichet, son of Plumback, one English Guinea : to Benjamin Todd, son of Benjamin Todd, one English Guinea ; to Levin Prichet, son of Plumback, a tract of Land called the Hope Lying to the southward of bounded pine Tree not to be sold or mortgaged out of the name Prichet; to Arthur, son of Plumback, a tract of land called Ringwood being a part of my now dwelling plantation, also a tract of land called Prichets Meadow containing 40 acres also part of the tract of land called the addition to the Hope that lyeth to the northward of the bounded pine, being the devision between the two brothers Levin and Arthur and the heirs of their body—in case of their death without male issues these lands to go to Thomas Prichet ye son of Plumback and to his heirs ; to Edward Prichet, son of Edward, deceased, 2 Guineas to be paid when he is 16 ; all not before mentioned to brother Plumback and his 2 sons Levin and Arthur, in case one should die Jates to have one equal part. Executors Plumback and two sons Levin and Arthur.

In 1743 Lot Pritchett, Planter, purchased a tract of land called Northampton (L. R. Old book No. 14) ; and in 1747 he purchased from John Stafford a tract called "Stafford's Oughtlett," containing one hundred acres. (L. R. Old book No. 14, p. 176.)

Abstract of Lot Pritchet's will made February 18, 1775, probated March 27, 1777.

"I give and bequeath to my son John Pritchett one tract of land called Canterbury Contain ninety-seven acres of land more or less, likewise one tract of land called Pritchett's Desire contain Ten acres . . . . . part of a tract called Robin Hood . . . . .

"I give and bequeath to my son Edward Pritchett part of a hundred acres of land called Robin Hood, likewise one hundred acres of Land more or less part of a Tract of land called Staffords Outlott to him and his heirs forever. likewise one mare colt named Fly.

"My will and desire is that my wife Ann Pritchett shall have the use of my dwelling plantation during her life, likewise all my movable estate during her life, and after her death to be equally divided between all my children."

Lot Pritchett [2] (John [1]) and Ann, his wife, had issue :—

    i. John Pritchett.
3. ii. Edward Pritchett.

They had other children but their names were not mentioned in their father's will.

May 20, 1778, the Council of Maryland issued to Edward Pritchett a commission as second lieutenant in the lower battalion of Militia in Dorchester County (*Arch.*, 21, 97), and on the 19th of June, 1778, it was ordered that the Treasurer of the Western Shore "pay to John Smoot three Pounds eighteen shillings and nine pence for the use of Edward Pritchard." (*Arch.*, 21, 140.)

EDWARD PRITCHETT [3] (Lot,[2] John,[1]) by his will made August 18, 1795, probated at Denton, Caroline County, January 8, 1796, left to his widow Prissilla the whole of his estates during her widowhood ; to his sons Collison and Edward, his dwelling plantation (about 100 acres) and about 33 acres of "Staffords Outlet "; to his son Lot fifty-four acres of land being part of "Dawsons Hazards"; to his daughters Araminta, Ann, Nelly and Prissilla all of his moveable estate to be equally divided between them ; to Abraham Pritchett, "one horse colt and suit of good close and three months schooling if in case he stays with my wife till he is of the age of Twenty one."

Edward Pritchett [3] married Prisilla (Collison) Minner, (widow) the daughter of William and Prissilla Collison ; they had issue :—

4. i.   COLLISON PRITCHETT, born 1789, married Ann Peters.
   ii. EDWARD PRITCHETT, Jr., married 1st. Nancy Wheeler, Jan. 12, 1813 ;
        2d. Sarah Hubbard, July 28, 1825 ; 3d. Ritty Hignutt, Jan. 21, 1832.
   iii. LOTT PRITCHETT, married Hester Shanahan (widow).
   iv. ARAMINTA PRITCHETT, married William Vickers, Jan. 16, 1800.
   v.   ANN PRITCHETT.
   vi. NELLY PRITCHETT, married Andrew Shepherd, Jan. 18, 1810.
   vii. PRISSILLA PRITCHETT.

COLLISON PRITCHETT [4] (Edward,[3] Lot,[2] John,[1]) married Nancy or Ann Peters, daughter of James and Sarah (Hignutt) Peters, February 27, 1809. He died intestate on the "Stafford Outlet " farm where he was born, August 27, 1830.

Collison Pritchett and Ann (Peters) his wife, had issue :—

   i.   FOSTER PRITCHETT, born 1808, married Sarah Hickey of Kent County,
        Delaware, and had issue. Died Dec. 21, 1884.
   ii. ELIZA ANN PRITCHETT, born 1810 ; died in infancy.
   iii. PETER BAYARD PRITCHETT, born 1813 ; married Sarah Ledenham,
        January, 1848, and had issue. Died Nov. 3, 1880.
   iv. EDWARD PRITCHETT, born March 11, 1816 ; married 1st. Lavenia E.
        Palmetry, Feb. 20, 1842, and had issue ; 2d. Wilhelmina Tatman,
        Dec. 21. 1858, and had issue. Died July 30, 1883.

v. JAMES WESLEY PRITCHETT, born July 13, 1818 ; married 1st. Katharine Adams, Nov. 14, 1850, and had issue ; she died Feb. 3, 1872 ; married 2d. Mrs. L. E. Perdue, Feb. 2, 1878, and had issue ; she died Sept. 15, 1898. He was a merchant at Harpersville, Ala., until the breaking out of the Civil War, when he enlisted in the Confederate Army as 1st Lieutenant ; afterwards promoted to Captain ; died Oct. 13, 1891.

5. vi. SARAH ANN PRITCHETT, born Jan. 9, 1820 ; married Solomon Downes Cranor, Jr., May 24, 1842, and had issue ; died Oct. 16, 1900.

vii. WILLIAM HUGHLETT PRITCHETT, born May 9, 1822 ; married Susan Roe, Nov. 7, 1867, and had issue ; died Nov. 26, 1894.

viii. ARAH ANN PRITCHETT, born Feb. 14, 1824 ; married Aaron Conrad of Wilmington, Del., July 20, 1858, and had issue ; died June 28, 1882.

ix. THOMAS BIRCHENAL PRITCHETT, born April 20, 1827 ; married 1st. Margaret Moore, May 12, 1853, and had issue ; 2d. Sarah Goodrich, no issue. He died April 16, 1892.

x. COLLISON PRITCHETT, born April 12, 1830 ; died unmarried Jan. 2, 1903.

Figures 1, 2, 3, 4, 5, indicate the branch followed.

SOME OLD BIBLE RECORDS OF THE RIDGELY FAMILY OF MARYLAND.

FRANCIS B. CULVER.

John Ridgely's Bible, printed in the year 1792, is owned by Mrs. Mary Ridgely Palmer, of "The Highlands," Baltimore County, Maryland. Through the kind permission of her daughter, Miss Elsie W. Palmer, the following transcripts were made by the contributor.

RIDGELY.

John Ridgely, Son of Jno. & Mary Ridgely, was born on the 24th of November, 1764.

Mary Emmit, Daughter of Abraham & Mary Emmit was born on the 1st of November, 1769.

John Ridgely was married to Mary Emmit, on the 15th of January, 1791. And on the 15th of October following (each day happening on a Saturday) Edward Ridgely their son was born.

John Ridgely their son was born on the 20th of April, 1793 and departed this Life on the 29th of January, 1795, between 12 and 1 o'clock A. M.

John Ridgely (2nd) their son was born on Monday, 21st of September, 1795, about 5 o'clock & christened (on the 13th of March, 1797) John William, by the Revd Mr. Bend.

Laming Ridgely their son was born on the 25th day of April, 1797, about 6 o'clock P. M.

Mary Ridgely their daughter was born on the 5th day of May, 1799 (happening to be Sunday) about 12 o'clock in the Day.

Charles Washington Ridgely was born on Friday the 9th day of January, 1801, about 1 o'clock A. M. and died on Tuesday, October 2nd, 1849, about 3 o'clock A. M. aged 48 years 8 mo. 22 days.

Mary Ann Ridgely was born on Friday the 12th day of November, 1802 (between 10 & 11 o'clock A. M.).

Eleanor Dall Ridgely was born on Thursday the 18th day of October, 1804 (about 3 o'clock A. M.).

Eliza Sophia Ridgely was born the 22d of November, 1807, between three and four o'clock A. M. and died on the 2d July, 1808, about 5 o'clock A. M.

William Ridgely Son of Jno. departed this life on Saturday evening the 11th of March, 1797.

Mary Ridgely daughter of John and Mary Ridgely departed this Life Jany. 27th, 1802—12 o'clock in the day.

John Ridgely died on Sunday, 26th of June, 1814, about 6 o'clock in the morning, aged 49 years. 7 months. 2 days.

Mary Ridgely (wife of the above named John Ridgely) departed this life on the 9th of September, 1833.

Edward Ridgely, Son of John and Mary Ridgely departed this Life November 3d, 1852, about 6 o'clock in the evening, aged 61 years 2 weeks & 5 days.

Laming Ridgely son of John and Mary Ridgely departed this life January 21st (29th?) 1860 about 2½ o'clock in the afternoon, aged 62 years 9 months 4 days.

Jno. W. Ridgely & Isabella Folger were married November 17th, 1818.

Mary Sophia, Daughter of the said Jno. & Isabella, was born on Friday the 22d October, 1819 and departed this Life Monday July 21st 1862, aged 42 years 9 months.

Eleanor their Daughter was born on Monday, November 12th, 1821 & christened Eleanor Laming.

Edward their Son was born on Wednesday the 21st day of April 1824 and christened by the Rev. Daniel Hall July 20th, 1828.

John Charles their Son was born on Tuesday September 26th, 1826 and died Thursday May 24th, 1827.

Anna Bella their Daughter was born on Sunday the 11th day of May 1828, christened by Doctr. Dan'l Hall, Sunday July 20th, 1828.

Emily their Daughter was born on Wednesday February 9th, 1831.

John Frederick their son was born 10th June 1834 and died

Tuesday December 28th, 1852, aged 18 years 6 months 2 weeks 4 days.

FOLGER.

Frederick Folger & Isabella Emmit were married on Thursday evening, the 7th of March 1782, by Rev. D^r. P. Allison.

Mary Folger, Daughter of the said Frederick & Isabella, was born on Thursday the 6th of March 1783, and died on Wednesday the 21st of January, 1784.

Franklin Folger, Son of said Frederick & Isabella, was born on the 17th of November 1784, and died April 21st, 1785.

Frederick Folger, Son of said Frederick & Isabella, was born March 21st, 1786.

Sophia Maria Folger, Daughter of said Frederick & Isabella, was born March 23^d. 1788; died 4 April 1814.

Thomas Cole Folger was born June 28th 1790 & died August 13th, '19.

Isabella Folger, Daughter of said Frederick & Isabella, was born on 7th September 1792.

Isabella Folger, mother of the above mentioned children, died 7th September 1794.

Capt. Frederick Folger,[1] father of the above mentioned children, died on 5th August 1797.

THE FAMILY OF COLONEL JAMES RIGBIE [1]

By HENRY CHANDLEE FORMAN

The name of Rigbie was familiar in many a Maryland household a little over a century ago, but is now almost unknown. A short genealogical sketch of this family is given below.[2] The Rigbie family of England lived chiefly in Lancashire at Burgh and Layton, at Middleton Hall, at Hartoke Hall and at Preston Wigan. The name had various spellings, such as Rigby, Rigbey, Rigbye, Rigbee. Since the records of the Parish Church of Wigan, Lancashire, possess the names of many persons by the name of James Rigby from 1580 onwards, it is possible, but of course by no means probable, that this was the branch of the family to which James Rigbie of Maryland belonged. Burke gives the arms of Rigby of Wigan as, *Argent, on a cross patonce sable, five mullets, pierced, or*, and Fairbairn gives the crest as, *An antelope's head erased or, guttée-de-sang*.

1. JAMES[1] RIGBIE and his wife Katherine Ceely came to Maryland in 1659, and for his services to Maryland he received the patent the same year for " Rigby," one hundred and twenty-five acres in Arundel County situated on the north side of Severn River and on the south side of Broad Creek (Annapolis, Liber 2, folio 213; Liber 4, folio 484; Liber 5, folio 53; Liber 6, folio 15). He also owned " Persimon Point," four hundred acres in Baltimore County patented to him in 1659; eighteen hundred acres on Kent Island; " Rigby's Marsh," three hundred acres in Talbot County patented to him in 1664; and " Cabin Neck," forty-three acres in the same county in 1669. In 1681 he died at " about " the age of fifty. In his will, dated 8 November 1680 and proved 30 April

---

[1] This article continues the story of Colonel James Rigbie which appeared in the *Magazine* for March, 1941.
[2] There were other Rigbies in Maryland who were not connected with the family of Colonel James Rigbie, as far as is known. The earliest Rigbie in Maryland was probably the Reverend Roger Rigbie, of the Roman Catholic mission in Maryland, 1640 (*Md. Hist. Mag.*, I, 307). In Talbot County Arthur Rigby married before 1677 Ellinor (Morris) Orem (d. 1743), widow of Andrew Orem, and had Arthur Rigbie II, who died in 1767. By his wife Mary LeCompte Arthur Rigbie II had Philip Rigbie, Moses Rigbie, Jonathan Rigbie, Elizabeth Rigbie and Eleanore Rigbie. In Calvert County John Rigbie (d. 1754) married Catherine, daughter of William Gray, and left issue. In Somerset County Lewis Rigbie married before 1733 Elizabeth, daughter of Peter Elzey.

1681 in Anne Arundel County (Annapolis, Liber 2, folio 140), he bequeathed to his wife Katherine Rigbie " the plantation I now live upon containing about one hundred and thirty acres by survey " [" Rigby "], and likewise his " silver tackard " and his " Silver Candle Cup and Cover."

" Mr " James Rigbie was a member of the House of Burgesses in 1678-9 (*Archives*, VII, 4, 11, 25), and also of the Society of Friends. In 1678 he was appointed not only to " look after " the orphans of the West River Friends' Meeting, but to make a report of collections and disbursements for his own Severn Meeting. At a Men's Meeting in 1679 at George Skipwith's house at West River he submitted satisfactorily these financial reports. In 1680 he left a legacy of £4 to the Meeting at West River (Friend's Records, Park Avenue, Baltimore).

After his death his widow Katherine married Henry Constable (died 1696; Annapolis, Liber 7, folio 220), who left to his stepson James [2] Rigbie, the three hundred acres of " Untried Friendship " on the Patapsco River. Katherine (Rigbie) Constable died in 1698 in Anne Arundel County. Her will, dated 17 April 1698, proved 26 May 1698 (Liber 7, folio 353), mentioned her son James [2] Rigbie and grandsons James [3] and Nathan [3] Rigbie, the sons of James [2] Rigbie, and her granddaughter Catherine [3] Ceely, and her son John [2] Rigbie. Her son John inherited land on Patapsco River and a lot in the town of Annapolis.

James and Katherine (Ceely) Rigbie had issue as follows:

2.   I. JAMES [2] RIGBIE, born before 1662 (since he had not reached 18 in 1680); died 1700 (*of whom later*).

  II. John [2] Rigbie, died 1700. His will, dated 26 October 1700 and proved 23 November 1700 (Annapolis, Liber 11, folio 28), mentions his father-in-law Richard Galloway, his mother-in-law Elizabeth Galloway, his brother-in-law Benjamin Lawrence, his brother James (Rigbie), his wife Eliza (Galloway) and his daughter Eliza, who married Peter Galloway (Annapolis, Accounts, Liber 1, folio 12). He inherited from his father three hundred acres of land on Patapsco River " bought of Robert Harwood."

  III. Mary [2] Rigbie, died 1690 or 1691. Her will was proved 14 February 1691 (Liber 6, folio 15). By the terms of

her father's will she was to inherit the home plantation
("Rigby") after the decease of her mother. She mar-
ried John Ceely (died 1691) of Anne Arundel County,
and had a daughter Katherine Ceely (Annapolis, Wills,
Liber 2, folio 213), who was in her minority in 1691.
IV. Elizabeth² Rigbie.

2. JAMES² RIGBIE (*James*¹) was born before 1662 in Anne
Arundel County, and died there in 1700. He married some time
before 18 September 1698 Elizabeth Smith, who was baptized in
that year at the age of twenty-five (St. James Parish Records,
1682-1869, p. 309). She was spoken of as "Elizabeth Rigbie wife
of Mr. James Rigbye of St. James Parish in Ann Arunˡˡ County."
In her will, dated 3 November 1700 and proved 8 December 1700
(Annapolis, Liber 11, folio 11), she left all her lands, except one
hundred acres, to her three "Deare" sons, Nathan,³ James,³ and
Thomas³ Rigbie. Fifty of these hundred acres were reserved as
a "Glebe" for the use of the minister of St. James' Parish and his
successors.

Elizabeth (Smith) Rigbie was the daughter of Nathan Smith
(II) of Anne Arundel County and his wife Margaret, who *later*
became the wife of Thomas Tench. The Rent Roll, 1707, Anne
Arundel County, gives the tract "Jericho" as belonging to Thomas
Tench Esquire "for ye orphans of James Rigbie whose wife was
daughter and heir of Nathan Smith." Nathan Smith (II) died in
1684. His will, dated 15 April 1684 and proved 1 September
1684 (Annapolis, Liber 4, folio 50), left "Smith's Delight" to his
wife Margaret, and "Dan" and "Jericho" to his son Thomas
Smith.

Margaret Smith in 1684 or 1685 married secondly Thomas
Tench Esquire of Anne Arundel County. On 8 October 1685 there
is notice of Thomas Tench and Margaret his wife (daughter-in-
law of Nathan Smith [I]) and the "espowsalls betwixt them
celebrated" (Annapolis, Prov. Ct. Judg., Liber DSA, folio 164).
In his will, dated 29 March 1708, with no probate date (Annapolis, Liber 12, folio 232), Thomas Tench gave and devised "unto
Nathan³ Rigbie son of James² Rigby & Grandson to my first wife
all my lands within this province." The name of the second wife
of Thomas Tench is not known. The will of Margaret (Smith)

Tench, mother of Elizabeth (Smith) Rigbie, is dated 25 March 1684 and was proved 20 June 1694 (Liber 7, folio 16). In his day Thomas Tench was an important figure in Maryland. He was Justice of Anne Arundel County, appointed 4 September 1686 (*Arch.*, XIII, 242), and member of the Governor's Council from 1692 to his death in 1708 (*ibid.*, VIII, 305 *et seq.*). At a Council held in Annapolis on 26 June 1702 he was appointed President of the Council, and was acting governor from the time of Blackiston's sailing for England in July 1702 until the arrival of Seymour in 1704 (*ibid.*, XXV, x, 122). On 3 April 1708, " Mr Thomas Tench president of her Ma^tys Councill " was noted as " being dead " (*ibid.*, XXV, 240), and he was buried in St. James' churchyard on 7 April 1708 (St. James' Register, 1682-1869, 333, Md. Hist. Soc.).

Both James Rigbie and his step father-in-law Thomas Tench were vestrymen of St. James' Parish. In 1694 a meeting of the vestry was held at the house of the " Honble Thomas Tench "; and in 1701 a petition of the vestrymen was read " praying an Act of Assembly to Oblige and Impower Thomas Tench Esqr to lay out & Ascertaine one hundred Acres of Land given the Church of that Parish by Mrs Elizabeth Rigby & her Husband Mr James Rigby " (Vestry Proceedings, 1695-1793, 2, 3, 70, 111, Md. Hist. Soc.).

The will of James Rigbie, dated 8 November 1700 and proved 4 December 1700 (Annapolis, Liber 11, folio 12), mentioned his (step) father-in-law Thomas Tench, and three sons not twenty-one years old, viz.: Nathan,[3] James,[3] and Thomas [3] Rigbie; and his cousins Catherine Ceely, Thomas and Nathan Smith.

The children of James and Elizabeth (Smith) Rigbie were orphans, of whom Thomas Tench was the guardian (Annapolis, Accounts and Inventories, Liber 32A, folio 82). They were as follows:

3.　I. NATHANIEL [3] RIGBIE, born 28 April 1695; died after 1753 (*of whom later*).

　　II. James [3] Rigbie, born 4 January 1696, baptized 26 June 1698 (St. James Parish Register, 1682-1869, p. 299). By his wife Elizabeth he had a son Nathan [4] Rigbie, born 8 January 1742 in Harford County, Maryland (St. George's Parish Register and Vestry Proceedings, 1681-1799, p. 349). There is record of a James Rigbie in 1709

giving twenty pounds sterling " to be laid out in good
and godly books " to the parochial library of St. James
Church, and it is presumed that James [3] Rigbie was
meant.

III. Thomas [3] Rigbie. In 1702 a Thomas Rigbie had an un-
patented certificate for " Dallams Neglect," one hundred
and fifty acres in Harford County (Annapolis, Cert.
113).

3. NATHANIEL [3] RIGBIE (*James,*[2] *James* [1]), the eldest son, was
born 28 April 1695, and died after 1753 (Annapolis, Adm.
Accounts, Liber 33, folio 350). From the records it is evident that
he married thrice. His first marriage was on 28 January 1715; the
girl's name is unknown (St. James Parish Register, 1682-1869, p.
291). In 1717 he married second, Cassandra Coale, Jr., at West
River Friend's Meeting (West River Records, 1677-1771, Book A,
Minutes, pp. 98, 100; Annapolis, Adm. Accounts, Liber 12, folio
393). By 1753 he had married third, Sabina Rumsey of Cecil
County, whose will was dated 16 October 1776 and proved 18
September 1779 (Bel Air, Liber AJ#R, folio 8; Annapolis, Adm.
Acc., Liber 33, folio 350). She was the widow of William Rumsey
and the daughter of Colonel Benjamin Bladenburg (" Account of
Colonel Nathan Rigbie by Albert Silver " (1895), *q. v.*).

It was Cassandra Coale, Jr., who was the mother of the ten
children of Nathaniel Rigbie. She was the daughter of Philip
Coale and Cassandra Skipwith, his wife, and she died in 1745
(*Narrative*). Philip Coale was the grandson of Lieutenant Philip
Thomas, a Parliamentary Commissioner governing Maryland
(1657) under Oliver Cromwell, Lord High Protector of England
(West River Records, p. 24; Annapolis, Warrants, Liber, A, folio
318; Wills, Liber 2, folio 350; Deeds, Liber 3, folio 260; *Arch.,*
X, 493-4). Cassandra Skipwith was the daughter of George
Skipwith, of " Silver Stone " in Anne Arundel County (*Gen. Soc.
Penna. Publ.,* X; Rent Rolls, Anne Arundel County).

In 1708 Nathaniel Rigbie inherited from his step grandfather-
in-law Thomas Tench " Phillips Purchase," a two-thousand-acre
tract originally surveyed 15 July 1683 for James Phillips, and in
1707 possessed by Thomas Tench. The tract lay on the west side
of the Susquehanna River at the present site of Darlington, Har-

ford County. In 1728 Nathaniel Rigbie sold five hundered acres of this land to Gerard Hopkins, one hundred to Thomas Jones, and in 1731 two hundred to Henry Coale. In 1739 he gave a small part of it to the Quakers for the building of their meeting-house at Deer Creek (Rent Rolls, Baltimore County; *Maryland Historical Magazine*, XVIII, 14). Nathaniel Rigbie also owned with his brother James the following properties in Baltimore County: "Rigby," "The Range," "Covell," "Untried [United] Friendship," "Smith's Desire," "Pole Minineck"; and in Anne Arundel County, "Jericho," "Dan," "Burrage," "Smith's Delight," "Lords County," "Poplar Ridge." He owned singly, "Brownton" in Anne Arundel County, and "Indian Fields," "Rigbie's Chance," and "Rigbie's Hope" in Harford County. In aggregate, these lands contained approximately seven and a half thousand acres.

In 1735, Nathaniel Rigbie was lieutenant-colonel of "all the Horse Militia" in Baltimore County, which at that time included the present Harford County as well (Annapolis, Deeds, Liber HWS#M, folio 312). In 1736 he was justice of the peace of Baltimore County (*Arch.*, XXVIII, 98) and in 1738 high sheriff of Baltimore County (*ibid.*, XL, 591). In 1744 he, and his son Nathaniel Rigbie, Jr., were signers of the treaty with the Six Nations of Indians at Lancaster (*Virginia Magazine*, XVIII, 397; *Arch.*, XLIV, 122).

Nathaniel and Cassandra (Coale) Rigbie had issue as follows:

4.   I. JAMES [4] RIGBIE, born 1720; died 6 January 1790 in his seventieth year (*of whom later*).

II. Nathaniel [4] Rigbie, Jr., born 18 June 1723 (St. George's Parish, Harford County, Register, p. 332, Md. Hist. Soc.); died 1784 (Bel Air, Wills, Liber AJR#8, folio 18, dated 8 December 1783, proved 10 June 1784). He married on 27 August 1747 Sarah Giles, daughter of Jacob and Joanna Giles of Harford County (Annapolis, Wills, Liber 2, folio 244; Nottingham M. M. Records), and had two daughters, Hannah [5] and Cassandra [5] Rigbie. About 1767 Cassandra [5] Rigbie married Jeremiah Sheridine. On 4 June 1767 she was disowned by Deer Creek Friend's Meeting (Deer Creek Records, Book A). They had a child, Nathan Rigbie Sheridine (Annapolis,

Wills, Liber 40, folio 403). Nathaniel [4] Rigbie, Jr., at one time was acting sheriff of Baltimore County in place of his brother, Colonel James Rigbie (*Narrative*), and was interested with his father-in-law Jacob Giles in the iron business in Pennsylvania. He was for many years part owner and manager of Cumberland Forge near Stafford. Wilson Mill on Deer Creek was built by him. His death occurred in his sixty-first year ("Account of Colonel Nathan Rigbie," by Albert Silver (1895), *q. v.*).

III. John [4] Rigbie, died 1767 in Cecil County. His will was dated 20 July 1766, and proved 20 May 1767 (Annapolis, Liber 35, folio 392). He married Henrietta Rumsey and had but one child, Nathan [5] Rigbie, who did not long survive (Bel Air, Wills, Liber AJ#R, folio 8).

IV. Thomas [4] Rigbie. He operated an iron forge on Deer Creek in Harford County.

V. Philip [4] Rigbie. He was mentioned in the will of his brother John [4] Rigbie.

VI. Skipwith [4] Rigbie, died about 1754. He was deputy surveyor of Baltimore County, 18 March 1749, and surveyor of Baltimore County in 1750 and 1754 (*Maryland Historical Magazine*, XV, XXIV, XXVI).

VII. Elizabeth [4] Rigbie. She married before 1748 William Smith.

VIII. Cassandra [4] Rigbie. She married in 1780 a Mr. Webster.

IX. Ann [4] (Anna) Rigbie, born 1 March 1735 (St. George's Parish, Harford County, Register and Vestry Proceedings). She was admitted a member of Deer Creek Friend's Meeting on 2 November 1762, and she married in 1768 Samuel Willits (Deer Creek M. M. Records).

X. Susan [4] Rigbie. She married William Rumsey. It is possible that she may have been the Susannah Rigbie who married 19 July 1759 in Harford County a man by the name of John Deaver.

4. JAMES [4] RIGBIE (*Nathaniel,*[3] *James,*[2] *James* [1]), author of the *Narrative,* was born in 1720 and died in Harford County on 6

January 1790 (Census of 1776; *Narrative;* "Some Account of Our Esteemed Friend James Rigbie . . .," *MS* at Park Avenue Friends' Meeting; Nottingham Friends' Records, Births and Deaths, 1691-1883, p. 69). His will is dated 3 October 1788 and was proved 24 January 1791. (Bel Air, Liber AJ#R, folio 31). He married first, in 1741, Elizabeth Harrison, the daughter of Samuel and Sarah (Hall) Harrison of "Holly Hill," one of the best examples of colonial mansions in Southern Maryland. The date of Elizabeth Harrison's marriage is given in the *Narrative.* Samuel Harrison (died 1733) was the son of Richard Harrison, one-time "lord" of Abbington Manor (1709) in Calvert County, and his wife Elizabeth Smith. Sarah (Hall) Harrison was the daughter of Elisha Hall and his wife Sarah Hooper Winggfield, and her will, dated 25 November 1741 and proved 23 February 1742 (Annapolis, Liber 22, folio 421), bequeathed all her "wearing apparel to be Equally Divided" among her daughters "Sarah Harrison, Elizabeth Wife of James Rigby & Mary Harrison."

After the death of his first wife, Elizabeth (Harrison) Rigby, on 22 July 1759 (Nottingham and Deer Creek Records), James Rigbie married second on 5 February 1761 Sarah Massey (born 1734, died 1783; Deer Creek Marriages), widow of Aquilla Massey, and daughter of Isaac Bolton, of Bucks County, Pennsylvania ("Account of Colonel Nathan Rigbie," by Albert Silver (1895), *q. v.; History of Byberry*: Nottingham M. M. Records). In 1752 Sarah Massey was acknowledged a Minister among Friends.

According to the *Narrative,* James Rigbie in 1740 was chosen to succeed his father as high sheriff of Baltimore County. There is record of his service as sheriff of this county for 1742 (*Maryland Historical Magazine,* XX, 264) and for 1744 and 1745 (*Arch.,* XXVIII, 387; XLII, 482; XLIV, 49, 353, 360, 494; L, 233). It is probable that he was sheriff from 1740 to 1745. In 1735 he was appointed lieutenant colonel of all the horse militia of Baltimore County (Annapolis, Deeds, Liber HWS#M, folio 312), and in 1744 he was colonel.

James Rigbie and his wife Elizabeth joined the Nottingham Friends in 1744, and he was soon (1745) appointed on a committee for the Meeting. In 1747 he was an overseer, and in 1748 a member of a committee to built the Bush River meeting-house. On 18 September 1749 the Bush River Preparative Meeting recommended him as a minister. But, as indicated in the *Narrative*, he had occasional lapses which did not always give the Friends satisfaction. On 7th month, 1757, East Nottingham Friends' Meeting noted that " as James Rigbie has several times neglected to give an account of his care when appointed on Business by this meeting, Wm Cox is appointed to speak for him, that he may give reasons for such Neglect." In 1760 Rigbie cared for the meeting at Susquehanna; in 1765 he obtained a certificate from his own Deer Creek Meeting to visit the Yearly Meeting in Virginia; and in 1769 he obtained a certificate for the Eastern Shore of Maryland.

The children of James and Elizabeth (Harrison) Rigbie were:

I. Nathan [5] Rigbie, born 5 November 1742 (Nottingham Friends' Records); died March 1767 (Deer Creek Records).

II. Sarah[5] Rigbie, born 22 June 1744 (Nottingham Records). She married Samuel Wallace (Bel Air, Deed, 11 May 1805). Her father in his will left her his " large trunk."

III. Cassandra [5] Rigbie, born 15 January 1746; died before 16 February 1799 (Deer Creek Births and Deaths, 1761-1823, p. 6; Cecil M. M. Records, pp. 934, 1242, Md. Hist. Soc.). She married in January 1771 (Bel Air, Deed, 11 May 1805) John Corse (born 18 September 1729, died 16 February 1807), son of John and Susannah (Hanson) Corse (Course, Coursey) of " Hebron," near Betterton, Kent County, Maryland (Cecil M. M., p. 29), and had issue: Sarah Corse, who married Joseph Turner, Sr., of " Hebron," and had fifty-four great-grandchildren, including C. Y. Turner, the mural painter (see *The Turner Family* by the writer) ; John Corse, Jr., who married Susannah Coale; and James Rigby Corse who married Rebecca.

IV. Elizabeth [5] Rigbie, born 11 July 1748, died 29 April 1813 (Nottingham Records). She married 18 May 1769 William Coale, son of Skipwith Coale (Bel Air, Deed, 11 May 1805), and had issue as follows, Rigbie, Margaret, Susannah, Sarah, Elizabeth, James, William and Hannah Coale (Deer Creek Marriages, p. 13; Family Bible of James Coale of Darlington, Harford County).

V. Susannah [5] Rigbie, born 2 March 1751, died May 1826 (Nottingham Records). She married 8 October 1784 Joseph Brinton, of Lancaster County, Penna. (Bel Air, Deed, 11 May 1805; Deer Creek Marriages).

VI. Mary [5] Rigbie, born 15 October 1755, died January 1756 (Nottingham Records).

VII. James [5] Rigbie, Jr., born 27 December 1756 (Nottingham Records). His father's will (1788) left him the sawmill with twelve acres adjoining. In 1786 he bought a negro and was disowned by the Deer Creek Friends' Meeting. In 1796 he held a patent for twelve acres called " Rigbies Saw Mill " in Harford County (Annapolis, Liber IC#K, folio 675).

The children of James [4] Rigbie, and his second wife, Sarah Massey, were:

VIII. Massey [5] Rigbie, born 7 July 1762; died 16 March 1767 (Deer Creek Records). Another(?) Massey Rigbie appears to have signed the marriage certificate of Susannah Rigbie and Joseph Brinton in 1784.

IX. Ann [5] Rigbie, born 12 February 1764. She married 3 October 1783 Aquilla Massey, son of Jonathan and Cassandra Massey (Deer Creek Records; Bel Air, Deed, 11 May 1805). Under terms of her father's will, she received two hundred pounds sterling, two beds and two

X. Mercy [5] Rigbie, born 17 March 1770 (Deer Creek chests of drawers.
Records). She was not mentioned in her father's will (1788) and in the deed (1805) above.

THE ROCKHOLDS OF EARLY MARYLAND.

By Nannie Ball Nimmo

Robert Rockhold, seated upon 250 acres of land in Nansemund County, Virginia, before the 3rd of November, 1647, came into Maryland about 1649, and with Richard Bennett, John Lordking, William Pell, and others, settled in " Towne

Neck," in Anne Arundel County, where for mutual security they took up small tracts of land, to the intent they might seat close together. (C. P., f. 174, 203). (Founders, f. 9).

In August of 1651, Robert Rockhold and John Scotcher, also from Virginia, were granted 400 acres of land in Calvert County, on top of the Cliffts, the former having transported himself, his wife Sarah, and his two sons Robert and Thomas into the province to inhabit. This land was laid out for Robert Rockhold of Anne Arundel County, gunsmith, and John Scotcher, cooper, on the west side of the Chesapeake Bay adjoining the land of William Parker. (P. B. 4, f. 94.)

The connection existing between the two, does not appear. The latter died in 1659, his estate being administered upon by his widow Rose Scotcher. His inventory included a silver cup, silver dram cup, and a dozen silver spoons. (Test. Pro. 1[b], f. 56, 64.)

In September of 1659, the above 400 acres was surveyed for Robert and John Rockhold, sons of the first named Robert Rockhold, and called " Rockhould," and in 1672, was resurveyed for them, as the boundary trees had fallen down. (P. B. 16, f. 608).

It is assumed that Robert Rockhould, Sr. (the name so spelled after their coming into Maryland), died before July the 30th, 1666, at which time 90 acres of land on Scotcher's Creek, bounded south by Fullers, was laid out for John Rockhould, of Anne Arundel County, orphan, and was the land upon which he was then living. This land about 1706, was assigned by Thomas Rockhold, son and heir of John Rockhold, to Thomas Homewood. The tract was " Rich Neck." (P. B. 10, f. 235.) (A. A. Rent Rolls.)

Edward Rockhould, probably the son of Robert Rockhold, Jr., married in 1699, Mary, widow of John Nelson of Charles County, while Anne Rockhould, sister of John Rockhold, married Stephen White, who died in 1676, leaving a son by the same name. She married second, William Hawkins. Their son William Hawkins, Jr., was remembered by John Rockhould in his will of 1698. (Test. Pro. 17, f. 303.) (Wills.)

It is suggested, but not proved, that John Rockhould married Mary, the daughter of Lawrence Richardson, whose will of 1666, names his sons, John, Thomas, Lawrence, and his daughters, Sarah, Elizabeth, Mary, to whom he leaves some of his stock, called Violett, Mayflower, etc., while to his two young sons he leaves 280 acres of Upper Taunton, maybe the name of the tract taken from Taunton, Somerset, England, for in 1653, Elizabeth Smith, of Taunton, Somerset, in her will designates her kinswoman Elizabeth Richardson, then residing with her, as the wife of Lawrence Richardson, of Taunton. (Gleanings in Eng.)

Lawrence Richardson, Jr., made over his interest in the above-named tract to Joshua Dorsey, husband of his sister Sarah Richardson, while the remaining 120 acres was possessed by John Young, for Rockhold's heirs, this land in John Young's possession being mentioned in the will of Mary Rockhould in 1703. (Deeds, Rent Rolls.) (Warfield's Founders, f. 59.)

Nothing has been found to indicate that John Rockhould possessed land through his wife Mary, but 200 acres of Richardson's Folly, surveyed 1661 for Lawrence Richardson, was possessed 100 acres by Thomas Bland, 100 acres by John Rockhold. Richardson's Levell, 207 acres, John Rockhold bought from Thomas Richardson, and he later bought Burntwood Common. (Deeds, Rent Rolls.)

Other lands too, were taken up by him, and from a warrant of 583 acres granted him, 243 acres were surveyed into Rockhould's Purchase, on the north side of Curtis Creek, and 186 acres into Rockhould's Search, on the south side of the Patapsco River.

Both John Rockhould and his wife Mary were persons of education, their signatures written. In 1667 a warrant for 100 acres of land was granted John Rockhould, which warrant in 1669, he made over to William Hopkins, writing on the back of the warrant: " I John Rockhould do convey and make over to William Hopkins all my right to the within named warrant of land. Wit. Samson Waring. (P. B. 12, f. 358.)

Signed, John Rockhould."

In 1684, Henry Hemslay of Anne Arundel County, gent, assigned to John Rockhould, gent, Rockhould's Range, on the north side of the Patapsco River on Rich Creek. (Liber 22, f. 9.)

No positions of State seem to have been held by John Rockhould, but he appraised, with Thomas Blackwell and Henry Sewell, a number of estates, went security, and witnessed wills. He was closely allied with the Dorseys and the Howards, was a witness for Edward Dorsey in his suit against Thomas Bland and Damaris, his wife, and with John Rockhould, Jr., and Thomas Blackwell, witnessed the will of Joshua Dorsey in 1687.

Thomas Blackwell married Sarah (Richardson), the widow of Joshua Dorsey, and in his will of 1700 names his wife Sarah, her son John Dorsey, and Mary Rockhold.

John Rockhould and Thomas Blackwell appraised the estate of John Howard Sr., while in 1698, Thomas Blackwell and John Howard appraised the estate of John Rockhould.

Letters of Administration were granted Mary Rockhould on the estate of John Rockhould, as is noted, " Came Mary Rockhould, relict and administratrix of the last will of John Rockhould late of A. A. Co. deceased." The said Mary with John Howard and Lancelott Todd, were executors. Philip Howard swore the appraisers, John Howard, Jr., and Thomas Blackwell.

The will of John Rockhould, made 17 Feb. 1698, fails to mention his daughters, and John, Jr., living in 1687, is probably dead, and is not mentioned.

To son Thomas and heirs " Rockhould's Purchase " on Curtis Creek, Baltimore County, son Charles and heirs 207 acres of " Richardson's Levell " on Saltpetre Creek, Baltimore County, son Jacob and heirs 180 acres of " Rockhould's Search " on south side of the Patapsco River. To wife Mary, extrx., dwelling, plantation and " Burntwood Common " during life; to revert to son Jacob at her decease. To two cousins (nephews) Stephen White and William Hawkins, Jr., personalty. Sons desired not to sell land until reaching age of

30 years.   Test. Lancelott Todd, Nathan Dorton and Thos. Ward.

Mary Rockhould outlived her husband about five years. Even before his death she was troubled, for on January the 25th, 1698, she wrote about it to Edward Batson, Deputy Comm.

" Mr. Batson,

Sir

These are to request you not to give letters of administration to any one for Nat Dotton's estate until I have seen you or sent you a ring.

All in trouble from your friend to command Mary Rockhould." (Test. Pro. 17, f. 267.)

Her will made March 2nd, 1703, probated May 15, 1704, bequeaths to dau. Sarah Rockhould ten pounds, to sons Charles and Jacob Rockhould each ten pounds, to 2 daus. Susan Crouch and Elizabeth Tod 5 pounds each, to dau. Sebrah Rockhould a feather bed and furniture, to son Thomas Rockhould all my sheep. I give to Lance Tod all my shoe leather and goods coming in the fleets. I give Lance Tod my spaid Mare toads paying my debts. I give my son Lance Tod my tobacco made on my plantation last year and all that is on bord of the ship, with the rent of the said Land that John Young owes me and all other tobacco debts, sd Lance Tod to pay my debts with all, and all the Rent that shall be due in the next four years. 2 sons Charles and Jacob to live with my son Lance Tod until they arrive at the age of 18 years. Lance Tod to be whole and sole exec. Wit. Elizabeth Dunklose, Wm. Roper and Mary Parmer. (Elizabeth Dunklose written Elizabeth Dunkin in probate.) (Will Book 1, f. 14, Baltimore.)

Her administration bond by Lancelott Todd, William Cromwell, and William Cockey. May 15, 1704. Administration Bonds. C. H. Baltimore.

Thomas Rockhould married.

Charles Rockhould married Elizabeth Wright, daughter of Henry.

Jacob married.

Susannah Rockhould married first John Howard, son of Matthew and Sarah (Dorsey) Howard, second William Crouch.

Elizabeth married Lancelot Dorsey, son of Thomas of Anne Arundel County.

Sebrah married Frizzel.

Sarah married 1704 John Garner (At. A. Paris Reg.).

Their descendants are found in Anne Arundel, Baltimore and Harford Counties.

Samuel Greniffe in 1703, left personalty to Sarah Rockhould, James Crouch, and Maurice Baker.

SEWALL FAMILY.

CHRISTOPHER JOHNSTON.

A very full genealogy of the Sewalls of New England and of the English ancestors of the family is given in Massachusetts Historical Collections, 5th Series, vol. v, pp. xvi–xviii. It is based largely on the work of the distinguished genealogist, the late Col. Joseph L. Chester, and has been freely utilized in the present genealogy. See also *Magazine* i, 190.

1. WILLIAM SEWALL [1] or SHEWEL, who married Matilda daughter of Reginald Horne of Pikesley in Shropshire, is the earliest ancestor of this family that has as yet been traced. The fact of his marriage is set forth in the Horne pedigree entered at the Visitation of Shropshire in 1623 (Harleian Society, vol. 28, p. 260), and also at the Visitation of Warwickshire in 1619 (*ibid.* vol. 12, p. 343). William Sewall and Matilda (Horne) his wife had issue :—

2.   i. HENRY SEWALL [2] b. about 1544 ; d. 16 April 1628.
    ii. WILLIAM SEWALL, Vintner, Mayor of Coventry in 1617 ; will dated 29 June 1624, proved 11 Sept. 1624. He married Ann (probably Wagstaffe) who died 20 Dec. 1609 aged 46, and was buried at St. Michael's, Coventry. They had three daughters all living in 1624.

2. HENRY SEWALL [2] (*William* [1]) was born about 1544, died 16 April 1628 aged 84 years, and was buried in St. Michael's Church, Coventry. He was an Alderman of Coventry, and was Mayor of the town in 1589 and 1606. His will, dated 1 Sept. 1624, was proved 30 June 1628. An abstract is given in *Water's Genealogical Gleanings in England*, pp. 153 ff. In it he leaves a bequest to " my cousin John Horne," and appoints " my loving kinsman Reginald Horne gentleman," one of his overseers. A reference to the Horne pedigree, cited above, readily establishes the testator's relationship. Henry Sewall married, about 1575, Margaret eldest daughter of Avery Grazebrook of Middleton, Co. Warwick. She was born about 1556 and, dying in 1629 was buried in St. Michael's. In her will, dated 7 May 1628 she states that she is " aged 72 and upwards." The

will was not admitted to probate until 13 June 1632, though administration on her estate was granted 23 November 1629. An abstract is given in *Water's Gleanings*, p. 811.

Henry Sewall and Margaret (Grazebrook) his wife had issue :—

    i. HENRY SEWALL[3] of Coventry, bapt. at St. Michael's 8 April 1576, emigrated to New England and died at Rowley, Mass., in 1657. He married Anne Hunt and was the ancestor of the New England Sewalls.

3. ii. RICHARD SEWALL of Nuneaton, d. 1638 ; of whom further.

    iii. ANNE SEWALL, mar. before 1 Sept. 1624, Anthony Power of Kenilworth, Co. Warwick, gent. He d. in 1632. Her will, dated 15 Jan'y, 1633, was proved 1 May following. Abstract in *Water's Gleanings*, p. 810.

    iv. MARGARET SEWALL, mar. Abraham Randall of Coventry, gent., who d. s. p. before 1646. Her will, dated 4 May 1646, was proved 22 May 1646. Abstract in *Water's Gleanings*, p. 1415.

3. **RICHARD SEWALL**[3] (*Henry,*[2] *William*[1]) of Nuneaton, Co. Warwick, died in the latter part of 1638 and letters of administration upon his estate were issued 2 January 1638/9. He married Mary daughter of John Dugdale of Shustoke, Co. Warwick, and Elizabeth Swynfen his wife, and sister of Sir William Dugdale (b. 12 Sept. 1605 : d. 10 Feb. 1685/6) the celebrated antiquary and author. She was baptized 7 December 1597, and died about 1648.

Richard Sewall and Mary (Dugdale) his wife had issue :—

    i. RICHARD SEWALL[4] of Nuneaton, will dated 11 Aug. 1642, proved 29 April 1648 ; a surgeon in Cromwell's Regiment in the Civil War.

4. ii. HENRY SEWALL, Secretary of Maryland, d. 1665, of whom further.

    iii. SAMUEL SEWALL, a minor in 1648 ; living in 1664.

    iv. MARGARET SEWALL, b. 1615 ; d. young.

    v. MARY SEWALL, b. 1616 ; living in 1642 ; wife of -—— Dudley.

    vi. ELIZABETH SEWALL, b. 1608 ; mar. Edmund Seare, Notary Public ; living in 1648.

    vii. ANNE SEWALL, living in 1648.

    viii. PRUDENCE SEWALL, living in 1648.

    ix. SARAH SEWALL, living in 1648.

4. **HENRY SEWALL**[4] (*Richard,*[3] *Henry,*[2] *William*[1]) was a minor and an apprentice in 1642, the date of his brother Richard's will. In 1652, then residing at Corley, Co. Warwick, he petitions the Committee for Compounding in regard to an estate in Corley, belonging to him, worth £30 a year which had been sequestered in 1644 for the delinquency of his elder brother Richard, now deceased. Richard however came in "upon Truro articles" with his horses, arms and "surgeons tools," and served in General Cromwell's regiment as a surgeon, finally dying in the service (Calendar of Committee for

Compounding, 2965). In 1661 Henry Sewall removed with
his family to Maryland. A warrant for 2000 acres was
issued, 12 Sept. 1661, to Henry Sewall of London, Esq.
(Land Office, Lit. 4, fol. 615), and, 10 April, 1663, he
entered rights for himself, his wife Jane, his children Nicholas, Elizabeth, and Anne, and three servants, and received
a warrant for 300 acres (ibid. Lib. 5, fol. 251). 20 August
1661, " Henry Sewall formerly of London, England, but now
of Calvert County, Maryland " was Commissioned Councillor,
Secretary, and Judge of the probate of Wills for the Province (Md. Archives iii, 439), and he held these offices until
his death. In his will, dated 25 April 1664, he states that
he intends to sail for England during the current year, and
at a Council Meeting held 6 Sept. 1664, "Henry Sewall
Esq. being called was returned absent in England " (Md.
Archives i, 509). His will was proved 17 April 1665. He
married, in England, Jane, daughter of Vincent Lowe of
Denby in Derbyshire, and sister of Col. Vincent Lowe, Member of Council and Surveyor General of Maryland. She
married secondly, in 1666, Charles Calvert then Governor of
Maryland, later the third Lord Baltimore.

Henry Sewall and Jane (Lowe) his wife had issue :—

5.   i. MAJ. NICHOLAS SEWALL,[5] b. 1655 ; d. 1737 ; of whom further.
    ii. ELIZABETH SEWALL, mar. 1°. Dr. Jesse Wharton (d. 1676), 2°.
        Col. William D. Digges (d. 1697) ; she d. 1710.
   iii. ANNE SEWALL, mar. 1°. Col. Benj. Rozer (d. 1681), 2°. Col. Ed-
        ward Pye.
    iv. MARY SEWALL, b. 1658, d. 12 March 1693/4 ; 1°. Col. William
        Chandler (d. 1685), 2°. 22 March 1687, Capt. George Brent of
        Woodstock, Stafford Co., Va.
     v. JANE SEWALL, b. 1664 ; mar. Philip Calvert, brother of Cecilius
        Calvert, second Lord Baltimore.

5.   MAJ. NICHOLAS SEWALL[5], (Henry[4], Richard[3], Henry[2])
was born in England in 1655, and died in St. Mary's
County, Md., in 1737. He came to Maryland with his
father in 1661, when about six years old, and in a deposition,
made in 1722, gives his age as 67 years (Chancery, Lib.
P. L., fol. 758). On the 5th of February 1682 he and John
Darnall were commissioned Secretaries of the province of
Maryland and took the oath of office the same day (Md.
Archives, xvii, 130–131). This office which carried with
it a seat in the Council, Maj. Sewall held until 1689. In
1684 Lord Baltimore, being about to leave the Province for
England, appointed his young son, Benedict Leonard Gov-

ernor of Maryland, but as the latter's extreme youth rendered the appointment purely formal, the real management of affairs was committed to a board of Deputy Governors. The commission to this board was issued in May 1684, and Maj. Nicholas Sewall was included in it (Md. Archives, xvii, 249). In consequence of the revolution of 1689 Maj. Sewall was obliged to vacate all his offices and retire to private life upon his estates in St. Mary's County. His will dated 16 April 1737, was proved 9 May following. He married Susanna, daughter of Col. William Burgess (b. 1622 ; d. 24 Jan. 1686/7) of Anne Arundel County, a member of the Council and one of the deputy Governors. Col. Burgess mentions in his will (dated 11 July 1685, and proved 19 Feb'y 1686/7) his daughter Susanna wife of Maj. Nicholas Sewall, and his grandchildren Charles and Jane Sewall (Baldwin's Calendar, ii, 12). Mrs. Susanna Sewall was living and joined her husband in a deed 11 Oct. 1705, but evidently died before him as she is not mentioned in his will.

Maj. Nicholas Sewall and Susanna (Burgess) his wife had issue :

6. i. CHARLES SEWALL [6], d. 1742, of whom further.
   ii. HENRY SEWALL, d. 1722 ; mar. Elizabeth . . . . . (who mar.2°. Philip Lee), and left issue.
   iii. NICHOLAS SEWALL, d. unmar. 1732.
   iv. CLEMENT SEWALL of Cecil Co., d. 1740 ; mar. Mary dau. of Col. John Smith of Calvert Co., and left issue.
   v. JANE SEWALL, b. before 1685 ; d. 1761 ; mar. Clement Brooke (b. 1676 ; d. 1737) of Prince George's Co., and had issue.
   vi. CLARE SEWALL, mar. 1°. Thomas Tasker (d. 1733), 2°. Wiliam Young (d. 1772). See Magazine, IV, 192.
   vii. ELIZABETH SEWALL, d. 1752, mar. Capt. Peregrine Frisby (b. 1688, d. 1738) of Cecil Co.
   viii. SUSANNA SEWALL, mar. George Douglas of Kent Co.
   ix. MARY SEWALL, mar. 1°. William Frisby (b. 1699, d. 1724) brother of Capt. Peregrine Frisby (see above), 2°. 3 Sept. 1725, Dominick Carroll of Cecil Co.
   x. ANNE SEWALL, d. 1789 ; mar. Joseph Douglas.
   xi. SOPHIA SEWALL, mar. John Cooke of Prince George's Co.

6. CHARLES SEWALL [6], (Nicholas [5], Henry [4], Richard [3]) was born before 1685, since he is named in the will of his grandfather Col. William Burgess. He was doubtless named for his father's stepfather, Charles Lord Baltimore. He lived at Eltonhead Manor, St. Mary's County. His will, dated 8 August 1741, was proved 27 April 1742. Charles Sewall married, after 1711, Eleanor widow of John Tasker of Calvert County, and daughter of Col. Thomas Brooke of Brookfield, Prince George's County, a member of the Council

of Maryland and its President in 1720. Her first husband,
John Tasker in his will dated 22 Sept. 1711 and proved 17
October following (Annapolis, Lit. 13, fol. 323) names his
wife Eleanor and his minor son Thomas Tasker. Col. Thomas
Brooke in his will dated 16 Nov. 1730 and proved 25
Jan'y following (Annapolis Lit. 20, fol. 125) mentions his
"daughter Eleanor Sewall wife of Mr. Charles Sewall" and his
eldest son Thomas Tasker. Charles Sewall of Eltonhead
Manor and Eleanor (Brooke) his wife had issue :—

7.   i. NICHOLAS SEWALL[7], d. 1798 ; of whom further.
     ii. CHARLES SEWALL, mentioned 1741, in his father's will.

7.   NICHOLAS SEWALL[7], (*Charles* [6], *Nicholas* [5], *Henry* [4]) of
Eltonhead Manor, died in 1798. In his will, dated 21
April 1797, proved 18 Dec. 1798, and recorded in St.
Mary's County, he states that he resided at Eltonhead Manor,
and mentions his sons Nicholas, Charles, and Robert, and his
granddaughter Katharine Kirwan. His sons Nicholas and
Robert are appointed executors. He had however several
other children not named in his will, and these are given
below, the information concerning them being derived from
family sources. Nicholas Sewall married Mary daughter of
Henry Darnall of Poplar Hill, Prince George's County, and
Ann Talbot his wife. Her brother Robert Darnall, died
without issue in 1803 and by will recorded in Prince
George's County, left Poplar Hill, to his nephew Dr. Robert
Sewall.

Nicholas Sewall and Mary (Darnall) his wife had issue :—

8.   i.   NICHOLAS SEWALL[8], d. 1813, of whom further.
     ii. CHARLES SEWALL.
     iii. DR. ROBERT SEWALL of Poplar Hill, Prince George's Co., d. in
          Washington D. C., 16 Dec. 1820. He mar. Mary (d. 23 July
          1822) dau. of Wm. Brent of Richland, Stafford Co., Va., and had
          a large family. His daughter, Mary Brent Sewall (b. Sept. 1808 ;
          d. 1 Jan'y 1831) was the first wife of Philip Barton Key, but had
          no issue.
     iv. HENRY SEWALL.
     v.   MARY SEWALL, d. 12 Jan'y 1791 ; mar. John Kirwan of Baltimore.
     vi. SARAH SEWALL, mar. —— Blake.
     vii. CATHERINE SEWALL, d. s. p. 1807 ; second wife of William Digges.

8.   NICHOLAS SEWALL[8], (*Nicholas* [7], *Charles* [6], *Nicholas* [5]) of
Eltonhead Manor and Cedar Point, St. Mary's County, died
in November or December 1813. His will, dated 18 November, proved 13 December, 1813, and recorded in St.

Mary's County, names his wife Mary, his children Henry L., Robert, Catherine, and Maria L. Sewall; and his brother Robert Sewall. His friends Raphael Neale and Lewis Ford are appointed executors. He married Mary (d. 1854) daughter of Edward and Ann (Hebb) Fenwick of St. Mary's County.

Nicholas Sewall and Mary (Fenwick) his wife had issue:—

   i. HENRY L. SEWALL [9], d. unmarried,
   ii. ROBERT SEWALL, mar. —— Herbert, and left two sons.
   iii. CATHERINE SEWALL. d. unmarried in Louisiana.
   iv. MARIA LAURA SEWALL, b. 7 June 1812; d. 10 Dec. 1897; mar. 25 April 1833, Philip Barton Key.

THE SEWALL ARMS.

An impression of a seal, in the possession of McHenry Howard, Esq., gives the arms of the Sewalls of Maryland as follows :

Arms. Sable, a chevron between three bees, argent.
Crest. A leopard's head affrontee.

The same arms, but with a bee volant for a crest, were borne by the New England branch of the family, and they are given in Hurd's engraved portrait of Rev. Joseph Sewall of Massachusetts in 1768. A writer in the American Quarterly Register for 1841 (p. 238) states that these arms have been handed down among the Sewalls of New England and Canada and, with a difference in the crest, among the Sewalls of the Southern States. This statement is borne out by the seal noted above. Burke's General Armory gives the same coat as the arms of Sewell of Newport, Isle of Wight, but the crest is an arm in armor holding an acorn. Another Sewell coat given in Burke is : Sable, a chevron between three butterflies argent.

SKINNER BIBLE RECORD

Publisher: Matthew Carey, Philadelphia, Pa.
Publication date: 1809
Present owner: Maryland Historical Society [photostat]
Copied by: Mary K. Meyer

MARRIAGES:

On the 22nd day of MARCH 1810 Zachariah Skinner led to the alter of hymen the amiable Miss Hannah Jones where the usual hymenial rites were performed by the reverend James Kemp.

BIRTHS:

[Willi]am Skinner son of [Zac]hariah Skinner and Hannah his wife was born on the 20th day of june in the year of our Lord Anno Domini 1811 at 3 Oclk in the afternoon.
2nd son. John Jones Skinner son of Zachariah Skinner and Hannah his wife was born on the 6th day of September 1813.
3rd son. Thomas Skinner Son of Zachariah Skinner and hannah his wife was Born on the 29th of November 1815.
Cassandra Johns Skinner was born 2nd day October 1817 [the 7 seems to have been written over an 8.] She departed this life 1820 [unclear] September 30 Aged 2 years wanten 2 days. first Daughter of Zachariah and Hannah Skinner.
4th son. A . . . illa: James Skinner son of Zachariah and Hannah his wife was born on the 15th of March [1820?]
Washington Hammond Skinner was born the 7th day of May 1823. 5th son of Zachariah and Hannah Skinner born 1823.
6th son. Zachariah H. Skinner was Born July 3th 1825.
2th dauthter. Mary E. Skinner then was born october 20th 1827.
7th son. Alexandra Summerfield Skinner was born December 26th 1829.
8th son. Richart Standly Skinner was Born May 25 1832.
Zachariah Skinner son of William Skinner and Elizabeth his wife was born on the 23rd day of March in the year of our Lord anno Domini 1787. Hannah Skinner consort of Zachariah Skinner was born on the 30th day of April 1794. [the date 179– is written twice then 1794 is subtracted from 1828 and 34 written underneath.]

DEATHS:

Cassandra John Skinner Departed this life September 30th 1820.
Mary Elizabeth Skinner Departed this life may 29 1831.
Richard Stanly Skinner Departed this Life june 29 1832.
Hannah Bonn Skinner departed this life June 18th 1846.
Zachariah Skinner Departed this Life May 19th 1864.

SMALLWOOD FAMILY OF CHARLES COUNTY.

ARTHUR L. KEITH.

James Smallwood, who arrived in Maryland in 1664, and his descendants were with a very few exceptions the sole bearers of the name in Maryland until comparatively recent times. One of these exceptions was a Thomas Smallwood who appears several times in the Baltimore County records from June, 1692, when he was a taxable on the south side of the Patapsco, to November, 1695. It is very improbable that he was identical with Thomas Smallwood, son of the above James, for during that period the latter Thomas appears in the Charles County records, as we shall see below. One Samuel Smallwood also appears in the Baltimore records June, 1713, and November, 1713. This Samuel encroaches upon the territory of James though there is nothing to indicate a relationship between the two. In one of his appearances in Charles County (Apr. 17, 1712) he is described as Samuel Smallwood of Baltimore County, carpenter, who with wife Martha sells land to Philemon Hemsley and to Mary, his wife. He may have been identical with the Samuel Smallwood who witnessed the will of Cornelius Brannon, St. Mary's County, Mch. 19, 1702. No closer contacts between him and James Smallwood have been found nor has any trace been discovered of later Smallwoods who might have descended from him.

A certain John Smallwell for some time proved a disturbing cause to the adjustments of the Smallwood genealogy. He settled in the immediate vicinity of James Smallwood and is found associated with the same families. It was easy to misread Smallwell into Smallwood. For instance, William Hutchinson and John Smallwell make indenture on May 5, 1691 (*La Plata,* Lib. R No. 1, fol. 232) yet in reference to this indenture he is called Smallwood (*Ibid.,* fol. 546). Baldwin's Calendar of Maryland Wills (Vol. II) gives his will as of John

Smallwood, Charles County, dated Nov. 6, 1695, prob. Jan. 3, 1695/6. But the name in the record at La Plata shows clearly as Smallwell. His line seems to have perished with himself and no confusion appears later because of the close resemblance of the two names.

The Prince George County records (Lib. T, fol. 157) show that Mr. John Smallwood, Hosier, of London on Aug. 27, 1734 appoints Capt. Postumus Thornton of Patuxent River, merchant, as his attorney. Aside from these exceptions the field is left pretty clear for the family of James Smallwood, at least prior to 1800.

All attempts to locate the English home of James Smallwood up to this writing have failed. The name appears in various parts of England for several centuries prior to 1664. Little effort seems to have been made by our English cousins of the name Smallwood to trace the family history.

The first mention of James Smallwood in Maryland is found in the Warrants at Annapolis (Lib. 9, fol. 439): May 24, 1666 Came James Smallwood and demands land for the transportation of himself and Hester, his wife, into this province, himself in 1664 and Hester in 1650. Warrant was then issued to James Smallwood to lay out 100 acres. From this record we learn that James Smallwood arrived in Maryland in 1664 and that he was of sufficient importance to provide for his own importation. He evidently arrived unmarried but before May 24, 1666 he had taken a wife Hester (or Esther) who had come into the province in 1650, probably as a child with parents or relatives. It does not appear why land was not taken for her before this date and it is difficult to see how James Smallwood, who certainly had no part in her transportation, was allowed to take 50 acres which represented the cost of her transportation.

Hester's family name has not been determined. However, an indication of her name may be found in the following record: Apr. 18, 1677. James Smallwood, Charles County, showed to the judge that John Evans, *his brother,* of said county, dec'd, had died intestate and prayed that the goods and chattels of said dec'd be committed to him. (*Test. Proc.* Lib. 9, fol. 59.) There are several ways in which James Smallwood and John Evans could have been brothers. John Evans's inventory seems to indicate an unmarried man (he had but one chair!). James Smallwood asks to take John Evans's effects to himself. No wife appears in the records of the settlement. The probability becomes strong that John Evans was a brother of James's wife Hester. On May 19, 1651 one John Nicholls of Charles County made gift of a cow to John Evans, son of William Evans, dec'd, whose widow John Nicholls had married. This John Evans is very probably identical with the John Evans of 1677, called brother of James Smallwood. If William Evans brought wife and two children John and Hester to the province in 1650 and died before May 19, 1651 he would have had slight opportunity for taking up land, and while the process appears irregular, James Smallwood in 1666 might be allowed to take land for Hester's importation which no one had yet claimed.

Hester was the mother of James's eleven children. She was still living on Aug. 9, 1692 on which date James Smallwood and Hester, his wife, sued Thomas Fowlkes for slander. (*La Plata,* Lib. R No. 1, fol. 456) (Case agreed out of court). She apparently died before Mch. 20, 1693 on which date her son John Smallwood made will, and as he mentions all his relatives, wife, daughter, brothers, sisters, father, brother's wife, and makes no mention of his mother, we may safely infer that she died before this date. Maj. James Smallwood in January and May, 1695 was the admr of Robert Thompson, Jr., dec'd, having intermarried Mary, relict of the dec'd. (*Test. Proc.* Lib. 15, fol. 63). She had previously been the wife of Giles Blizard of Charles County. After James Smallwood's death in 1714-15 she married a fourth time, to Alexander Herbert.

The land transactions of James Smallwood were numerous, in almost all of which he appears as warrantee or grantee. The warrant for 100 acres mentioned above, dated May 24, 1666, he assigned on Sept. 20, 1666 to Thomas Hussey (*Annapolis,* Lib. 10, fol. 257), On Feb. 7, 1669/70 he received assignment from Daniel Johnson (part of warrant for 550 acres) for 150 acres (*Annapolis,* Lib. 12, fol. 467) on which he was allowed grant of "Goates Lodge", 150 acres, lying in Charles County, Mch. 16, 1669/70 (Lib. 12, fol. 467). On Mch. 5, 1677 James Smallwood bought from John Duglas, Gent., land called "Welcome", 200 acres (*La Plata,* Lib. G No. 1, fol. 125). On June 8, 1681 Rand. Brandt assigned to James Smallwood 75 acres due on warrant. (*Annapolis,* WC No. 4, fol. 53). This land was surveyed the same year, 1681, but not patented until Oct. 26, 1694, and was given the name "Eltham". The date of the patent is given as Nov. 10, 1695 in a deed dated Mch. 10, 1718 in which James Smallwood conveys this land to John Smallwood (*La Plata,* Lib. H No. 2, fol. 231). On Apr. 20, 1687 Edmond Lindsey sold to James Smallwood land called "May Day", 300 acres, (*La Plata,* Lib. N, No. 1, fol. 210). On May 20, 1688, Cornelius Maddock, merchant, and Mary, his wife (she was the daughter of James Smallwood), sold to James Smallwood "Tatshall", 60 acres. On Mch. 15, 1688/9 James Smallwood had land surveyed, 110 acres, by virtue of a warrant to William Hutchinson for 1000 acres and by him assigned to James Smallwood. This tract was named "Porke Hall", sometimes more elegantly called "Park Hall". There must have been a conflicting claim to this land for on Aug. 10, 1694 William Griffin sold to Maj. James Smallwood, Sr for 10000 lbs of tobacco his right to "Porke Hall", 113 acres, more or less. (*La Plata,* Lib. S No. 1, fol. 344). On Oct. 17, 1694 "Batchellors Hope" was surveyed for James Smallwood, patented for 184 acres (*Annapolis,* Lib. C No. 3, fol. 166 and *Charles County Rent Rolls*). "Batchellors Delight", 235 acres, was surveyed Sept. 7, 1694 for Matthew Smallwood and Thomas Smallwood (they were sons of James) (*Annapolis, Charles County Rent Rolls.*) On May 14, 1695 warrant was issued to James Smallwood for 581 acres, due to him by renewment of that quantity, being remainder of a warrant for 1000 acres granted him on July 28, 1694 (*Annapolis,* Lib. A, fol. 5 and 39). William Diggs is his caution. It will be observed that the sum of the last two tracts mentioned equals 419 acres, which exactly represents the used part of this warrant. There seems to be no record showing how James Smallwood used the balance, 581 acres, due on his warrant, but since he was providing for his other sons it is reasonable to suppose that the land held later by his son James was part of the remainder. James Smallwood, Jr was in 1704 the possessor of "Hopewell", which was surveyed Aug. 29, 1696 for William Dent, 521 acres. Of this tract 495 acres were included in the lines of "Friendship" (*Annapolis, Charles County Rent Rolls*). James Smallwood, Jr in his will 1723, refers to land bought of Maj. William Dent and his will shows that he was at that time involved in a lawsuit with Dent's heirs regarding this land. After his death adjustments seem to have been made and his heirs remain in possession of 433 acres of "Friendship".

On Dec. 6, 1695 William Forster and Dorothy, his wife, exor of Michael Minoake, sold to James Smallwood, land called "St. Edmonds", 150 acres at head of Port Tobacco Creek, joining John Duglas, Gent. On Aug. 11, 1696 Thomas Whichaley and Elizabeth, his wife, sold to Pryor Smallwood and Bayne Smallwood (the price of 10000 lbs of tobacco being paid therefor by James Smallwood, Sr) part of Christian Temple Manor, 200 acres, lying on Mattawoman or St. Thomas Creek. (*La Plata,* Lib. Q No. 1, fol. 97). This transaction properly belongs to James Smallwood, Sr as neither Pryor or Bayne could have been over 16 years of age at the time. Warrant was granted July 6, 1696 to James Smallwood, Sr for 400 acres (*Annapolis,* Lib. A, fol. 110). On July 29, 1696 "Bayne",

100 acres, was surveyed for James Smallwood (*Annapolis, Charles County Rent Rolls*). The Rent Rolls show that " this land is now disclaimed ". The quantity is given as 100 acres but the rent asked, 16 shillings, indicates a larger tract. The 100 is probably an error for 400. No later warrants, surveys, or sales to James Smallwood have been found. By the proceding acquisitions he was able to make generous provision for his eleven children. Most of these tracts remained in possession of his descendants for several generations and are sometimes the only means we have of determining the family connections. " Batchellors Hope " apparently did not satisfy the original hope and was disclaimed. For some reason " Bayne " was also disclaimed. " Goates Lodge" seems to disappear from the Smallwood holdings unless perhaps it changed its name. John Smallwood, son of James, according to his will, 1693-94, owned 300 acres. There is no record of his receiving land either by sale or original grant. He very probably received his land from his father. " Goates Lodge ", 150 acres, may have been part of his plantation, to which he gives no name in his will.

James Smallwood was a very useful man in his community. His name is very frequent in the records of Charles County. Only a few instances will be given here. In 1676 James Smallwood and Ralph Shaw were apprs of the estate of Giles Cole (*Maryland Hist. Mag.*, Vol. XIX, 339). On Sept. 24, 1677 James Smallwood and Ralph Shaw were apprs of Edward Lindsay. In 1696 James Smallwood was one of the apprs of Col. Edward Pye. On Oct. 4, 1697 James Smallwood and Anthony Neale appraised the estate of Col. William Digges, and acted as security for the exors, Elizabeth Digges and Edward Digges. In 1698 James Smallwood assisted in appraising William Chandler's estate. In 1699 he was overseer of Hugh Teares's will, in 1701, trustee of John Bayne's will. This association with the Bayne or Bean family (so far as we know there was no kinship) was responsible for the name Bayne among the sons of James Smallwood, a name which persisted in the Smallwood family for several generations. In 1682 James Smallwood had business relations with John Pryor, merchant, at Westwood, and this contact was no doubt responsible for the name Pryor in the Smallwood family. On Jan. 30, 1687/8 Nicholas Lidstone (also Lydestone), mariner, of Dartmouth in the county of Devon, England, and William Hayne of the same place appointed James Smallwood of Charles County Maryland as their attorney (*La Plata,* Lib. N, No. 1, fol. 319). This association provides the explanation for another name in the Smallwood family, namely, Ledstone or Leadstone which also persisted for several generations.

The many plantations of James Smallwood suggest that he was chiefly a planter. But at least once he tried his hand at something else. On Dec. 14, 1686 James Smallwood was licensed and admitted to keep an ordinary at Chandlertown (*La Plata,* Lib. N, No. 1, fol. 7).

But in a public capacity James Smallwood was still more conspicuous. In 1676 he was appointed " post " to convey all public intelligence in Charles County, from thence to his Lordship and his Council (*Richardson, Side-Lights on Maryland History,* Vol. I, 96). As this service fell within the troublous period of Indian disturbances, the appointment as " post " involved considerable danger and distinction. In 1683 he was a commissioner of Charles County (*Md. Archives,* Vol. VII, 611). As a Protestant freeholder of Charles County he joined in a petition to the crown in 1689. In 1694 he signed with others the usual disclaimer of belief in transubstantiation. In the same year he contributed 800 lbs of tobacco toward the support of a free school. In 1694 he was high sheriff of Charles County (*Md. Archives,* Vol. XX, 68). In 1689 Mr. James Smallwood was appointed Major of foot in room of Maj. John Wheeler (*Md. Archives,* Vol. XIII, 242) and was named as one of a number to regulate the civil affairs in Charles County (*ibid.,* 243). On April 8, 1692 Major James Smallwood of

Charles County was appointed to deal with Indians as a near neighbor unto and well acquainted with most or all the Indians of the said county (*ibid.* Vol. VIII, 307). In 1692 Major James Smallwood was authorized to raise his company on the east side of Port Tobacco Creek and on north side of Potomac River within the bounds of Port Tobacco Parish (*La Plata, Lib, R, No. 1, fol. 460*). On June 9, 1700 he is called Lt. Col. James Smallwood (*La Plata, Lib. A, No. 2, fol. 65*), and shortly after that date to his death his name is regularly pre-- fixed with the title, Colonel. In 1694 and later he was a member of the quorum of Charles County. On Sept. 4, 1708 Joseph Manning, James Smallwood, and William Stone sign bond to make true account of her Majesty's lands in Charles County (*Annapolis, Prov. Ct. Rec.,* Vol. PL No. 3, fol. 103). From 1692 until his death he represented Charles County in the Maryland Assembly and the published archives of that period are replete with references to him.

Col. James Smallwood's will is dated Sept. 16, 1712, prob. in Charles County, Jan. 12, 1714/5. This indicates that he died near the close of 1714 or the beginning of 1715. He styles himself as of Charles County yet his will indicates that he was living at the time on his wife's plantation Bew (or Beau) Plains in Prince George County. His wife Mary was named as extx (in the execution of this will she appears as wife of Alexander Herbert, her fourth husband). He names children James, Thomas, Prier, and Leadstone Smallwood, and Mary Tayler and Sarah More. Aside from these children Col. James had five other sons, three and probably four of whom had predeceased him. A fifth son was for some reason not named in his father's will though he lived until 1737. Of Col. James's nine sons seven left wills on record in Charles County (three of them earlier than their father's will), an inventory marks the death of another (Benjamin), and the ninth (Matthew) passes away unnoticed by the records. The names of all (apparently) the children can be determined from the will of John Smallwood who died in 1694. The order of all these children is not certain. Dates of birth have been found for some, depositions show the approximate birth of others, and the remainder are placed according to other indications. James Smallwood and wife Hester had the following children:

1. John Smallwood, born January, 1666/7, died 1694.
2. James Smallwood, born October, 1668, died 1723.
3. Mary Smallwood, born Nov. 2, 1670, md 1. Cornelius Maddocks, 2. ——Tayler (Taylor).
4. Matthew Smallwood, born April, 1673. Probably died before 1712 (mentioned in his brother John's will, 1694, but not in his father James's will, 1712).
5. Thomas Smallwood (old enough to act as exor of his brother John's will, 1694), died May 4, 1734.
6. William Smallwood (married in 1693 or before), died 1706.
7. Prior Smallwood, born about 1680 (42 years old in 1722), died 1734.
8. Benjamin Smallwood (not mentioned in his father's will), died 1737.
9. Bayne Smallwood, died 1709.
10. Leadstone Smallwood, born about 1687 (58 years old in 1745), died 1755.
11. Sarah Smallwood, married Henry More, still living in 1736.

1. John Smallwood (son of Col. James) was born Jan. 1666/7, made will Mch. 20, 1693/4, prob. Aug. 6, 1694. He mentions wife Lettis who is to have use of his plantation of 200 acres (unnamed) until she marries, in which case she is to have but 50 acres. Said plantation is to pass to daughter

12. i. Ester Smallwood (so in record at Annapolis but plainly Eliza at La Plata. Ester is correct).

The testator makes bequests to father Smallwood, brothers James, Matthew, Thomas, William, brother William's wife, sister Sarah, Henry Moore (relationship not shown), brothers Ledstone, Benjamin, Bayne and Pryor (who is to receive 50 acres joining "my daughter's land"), sister Mary Maddocks (who is to receive the other 50 acres joining Pryor's land), brother-in-law Cornelius Maddocks. Brothers James Smallwood and Thomas Smallwood are appointed exors. (Baldwin in Cal. of Md. Wills, Vol. II, erroneously represents the Ledstone, Pryor, and Bayne of the above will as surnames).

James Smallwood renounces his part in the execution of the will and Thomas Smallwood appears as sole exor. The court allowed him upon his administration of John Smallwood's estate one penny upwards in tobacco, Sept. ? 11, 1694 (*La Plata,* Lib. S, No. 1, fol. 342 ?).

2. James Smallwood (son of Col. James) was born October, 1668, made will Nov. 13, 1723, prob. Dec. 12, 1723. He had wife Mary Griffin as early as Aug. 10, 1703 (*La Plata,* Lib. A, No. 2, fol. 249) who was the mother of his children. He seems to have recently married her at this date. If he had any earlier wife no record thereof has been found. His wife Mary was the daughter of John Boyden and at the time of her marriage to James Smallwood was a widow Griffin. By her first husband she had son James Griffin (*La Plata,* Lib. M, No. 2, fol. 280 and Lib. 40 (or Y No. 2), fol. 336, deed of Mary Smallwood, als Mary Boyden, heir of John Boyden, and her son James Griffin to John Hamill, Feb. 22, 1731; the deposition of James Griffin, June, 1745, in which he calls James Smallwood, dec'd, his father-in-law. James Smallwood and wife Mary had seven children of whom one, Anne, was not named in his will, probably because already married. These children were as follows:

13.   i. Ann Smallwood.
     ii. Elenor Smallwood.
14. iii. John Smallwood.
15. iv. William Smallwood.
16. v. Matthew Smallwood (under 18).
17. vi. James Smallwood (under 18).
31. vii. Lydia Smallwood (under 16).

3. Mary Smallwood (daughter of Col. James) was born Nov. 2, 1670. She married (1) Cornelius Maddocks, merchant, (2) ———— Taylor. Her first marriage occurred before she was 16, for on Mch. 16, 1685/6 James Smallwood made gift of one cow and one mare to daughter Mary Maddocks (*La Plata,* Lib. M No. 1, fol. 27). Cornelius Maddocks died before Feb. 25, 1705/6. This inventory was presented Mch. 9,

1705/6. His widow Mary married ———— Taylor before
Sept. 16, 1712 (date of her father's will). By her first husband she had the following children:

    i. John Maddox.
    ii. Edward Maddox.
    iii. Benjamin Maddox.
    iv. Phoebe Maddox, md Joseph Clements.

By her second husband she had

  18. v. William Smallwood Taylor.
      vi. Anne Taylor (her inventory at Annapolis, Aug. 10, 1745, is
         the source of information for her mother's children living
         then).
      vii. Elizabeth Taylor.

4. Matthew Smallwood (son of Col. James) was born April,
1673. He married Grace Robertson as early as Dec. 10, 1703
(*La Plata*, Lib. A No. 2, fol. 326). He probably died soon
after without will or other record to mark his departure. He
is not mentioned in his father's will. No issue has been certainly found for him but it is worthy of note that the Rent
Rolls of Charles County show that in 1753 one Smallwood
Beane owned 117½ acres, one half of "Batchellors Delight",
which was the amount that belonged to Matthew Smallwood
by virtue of the survey of 1694. Matthew Smallwood might
have left a daughter who became the mother of a Smallwood
Beane, rightful heir to his portion in 1753.

5. Thomas Smallwood (son of Col. James) was old enough
to have his mark of cattle and hogs recorded, June 28, 1692.
He was exor of his brother John's will in 1694. In Prince
George County, June, 1717, he sued Alexander Herbert and
his wife Mary, extx of James Smallwood, claiming that at the
instance of the said James, he (Thomas) had taken into his
home a certain John and Anne Smallwood (they were the
children of his dec'd brother William) to board and lodge,
for which service the said James had promised 2000 lbs of
tobacco, which had never been paid. Through his attorney

Daniel Dulany, Thomas won the suit (*Marlboro, Court Proc.*
H, fol. 250). On June 10, 1718 Thomas Smallwood brought
suit against William Bagg for libelling himself and family,
and summons was issued for Thomas's evidences, namely,
Stephen Cawood, Jr, Mary Cawood, Jr, Elizabeth Harris, John
Smallwood, Jr, Mary Smallwood, and John Maddox (*La
Plata,* Lib. I No. 2, fol. 74). The John Smallwood, Jr was
not identical with the John whom Thomas had taken to board
but was the son of James, the second, though he could not have
been over 13 years old at the time. The Mary Smallwood,
summoned as witness, was very probably the mother of John
Smallwood, Jr and wife of James, the second; but she may have
been the wife of John, the son of William, who married about
this time to Mary Macknew. The outcome of this suit seems
not to be recorded. On May 28, 1718 Thomas Smallwood surveyed " Smallwoods Plains ", 300 acres. On Nov. 16, 1723
he surveyed " Smallwoods Addition ", 100 acres (patented
Sept. 7, 1744 to James Smallwood, son of Thomas, dec'd).
In 1728 he surveyed " Amendment ", 250 acres. On Nov. 30,
1732 (?), Thomas Smallwood, Sr, Gent., of Charles County
bought from Henry Moore and wife Sarah of Prince George
County, 200 acres lying in Prince George County, called
" Wheelers Choice " (*Marlboro,* Lib T, fol. 50). The name of
this tract was changed to " Moores Rest " (*Baldwin, Cal. Md.
Wills,* Vol VII, 161). Thomas Smallwood died May 4, 1734
but owing to a caveat filed by his son James the will was not
probated until April 9, 1735. It was dated Apr. 14, 1734.
He named wife Alice as extx but on Sept. 17, 1735 the exor
was Thomas Middleton who had married Alice Smallwood, the
widow of Thomas, the said Alice being at this date also
deceased. No other mention has been found of Alice. She
may have been the mother of Thomas's children but since there
was a marked tendency to perpetuate family names in the
Smallwood family and since the name Alice does not appear
among the many daughters and granddaughters of Thomas I

suspect that Thomas had been married before. Thomas Smallwood according to his will had the following children:

19. i. James Smallwood.
20. ii. Thomas Smallwood.
21. iii. Pryor Smallwood.
22. iv. Elizabeth Smallwood, md Cawood.
      v. Sarah Smallwood, md Roby.
23. vi. Esther Smallwood, md Harrison.
24. vii. Charity Smallwood, md Davy.
25. viii. Mary Smallwood (deceased at making of the will) md Berry.

6. William Smallwood (son of Col. James) had wife (not named), Mch. 20, 1693/4 (date of his brother John's will). On Jan. 13, 1701/2 Thomas Hunt sued William Smallwood and Elizabeth his wife, for slander (*La Plata,* Lib. Y No. 1, fol. 358). The defendants were acquitted. Wife Elizabeth died before June 5, 1705 on which date William Smallwood, Gent., signed articles of agreement with Elinor Tubman, who was about to become his wife (*La Plata,* C No. 2, fol. 129). (This Eleanor was the daughter of Henry Hawkins of Charles County, who died in 1699. She md. (1) Rev. George Tubman, (2) William Smallwood, (3) Edward Philpott). William Smallwood made will Feb. 17, 1705/6, prob. June 12, 1706. He mentions wife Eleanor, clearly not the mother of his children, and children

      i. Jane Smallwood (not heard of later).
26. ii. John Smallwood
27. iii. Ann Smallwood.

To son John he left two tracts of land (unnamed but apparently " Eltham " and " Tatshall " which are found later belonging to the said John). Mention is made of brother Pryor Smallwood. Wife Eleanor and brother James Smallwood are named as exors. On Aug. 3, 1709 the inventory of Capt. William Smallwood was presented, at which time Eleanor, widow of William Smallwood, was the wife of Edward Philpott.

7. Pryor Smallwood (son of Col. James) was born about

1680. In Aug. 1720 he deposed that he was 40 years or thereabouts (*La Plata*, Lib. M No. 2. fol. 122). On July 2, 1708 Pryor Smallwood had wife Elizabeth, extx and relict of Peter McMillion (whose will was probated in Charles County, July 27, 1706). On Aug. 9, 1720 Pryor Smallwood sold to Daniel Bryan of Stafford County, Va. land called " St. Bridgetts " in Charles County. Wife Elizabeth gave consent (last mention found of Elizabeth) (*La Plata*, Lib. H No. 2, fol. 377). Prior Smallwood made will Feb. 23, 1732/3, prob. Mch. 29, 1734. To son William Smallwood he left 200 acres, part of Christian Temple Manor. To son Bayne Smallwood he left all his remaining lands excepting that daughters Ann and Elizabeth Smallwood are to have use of " Bayne " and " My New Design " while single. Daughter Hester is mentioned for whom the exor is to buy as speedily as possible a negro boy or girl. Son Bayne is appointed exor. His inventory, which shows that he had accumulated considerable wealth, was signed by Ledstone Smallwood and Matthew Stone, Senr, as next of kin. The nature of Matthew Stone's relationship to Prior Smallwood has not been determined, but if known it might throw light upon the family name of Elizabeth, wife of Prior. Prior Smallwood and wife Elizabeth had the following children:

    28. i. Bayne Smallwood, born about 1711.
    29. ii. William Smallwood.
        iii. Ann Smallwood.
        iv. Elizabeth Smallwood.
    30. v. Hester Smallwood.

8. Benjamin Smallwood (son of Col. James) receives scant notice in the records. On Apr. 1, 1701 he sued John Wynn (who later married his niece) for the recovery of a horse. There is no record of his father having provided him with land nor is he mentioned in his father's will. On June 24, 1737 the inventory of Benjamin Smallwood of Prince George County, showing only a small estate, was signed by Elizabeth Cawood and Charity Davy, as next of kin. James Small-

wood, Thomas Smallwood, and Pryor Smallwood make oath
that the inventory is correct. In these names we recognize five
of the children of Thomas Smallwood, brother of Benjamin.
He probably died unmarried and without issue.

9. Bayne Smallwood (son of Col. James) is mentioned in
the will of John Bayne (1700) as godson.   He married
Charity Courts, daughter of Col. John Courts.   He made will
June 28, 1709 (?), prob. Dec. 2, 1709 in which he appoints
brother James Smallwood as exor.   He had no issue.

10. Leadstone Smallwood (the last surviving son of Col.
James) was born about 1687.   He deposed Sept. 5, 1738 that
he was 51 years old or thereabouts (La Plata, Lib. 38 T No. 2,
fol. 516).   This age is confirmed by two later depositions, 1749
and 1755, in which he gives his age as 62 and 68.   However,
in a deposition made Dec. 22, 1718 his age is given as 36 years
(La Plata, Lib. M No. 2, fol. 41), which would carry his birth
back to 1682.   The agreement of the other three depositions
guarantees their accuracy.   On Jan. 12, 1726 he surveyed and
on Mch. 20, 1732 he patented " Addition to May Day ", 131
acres, which he sold on Mch. 14, 1744 to Francis Goodrich,
Gent., being called in the deed Leadstone Smallwood, Gent.
Wife Elizabeth joined in the deed (La Plata, Lib. O No. 3,
fol. 25).   On Apr. 7, 1731 he surveyed " The Gore ", 23 acres,
which he patented Nov. 11, 1737.   In 1735 William Smallwood and Leadstone Smallwood signed as next of kin the
inventory of John Smallwood (son of the William who died
in 1706).   At the final accounting of his estate by Mary
Smallwood, the extx, Mch. 4, 1740 Ledstone Smallwood, Senr
and Thomas Cawood were her sureties.   On June 17, 1736
Leadstone Smallwood and Elizabeth, his wife, made deed
of gift to son Will Smallwood, 100 acres, part of " May Day ".
On June 12, 1740 Ledstone Smallwood, Gent., and Elizabeth,
his wife, and William Smallwood, Gent., and Ledia, his wife,
sold to Arthur Westman a lot in Charlestown.

Leadstone Smallwood married Elizabeth Garland, daughter of Randolph Garland of Charles County, whose will dated Aug. 27, 1722, prob. Sept. 27, 1722, mentions daughter Elizabeth Smallwood and grandchildren Charity, Ann, Mary, Henrietta, Ledstone, and William Smallwood. Ledstone Smallwood and wife Elizabeth had at least two other children not named in this will, apparently being born later than the date of the will. One was John Smallwood who will be mentioned in his father's will of 1755, and the other was James Smallwood, called the son of Ledstone in June, 1749 (*La Plata,* Lib. 42, fol 340) and in Aug. 1749 (*Ibid.* fol. 410). He is not found elsewhere. He was probably born after 1722 and died before 1755. Leadstone Smallwood made will Jan. 20, 1755, prob. Feb. 22, 1755. To son Leadstone Smallwood he left "May Day", 200 acres, and a portion of "Addition to May Day". To son John Smallwood he left "Welcome". He also made bequests to daughter Susannah Smallwood, son William Smallwood, daughters Charity Mitchell, Mary Godfrey, Henrietta Newland, and Elizabeth Smallwood, and to granddaughter Elizabeth Noland. The children of Leadstone Smallwood and his wife were as follows:

31.   i. William Smallwood.
32.   ii. Leadstone Smallwood.
33.   iii. John Smallwood.
      iv. Charity Smallwood, md —— Mitchell.
      v. Mary Smallwood, md —— Godfrey.
      vi. Susannah Smallwood.
34.   vii. Henrietta Smallwood, md —— Noland.
      viii. Elizabeth Smallwood.
      ix. James Smallwood.

11. Sarah Smallwood (daughter of Col. James) is mentioned in her brother John's will, 1693, as is also the man whom she married later, Henry More. It does not appear why the latter was mentioned by John Smallwood. If he was Sarah's betrothed, we shall have to place her birth elsewhere than among the youngest children of her father. Henry Moore of Prince George County and Sarah, his wife, on Nov. 30, 1732 (?)

sold to Thomas Smallwood, Sr, Gent., of Charles County
"Wheeler's Choice", 200 acres. Deed was signed by Henry
Moore, his mark, and Sarah More (*Marlboro,* Lib. T, fol. 50).
Henry Moor (sic) of Prince George County made will Mch. 17,
1732/3, prob. Feb. 17, 1735/6. He mentions wife Sarah;
also the following children:

      i. Sarah.
      ii. Esther.
      iii. Charity.
      iv. Ann Davis.
35. v. Benedictor.
      vi. Elizabeth.
      vii. William (Moore).
      viii. Henry (Moore) (under 18).

12. **Esther Smallwood** (daughter of John Smallwood who
died 1694) married Benjamin Adàms. On June 9, 1742
Benjamin Adams of Charles County and Hester, his wife, sold
to James Smallwood, planter, their right to "Pork Hall", 110
acres (*La Plata,* Lib. O No. 2, fol. 479). Pryor Smallwood,
brother of James, had received "Poor Call" (Pork Hall) by
the terms of his father Thomas's will, 1734. Pryor had died
only a few months before this deed. Evidently James is trying
to secure all right to this land, which he maintained until he
was dispossessed in 1762. Hester Adams, widow, in January,
1763 sold to William Smallwood 100 acres, called "May —— "
(*La Plata,* Lib. L No. 3, fol. 220). (William Smallwood sold
"May Day" a few days later, Feb. 4, 1763, to James Craik,
physician. The preceding transaction apparently was to
enable him to furnish a good title). These properties had been
for many years in the Smallwood family and there is no other
way to account for Hester Adams's interest in them than to
make her the daughter of John Smallwood. Benjamin Adams,
Sr, made will July 14, 1756, prob. Nov. 13, 1758 in Charles
County. He makes bequests to wife Easter and names the following children:

      i. James Adams.
      ii. Leonard Adams.

iii. Ann Adams, wife of Thomas Wheeler.
iv. Verlinda Adams, wife of Charles Brooke.
v. Thomas Adams.

13. Ann Smallwood (daughter of James who died 1723) married William Coghill. He made will Apr. 24, 1729, prob. June 4, 1729 in Prince George County. He mentions wife Ann and children Smallwood, Mary and Lidia. In event of wife Ann's death, the children are to be placed under the care of Mrs. Mary Smallwood. Wife Ann was named extx. Her bond was signed June 25, 1729 by John Smallwood, William Smallwood, and Henry Acton. Anne Cogghill of Charles County made will Nov. 24, 1729, prob. Mch. 18, 1730. She mentions son Smallwood Coghill (under 16) and daughters Mary and Lidia (both under 16). Mother Mary Smallwood is appointed extx and in the event of her death, brother Matthew Smallwood. The will was witnessed by Henry Acton, Sr, and Henry Acton, Jr. Mary Smallwood's bond was signed by Thomas Smallwood, Gent., and Henry Acton, Sr., Gent. The children of William Coghill by his wife Anne Smallwood were as follows:

i. Smallwood Coghill.
ii. Mary Coghill.
iii. Lidia Coghill.

Smallwood Coghill was warden of Broad Creek Church in 1759. He made will July 23, 1759, prob. Aug. 27, 1759 in Prince George County. He made bequests to wife Keziah Coghill, extx and to cousin Isaac Smallwood Middleton. No children named. The manner of Isaac Smallwood Middleton's relationship to the testator has not been determined. Smallwood Coghill's inventory was signed by Mary Middleton and John Smallwood, Jr, next of kin.

14. John Smallwood (son of James who died in 1723) was born about 1705. He deposed in 1745 that he was 40 years old or thereabouts (La Plata, Lib. 40, fol. 465). He was undoubtedly the oldest son of his father since the latter's will

enjoins his sons to make no arrangements without consent of their brother John, and he is authorized to continue the suit against the Dents in which the testator was then involved. The Charles County Debt Books show John Smallwood in possession of 100 acres of " Friendship " in 1753. We have already seen that " Friendship " and " Hopewell " overlay each other. Probably James Smallwood's suit with the Dents arose from conflicting claims resulting from this complication. The matter seems to have been adjusted after his death by two deeds, one dated Mch. 17, 1724, in which John Cofer, Jr, of Charles County, son and heir of Elizabeth Cofer, and one of the co-heirs of Hugh Thomas, late of Charles County, sold to Mary Smallwood. widow and extx of James Smallwood, for use of Mary Smallwood and the devisees of James Smallwood, all of Cofer's right claimed by him in " Friendship ", 100 acres (*La Plata,* Lib. L, No. 2, fol. 217) ; the other dated Aug. 18, 1725, in which William Hoskins, Gent., of Charles County, sold to Mary Smallwood, widow and extx of James Smallwood for use of Mary Smallwood and the devisees of James Small-wood, " Friendship ", 333 acres, lying on south side of Matta-woman fresh, joining land called " Hopewell ", which the said James Smallwood bought of William Dent (*La Plata,* Lib. L No. 2, fol. 231). On Mch. 27, 1742 Mary Smallwood made deed to John Smallwood, William Smallwood, Matthew Small-wood and James Smallwood of land called " Friendship ". This deed does not seem to appear in the Charles County records but is referred to in a deed made Oct. 29, 1793 by John Smallwood to Nicholas Blacklock of a part of " Friendship " (*La Plata,* Lib. No. 4, fol. 244). The Debt Books of Charles County, 1753, show 433 acres of " Friendship " in the posses-sion of the above named Smallwoods. John Smallwood's wife is not known. He made will Mch. 28, 1768, prob. Nov. 3, 1770. To son John Smallwood he left part of " Friendship ", also " Smallwood's Meadows " ; to son Luke Smallwood he left part of " Friendship " ; he makes bequests also to son James

Smallwood, son George Smallwood, daughter Sarah, wife of Seth Johnson; to grandson Kensey Johnson " if ever said Kensey should return to Maryland ", to grandson Randolph Marlow, son of daughter Charity, late wife to Richard Marlow (in the settlement Randolph appears as Rudolph). Sons John and Luke Smallwood are named exors. That James Smallwood was the oldest son of John is shown by a note appended to the probate stating that James Smallwood, Jr, the heir at law, consents to the probate of the will. John Smallwood had the following children:

    36. i. James Smallwood.
    37. ii. John Smallwood.
    38. iii. Luke Smallwood.
    39. iv. George Smallwood.
    40. v. Sarah Smallwood, md Seth Johnson.
    41. vi. Charity Smallwood, md Richard Marlow.

15. William Smallwood (son of James who died in 1723) was born about 1710. On Aug. 14, 1733 William Smallwood and James Smallwood of Charles County sold to John Holly of Prince George County, 2 acres of " Friendship ". Mary, wife of William Smallwood, gives consent. No wife comes for James. On Aug. 5, 1747 William Smallwood surveyed and patented " Smallwood's Meadows ", 85 acres. In 1753 he owned this tract, also " Friendship ", 100 acres, and " Hopewell," 26 acres. On Dec. 13, 1755 he hold to James Edelen part of " Friendship ", 39 acres, also " Smallwoods Meadows ", 32 acres, and part of " Hopewell ", 17 acres, a total of 98 acres. This total does not agree with the sum of the various parts. William Smallwood on the same day, Dec. 13, 1755, sold to John Smallwood, Gent., part of " Friendship ", 66 acres, also part of " Smallwoods Meadows ", 42 acres. It is impossible to make the acreage in these deeds agree with his holdings of 1753. Wife Mary consents to both deeds (*La Plata,* Lib. A No. 3, part 2, fol. 421). After this date William Smallwood is not found in the land records. He lingers on in the court records for some years. No will or

account has been found for him. It is a curious fact that about this time and later there were four and probably five William Smallwoods living in Charles County all old enough to own land but not one has left a will nor has any administration account been found for any except for General William Smallwood in 1792. Many of our genealogical difficulties would disappear if they had left wills. The account of Bayne Smallwood, Oct. 13, 1768, shows amounts due the estate from William Smallwood, Sr, and from John Smallwood, son of William Smallwood, Sr. This William with the title Sr is almost certainly the son of James who died in 1723. If so, we have the name of one of his sons. We can certainly ascribe to him another son, named James, who in a record of a suit brought against him by John Jordan in Nov., 1755 is designated as James Smallwood, son of William (*La Plata,* Lib. E No. 3, fol. 365). We may assign to William Smallwood two sons, namely,

    i. John Smallwood (with some slight reservation).
42. ii. James Smallwood.

16. Matthew Smallwood (son of James who died in 1723) married Mary Marbury, daughter of Francis Marbury, of Prince George County who made will Jan. 11, 1734/5, prob. Jan. 22, 1734/5. To daughter Mary Marbury he left land called " School House ". The account of his estate, May 22, 1738, shows amount paid to Matthew Smallwood in right of his wife, daughter of the dec'd. On Feb. 19, 1739 Matthew Smallwood of Charles County and Mary, his wife, sold to Smallwood Coghill of Prince George County land called " School House " (*Marlboro,* Lib. Y, fol. 127). On May 6, 1740 Matthew Smallwood of Prince George County (error for Charles County or perhaps he did live in Prince George County for a short time) and Mary, his wife, sold to Catharine Playfair of Prince George County land called " Marbury's School House ", 66 acres, on south side of main branch of the Piscataway " bequeathed by Francis Marbury to Mary, wife of Matthew Smallwood "; also land called " Long Court ". On

Jan. 9, 1742 Matthew Smallwood signed inventory of Pryor Smallwood as creditor. In 1753 he owned 133 acres of " Friendship ". Matthew Smallwood made will in Charles County Nov. 5, 1760, prob. Jan. 4, 1764. No wife is mentioned. To son Beane Smallwood he left " Friendship ". Other children mentioned are Francis Green Smallwood, Martha Smallwood, Benjamin Smallwood, Philip Smallwood, James Smallwood, and Priscilla Smallwood. Son Beane, daughter Priscilla, and Joshua Harris were named as exors. The census of St. John and St. George Parish, Charles County, 1776, gives the age of Philip Smallwood as 32, of Francis Smallwood as 23, of Benjamin Smallwood as 17 (apparently Matthew Smallwood's wife died in 1759 or 1760), of Precilla Smallwood as 30, and of Martha Smallwood as 20. Matthew Smallwood and wife Mary had the following children:

> i. Beane Smallwood (sold " Friendship," 100 acres, Aug. 14, 1771, to Philip Thomas, wife Mary consenting).
> ii. Philip Smallwood, born about 1744.
> iii. Priscilla Smallwood, born about 1746.
> iv. Francis Green Smallwood, born about 1753.
> v. Martha Smallwood, born about 1756.
> vi. Benjamin Smallwood, born about 1759.
> vii. James Smallwood.

17. James Smallwood (son of James who died in 1723) was called Jr to distinguish him from James, son of Thomas. In 1753 he owned ' Friendship ", 100 acres. He married Susannah Marbury, sister of Mary who married his brother Matthew. This marriage occurred between Jan 11, 1734/5 (date of Francis Marbury's will) and May 22, 1738 on which date Marbury's account shows payment of legacy to James Smallwood in right of his wife. James Smallwood, Jr, made will Nov. 27, 1766, prob. Jan. 17, 1767. He appoints wife Susannah as extx., who is to receive " Friendship ", which at her death is to be equally divided between sons Walter Bayne Smallwood and Francis Heard Smallwood. He also mentions children Henry Smallwood, James Bidon Smallwood, William Marbury Smallwood, Samuel Smallwood, Susannah Smallwood,

and Frances Ann Smallwood; also grandchildren Lucretia
Wilson and James Smallwood Wilson (their mother not mentioned, apparently dec'd). Susannah Smallwood (widow of
James) appears in the 1790 census. On Sept. 15, 1790 she
sold a negro to Hezekiah Berry. On Jan. 11, 1800 she sold
a negro girl to her daughter Chloe Turtur (?), wife of George.
But in her will, 1796, she has daughter Chloe, wife of William
Richards. Susannah Smallwood made will Sept. 24, 1796,
prob. Feb. 1, 1803. She mentions son Walter Bayne Smallwood who is to receive " Hopewell ", daughters Lucy Acton,
Sally Nelson, Chloe Richards, Susannah Berry, granddaughters Sally Berry and Nelly Berry; the three daughters of my
son Luke Smallwood, namely, Susannah Marbury, Ann and
Teresa Smallwood; son William M. Smallwood. Hezekiah
Berry is to keep mulatto girl Letty until testator's granddaughters Sally and Nelly are of age. Son William M. Smallwood and son-in-law William Richards are named as exors.
It is strange that there are four children named in Susannah's
will, 1796, not named in James's will, 1766. From these two
wills we obtain the following as the children of James Smallwood by his wife Susanna Marbury:

43.   i. daughter, md ——— Wilson.
44.   ii. Henry Smallwood.
45.   iii. Walter Bayne Smallwood.
46.   iv. James Bidon Smallwood.
47.   v. William Marbury Smallwood.
48.   vi. Samuel Smallwood.
49.   vi. Susannah Smallwood.
50. viii. Luke Smallwood.
     ix. Frances Ann Smallwood.
     x. Lucy Smallwood, md ——— Acton.
    xi. Sarah Smallwood, md William Nelson, Apr. 13, 1779.
    xii. Chloe Smallwood, md William Richards, Jan. 24, 1790
        (probably later md George Turtur (?).
   xiii. Francis Heard Smallwood, bapt. May 25, 1766.

31. Lydia Smallwood (daughter of James who died 1723).
See under William Smallwood, son of Ledstone.

18. William Smallwood Taylor (son of Mary Smallwood by

her second husband, ——— Taylor) married Mary Sanders, daughter of John Sanders of Charles County. In 1753 he owned 100 acres of Christian Temple Manor. His inventory was signed June 15, 1765 by Barton Brawner and Ann Taylor, kin. His final account by John Maddox, admr, is dated Oct. 30, 1767. No mention is made of wife but the children of the dec'd are given as follows:

    i. Elizabeth Taylor, of age in 1767.
    ii. Mary Taylor, of age in 1767.
    iii. Ann Taylor, of age in 1767.
    iv. William Taylor, born Oct., 1747.
    v. Robert Taylor.
    vi. Sarah Taylor.

19. James Smallwood (son of Thomas who died in 1734) was called Sr. to distinguish him from James, the son of James, sometimes called Piney James because he lived on Piney Creek. In June, 1745 he deposed that he was 48 years old or thereabouts and that about 23 or 24 years ago he had seen William Hoskins make notches on a certain tree (*La Plata,* Lib. 40 (or Y No. 2), fol. 336). In Nov. 1745 James Smallwood deposed that he was 45 years or thereabouts and refers to what he had seen William Hoskins do about 25 years ago (*La Plata,* Lib. 40 (or Y No. 2), fol. 464). In spite of the difference in the ages given, the circumstances are such as to indicate that the depositions belong to the same man and that he, James, son of Thomas, was born about 1697-1700. According to all indications, James, son of James, was born at least ten years later. James Smallwood, son of Thomas, received from his father's will, 1734-35, a part of " Poor Call " (Pork Hall) and is to receive all of it in case his brother Pryor dies without heirs. In 1753 James Smallwood claims all of " Porkhall ", 110 acres; also " Batchellors Delight ", 117½ acres, which had also been left to Pryor; also " Stewart's Oversight ", 45 acres (warrant and patent for same issued to James Smallwood, Nov. 26, 1729 and Nov. 4, 1737); also " Smallwood's Addition ", 100 acres (surveyed Nov. 16, 1723 for Thomas Smallwood and patented by his son James, Sept. 7, 1744); and " Smallwood's Gore ",

46 acres (a grant by renewment to James Smallwood, May 25,
1730). On Mch. 4, 1768 James Smallwood and wife Ann sold
to son-in-law Richard Tubman part of " Stewart's Oversight ";
on the same day they sold part of the same tract to James
Smallwood, Jr; likewise on same day they sold to Henry Acton,
Jr, of Prince County land called " Smallwood's Grubb ", which
must have been a new name for part of " Stewart's Oversight "
for Henry Acton, Jr, is listed in 1769 as possessor of 103½
acres of " Stewart's Oversight ". James Smallwood, Sr, made
will May 1, 1775, prob. July 17, 1775. He mentions wife
Ann, grandsons Francis Acton, Been Smallwood, George
Magruder Tubman, John Smallwood, son of James; and his
four children:

    51. i. Thomas Smallwood.
    52. ii. James Smallwood.
    53. iii. Easter Smallwood (born about 1731), md Henry Acton.
        iv. Ann Smallwood, md Richard Tubman.

20. Thomas Smallwood (son of Thomas who died 1734)
received by his father's will " Moore's Rest ", 200 acres, which
he owned till his death. On Aug. 13, 1764 he bought " Atcherson's Woodyard " (identical with " Atchison's Hazard ").
Pryor Smallwood, son of the above Thomas, on Apr. 11, 1785
bought William Atcherson's right in this land in order to confirm title (*La Plata,* Lib. Z No. 3, fol. 137). On July 17,
1749 Thomas Smallwood and John Cawood, Jr, planters, were
sureties for John Cawood, admr of Mary Cawood. On Aug. 4,
1750 Thomas Smallwood and John Atchison were sureties for
John Cawood, exor *de bonis non* of Stephen Cawood. In
Mch., 1739 Thomas Smallwood and Henry Moore of Prince
George County, signed an agreement to pay to Elizabeth and
Sarah Maggatee (McAtee) the portion due them from the estate
of their father Edmd Maggatee (*Marlboro,* Lib. X, fol. 274).
Thomas Smallwood received bequest by Samuel Williams's will,
Prince George County, Dec. 20, 1737 (no relationship shown).
In a suit brought by Stephen Cawood, Jr, against Samuel
Williams, Nov. 14, 1728, the defendant losing, Thomas Small-

wood becomes his "main person" (bail?). Thomas Smallwood made will July 16, 1778, prob. Aug. 23, 1778. Wife
Mary and son Bayne are appointed exors. The children of
Thomas Smallwood and wife Mary (named in the will) are as
follows:

54.   i. Thomas Smallwood.
55.   ii. Bayne Smallwood.
     iii. Prior Smallwood.
56.   iv. Hezekiah Smallwood.
57.   v. Benjamin Smallwood.
     vi. Eleanor Smallwood, md —— Brawner.
     vii. Mary Smallwood, md John Ward.
     viii. Ann Smallwood, md William Jackson.

21. Pryor Smallwood (son of Thomas who died in 1734)
received by the terms of his father's will part of "Poor Call"
(Pork Hall) and "Batchellors Delight", but if he should die
without heirs these tracts were to pass to his brother James.
We find James possessing these lands in 1753, hence we might
infer that Pryor died childless. Pryor Smallwood's inventory
is dated Jan. 9, 1741/2. It appears on record again, Feb. 17,
1741/2, signed by Walter Bayne and Winifred, his wife, admx
of Pryor. Pryor Smallwood, therefore, married Winifred
———, died before Jan. 9, 1742, and his widow soon after
married Walter Bayne. But Pryor certainly left issue. In
April, 1759, Sept., 1759, and later, Richard Harrison, and
Elizabeth, his wife, and Sarah Smallwood brought suit in the
Provincial Court against James Smallwood in regard to the
possession of disputed land (*Annapolis* Judg. BT No. 5, fol.
193 and 496, D. D. No. 1, fol. 208). The outcome of the
suit was agreement, and a deed in Charles County shows the
manner of the agreement. On July 13, 1762 James Smallwood and wife Ann sold to Richard Harrison, Jr, and to Elizabeth, his wife, and to Sarah Smallwood part of "Batchellors
Delight" and "Porkehall", 150 acres lying on the north
side of Piney. These are the tracts left to Pryor Smallwood
by his father Thomas in 1734. The will, the suit for evic-
tion, and the deed can mean but one thing, namely, that James

Smallwood upon the death of his brother Pryor took possession of this land as his own. We have seen above that James filed a caveat against the probate of his father's will and in 1742 bought the right claimed in " Pork Hall " by Hester Adams. Pryor's children upon coming to maturity had entered a suit for ejectment. To Pryor Smallwood we may confidently assign two children:

58. i. Elizabeth Smallwood, md Richard Harrison, Jr.
    ii. Sarah Smallwood (Sarah Smallwood, aged 38, was in Prince George County, 1776. Sarah Smallwood, buried in Piscataway Parish, Aug. 20, 1792. Both probably identical with this Sarah).

22. Elizabeth Smallwood (daughter of Thomas who died in 1734) married John Cawood. They had at least four children:

    i. Benjamin Cawood (had son Smallwood Cawood and others).
    ii. John Cawood.
    iii. Stephen Cawood (born Aug. 6, 1724).
    iv. Moses Cawood (had son Smallwood Cawood and others).

(The Cawoods will be treated in extenso in my forthcoming article on Cawoods).

23. Esther Smallwoodd (daughter of Thomas who died in 1734) married Richard Harrison. He made will in Charles County, Mch. 25, 1733/, prob. June 19, 1734. He names wife Ester extx; sons Richard, Thomas, Joseph; daughters Mary and Elizabeth (both minors). Ester Harrison died Aug. 19, 1776 (Annapolis, Judg. Lib. 88, fol. 122). She made will Dec. 21, 1771, prob. Nov. 26, 1776 in Charles County. She mentions daughters Mary Reeder and Elizabeth Elgin; grandchildren Virlinda Harrison, Thomas Smallwood Harrison, Joseph Harrison, Esther Harrison, Mary Harrison, Richard Harrison and Francis Harrison (without indicating parentage). She appoints sons-in-law Rich'd Robins Reeder and William Elgin as exors. To Richard Harrison and his wife Esther Smallwood Harrison may be assigned the following children:

58. i. Richard Harrison, md Elizabeth Smallwood.
    ii. Thomas Harrison.
    iii. Joseph Harrison.

iv. Mary Harrison, md Rich'd Robins Reeder.

v. Elizabeth Harrison, md William Elgin.

vi. Hezekiah Harrison, probably the oldest son, not mentioned either in his father's or his mother's will but mentioned in the will of his grandfather, Capt. Joseph Harrison, Dec. 24, 1726, prob. May 5, 1727, in which he bequeathes to him "Christian Milford", 150 acres. Richard Harrison, Jr., in his will made Dec. 11, 1771 (see below) mentions land heired from his brother, Hezekiah Harrison, dec'd. He probably died without issue.

24. Charity Smallwood (daughter of Thomas who died in 1734) married ——— Davy and had the following children named in Thomas Smallwood's will:

i. Ann Davy.

ii. Eleanor Davy.

25. Mary Smallwood (daughter of Thomas who died in 1734) married Humphrey Berry. She predeceased her father. Her two children are named in Thomas Smallwood's will:

35. i. Humphrey Berry, Jr.

ii. Thomas Berry, died without issue in 1779 or before.

26. John Smallwood (son of William who died in 1706 on Mch. 10, 1718/9 bought for 5 shillings of James Smallwood land called "Tatshall", 60 acres, and "Eltham", 75 acres. These land apparently represent his inheritance from his grandfather Col. James Smallwood, and were evidently the lands to which William Smallwood referred in his will of 1706 (*La Plata,* Lib. H No. 2, fol. 231). For some reason not known one Michael Ashford of Stafford County, Va. claimed right to "Tatshall" and on Apr. 14, 1726 he sold this right to John Smallwood for 600 lbs. of tobacco. (*La Plata,* Lib. L No. 2, fol. 264). John Smallwood married about 1720 to Mary Macknew, daughter of Jeremiah Macknew of Prince George County (*Annapolis, Admn Accts,* Lib. 15, fol. 59). John Smallwood made will Dec. 21, 1734, prob. Feb. 19, 1734/5. In this will he mentions wife Mary, extx, and children William and Ann Smallwood. His inventory, dated May —, 1735, was signed by William Smallwood and Ledstone Smallwood,

relations. Mary Smallwood's final account (with Ledstone Smallwood, Sr, and Thomas Cawood as sureties) was presented Mch. 4, 1740/1 and states that the heirs are a widow and six children (not named). Mary Smallwood from 1753 to 1762 was the possessor of " Eltham " and " Tatshall ". In June, 1757, Mary Ann Lovely, daughter of William Lovely, aged 5 years on the 2nd day of last October, was placed under the guardianship of Mary Smallwood (*La Plata,* Lib. F No. 3, fol. 488). Mary Smallwood made will Apr. 28, 1757, prob. Dec. 8, 1762. She makes bequest to daughter Elizabeth Smallwood, who is to have keeping of granddaughter Mary Ann Lovely; to son William Smallwood; to daughters Ann Hopewell and Mary Ann Smallwood. If daughters Elizabeth and Mary Ann Smallwood should die, " then my other two daughters etc ". From these records we make the children of John Smallwood by wife Mary as follows:

59 i. William Smallwood.
  ii. Ann Smallwood, md —— Hopewell.
  iii. Elizabeth Smallwood.
  iv. Mary Ann Smallwood.
  v. daughter, md William Lovely and had daughter Mary Ann Lovely, born Oct. 2, 1751.
  vi. daughter living when Mary Smallwood made will but name not given.

27. Ann Smallwood (daughter of William who died in 1706) was born in 1700/1, married John Winn (Wynn) in St. John's Parish, Prince George County, Feb. 5, 1717. This John Wynn was born in 1680 and was the son of Dr. John Wynne of St. Mary's County (*Baldwin, Cal. Md. Wills,* Vol I, 136). John Winn was chosen vestryman of St. John's of Piscataway Parish, Apr. 2, 1711. John Wynn, Sr, died Mch. 21, 1752. His wife Ann Smallwood Wynn died Feb. 20, 1752, aged 51 years. Their children were as follows:

  i. Mary Ann Winn, died Mch. 21, 1721/2 (?).
60. ii. John Winn, born Jan. 27, 1720/1.
  iii. Annake Winn, born June 10, ——, died 172—.
  iv. Eliza Winn, born Nov. 27, 1722.
61. v. Josiah Winn, born Feb. 1, 1726.
  vi. William Winn, born Oct. 18, 1728.

(The above records are from the St. John's of Piscataway Parish records. The following names are added from John Wynn's will, dated Mch. 21, 1752, prob. in Prince George County, Apr. 11, 1752. Eliza and William are not mentioned in the will).

  vii. Ann Wynn.
  viii. Jemima Wynn.
  ix. Jean Wynn.
  x. Mary Wynn.
  xi. Martha Wynn.
  xii. Susannah Wynn.

28. Bayne Smallwood (son of Pryor who died in 1734) was born about 1711. He deposed Aug. 11, 1760 that he was 49 years old (*La Plata,* Lib K No. 3, fol. 3). He represented Charles County in the Maryland Assembly in 1742. He was a large landholder and was a party in many transfers. He is said to have married Priscilla Heabard of Virginia. I have been unable to find any contemporary record by which this may be proved but I have no doubt as to the accuracy of the tradition. The writer examined many deeds of this Bayne at La Plata but found no wife signing. Bayne Smallwood died intestate in 1768. He had the following children:

  i. William Smallwood, born 1732, died Feb. 14, 1792. He was Major General in the Revolution and distinguished himself for gallantry. After the war he was elected to the American Congress and later became Governor of Maryland. He died unmarried. (See *Maryland Historical Magazine,* Vol. XIX, 304).
62. ii. Lucy Heabard Smallwood, md John Truman Stoddert.
  iii. Elizabeth Smallwood, md James Leiper.
  iv. Margaret Smallwood, md Walter Truman Stoddert.
  v. Heabard Smallwood (See Tyler's Quarterly Magazine, Vol. VIII, page 119).
  vi. Priscilla Smallwood, md John Courts.
63. vii. Eleanor Smallwood, md William Grayson.

29. William Smallwood (son of Prior who died in 1734) received by the terms of his father's will 200 acres of " Christian Temple Manor ". In 1753 this tract is ascribed to his brother Bayne Smallwood. No record of its transfer from

William to Bayne has been found. During this period the name of William Smallwood appears very frequently in the Charles County records but not once can it be identified with this William. However, I believe that this William married and left heirs. Prior Smallwood and Bayne Smallwood, father and brother of this William, both had dealings with Stafford County. The Stafford records are very incomplete, but they do show that one William Smallwood of that county was exor in 1765 of William Travis (great-grandfather of Col. William Barrett Travis of Alamo fame). Furthermore, a Barrett Travis who came from this part of Virginia to Edgefield County, South Carolina, where he died in 1814, is said to have married Ann Smallwood, and among their sons was one named Prior Smallwood Travis. The name Smallwood also appears twice among their grandchildren. This William Smallwood of Stafford County is probably identical with William, son of Prior.

30. Hester Smallwood (daughter of Prior who died in 1734) married Jacob Smith. Her father in his will directs that his exor buy as speedily as possible a negro boy or girl and give to his daughter Hester. His account by Bayne Smallwood, June 4, 1736, shows payment of a negro girl to Jacob Smith, as a legacy.

31. William Smallwood (son of Ledstone who died in 1755) on June 17, 1736 received deed of gift ("May Day", 100 acres) from his father Ledstone Smallwood, wife Elizabeth consenting (*La Plata*, Lib. O No. 2, fol. 132). On June 12, 1740 Ledstone Smallwood, Gent., and Eliza, his wife, and William Smallwood, Gent., and Ledia, his wife, sold to Arthur Westman. On May 29, 1750 William Smallwood, son of Ledstone, sold to John Hanson land called "May Day", 100 acres (*La Plata*, Lib. Z No. 2, fol. 488). No wife signs. However, this land is recorded as belonging to William Smallwood in the Charles County Debt Books from 1753 to 1768. On Feb. 4, 1763 (a few days after buying from Hester Adams, widow, her

interest) William Smallwood, planter, sold to James Craik, physician, "May Day", 100 acres (*La Plata,* Lib. L No. 3, fol. 279). This is the last certain reference to William Smallwood as living. He is mentioned as deceased in a deposition of Ledstone Smallwood, Nov. 19, 1782 (*La Plata,* Lib. Z No. 3, fol. 5). We are able to give William's wife and the names of two of his children from two deeds of gift. The first is dated Sept. 18, 1747 and records that Mary Smallwood makes deed of gift (negroes) to her granddaughter Anne Smallwood, daughter of William Smallwood, son of Ledstone Smallwood (*La Plata,* Lib. Z No. 2, fol. 181). The other deed, dated Sept. 18, 1750, records that Mary Smallwood, widow, makes deed of gift (negro) to her granddaughter Eleanor Smallwood, daughter of William Smallwood (*La Plata,* Lib. Z No. 2, fol. 425). In neither deed does she call William Smallwood *her* son. Mary Smallwood, widow, could not be Ledstone's wife, for Ledstone himself did not die until 1755, and his wife was Elizabeth (not Mary) at least down to Mch. 14, 1744. Mary Smallwood of these deeds must have been the widow of James Smallwood who died in 1723. This Mary had a daughter Lydia, and William, son of Ledstone, had wife Ledia in 1740. She probably died in 1747 or before as otherwise she would probably have been named in these deeds. No wife signs with William in the deeds of 1750 and 1763. William Smallwood married his cousin Lydia Smallwood, daughter of James, and they had the following children:

> i. Anne Smallwood.
> ii. Eleanor Smallwood.

32. Ledstone Smallwood (son of Ledstone who died in 1755) was born about 1720 and married Susannah Burch, born about 1711, daughter of Justinian Burch, according to deposition made Nov. 19, 1782 (*La Plata,* Lib. Z No. 3, fol. 5). On Jan. 3, 1771 Ledstone Smallwood and wife Susannah sold to William Rody Luckett "May Day", 200 acres and "Addition to May Day", 11 acres (*La Plata,* Lib. S No. 3, fol. 105). Ledstone Smallwood's inventory was presented Dec. 29, 1794,

signed by Mary Smallwood and Bayn Smallwood, kin. Sarah
Smallwood was admx (*La Plata,* Inventories 1791-97, fol.
260). His wife Susannah Smallwood made will Oct. 27, 1805,
prob. Jan. 7, 1806 (she must have been in her 96th year).
She mentions daughter Mary Clements and son Ledstone
Smallwood, exor. Ledstone Smallwood and wife Susannah had
the following children:

64.   i. Ledstone Smallwood.
     ii. Pryor Smallwood (mentioned as son of Ledstone in the
         1790 census).
    iii. Mary Smallwood, md —— Clements.
     iv. Sarah Smallwood (?).

33. John Smallwood (son of Ledstone who died in 1755)
on Mch. 14, 1759 sold to Roger Smith " Welcome ", 200 acres.
No wife signs. (*La Plata,* Lib. G No. 3, fol. 369).

34. Henrietta Smallwood (daughter of Ledstone who died
in 1755) married —— Noland and had.

i. Elizabeth Noland (mentioned in her grandfather's will).

35. Benedictor More (daughter of Henry and Sarah Small-
wood More) married Humphrey Berry (son of Humphrey
Berry, Sr, by his wife Mary Smallwood, daughter of Thomas).
Humphrey Berry made will Oct. 12, 1794, prob. Oct. 20, 1794.
He makes bequests to wife Benictor (sic) Berry; to sons Henry
More Berry (exor), James Smallwood Berry, Benjamin Berry,
and " my other six children ". Benedictor Berry made will
July 18, 1811, prob. Feb. 4, 1812. She mentions sons Henry
M. Berry (exor), Pryor Berry, Samuel Berry, Benjamin Berry,
and James S. Berry. To these names we may add that of
Thomas Berry, who on Jan. 30, 1795 (described as son of
Humphrey) joined with Ledstone Smallwood and Ann Small-
wood in deed of negro to Thomas Smallwood (*La Plata,* Lib. N
No. 4, fol. 340). (What relationship is disguised in this deed
I can not make out). The children of Humphrey Berry and
his wife Benedictor More (they are twice descended from the
Smallwood family) are as follows:

i. Henry More Berry.

65. ii. James Smallwood Berry.

iii. Benjamin Berry.

66. iv. Pryor Berry.

v. Samuel Berry.

vi. Thomas Berry.

vii, viii and ix, Three others, names not learned.

36. James Smallwood (son of John who died in 1770) on Oct. 4, 1764 with Elizabeth, his wife, sold to Oliver Burch lands called " Burches Addition ", 18 acres, " Bowlings Plains ", 19 acres, also another part of " Bowling Plains ", 40 acres, where the said James and Elizabeth Smallwood now live, including the spring now used by James Smallwood and family; James and Elizabeth for their heirs, and Elizabeth for her heirs, guarantee, etc. (*La Plata*, Lib. L No. 3, fol. 550). " Bowlings Plains " was willed by Oliver Burch to his son Benjamin Burch in 1727. Elizabeth, wife of James Smallwood, clearly had a right in this land not dependent upon her marriage with James Smallwood. It is practically a certainty that she was a Burch before marriage. On Mch. 29, 1771 James Smallwood, son of John, sold to Luke Smallwood, son of John, his interest in land bequeathed to Luke by their dec'd father, " Friendship ", 100 acres. Elizabeth, wife of James, consents (*La Plata*, Lib. S No. 3, fol. 158). Likewise on May 18, 1771 James Smallwood, son of John, sold to John Smallwood, son of John, " Friendship " and " Smallwoods Meadows ", wife Elizabeth consenting (*La Plata*, Lib. S No. 3, fol. 160). He appears in the Charles County census, 1775-78, as James Smallwood, son of John. He is probably identical with the James Smallwood, Sr, whose inventory was presented May 8, 1792 with Smallwood Thompson and John Berry, apprs, James Smallwood, relation, and Thomas Smallwood, Sr, as admr. On same day the inventory of Ann Smallwood was presented with the same persons signing as apprs, relation, and admr (*La Plata*, Inventories 1791-97, fol. 73-4). James, the son of James, was still living at this time, and the only other James who could be called Senior in his life time must

be James, son of John. The Ann Smallwood, so closely linked with his name by the above records, may be a second wife.

37. John Smallwood (son of John who died in 1770) on Mch. 11, 1775 sold " Friendship ", 66 acres, and " Smallwoods Meadows ", 42 acres, to Rich'd Willett, wife Ann consenting (*La Plata,* Lib. S No. 3, fol. 707). This Ann was the daughter of James Grant (*La Plata,* Lib. No. 6, fol. 305). Ann Smallwood, widow of John Smallwood, appears in the Charles County census, 1790. We have no record of John's death but it must have been before 1790. Ann Middleton Smallwood, daughter of John and Ann Smallwood, who was born June 25, 1755 (recorded in Piscataway Parish records, Prince George County) may have been their child but another John Smallwood with wife Ann was living in this parish at this time or only a little later.

38. Luke Smallwood (son of John who died in 1770) on Oct. 31, 1786 (described in deed as of Loudoun County, Virginia) sold to Benjamin Cawood land called " Friendship ", 100 acres, and 4 acres to the west of said tract, lying in Charles County, Maryland. Luke Smallwood and Bane Smallwood appear among the tithables of Loudoun County, Virginia, in 1788 and later. Luke Smallwood and Bayn Smallwood sign a petition from Loudoun County, Oct. 6, 1792 (*Richmond, Department of Archives, Tithables and Petitions*). The estate of Luke Smallwood, dec'd, was appraised in Loudoun County, Feb. 10, 1794 (*Leesburg,* Estate Accts E, fol. 163). The relation of Bayn to Luke has not been ascertained.

39. George Smallwood (son of John who died in 1770) has unimportant mention in the Court Proceedings of Charles County in Aug. 1756 and Nov. 1757. He is undoubtedly identical with the George Smallwood who bought land of James Loyd in Frederick County, Virginia on Sept. 3, 1764 (*Winchester,* Lib. 9, fol. 371). In this county on Aug. 2, 1769 the court ordered Stephen Cawood (he was the son of John Cawood who married Elizabeth Smallwood) to pay 200 pounds

of tobacco to George Smallwood for his service as witness; and on Oct. 6, 1772 George Smallwood was a witness in the same county in the case of John Keywood (either father or brother of the above Stephen Cawood) vs Ulrick Spoar. George Smallwood lived in that part of Frederick County which was set off into Berkeley County. In this latter county he was one of the apprs of the estate of Rich'd Locke, Sept. 11, 1775, of Robert Tabb, May 21, 1776, and of John Goddart, Nov. 1777. In the same county on Mch. 18, 1797 George Smallwood bought land of George Hite and wife Deborah (which land had formerly belonged to Dr. John Briscoe and had been willed by him to his son Hezekiah Briscoe) (*Martinsburg*, Lib. 13, fol. 333). On May 18, 1801 George Smallwood bought land of John Potts and Elizabeth, his wife, and of William Hall and Miriam, his wife (*Martinsburgh*, Lib. 18, fol 195 and 198). Both deeds were delivered to Gabriel Smallwood (probably son of George).

40. Sarah Smallwood (daughter of John who died in 1770) married Seth Johnson and had son

 i. Kensey Johnson.

41. Charity Smallwood (daughter of John who died in 1770) married Richard Marlow and had son.

 i. Randolph Marlow (but called Rudolph in the account). She predeceased her father.

42. James Smallwood (son of William, son of James who died in 1723) and wife Jemima had son Hepburn Smallwood, born Mch. 1, 1760 in Rock Creek Parish, Prince George County. He is undoubtedly identical with the James Smallwood who in Frederick County, Virginia on Feb. 8, 1769 brought suit against Benjamin Berry (agreed out of court). James Smallwood and William Smallwood signed petition from Frederick County, Virginia in 1776. The census of this county for 1782 gives four Smallwoods as heads of families living in the same vicinity (that is, in the same list), namely, James Smallwood, William Smallwood, Hebbern (sic) Small-

wood, and the inevitable Bean Smallwood. The tax-lists of the same county for 1784 show a Mimey Smallwood with no tithable. This gives us a date before which James Smallwood must have died. The tax-lists of 1786 show Jeremiah Smallwood with no tithable (undoubtedly error for Jemimah). Other Smallwoods appearing in these lists prior to 1800 are Van, Elijah, and David Smallwood. Hepburn appears in numerous spellings (Hebron, Hebbern, Hebborn, etc.) (*Richmond,* Department of Archives, Tax-lists).

43. Daughter (of James Smallwood who died in 1767) married ———— Wilson and had

    i. Lucretia Wilson.
    ii. James Smallwood Wilson.

44. Henry Smallwood (son of James who died in 1767 married (1) ———— and had two children:

    i. Samuel Smallwood, of full age in 1806.
    ii. Anastasia Smallwood, of full age in 1806 and married to Cornelius Smith of Washington, D. C.

Henry Smallwood married (2) Verlinda, widow of Joshua Tench and daughter of James Smallwood whose will was probated Jan. 12, 1795, and they had.

    iii. Colbert Smallwood, aged 5 in 1806.
    iv. Mary Smallwood, aged 4 in 1806.

(*Annapolis,* Chancery Papers, Bundle 363; *La Plata,* Court Proc. Lib. Acct of Sales and Bonds, 1797-99, fol. 252; and will of James Smallwood, 1795).

45. Walter Bayne Smallwood (son of James who died in 1767) served in the Revolution from Prince George County in 1781, giving his age as 18 years. He married Elizabeth Noble, Apr. 30, 1796.

46. James Bidon Smallwood (son of James who died in 1767) married Jemima ————. His inventory is dated 1783. At a court held in Feb., 1788, Smallwood Thompson brought

suit against Elisha Robertson, and Jemima, his wife, admx of James B. Smallwood, demanding that they show why they should not furnish counter security.

47. William Marbury Smallwood (son of James who died in 1767) married Grace Harmon, widow of John Harmon in 1772 or before. He made will Mch. 19, 1806, prob. Aug. 26, 1809, in which he mentions the following children:

    i. Daniel Smallwood (born Apr. 23, 1773, married Mary ——).
    ii. Ann Smallwood, md —— Robey.
    iii. Elizabeth Smallwood, md —— Adams.

and grandchildren Harriet Robey, Grace Robey, Walter Robey, Garrett Robey, and Leonard S. Robey. Tradition insists that William Marbury Smallwood also had children

    iv. William Smallwood.
    v. Leonard Smallwood.

48. Samuel Smallwood (son of James who died in 1767) married about 1771 to Martha Ann Berry, daughter of Humphrey Berry, Sr, by his second wife. (Martha Smallwood who married Robert Abercromby in Prince George County on Aug. 5, 1787, is probably the widow of Samuel). Samuel Smallwood's will, made ——, 1784, prob. ——, 1785, mentions wife Martha Ann and children:

67.   i. Samuel Nicholas (or Nicholls) Smallwood.
    ii. Letty (Letitia) Smallwood (testator mentions property left to her by her grandfather, Humphrey Berry).
    iii. Rebecca Smallwood (md George Lovejoy, June 10, 1794, in Prince George County).
68.   iv. Felder Smallwood.
    v. Unborn child.

49. Susannah Smallwood (daughter of James who died in 1767) married Thomas Berry, Aug. 25, 1781, and they had at least two children:

    i. Sarah (Sally) Berry.
    ii. Nelly Berry.

50. Luke Smallwood (son of the James who died in 1767) had three children:

    i. Susannah Smallwood, md —— Marbury.
   ii. Ann Smallwood.
  iii. Teresa Smallwood.

51. Thomas Smallwood (son of James who died 1775) on July 17, 1775 joined his mother Ann Smallwood, widow, in a deed of " Smallwoods Addition ", 100 acres, to Josias Beall (*La Plata,* Lib. V No. 3, fol. 13). On Sept. 7, 1779 Thomas Smallwood sold to Humphrey Berry his right and interest in " Smallwoods Plains ", which right Thomas bases upon the fact that he is the grandson and heir at law of Thomas Smallwood who bequeathed the land in 1734 to Humphrey Berry, at whose death it was to be equally divided between the latter's two sons, Humphrey and Thomas Berry (by his first wife Mary Smallwood) and since Thomas Berry had died without issue, Thomas Smallwood now claims a moiety in said land. This Thomas appears in the 1790 census as Capt. Thomas Smallwood, thus being distinguished from Thomas, son of Thomas. He was older than his cousin for he is called Sr in a deed of Nov. 11, 1793, in which he sold to Henry Green land called " Smallwood's Gore ". On Mch. 22, 1796 he sold to Ledstone Smallwood " Pork Hall " and " Batchellors Delight ". On May 14, 1792 Thomas Smallwood, son of James, sold a negro to son Richard Smallwood (*La Plata,* Lib. K No. 4, fol. 426). On Jan. 30, 1795 Ledstone Smallwood, Ann Smallwood, and Thomas Berry, son of Humphrey, sold back to Thomas Smallwood the negro which he had sold to his son Richard Smallwood during the life time of said Richard. (*La Plata,* Lib. N No 4. fol. 340). Apparently, Richard Smallwood, son of Thomas, died before 1795, and the three grantors in the last deed had acquired a claim to his slave by right of inheritance but on what relationship that right was based I am not yet prepared to say. We may certainly say that Thomas Smallwood had son

    i. Richard Smallwood, born 1767 (?),

probably identical with the Richard Smallwood, aged 9 years in 1776, living in the home of Henry Acton, Prince George

County, who had married Thomas Smallwood's sister. We may infer that Thomas's wife (name not known) died in 1776 or before. He is probably identical with Thomas Smallwood, Charles County, inventory 1801, Ledstone Smallwood, exor.

52. James Smallwood (son of James who died in 1775) married Eleanor ———. He made will Dec. 19, 1794, prob. Jan. 12, 1795, in which he mentions wife Elenor and children:

69. i. John Smallwood.
 ii. Henry Acton Smallwood.
 iii. Calvert Acton Smallwood.
 iv. James Smallwood.
 v. Leney (or Linny) Smallwood, md —— Tench.
 vi. Elenor Smallwood (md Walter Boswell, Oct. 14, 1779).
 vii. Elizabeth Smallwood.
 viii. Ann Smallwood, md —— Thompson.
 ix. Sarah Smallwood, md —— Moore.
 x. Mary Smallwood, md (Benjamin) Bean.
 xi. Chloe Smallwood.

53. Easter (Hester) Smallwood (daughter of James who died in 1775) married Henry Acton about 1754. The names of their children are found in the Prince George Census of 1776 with ages by which we arrive at the approximate dates of their birth. They are as follows:

i. Henry Acton, Jr., born about 1755.
ii. Smallwood Acton, born about 1759, served in the Revolution.
iii. Nancy Smallwood Acton, bapt. Jan. 19, 1766.
iv. Ann Acton, born about 1767.
v. Elizabeth Acton, born about 1769.
vi. Mary Acton, born about 1772.
vii. Francis Acton, named in his grandfather's, James Smallwood's, will, 1775.

54. Thomas Smallwood (son of Thomas who died in 1778) before Mch. 4, 1777, married Ann Macatee, widow and admx of Thomas Macatee. On Apr. 5, 1787 Thomas Smallwood, son of Thomas, and wife Ann sold " Moore's Rest " to Hezekiah Smallwood.

55. Bayne Smallwood (son of Thomas who died in 1778)

was baptized in St. John's of Piscataway Parish, Mch. 1, 1752. On Dec. 3, 1782 he married Chloe McAtee. In deed made Aug. 7, 1787 by Bayne and Hezekiah Smallwood, Bayne's wife is given as Clotilda (probable the same as Chloe), and Hezekiah's wife as Catherine.

56. Hezekiah Smallwood (son of Thomas who died in 1778) married Catharine ——— and they had son

i. Bean Smallwood, born May 14, 1796.

57. Benjamin Smallwood (son of Thomas who died in 1778) married Lydia Hutchinson and they had the following children:

i. Chloe Smallwood, md Henry Russell, Nov. 10, 1782.
ii. Samuel Smallwood.
iii. Hezekiah Smallwood, moved to Hardin County, Kentucky, about 1800.
iv. William Smallwood, moved to Missouri.
v. Pryor Smallwood, moved to Kentucky.

58. Richard Harrison (son of Richard Harrison by his wife Esther Smallwood) married Elizabeth Smallwood (daughter of Pryor, son of Thomas). He made will Dec. 11, 1771, prob. Mch. 14, 1772. He mentions his mother Esther Harrison as still living, refers to land inherited from his dec'd brother Hezekiah Harrison, and names the following children (all minors):

i. Joseph Harrison.
ii. Virlinda Harrison.
iii. Thomas Harrison.
iv. Mary Harrison.
v. Richard Harrison.
vi. Francs Harrison.

59. William Smallwood (son of John who died in 1736) was born about 1721. The 1776 census of Prince George County gives William Smallwood, aged 54, living in St. John and St. George Parish as a neighbor of John Winn, John Winn, Jr, and John Berry. His wife Mary is 56 years old. There are also in the family another male aged 19 and two females aged 20 and 14, names not given. In Aug. 1780 William

Smallwood, Senr, son of John, aged 59 years or thereabouts, deposed in regard to the bounds of " Tatshall ", " Eltham ", and " Moore's Ditch " that about 40 years ago the deponent's mother Mary Smallwood, since dec'd, showed him the stump on which a rock is now fixed and engraved 1774, and the words " Mount Pleasant's beginning " (*La Plata,* Lib. Y No. 3, fol. 596). On Mch 13, 1759 William Smallwood, Jr, planter, (wife Mary Ann consenting) sold to Samuel Marshall land called " Tatshall ", 60 acres (*La Plata,* Lib. G No. 3, fol. 309). On Mch. 24, 1759 Samuel Marshall sold to William Smallwood, Jr, land called " Griffins Seat ", 112 acres (*Ibid.* fol. 312). On June 13, 1764 William Smallwood, Jr, (wife Mary Ann consenting) sold " Griffins Seat ", 112 acres, to George Maxwell.   On Oct. 24, 1778 Thomas Berry of Charles County in his will directs that William Smallwood, son of John, be allowed to have use of his upper plantation in Prince George County so long as he conducts himself properly as a tenant.   The record of his death and the names of his children have not yet been learned but I feel confident that some of the unplaced Smallwoods belong to him.

60. John Wynn (Winn) (son of John Winn by his wife Ann Smallwood) was born Jan. 27, 1721/2. He married Sarah Robey, Aug. 24, 1738 (she was born about 1723, died May 22, 1777). In 1779 he had married Ann Smallwood (widow of John Smallwood, Jr, who died in 1765, and daughter of Ralph Marlow). By his wife Sarah he had the following children:

    i. John Wynn, born July 23, 1739, md Mary ——.
    ii. Elizabeth Wynn, born May 30, 1741.
    iii. Hezekiah Wynn, born Sept. 12, 1742.
    iv. Sarah Ann Wynn, born Dec. 9, 1744.
    v. Violender Wynn, born Sept. 13, 1746, died Oct. 12, 1748.
    vi. Easter Wynn, born Apr. 15, 1748, died Apr. 8, 1753.
    vii. Anaka Wynn, born Jan. 24, 1750.
    viii. Hannah Wynn.
    ix. Easter Verlinda Wynn, born Aug. 10, 1755.
    x. William Smallwood Wynn, born Aug. 9, 1757 (?), served in the Revolution; married Milicent Smallwood in Prince George County, May 20, 1778, her parentage not known.

xi. Hezekiah Wynn, born Oct. 22, 1759, married Rebecca M.
Smallwood, Jan. 12, 1779, in Prince George County, her
parentage not known.
xii. Ann Wynn, born Apr. 22, 1761, married Robert Ogden,
Oct. 17, 1778.
xiii. Lucy Ann Wynn, born Sept. 26, 1762, married George
Alder, Oct. 31, 1778.
xiv. Priscilla Ann Wynn, born Apr. 16, 1764.
xv. Eleanor Ann Wynn, born Nov. 13, 1767.
(The births in the above records taken from Piscataway Parish records.)

61. Josiah Wynn (son of John Wynn by his wife Ann
Smallwood) was born Feb. 1, 1726, married Ann Downing in
1750 or before. His will is dated Sept. 30, 1763, prob. Dec.
21, 1763, Prince George County. He mentions wife and all
my children (not by name), and in particular two sons:

i. William Wynn.
ii. Josiah Wynn, born Mch. 27, 1762.
He also had daughters:
iii. Elizabeth Bread Wynn, bapt. Apr. 28, 1751.
iv. Ann Wynn, born Apr. 30, 1755.

62. Lucy Heabard Smallwood (daughter of Bayne who died
in 1768) married John Truman Stoddert. She made will in
Charles County Nov. 2, 1767, prob. Oct. 27, 1768, in which
she names her father Bayne Smallwood, brother William Smallwood, sisters Elizabeth Leiper, Margaret Stoddert, Eleanor
Smallwood, and Priscilla Smallwood, and one son

i. William Truman Stoddert.

63. Eleanor Smallwood (daughter of Bayne who died in
1768) married Col. William Grayson. He served under
Washington in the Revolution and was one of the first two
U. S. Senators from Virginia. He died in 1790. By his
wife Eleanor Smallwood he had the following children:

i. William Grayson.
ii. George W. Grayson.
iii. Robert Hanson Harrison Grayson.
iv. Heabard S. Grayson.
v. Alfred Grayson.

(The Carter Henry Harrisons of Chicago, father and son, mayors, descend from this Grayson-Smallwood marriage. For other descendants of Col. Wm. Grayson see Tyler's Quarterly Magazine, Vol. VIII, page 119.)

64. Leadstone Smallwood (son of Leadstone by his wife Susannah Burch) made deed of gift Aug. 22, 1816 to son

    i. Richard Leadstone Smallwood.

Leadstone Smallwood made will Apr. 23, 1832, prob. May 1, 1832, in which he mentions wife Jane only.

65. James Smallwood Berry (son of Humphrey Berry who died in 1794) married Elizabeth Heard and had son

    i. Judson Heard Berry, born Nov. 25, 1786.

66. Pryor Berry (son of Humphrey Berry who died in 1794) made will Apr. 28, 1820, prob. July 21, 1820, in which he mentions wife (not by name) and the following children:

    i. Permelia Marlow.
    ii. John Berry.
    iii. Mary E. Gates.
    iv. Meaky A. Giddens.
    v. Nathaniel Berry.
    vi. Thomas Humphrey Berry.
    vii. Thomas Smallwood Berry.

67. Samuel Nicholls Smallwood (son of Samuel who died in 1785) was born in 1772, married Ruth Beall, Mch. 5, 1801. He was at one time mayor of Washington. He had son

    i. William Augustin Smallwood, born Dec. 13, 1804, trained first as lawyer and next as Episcopal clergyman. He was once elected Bishop of Indiana but declined.

68. Felder Herd Smallwood (son of Samuel who died in 1785) gave his age as 16 when he apprenticed himself to Jonathan Jackson, carpenter, of Montgomery County, Mch. 17, 1799 (therefore, born about 1783). He made will in Charles County, Mch. 9, 1813, prob. Aug. 13, 1816, in which he mentions wife Christeny, at whose death certain property is to be

divided equally between Elizabeth Innocent Berry (relationship not given) and son

i. Enoch Washington Smallwood.

69. John Smallwood (son of James who died in 1794-5) died before Mch. 9, 1796 on which date his inventory was presented, signed by Benj. Bean and Henry A. Smallwood, kin, with Elizabeth Smallwood, admx.

I give next records of Smallwoods of Charles and Prince George Counties who certainly belong to the line of Col. James Smallwood though their exact place is not yet known.

John Smallwood, Jr, of Prince George County sold a negro to John Wynn, Nov. 26, 1763. His inventory was presented in Prince George May 17, 1765 with John Marlow as admr, and James Smallwood, Jr, and John Smallwood as kin, and John Wynn as creditor. His wife was Ann Marlow, daughter of Ralph Marlow, whose will, June 30, 1770, mentions daughter Ann Smallwood. It was certainly this Ann Smallwood, widow, who in about 1779 married John Wynn. I suggest that John Smallwood, Jr, was the son of James who died in 1775. Ann Smallwood, aged 41, appears in the Prince George County census in 1776 with two females, aged 17 and 7. The Piscataway Parish records show that Ann Middleton Smallwood, daughter of John and Ann Smallwood, was born June 25, 1755. She may have been the daughter of the John Smallwood, Jr, who died in 1765, but there was another John living at this time with wife Ann who may have been her father.

The inventory of one Prior Smallwood was presented in Charles County, Dec. 1797 and Mch. 1798 with Casana (or Caesaria ?) Smallwood as admx and Samuel Smallwood and Susannah Smallwood, kin. Her bond was signed by Bayne Smallwood and Bayne Smallwood, son of John, as sureties. The size of her bond, 5000 pounds current money, would indicate that Prior was a man of some importance. I have no suggestion either in regard to Prior or to the two Baynes.

Basil Smallwood married Mary Gareff (?) in Piscataway

Parish, May 13, 1787.   He appears in the 1790 census of
Charles County.   In Piscataway Parish, Mary Ann, daughter
of Basil Smallwood and *Susanna,* his wife, was born Jan. 16,
1792.

Bean Smallwood appears in the 1790 census of Charles
County, called " son of Pryor " (so as to distinguish him from
Bean, son of Thomas).   There were two Pryors at this time,
one, the son of Thomas, and the other, the son of Ledstone.
This Bean of 1790 is almost certainly identical with Bayne
Smallwood of Charles County who made will Sept. 22, 1807,
prob. Oct. 6, 1807.   Ledstone Smallwood was one of the wit-
nesses.   The testator mentions no wife or children, but names
sisters Priscilla Smallwood, Ann Haislep, Sarah Hamilton,
Elizabeth Tydings, brothers Benjamin Smallwood and John
Smallwood.   These appear to be the names (along with Bayne)
of the children of some Pryor Smallwood, but which Pryor
I am not prepared to say.

John Smallwood married Cloe Wilson in Prince George
County, Dec. 16, 1787.   He bought " Refuse " in Prince
George County of William Alexander Wilson on Aug. 28,
1804; also part of " Refuse " of Nathaniel Wilson, Apr. 4,
1809.   He made will July 23, 1811, prob. June 4, 1812 in
Prince George County.   He mentions wife Chloe and chil-
dren Aquilla Wilson Smallwood (eldest son), Nathaniel Gusta
Smallwood (second son), Jerusha Ann Smallwood, Elizabeth
Burch Smallwood, Henrietta Maria Smallwood, Lucy Harriet
Smallwood, Chloe Ann Smallwood, and John Randolph Small-
wood.   We have already seen that James Smallwood (son of
John who died in 1770) almost certainly married Elizabeth
Burch.   This John is most probably their son.   I also regard
him as identical with the John Smallwood of Prince George
County (there was only one John Smallwood in this county in
1790) who sold 9 acres of " Friendship ", lying in Charles
County, to Nicholas Blacklock on Oct. 29, 1793, according to
the lines laid down in the deed of Mary Smallwood, Mch. 27,
1742 (which deed appears not to be on record).   No wife

signs with John, though he had wife Chloe at this time if he is identical with the John named above (*La Plata*, Lib. M No. 4, fol. 244). This deed has a close connection with the following record:

On Nov. 12, 1793, at the request of Nicholas Blacklock the following assignment of Benjamin Cawood was recorded:

"Whereas I am largely indebted to Nicholas Blacklock (my Cawood genealogy will show that he was Blacklock's father-in-law)—and whereas I have made considerable building and improvements on land the fee simple of which is in a certain John Smallwood, supposing the said land to be my own right in fee—and whereas I may be entitled to a compensation for the said buildings, etc—therefore, I, Benjamin Cawood, sell to Nicholas Blacklock my title in land held by John Smallwood" (*La Plata*, Lib. N No. 4, fol. 171). Benjamin Cawood bought "Friendship," 100 acres, and 4 acres west of said tract, of Luke Smallwood in 1786. Shortly after that time he had some resurveys made by which undoubtedly a longstanding error was discovered. We have already seen that John Smallwood who died in 1770 left "Friendship" to his sons John and Luke. The records show plainly that his son James was the oldest son and the natural heir at law. Benjamin Cawood's resurvey evidently disclosed that John Smallwood possessed 9 acres more than he was aware of and which he did not will away. His son James became the rightful owner of this land and from him (for this James died in 1792) the title would pass to his eldest son, namely, John Smallwood of this deed.

There are two other records which seem to have some connection with this deed of John Smallwood and with Benjamin Cawood's assignment. On Oct. 31, 1793, Ann Smallwood sold to Catharin Smallwood, Emily Smallwood, and Smallwood Cawood one negro and sundry personals for 45 pounds, 7 shillings, and four pence. On same date Smallwood Cawood, Emally Smallwood, Catharine Smallwood, and Ann Smallwood, all of Charles County, sold for same amount two negroes to Stephen Cawood (*La Plata,* Lib. N. No. 4, fol. 172-3). The Smallwood Cawood and Stephen Cawood of this record were half-brothers of Benjamin Cawood of the preceding record. Smallwood Cawood had married Elizabeth Smallwood in Prince George County, June 18, 1787. Elizabeth, Catharine, and Emily Smallwood seem to have been sisters, perhaps also Ann Smallwood, but their relationship with John Smallwood who sold to Nicholas Blacklock on almost the same day, and their parentage have not been as yet determined. The Catharine Smallwood of this record may be the one who married John Rowling in Prince George County, June 10, 1794.

Another John Smallwood died in Charles County about 1788. His inventory, 1788, is signed by Bayne Smallwood, kin, and Ledstone Smallwood and Mary Smallwood, admrs.

Vermillion, South Dakota, September 25, 1926.

SMITH FAMILY OF CALVERT COUNTY.

CHRISTOPHER JOHNSTON.

1. RICHARD SMITH,[1] the ancestor of this family, enters rights,
7 October 1662, for himself in February 1649 and his wife
Eleanor in August 1651 (Land Office, Lib. 5, fol. 188). He
lived in Calvert County, and owned land on St. Leonard's
Creek and in the neighborhood of Lyon's Creek. He was
a lawyer by profession and he frequently appears in this
capacity in the records of the Provincial Court. He was
commissioned Attorney General of the Province, 28 September 1657 (*Md. Arch.*, x, 542) and held office under Fendall's
administration until 1660. In the commission he is styled
"Lieutenant Richard Smith," doubtless indicating that he
held this rank in the Provincial militia. He was elected, 10
April 1658, one of the Burgesses for Calvert County (Lib. S.,
fol. 26). He was not a member of the House which met 28
February 1659/60 (*Md. Arch.*, i, 382), but he represented
Calvert County in the Assembly which met in April 1661,
and sat successively until 1667 (*Md. Arch.*, i, 396, 426 ; ii, 8).
In 1665 he was Foreman of the Grand Jury of the Province
(Lib. FF, fol. 64). 30 February 1671, "Richard Smith of
Calvert County " was summoned as a juror by the Provincial
Court and, not appearing, was fined 500 lbs. tobacco (Lib. JJ,
fol. 264). In the levy of November 1678, "Mr. Richard
Smith Senior " had a credit of 900 lbs. tobacco in Calvert
County (*Md. Arch.*, vii, 103), and, 22 May 1679, "Richard
Smith Senior " of Calvert County was cited to appear at St.
Mary's on the 6th of July following to testify in regard to the
will of John Gnammar deceased. The citation was returned
"served," 4 June 1679 (Test. Proc., Lib. 11, fol. 92). In
November 1683 an act was passed establishing a port on

Richard Smith's land at St. Leonard's Creek, and by the
same act Richard Smith *Junior* was appointed one of the
Commissioners for laying out towns and ports in Calvert
County (*Md. Arch.*, vii, 609, 611). Richard Smith Senior
was probably living in 1689 when his son Richard is styled
"Richard Smith Junior" (*Md. Arch.*, xiii, 242), but neither
his will nor any record of the administration of his estate
appears on record. He probably died not long after 1689,
when the records were very badly kept in consequence of the
Revolution. A list of the Provincial Archives, compiled in
1695, states that from 13 July 1689 to 14 June 1692 no
testamentary records were in existence (*Md. Arch.*, xx, 200).
Eleanor wife of Richard Smith joined her husband, in 1665,
in a deed conveying land in Calvert County. 18 February
1671, Richard Smith sues James Veitch about a tract called
Smith's Joy, on St. Leonard's Creek, which the said Richard
Smith and Eleanor his wife conveyed to the said James
Veitch by deed dated 18 January 1664/5 (Lib. JJ, fol. 280).
18 December 1669, Mrs. Eleanor Smith was one of the
ladies of Calvert County who petitioned the Provincial Court
for a respite of the sentence of an unfortunate woman convicted of child murder, she having concealed the birth of her
child. The petition was granted and the prisoner respited
until the 18th of October following.

Richard Smith and Eleanor his wife had (with perhaps other
issue) two sons :—

2.　i.　CAPT. RICHARD SMITH,[2] d. 1714.
3.　ii.　COL. WALTER SMITH,[2] d. 1711.

2.　CAPT. RICHARD SMITH [2] of St. Leonard's, Calvert County,
died in 1714, and his will (dated 31 July 1710, proved 23
Feb'y 1714) affords proof of his parentage. In it he appoints "my loving brother Walter Smith" sole executor and,
among other dispositions, leaves to his son Walter "my
dwelling house with all the lands belonging to it as my
father bought of Mr. Stone." This was a tract of 350 acres,
called St. Leonards, at the mouth of St. Leonard's Creek.
9 September 1663, Thomas Stone of Charles County and
Mary his wife convey to Richard Smith of Calvert County
a tract of 350 acres at the mouth of St. Leonard's Creek
(Lib. BB). In the Calvert County Rent Roll it is entered as
follows : "*St. Leonards*, 350 acres—Surveyed 15 July 1651
for Thomas Stone Gent., near St. Leonard's Creek. Possessor

(1707) Richard Smith." In November 1683, Richard Smith
Junior was appointed one of the Commissioners for laying
out towns and ports in Calvert County (*Md. Arch.*, vii, 611).
In the revolution of 1689 he sided with Lord Baltimore's
government and took an active part against the revolutionists.
Being captain of a company of foot, he gathered his men and
marched with them, under orders from the Council, to Mattapany, where the government was then seated. But the
revolutionists appeared in overwhelming force and the gar-
rison of Mattapany was compelled to capitulate. Later, the
revolutionary party issued writs for an election of Burgesses,
but Captain Smith strongly urged the people of Calvert to
hold no election, alleging that the writs were not issued
under proper authority, and that the new Assembly was
merely intended to approve the illegal acts of Coode and his
associates. Michael Taney, High Sheriff of the County, and
Capt. Thomas Clagett, the coroner, both refused to hold an
election. Richard Smith, Michael Taney, and Cecilius Butler,
who had also taken an active part against the revolutionary
proceedings, were all imprisoned (*Md. Arch.*, viii, 147–149).
Richard Smith made a strong protest against his illegal arrest
(*ibid.*, 149–151), and his wife Barbara went to England
where she presented, 30 December 1689, a petition to the
Commissioners for Trade and Plantation, with a narrative of
the troubles in Maryland (*ibid.*, 153–155). Under the new
government Capt. Smith was deprived of his commission as
captain in the Calvert County militia, and Thomas Tasker
was appointed in his place (*Md. Arch.*, xiii, 242). Capt.
Smith was Surveyor General of Maryland 1693–94 (*Md.
Arch.*, xix, 58 ; xx, 34, 37). Richard Smith was thrice married. His first wife, married before 1679, was Elizabeth,
daughter of Robert and Mary (Mainwaring) Brooke who,
with her twin brother Henry, was born at Brooke Place
Manor, Calvert County, 28 November 1655 (*Magazine*, i,
69). Under date of 2 December 1679, Christopher Baines
and Ann his wife, and Richard Smith and Elizabeth his wife,
obtain a warrant of resurvey for a tract called Brooke Ridge,
devised to the said Ann and Elizabeth by the will of their
brother Charles Brooke late of Calvert County, Gent., (Land
Office, Lib. 20, fol. 285). An abstract of the will of Charles
Brooke is given in *Baldwin's Calendar*, i, 64. Richard Smith
married secondly, 13 July 1686, Barbara widow of John
Rousby of Calvert County and daughter of Henry Morgan

of Kent County (*Magazine*, ii, 374). In 1697 Richard Smith was married, at Christ Church, Calvert County, to his third wife Maria Johanna widow of Col. Lowther, and daughter of Charles Somerset Esq. of Acton Park, Co. Middlesex, and Ross in Hertfordshire, third son of Lord John Somerset, son of the first Marquis of Worcester (Chancery, Lib. PC., fol. 849–50).

Richard Smith and his first wife, Elizabeth Brooke, had issue :—

    i. RICHARD SMITH,[3] mar. Elizabeth widow of Roger Brooke Jr. and daughter of Francis Hutchins (*Magazine*, i, 187). They had a daughter Margaret Smith[4] who mar. Thomas Wilson.
    ii. ANNE SMITH, mar. William Dawkins.
    iii. ELIZABETH SMITH, mar. William Tom.

By his second wife, Barbara, he had :—

4.   i. WALTER SMITH of St. Leonard's, d. 1748.
    ii. FRANCES SMITH.
    iii. SUSANNA SMITH.
    iv. BARBARA SMITH, b. 1693; d. 1764; mar. 1°. 1 Jan'y 1712, Thomas Holdsworth, 2°. about 1720, Benjamin Mackall.

Richard Smith and Maria Johanna his third wife, had issue :—

5.   i. CHARLES SOMERSET SMITH of Charles Co., b. Feb'y 1698; d. 1738.

3. COL. WALTER SMITH[2] of Hall's Craft, Calvert County, died in 1711. His will, dated 16 February 1710/1, was proved 4 June 1711. He signed the "Declaration of Calvert County for not choosing Burgesses," 20 August 1689 (*Md. Arch.*, viii, 111),* and the "Address from the Protestants of Calvert County to His Majesty" (*ibid.*, 131). He was commissioned, 4 September 1689, captain of foot in the Calvert County militia (*Md. Arch.*, xiii, 242), and was commissioned Major of the County 17 August 1695 (*Md. Arch.*, xx, 281). After 1706 he is styled "Colonel." By act of Assembly, 17 April 1706, "Col? Walter Smith" and Capt. Richard Smith are appointed members of the commission for laying out towns and ports in Calvert County (*Md. Arch.*, xxvi, 638). Walter Smith represented his County in the Assembly from 1696 to 1704, and from 1708 to 1711 (*House Journals*). He was elected a vestryman of All Saints Parish, Calvert County, at the organization of the parish, 7 February 1692/3 (*Md.*

---

* In the printed Archives his name erroneously appears as "Wm Smith," instead of "W^t Smith" as in the original.

Arch., viii, 473), and held the position until his death. He was present at a vestry meeting 2 April 1711 (Vestry Book), and his will was proved 4 June following, so that he must have died in April or May. He was commissioned one of the Justices of Calvert County 16 May 1694 (*Md. Arch.*, xx, 64) and again 16 October following (*ibid.*, 138). He was added to the Quorum 10 July 1696 (*ibid.*, 465) and was made Presiding Justice of the County 10 May 1699 (*Md. Arch.*, xxv, 75, 108). He was appointed, 1 June 1697, by the Assembly, one of the Commission to treat with the Piscataway Indians (*Md. Arch.*, xix, 530). It would seem that Col. Smith had Jacobite tendencies, since in July 1698 he was required to give security to appear at the next Provincial Court for drinking King James' Health (*Md. Arch.*, xxiii, 461, 468, 469). Col. Walter Smith married in 1686 Rachel, daughter of Richard Hall of Calvert County (d. 1688), who was one of the Burgesses for the County 1666–1670, and 1674–85. Her father names in his will "my daughter Rachel now wife of Walter Smith," and leaves her a tract of 300 acres called Aldermason (*Baldwin's Calendar*, ii, 32). This tract is devised by the will of Col. Walter Smith to his daughters Rebecca and Elizabeth. Mrs. Rachel Smith was born in 1670 and died 28 October 1730. The following entry is found in the Greenfield family Bible:— "Mrs. Rachel Smith wife & Relict of Col. Walter Smith late of Calvert Co. dec^d departed this life Oct: ye 28th 1730 in ye 60th year of her age & was Interred the 6th of Nov: following." Her will, dated 28 October 1730, was proved 3 February 1730/1.

Col. Walter Smith and Rachel (Hall) his wife had issue :—

6.   i.   WALTER SMITH [3] of Hall's Craft, b. about 1692 ; d. 1734.
7.   ii.   RICHARD SMITH of Lower Marlboro, d. 1732.
     iii.   LUCY SMITH, b. 1688 ; d. 15 April 1770 ; mar. 9 May 1705, Thomas Brooke (*Magazine*, i, 285).
     iv.   ELEANOR SMITH, b. 1690 ; d. 19 Jan'y 1761 ; mar. 7 June 1709, Col. Thomas Addison of Pr. George's Co.
     v.   ANNE SMITH, b. about 1694 ; d. 1759 ; mar. 1°. Francis Wilkinson (d. 22 Feb'y 1724/5), 2°. 5 Aug. 1725, Col. Thomas Truman Greenfield (b. 1682 ; d. 1733) of Pr. George's Co.
     vi.   REBECCA SMITH, b. 1696 ; d. 18 March 1737 ; mar. Daniel Dulany of Annapolis.
     vii.   ELIZABETH SMITH, mar. 1°. Thomas Jennings of Pr. George's Co., 2°. Humphrey Batt of same County.
     viii.   MARY SMITH.

4.   WALTER SMITH [3] of St. Leonards, died in 1748. His will, dated 1 Sept. 1748, was proved 18 October following. He

was School Commissioner for Calvert in 1723, and represented the County in the Assembly from 1724 to 1744 (*House Journals*). He married Alethea, daughter of Nathaniel and Mary Dare of Calvert County. Mrs. Mary Dare mentions her daughter Alethea Smith in her will (dated 17 June, proved 17 December, 1748), and Richard Smith, son of Walter and Alethea, mentions his grandfather Nathaniel Dare in his will (dated 21 September, proved 22 October, 1748). Mrs. Alethea Smith married, secondly, Rev. George Cooke and died 30 January 1753 (*Md. Gazette*, 1 Feb'y 1753).

Walter Smith of St. Leonards and Alethea (Dare) his wife had issue :—

    i. RICHARD SMITH [4] of St. Leonards, d. unmarried 1748.

8.   ii. WALTER SMITH of Parker's Creek, d. 1748.

   iii. JOHN SMITH, d. unmarried 1754.

   iv. NATHANIEL SMITH, d. unmarried 1752.

   v. CHARLES SMITH, d. unmarried 1750.

   vi. ALETHEA SMITH, mar. —— Parker.

5. CHARLES SOMERSET SMITH [3] of Charles County was born in 1698 and died in 1738. He gives his age as twenty years in a deposition made in 1718 (Chancery, Lib. PL, fol. 849) and his will, dated 17 November 1738, was proved 20 February 1738/9. His first wife was Jane, daughter of Thomas Crabb of Charles County, who in his will (dated 3 Jan'y, proved 8 March, 1719) mentions "my son-in-law Charles Somerset Smith who married my daughter Jane." His second wife, according to family account, was Margaret, daughter of William Smith. She survived him and married 2°. —— Parrie and 3°. Allen Davies. The account of Margaret Parrie, executrix of Capt. Charles Somerset Smith, late of Charles County deceased, was recorded 28 February 1744, and there is a deed, dated 4 September 1759, from Charles Somerset Smith (son of Charles Somerset Smith late of Charles County deceased, and brother of Richard Smith late of said County deceased) to Allen Davies and Margaret his wife, who was the widow and relict of the said Charles Somerset Smith deceased (Charles Co., Lib. 51, fol. 391). Charles Somerset Smith in his will appoints his wife executrix and names his sons Richard and Charles Somerset, and his daughters Elizabeth, wife of Francis Wilkinson, and Anne, Dicandia, Mary, and Jane. Of these, Elizabeth was evidently the daughter of the first wife, while the two sons were, according to family record, the children of the second wife. With regard to the remaining four daughters the case

is not so clear, though they were probably the children of the first marriage. With this reservation, the issue of Richard Smith and Jane (Crabb) his first wife was :—

    i. ELIZABETH SMITH,[4] mar. 1°. Francis Wilkinson Jr. of Calvert Co. (d. 1740), 2°. Young Parran of Calvert Co. (b. 1711; d. 1772).
    ii. ANNE SMITH, mar. Samuel Parran (brother of Young Parran).
    iii. DICANDIA SMITH.
    iv. MARY SMITH.
    v. JANE SMITH.

Charles Somerset Smith and Margaret (Smith) his second wife had issue :—

    i. RICHARD SMITH (twin) b. 13 Oct. 1733; d. in London, unmarried, 1 April 1759.
9.   ii. CHARLES SOMERSET SMITH (twin) b. 13 Oct. 1733; d. 1781.

6. WALTER SMITH [3] of Hall's Craft, also called "of the Freshes," since Hall's Craft was in the Freshes of the Patuxent not far from Lower Marlboro', was born about 1692 and died in 1734. His will, dated 22 March 1731, was proved 13 March 1733/4. He represented Calvert County in the Assembly from 1719 to 1722 (*House Journals*), was High Sheriff in 1725, and was a Justice of the County from 1726 until his death. He was Deputy Commissary of Calvert from 1722 to 9 May 1730, when he resigned (Test. Proc.). He was elected church warden of All Saints Parish 10 Nov. 1715, and was vestryman from 7 April 1729 till 4 April 1732, when he was succeeded by his brother Richard (All Saints Vestry Book). Walter Smith married, about 1714, Susanna daughter of Clement Brooke and Jane his wife, daughter of Maj. Nicholas Sewall (*Magazine*, i, 187, 190). Mrs. Susanna Smith married, secondly, Hyde Hoxton (d. 1754) of Pr. George's County, and had a son Walter Hoxton. She survived her second husband and died in 1767. Her will, dated 23 June 1767, was proved 23 October following.

Walter Smith of Hall's Craft and Susanna (Brooke) his wife had issue :—

10.   i. WALTER SMITH,[4] b. about 1715; d. 1743.
11.   ii. D? CLEMENT SMITH, d. 1792.
    iii. D? RICHARD SMITH, d. 1794 ; mar. Elizabeth, dau. of Henry Darnall of Portland Manor, but had no issue.
    iv. DOROTHY SMITH, b. 1716 ; mar. 13 Nov. 1735, Alexander Lawson (b. 1710; d. 14 Oct. 1760) of Calvert Co., later of Baltimore Town.
    v. RACHEL SMITH, b. 1720; d. 7 Jan'y 1787 ; mar. Richard Harrison (d. 1761) of Anne Arundel Co.
    vi. JANE SMITH.

7. RICHARD SMITH [3] of Lower Marlboro', Calvert County, died in 1732. His will, dated 23 October 1732, was proved 29 December following. He was a vestryman of All Saints Parish from 15 April 1723 till 7 April 1729, and was re-elected 4 April 1732 (All Saints Vestry Book). He married Eleanor, daughter of Col. Thomas Addison of Prince George's County, by his first wife Elizabeth daughter of Thomas Tasker. She was born 20 March 1705 and had four husbands :—1°. Bennett Lowe of St. Mary's County, 2°. Richard Smith (d. 1732), 3°. Capt. Posthumus Thornton of Calvert Co. (d. 1738), 4°. Corbin Lee (married 31 Jan'y 1754).

Richard Smith and Eleanor (Addison) his wife had issue :—

12. i.   WALTER SMITH,[4] d. Jan'y 1755.
     ii. RICHARD SMITH.
13. iii. JOHN ADDISON SMITH, of Baltimore Town, d. 8 May 1776.
     iv. REBECCA SMITH, d. 1775; mar. Roger Boyce (d. 1772).
     v.   RACHEL SMITH.

8. WALTER SMITH [4] of Parker's Creek, Calvert County, died in 1748, leaving a will dated 28 August and proved 22 October of that year. His wife was named Sarah, as appears from the register of Christ Church, Calvert County, whence the dates of birth of his children are derived.

Walter Smith and Sarah his wife had issue :—

14. i.   WALTHER SMITH, b. 12 August 1747.
     ii. ALETHEA SMITH, b. 23 October 1748.

SMITH FAMILY OF CALVERT COUNTY.

CHRISTOPHER JOHNSTON.

---

9. CHARLES SOMERSET SMITH [4] was born, with his twin brother Richard, 13 October, 1733 (family record), and died in Charles County in 1781. His will, dated 17 Nov., 1780, was proved 18 June, 1781. In it he names his children as given below, and leaves a bequest to Margaret Selwood and her daughter Elizabeth. Charles Somerset Smith and . . . . . his wife had issue:—

   i. WALTER SMITH,[5] d. s. p. will proved in Charles Co. 19 Aug. 1802.

   ii. CHARLES SOMERSET SMITH, mar. Ann Sothoron, and left issue.

   iii. HENRY ARUNDEL SMITH, mar. in 1795 his cousin Dicandia Garland, but d. s. p.

   iv. MARGARET SMITH.

   v. MARY SMITH.

10. WALTER SMITH,[4] of Halls Croft, was born about 1715 and died in 1743. His will was proved in Calvert County, 1 Feb., 1743/4. He married Elizabeth Chew (who married, secondly, ... Hunt) and had one son:—

   i. WALTER SMITH,[5] b. Jan'y 1739 ; d. unmar. 18 Feb. 1772.

11. DR. CLEMENT SMITH,[4] of Calvert County, was born about 1718, and died in 1792. His will, dated 10 Jan'y, 1787, was proved 28 Sept., 1792. According to family tradition he was educated and received his medical degree in England. He was elected a vestryman of All Saints Parish, 16 April, 1750 (Vestry Book), was Deputy Commissary of Calvert County from 1752 to 1777 (Commission Book), and was High Sheriff of the County from 16 Sept., 1772 to 9 Dec., 1775. He married his cousin Barbara Sim, daughter of Dr. Patrick Sim of Prince George's County and Mary his wife daughter of Col. Thomas Brooke. Mrs. Barbara Smith was therefore a grand niece of Clement Brooke, the maternal grandfather of her husband Dr. Clement Smith.

Dr. Clement Smith and Barbara (Sim) his wife had issue (order of birth uncertain) :—

15.   i. PATRICK SIM SMITH,[5] b. 1742 ; d. 1792.

16.   ii. DR. WALTER SMITH of Georgetown, d. 29 Aug. 1796.

17.   iii. RICHARD SMITH.

18.   iv. LT.-Col. ALEXANDER LAWSON SMITH, b. 1754 ; d. Jan'y 1802.

     v. DR. CLEMENT SMITH of Prince George's Co., b. 1756 ; d. 10 Dec. 1831 ; was married but left no male issue.

19.   vi. DR. JOSEPH SIM SMITH, d. 5 Sept. 1822.

    vii. JOHN ADDISON SMITH, a sea captain ; d. unmarried.

   viii. MARY SIM SMITH, mar. Henry Huntt of Calvert Co.

    ix. SUSANNA SMITH, d. unmar. 1824.

    x. RACHEL SMITH, d. unmar. 1824

SMITH FAMILY OF CALVERT COUNTY.

CHRISTOPHER JOHNSTON.

12. WALTER SMITH[4] died in January, 1755. He married Christian, widow of Thomas Lee (d. 1749) and daughter of Dr. Patrick Sim and Mary (Brooke) his wife. The will of Walter Smith, dated 3 January, 1755, was proved 18 February following—that of his widow, Mrs. Christian Smith, is dated 12 February and was proved 24 March, 1762. By her first husband she was the mother of Thomas Sim Lee, Governor of Maryland, 1779–83 and 1792–94, and Delegate to Congress, 1783–84. Walter Smith and Christian (Sim) his wife had issue:—

  i. ELEANOR ADDISON SMITH,[5] mar. John Robert Hollyday of Epsom, Baltimore County, High Sheriff of his County in 1770.

13. JOHN ADDISON SMITH,[4] of Baltimore Town, died 8 May, 1776. He married, 17 October, 1765, Sarah, daughter of William and Sarah Rogers of Baltimore Town. She married, secondly, 9 December, 1777, John Merryman. John Addison Smith and Sarah (Rogers) his wife had issue:

  i. ELEANOR ADDISON SMITH,[5] b. 14 Nov., 1766; mar. Nicholas Merryman Bosley, but d. s. p. 3 Feb'y, 1855.
  ii. CATHERINE ROGERS SMITH, b. 9 Sept., 1768; d. 18 Aug., 1769.
  iii. REBECCA SMITH, b. 4 June, 1770; mar. Henry Nichols, and d. s. p.
  iv. RICHARD SMITH, b. 26 March, 1772; lost at sea s. p.
20. v. WILLIAM ROGERS SMITH, b. 25 Nov., 1774; d. 10 June, 1818.

14. WALTER SMITH[5] was born 12 August, 1747, and died in 1804. He married Ann Mackall (b. 12 March, 1753) of Godsgrace, Calvert County, and had issue:—

  i. WALTER SMITH,[6] d. unmar.
  ii. COL. RICHARD SMITH, U. S. Marine Corps.
  iii. JOSEPH SMITH, planter in Miss.; mar. ...... Stockett, niece of Gov. Johnston of La., but d. s. p.

iv. SARAH SMITH, mar. ...... Hillen of Calvert Co.
v. MARY SMITH, mar. Samuel Chew; d. s. p.
vi. ELIZABETH SMITH, d. 1825; mar. Thomas Holland Chew (b. 1781;
d. 1840), and left issue.
vii. MARGARET MACKALL SMITH, b. 1787; d. 14 Aug., 1852; mar. 18
June, 1818, Zachary Taylor, then Major of Infantry, U. S. A., later
Major-General, and President of the United States.

15. PATRICK SIM SMITH [5] was born in 1742 and died in 1792.
He was commissioned a Justice of Calvert County 24 Aug.,
1773 (Com. Book), was a member of the County Committee
of Observation in November, 1774, and was a member of
the Maryland Convention which met at Annapolis, 7 December, 1775, (Force's *Amer. Archives*). He was Second Major
of Militia for Calvert County in 1776. Later he removed
to Frederick County, which he represented in the State
Legislature in 1791 (Assembly Proceedings). He married
1 December, 1768, Anne Truman Greenfield, daughter of
James Truman Greenfield and Elizabeth his wife, and
granddaughter of Thomas Truman Greenfield and his
second wife, Anne, daughter of Col. Walter Smith. Patrick
Sim Smith and Anne Truman (Greenfield) his wife had
issue :—

i. WALTER SMITH,[6] b. 14 Sept., 1769.
ii. CHRISTIAN SIM SMITH, b. 2 Dec., 1770; married her cousin Anthony
Sim of Frederick Co.
iii. ANNE SMITH.
iv. BARBARA SMITH.
v. MARY SMITH.
vi. SUSANNA SMITH.
vii. HARRIET SMITH.
viii. PATRICK SIM SMITH.

16. DR. WALTER SMITH,[5] of Georgetown, D. C., died in
Georgetown 29 August, 1796. In the Revolution he was
a surgeon in the Maryland Militia, 1776–77 (Heitman's
Register). He married Esther Belt (b. 1744; d. 21 March,
1814) daughter of Col. Joseph Belt (b. 1716; d. 16 June,
1793) of Montgomery County, and Esther his wife (b.
1722; d. 12 July, 1796) daughter of William Smith of
Prince George's County. Dr. Walter Smith and Esther
(Belt) his wife had issue :—

i. WALTER SMITH,[6] mar. Sallie Hoffman and had one daughter; Sallie
Smith [7] mar. Hon. William Hunter.
ii. CLEMENT SMITH, mar. 1809, Margaret Clare, daughter of John and
Mary (McCubbin) Brice, and had issue.

iii. ELIZABETH SMITH, mar. Richard Ringgold and had issue.
iv. BARBARA SMITH, b. 1779 ; d. 16 March, 1837 ; mar. Peregrine Ringgold and left issue.
v. RICHARD SMITH, mar. Covington Mackall and left issue.
vi. MATILDA BOWEN LEE SMITH, mar. 4 Sept., 1800, John Cox and left
issue.
vii. SOPHIA SMITH, b. 1783 ; d. unmar. 30 Nov., 1860.
viii. JOSEPH SMITH, d. unmar.

17. RICHARD SMITH[5] was living in Frederick County in 1775.
In the *Maryland Gazette* of 30 March, 1775, he inserted an
advertisement (dated Frederick, March 14th) announcing
that he will sell to the highest bidder his property of Hall's
Craft, containing 140 acres, and that his brother Patrick
will show it to any one desiring to inspect it. Richard
Smith married Mary Peter and had issue :—

i. BARBARA SIM SMITH,[6] b. 21 Oct., 1778 ; d. 15 Sept., 1863 ; mar.
John Suter.
ii. CASSANDRA SMITH, mar. Benj. Gott of Montgomery Co. and d. s. p.
iii. ROBERT SMITH, d. unmar.
iv. SARAH SMITH, mar. Capt. John Wailes of Calvert Co.
v. HARRIET SMITH, d. unmar. 4 June, 1875.
vi. CLEMENT SMITH, d. unmar.

18. LIEUT.-COL. ALEXANDER LAWSON SMITH[5] was born in
1754 and died in January, 1802. He was commissioned
Captain in the Maryland Line 13 July, 1776, and was promoted to Major in 1778. In 1784 he petitioned the Maryland Legislature, and the Committee to whom his claim was
referred, report, 7 January, 1785, as follows :—That being
Lieut.-Colonel in the Federal Army he resigned his commission in 1780 and accepted a commission of Lieut.-
Colonel commandant in a regiment extraordinary raised by
the State of Maryland in 1780, with which he joined the
Southern Army and continued in the service until recalled
by Act of Assembly of this State, passed at October Session,
1780, disbanding the regiment and calling home the officers
(Votes and Proceedings of Maryland House of Delegates,
1785). After the war he settled in Harford County and
was buried there 26 January, 1802 (*St. George's Register*).
He married Martha Griffith (b. 16 September, 1771 ; d. 4
August, 1847), daughter of Samuel Griffith of Harford
County, and Frenetta (Garretson) his wife. Mrs. Martha
(Griffith) Smith married, secondly, Samuel Jay. Lieut.-Col.

Alexander Lawson Smith and Martha (Griffith) his wife had issue:—

   i. SAMUEL GRIFFITH SMITH,[6] b. 25 Dec., 1794; d. unmar.
   ii. FRANCINA FRENETTA SMITH, b. 10 Nov., 1797; d. unmar. 10 Feb'y, 1860.
   iii. MARIA MATILDA SMITH, b. 1 July, 1799; d. unmar. 14 Sept., 1860.

19. DR. JOSEPH SIM SMITH [5] was born in Calvert County and died in Frederick County 5 September, 1822. In November, 1789, he presented a petition to the Maryland Legislature stating that he acted as Surgeon's Mate in the Maryland Line until appointed Cornet in the Partizan Legion, where he continued till the end of the war, and praying to be allowed the same bounty land as the officers of the Maryland Line were entitled to, &c. (Votes and Proceedings, Md. House of Delegates, November Session, 1789). Heitman's *Register* (p. 372) shows that he served, from 1780 till 1782, as Cornet in the First Battalion of Cavalry, Armand's Partizan Corps. After the war he practiced medicine in Frederick County and lived at Taneytown. He was one of the incorporators of the Maryland Medical and Chirurgical Faculty in 1799 (*History of the Faculty*), and was one of its Censors in 1803 (*Ibid.*). On the organization of the Maryland Militia in 1793, Dr. Joseph Sim Smith was appointed Major (Scharf's *Western Md.*, p. 164), and he was one of the Justices of Frederick County, 1802–07, 1814 and 1819 (*Ibid.*). The *Frederick Town Herald* of 14 Sept., 1822, has the following obituary notice:—"DIED. At Taney Town, on Friday, the 5th inst., Doct. Joseph Sim Smith, a patriot of '76 and an officer of the Revolution. Doct. Smith fulfilled the various duties of a good citizen with honour to himself and advantage to the community; and by his worth and usefulness had secured the affection and esteem of a wide extended circle of relations and friends, by whom his memory will long be cherished with tenderness and regret." Dr. Joseph Sim Smith married Elizabeth Price (b. 3 August, 1765), daughter of Col. Thomas Price of Frederick County, and Mary his wife, and had issue:—

   i. ELIZA SMITH,[6] d. unmar.
   ii. JOHN ADDISON SMITH of Washington, D. C., b. 27 June, 1792; d. July, 1868; mar. his cousin Sally Cox and left issue.
   iii. MARY SMITH, d. unmar. 1859.
   iv. DR. SAMUEL PRICE SMITH, b. 21 Dec., 1795; d. s. p. 2 March, 1882; mar. Margaret Watson.

    v. THOMAS SMITH, d. unmar.
   vi. REBECCA SMITH, b. 1798 ; d. 12 July, 1879; mar. Reuben M. Worth-
        ington and left issue.
  vii. BENJAMIN PRICE SMITH, b. 3 Dec., 1800 ; d. 15 June, 1862 ; mar.
        his cousin Matilda Rebecca Price and left issue.
 viii. MATILDA SMITH, b. 1802 ; mar. Col. Henry Naylor and left issue.
   ix. CLEMENT SMITH, d. unmar.
    x. GEORGE SMITH, d. in youth.

20. WILLIAM ROGERS SMITH [5] was born 25 November, 1774,
and died 10 June, 1818. He married, 2 October, 1798,
Margaret (b. 13 April, 1780), daughter of Cumberland
Dugan of Baltimore, and his first wife Abigail May. They
had issue;—

    i. REBECCA SMITH,[6] mar. James C. Gittings.
   ii. ELEANOR ADDISON SMITH, mar. John Sterett Gittings.
  iii. JOHN MERRYMAN SMITH, d. unmar.

SPRIGG FAMILY.

CHRISTOPHER JOHNSTON.

1. THOMAS SPRIGG,[1] the ancestor of this family, was born in
1630 and died in 1704. In a deposition, made in 1665,
" Mr. Thomas Sprigge " gives his age as 35 years (*Prov.
Court,* Lib. FF, fol. 91), and in another deposition, made
in 1694, his age is stated as 64 years (*ibid.,* Lib. W. R. C.,
no. 1, fol. 696). His will was proved 29 Dec. 1704. He
appears as party to a suit in the Provincial Court in
October 1657 (*Arch.,* x, 546), and may have been a resident
of Maryland for some years previously. 18 January 1658,
a patent issued to Thomas Sprigg, who had transported to
Maryland " himself, Catherine his wife, Verlinda Roper,
Edward Bushell, Nathaniel Sprigge, and Hugh Johnson,"
for a tract of 600 acres called " Sprigley " in Chester
River (Land Office, " Torn Book "). In the opinion of
the late George L. L. Davis, the author of the " Day Star
of American Freedom," and a very able and conscientious
genealogist, Thomas Sprigg arrived about 1655 and probably
came from Northamptonshire, in England. Mr. Davis
points out that one of the tracts taken up by him was called
" Kettering," and that he held another tract called " Northampton " (*Day Star,* p. 265). The records of the Maryland
Land Office show that he obtained grants for a large amount
of land. He lived on or near Resurrection Manor, in Calvert County, a district later included in Prince George's,
and he was twice married. His first wife, Catherine, was
living in 1661 and executed a deed with her husband in
that year. 17 August 1661, Thomas Sprigg of Resurrection
Manor, Calvert County, and Catherine his wife convey to
Simon Carpenter 600 acres in Worrell Hundred, Talbot
County (*Prov. Court,* Lib. B. B., fol. 176). Mrs. Catherine
Sprigg may have been a sister of Gov. William Stone,
or the latter may have married a sister of Thomas Sprigg.
Gov. Stone in his will, dated 3 Dec. 1659 and proved 21
Dec. 1660 (Annapolis, Lib. 1, fol 89), mentions " my

brother Sprigg," and Thomas Stone, son of the governor,
executes an assignment, 3 August 1662, of his right to 100
acres of land to "my uncle Thomas Sprigg" (Land Office,
Lib. 5, fol. 182). Mrs. Catherine Sprigg seems to have
died without issue and, before 1668, Thomas Sprigg married
Eleanor, daughter of John Nuthall. In September 1668,
the Council of Maryland passed an order dividing the estate
of John Nuthall, deceased, among his three children John
and James Nuthall, and Eleanor wife Thomas Sprigg
(*Arch.*, v, 34). Mrs. Eleanor Sprigg was living in 1696,
when she joined her husband in a deed. 2 July 1696,
Thomas Sprigg and Eleanor his wife convey to John Nuthall of St. Mary's County, 250 acres in Resurrection Manor,
purchased by the said Thomas Sprigg from Capt. Thomas
Cornwallis; John and Elias Sprigg witness the deed (*Prov.
Court*, Lib. W .R. C. no. 1, fol. 760. 771). She was probably dead before the date of the following deed, in which
she does not join. 16 March 1700/1, Thomas Sprigg of
Prince George's County, Gent., to his eldest daughter Sarah
Pearce, his grandson John Pearce, only son of said Sarah,
and Sarah wife of John Bell daughter of said Sarah Pearce:–
gift of certain lands (parts of Northampton, Kettering, etc.)
lately in the tenure and occupation of John Sprigg deceased
(Pr. Geo. Co., Lib. A., fol. 362). Thomas Sprigg was
one of the Justices of Calvert County, and of the Quorum,
in 1658, 1661, 1667, 1669-70, 1674 (*Arch.*, iii, 424; v, 14.
61; xv, 37; Lib. S., 54; Lib. C. D., 412). In 1661 his
name stands at the head of the Commission showing that
he was Presiding Justice of the County (*Arch.*, iii, 424).
He was commissioned High Sheriff of Calvert County 1
April 1664 and held office until 4 May 1665 (*Arch.*, iii,
490. 491. 520). The following is a brief abstract of his
will. Thomas Sprigg Sen'r. of Prince George's County—
will dated 9 May 1704, proved 29 Dec. 1704 (Pr. Geo. Co.,
Lib. 1, fol. 23). Mentions daughter Sarah Pearce; son
Thomas Sprigg; daughters Martha Prather, Eleanor Nuthall, Elizabeth Wade, and Anne Gittens; Thomas Stockett
and my grandson Thomas Stockett; Eleanor Stockett; my
son Thomas Sprigg and my sons-in-law James Wade, Philip
Gittens, and Thomas Prather executors. The name *James*
Wade is evidently a clerical error for Robert Wade. No
James Wade appears in the records, and the following ex-

tract is conclusive: 5 January 1704/5, ¹ d of Robert Wade, of Pr. George's County, as one of the executors of Thomas Sprigg, late of said County deceased, in the sum of £600 sterling; sureties Philip Gittings, Thomas Prather, and Samuel Magruder all of Pr. George's County (*Test. Proc.*, Lib. 10, fol. 18).

Thomas Sprigg and Eleanor (Nuthall) his wife had issue:

2.   i.   COL. THOMAS SPRIGG.
   ? ii.   JOHN SPRIGG, d. about 1700.
   ? iii.   ELIAS SPRIGG.
    iv.   SARAH SPRIGG, mar. . . . Pearce.
    v.   MARTHA SPRIGG, mar. Thomas Prather.
    vi.   ELEANOR SPRIGG, mar. 1°. Thomas Hilleary (d. 1697), 2°. her cousin John Nuthall, son of her uncle John Nuthall of St. Mary's County.
    vii.   ELIZABETH SPRIGG, mar. Robert Wade.
    viii.   ANNE SPRIGG, mar. Philip Gittings.
    ix.   MARY SPRIGG, d. 27 Jan'y 1694; mar. 12 March 1689, Thomas Stockett of Anne Arundel Co. (*Stockett Genealogy*, pp. 14-15).
NOTE.   John and Elias Sprigg were probably sons of Thomas. Elias witnesses a deed of Thomas and Eleanor Sprigg in 1696 (see above), and in another deed, cited above, John Sprigg deceased is mentioned. The following extracts refer to him: 27 Sept. 1705, bond of Thomas Sprigg for the administration of the estate of John Sprigg late of Pr. George's County deceased, in the sum of £100 sterling; surety, Dr. Richard Pile (*Test. Proc.*, Lib. 19, fol. 90). 10 Dec. 1705, inventory of John Sprigg late of Cecil (sic!) County deceased, amounting to £500: 9: 00; likewise account of estate by Thomas Sprigg administrator (*ibid.*, fol. 115).

2. COL. THOMAS SPRIGG ² (*Thomas* ¹) was probably born not far from the year 1670, calculating from the ages of his children and from other circumstances. He was living in 1736, when he executed a deed, but he left no will, and the records of the Prerogative Court do not show that letters of administration were ever issued on his estate. He was probably dead in 1739, when letters on the estate of his wife Margaret were taken out by Osborn Sprigg. In 1722, Col. Sprigg deeded lands in Pr. George's County to his sons Thomas, Osborn, and Edward Sprigg, and, in 1728, he executed a conveyance to his daughter-in-law Margery Sprigg, widow of his eldest son Thomas who died in 1725. Margaret, wife of Col. Thomas Sprigg joined her husband in this last deed. She was the daughter of Edward and Honor Mariarte of Anne Arundel County, and proof of her parentage will be found in the *Maryland Historical Maga-*

zine, vol. i, p. 381; vol. ii, p. 179. Mrs. Margaret Sprigg died intestate in 1739, before 27 November when her son Osborn Sprigg gave bond for the administration of her estate in the sum of £600, with Thomas and Basil Waring as his sureties (Pr. Geo. Co. Records). At June Court 1697, " Mr. Thomas Sprigg Jun'r." being first duly sworn, took his seat as one of the Justices of Prince George's County (Pr. Geo. Co., Lib. A, fol. 169), and subsequent entries prove that he sat as a member of the Court from this date until 1704. From 1712 to 1715 he represented Prince George's County in the Maryland Assembly (*Ms. House Journals*). In the *Journals* for 1713 and 1714 he is styled " Major Thomas Sprigg," while in 1715 his name is entered as " Lieut. Coll. Thomas Sprigg." It is therefore evident that in 1714 or 1715 he was promoted from Major to Lieutenant-Colonel of the County militia. The deed executed in 1728 to his daughter-in-law Margery Sprigg is acknowledged by " Col. Thomas Sprigg " and Margaret his wife.

Col. Thomas Sprigg and Margaret (Mariarte) his wife had issue:

3.   i.   THOMAS SPRIGG,³ d. 1725.
4.   ii.   COL. EDWARD SPRIGG, b. 1697; d. 30 Nov. 1751.
5.   iii.   OSBORN SPRIGG, b. 1707(?); d. 7 Jan'y 1750.
    iv.   PRISCILLA SPRIGG, mar. 22 Aug. 1716, Ralph Crabb.
    v.   MARGARET SPRIGG, mar. 26 Sept. 1717, Francis King.
    vi.   ELEANOR SPRIGG, mar. about 1716, Henry Wright.

3.   THOMAS SPRIGG ³ (*Thomas,*² *Thomas* ¹) died intestate in 1725. His widow, Margery, administered on his estate and filed her bond, 15 Nov. 1725, in the sum of £4,000, with Thomas Gantt, Edward Sprigg, and John Wight as her sureties (*Test. Proc.,* Lib. 27, fol. 232). Mrs. Margery Sprigg was the daughter of Capt. John Wight of Prince George's County who died in 1705 intestate, and Ann his wife, widow of Thomas Gantt of Calvert County who died in 1692. Mrs. Ann Wight died in 1726, and in her will, dated 15 Sept. 1725, proved 26 May 1726 (Annapolis, Lib. 18, fol. 518), mentions her daughter Margery Sprigg, and her grandchildren Thomas, Anne, and Edward Sprigg. In 1728, Col. Thomas Sprigg conveys to his daughter-in-law " Margery Sprigg widow and administrator of Thomas Sprigg, Gent., eldest son and heir of the said Thomas Sprigg " the grantor, a water mill in Prince George's County

(Pr. Geo. Co., Lib. M., fol. 350). Before 1737, she married Col. Joseph Belt whose daughters, by a former marriage, Rachel and Mary, married Osborn and Edward Sprigg respectively. 30 June 1737, Joseph Belt and Margery his wife " widow and administratrix of Thomas Sprigg, late of Prince George's County deceased," rendered an additional account of the said deceased's estate (*Accounts,* Lib. 15, fol. 341). She died in 1783 leaving a will recorded in Prince George's County. Thomas Sprigg and Margery his wife had issue:

6. i. THOMAS SPRIGG,[4] b. 1715; d. 29 Dec. 1781.
   ii. JOHN SPRIGG, b. 26 Nov. 1716.
   iii. EDWARD SPRIGG, mentioned, 1725, in his grandmother's will; living 1772, and had a son Richard.
   iv. ANNE SPRIGG, mar. Joseph Belt, Jr., son of her step-father, Col. Joseph Belt.
   v. MARY SPRIGG, b. 15 Dec. 1723; mar. 21 June 1746, Jeremiah Belt.

4. COL. EDWARD SPRIGG [3] (*Thomas,*[2] *Thomas* [1]), was born in 1697, and died 30 Nov. 1751. His age is given in depositions as 50 years in 1747/8, 52 in 1748/9, and 53 in 1750 (Pr. Geo. Co., Lib. E. E., fol. 466. 629; Lib. P. P., fol. 88). He was one of the Justices of Prince George's County 1726-1732, 1747-1751, was Presiding Justice 1747-1751 (Commission Book), and was commissioned, 29 April 1732, one of the Justices of the Provincial Court of Maryland, the highest judicial tribunal in the Province (*ibid.*). He represented Prince George's County in the Assembly 1729-1751, and was Speaker of the House 1742-1748 (*Ms. Journals*). In the *House Journals* he is styled " Captain " from 1730 to 1735, " Major " from 1735 to 1742, and " Colonel " from 1742 to 1751, showing that he held these successive ranks in the militia of his County. The *Maryland Gazette* of 4 Dec. 1751 has the following obituary notice: " On Saturday last (30 November) died, in Prince George's County, after a short illness of 20 hours, Col. Edward Sprigg, who was for more than 22 years past one of the Representatives for that County in the House of Delegates of this Province; was for several years the Honourable Speaker of that House; and presided as chief of the Commission of the Peace for the said County, and continued in that Station until he died. Col. Sprigg was twice married. His first wife, married 26 April 1720, was Elizabeth

daughter of Dr. Richard Pile. The marriage is recorded in
the register of Queen Anne Parish. His second wife was
Mary (b. 24 Dec. 1722) daughter of Col. Joseph Belt.
After the death of Col. Sprigg, she married Thomas Pindle.
Col. Edward Sprigg and Elizabeth (Pile) his first wife
had issue:

    i. RICHARD SPRIGG,[4] b. 28 April 1721.
    ii. EDWARD SPRIGG, b. 12 June 1723.
7. iii. JAMES SPRIGG, b. 27 Jan'y 1724/5; d. 1778.
    iv. THOMAS SPRIGG, b. 21 Feb'y 1726/7.
    v. ELIZABETH SPRIGG, b. 21 July 1728.
    vi. GILBERT SPRIGG, b. 11 August 1730.
    vii MARY SPRIGG, b. 17 August 173—.
    viii. MARGARET SPRIGG.

Col. Edward Sprigg and Mary (Belt) his second wife
had issue:

    ix. JACOB SPRIGG, d. s. p. 1770.
    x. FREDERICK SPRIGG.
    xi. LUCY SPRIGG, b. 1752; a posthumous child.

5. OSBORN SPRIGG [3] (*Thomas,*[2] *Thomas* [1]) of Prince George's
County, is said to have been born in 1707. In a deposition
made in 1745 (Chancery, Lib. I. R., no. 4, fol. 591) his age
is given as 38 years. If this be correct, he was only twenty
years old in 1727 when he married his second wife. It is
possible, however, that there may be a clerical error here,
and that he was really born some years earlier. In February 1722 he received from his father a gift of parts of
Northampton, Brook Grove, Kettering, and Addition to
Kettering, though he was not to enter into possession until
after the death of his mother Mrs. Margaret Sprigg (Pr.
Geo. Co., Lib. I, fol. 368). Osborn Sprigg represented
Prince George's County in the Assembly 1739-1744 (*House
Journals*), and was High Sheriff of the County from 18
Sept. 1747 until his death (*Commission Book*). He died
7 January 1750, and the *Maryland Gazette,* three days later,
has the following notice: " We have just received the melan-
choly News of the Death of Osborn Sprigg, Esq.; High
Sheriff of Prince George's County, on Monday last." Osborn Sprigg was twice married. His first wife, Elizabeth,
died in 1726/7 leaving an infant daughter, Margaret. The
register of Queen Anne Parish records the birth, 20 March
1726/7, of Margaret " daughter of Osborn and Elizabeth
Sprigg." The marriage of Osborn Sprigg to his second

wife, Rachel daughter of Col. Joseph Belt took place 11 July 1727, and is recorded in the same parish register. Mrs. Rachel Sprigg was born 13 December 1711 (Queen Anne Par. Reg.). Osborn Sprigg and Elizabeth his first wife had a daughter:

    i. MARGARET SPRIGG,[4] b. 20 March 1726/7; d. October 1804. She mar., about 1745, Capt. William Bowie of Pr. Geo. Co., and their son, Robert Bowie (b. 1750; d. 1818) was Governor of Maryland 1803-1806, and 1811-1813.

Osborn Sprigg and Rachel (Belt) his second wife had issue:

8. ii. JOSEPH SPRIGG, b. 1736; d. 1800.
    iii. OSBORN SPRIGG, mar. 8 April, 1779, Sarah dau of Thomas Gantt of Pr. Geo. Co.
    iv. GEN. THOMAS SPRIGG, b. 1747; d. in Washington Co., 13 Dec. 1809; Mem. Congress 1793-1796. His wife, Mrs. Elizabeth Sprigg, d. 28 July 1808.
    v. LUCY SPRIGG, b. 9 Jan'y 1728/9.
    vi. ESTHER SPRIGG, b. 16 Feb'y 1730; mar. Thomas Bowie, and d. s. p.
    vii. RACHEL SPRIGG, b. 1 June 1733.
    viii. PRISCILLA SPRIGG, b. 26 Sept. 1735; mar., 28 Nov. 1762, Col. Barton Lucas.
    ix. ELIZABETH SPRIGG.
    x. ANNE SPRIGG.

6. THOMAS SPRIGG,[4] (*Thomas,*[3] *Thomas,*[2] *Thomas* [1]) of Anne Arundel County, was born in 1715 and died 29 December 1781. He gives his age as 30 years in a deposition made in 1745 (A. A. Co., Lib. I. B. no. 1, fol. 212), and as 52 years in 1767 (Chancery, Lib. 1774-83, fol. 20). He married, 14 December 1737, Elizabeth (b. 16 Jan'y 1721/2) daughter of Richard Galloway (d. 1741) of Anne Arundel County and Margaret (Smith) his wife. They had a son:

9. i. RICHARD SPRIGG,[5] b. 16 Dec. 1739; d. 24 Nov. 1798.

7. JAMES SPRIGG [4] (*Edward,*[3] *Thomas,*[2] *Thomas* [1]) was born in Prince George's County, Maryland, 27 January 1724/5 (Qu. Anne Par. Rec.) and died in Montgomery County, in 1778. His will, dated 2 April 1778, and proved 14 May following, is recorded in Montgomery County (Lib. A., fol. 47). It mentions his wife Elizabeth and the children named below. James Sprigg and Elizabeth his wife, who died in 1811, had issue:

    i. JOHN SPRIGG.[5]
    ii. LEVIN SPRIGG, b. 14 March 1762; apparently d. young.

iii. REGIN SPRIGG, b. 31 August 1766.
iv. ELEANOR SPRIGG, mar. 1°. Thos. Stillings, 2°. Joseph Stillings.
v. MARY SPRIGG, b. 4 Sept. 1768; mar. . . . Lawman.
vi. ELIZABETH SPRIGG, mar. . . . Markham.
vii. LUCY SPRIGG, mar. . . . McTee.
viii. MARGARET SPRIGG.

8. JOSEPH SPRIGG [4] (*Osborn*,[3] *Thomas*,[2] *Thomas* [1]) was born in 1736 and died in 1800. In a deposition, made in 1774, he gives his age as 38 years (Chancery, Lib. 1774-83, fol. 111), and his will was proved 8 Nov. 1800. With Hannah his wife he conveyed, 24 Nov. 1760, to William Bowie, 310 acres part of Darnall's Grove, which he had purchased from the estate of Osborn Sprigg deceased, the said land having been mortgaged as security for a bond given by said Osborn Sprigg to the Commissioners or Trustees for emitting Bills of Credit (Pr. Geo. Co., Lib. R. R., fol. 107). 6 Sept. 1773, "Joseph Sprigg of Prince George's County, Gent., eldest son and heir of Osborn Sprigg late of said County, deceased," and Thomas Williams, grandson and heir at law of Thomas Williams deceased, convey to two daughters of Jeremiah Berry a tract of land deeded, 22 July 1747, by Benj. Berry to the said Osborn Sprigg and Thomas Williams (Pr. Geo. Co., Lib. B. B. no. 1, fol. 339). In February 1774, Joseph Sprigg of Prince George's County, Gent., and Hannah his wife convey to Thomas Sprigg of the same County " all that tract whereon my late father Mr. Osborn Sprigg dwelt, called Northampton," and also parts of Kettering, Addition to Kettering, and Hearts Delight (Pr. Geo. Co., Lib. B. B. no. 1, fol. 473). At the same time they convey other lands to Jeremiah Magruder (*ibid.,* fol. 366). Before November following Joseph Sprigg had removed from Prince George's County, and settled in that part of Frederick County which was later included in Washington County, created by Act of Legislature 6 Sept. 1776 (Scharf's *Western Maryland,* p. 973). Joseph Sprigg was one of the Justices of Prince George's County from 1766 to 1774, and was of the Quorum 1773-74 (*Commission Book*). 18 Nov. 1774, he was elected a member of the Committee of Correspondence of Frederick County (*Md. Gazette,* 24 Nov. 1774). He was commissioned Judge of the Orphans' Court for Washington County 4 June 1777 (*Arch.* xvi, 275), and again in 1778 (*Commission Book*). In 1778 and 1782 he was one of the Justices of Washington County (*ibid.*). Ac-

cording to family tradition Joseph Sprigg is said to have been several times married. It can be proved that he married twice. His first wife Hannah was the daughter of Hon. Philip Lee, Member of the Council of Maryland, and widow of Thomas Bowie. His second wife was Margaret daughter of James Weems of Calvert County, and widow of —— Elzey. They were married 8 April 1781, and she died in 1783. In 1785, Joseph Sprigg, as her administrator, together with other heirs, filed a bill in Chancery against John Weems executor of her father James Weems. The case went on from term to term, and it appears from the records that Joseph Sprigg was dead in 1804, before the termination of the suit, which was carried on by his son Joseph. The will of Joseph Sprigg was proved in Calvert County 8 November 1800. By Hannah (Lee) his first wife he had issue:

10. i. JOSEPH SPRIGG,[5] b. 1760; d. 5 Dec. 1821.
11. ii. OSBORN SPRIGG.
  iii. PHILIP SPRIGG, named in the will of his half brother, Capt. Daniel Bowie.
  iv. CORBIN SPRIGG.
  v. THOMAS SPRIGG, a sea captain; d. 10 July 1810..
  vi. WILLIAM SPRIGG, Judge of Supreme Court of Ohio, 1803; U. S. Judge for Territory of Michigan 1805, for Orleans 1806, for Louisiana 1812, and for Illinois 1813; District Judge of State of Missouri.
  vii. ANNE SPRIGG, mar. Charles Carroll of Bellevue.
  viii. LETTICE SPRIGG, named in Capt. Daniel Bowie's will.
  ix. Hannah Sprigg.

By his second wife, Margaret (Weems) Joseph Sprigg had a son:

12. x. SAMUEL SPRIGG, d. 21 April 1855; Governor of Maryland.

9. RICHARD SPRIGG [5] (*Thomas,*[4] *Thomas,*[3] *Thomas,*[2] *Thomas*[1]) of Cedar Park, Anne Arundel County, was born 16 Dec. 1739, and died 24 Nov. 1798. He married, 1 August 1765, Margaret daughter of John Caille and Rebecca (Ennalls) his wife, and she died 13 July 1796. They had issue:

  i. SOPHIA SPRIGG, b. 1766; d. 1812; mar. 1785, Col. John Francis Mercer.
  ii. REBECCA SPRIGG, b. 1767; d. 1806; mar. 1787, Dr. James Steuart.
  iii. ELIZABETH SPRIGG, b. 1770; d. 1813; mar. 1795, Hugh Thompson.
  iv. HENRIETTA SPRIGG, b. 1775; d. 1791.
  v. MARGARET SPRIGG, b. 1790; d. 1864.

10. JOSEPH SPRIGG [5] (*Joseph,*[4] *Osborn,*[3] *Thomas,*[2] *Thomas*[1]) was born in Prince George's County in 1760. In 1774 he

went with his father to Washington County (then a part of Frederick County, and lived there until 1816, when he removed to Illinois. He died 5 Dec. 1821, in the 62nd year of his age. About 1789, he married Ann Taylor daughter of Major Ignatius Taylor of Washington County. It is said that the marriage took place on the same day that Major Taylor was married to Joseph Sprigg's half-sister Barbara. Joseph Sprigg and Ann (Taylor) his wife had issue:

13.   i.   DANIEL SPRIGG⁶ of Baltimore, b. 1790; d. 21 Jan'y 1871.
      ii.   JENIFER SPRIGG.
     iii.   ANN SPRIGG.
     iv.   HANNAH SPRIGG.
      v.   MARGARET SPRIGG.
14.   vi.   IGNATIUS SPRIGG of Randolph Co., Illinois.
     vii.   CAROLINE SPRIGG.
    viii.   ELIZABETH SPRIGG, mar. . . . Blackwell.
     ix.   LUCRETIA SPRIGG.
      x.   FRANCIS SPRIGG.
     xi.   MARIA BARBARA SPRIGG, b. 25 Aug. 1808.
     xii.   JOHN CHAMBERS SPRIGG, b. 27 Jan'y 1811.
NOTE.   The births of the last two children are recorded in St. John's Parish, Washington Co., Md.

11. OSBORN SPRIGG⁵ (*Joseph,*⁴ *Osborn,*³ *Thomas,*² *Thomas*¹), married Sarah doughter of Capt. Michael Cresap, and grand-daughter of Col. Thomas Cresap. They had issue:

      i.   MICHAEL CRESAP SPRIGG,⁶ b. 1 July 1791; d. 18 Dec. 1845. Mem. Md. Legislature; President C. & O. Canal; Mem. Congress 1827-1831; married, 27 April 1815, Mary Lamar.
     ii.   JOSEPH SPRIGG, b. 24 Feb'y 1793; d. 1864; mar. Jane D. McMahon.
    iii.   OSBORN SPRIGG, b. 6 Aug. 1795.
     iv.   JAMES CRESAP SPRIGG, b. 1 May 1797; d. in Kentucky 3 Oct. 1852. Member of Congress from Kentucky, 1841-1843.

12. SAMUEL SPRIGG⁵ (*Joseph,*⁴ *Osborn,*³ *Thomas,*² *Thomas*¹) was Governor of Maryland 1819-1822, and died 21 April 1855. He married, 1 Jan'y 1811, Violetta daughter of Thomas Lansdale (d. 1802) of Prince George's County and Cornelia (van Horne) his wife. They had issue:

      i.   SARAH SPRIGG,⁶ b. 27 March 1812; mar. her cousin William Thomas Carroll.
15.   ii.   OSBORN SPRIGG, b. 7 Nov. 1813; mar. 22 Dec. 1840, Caroline Lansdale Bowie.

13. DANIEL SPRIGG⁶ (*Joseph,*⁵ *Joseph,*⁴ *Osborn*³) was born in Washington County, Md., in 1790, and died in Baltimore, Md., 21 Jan'y 1871, in the 81st year of his age. In 1814, he came from Hagerstown as a member of Capt.

Quantrell's Company, and took part in the defense of
Baltimore against the British attack. He was for a number of years cashier of the Hagerstown Bank, and was a
vestryman of St. John's Church, Hagerstown, from 1816
to 1831. Not long after the latter date he removed to
Buffalo, New York, where he was cashier of the Branch
Bank of the United States. On the establishment of the
Merchants Bank of Baltimore, he was invited to become
its cashier. He accepted this position and held it from
1835 until his death in 1871. He was at one time elected
to the Maryland State Senate by the Senatorial Electors,
but declined the honor. Daniel Sprigg married Elizabeth,
daughter of Alexander Chesley of Hagerstown, and had
issue:

   i. GEORGE HARRY SPRIGG,[7] mar. 1°. Ellen Compton, 2°. Elizabeth
      Smith.
   ii. ANN TAYLOR SPRIGG, mar. Michael Sanderson Newman.
  iii. JOSEPH ALEXANDER SPRIGG, mar. Ann dau. of Thomas Phenix,
      but had no issue.
   iv. WILLIAM SPRIGG.
   v. REV. DANIEL FRANCIS SPRIGG of Washington, D. C.; mar.
      Emily Rutter.
   vi. ELIZABETH SPRIGG, d. young.
  vii. VIOLETTA SPRIGG, d. 14 March 1870; mar. John F. Pickrell.
 viii. MARY ELIZABETH SPRIGG, mar. William Donnell of Baltimore,
      Md.
   ix. SARAH CHESLEY SPRIGG, mar. Oliver Beirne.
   x. CHARLES CARROLL SPRIGG, d. young.

Mrs. Elizabeth Sprigg, wife of Daniel Sprigg, died in
Baltimore, 19 April 1870, aged 76 years.

14. IGNATIUS SPRIGG [6] (*Joseph,*[5] *Joseph,*[4] *Osborn* [3]) removed
to Illinois with his father in 1816. He was married, 6
November 1820, in Randolph County, Illinois, to Mary
Adkins, and they had a daughter.

   i. MARY SPRIGG,[7] b. 12 Sept. 1833; mar. 28 June 1855, Andrew
      B. Skidmore.

15. OSBORN SPRIGG [6] (*Samuel,*[5] *Joseph,*[4] *Osborn* [3]) was born 7
November 1813. He married, 22 Dec. 1840, Caroline
Lansdale Bowie (b. 5 February 1820) daughter of Robert
W. Bowie, and had issue:

   i. MARY BOWIE SPRIGG,[7] b. August 1842; mar. April 1876, James
      Anderson of Rockville, Md., and died without surviving issue.
   ii. VIOLETTA LANSDALE SPRIGG, b. 30 June 1844; d. unmarried.
  iii. CATHERINE LANSDALE SPRIGG, b. 30 August 1846; d. in infancy.
   iv. SAMUEL SPRIGG, b. 27 Sept. 1849; mar. Mlle. Dubois of Cannes,
      France; d. s. p. 2 Nov. 1882.

STANSBURY FAMILY.

CHRISTOPHER JOHNSTON.

1. DETMAR STERNBERG,[1] the ancestor of this family, came to Maryland, in 1658, with his wife Renske and his son Tobias. The following record of his arrival has been preserved: "1663. I Detmoore Stairnber do assign over unto Thomas Bradley or his assigns all my right and Title of land due unto me for . . . myself who came in the year 1658, my wife Renscoe in 1658, John Dowlin in 1663. Witness my hand this 19th of November 1663, and also my son Tobias in 1658."

(Signed)   Detmorus Sternberge.

(*Land Office,* Lib. 6, fol. 82.)

15 December 1663, Thomas Bradley assigns to Henry Sewall, Esq. the rights of a large number of persons, including "Datmorus Sternber, Renscoe and Tobias Sternber in 1658" (*ibid.* fol. 84). While the name Sternberg is German, it should be borne in mind that similar names frequently occur in Holland, whither many families migrated from adjacent German territory. The name "Detmoore" or, in the Latinized form "Detmorus," evidently stands for the well known Low German name Detmar. The name of the immigrant's wife "Renscoe" must stand for

"Renske," the Low German or Dutch diminutive of Catherine. Detmar Sternberg settled in Baltimore County, and was living there in 1678. He is evidently the "Dodman Sternbrough" to whom there is entered a credit of 40 lb. tobacco in the Baltimore County levy of 1678 (*Md. Arch.*, vii, 96). After this no further mention of him occurs, and no will or administration appears on record. He appears to have owned no land, and such estate as he possessed was probably settled by family arrangement. Detmar [1] and Renske Sternberg had a son:—

2.   i. TOBIAS STERNBERG [2] or Starnborough, as the name appears on the records.

2.   TOBIAS STARNBOROUGH [2] (Detmar [1]) was brought to Maryland by his parents in 1658. He was certainly a minor at the time, since his father enters and disposes of his land rights, and he was probably quite young. 26 April 1707, Tobias Starnborough, "aged 44 years or thereabouts," deposes that when he first "went a ranging," some twelve years previously, one Daniel Welch told him that a certain tract of land was called Maiden's Choice (*Balto. Co. Resurveys*, fol. 21). This record, which would place the birth of Tobias in 1662 or 1663, can hardly be correct, since it has been shown above that he was born before 1658, and besides the latter date does not accord with the fact that his twin sons, Daniel and Thomas, were born in 1678. It is to be noted, however, that in these depositions the age of the deponent was often very perfunctorily recorded, as it did not form a material part of the evidence. A number of cases can be cited from the Chancery and other records where there is a discrepancy of at least ten years. If, in the present case, a similar error be assumed, and 54 years be read in the deposition instead of 44, the birth of Tobias would be placed in 1652 or 1653, and with this all the other data harmonize. Assuming, therefore, that Tobias was born in 1652-3, he would seem to have acquired land at the age of about 17 years, no unusual circumstance for an energetic lad at that time. 16 January 1670/1, by virtue of a warrant, dated 31 December 1670, to George Yate of Anne Arundel County for 150 acres, whereof 100 acres were assigned by the said Yate to Tobias Sternberge, a certificate of survey issued to the said Tobias for 100 acres in Balti-

more County called Poplar Neck. The patent which folowed is dated 10 July 1671 (*Land Office,* Lib. 16, fol. 148). It is, of course, possible that Detmar Sternberg, who was then living, purchased the assignment from Yate in his son's name. In the Baltimore County Rent Roll, the date of survey of Poplar Neck, which lay on the south side of Bear Creek, is given as 16 January 1672, and the possessor (about 1712) was Daniel Stansbury. In 1681, Tobias Stanborrow is credited with 270 lb. tobacco due to him in the levy of Baltimore County (*Md. Arch.,* vii, 210). Tobias Starnborough was a member of the Grand Jury of Baltimore County at March Court 1683/4 (*Balto. Co.,* Lib. D., fol. 129). Under the existing law of the Province he must have been a freeholder, and ought to have been at least 25 years of age. A few years later he acquires more land. 29 June 1688, a tract of 135 acres called Huntington, on the north side of Patapsco River in Baltimore County, was surveyed for Tobias Sternbridge (*Balto. Co. Rent Roll*). This land was conveyed, 8 July 1695, by Tobias Starnborough planter, of Baltimore County, and Sarah his wife, to Richard Thompson of the same county (*Balto. Co.,* Lib. RM. No. HS, fol. 479). In 1692, Tobias Starnbarrow appears on the list of taxables for the north side of the Patapsco (Balto Co., Lib. F, no. 1, fol. 227). In 1694 his residence is more precisely located. In that year the name of Tobias Starnborrow is found on the list of taxables for Patapsco Hundred, on the south side of Bear Creek (Balto. Co., Lib. G, no. 1, fol. 274). 30 July 1695, a tract of 185 acres called Strife was surveyed for Tobias Sternbrow " between the branches of Back River and Gunpowder " (Balto. Co. Rent Roll). In this year he became a "ranger" under Capt. John Oldton (*Md. Arch,* xx, 205), a member of the force maintained by the Province to range or patrol the outlying districts as a protection against Indians. In October 1695, Tobias Standborrow of Baltimore County has an allowance of 4200 lb. tobacco for seven months service as ranger (*Md. Arch,* xix, 266). An allusion to his position as a ranger will be found in his deposition cited above. He died in 1709. The inventory of Tobias Starnbrough's estate was filed from Baltimore county 3 August 1709 (*Test. Proc.,* Lib. 21, fol. 175). It is recorded at Annapolis in Inventories and Accounts, Lib. 29, fol. 408, and is

signed by Robert Gorsuch as chief creditor, by Sarah Starnbrough as administratrix, and by Luke Raven " brother to
ye administratrix." At July Court 1710, Sarah Starnbrough administratrix of Tobias Starnbrough filed her
administration bond (dated 23 April 1709) in common
form, with Wm. Farfare and John Barrett as her sureties
(*Test. Proc.*, Lib. 21, fol. 254). Shortly after this the
administratrix married Enoch Spinks and, at October Court
1710, citation issued to said Enoch Spinks and his wife, the
administratrix of Tobias Starnbrough, to give new security
for the administration of the deceased's estate (*ibid.* fol.
281). 15 July 1712, Sarah Spinks, administratrix of
Tobias Standburrough deceased, filed her account, and at
August Court 1714, she gave bond to Samuel and Tabitha
Stansbury, orphans of Tobias Stansbury late of Baltimore
County deceased, for their filial portion of their father's
estate (Baltimore County, Court Record). Daniel, the
eldest son of Tobias Stansbury, and his twin brother
Thomas were born in 1678, while the next child, Luke, was
not born until 1689. It is possible, therefore, that the two
elder sons were the offspring of a former wife, but there is
no other evidence that Tobias Stansbury was married more
than once, and Sarah was undoubtedly the mother of all
the rest.

Tobias Starnborough [2] had issue:—

3.   i.   DANIEL STANSBURY,[3] b. 1678; d. April 1763.
4.   ii.   THOMAS STANSBURY, twin of Daniel, b. 1678; d. 1766.
5.   iii.   LUKE STANSBURY, b. 1689; d. 1742.
6.   iv.   TOBIAS STANSBURY, b. 1691; d. 1764.
7.   v.   SAMUEL STANSBURY, a minor in 1714.
    vi.   TABITHA STANSBURY, a minor in 1714.

3.   DANIEL STANSBURY [3] (Tobias,[2] Detmar [1]) of Baltimore
County, the eldest son of his father, was born in 1678, and
died in April 1763. The *Annapolis Maryland Gazette* of
7 April 1763, has this obituary: " Last week, died very suddenly in Baltimore County, Mr. Daniel Stansbury, a native
of that place, in the 85th year of his age. He had eat a
hearty supper the evening before he died; and has left a
twin brother." The twin brother can only be Thomas, since
all the other brothers are accounted for. 24 November 1713,
Daniel Stansbrough executed a deed of gift to his brother
Thomas Stansbrough, of Daniel's Gift, 40 acres, " being
part of a tract called Strife " (Balto Co., Lib. T. R. no. A,

fol. 252). 7 November 1714, by virtue of a warrant to Daniel Starborrough and Thomas Starborrough, both of Baltimore County, dated 8 September 1714, to resurvey a tract in said county called " Strife," which was formerly granted to their father, Tobias Starnborrough deceased, a certificate issued to said Daniel for " Strife " now laid out for 268 acres. On the same date and by virtue of the same warrant, and " whereas the said Daniel, as eldest son and heir to his father, out of his fraternal love and affection for his brother Thomas " did grant to him by deed, dated 24 Nov. 1713, 40 acres part of Strife,—a certificate of resurvey issued to said Thomas for Daniel's Gift now laid out for 127 acres (Original Certificates in Land Office). The following children of " Daniel and Elizabeth Stansbury " are entered in the register of St. Paul's, Baltimore County, with exception of William whose dates are derived from his epitaph. Daniel [3] and Elizabeth Stansbury had issue.

8.   i.   WILLIAM STANSBURY,[4] b. 20 Jan'y 1716; d. 3 Nov. 1788.
9.   ii.   RICHARDSON STANSBURY, b. 20 May 1723; d. 1797.
10.   iii.   RICHARD STANSBURY, b. 22 May 1725; d. 1791.
11.   iv.   DANIEL STANSBURY, b. 23 July 1727.
      v.   ELIZABETH STANSBURY, b. 21 Oct. 1730; m., 14 Jan'y 1749/50, Aquilla Gostwick.
      vi.   ANNE STANSBURY, b. 26 Dec. 1735.

4.   THOMAS STANSBURY,[3] (Tobias,[2] Detmar [1]) was born in Baltimore County in 1678, being the twin of his brother Daniel, and died 4 May 1766 (St. Paul's register). His brother's deed of gift, containing proof of his affiliation has already been cited, and the Baltimore County Rent Roll shows that a tract of 268 acres, called " Stansbury," was surveyed for him, 5 April 1724, on the west side of Little Falls of Gunpowder. His will, dated 21 Feb'y 1748, confirmed 9 March 1763, and proved 4 June 1766 (Baltimore, Lib. 3, fol. 44) and the Baltimore County land records show that he acquired a very considerable landed estate. Thomas Stansbury [3] and Jane (Dixon) his wife had issue (dates of birth, &c., from St. Paul's) :—

12.   i.   JOHN STANSBURY,[4] b. 1710; living 1785; named in his father's will as eldest son.
13.   ii.   THOMAS STANSBURY, b. 24 April 1714; d. 1798.
14.   iii.   DANIEL STANSBURY of Anne Arundel Co., d. 1770.
15.   iv.   DIXON STANSBURY, b. 6 Dec. 1720; d. 1805.
16.   v.   EDMUND STANSBURY, b. 13 Jan'y 1724; d. 22 April 1780.
      vi.   JEMIMA STANSBURY, b. 19 July 1727; m., 16 Aug. 1747, Roebuck Lynch.

5. LUKE STANSBURY [3] (Tobias,[2] Detmar [1]) was born in 1689, and died in 1742. He gives his age as 44 years in 1733 (Balto. Co., Lib. H. W. S. no. 3, fol. 188), 48 in 1737 (*ib.* H. W. S. no. 4, fol. 21), and 50 in 1739 (*ibid.,* fol. 50). His will, dated 25 March 1742, was proved 7 May following (Balto., Lib. 1, fol. 345). 14 Dec. 1709, the year of his father's death, Sarah Stansbury assigns to her " son Luke Stansbury " all her right and title to a tract of 105 acres in Baltimore County called " The Lot," for which Tobias Starnborough had a certificate dated 19 June 1705, and a patent issued, 1 Nov. 1710, to Luke Stanborough, "son of the said Tobias" (*Land Office,* Lib. D. D. no. 5, fol. 634). The patent recites that Tobias Stanborough, of Baltimore County deceased, had surveyed for him, 16 June 1705, a tract of 105 acres, by virtue of an assignment for that amount from James Crooke, out of a warrant for 500 acres granted to the said Crooke 20 Dec. 1704; that Sarah Stanborough, administratrix of the said Tobias, assigned her right and title to Luke Stanborough; and that the said 105 acres is now patented to said Luke under the name of " The Lot " (*Land Office,* Lib, P. L. no. 3, fol. 263). Jane, wife of Luke Stansbury, survived her husband and died in 1759. Her will, dated 16 April 1759, was proved 9 May following (Balto., Lib. 2, fol. 304). They had issue:—

17.　i.　CAPT. TOBIAS STANSBURY,[4] b. 23 March 1718/19; d. Oct. 1757.
　　ii.　LUKE STANSBURY, b. 26 Dec. 1735.
　　iii.　ELIZABETH STANSBURY, m. William Bond.
　　iv.　BETHIA STANSBURY, b. 1726; d. 10 July 1780; m., 9 Aug. 1743, Capt. John Hall of Cranberry.
　　v.　RUTH STANSBURY, b. 20 Jan'y 1728/9.

6. TOBIAS STANSBURY [3] (Tobias,[2] Detmar [1]) was born in 1691 and died in 1764. He gives his age, in depositions, as 42 years in 1733 (Balto. Co., Lib. H. W. S. no. 3, fol. 187), as 56 in 1746 (*ib.* Lib. H. W. S. no. 4, fol. 128), and as 60 in 1746 (*ibid.,* fol. 142, 160). In the last deposition cited, he states that he was with his " uncle Luke Raven " when he ran a certain survey &c., and the fact that he was a nephew of Luke Raven affords proof of his parentage. His will, dated 6 Jan'y 1762, was proved 7 August 1764 (Balto., Lib. 2, fol. 167). Tobias Stansbury [3] and Honor (Bowen) his wife had issue (dates from St. Paul's register) as follows:—

18.   i.   TOBIAS STANSBURY⁴ of Patapsco Neck, b. 11 Feb'y 1726/7; d.
            10 Dec. 1799.
19. ii.   GEORGE STANSBURY, b. 3 July 1732; d. 1789.
    iii.   BOWEN STANSBURY.
     iv.   AVERILLA STANSBURY, b. 9 Oct. 1723.
      v.   HONOR STANSBURY, m. — Gambrill.
     vi.   SOPHIA STANSBURY, m. — Robinson.

7.   SAMUEL STANSBURY ³ (Tobias,² Detmar ¹) was, with his
sister Tabitha, a minor in 1714, and their mother Sarah,
who had married her second husband, Enoch Spinks, gave
bond for the payment of their filial portions of their father's
esate.   20 November 1719, Samuel Stansbury of Baltimore
County had a certificate for 100 acres on the south side of
the Great Falls of Gunpowder River in Baltimore County,
by virtue of a warrant issued to the said Samuel 29 Sept.
1719 (Land Office, Lib. I. L. no. A, fol. 24).   This tract,
under the name Long Island, was surveyed 20 Nov. 1720
(Balto. Co. Rent Roll).   Samuel Stansbury's will, dated
19 April 1783, was proved 9 May following (Balto., Lib. 3,
fol. 547).   He leaves to his grandson Wm. Welch, after
his mother's decease part of The Addition, on the south side
of Towson's River.—Remainder of said tract to Solomon
Stansbury.—£50 to John Ensor Stansbury, son of William
Stansbury.—To my son Jasper Stansbury Colston and my
daughter Ruth Stansbury Colston, £50.—To my daughter
Tabitha Cross, £100.—To Delia Standifer, £50.—To
Zebedee Hicks, £50.—To Solomon and Luke Stansbury, £50
each.—To Matthias Galloy and Ruth Hicks, each one shilling.—To my daughter Polly Stansbury Colston, £20.—
John Ensor Stansbury executor.—Witness: Benj. Stansbury, John Talbot Risteau, William Stansbury.   John
Ensor Stansbury, who is appointed executor, was the son of
William ⁴ (Daniel,³ Tobias,² Detmar ¹) and the great
nephew of the testator.   Tabitha Cross was doubtless Samuel's daughter, but the Colstons, whom he calls his son and
daughters, seem rather to have been his grandchildren.   As
for the other legatees, it is difficult to trace their connection
with the testator, and it is probably safer to attempt no
further interpretation of the will without additional information.

8.   WILLIAM STANSBURY ⁴ (Daniel,³ Tobias,² Detmar ¹) was
born 20 January 1716, and died 3 November 1788 in his

73rd year (Epitaph). His father dying intestate, William, as son and heir, made provision for two of his brothers. 25 April 1763, William Stansbury of Baltimore County, planter, son and heir-at-law of Daniel Stansbury, late of said county deceased, and Elizabeth, wife of said William, convey to Richard Stansbury, son of said Daniel deceased, tract Poplar Neck, 100 acres, on Bear Creek, in Baltimore County (Balto. Co., Lib. B. U. no. L, fol. 350). Also 25 April 1763, the same parties convey to Daniel Stansbury, another son of said Daniel deceased, tract Prospect, 80 acres, on Back River, in Baltimore County (*ibid.* fol. 353). William Stansbury married, 14 Feb'y 1739/40, Elizabeth daughter of John Ensor. She was born 12 July 1721, and died 10 Sept. 1799 (Epitaph). Her father in his will, dated 10 April 1771, and proved 11 March 1773 (Balto., Lib. 3, fol. 240), leaves a bequest to his "grandson John Ensor Stansbury, son of my daughter Elizabeth Stansbury." William Stansbury [4] and Elizabeth (Ensor) his wife had issue:—

   i.   WILLIAM STANSBURY,[5] b. 4 April 1746; d. 1826; m. Belinda — (b. 1750; d. 7 April 1830).
20. ii. ABRAHAM STANSBURY, b —; d. 1811.
  iii. ISAAC STANSBURY, b. 2 July 1752; d. Oct. 1792.
  iv. JACOB STANSBURY, b. 14 March 1755; d. 22 Feb'y 1812.
   v. ELIJAH STANSBURY, m. 1°, 27 Dec. 1779, Sarah Gorsuch, 2°, 15 Nov. 1783, Elizabeth Gorsuch.
  vi. JOHN ENSOR STANSBURY, b. 1760; d. 30 April 1841; m. 1°, Mary — (b. 1777; d. 1800), 2°, Ann — (b. 1783; d. 1 April 1815).
  vii. RUTH STANSBURY, b. 28 April 1744.
 viii. ELIZABETH STANSBURY, m. James Edwards.

9. RICHARDSON STANSBURY [4] (Daniel,[3] Tobias,[2] Detmar [1]) is doubtless correctly placed here, but a word of explanation is necessary. The register of St. Paul's Parish records that Richard Stansbury, son of Daniel and Elizabeth, was born 20 May 1723. A later hand has converted "Richard" into "Richardson." That the clerk who made the original entry accidentally dropped the final syllable "son," is probable enough, as it is an error specially easy to make; and the person who made the correction seems to have been well informed. Richardson Stansbury lived in Back River Neck with the other sons of Daniel. He was undoubtedly a grandson of Tobias, and a careful examination fails to to find a place for him elsewhere than among the sons of

Daniel. In a deposition, made in 1773, he gives his age as 50 years (Balto. Co., A. L. No. R, 272) which agrees precisely with the record of birth in St. Paul's register. Richardson Stansbury married, 23 February 1747, Mary daughter of Isaac Raven (d. 1757) of Baltimore County, and Letitia his wife daughter of Joseph Ward (d. 1754) of Back River Neck. The will of " Richardson Stansbury of Back River Neck, in Baltimore County " is dated 30 January 1797, and was proved 22 April following (Balto., Lib. 5, fol. 507). In it he names the children given below, makes his grandson William Boswell one of his residuary legatees, and appoints his son Isaac his executor. Richardson Stansbury [4] and Mary (Raven) his wife had issue:—

     i.   JOSEPH WARD STANSBURY,[5] b. 24 Jan'y 1749; living 1797.
     ii.   ISAAC STANSBURY, executor of his father's will, 1797.
21.   iii.   RICHARDSON STANSBURY, of Middle River Neck, d. 1819.
     iv.   DRUSILLA STANSBURY, m. Charles Pearce.
     v.   SARAH STANSBURY, m. — Shaw.
     vi.   DEBORAH STANSBURY.
     vii.   CASSANDRA STANSBURY, b. 13 April 1761; m. — Bonfield.

10. RICHARD STANSBURY [4] (Daniel,[3] Tobias,[2] Detmar [1]) was born 22 May 1725, and died in 1791. He had a deed of gift, 25 April 1763, from his brother William of a tract of 100 acres in Baltimore County called Poplar Neck, and this tract was, at Richard's death, divided among his four sons by deed of partition recorded in Baltimore County. His will, dated 28 May 1791 and proved 6 October following (Balto. Lib. 5, fol. 11), names his wife Sarah and the four sons and three daughters given below. *The Maryland Journal* of 2 July 1782 has this obituary: " Died. In the prime of life, Mr. Solomon Stansbury and his two sisters, viz: Sarah and Elizabeth, son and daughters of Richard Stansbury of Patapsco Neck, a few days ago were drowned by the oversetting of a canoe in the River " &c. &c. In addition to these three, Richard Stansbury and Sarah his wife had issue:—

     i.   DANIEL STANSBURY.[5]
     ii.   THOMAS STANSBURY, b. 2 Sept. 1770.
22.   iii.   JOSIAS STANSBURY, d. 26 April 1825.
     iv.   JOSHUA STANSBURY.
     v.   KEZIAH STANSBURY.
     vi.   TABITHA STANSBURY.
     vii.   PRISCILLA STANSBURY.

11. DANIEL STANSBURY [4] (Daniel,[3] Tobias,[2] Detmar [1]) of Patapsco Neck, Baltimore County, was born 23 July 1727, and died in October or November 1803. His father, Daniel, having died intestate, and therefore without making provision for his younger sons, his eldest brother, William, conveyed to him by deed of gift, dated 25 April 1763, a tract of 80 acres called Prospect, on Back River (Balto. Co., Lib. B. no. L, fol. 353), and 20 April 1768, Aquilla Gostwick and Elizabeth his wife conveyed to "Daniel Stansbury son of Daniel" a tract of 100 acres called Adventure (*ib.* Lib. A. L. no. A, fol. 39). In his will, dated 26 October, and proved 26 November, 1803 (Balto. Lib. 7, fol. 256), he leaves to his eldest son Daniel the tract "Adventure which I purchased of Aquilla Gorsuch" (sic!); to his son William, the tract Force "which I now live on"; and leaves legacies to his daughters Rebecca Bowen and Elizabeth Phipps, and to his granddaughter Averilla Bowen. The witnesses are Josias Stansbury, Joshua Stansbury, and Thomas Jones, the first two being his nephews, sons of his brother Richard. Testator's wife is not mentioned and was presumably dead. Daniel Stansbury [4] had issue:

    i. DANIEL STANSBURY.[5]
    ii. WILLIAM STANSBURY.[5]
    iii. REBECCA STANSBURY, m. — Bowen.
    iv. ELIZABETH STANSBURY, m. — Phipps.

12. JOHN STANSBURY [4] (Thomas,[3] Tobias,[2] Detmar [1]) is named in his father's will as his eldest son. In a deposition made in 1785 he gives his age as 75 years and mentions his father Thomas Stansbury (Balto. Co., W. G. no. Y, 190). He was born, therefore, about 1710, and he probably died not many years after 1785. He married, 12 Feb'y 1734, Ann Ensor, and had issue (with perhaps others):—

    i. JANE STANSBURY,[5] b. 26 June 1736.
    ii. JOHN STANSBURY, b. 23 Jan'y 1737/8.
    iii. ELIZABETH STANSBURY, b. 25 Feb'y 1739.

13. THOMAS STANSBURY [4] (Thomas,[3] Tobias,[2] Detmar [1]) was born 24 April 1714, and died in 1798. In his will, proved 30 June 1798 and recorded in Baltimore, he names the children given below. He married, 2 March 1735, Hannah daughter of Charles Gorsuch and Sarah Coale his wife. They had issue (order of birth uncertain):

    i. CHARLES STANSBURY, b. 24 Jan'y 1736.
    ii. LUKE STANSBURY, dead in 1798, leaving a widow Catherine.
   iii. BENJAMIN STANSBURY.
   iv. JOHN DIXON STANSBURY.
    v. WILLIAM STANSBURY.
   vi. DAVID STANSBURY.
   vii. SARAH STANSBURY.
  viii. HANNAH STANSBURY, b. 20 April 1743; m. Henry Sater (b. 1745).
   ix. JANE STANSBURY, b. 14 April 1750; d. 10 June 1798; m., 14 July 1774, William Wilson (b. 1749; d. 30 March 1824).
    x. RACHEL STANSBURY, m. — Lemon.

14. DANIEL STANSBURY [4] (Thomas,[3] Tobias,[2] Detmar[1]) of Anne Arundel County was probably born about 1716-18, though this is largely conjectural, and died in December 1769. His will, dated 22 December 1769, was proved 29 January 1770 (Annapolis, Lib. 37, fol. 487) and mentions testator's wife Elizabeth and his children as given below. He married, about 1740, Elizabeth (b. 24 Dec. 1718) daughter of John Ashman (d. 1737) of Anne Arundel County and Constant his wife daughter of John Wilmot (d. 1719) of Baltimore County. Daniel Stansbury [4] and Elizabeth (Ashman) his wife had issue (dates from St. Margaret's, A. A. Co.):

23.   i. EZEKIEL STANSBURY,[5] b. 13, March 1740/1; d. December 1789.
24.   ii. EMANUEL STANSBURY, b. 21 Feb'y 1743/4; d. 1790.
25. iii. JOSEPH STANSBURY, b. 19 Feb'y 1745/6; d. Dec. 1798.
    iv. CHARITY STANSBURY, b. 31 January 1747/8; d. 1777; m. George Presstman of Balto. Co.
    v. ELIZABETH STANSBURY, b. 9 April 1750.
   vi. BENJAMIN STANSBURY, b. 9 Dec. 1754.
  vii. PATIENCE STANSBURY, b. 14 July 1757.

15. DIXON STANSBURY [4] (Thomas,[3] Tobias,[2] Detmar[1]) was born 6 Dec. 1720, and died in 1805. He married, 4 January 1740/1, Penelope (b. 27 Nov. 1724) daughter of Stephen and Elizabeth Body (St. Paul's, Balto. Co.). His will, dated 19 March 1805, was proved 4 December following (Balto., Lib. 8, fol. 10). His wife is not mentioned in it, and she was doubtless dead at the time. Dixon Stansbury [4] and Penelope (Body) his wife had issue:

    i. DIXON STANSBURY,[5] b. 22 July 1744; living 1805.
26.   ii. CAPT. EDMUND STANSBURY, b. 6 Oct. 1746; d. 1801.
   iii. ELIZABETH STANSBURY, b. 7 June 1749; m., 16 Jan'y 1770, William Slade.
   iv. JAMES STANSBURY, b. 7 Nov. 1751; m., 7 Feb'y 1789, Jemima Gorsuch.

16. EDMUND STANSBURY [4] (Thomas,[3] Tobias,[2] Detmar [1]) was born 13 January 1724/5, and died 22 April 1780. He died intestate, and letters of administration were issued, 12 January 1781, to Joseph Cromwell, with Wm. Cromwell and Thomas Miles as sureties (Balto. Administrations, Lib. 1, fol. 181). Edmund Stansbury married, about 1775, Keziah Gostwick (b. 1753, d. 7 July 1809) who survived him and married, secondly, Joseph Cromwell (b. about 1743, d. 12 Nov. 1800). Edmund Stansbury [4] and Keziah Gostwick his wife had issue:

   i. JANE STANSBURY,[5] b. 3 Oct. 1776.
   ii. MARY STANSBURY, b. 30 Oct. 1778.
   iii. KEZIAH STANSBURY, b. 22 Feb'y 1780.

17. CAPT. TOBIAS STANSBURY [4] (Luke,[3] Tobias,[2] Detmar [1]) was born 23 March 1718/9, and died in October 1757. *The Annapolis Maryland Gazette* of 20 October 1757 has the following brief obituary: " A few days ago died, in Baltimore County, Capt. Tobias Stansbury." He doubtless held a commission as Captain in the County militia. His will dated 6 October 1757, was proved 31 March 1758 (Balto., Lib. 2, fol. 68). Tobias Stansbury married, 27 April 1746, Mary Hammond, daughter of Thomas Hammond of Queen Anne County and Catherine Emerson his wife. Thomas Hammond, born 19 Dec. 1693, was the son of William, and the grandson of Maj. Gen. John Hammond. The record of Tobias Stansbury's marriage and of the births of his children may be found in the register of St. Paul's, Baltimore, with exception of Gen. Tobias Emerson Stansbury, whose birth is not entered. There is, however, ample proof that Gen Stansbury was the unborn child mentioned in his father's will. Capt. Tobias Stansbury [4] and Mary (Hammond) his wife had issue:

   i. HENRIETTA STANSBURY,[5] b. 26 Feb'y 1747/8.
   ii. CATHERINE STANSBURY, b. 28 March 1749.
   iii. REBECCA STANSBURY, b. 22 April 1751; m. Thomas E. Bond.
   iv. JANE STANSBURY, b. 9 June 1753.
   v. MARY STANSBURY, b. 12 Sept. 1755. } Twins
   vi. SARAH STANSBURY, b. 12 Sept. 1755. }
27. vii. GEN. TOBIAS EMERSON STANSBURY, b. 1757; d. 25 Oct. 1849.

18. TOBIAS STANSBURY [4] (Tobias,[3] Tobias,[2] Detmar [1]) of Patapsco Neck was born 11 Feb'y 1726/7, and is said to have died in 1799. His wife's name was Blanche and they had issue:

28.   i,   REV. TOBIAS STANSBURY,⁵ d. about 1811.
      ii.   NATHANIEL STANSBURY, b. 10 March 1759; d. unmar. about 1808.
      iii.   CATHERINE STANSBURY, b. 4 July 1754; m.—Partridge.
      iv.   SARAH STANSBURY, b. 20 Oct. 1756; m. 1°—Bowen, 2° John M.
             Gorsuch.
      v.   ELLEN STANSBURY.

19. GEORGE STANSBURY ⁴ (Tobias,³ Tobias,² Detmar ¹) was
    born 3 July 1732, and died in 1789. His wife was named
    Mary and they had issue (order of birth uncertain):

29.   i.   GEORGE STANSBURY,⁵ b. 18 April 1771.
      ii.   ELISHA STANSBURY.
      iii.   DARIUS STANSBURY.
      iv.   WILLIAM STANSBURY.
      v.   RUTH STANSBURY, b. 9 Nov. 1760; m., 10 Feb'y 1781, William
             Lynch.
      vi.   CATHERINE STANSBURY, m. Joseph Green.
      vii.   ELLIN STANSBURY, m., 1 May 1787, John Battie.
      viii.   REBECCA STANSBURY.
      ix.   MARY STANSBURY.
      x.   SARAH STANSBURY.

20. ABRAHAM STANSBURY ⁵ (William,⁴ Daniel,³ Tobias ²) died
    in 1811. His will, dated 19 August 1811, was proved 2
    October following (Balto., Lib. 9, fol. 174). His wife was
    named Elizabeth, as appears from the register of St. James'
    Parish, Baltimore County, where the births of four of their
    children are recorded, but her surname is unknown. She
    may, however, have been an Edwards, as may be conjec-
    tured from the fact that no less than three of their nine
    children bear this name. Abraham Stansbury ⁵ and Eliza-
    beth his wife had issue:—

      i.   WILLIAM STANSBURY.⁶
      ii.   ISAAC STANSBURY.
      iii.   CHARITY STANSBURY, m. George C. Collins.
      iv.   ELIZABETH STANSBURY, m. Thomas Cowley.
      v.   JACOB STANSBURY, b. 10 Nov. 1789.
      vi.   RUTH EDWARDS STANSBURY, b. 11 May 1782; d. young.
      vii.   PRUDENCE STANSBURY, m. Josias Bowen.
      viii.   RUTH JAMES EDWARDS STANSBURY, b. 20 Sept. 1794; m. Isaac
             Hollingsworth.
      ix.   JAMES EDWARDS STANSBURY, b. 26 Feb'y 1799.

21. RICHARDSON STANSBURY ⁵ (Richardson,⁴ Daniel,³ Tobias ²)
    of Middle River Neck, Baltimore County, died in 1819.
    His will, dated 17 July 1815, was proved 20 October 1819
    Balto., Lib. 11, fol. 71). He married, 14 April 1791,
    Sarah daughter of Luke Raven (d. 1798) and Anne Rigbie
    his wife. They had issue:—

i. JAMES STANSBURY.[6]
ii. ANNE STANSBURY, m. William Sinclair.

22. JOSIAS STANSBURY [5] (Richard,[4] Daniel,[3] Tobias [2]) died 26
April 1825. He married 1[0]. Sarah Colegate, who died 17
June 1822, and 2[0]. Keziah Bowen. By the first marriage
he had issue:—

Twins:
   i. BENJAMIN STANSBURY, b. 28 Sept. 1810; d. 10 April 1811.
   ii. JOSIAS STANSBURY, b. 28 Sept. 1810; d. 11 June 1811.
Twins:
   iii. RICHARD COLEGATE STANSBURY, b. 18 March 1814; d. 11 May
      1857; m. Ellen Bond.
   iv. SARAH COLEGATE STANSBURY, b. 18 March 1814; d. 22 July 1868.
   v. ELIZABETH COLEGATE STANSBURY, b. 25 Oct. 1816; m. George B.
      Graves.

By the second marriage Josias Stansbury had issue:—

   vi. REBBECA ALLEN STANSBURY, d. an infant.

23. EZEKIEL STANSBURY [5] (Daniel,[4] Thomas,[3] Tobias [2]) of
Baltimore County was born 13 March 1740/1 (St. Margaret's, A. A. Co.) and died in December 1789. He married Keziah Wood, who survived him, and married secondly, 28 August 1796, Thomas Greenwood. Ezekiel
Stansbury died intestate, and his widow Keziah filed her
bond for the administration of his estate 5 January 1790
(Balto. Admin. Bonds, Lib. 7, fol. 242), her sureties being
Emanuel Stansbury and John Eager Howard. From the
date of the bond, it would appear that Ezekiel had died in
the course of the preceding month, December. Ezekiel
Stansbury [5] and Keziah his wife had issue:—

   i. ELIZABETH ANN STANSBURY,[6] b. 15 March 1772; d. 1862; m., 23
      Dec. 1792, George Dutroc.
   ii. MARY STANSBURY, m.—, Elder.
   iii. THOMAS STANSBURY, b. 5 April 1778; m., 20 Dec. 1801, Eliza-
      beth Skelton.
   iv. WILLIAM STANSBURY, m. and left issue.
   v. CHARITY STANSBURY, b. 28 Oct. 1782; m., 8 April 1804, Abraham
      Jones.
   vi. REV. DANIEL STANSBURY (M. E. Church), d. 26 Oct. 1828; m., 13
      June 1816, Elizabeth Hunt.
   vii. SUSANNA ATLEE STANSBURY, b. 22 Jan'y 1786; d. 21 Nov. 1869;
      m., 20 April 1806, Col. Joshua Lee.
   viii. PATIENCE STANSBURY, b. 20 Sept. 1789.

24. EMANUEL STANSBURY [5] (Daniel,[4] Thomas,[3] Tobias [2]) was
born 21 Feb'y 1743/4, and died in 1790. He married, 25
March 1778, Roche Pumphrey and had issue:—

i. EMANUEL STANSBURY.⁶
ii. ANNE STANSBURY.
iii. SUSANNA STANSBURY..

25. JOSEPH STANSBURY ⁵ (Daniel,⁴ Thomas,³ Tobias ²) was born 19 Feb'y 1745/6, and died in December 1798. He was commissioned, 25 May 1776, Ensign in the Gunpowder Battalion of Baltimore County. He married first, 12 Dec. 1773, Jane Long, and secondly, 1 March 1796, Frances widow of Philipps Gough. By the first marriage he had issue:—

i. ELEANOR STANSBURY,⁶ d. 24 Nov. 1792.

By the second marriage:—

ii. JOHN STANSBURY, b. 16 January 1797.
iii. REBECCA STANSBURY.
iv. NANCY STANSBURY, m. — Grundy.
v. ELIZABETH STANSBURY, m. — Dew.

26. CAPT. EDMUND STANSBURY ⁵ (Dixon,⁴ Thomas,³ Tobias ²) was born 6 October 1746, and died in 1801. He was commissioned, 3 Sept. 1777, 1st. Lieutenant in Capt. Standiford's Company, Gunpowder Battalion, militia of Baltimore County (*Md. Archives,* xvi, 359). He is usually styled Captain, and was probably promoted before the close of the war. He married Belinda, widow of Thomas Talbot (d. 1773) of Baltimore County, and daughter of William Slade and Elizabeth Dulany his wife. She was married to her first husband, Thomas Talbot, 21 January 1766. Capt. Edmund Stansbury ⁵ and Belinda his wife had issue:—

30. i. MAJ. DIXON STANSBURY ⁶ U. S. A., b. about 1783; d. 5 June 1841.

27. GEN. TOBIAS EMERSON STANSBURY ⁵ (Tobias,⁴ Luke,³ Tobias ²) was born in 1757, and died 25 October 1849. He was commissioned 6 December 1809, Brigadier-General commanding the 11th Brigade, which comprised the 7th, 15th, 36th, 41st, and 46th regiments of Baltimore County, and served with his brigade in the defense of Maryland against the British Invasion of 1814. Gen. Stansbury was thrice married. His first wife Mary was born 3 August 1760, and died 21 April 1809 aged 48 years, 8 months,

and 18 days. His second wife, Anna D. Steenback, was born 1784, and died 9 July 1839. His third wife is said to have been Rose (?) Dew. The second and third wives appear to have had no issue.

Gen. Stansbury and Mary, his first wife, had issue (order of birth uncertain) :—

  i. WILLIAM STANSBURY,[6] d. before 1850; had two daughters.
  ii. EMERSON STANSBURY, lived in St. Louis, Mo.
  iii. CARVELLE S. STANSBURY, m. Harriet Louisa Stansbury, dau. of his brother William.
  iv. JOHN LIGHTFOOT STANSBURY, d. 1888; married, but no surviving issue.
  v. EDWARD H. STANSBURY, m. Elizabeth Johnson, and left issue.
  vi. TOBIAS EMERSON STANSBURY JR., was commissioned, 1st Lieut. in 6th Cavalry District, 26 April 1812; Captain, 8 July 1814. He mar. & left issue.
  vii. HAMMOND N. STANSBURY, 3rd. Officer in the privateer Chasseur, war of 1812; mar. & left issue.

28. REV. TOBIAS STANSBURY [5] (Tobias,[4] Tobias,[3] Tobias [2]) was a minister of the Methodist Episcopal Church, and is said to have died in 1811. He maried 10 December 1799, Ariana daughter of Thomas Sollers (d. 1783) Naval Officer of Baltimore and Ariana Dorsey his wife. Their issue:—

  i. NATHANIEL STANSBURY,[6] b. 1804.
  ii. CATHERINE PARTRIDGE STANSBURY.
  iii. SARAH BOWEN STANSBURY.

29. GEORGE STANSEURY [5] (George,[4] Tobias,[3] Tobias [2]) was born 18 April 1771. He is said to have married and left a son:—

  i. GEORGE STANSBURY,[6] who m. Elizabeth Sollers and had: a) Darius Stansbury,[7] b) Eliza Stansbury, c) Catherine Stansbury, m. Nathaniel Stansbury, d) Mary Ann Stansbury.

30. MAJ. DIXON STANSBURY [6] U. S. A. (Edmund,[5] Dixon,[4] Thomas [3]) was born in 1783, and died 5 June 1841. He was commissioned 1st Lieutenant in the 13th U. S. Infantry, 20 January 1813, was promoted to Captain 30 June 1814, and resigned 31 January 1815. He is usually styled Major, and probably held this rank by brevet. Major Stansbury was twice married, but had no issue by his second wife, Sarah McComas. His first wife, Sophia daughter of

Sampson Levy, to whom he was married in 1817, was born in 1791, and died 12 October 1831. Their issue:—

   i. SAMPSON STANSBURY.[1]
   ii. THOMAS STANSBURY.
   iii. EDMUND STANSBURY.
   iv. ELIZABETH STANSBURY, m. Victor Holmes.
   vi. SOPHIA STANSBURY, d. unm'd.
   vi. ARABELLA STANSBURY, m. Thomas Edward Hambleton.

NOTE.—In concluding this genealogy, the compiler desires to express his indebtedness to Mrs. Walter Damon Mansfield of San Francisco, California, Corresponding Secretary of the California Society, Colonial Dames of America, for kindly and generously placing at his disposal her extensive Stansbury collections, which have been freely utilized. It is to be hoped that other Stansbury descendants will add to the completeness of the genealogy by sending to the editor such additions, especially in the earlier portion, as they may be able to make.

STANSBURY FAMILY.

FRANCIS B. CULVER.

In the genealogical contribution by Dr. Christopher Johnston treating of the Stansbury family, in the March 1914 issue of The *Maryland Historical Magazine,* (Vol. IX, No. 1), certain errors occur with reference to the section relating to Gen. Tobias Emerson Stansbury (1757-1849) on pages 86 and 87. The corrections are herewith submitted.

General Stansbury was thrice married. His first wife was Mary *Buffington,* born 3 August 1760, and died 21 April 1809. Marriage license issued to Rev. West [William West, of Old St. Paul's parish] on 1 May 1784 (see Balto. County Marriage Licenses: *Baltimore American,* 24 April 1809: *Baltimore Whig,* 24 April 1809). His *second* wife was *Ann* Dew. Marriage license issued 8 Jan'y 1811. (See Balto. County Marriage Licenses.)

His *third* wife was the widow Anna Dorothea Steinbeck, relict of John C. Steinbeck, whose will was probated 3 Jan'y 1821. (See Balto. County Wills, Liber No. 11, fol. 209). Marriage license issued 27 April, 1824 to Rev. Soule. She died 9 July 1839 in her 55th year, and "was the sister of John G. Wender [Wendell?] of New York." (See *Baltimore Sun,* 16 July 1839).

General Stansbury had issue by his first and second wives, and the following is believed to be the order of birth of the children, based upon family records and certain other data.

Issue by first wife, Mary Buffington :—

    i. HENRIETTA STANSBURY, married in Balto. Co., James C. Dew (license 26 Sept. 1807).
    ii. TOBIAS EMERSON STANSBURY, JR., married in Balto. Co., Elizabeth Divers (lic. 2 June 1813). He died in Ascension Parish, La., in Apl. 1828, aged 40 and left issue.
    iii. HAMMOND N. STANSBURY, married in Balto. Co., and died there 7 June 1836, aged 46, leaving issue.
    iv. WILLIAM STANSBURY, married in Balto. Co., Maria Norwood (lic. 17 Mch. 1819), died in Ascension Parish, La.: had a son who died young (perhaps, others).
    —— STANSBURY. Uncertain as to name of fifth child. The *Baltimore Whig* of 24 April 1809 states that Mrs. Mary Stansbury left a husband and five children.

Issue by second wife, Ann Dew :—

    v. EMERSON STANSBURY, lived in St. Louis, Mo.
    vi. JOHN "LIGHTFOOT" [LEWIS?] STANSBURY (twin), b. 1817, married in Balto. Co., Mary Jones (license 17 Feby. 1840), died in Virginia.
    vii. CARVELL S. STANSBURY (twin), b. 1817, married Harriet Louisa Stansbury, daughter of William, his step-brother: had issue. He died in Baltimore, 2 April 1865 in his 49th year (*Baltimore Sun,* 3 April 1865).
    viii. EDWARD H. STANSBURY, married Elizabeth Johnson and left issue.

THE SWEETSER FAMILY OF MARYLAND.

By Lester Durand Gardner.

Many descendants of New England families migrated in the Eighteenth Century to Maryland where a more temperate climate and better trade conditions were to be found. Seth Sweetser, whose Puritan ancestry embraced such well known families as the Spragues, Breeds, Wigglesworths and Rhodes came from Malden, Mass., and settled at Annapolis, later moving near to Baltimore where he built the Sweetser Bridge across the Patapsco River. His home and toll house are still standing at Linthicum, the home and land development of several members of the Linthicum family, his descendants. This study traces the ancestry of Seth Sweetser in New England and gives, as far as could be learned, the record of his descendants who are to be found among many well known Maryland families.

The earliest known Sweetser of this family was James Sweetser of Tring, Hertfordshire, England. He was apparently married three times, his third wife being Jane Stowell. Their issue were John, Elizabeth, James, Benjamin and *Seth* who was born May 18, 1605. Seth, the youngest son emigrated to Charlestown, Mass., and was listed as an inhabitant in 1637 and at that time he was one of the proprietors. He was listed as a freemen, March 14, 1638-9; constable, Jan. 3, 1652; sealer of

416

leather, Jan. 2, 1653 and surveyor of highways, Jan. 2, 1659. He owned a ten acre lot on the Mystic River. On Jan. 31, 1630, he was married to Bethia Cooke and later, in April, 1661, to Elizabeth Oakes. His children with Bethia Cooke were *Benjamin,* Sarah, Mary, Hannah, Elizabeth and Anna.

Benjamin (James, Seth) Sweetser was baptised Dec. 7, 1633 at Tring. He died on July 22, 1718 and was buried in the Phipps Street Burying Ground, Charlestown, Mass. He married Abigail Wigglesworth (see note at end of article). Benjamin Sweetser served in King Phillips War (*N. E. Hist. Reg.,* Vol. 43, pp. 271, 354). He served under Lieut. John Floyd and received an allowance for his family while he was away. He was admonished and fined £10 by the General Court of Mass. in 1671 for circulating a petition to have three Baptists released from prison. His deed to property and Will are given in Wyman, "Genealogies and Estates of Charlestown, Mass.," p. 921. Issue: Abigail, Bethia, Benjamin, Seth, Joseph, *Samuel,* Wigglesworth.

Samuel (James, Seth, Benjamin) Sweetser, b. Nov. 1, 1673 at Charlestown, Mass., d. July 18, 1757 at Malden, Mass. He married Elizabeth Sprague (see note). Issue: Elizabeth, Abigail, Samuel, John, Jacob, Michael, Joseph, Lydia, Stephen, *Phinehas,* Mary. It is the descent of Phinehas from Samuel that has given much trouble as his name is omitted from the list of children of Samuel given by Wyman on p. 921 referred to above.

Phinehas (James, Seth, Benjamin, Samuel) Sweetser, b. Sept. 10, 1718 at Malden, Mass. and d. Sept. 24, 1764 at Stoneham, Mass. His Bible giving the dates of his birth and death and the births and deaths of his Children has been presented by Dr. G. Milton Linthicum of Baltimore to the Maryland Historical Society for its collection of Maryland genealogies. Phinehas married Mary Rhodes (see note). Issue: Elizabeth, Samuel, Thomas, Phinehas, Mary, Elizabeth, *Seth,* Johanna.

A comprehensive history of the Sweetser Family is being

prepared by Mr. Philip Sweetser of Waban, Mass., and when it is completed it will give all that is known of the entire family. He writes about the descent of Phinehas from Samuel Sweetser as follows: " Phinehas was buried in the Old Burying Ground at Stoneham, Mass. According to the gravestone inscription he died in his 46th year and married, Sept. 10, 1747 Mary Rhodes of Lynn, Mass., daughter of Thomas and Elizabeth (Burrage) Rhodes. Search of the town or church records has failed to disclose any record of his birth. His name is not mentioned in his father's will, dated Sept. 28th, 1752, nor can any deed be found with him as grantee or grantor. There is nothing in the official records to establish his parentage. Eaton in " History of Reading, Mass.," p. 341 states that Phinehas ' lived on the Pierce Farm now so-called in Stoneham and was the brother of Michael Sweetser who lived where Asa N. Sweetser now lives '. Private records have also been located in two separate branches of Phinehas' descendants."

" The covers of Phinehas Sweetser's own Bible which come down from Elizabeth Sweetser contain a complete record of Phinehas' family. The fact that this record states that Phinehas was born in ' Maltin ' (Malden) is excellent corroboration that he was the son of Samuel. The record of his birth is not shown as the page is torn but his descendants give it as Sept. 10, 1718."

" The other family record of Phinehas was located in the possession of Prof. Ephraim Emerton of Cambridge, Mass., (retired Harvard Professor) whose grandmother was Hannah Sweetser, daughter of Samuel of Salem and granddaughter of Phinehas. This record states: ' A copy of the Family Record of Samuel Sweetser of Salem. Samuel Sweetser was born in Lynn and was the oldest son of Phinehas Sweetser who died in Stoneham in 1764 in the 46th year of his age. Said Phinehas was the youngest son of my grandfather Samuel Sweetser of Malden which the name of Sweetser sprang from.' Although evidence from official sources is lacking, the evidence from these sources definitely establishes the parentage of Phinehas beyond all doubt."

Seth Sweetser, son of Phinehas, moved to Annapolis as stated at the beginning of this article. He was born at Stoneham, Mass., June 5, 1762 and died July 19, 1828. He married, Nov. 9, 1790, Ann Valliant, b., Royal Oak, Talbot Co., Md. Dec. 11, 1765; d. Sept. 10, 1823. She was the daughter of John Valliant and Ann Robinson of Royal Oak and granddaughter of John Valliant of Tred Avon formerly called Third Haven Creek in the Great Choptank River, Talbot Co. Will dated Jan. 13, 1721, Talbot Co. This John Valliant was the grandson of the immigrant whose history is given in *Biographical Encyclopedia of Maryland,* 1874, p. 382.

ISSUE: Seth Sweetser and Ann-Valiant.

(1) Samuel Sweetser, b. Annapolis, Jan. 28, 1792; d. Jan. 8, 1881; m. May 7, 1816, Mary Ann Oldham; b. Baltimore, Aug. 3, 1793; d. Fairhaven, N. J., July 29, 1876.

(2) Mary Sweetser, b. April 7, 1793 at Annapolis; d. Dec. 29, 1873 at Baltimore; m. April 22, 1818, William Rogers, b. Aug. 14, 1794; d. Oct. 3, 1862.

(3) Seth Sweetser, b. Jan. 24, 1796; d. Sept. 13, 1848. He was in the Battle of North Point in 1814. Later in life he moved to Guayaquil, Equador, S. A., and became an exporter and partner in the firm Icaza, Sweetser & Co. He was American Consul at Guayaquil from May 5, 1834 until his death. He married Carmencita Rica and had children but a letter from the present Consul (1932) states that there are no living descendants so far as he could learn, the last son dying fifteen years ago.

(4) Ann Sweetser, b. Feb. 10, 1798, d. 1882; m. James Hance b. 1786, d. 1865, an Old Defender of Baltimore.

(5) Elizabeth Sweetser, b. Aug. 23, 1800; d. Dec. 22, 1875; m. William Linthicum. For issue, see *Maryland Historical Magazine,* Sept. 1930, p. 281.

(6) Thomas Washington Sweetser, b. Sept. 5, 1802; d. Aug. 5, 1803.

(7) Maria, b. June 11, 1804; m. Samuel Thomas.

(8) Susan Bunn Sweetser, b. Nov. 13, 1807; d. 1900; m. David Edward Thomas.

(9) Thomas Washington Sweetser, b. Jan. 25, 1810; d. Aug. 21, 1811.

The issue of (1) Samuel, (2) Mary, (4) Ann, (7) Maria, and (8) Susan Bunn Sweetser follow:

(1) Samuel Sweetser, son of Seth and Ann, was an "Old Defender" of Baltimore of the War of 1812. An affidavit made

by David Thomas Carter of Baltimore states that his grandmother Susan Bunn Sweetser told him the following about Samuel's service at the Battle of North Point: " Just before the battle, my brother (3) Seth who was eighteen, was drafted to aid in the defense of Baltimore. As Seth was young, my older brother (1) Sammy bought a uniform and said that he would also go along to take care of Seth. After the battle was over Seth came home but Sammy did not put in an appearance. My father, thereupon, hitched up his gig and drove to the battlefield to search for Sammy. They eventually found Sammy in a ravine with a shot wound across his mouth. Before leaving the field they picked up another wounded man, who, on account of the crowded condition of the gig, rode on the shafts. This man's name was Jesse Hunt and he afterwards became Mayor of Baltimore." Descendants of Samuel remember that he carried the bullet in his cheek until his death. The record of the services of Samuel and Seth Sweetser often appear under the names Switzer and Swetzer, variable spellings of the name. The Adjutant General of the Army in a letter to the writer dated April 3, 1931 gave the full records of the services of both in Capt. A. R. Levering's 5th Company, Maryland Militia from Sept. 7th, 1814 to Nov. 18, 1814. (See " Citizen Soldiers at North Point and Ft. McHenry ", p. 33). Samuel received a pension on May 8th, 1871. He is buried in Greenwood Cemetery, Brooklyn N. Y.

ISSUE: Samuel Sweetser and Mary Ann Oldham Sweetser.

(1) John O., m. Frances Tanner; issue: Samuel Charles, Carroll.

(2) Edw. Francis.

(3) Samuel.

(4) Laura, b. Baltimore, 1825; d. Royal, France, July 31, 1905; m. John E. Forbes, d. Oct. 5, 1864, age 52; issue: 1. Lelia S., b. Dec. 20, 1847, d. May 28, 1930; m. John McKesson, Jr. and had Irving, Donald, Berkley, Grover, John, Clifford; 2. Cora S., m. Arnold C. Saportas; 3. Laura S., m. Geo. Temple Mayo; 4. John E., m. Bertha E. Tompkins; 5. Louise E., m. Julius F. Buchler; 6. Samuel S.

(5) Eleanor, d. circ. 1852, m. John Bishop; issue: 1. Eleanor S., b. 1852, d. March 7, 1909, m. Thomas E. O. Marvin.

(6) Eliza, b. 1838, d. June 18, 1888, m. Wm. J. Osborne (1837-1897); issue: 1. Louis Huber; 2. Wm. J.; 3. Lillian, m. Joseph P. Topping.

(7) Henry Clay.

(8) Ada, d. Aug. 3, 1902, age 70.

(9) Victoria, b. Philadelphia, Pa., July 15, 1838, d. Nov. 16, 1921, m. Orville Oddie (b. Aug. 1833); issue: 1. Fred; 2. Orville; 3. Albert; 4. Victoria Adelaide, b. March 24, 1868, d. June 21, 1911, m. Ivan T. Mead.

(2) Mary Sweetser married William Rogers a merchant of Baltimore and lived there all her life. She and her husband and children are buried in the Rogers Vault at Green Mount Cemetry, Baltimore.

ISSUE: Mary Sweetser Rogers and William Rogers.

(1) Eliza Ann, b. April 5, 1819, d. Dec. 6, 1885; m. May 28, 1839, Borius Fahnestock Gardner, b. York Springs, Pa., April 19, 1808, d. Jan. 28, 1885; issue: 1. William R., b. Sept. 28, 1840, d. Feb. 2, 1900, m. July 2, 1883, Ella McNeal; 2. Helen, b. Aug. 8, 1842, d. Dec. 12, 1854; 3. Theodore, b. July 20, 1844, d. Dec. 12, 1880, m. Agnes Stoddard; 4. Amelia, b. April 17, 1846, d. Dec. 31, 1852; 5. Mary Joseba, b. Nov. 10, 1848, d. Jan. 3, 1853; 6. Harry, b. Feb. 12, 1851, d. May 3, 1922, m. (1) Nov. 2, 1874 Frances Scott of Ironton, O. and had Lester Durand Gardner (see Who's Who in America); m. (2) Minnehaha Hawthorne and had Lawrence; 7. Elizabeth, b. May 17, 1853, m. Dr. David M. A. Culbreth; 8. Charles, b. Sept. 18, 1855. d. Feb. 24, 1914, m. (1) Sarah Frank; m. (2) Marion Miller; 9. Mary R. b. Sept. 9, 1858, d. April 30, 1862; 10. Anna Roberts, b. Dec. 2, 1861, d. May 5, 1924, m. Dec. 2, 1884, Albert Marburg; 11. John Buckler, b. May 18, 1864, d. Aug. 1864.

(2) Amelia, b. July 15, 1821, d. March 8, 1846; m. Robert Wesley Dryden; issue: 1. Meredith; 2. Mary, m. Thomas Kensett; 3. Annie, m. John R. Kensett and had 1. John, 2, Mary who m. W. H. Dempsey.

(3) James, b. 1828, d. 1883.

(4) Charles, b. Nov. 8, 1832, d. April 24, 1863.

(5) Philip, b. Aug. 14, 1835, d. Jan. 7, 1889.

(6) Henry, b. June 8, 1840, d. Feb. 21, 1875.

(7) Sarah, d. July 28, 1877, m. Phillip Hiss.

(8) Jacob, d. Oct. 4, 1862.

(9) Seth.

(10) William.

(4) Ann Sweetser married James Hance,

ISSUE:

(1) Seth m. Eliza Kirk, issue, Frank.

(2) Ann S. d. s. p.

(3) James, Jr., d. s. p.

(4) Maria S., m. (1) Thomas Anderson Dorsey of Baltimore; issue: 1. Rev. James Owen Dorsey, b. Oct. 31. 1848. d. Feb. 4. 1895, an

ethonologist and authority on the American Indian language, m.
April 18, 1876, Clara Virginia Wynkoop and had Virginia, b. 1880,
m. Jas. Herndon Lightfoot; 2. Thomas Anderson, Jr., m. Bettie
Claybaugh and had George B. and Lawrence A.; m. (2) Leven Stan-
forth of Calvert Co., Md.

(5) Sarah S., d. s. p.

(6) Christina Virginia, m. Henry Allnut.

(7) Maria Sweetser married Samuel Thomas, a widower with
three children.

ISSUE:

(1) Mary Rogers, m. Nikolas Brice Medairy (Madeira), issue: 1. Cora
m. Percy Guard; 2. Samuel Thomas; 3. Edwin; 4. Anna Louise, m.
Robert Lucas Chamberlaine.

(2) Anna Maria, m. Rev. Charles W. Baldwin.

(3) Amelia S.

(8) Susan Bunn Sweetser married David Edward Thomas,

ISSUE:

(1) Florence, m. John M. Carter; issue: 1. John M. Jr.; 2. Mable; 3.
David E. T.; 4. Mary Christine m. Herbert Bagg and had Herbert
B. Jr.

(2) Mary Rogers, m. Charles Green Summers; issue: 1. Charles G. Jr.
m. Anna Strand McAuley; 2. Walter Penrose m. Grace Hubbard;
3. Grace, m. David Hays Stevenson.

(3) Grace, d. young.

The General Society of the War of 1812 have accepted the
service of Seth and Samuel Sweetser of Baltimore, sons of Seth
of Annapolis and all descendants are eligible to membership.
The following ancestors of Seth Sweetser of Annapolis have
been accepted by the Society of Colonial Wars for their colonial
war service and all his descendants are eligible to Colonial
patriotic societies under their service: Ralph Sprague, John
Sprague, (1624-1682), John Sprague, (1651-1703), Benjamin
Sweetser, Thomas Burrage, Henry Rhodes.

As the foregoing was prepared almost entirely from family
records, the compiler will be glad to receive corrections and
additions to be placed with the original papers in the New York
Geneological and Biographical Society.

REFERENCES AND NOTES.

Sweetser Family.

For those who wish to refer to the original sources on the Sweetser Family the following references are given: " Pioneers of Mass.," Pope, p. 443; " Old Charlestown ", Sawyer, p. 368. The Will of Seth Sweetser, I, has been photostated and is to be found in the Sweetser Family collection in the library of the N. Y. Genealogical and Biographical Society, 122 East 58th St., New York. This collection contains a large number of letters and photostats from which much of the material in this article has been taken. The library is open to the public. " Stoneham Vital Records," p. 65; Bodge, " Soldiers of King Philips War ", pp. 232-4; " Genealogy of the Wells Family " by G. W. W. Cushing, gives sketch of the Sweetser Family; " History of Charlestown, Mass.," p. 87; *New England Hist. Reg.,* Vol. 18, p. 29; Vol. 54, p. 356, Vol. 43, p. 276.

Wigglesworth Family.

For Abigail Wigglesworth, dau. of Edward Wigglesworth of New Haven, see "Genealogy of the Wells Family" by Cushing, p. 169; *New England Hist. Reg.,* Vol. 17, 1863, p. 130; "Genealogies and Estates of Charlestown," Wyman, p. 1029; "History of New Haven", Atwater, p. 531; *New England Hist. Reg.,* Vol. 18, p. 29, Vol. 2, 1857, pp. 110-11, "Certain Comeovers" by W. H. Crapo, Vol. 2, p. 689.

Rhodes Family.

For the genealogy of Mary Rhodes, b. March 4, 1727, d. March 27, 1813 who m. Phinehas Sweetser see *Lynn Vital Statistics,* Vol. I; " History of Lynn," A. Lewis, pp. 190, 281 2, 293; " Colonial Families of America ", Rhoades, p. 394-5; " Society of Colonial Wars " 1922, p. 396. She was descended from Henry Rhodes who was Representative of the General Court of Mass. and served in King Philips War. Mary Rhodes' mother was Elizabeth Burrage who was descended from the

Burrage and Breed Families. For Burrage Family, see " The Burrage Memorial ", by Alvah Burrage, 1877, p. 160. For Breed Family, see *Essex Antiquarian,* Vol. XI, No. 4, p. 1 and the publications of the Breed Family Association, of Lynn, Mass.

Sprague Family.

Samuel Sweetser m. Elizabeth Sprague, b. 1676, d. March 12, 1572. For a complete history of her ancestry see " The Sprague Family of Malden, Mass.," by Chamberlain. Two of her ancestors served in King Philips War.

TASKER FAMILY.

1. CAPT. THOMAS TASKER[1] was commissioned one of the Justices of Calvert County 30 May 1685 (*Md. Arch.*, xvii, 379), and was also in the commission from 1689 to 1692 (*Md. Arch.*, viii, 145 ; Test. Proc., xvi, 8, 28, 44). In 1689 he signed the Declaration of the inhabitants of Calvert County for not choosing Burgesses (*Md. Arch.*, viii, 110). He represented the County in the Assembly from 1692 till 1697 (*Md. Arch.*, xiii, 351 ; xix, 355) and was a member of Council from 18 March 1698/9 (*Md. Arch.*, xxv, 55) until his death. He was commissioned a Justice of the Provincial Court 17 Oct. 1694 (*Md. Arch.*, xx, 137), and was Treasurer of the Province in 1695 (*ibid.*, 274). 4 September 1689 he was commissioned Captain of Foot in the Calvert County Militia (*Md. Arch.*, xiii, 242), and is frequently designated by his military title. He attended a Council meeting 18 July 1700 (*Md. Arch.*, xxv, 101), and his will was proved 31 August following, so that he apparently died in August 1700. In the year 1736 a commission was appointed to perpetuate testimony in regard to the Tasker pedigree (Chancery, IR., No. 3, fol. 800 ff.). It was in evidence before this commission that Thomas Tasker married in 1676 a widow, Mrs. Brooke, who died about 1695, but her identity is not further established. In his will (dated 16 March 1699, proved 3 August 1700) he makes provision for his mother, Mrs. Ann Tasker.

Capt. Thomas Tasker[1] and —— Brooke his wife, had issue :—

    i. THOMAS TASKER,[2] d. unmar. in England, about 1696.
2.   ii. JOHN TASKER, d. 1711.
3.   iii. HON. BENJAMIN TASKER, b. 1690 ; d. 19 June 1768.
    iv. ELIZABETH TASKER, b. 1686 ; d. 10 February 1706 ; married 21 April 1701, Col. Thomas Addison of Prince George's Co.

2. JOHN TASKER[2] (Thomas[1]) of Calvert County, died in the year 1711. In his will dated 22 September 1711, and proved 17 October following (Annapolis, Lib. 13, fol. 233) he mentions his wife Eleanor, his son Thomas Tasker (under 18 years old), his aunt Elizabeth Sury, and his brother Benjamin Tasker. He married Eleanor, daughter of Col. Thomas Brooke of Brookfield, Prince George's County, and she married secondly Charles Sewall (d. 1742) of Eltonhead Manor,

St. Mary's County (*Magazine*, i, 186) Her father's will mentions "my daughter Eleanor Sewall (wife of Mr. Charles Sewall)" and her eldest son Thomas Tasker.

John Tasker and Eleanor (Brooke) his wife, had issue:—

i. THOMAS TASKER,[3] d. 1734; mar. Clare, dau. of Major Nicholas Sewall, and had an only child John,[4] who died young, about 1736 (Chancery, IR., No. 3, 800 ff.). Mrs. Clare Tasker mar. 2°. Wm. Young.

3. HON. BENJAMIN TASKER [2] (Thomas [1]) was born in 1690 according to a deposition made in 1741, wherein he gives his age as 51 years (IR., No. 4, 365). He was a Justice of Anne Arundel County 1714–17, and High Sheriff of the County 1717–18 (A. A. Co., Court Record). He was a member of the Council of Maryland from 4 November 1722 until his death in 1768 (*U. H. Journals*), and 1752–53, as President of the Council, he was Acting Governor of the Province (*ibid.*). The inscription on his tombstone, in St. Ann's Church yard, Annapolis, states that he was President of the Council for thirty-two years, Agent and Receiver General of the Province, and Judge of the Prerogative Court. He was a Justice of the Provincial Court, and member of the Quorum, from 1729 to 1732 (Commission Book), and he was Mayor of Annapolis 1721, 1726, 1750, 1754 and 1756 (Riley's *Ancient City*). He died on Sunday, 19 June 1768, in the 79th year of his age, and the *Maryland Gazette* of the 23rd inst. gives a lengthy obituary. He married, 31 July 1711, Ann, daughter of Hon. William Bladen (b. 1673; d. 1718), Secretary of Maryland 1701, Attorney General 1707, and Commissary General 1714. Her brother, Col. Thomas Bladen (b. 1698; d. 1780), Governor of Maryland 1742–47 and later member of Parliament, married Barbara Janssen, daughter of Sir Theodore Janssen, Bart., and sister of Mary Janssen, wife of Charles, fifth Lord Baltimore.

Benjamin Tasker and Ann (Bladen) his wife, had issue:—

i. WILLIAM TASKER,[3] b. 3 July 1713; d. 18 March 1715.
ii. BENJAMIN TASKER, b. 29 Sept. 1717; d. 13 Nov. 1717.
iii. BLADEN TASKER, b. ....; d. 17 Jan'y 1721.
iv. COL. BENJAMIN TASKER, b. 14 Feb'y 1720; member of Council 1744–60, and Secretary of Maryland; d. unmar. 17 Oct. 1760, and is buried at St. Ann's, Annapolis.
v. BLADEN TASKER, b. 28 June 1722; d. 22 Aug. 1723.
vi. ANN TASKER, b. 7 Oct. 1728; mar. Gov. Samuel Ogle.
vii. REBECCA TASKER, b. 4 Nov. 1724; mar. 16 Sept. 1749, Hon. Daniel Dulany.
viii. ELIZABETH TASKER. b. 4 Feb'y 1726; d. 19 Sept. 1789; mar. 14 May 1747, Christopher Lowndes.
ix. BLADEN TASKER, b. 4 Feb'y 1730; d. young.
x. FRANCES TASKER, mar. 2 April 1754, Robert Carter of Nominy, Westmoreland Co., Va.

CAPTAIN PHILLIP TAYLOR AND SOME OF HIS
DESCENDANTS.

By EMERSON B. ROBERTS.

Captain Phillip Taylor was a Virginian, and one of that gallant band under the command of Captain William Claiborne, who established the first settlement of Englishmen within the bounds of Maryland on Kent Island, August 17, 1631, nearly three years before the arrival of The Ark and The Dove at St. Mary's, March 25, 1634. Phillip Taylor came with the first of Claiborne's men, and is, therefore, not antedated by any person as a Maryland settler. He was born about 1610, in the village of Marden in Herefordshire, and was the son of another Phillip Taylor. Coming to the Province of Virginia, in the ship *Africa*, he established himself in Northampton and Accomac Counties on the eastern shore. There is a Virginia record of 1637 that —— Taylor was brought in by her husband, Phillip Taylor of Accomac County (Greer: *Virginia Immigrants*), and another record of a petition for land by Phillip Taylor, 1643, for the transportation of Jane Taylor. Yet another Virginia record tells of the transportation of Phillip Taylor, Sr., 1643, by Phillip Taylor. In 1642-43 Phillip Taylor was returned to the Assembly of Virginia as the Burgess for Northampton County (*Minutes of the Council and General Court of Colonial Virginia*). Earlier in the same minutes, under date of December 15, 1640, there is this : " The Council hath ordered that a patent shall be granted to the Indians of Accomac County for fifteen hundred acres of land upon the eastermost shore of the seaboard side, and that a new survey thereof be made at the appointment and direction of Mr. Yeardley and Mr. Littleton, and that the right of two hundred acres there already granted unto Phillip Taylor be not thereby infringed, and after a true survey be taken thereof, a patent be made for the said land, for the use of the said Indians " (*Minutes of Council and General Court*, p. 478).

In the Accomac records there are frequent references to Captain Taylor. In 1640 he was admonished not to molest certain Indians. The Letters of Marque and Reprisal issued by Claiborne are addressed to Captain Phillip Taylor as his chief lieutenant. In 1642 Phillip Taylor was one of the original justices for the then newly formed County of Northampton. At the first court he was directed to proceed against a certain Indian town and to do what seemed best for the welfare of the county. Again in 1643, as sheriff, he presented the petition that the county be provided with a gaol (Northampton County Records. See also Wise: *Ye Kingdome of Accawmacke*).

In this study of the Taylor genealogy, there is no concern with the merits of the Baltimore-Claiborne controversy over the legal status of the Kent Island trading post, or the exact meaning of *hactenus inculta*, or the precedence of the Broad Seal of England over the Scottish Signet, or what the King had in mind when he granted Lord Baltimore his charter, around all of which issues the controversy raged in Maryland, in Virginia, and in the councils of King Charles. We are alone concerned that Phillip Taylor came " at the first," was one of the leading spirits among the Claiborne forces, regarded himself as a Virginian, was captain of one of the boats engaged in the service of supply, and engaged in the pitched battle that was fought in the mouth of the Wicomico River—the first battle between English forces in the New World. Fortunately, there is, for his descendants, his own account of the events of those years, and the part he played, or saw, as an eye-witness. One of the supporting documents presented by Captain Claiborne when he submitted his cause to the King in 1640, was a deposition of Phillip Taylor. This document, recorded in full in *Archives of Maryland*, Vol. V, p. 220, is of great interest as a source of information regarding life and activity on Kent Island, and of the point of view of the Kent Islanders. It begins:

> Phillippus Taylor de Accomacke in Colonia de Virginia etatis 30 annor. aut eo circiter natur infra pochiam de Marden in Com. Hereford.

The document reveals Philip Taylor as the commander of one of the pinnaces used in the trading operations between Kent Island and Virginia. Until 1643 or afterwards, he seems to have held his property and residence in Virginia, but later came permanently to Maryland.

The armed conflict between Captain Taylor and his crew and the Maryland forces under Captain Cornwalleys in the mouth of the Wicomico River in 1635 is pictured in detail, colored, of course, with the Maryland point of view of the affair, in the inquest before the Provincial Court, 1637. This bill is recorded in Liber Z, Court and Testamentary Business, 1637 (*Archives of Maryland*, Vol. IV, p. 23).

It is a matter of surmise that Phillip Taylor may have had issue by his first wife, Jane. The records are not clear. If there was such issue, however, Phillip Taylor is probably the forebear of those Taylors who became powerful at a very early date in the affairs of Dorchester County.

The death of Jane Taylor, first wife of Phillip Taylor, is not recorded, nor is it known that she survived until the permanent settlement on Kent Island. His second wife was also Jane, and there is some evidence to indicate that she was the sister of Cuthbert Fenwick, who was first a Virginian, then a Marylander, and the Lord of Fenwick Manor. It is established, however, that she was born about 1617 (*Archives of Maryland,* Vol. X, p. 560). Her life was fraught with all the tragedy of troublous times. Thrice married, she lost her first and third husbands by execution; one, for the part he had as a Virginian in the opposition to Lord Baltimore and the authority of St. Mary's; the third, at the hands of the men of Providence, for loyal support of the constituted authority of Lord Baltimore in Maryland.

Her first husband was that Captain Thomas Smith, gentleman, a commander in Claiborne's forces in the Battle of Wicomico, May 10, 1635, who won the battle and drove off the Marylanders. Three years later, Lord Baltimore, in settling the disturbed affairs of Kent Island, caused the arrest of Captain Smith, with others. Smith was taken to St. Mary's, tried, and convicted, and there is evidence of the sentence to death by hanging having been carried out (Andrews: *History of Maryland,* pp. 119, 121, and 131). The evidence of Jane Taylor's marriage to Smith is embraced in some testimony in the Allen case to which more detailed subsequent reference will be made. At the time of the trial of the Allen case, she was married to William Eltonhead, who testified that his wife, at the time in question, was " the relict of Smith."

Second, Jane married Captain Phillip Taylor, and became the mother of his children, Thomas and Sarah.

The conjecture that Jane was by birth a Fenwick and the sister of Cuthbert Fenwick, rests not alone upon the fact that she undoubtedly bore a close relationship to the Fenwicks, but upon a deposition she made, June 6, 1653, to the effect that " she was in company with her brother and sister Fenwick . . ." (*Archives,* Vol. X, p. 496). Dr. William Hand Browne, then editor of the *Archives,* indexed " brother " as " Cuthbert Fenwick," but whether he was closer as a brother than the husband of her deceased husband's sister, remains a matter of surmise.

Others who have studied the matter—among them the late Mr. Samuel H. Troth—have also concluded that she was born Jane Fenwick (Letter of Mr. S. H. Troth, March 14, 1909, in papers owned by Dr. Julian Sears, Washington, D. C.).

Direct evidence of the children of Captain Phillip Taylor is embraced in the registry of their mark for cattle and hogs, and this same record affords us all we know of the date of the death of their father. The record runs: " September 29, 1649, Thomas and Sarah Taylor, the children of Captain Phillip Taylor, deceased, their mark . . . (*Archives*, Vol. IV, p. 507). At this date, they were residents of Kent Island, and the above is a Kent record.

After the death of Captain Taylor, his widow married William Eltonhead, Gentleman, Lord of Eltonhead Manor, and Secretary of the Council. His life was sacrificed in illegal execution after the defeat of the Maryland party by the Puritans of Providence, at the " Battle of Severn." While a resident of Calvert County, he was known and was doing business on Kent Island as early as 1648. On June 7, 1648, he, with Giles Brent, Lord of Kent Fort Manor, witnessed a release of Mistress Margaret Brent by Thomas Gerrard for certain debts, in the affair of her celebrated administration of the estate of Leonard Calvert (*Archives*, Vol. IV, p. 428). The ties between Lord Baltimore and William Eltonhead were strong, and express mutual confidence. It appears that at least twice—June, 1642, and again in 1648—William Eltonhead made a trip to London in the interest of Baltimore's affairs (*Archives*, Vol. IV, p. 210). When an ordinance was presented before the House of Lords for the removal of Lord Baltimore and the appointment of a Protestant, January 20, 1646, William Eltonhead was one of those who signed an oath of fealty (*Archives*, Vol. III pp. 173-74). In 1649, Cecilius Calvert issued a special commission " to our trusty and well beloved William Eltonhead, To Be one of Our Privy Council of State within our Province of Maryland." On July 22, 1650, William Eltonhead took the Oath of Councillor (*Archives*, Vol. III, p. 256). Subsequently, he was chosen Secretary of Council, and in this relation his name is much in the public record of the day.

The feelings of Lord Baltimore toward the affair at Severn are well-known.

In the Proceedings in the Fendall case, at the Court at St. Mary's, November 29, 1660, the record runs: "Then came Josias Fendall and submitted himself to the government of the Lord Proprietary, and proffessed to do in the future for the good . . . [and the letter of His Lordship, August 24th, was introduced] . . . ' I would have you proceed against such of them as you shall not see fit to pardon . . . upon no terms pardon Fendall so much as his life . . . nor . . . pardon . . . any of those that sat in the Council of Warr at Anne Arundel, and Concurred in the Sentence of Death against Mr. William Eltonhead, or any of my honest friends then and there murthered . . . but do justice upon them, and I shall justify you in it. . . .' " In another letter to his governor, Lord Baltimore directs the Governor and Council " to doe especial care of those Widdows who have lost their husbands in and by occassion of the late trouble vizt: Mrs. Hatton, Mrs. Lewis, and Mrs. William Eltonhead, whom his Lordship would have his said Lieutenant to cause to be supplied out of such rents and other proffitt as are due to his Lordship " (*Archives*, Vol. III p. 326).

William Eltonhead was adjudged by Council to have left a nuncupative will, the action having been taken on a deposition of John Anderton (*Archives*, Vol. XLI, pp. 179, 180). Letters of administration were issued at Patuxent by the Provincial Court, May 14, 1657, to Mrs. Jane Eltonhead.

After reading the record of the Allen case, there can be no doubt of the identity of the Jane who married Phillip Taylor, with the widow, Jane Taylor, who married William Eltonhead. Thomas Allen, of Kent Island, died in 1648 (His will, *Maryland Calendar of Wills*, Vol. I). " At the Court at St. Maries die Jovis, 15th November, 1649, William Eltonhead, Gent.," in right of his wife as plaintiff, brought a suit against the administrators of the estate of Thomas Allen, deceased, and in the record of the case occurs this significant statement, " where-upon the deft. Alleadged that 380 pounds of Tobacco . . . and produced a Receipt thereof under the hand of one Giles Bashawe whom Mrs. Eltonhead present in the Court acknowledged was the Atty of Capt. Phillip Taylor, her former husband . . ." (*Archives*, Vol. IV, p. 527). Giles Bashaw was a Kent Islander, and had come to Northampton County with the Taylors, and had been one of Claiborne's band. Further in the suit this " William Eltonhead, pltf, sues to be relieved of tobacco due upon two bills, by one of which it appears that the decedent Allen was engaged unto the plaintiff's wife—then the relict of Smith, Gent., for payment of 600 pounds of tobacco to her in November, 1639. . . ." Hence, the conclusions previously drawn as to the several marriages of Jane, whom we now write as Jane (Fenwick?) Smith Taylor Eltonhead (*Archives*, Vol. IV, pp. 496 *ff.*).

After the tragic death of her third husband, the widow, Jane Eltonhead, continued to reside on the Eltonhead lands in Calvert, near the mouth of the Patuxent, even though they were in litigation. As late as March 23, 1656, there was an Order in Council which had to do with strengthening the militia, and the appointment of officers to fill vacancies. Among other places mentioned " downward on both sides the river and creek to the mouth of the River, including the Plantation of Mrs. William Eltonhead."

Jane Eltonhead survived until 1659. Her will, recorded at St. Mary's, February 28, 1659, mentions her eldest son, Thomas Taylor, and to him she devised " Cedar Point." Her daughter, Sarah, is also mentioned in the will, as also her grandchild, Roger Anderton, leading to the almost inevitable conclusion that her daughter, Sarah, married that John Anderton who attended William Eltonhead in his last hours in prison, and received his last will and testament. Further, she says the debts of William Eltonhead are to be paid.

The circumstances surrounding the death of William Elton-head resulted in recriminations and litigations that involved the several branches of the family for a number of years. In these court cases the cards appear to have been stacked against Thomas Taylor, and it seems hardly beyond doubt that the feelings resultant, together with the loss of his property, were the causes of his permanent removal to Kent Island and the eastern shore. In brief this litigation is sketched:

Before the Provincial Court, Wednesday, February 29, 1659, Thomas Taylor, of Patuxent River, aged about sixteen or seventeen years, showed that his mother, Mrs. Jane Eltonhead, Relict of William Eltonhead, Esq., being lately deceased . . . chose as his guardian his mother, Mrs. Jane Eltonhead (*Archives*, Vol. XLI, p. 345).

Before the Court, " Thursday, April 13, 1661. This day came Thomas Taylor, and desired liberty to choose his . . . [the words are lost, but presumably ' guardian '] whereupon he made choice of Phillip . . ." (again the last name is lost here, but subsequent record renders it clear that it is ' Philip Calvert ') (*Archives*, Vol. XLI, p. 447).

" August 6, 1661, Captain Josias Fendall demands a writt to arrest Thomas Taylor in an action of detenue," and the warrant was issued to the Sheriff of Calvert County (*Archives*, Vol. XLI, p. 490).

April 1662 an order was issued by the Upper and Lower Houses, directed to the Sheriff of Calvert County, for the appearance of Thomas Taylor to answer suit by Cuthbert Fenwick. The suit was for the recovery of certain lands on the basis that the Court had declared all the heirs-at-law of William Eltonhead barred all claim of land as heirs of William Eltonhead (*Archives*, Vol. I, p. 432).

August 17, 1663. Thomas Taylor, through Phillip Calvert, his guardian, sued for rent due from John Anderton (*Archives*, Vol. XLI, p. 99).

On the same date he entered another suit against Anderton.

September 17, 1663. Thomas Taylor, Cuthbert Fenwick, and John Bogue and William Mills as guardians for Robert and Richard Fenwick, join in a petition before the Provincial

Court in which Thomas Taylor relinquished "for love and affection . . . two hundred acres of land . . . he now liveth on . . . for which free gift . . . Cuthbert Fenwick, John Bogue and William Mills, guardians for Robert and Richard Fenwick release, acquit and discharge Thomas Taylor " (*Archives*, Vol. I, pp. 467, 481).

Before the Court, January 11, 1663-4, a petition of Thomas Taylor by his guardian, Philip Calvert, sets forth that Thomas Taylor is the son and heir of Jane Eltonhead and has occupied in fee simple the Manor of 'Little Eltonhead' in Calvert since the death of his mother . . . (*Archives*, Vol. XLIX, p. 99).

March 29, 1664. Thomas Taylor records an assignment of a portion of 'Little Eltonhead' to his brother-in-law, Thomas Courtney and his wife Sarah (*Archives*, Vol. XLIX, p. 211).

Before the Court, April 5, 1664, Thomas Taylor is declared to be of age.

Before the Court, April 12, 1664, a deposition of John Anderton sets forth the nuncupative will of William Eltonhead by which his land and personal estate was to be his wife's at her disposing, and his desire for her to bestow on Robert and Richard Fenwick something as a remembrance of him (*Archives*, Vol. XLIX, p. 207).

From these fragments then we are able to piece together some story of Thomas Taylor and to draw some highly probable conclusions from them.

Thomas Taylor, son of Captain Phillip Taylor and Jane, his wife, was born about 1643, probably upon Kent Island. He had property rights there, but in his boyhood resided with his widowed mother on his step-father's lands, near the mouth of the Patuxent in Calvert County in the Quaker colony. After he became of age he returned to the eastern shore probably because he had property rights there and because he had lost through litigation whatever property rights he may have had in Calvert.

When and under what circumstances Thomas Taylor became a Quaker is not clear. There can be only surmise that his father

Phillip Taylor and his mother Jane were of the Establishment. The Fenwicks were Roman Catholics. ' Little Eltonhead ' was in the Quaker area. Indeed there may be, between the lines in some of the subsequent Quaker records of him, the implication that he was, while of Quaker identification, less orthodox Quaker than some of the Friends. He is mentioned as " the man who wrote for the Friends." Does the phrase indicate complete identification with the Society?

Be that as it may, Thomas Taylor married Elizabeth Marsh, a Quakeress, of Severn, daughter of Thomas and Margaret Marsh, April 1, 1669 " at the house of John Pitt of Patoxon " (Third Haven Records). They may have gone at once to Kent Island or Thomas may have been residing there before his marriage[1]. Their home became a focus of Quaker enthusiasm. George Fox, the apostle of the Friends, was entertained there on his trip to Maryland.

Certainly as late as 1672, their residence was still on the island. Afterwards they removed to Talbot, into the Chapel District, near King's Creek. Third Haven Records show (Vol. I, pp. 3, 4) : " Att a Mens Meeting att John Pittes the 8th day of the 7th Month 1676. . . . It is agreed by the Meeting that Thomas Taylor doe keepe Friends books and write the concerns

---

[1] Col. Tilghman in his *History of Talbot County* (Vol. I, p. 107) in introducing the early " Quaker worthies of Talbot " comes to this Thomas Taylor, and after speaking of his early residence on Kent Island, his removal into the Chapel District near King's Creek, and later yet removal into Baily's Neck, asks the question: " Was this Thomas Taylor the son and biographer of that Thomas Taylor who surrendered his benefice at Richmond in Yorkshire to become an unpaid minister among the despised Friends, and who rather than take an oath suffered an imprisonment of ten years and a half, the loss of his real estate for life, and his personal forever, and the deprivation of the protection of law? "

While the answer to the question is not what Col. Tilghman thought it might be the question itself was among the incentives to this study. Thomas Taylor was only one among a number of early Calvert residents who crossed via the islands to those areas of Kent County that are now within the borders of Talbot, Queen Anne's and Dorchester. If subsequent papers of this series are published, they will trace the migration of several of these families—among them the Marshes, the Dixons, the Harwoods, the Stevenses, the Gareys, the Sharps, the Kemps and others.—AUTHOR.

of friends in their Mens Meetings." This office, he appears to have filled for years, and to have been succeeded in it by his son or grandson. The records of Third Haven are replete with references to his actions. As "the man who wrote for the Friends" much of the spelling and misspelling of the proper names of the day can be traced to him. For example, Tredaven, Tredhaven, Tredavon, Third Haven, Trade Haven, Treadhaven, and even Trad Haven, in the records precede the present Tred Avon, and Thomas Taylor is responsible for using a number of them, though he usually seemed to prefer Trad-Haven. He was the keeper of the books, and it was he who received, recorded, and took custody of the "parcel of books, which came from our dear friend and brother, George Fox, before his death, as a token of love." This has been referred to as the germ of the first public library in America. Along with others, he subscribed four hundred pounds of tobacco for the purchase of books for the good of the Meeting.

In 1678-9 Thomas Taylor, with William Sharp and the widow Elizabeth Christison, administered on the estate of Wenlock Christison.

The high character sustained by Thomas Taylor and his wife, Elizabeth, is a matter of testimony in the will of their son, Thomas. In disposing of his personal property, he says, "Ye four (silver spoons) marked ' T T E ' to my four sons, each one, for to be kept in ye remembrance of their honest grandfather and mother, who lived and died in Ye Truth, and left a good savor behind."

Thomas Taylor died in 1684 or 1685. His will, a Talbot County document (Liber 4, folio 92, Annapolis), dated July 30, 1684, and probated March 25, 1684-5, mentions his wife, Elizabeth, who is to have " the plantation on which I now dwell as far as ' Poplar Neck.' " The Third Haven Record of the death of Thomas Taylor (Vol. T. f 128-130—12 mo. 13th 1684) show that a part of Thomas Marsh's estate was in his hands at that date. The children mentioned in his will are:

1. Thomas, to whom was devised " Terby Neck."

2. James, to whom " Kingsburry " and " Kingsburry Addition " were devised.

3. John, to whom "Taylor's Chance " was devised. And daughters,

4. Sarah and

5. Elizabeth, and an unborn child.

Of these children we take notice, treating each and some of his descendants in the following paragraphs.

Thomas Taylor (1), second of the name, was under age at the time of his father's death, in 1684. There is a minute in the Third Haven Records, that he appeared before the Meeting, 2nd of the 9th month, 1688, and was advised to go home with his uncle, John Pitt. In 1690, William Sharp and John Pitt proposed to place him with Peter Harwood, to learn the trade of cooper and carpenter (Third Haven Records, Vol. I, p. 199). In adult life, he continued to reside on the lands in King's Creek devised him by his father's will, devising the same property in his own will, made December 16, 1709, probated April 30, 1711 (Annapolis, Liber 13, folio 292) saying " which I now live on." He married before 1707, Elizabeth, to whom some evidence points as the widow of William Sharp (Test. Proc. Liber 19, folio 250). After the death of Thomas Taylor, she married John MacCarthy, May 29, 1718 (St. Peter's Parish Records, p. 92 and Accounts CVII, folio 352). She died about 1726 or 1727, leaving four sons, all by her second husband, Thomas Taylor, second. These were:

Thomas Taylor, third, who probably married in 1718, Ellinor (or Elizabeth), the widow of John Ennalls, of Dorchester County (Adm. Accts., Liber I, folio 228). This Thomas Taylor died, probably in 1727, and was, at the time of his death, clerk of Third Haven Meeting. In Volume II, page 295, Third Haven Records, is this minute: " At a Monthly Meeting at our Meeting House at Treadhaven, the 8th of the 6th month 1727. . . . Our friend Thomas Taylor being Removed by death and being one appointed to give acct. of the said Meeting the meeting leaves the Consideration of appointing one in that place to the next

Monthly Meeting." In the accounting on the estate, the widow, Ellinor (or Elizabeth), mentions her Ennalls children:

John Taylor, under age in 1709.
William Taylor, under age in 1709.
Mordecai Taylor, under age in 1709.

James Taylor (2), son of Thomas and Elizabeth Taylor, inherited from his father " Kingsburry " and " Kingsburry Addition." He married, in 1689, Isabella Atkinson (Third Haven Records).

James Taylor's will was made November 8, 1718, probated May 19, 1719 (Annapolis, Liber 15, folio 109). James, the eldest son, was under 21, but on becoming of age was to divide the dwelling plantation with his brother, Thomas. Joseph was to inherit " Taylor's Chance." A daughter, Elizabeth, is mentioned, as also the wife Isabel as executrix.

John Taylor (3), son of Thomas and Elizabeth Taylor, inherited a portion of " ' Taylor's Chance,' two hundred acres on the other side of King's Creek." He appears to have been born in 1684, or slightly earlier, for in 1738, his age was recorded about fifty-four years (Chancery Records I R 3, folio 447).

Sarah Taylor (4), daughter of Thomas and Elizabeth Taylor, received, under her father's will, one-half of certain lands, jointly with her sister, Elizabeth. She married (possibly Henry) Parrott.

Elizabeth Taylor (5), eldest child of Thomas and Elizabeth Taylor, was born November 6, 1669 (T. A. Meeting, Vol. IV—132). By the will of her father, she received one-half of the land at the head of the river, which must have been " Taylor's Desire," and four hundred acres, " Ye Addition." She married, at Tuckahoe Meeting, July 20, 1690, Peter Harwood (T. A. Meeting, Vol. VI, folio 347). These are the parents of Elizabeth Taylor, who married, at Third Haven Meeting, 1710, Isaac Dixon. The descendants of Isaac Dixon and his wife, Elizabeth Taylor are the subjects of a monograph on which the writer is engaged.

Taylor.

Phillip Taylor, Sr., of Marden, County Hereford
to Virginia 1643.

Phillip Taylor, of Marden, of Accomac, Virginia;
and of Kent Island, Maryland.
b. cir. 1610, d. cir. 1649
m. 1 Jane ——, and possibly had issue.
m. 2 Jane (Fenwick?) her 2nd marriage, d. 1659.
    she m. 1 Thomas Smith, Gent., executed
      1638, but no issue.
    she m. 3 William Eltonhead, Gent., Lord
      of Eltonhead Manor, Secretary of
      Council, executed, but no issue.

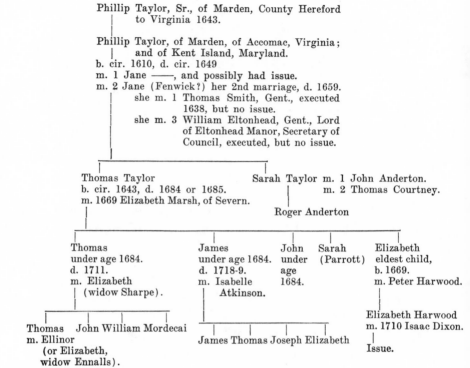

Thomas Taylor
b. cir. 1643, d. 1684 or 1685.
m. 1669 Elizabeth Marsh, of Severn.

Sarah Taylor m. 1 John Anderton.
          m. 2 Thomas Courtney.

Roger Anderton

Thomas
under age 1684.
d. 1711.
m. Elizabeth
(widow Sharpe).

James
under age 1684.
d. 1718-9.
m. Isabelle
Atkinson.

John
under
age
1684.

Sarah
(Parrott)

Elizabeth
eldest child,
b. 1669.
m. Peter Harwood.

Thomas John William Mordecai
m. Ellinor
(or Elizabeth,
widow Ennalls).

James Thomas Joseph Elizabeth

Elizabeth Harwood
m. 1710 Isaac Dixon.

Issue.

CAPTAIN PHILLIP TAYLOR AND SOME OF HIS DESCENDANTS:
A CORRECTION

A. RUSSELL SLAGLE

In the *Maryland Historical Magazine* for the year 1938 there is an interesting article, "Captain Phillip Taylor and Some of His Descendants," by Emerson B. Roberts. This article shows Thomas Taylor, son of Captain Phillip Taylor as marrying on April 1st 1669 Elizabeth Marsh of Severn, a Quakeress, daughter of Thomas and Margaret Marsh.[1] We believe this statement to be incorrect. Apparently a Thomas Taylor, a Quaker, did marry on April 1st 1669 Elizabeth Marsh, a Quakeress, daughter of Thomas and Margaret Marsh; but we purport to show it was not Thomas Taylor, son of Captain Phillip; unless Phillip had two sons named Thomas, which is unlikely. We propose to show that Thomas Taylor, son of Captain Phillip had a wife *Frances,* a Protestant, and a Colonel.

We agree with Mr. Roberts where he shows Thomas Taylor to be a son of Phillip Taylor by his second wife Jane (Fenwick?), widow of Thomas Smith, who after the death of Phillip Taylor married as her third husband, William Eltonhead. However, Mr. Roberts apparently did not find the following item in Warrants Lib. 12, fol. 206 from which we quote: "20th March 1669 between Thomas Taylor of Petuxent in the county of Calvert, gent. and Hon. Charles Calvert, esq. Lieut. and Chief Gov. of same province for 30,000 lbs. of tobacco-land lying near mouth of Petuxent River in the province aforesaid commonly called by name of the Mannor of Eltonhead late in the tenure or occupancy of William Eltonhead, gent. deceased; bounded on west with land of Capt. William Hawley and a creek called St. James Creek, on north with Petuxent River and East side with bay of Chesapeake—2,000 acres . . . signed: Thomas Taylor and *Francis* [sic] his wife."[2]

Thus, we see that on 20 March 1669 Thomas Taylor, son of Captain Phillip had a wife, *Frances* and not Elizabeth, as Mr. Roberts concludes. We plan to show later that his wife, Frances, was still living when he made his will October 2, 1696 as Thomas Taylor, gent., of Dorchester County.

By studying the very numerous records of the Maryland Archives, we can easily trace the rise of Thomas Taylor, son of Captain Phillip from Sheriff to Major, to Lieut. Colonel, and finally Colonel.[3] We also agree with Mr. Roberts when he says Thomas Taylor "resided with his widowed mother on his step-father's land, near the mouth of the Petuxent in Calvert Co."[4] However, he owned property in Dorchester County in 1669, for on February 27 of that year he and his wife, *Frances,* sold Taylor's inheritance to Arthur Wright—1200 acres more or less on

---

[1] Emerson B. Roberts, "Captain Phillip Taylor and Some of his Descendants," *Md. Hist. Mag.,* XXXIII (1938), pp. 280 293.

[2] Land Office, Warrants, Lib. 12, fol. 206, Hall of Records, Annapolis.

[3] William Hand Browne, et al., ed., *Archives of Maryland* (Baltimore, 1883   ), II, pp. 193, 513, 514; V, pp. 310, 460.

[4] Roberts, "Captain Phillip Taylor," p. 288.

an island, Slaughter Creek and St. Johns Creek.[5] An interesting deed showing Thomas Taylor's connection with Dorchester County on the Eastern Shore and the Petuxent [sic] River on the Western Shore is the following: "on the back of warrant to Thomas Taylor of Dorchester Co., gent.—for 1500 acres bearing date Aug. 20, 1667 was written (viz.): know all men by these presents that I Thomas Taylor of Petuxent River do assign over unto James Clifton his heirs or assigns all my rights title of this within specified-witness my hand this 12 day of Dec. 1667 signed Thomas Taylowe [sic]."[6]

Colonel Thomas Taylor was one of the most prominent men in southern Maryland at that early date, as, for instance, from the *Maryland Archives* we quote: "a conference held between the right Honorable the Lord Baltemore Proprietor and William Pen Esq. Proprietary of Pensilvania at the house of Colonel Thomas Tailler on the ridge in Ann Arrundell County Wednesday the 13th of December 1682."[7]

About 1686 this Thomas Taylor, then a Major, moved to Cambridge, Dorchester County: "Maj. Thomas Taylor of Dorchester Co.—April 28, 1686;"[8] and "Major Thomas Taylor, officer in Cambridge, Dorchester Co. Sept. 15, 1686."[9] Also from *Maryland Archives* we quote: "was then taken into consideration the great inconveniency and prejudice caused by the remoteness of living and want of due attendence of Major Thomas Taylor or Deputy Surveyor General att his office whereby the publick business of this Province is much impeded . . . Henery Brent of Calvert Co. put in place of Thomas Taylor—18 May 1687."[10] The "remoteness" was from St. Marys. So now we find Col. Thomas Taylor, often mentioned as "gent," living in Dorchester County.

That Col. Thomas Taylor was a Protestant and a colonel we quote from *Maryland Archives:* "Coll. Thomas Taylor a Protestant commands the horse of Baltimore, Anne Arundel and part of Calvert Co."[11]

Thomas Taylor's wife, Frances, was still living on October 2, 1696, when he made his will: "Thomas Taylor, gent. of Dorchester Co. to his 4 sons John Taylor, Thomas Taylor, Phillip Taylor, and Peter Taylor,—all his property—sons to provide for their father and mother, Thomas and *Frances* Taylor, their two youngest sisters Frances and Mary, untill married and to their sister Aloysia Taylor 400 acres on Hunting Creek when she shall require it. Wit: Francis Anderton and John Dyer."[12]

Thus, we find that Thomas Taylor, son of Captain Phillip was a different man from the Thomas Taylor who married April 1, 1669 Elizabeth Marsh, a Quakeress of Severn, daughter of Thomas and Margaret Marsh. This latter couple had children: Thomas, James, John, Sarah and Elizabeth;[13] and we see that the descendants of Thomas Taylor with wife Elizabeth Marsh are not descended from Capt. Phillip Taylor.[14]

[5] James A. McAllister, Jr., *Abstracts From the Land Records of Dorchester County, Maryland* (hereinafter called McAllister's Abstracts) Vol. 1, p. 1-1 old 4.

[6] Land Office, Patent Book 12, p. 390.

[7] *Archives of Maryland*, V, p. 382.

[8] *Ibid.*, V, p. 460.

[9] *Ibid.*, V, p. 503.

[10] *Ibid.*, V, p. 542.

[11] *Ibid.*, V, pp. 309, 310, 354.

[12] McAllister's *Abstracts* (1961), Vol. 3, pp. 42–45, old 85. 2 October 1696.

[13] Roberts, "Captain Phillip Taylor," p. 293.

[14] Note: An interesting book which shows how close Captain Phillip Taylor and Captain Thomas Smith, the former married the latter's widow, were to William Claiborne is *Virginia Venturer* (1951) by Nathaniel C. Hale.

TILGHMAN FAMILY.

A pedigree of this family, entered at the Visitation of Kent in 1619, is published in the Harleian Society's *Publications*, vol. 42, p. 37, and in Berry's *Kent Genealogies*, p. 70, but it contains serious errors, the heralds having apparently put their notes together with little care and confused some of the generations. Among the manuscript collections of the Pennsylvania Historical Society is a very carefully prepared pedigree, gathered from wills and other English records by two well-known Philadelphia genealogists, Messrs. Charles R. Hildeburn and Charles P. Keith, for the late William M. Tilghman of Philadelphia. This pedigree, for a copy of which the writer is indebted to the courtesy of Mr. Samuel Troth of Philadelphia, forms the basis of the earlier portion of the present genealogy. An important source of information is the manuscript journal of William Tilghman (b. 1518; d. 1594) of Holloway Court, which is still preserved by his descendants. Beginning in 1540, it contains, together with a number of accounts and miscellaneous entries, a record of the births of William Tilghman's children, and the book has served as a family register for many successive generations. In it the first possessor has entered his arms, neatly tricked, with the date "xix die Aprilis Anno dñi. 1540" and the subscription "Arma Willmi Tilman als. Tilghman." The crest is wanting, but arms and crest were recorded at the Visitation as follows :—

Arms.—Per fess sa. and arg., a lion rampant regardant, double queued, counter-changed, crowned or.

Crest.—A demi lion issuant, statant, sa., crowned or.

1. RICHARD TILGHMAN,[1] of Holloway Court, Snodland, Kent, living about 1450, and Dionysia his wife had issue :—

    2. i. THOMAS TILGHMAN[2] of Holloway Court.
        ii. WILLIAM TILGHMAN of London, mar. Margaret Saunders. In his will, dated 15 Sept. 1493 and proved in 1494, he leaves a bequest for masses for the souls of his deceased parents Richard and Dionysia.

2. THOMAS TILGHMAN[2] (*Richard*[1]), of Holloway Court, and Joan his wife had issue :—

    3. i. WILLIAM TILGHMAN,[3] d. 27 Aug. 1541.
        ii. RALPH TILGHMAN.
        iii. JOHN TILGHMAN.

3. WILLIAM TILGHMAN [3] (*Thomas*,[2] *Richard* [1]), of Holloway Court, died 27 August 1541. A brass in Snodland Church bears the following inscription : " Pray for the Soules of William Tilghman the elder, and Isabell and Joan his wives, which William decessyd the xxvii day of August, Anno Domini mcccccxli, on whose Soules Jesu have mercy. As you are so was I, and as I am so shalt you be." The will of William Tilghman was proved 22 November 1541. His two wives were 1. Isabel Avery, and 2. Joan Amherst. By his first wife, Isabel Avery, he had a son :—

    4. i. RICHARD TILGHMAN,[4] d. 1518.

4. RICHARD TILGHMAN [4] (*William*,[3] *Thomas*,[2] *Richard* [1]), of Snodland, died in 1518 in his father's life time. His will was proved 12 November 1518. By his wife Julyan, daughter of William Pordage, he had a son :—

    5. i. WILLIAM TILGHMAN,[5] b. 1518 ; buried 24 February 1593/4.

5. WILLIAM TILGHMAN [5] (*Richard*,[4] *William*,[3] *Thomas*,[2] *Richard* [1]), of Holloway Court, was born in 1518 and was buried, according to the Snodland register, 24 February 1593/4. His will was proved 24 April 1594. William Tilghman had four wives. His first wife was Mary, daughter of John Bere of Rochester. His second wife, Joan . . . ., was buried 20 September 1563 (Snodland register). He was married to his third wife, Dorothy Reynolds, 11 August 1567, and she was buried 21 November 1572. About 1575, William Tilghman married his fourth wife, Susanna Whetenhall, daughter of Thomas Whetenhall of Hextall's Court, East Peckham, Kent, and Dorothy his wife, daughter of John Fane. This marriage is recorded both in the Tilghman pedigree and in the very accurate Whetenhall pedigree in Harleian MSS. 1548, fol. 121. Susanna Whetenhall, through her grandmother Alice Berkeley (wife of George Whetenhall), whose mother Elizabeth Neville (wife of Thomas Berkeley) was a daughter of Sir George Neville Baron Abergavenny (d. 1492), was a lineal descendant of King Edward III. By his second and third wives William Tilghman appears to have had no issue.

    By his first wife, Mary Bere, he had :—

      i. JOAN TILGHMAN,[6] b. 15 Dec. 1540.
    6. ii. EDWARD TILGHMAN, b. 15 April 1542 ; buried 23 Dec. 1611.
      iii. HENRY TILGHMAN, b. 11 Jan. 1543/4.
      iv. DOROTHY TILGHMAN, b. 4 Feb. 1545.

By his fourth wife, Susanna Whetenhall, William Tilghman had issue :—

7. i. WHETENHALL TILGHMAN, b. 25 July 1576.
    ii. DOROTHY TILGHMAN, b. 11 Jan. 1577/8 ; d. 18 Sept. 1605 ; mar. Thomas St. Nicholas (b. 1567 ; d. 1626) of Ashe, Kent, and had six children. See Planché, *A Corner of Kent*, p. 372.
8. iii. OSWALD TILGHMAN, b. 4 Oct. 1579 ; d. 1628.
    iv. CHARLES TILGHMAN, b. 13 Oct. 1582 ; buried 25 May 1608.
    v. LAMBARD TILGHMAN, b. 10 April 1584 ; d. young. He was baptized 12 April 1584, one of his godfathers being William Lambard, author of the *Perambulation of Kent*.
    vi. LAMBARD TILGHMAN, bapt. 18 August 1586 ; buried 21 Nov. 1586. His birth is not entered by his father, but his baptism and burial are recorded in the Snodland register.

6. EDWARD TILGHMAN [6] (*William*,[5] *Richard*,[4] *William*,[3] *Thomas*,[2] *Richard*[1]), of Holloway Court, was born 15 April 1542, and was buried 23 December 1611 (Snodland register). His will was proved 24 April 1612. He married Margaret, daughter of . . . . Brewer of Ditton, who survived him and was buried 23 October 1613.

   Edward Tilghman and Margaret (Brewer) his wife had a son :—

   i. FRANCIS TILGHMAN,[7] mar. 15 June 1615, Margery, daughter of Sir Adam Sprackling of Ellington, in Thanet, and had two children, Francis,[8] who died young, Catherine,[8] an infant in 1619. Francis Tilghman inherited Holloway Court, which he sold in the reign of James I.

7. WHETENHALL TILGHMAN [6] (*William*,[5] *Richard*,[4] *William*,[3] *Thomas*,[2] *Richard*[1]) was born 25 July 1576. In 1650, being then advanced in years, he petitioned the Committee for Compounding Royalists' estates, stating that, in 1606, he had purchased of Edward Neville, Lord Abergavenny, for £120, an annuity of £20 on Rotherfield Manor, Sussex, and that the annuity is now in arrears through the sequestration of the manor. In 1652, the Committee decided that he must try his title at law with Lord Abergavenny (Cal. Com. for Compounding, p. 872). Whetenhall Tilghman married Ellen daughter of Richard Renching of London and Susan his wife daughter of Robert Honywood of Charing, Kent, and Marks Hall, Essex. They had issue :—

   i. SAMUEL TILGHMAN,[7] d. young.
   ii. MARY TILGHMAN, bapt. 11 Dec. 1608.
   iii. ISAAC TILGHMAN, b. 1615 ; d. 21 Dec. 1644.
   iv. NATHANIEL TILGHMAN, b. 1616.
   v. SAMUEL TILGHMAN, b. 1618.
   vi. JOSEPH TILGHMAN, bapt. 2 Jan. 1625.
   vii. SUSAN TILGHMAN.
   viii. BENJAMIN TILGHMAN, bapt. 25 Jan. 1633.

Mrs. Ellen Tilghman, wife of Whetenhall Tilghman, was buried 30 December 1632, having probably died at the birth of her son Benjamin. The names of Whetenhall Tilghman's children are derived from the Visitation of Kent (1619), from the Snodland register, and from *Familiae Minorum Gentium*, p. 1300.

8. OSWALD TILGHMAN[6] (*William*,[5] *Richard*,[4] *William*,[3] *Thomas*,[2] *Richard*[1]) was born, according to his father's careful record, on Sunday, October 4th, 1579, between 1 and 2 o'clock a. m., and was baptized, according to the Snodland register, 11 October 1581, his godparents being Thomas Colepeper and Thomas Shakerly, Gents., and his aunt Lydia Whetenhall. He was a member of the Grocers Company of London and died in 1628, his will being proved 22 January of that year. Oswald Tilghman was twice married. He married first, 13 January 1611/2, Abigail Tayler (then aged 26), daughter of the Rev. Francis Tayler, Vicar of Godalming, Surrey (Harl. Soc. xxvi, 8). His second wife, Elizabeth Packnam, was married to him 15 November 1626 (Harl. Soc. xxv, 179) and is named in his will.

By his first wife Oswald Tilghman had a son:—

i. DR. RICHARD TILGHMAN,[7] b. 3 Sept. 1626; d. 7 Jan. 1675; came to Maryland, in 1661.

TILGHMAN FAMILY.

9. DR. RICHARD TILGHMAN[7] (*Oswald*,[6] *William*[5]) was born 3rd September, 1626, and came to Maryland with his family, in 1661, in the ship *Elizabeth and Mary*. It is not unlikely that he was induced to do so by Samuel Tilghman, probably the son of Whetenhall Tilghman, and therefore the cousin german of Richard, who had long commanded a vessel trading to Maryland and was commissioned, 15 July, 1658, "admiral" of the Maryland fleet (*Calvert Papers*, No. 205). At all events patents were issued, 17 January, 1659, in identical terms to Samuel Tilghman of London, mariner, and to Richard Tilghman, citizen and chirurgeon, of London, each of whom had undertaken to transport into the province twenty persons of British descent (Md. Land Office, Lib. 4, fol. 416. 420). Each patent was for 1000 acres of land on Tredavon Creek. 28 July, 1663, "Richard Tilghman of the Province of Maryland and Continent of Virginia, Doctor in Physick," purchased from James Coursey of Lincoln's Inn, in the County of Middlesex, Gent., a tract of 400 acres near the mouth of Chester River (*ibid.*, Lib. 10, fol. 447), and other records show that Dr. Tilghman, partly by grant and partly by purchase, acquired a very considerable landed estate. He was commissioned, 1 May 1669, High Sheriff of Talbot County and served until 17 June 1671 (Lib. C. D., fol. 404. 438). During his residence in Maryland he was actively engaged in the practice of his profession (*Old Kent*, p. 229). He died 7 Jan. 1675/6 and is buried at The Hermitage, Queen Anne County, where his tomb is still to be seen, though the inscription is now illegible. His will, dated 5 Oct. 1673 and proved 6 March 1675/6, leaves to his son William, Tilghman's Hermitage (now known as The Hermitage) and Tilghman's Addition to the Forlorn, on Chester River; to his son Richard, Tilghman's Farm, Tilghman's Choice and Tilghman's Discovery; and to his daughter Rebecca, Poplar Hill. His wife Mary is appointed executrix. The inventory of his personal estate, filed 28 August 1676, showed a total of 187,289 pounds of tobacco. Dr. Tilghman married, in

England, Mary Foxley, who survived him and died between
1699 and 1702. In August 1683, in behalf of her son
William Tilghman, then deceased, she acknowledged a deed
executed by the said William 17 Oct. 1682 (Talbot Co., Lib.
4, fol. 213). 18 Jan. 1688, Mary Tilghman of Talbot Co.
widow, conveys to her "son and daughter" Simon Wilmer
and Rebecca his wife, 1000 acres part of Tilghman and
Foxley Grove (Kent Co., Lib. M., fol. 1), and in a deed to
her son Richard Tilghman, dated 20 Sept. 1699, she mentions
her "well beloved daughter Rebecca Wilmer," and her "son-
in-law Mr. John Lillingston and his present wife" (Talbot
Co., Lib. 7, fol. 219. 271). 29 August 1702, her son,
Richard Tilghman, confirms the deed of his mother "Mary
Tilghman, late of Talbot County, widow, deceased" to his
sister Rebecca Wilmer, widow, and her children Simon and
Rebecca Wilmer, for 1000 acres part of Tilghman and Foxley
Grove (Kent Co., Lib. N., fol. 71).

Dr. Richard Tilghman and Mary (Foxley) his wife had
issue :—

i. SAMUEL TILGHMAN,[8] b. 11 Dec. 1650 ; d. young.
ii. MARY TILGHMAN, b. Feb. 1655 ; mar. Matthew Ward (d. 1677)
of Talbot Co. Her only son, Maj.-Gen. Matthew Tilghman Ward
(b. 1677 ; d. 25 May 1741), was Speaker of the Md. Assembly,
1716–18 ; Chief Justice of the Provincial Court, 1729–32 ; Member
of Council, 1719–41, and at the time of his death its President. He
was commissioned, 22 Jan. 1739, Major-General, Commanding the
militia of the Eastern Shore. He was twice married, but left no
issue.
iii. WILLIAM TILGHMAN, b. 16 Feb. 1658 ; d. unmarried 1682.
iv. REBECCA TILGHMAN, d. 1725 ; mar., about 1681, Simon Wilmer (d.
1699) of Kent Co.
v. DEBORAH TILGHMAN, b. 12 March 1666.
10. vi. RICHARD TILGHMAN, b. 23 Feb. 1672 ; d. 23 Feb. 1738.

10. COL. RICHARD TILGHMAN[8] (*Richard,*[7] *Oswald,*[6] *William*[5])
was born at The Hermitage, then called Tilghman's Hermitage, 23 Feb. 1672, and died there 23 Feb. 1738. His
will, dated 25 April 1737 and proved 14 March 1738, after
disposing of more than 10,000 acres in portions to his younger
children leaves "the rest of my lands" to his eldest son
Richard. Col. Tilghman represented Talbot County in the
Maryland Assembly from 1698 to 1702 (House Journals),
and was a Member of Council from 1711 until his death (U.
H. Journals). In 1722, he was Chancellor of the Province
(*Calvert Papers*, No. 275). He married, 7 January 1700,
Anna Maria (b. 1676 ; d. Dec. 1748), daughter of Col.

Philemon Lloyd of Talbot County and Henrietta Maria, his wife, daughter of Capt. James Neale and widow of Richard Bennett, Jr (See *Mag.* pp. 73–75). Col. Richard Tilghman and Anna Maria his wife, are buried at The Hermitage, which is now possessed by their descendant, Miss Susan Williams. They had issue :—

  i. MARY TILGHMAN,[9] b. 23 Aug. 1702 ; d. 10 Jan. 1736 ; mar., 12 Oct. 1721, James Earle.
  ii. PHILEMON TILGHMAN, b. 1704 ; d. young.
11. iii. RICHARD TILGHMAN, b. 28 April 1705 ; d. 9 Sept. 1766.
  iv. HENRIETTA MARIA TILGHMAN, b. 18 Aug. 1707 ; d. 7 Nov. 1771 ; mar. 1°, 22 April 1731, George Robins, 2°, 1747, William Goldsborough.
  v. ANNA MARIA TILGHMAN, b. 15 Nov. 1709 ; d. 30 Aug. 1763 ; mar. 1° William Hemsley, 2° Col. Robert Lloyd.
12. vi. WILLIAM TILGHMAN, b. 22 Sept. 1711 ; d. 1782.
13. vii. EDWARD TILGHMAN, b. 3 July 1713 ; d. 9 Oct. 1786.
14. viii. JAMES TILGHMAN, b. 6 Dec. 1716 ; d. 24 Aug. 1793.
15. ix. MATTHEW TILGHMAN, b. 17 Feb. 1718 ; d. 4 May 1790.

11. COL. RICHARD TILGHMAN [9] (*Richard,*[8] *Richard,*[7] *Oswald,*[6] *William*[5]) of the Hermitage, Queen Anne Co., was born 28 April 1705, and died 9 Sept. 1766. He was a Justice of the Provincial Court of Maryland 1746 to 1766, and was of the Quorum of that body from 1754 (Commission Book). He married Susanna (b. 19 June 1718) daughter of Peregrine Frisby (d. 1738) of Cecil County and Elizabeth his wife, daughter of Maj. Nicholas Sewall of St. Mary's County. Mrs. Elizabeth Frisby mentions her daughter Susanna Tilghman in her will (dated 15 April 1751, proved 22 April 1752).

  Col. Richard Tilghman and Susanna (Frisby) his wife had issue :—

16. i. RICHARD TILGHMAN,[10] b. 11 May 1739.
17. ii. PEREGRINE TILGHMAN, b. 24 Jan. 1741; d. 1807.
18. iii. JAMES TILGHMAN, b. 2 Aug. 1743 ; d. 19 April 1809.
19. iv. WILLIAM TILGHMAN, b. 11 March 1745 ; d. Dec. 1800.
  v. EDWARD TILGHMAN.
20. vi. ELIZABETH TILGHMAN, b. 24 April 1749 ; d. 1836 ; mar. William Cooke.
  vii. SUSANNA TILGHMAN, b. 1751.
  viii. ANNA MARIA TILGHMAN, b. 1759 ; d. 1834 ; mar. Henry Ward Pearce of Cecil Co.

12. WILLIAM TILGHMAN [9] (*Richard,*[8] *Richard,*[7] *Oswald,*[6] *William*[5]) of Grosses, Talbot County, was born 22 Sept. 1711, and died in 1782. His will dated 20 Dec. 1761 (with codicil 15 Nov. 1769), was proved in Talbot County 31 Oct. 1782. He was one of the Justices of Queen Anne County

1734-36, 1737-39, 1743-45, 1747-51, and 1754-60; was of the Quorum from 1737; and was Presiding Justice from 1755 to 1760 (Commission Book). He represented Queen Anne County in the Assembly from 1734 to 1738 (House Journals). He married, 2 Aug. 1736, his cousin Margaret Lloyd (b. 16 Feb. 1714) daughter of his uncle James Lloyd (b. 7 March 1680; d. 27 Sept. 1723) and Ann Grundy (b. 25 April 1690) his wife. James Lloyd was one of the representatives for Talbot County in the Maryland Assembly 1712-14 and 1716-22 (House Journals) and was a member of Council from 4 Nov. 1722 to 27 Sept. 1723 (U. H. Journals).

William Tilghman and Margaret (Lloyd) his wife had issue:—

    i. ANNA MARIA TILGHMAN,[10] b. 3 Nov. 1737; d. 4 Feb. 1768; mar., 3 Sept. 1764, Charles Goldsborough (b. 2 April 1740; d. 25 Feb. 1769). Their son, Hon. Charles Goldsborough, was Governor of Maryland in 1818.

21. ii. RICHARD TILGHMAN, b. 6 April 1740; d. 12 April 1809.
    iii. JAMES TILGHMAN, b. 10 April 1742.
    iv. MARGARET TILGHMAN, b. 24 Dec. 1744; mar. her cousin Richard Tilghman (son of Matthew).
    v. HENRIETTA MARIA TILGHMAN, b. 18 Oct. 1749.
    vi. MARY TILGHMAN, b. 28 June 1753; mar. Edward Roberts of Talbot Co.

13. EDWARD TILGHMAN[9] (*Richard,*[8] *Richard,*[7] *Oswald,*[6] *William*[5]) of Wye, Queen Anne County, was born 3 July 1713, and died 9 Oct. 1786. He was High Sheriff of Queen Anne County from 5 Nov. 1739 to 5 Nov. 1742, and was one of the Justices of the County from 1743 to 1749 (Commission Book). He represented the County in the Assembly from 1746 to 1750, when he was commissioned Keeper of the Rolls for the Eastern Shore (House Journals). In 1754 he was again elected to the Assembly and served until 1771, being Speaker of the House during the sessions of 1770 and 1771 (*ibid.*). In the House Journals he is styled Captain in 1746, and Colonel in 1756, indicating that he held these ranks in the militia of his County. In 1765 he was a member of the Stamp Act Congress and one of the Committee which drew up the remonstrance to Parliament. His will was proved 31 Oct. 1786. Col. Tilghman was thrice married. His first wife was Anna Maria Turbutt, daughter of Maj. William Turbutt of Queen Anne County. His second wife, whom he married in 1749, was Elizabeth (b. 25 Nov.

1720), daughter of Samuel Chew of Dover and Mary (Galloway) his wife. The third wife of Col. Tilghman, married 25 May 1759, was Juliana (b. 3 Jan. 1729) daughter of Dominick Carroll of Cecil County and Mary his wife, daughter of Maj. Nicholas Sewall of St. Mary's County.

Col. Edward Tilghman and Anna Maria (Turbutt) his first wife had issue :—

  i. ANNA MARIA TILGHMAN,[10] mar. Bennet Chew.

By his second wife, Elizabeth Chew, Col. Tilghman had issue :—

22. i. RICHARD TILGHMAN.
22 ii. EDWARD TILGHMAN, b. 11 Feb. 1750/1 ; d. 1 Nov. 1815.
  iii. BENJAMIN TILGHMAN.
  iv. ELIZABETH TILGHMAN, mar. her cousin Richard Tilghman (son of Richard) of The Hermitage.
  v. ANNA MARIA TILGHMAN, mar. 1° Charles Goldsborough (b. 1744; d. 1774), 2° Rt. Rev. Robert Smith, Bishop of South Carolina.

Col. Edward Tilghman and his third wife, Juliana Carroll, had issue :—

23. i. MATTHEW TILGHMAN,
  ii. BENJAMIN TILGHMAN, b. Dec. 1764.
  iii. MARY TILGHMAN, mar. her cousin Richard Tilghman, (son of Matthew).
  iv. SUSANNA TILGHMAN, mar. Richard Ireland Jones.

(*To be Continued.*)

TILGHMAN FAMILY.

14. JAMES TILGHMAN[9] (*Richard*,[8] *Richard*,[7] *Oswald*[6]) was born 6 December 1716. He was a lawyer and began the practice of his profession in Talbot County, which he represented in the Maryland Assembly for the years 1762 and 1763, (House Journals). Shortly after this he removed to Philadelphia. Gov. Sharpe, in a letter dated 8 May 1764, alludes to him as "Mr. James Tilghman lately Burgess for Talbot and one of our first-rate lawyers, but now settled in Philadelphia" (Md. Archives, xiv, 160). James Tilghman was elected a Common Councilman of Philadelphia, 2 October, 1764 (Penna. Archives, 2nd Ser., ix, 733), was a member of the Council of Pennsylvania 1767–76 (*ibid.* 625), and was commissioned Secretary of the Pennsylvania Land Office, 1 January 1769 (*ibid.* 628). He returned to Maryland in 1777 and settled at Chestertown, where he died 24 August 1793. He married Anna, daughter of Tench Francis of Fausley, Talbot Co., Md., and had issue :—

24. i. TENCH TILGHMAN,[10] b. 25 Dec. 1744; d. 18 April 1786.
     ii. RICHARD TILGHMAN, b. 17 Dec. 1746; d. unmarried 24 Nov. 1796.
25. iii. JAMES TILGHMAN, b. 1 Jan. 1748; d. 24 Nov. 1796.
26. iv. WILLIAM TILGHMAN, b. 12 Aug. 1756; d. 30 April 1827.
27. v. PHILEMON TILGHMAN, b. 29 Nov. 1760; d. 11 Jan. 1797.
     vi. THOMAS RINGGOLD TILGHMAN, b. 17 Aug. 1765; d. unmarried 29 Dec. 1789.
     vii. ANNA MARIA TILGHMAN, mar. William Hemsley, and d. s. p.
     viii. ELIZABETH TILGHMAN, mar. Maj. James Lloyd of Kent Co.
     ix. MARY TILGHMAN, d. unmarried.
     x. HENRIETTA MARIA TILGHMAN, b. 26 Feb. 1763; d. 2 March 1796; mar. her cousin, Lloyd Tilghman (son of Matthew).

15. MATTHEW TILGHMAN [9] (*Richard*,[8] *Richard*,[7] *Oswald*,[6]) *clarum et venerabile nomen*, was born 17 February 1718. He was adopted at the age of fifteen by his childless cousin, Maj. Gen. Matthew Tilghman Ward (*Mag.*, p. 281), from whom he inherited the handsome estate of Bayside in Talbot County. According to the statement of his daughter, Mrs. Anna Maria Tilghman, he was commissioned in 1741, Captain of a troop of horse organized to protect the outlying settlements of the Eastern Shore from Indian incursions. The same year he was commissioned one of the Justices of Talbot County and was continuously a member of the County Court from that date until 1775, being one of the Quorum from 1749, and Presiding Justice from 1769 (Commission Book). He represented Talbot County in the Maryland Assembly from 1751 to 1758, sat for Queen Anne County from 1760 to 1761, and again for Talbot from 1768 to 1774. In 1773 and 1774 he was Speaker of the House (House Journals). Throughout the Revolution he played a leading part in the affairs of Maryland. He was chosen Chairman of the Committee of Correspondence in December 1774, and of the Council of Safety in July 1775. He was President of the Maryland Convention from 1774 to 1776, and headed every delegation sent by the Convention to Congress. In June 1776 he was summoned from Congress to attend the Convention at Annapolis, and was President of the new Convention which met August 14th to prepare a new form of government for the State. It was this alone which prevented his signing the Declaration of Independence. He was member of Congress from 1774 to 1777, when he resigned his seat to take his place as Senator from Talbot in the first Assembly held under the new Constitution of Maryland. He continued to serve in this capacity until 1781, when he was again chosen Senator but did not serve out his term. After the declaration of peace in 1783, feeling the infirmities of advancing age, he resigned all his public trusts, and retired to his estate in Talbot County to enjoy a well earned repose. He died of a paralytic stroke 4 May 1790. As a statesman Matthew Tilghman takes high rank. He exerted a profound influence upon the policy of Maryland during the trying times of the Revolution, and upon the formation of the constitution of the State. He has justly been called by McMahon "the patriarch of the colony." He married, 6 April 1741, Anna Lloyd (b. 13 Feb. 1723; d. 15 March 1794) daughter of

James Lloyd and sister of his brother William Tilghman's
wife (*Mag.* 283). They had issue :—

   i. MARGARET TILGHMAN,[10] b. 13 Jan. 1742 ; d. 14 March 1817 ; mar.
     23 June 1763, Charles Carroll Barrister (b. 22 March 1723 ; d. 23
     March 1783), and had two children, twins, who died in infancy.
   ii. MATTHEW WARD TILGHMAN, b. 1743 ; d. 17 March 1753.
28. iii. RICHARD TILGHMAN, b. 28 Jan. 1746 ; d. 28 May 1805.
29. iv. LLOYD TILGHMAN, b. 27 July 1749 ; d. 1811.
   v. ANNA MARIA TILGHMAN, b. 17 July 1755 ; d. 17 Jan. 1843 ; mar.
     1783, her cousin, Col. Tench Tilghman.

16. LIEUT. COL. RICHARD TILGHMAN [10] (*Richard,*[9] *Richard,*[8]
Richard,[7] *Oswald*[6]) of the Hermitage, Queen Anne County,
was born 11 May 1739, and died in 1810. He was commissioned, 6 Jan. 1776, Lieut. Col. of the Lower Battalion
of Queen Anne Co. (Journal of Convention of 1776, p. 80).
He married his cousin Elizabeth Tilghman (b. 5 Dec. 1748 ;
d. 7 June 1767) daughter of his uncle, Col. Edward Tilghman, and had an only son

   i. RICHARD EDWARD TILGHMAN,[11] d. before his father, unmarried.

17. COL. PEREGRINE TILGHMAN [10] (*Richard,*[9] *Richard,*[8] *Richard,*[7]
Oswald[6]) of Hope, Talbot County, was born 24 Jan. 1741
and died in 1807. He was member, for Talbot Co., of the
Maryland Convention of 1775 (Md. Arch. xi. 3), was com-
missioned, 9 April 1778, Colonel of the 4th Battalion of
Talbot Co. (*ibid.* xxi, 24), and was member of the State
Senate 1787–88 (Senate Journals). He married Deborah
daughter of Col. Robert Lloyd of Hope and Anna Maria
Tilghman his wife (*Mag.,* p. 282) and had issue :—

   i. ROBERT LLOYD TILGHMAN,[11] b. 13 May 1778; d. 12 June 1823; mar.
     16 April 1807, Henrietta Maria, daughter of Col. Joseph Forman
     and Mary Hemsley, his wife.
   ii. ANNA MARIA TILGHMAN, mar. James Earle of Easton.
   iii. TENCH TILGHMAN, b. 18 April 1782 ; d. 16 April 1827 ; mar. Mar-
     garet, daughter of Col. Tench Tilghman.
   iv. WILLIAM HEMSLEY TILGHMAN, b. 16 Dec. 1784; d. Dec. 1863; mar.
     Maria Lloyd, daughter of Philemon Hemsley, but had no issue.
   v. ELIZABETH TILGHMAN, mar. John Custis Wilson of Somerset Co.

18. JAMES TILGHMAN [10] (*Richard,*[9] *Richard,*[8] *Richard,*[7] *Oswald*[6])
of Melfield, Queen Anne County, was born 2 August 1743
and died 19 April 1809. He represented his county in the
Convention of 1775 (Md. Arch. xi, 3), was member of
the Council of Safety in 1776 (*ibid.* 103, 447), and was
commissioned, 7 August 1777, Attorney General of Maryland (Md. Arch. xvi. 327). He was member of Legislature

1788–89, and in 1791 was appointed Chief Judge of the judicial district composed of Cecil, Kent, Queen Anne, and Talbot Counties. From 1804 to 1809 he was judge of the Court of Appeals. He married, for his first wife, 19 Jan. 1769, Susanna (d. 24 Oct. 1774) daughter of Dr. George Steuart of Annapolis. He married, secondly, 19 Feb. 1778, Elizabeth daughter of Kinsey Johns of West River. Judge Tilghman had issue by his first wife Susanna Steuart:—

i. GEORGE TILGHMAN,[11] b. 11 Oct. 1771; d. 30 July 1792.
ii. FRISBY TILGHMAN, b. 4 Aug. 1773; d. 14 April 1847; mar. 1°., 24 Feb. 1795, Anna Maria Ringgold (d. 21 Feb. 1817), 2°., 3 Sept. 1819, Louisa Lamar.
iii. SUSANNA TILGHMAN, b. 1774.

By his second wife, Elizabeth Johns, he had :—

i. ANNA MARIA TILGHMAN, b. 10 March 1779 ; mar. Peregrine Blake.
ii. SAMUEL TILGHMAN, b. 30 Aug. 1781 ; d. 19 Aug. 1782.
iil. MARY TILGHMAN, b. 6 Feb. 1783; mar. 3 Dec. 1801, Judge Richard Tilghman Earle (b. 23 June 1767 ; d. 8 Nov. 1843), whose accurate memoir of the Tilghman family, compiled in 1839, has been a valuable aid to the writer of this Genealogy.
iv. JOHN TILGHMAN, of Centreville, b. 8 March 1785 ; mar. 1° Anna Katherine Tilghman, daughter of Richard[10] (Matthew[9]), 2° Ann, daughter of Lloyd Tilghman[10] (Matthew[9]).
v. CHARLES CARROLL TILGHMAN, b. 26 Feb. 1788 ; d. Dec. 1861; mar. Mary Lloyd Tilghman, daughter of Richard[10] (Matthew[9]).
vi. PEREGRINE TILGHMAN, b. 31 March 1790 ; d. 1874; mar. Harriet Haddaway.

19. WILLIAM TILGHMAN[10] (*Richard,*[9] *Richard,*[8] *Richard,*[7] *Oswald*[6]) of the White House, Queen Anne Co., was born 11 March 1745 and died in December 1800. He was thrice married. His first wife, Ann Kent, had no children. His second wife, Anna Maria daughter of Col. Robert Lloyd of Hope (*Mag.*, p. 282) had one child who died young. By his third wife, Eleanor widow of Thomas Whetenhall Rozer and daughter of Francis Hall, he had an only daughter,

i. ANNA MARIA TILGHMAN,[11]' mar. Edward Tilghman[11] (Matthew,[10] Edward[9]).

20. ELIZABETH TILGHMAN[10] (*Richard,*[9] *Richard,*[8] *Richard,*[7] *Oswald*[6]) was born 24 April 1749, and died in 1836. She married, 29 April 1771, William Cooke of Annapolis (d. 1817), son of John Cooke of Prince George's Co. and Sophia his wife daugher of Maj. Nicholas Sewall of St. Mary's Co., and had issue :—

    i. RICHARD COOKE,[11] b. 10 May 1772, took the name of Tilghman in compliance with the will of his uncle, Richard Tilghman. He married 1° Elizabeth Van Wyck, of Baltimore, 2² her sister, Frances Van Wyck, and left issue by his first wife.

    ii. CATHERINE COOKE, b. 6 Aug. 1774; d. 4 Aug. 1849; mar. 7 Dec. 1793, Jonas Clapham (b. 31 May, 1763; d. 28 Aug. 1837).

    iii. WILLIAM COOKE, b. 29 March. 1776; mar. Elizabeth, daughter of Edward Tilghman[10] (Edward[9]) of Philadelphia.

    iv. ANNA MARIA COOKE, b. 20 April, 1777; mar. Benjamin Ogle, son of Hon. Benjamin Ogle, Governor of Maryland, 1798–1801.

    v. ELIZABETH COOKE, b. March 1783; mar. Robert Gilmor and d. s. p.

    vi. SOPHIA COOKE, b. 5 Jan. 1785; d. unmarried.

    vii. SUSANNA FRISBY COOKE, b. 27 Aug. 1786; mar. William Elie Williams of Frederick Co., son of Gen. Otho Holland Williams. Their grand-daughter, Miss Susan Williams, daughter of Otho Holland Williams, is the present owner of the Hermitage.

    viii. FRANCIS COOKE, d. 1843.

    ix. GEORGE COOKE, b. 25 Aug. 1791; d. 7 Oct. 1849; mar. 21 June 1814, Eleanor Addison Dall (b. 5 Nov. 1795; d. 22 Feb. 1853).

21. RICHARD TILGHMAN[10] (*William,*[9] *Richard,*[8] *Richard,*[7] *Oswald*[6]) of Grosses, Talbot Co., was born 6 April 1740 and died 12 April 1809. He married, 2 August 1784, Mary (b. 21 Sept. 1766; d. 1 Dec. 1790) daughter of John Gibson of Talbot Co., and had issue :—

    i. WILLIAM GIBSON TILGHMAN,[11] b. 24 Sept. 1785; d. 20 June 1844; mar. 13 Dec. 1808, Anna (b. 14 March 1788; d. 29 Sept. 1860), daughter of Daniel Polk of Sussex Co., Del.

    ii. JOHN LLOYD TILGHMAN, b. 21 May 1788; mar. Maria, daughter of John Gibson of Magothy, A. Arundel Co.

    iii. RICHARD TILGHMAN, b. 26 March 1790; d. in infancy.

22. [1] EDWARD TILGHMAN[10] (*Edward,*[9] *Richard,*[8] *Richard,*[7] *Oswald*[6]) of Philadelphia, was born 11 Feb. 1750/1, and died 1 Nov. 1815. He married, 26 May 1774, Elizabeth (b. 10 Nov. 1751) daughter of Chief Justice Benjamin Chew of Pennsylvania, and had issue :—

    i. EDWARD TILGHMAN,[11] b. 27 Feb. 1779; mar. Rebecca Waln.

    ii. BENJAMIN TILGHMAN, b. 1 Jan. 1785; mar. Anna Maria McMurtrie.

    iii. ELIZABETH TILGHMAN, mar. 24 Jan. 1804, William Cooke of Baltimore (see above).

    iv. MARY ANNA TILGHMAN, mar. William Rawle of Philadelphia.

23. MATTHEW TILGHMAN[10] (*Edward,*[9] *Richard,*[8] *Richard,*[7] *Oswald*[6]) was born 5 June 1760. He was member of Legislature for Kent County 1789, and 1793–94, and was Speaker of the House in 1794 (House Journals). He married, in 1788, Sarah daughter of Thomas Smyth of Chestertown, and had issue :—

---

[1] On p. 284 the running number 22 should be prefixed to the name of **Edward**, and not to that of his brother **Richard**.

i. EDWARD TILGHMAN,[11] mar. Anna Maria, daughter of William Tilghman of the White House, and had one daughter, Eleanor Sarah Tilghman.[12]

ii. HENRY TILGHMAN, mar. Martha, daughter of Dr. Benj. Hall; no issue.

iii. SARAH TILGHMAN, mar. Francis Hall of Queen Anne Co., no issue.

24. COL. TENCH TILGHMAN [10] (*James,*[9] *Richard,*[8] *Richard,*[7] *Oswald* [6]) of Plimhimmon, Talbot Co., was born 25 Dec. 1744. He was commissioned, in June 1776, Captain of a Pennsylvania battalion of the Flying Camp; was on duty at Washington's headquarters as Military Secretary from 8 August 1776; and was commissioned Lieutenant Colonel, Aide de Camp, and Military Secretary to Gen. Washington 1 April 1777. A brave and efficient officer, he was selected to bear to Congress the news of the surrender of Cornwallis at Yorktown. By act of Congress, 29 October 1781, it was "Resolved, that the Board of War be directed to present to Lieut. Colonel Tilghman, in the name of the United States in Congress assembled, a horse properly caparisoned and an elegant sword in testimony of their high opinion of his merit and ability." Col. Tilghman served until 23 Dec. 1783. He died 18 April 1786 leaving, in the words of Gen. Washington, "as fair a reputation as ever belonged to a human character." He married, in 1783, Anna Maria Tilghman daughter of his uncle Matthew, and had issue :—

i. MARGARET TILGHMAN,[11] b. 1784; mar. Tench Tilghman [11] (Peregrine [10]) of Hope.

ii. ELIZABETH TENCH TILGHMAN, b. 11 Oct. 1786; d. May 1852; mar. 25 April 1811, Nicholas Goldsborough of Oxford Neck.

25. JAMES TILGHMAN [10] (*James,*[9] *Richard,*[8] *Richard,*[7] *Oswald* [6]) was born 2 January 1748, and died 24 November 1796. He represented Talbot County in the Legislature 1787–91, and was Associate Judge of the Talbot Co. Court. He married Elizabeth Buely and had issue :—

i. JAMES TILGHMAN,[11] b. 1 May 1792; d. unmarried 22 March 1824.

ii. MARIA TILGHMAN, d. unmarried.

iii. ELIZABETH TILGHMAN, mar. Thomas Hemsley, son of Wm. Hemsley of Cloverfield.

iv. ANN TILGHMAN, mar. Robert Browne of Queen Anne Co.

v. MARGARET TILGHMAN, mar. 1° Henry Goldsborough, 2° John Goldsborough.

26. WILLIAM TILGHMAN [10] (*James,*[9] *Richard,*[8] *Richard,*[7] *Oswald* [6]) was born 12 Aug. 1756, and died 12 Aug. 1827. He was a member of the Maryland Convention to ratify the Federal

Constitution, and represented Kent County in the Legislature 1788–90. He was a member of the State Senate 1791–92, and in 1793 removed to Philadelphia. He was appointed, 3 March 1801, Presiding Judge of the Third Circuit, comprising part of Pennsylvania, New Jersey and Delaware, and, in May 1805, President of the Court of Common Pleas in the First District. He was made Chief Justice of Pennsylvania, 26 Feb. 1806. In 1824, he was elected President of the American Philosophical Society. Judge Tilghman married Margaret Elizabeth Allen of Philadelphia and had issue :—

    i. ELIZABETH TILGHMAN,[11] d. 17 June 1817 ; mar. Benjamin Chew and had an only daughter, who died in infancy.

27. PHILEMON TILGHMAN [10] (*James*,[9] *Richard*,[8] *Richard*,[7] *Oswald*[6]) was born 29 Nov. 1760. He was an officer in the British Navy, but returned to Maryland after the war, and died at his farm, called the Golden Square, in Queen Anne Co., 11 Jan. 1797. He married Harriet Milbanke, daughter of Admiral Mark Milbanke, R. N., third son of Sir Ralph Milbanke, Bart., and had issue :—

    i. RICHARD TILGHMAN,[11] mar. Augusta Elphinstone.
    ii. HARRIET TILGHMAN, d. s. p. 1856 ; mar. Rev. Richard Cockburn, Prebend of Winchester Cathedral and Vicar of Boxley, Kent.
    iii. EMILY TILGHMAN, d. 1818 ; mar. Jeremiah Hoffman of Baltimore.
    iv. CAROLINE TILGHMAN, d. unmarried 1868.
    v. CHARLOTTE TILGHMAN, d. 26 June 1838 ; mar. 30 Aug. 1813, Sir Molyneux Hyde Nepean, Bart.

28. MAJ. RICHARD TILGHMAN [10] (*Matthew*,[9] *Richard*,[8] *Richard*,[7] *Oswald*[6]) was born 28 Jan. 1746, and died 28 May 1805. He was commissioned, 8 May 1777, First Major of the 5th Battalion of Queen Anne Co. (Md. Arch. xvi, 243). He married 1°, Margaret Tilghman (b. 24 Dec. 1744 ; d. 24 Dec. 1779) daughter of his uncle William of Grosses (*Mag.*, p. 283), and 2°, Mary Tilghman (b. 8 Sept. 1762 ; d. 18 Oct. 1793) daughter of his uncle Col. Edward of Wye (*Mag.*, p. 285). By his first wife Maj. Tilghman had issue :—

    i. ANNA MARIA TILGHMAN,[11] b. 20 Aug. 1774 ; d. 15 Dec. 1858 ; mar. 5 Dec. 1797, Judge Nicholas Brice (b. 23 April 1771 ; d. 9 May 1851).
    ii. MATTHEW TILGHMAN, b. 20 Sept. 1779 ; d. 21 Oct. 1828 ; mar. 1° Eleanor, daughter of Thos. Whetenhall Rozer, 2° Harriet Hynson of Kent Co.
    iii. ELIZA TILGHMAN, b. 22 Nov. 1779 ; mar. 1799, George Hoffman of Baltimore ; d. s. p.

Maj. Tilghman had issue by his second wife :—

   i. JULIANA TILGHMAN, b. 6 Dec. 1783 ; mar. 23 Oct. 1800, John Philemon Paca of Wye Island.

   ii. HARRIET TILGHMAN, b. 6 Dec. 1785 ; mar. Henry Brice of Baltimore, brother of Judge Nicholas Brice.

   iii. ANNA CATHERINE TILGHMAN, b. 26 April 1787 ; first wife of John Tilghman [11] (James [10]) of Centreville.

   iv. MARY LLOYD TILGHMAN, b. 24 Nov. 1789 ; mar. 20 Nov. 1820, Charles Carroll Tilghman [11] (James [10]).

29. LLOYD TILGHMAN [10] (*Matthew,*[9] *Richard,*[8] *Richard,*[7] *Oswald*[6]) was born 27 July 1749, and died in 1811. He married, 22 Jan. 1785, Henrietta Maria Tilghman (b. 26 Feb. 1763 ; d. 2 March 1796) daughter of his uncle James, and had issue :—

   i. JAMES TILGHMAN, [11] b. 5 Feb. 1793 ; mar. Ann Shoemaker of Philadelphia.

   ii. LLOYD TILGHMAN.

   iii. MATTHEW WARD TILGHMAN.

   iv. ANNA TILGHMAN, b. 31 Dec. 1785 ; second wife of John Tilghman [11] (James [10]) of Centreville.

   v. HENRIETTA MARIA TILGHMAN, b. 30 March 1787 ; mar. Alexander Hemsley.

   vi. MARY TILGHMAN.

   vii. ELIZABETH TILGHMAN, d. in infancy.

THE TODD FAMILY OF ANNE ARUNDEL COUNTY

CHRISTOPHER JOHNSON.

1. THOMAS TODD,[1] the immigrant ancestor of this family
came to Maryland in 1651 and settled on the Severn River,
near Annapolis, 8 July, 1651, a tract of 100 acres, called
Todd, was surveyed for him on the South side of Severn
River, and 27 October 1651 there was laid out for " Thomas Todd of Anne Arundel County, planter " 200 acres on
the West side of Chesapeake Bay adjoining the land of
Leonard Givins (L. O., A. B. & H., 258, 259). 23 July
1658, he demanded land, partly by his rights on record in
Anne Arundel County, and partly for the transportation
of certain persons whose names are given, and received
a warrant for 1040 acres to be laid out in one or more
parcels (L. O., Q., 73). It was doubtless part of this
large warrant that formed the tract Todd's Range, containing 120 acres, surveyed for him, 18 Dec. 1662, on the
South side of Severn River (Rent Roll). He also appears to have taken up land in Baltimore and Talbot Counties. Thomas Todd was commissioned, 12 July 1658,
one of the Justices of Anne Arundel County (*Md. Arch.*
iii, 348), and was again commissioned 14 June 1661
(*ibid.* 424). He was certainly living in 1662 when he
took·up Todd's Range, and he was certainly dead in 1671
when his son John was a minor under the guardianship
of Lancelot Todd (John's brother) and Cornelius Howard.
In all probability he died about 1669 or perhaps somewhat earlier. The name of his wife is unknown, but he
had at least three sons, viz:—

2.   i.   THOMAS TODD,[2] d. 1677; m. Sarah —.
3.   ii. LANCELOT TODD, d. 1691; m. Sarah Phelps.
4.   iii. JOHN TODD, d. 1677.

2. THOMAS TODD [2] (*Thomas* [1]) was the eldest son of his father and died in 1677. According to the Rent Roll for
Anne Arundel County, a tract of 120 acres, called Todd's
Harbor was surveyed, 16 Dec. 1670, for Thomas Todd,
on the South side of Severn River. There is a bare

chance that it was the elder, and not the younger Thomas, who took up this land, but it is extremely improbable. It was certainly the younger Thomas for whom was surveyed, 16 Nov. 1674, the tract Todd's Pasture (29 acres) " in Todd's Neck in the town of Annapolis " (Rent Roll). In 1713, Lancelot Todd, son and heir of the younger Thomas conveyed all the Todd tracts to Bordley and Larkins, and a law suit arose which was tried in Chancery in 1736. The testimony of the witnesses is extremely confused and contradictory, and only a few salient point can be picked out. Abraham Child, of Anne Arundel County, who gives his age as 90 years in 1736, and was therefore 31 years old at the death of the younger Thomas Todd in 1677, testifies that he did not know Thomas Todd Senior, but that he well remembers several of his children, and particularly one named Thomas (L. R. No. 3, 476). It is also in evidence that, by deed dated 1 May 1672, Robert Busby bought certain land from Thomas Todd *son* of Thomas Todd the patentee. Thomas Todd the younger died, as above stated, in 1677, leaving a widow Sarah who married, secondly, William Stafford. 18 April 1677, Sarah Todd of Anne Arundel County was granted administration on the estate of her husband, Thomas Todd late of said County, deceased (*Test. Proc.*, ix, 54). 24 Sept. 1678, Lancelot Todd of Anne Arundel County files a petition alleging that his brother Thomas Todd left a widow Sarah who has since married William Stafford, who wastes the orphans' estate (*Test. Proc.* x, 282). Thomas Todd [2] and Sarah his wife had issue:—

5. i. Capt. LANCELOT TODD,[3] b. c. 1674; d. 1735; Elizabeth Rockhold.
6. ii. RICHARD TODD, b. c. 1676; d. 1718; m. Margaret—

3. LANCELOT TODD [2] (*Thomas* [1]) of Anne Arundel County was apparently the second son of Thomas, the immigrant, and was of age before 1671, when he was guardian to his brother John. 14 Sept. 1671, Lancelot and Cornelius Howard of Anne Arundel County, guardians to John Todd, brother to said Lancelot, convey to Thomas Furley of Talbot County, the tract Todd upon Darvan, containing 400 acres, on St. Michael's River (Talbot Co., i, 173). 15 April 1680, Lancelot Todd was a witness to the will of Cornelius Howard, to whom he seems to have been related in some way. In 1683, Lancelot Todd of Anne Arundel

County and Sarah his wife, daughter of Thomas Phelps (d. 1674), late of Anne Arundel County deceased, convey to Edward Philkes of said County, a tract of 150 acres called Wolf's Neck, on Gunpowder River (Balto. Co., R. M. No. H. S., 116). The will of "Lancelot Todd of Anne Arundel County, planter," dated 28 Feb'y 1690, was proved 10 Nov. 1691 (Annapolis, ii, 219). After providing for his wife Sarah, he leaves to his son John, at the age of 18 years, "the plantation I now live on and one half Philk's (*sic!*) Rest"—to his daughter Mary, the other half of Philk's Rest—Bequests to daughters Elizabeth and Eleanor. His wife Sarah and his friend John Hammond are appointed executors—Testator's kinsman, Lancelot Todd to be of age at 18 years—His daughter Mary to have the cow her aunt Elizabeth Howard gave her. Lancelot Todd [2] and Sarah (Phelps) his wife had issue:—

7. i. JOHN TODD,[3] d. 11 July, 1733; m., 1710, Kath. Smith.
   ii. MARY TODD.
   iii. ELIZABETH TODD.
   iv. ELEANOR TODD.

4. JOHN TODD [2] (*Thomas* [1]) first appears 25 Jan'y 1669 when with Cornelius Howard, he witnesses the will of John Minter of Anne Arundel Court. It is probable that, at this time his father was dead, and that he was under the guardianship of his brother Lancelot and of Cornelius Howard. This was certainly the case in 1671, as is proved by the Talbot County deed cited above. John Todd died in 1677 intestate and apparently unmarried. 8 Feb'y 1677, Lancelot Todd of Anne Arundel County was granted administration on the estate of his brother John Todd deceased intestate and without issue (*Test. Proc.* ix, 457). 28 March 1678, Lancelot Todd of Anne Arundel County, administrator of his brother John Todd, late of said County deceased, returned an inventory of his said brother's estate (*Test. Proc.*, x, 13).

5. CAPT. LANCELOT TODD [3] (*Thomas,* [2] *Thomas* [1]) was born about 1674, and died in 1735. His uncle Lancelot Todd, in his will dated 28 Feb'y 1690, directs that his "kinsman Lancelot Todd" shall be of age at 18 years, so that he must have been born after 1672. But his father died in

1677 and he had a younger brother Richard, and therefore, taking into consideration all the attendant circumstances, the date of his birth can be pretty confidently set
down as 1674. In the year 1695, there is an allowance
to his credit, in the public levy, of 600 lb. tobacco for
building or repairing the Court House fence at Annapolis
(*Md. Arch.*, xix, 201), and he was a Provincial grand
juror in 1698 (*ibid.* xxiii, 530; xxv, 9). 12 April 1698,
he conveyed to Samuel Norwood of Anne Arundel County,
100 acres part of Todd's Range (120 acres) on South side
of Severn River (A. A. Co., W. H. No. 4, 42). This land,
it will be observed, was taken up by Lancelot's grandfather
Thomas, and he now disposes of it as heir at law. Soon
after this he removed to Baltimore County and, 10 March
1713, Lancelot Todd of Baltimore County, Gent., conveys
to Messrs. Thomas Bordley and Thomas Larkin of Anne
Arundel County, Gents., the following tracts, viz:—Todd's
Pasture 29 acres, Todd's Harbor 120 acres, Todd's Range
120 acres (except 100 acres sold to Samuel Norwood),
and 100 acres surveyed 8 July 1651 for Thomas Todd, on
the South side of Severn River (Anne Arundel Co. Rec.):
All these tracts are conveyed by Lancelot as son and heir
of Thomas Todd, and therefore this deed furnishes positive
proof of his descent. Lancelot Todd was one of the Justices of Baltimore County 1719-1726 (Court Minutes),
and, returning at this time to his native County, was a
Justice of Anne Arundel County 1727-1832 (Commission
Book). In 1723, and also later, he is styled " Captain "
in the record, and doubtless held this rank in the Provincial militia. He married Elizabeth daughter of John and
Mary Rockhold of Anne Arundel County. John Rockhold made his will 17 Feb'y 1698 (Annapolis, vi, 20) and
names in it his sons Thomas, Charles, and Jacob; his wife
Mary, who is constituted executrix; and his cousins Stephen White and Wm. Hawkins Jr. Lancelot Todd is one
of the witnesses. The will of Mary Rockhold, widow of
John, is dated 2 March 1703, and was proved 15 May
1704 (Annapolis, iii, 248). In it she mentions her
daughter Sarah Rockhold; her sons Thomas, Charles, and
Jacob Rockhold; her daughter Sebrah Rockhold; and her
daughters Susanna Crouch, and Elizabeth Todd. Her
son-in-law Lancelot Todd is constituted executor. The
will of Lancelot Todd, dated 6 May 1735, was proved 16

June following (Annapolis, xxi, ɔɔɔ), while that of his
wife, Elizabeth Todd, is dated 19 June, and was proved
13 Aug., 1741 (Annapolis, xxii, 373). Lancelot Todd [3]
and Elizabeth (Rockhold) his wife had issue:—

8. i. THOMAS TODD;[4] m. Sophia —
9. ii. LANCELOT TODD, b. 1716, living, 1775; m., 10 April, 1744,
   Eleanor Ford.
iii. JOHN TODD, m., 10 June, 1756, Elizabeth Linstead.
iv. NATHAN TODD.
v. SARAH TODD, m. Edward Dorsey (d. 1767).
vi. RUTH TODD, m., 10 Aug. 1733, Michael Dorsey (d. 1777).

6. RICHARD TODD [3] (*Thomas,*[2] *Thomas* [1]) was born about
1676, and died in 1718. He was certainly the younger
brother of Capt. Lancelot, though the proof is rather in-
ferential than direct. In his petition, 24 Sept. 678, Lancelot Todd states that Sarah, the widow of his brother
Thomas, has married a certain Wm. Stafford " who wastes
the orphans' estate." The word " orphans' " is plural, so
that there must have been another son beside Lancelot, and
this son, from all the circumstances of the case, can be no
other than Richard. 4 March 1693/4, he witnessed the will
of John Pettybone of Anne Arundel County, and he also
witnessed the will of Richard Baly, 26 Feb'y 1696, and of
Joseph Pettybone, 10 Sept. 1698. His wife, Margaret,
gives her age as 50 years in a deposition made in 1720
(A. A. Co., I. T. No. 5, 48), so that she was born in 1670
and was therefore some years older than her husband.
The will of " Richard Todd of Westminster Parish, Anne
Arundel County" is dated 10 October 1718, and was proved
10 March 1718/9 (Annapolis, xv, 4). He names in it
his eldest son Richard; his son Lance; his daughters Elizabeth and Mary; his youngest daughter Anne; and his wife
Margaret who is appointed executrix. The dates of birth
&c. given below are from the register of St. Margaret's
Parish, Anne Arundel County. Richard Todd [3] and Margaret his wife had issue:—

i. ELIZABETH TODD,[4] b. 31 Jan'y, 1694.
ii. MARY TODD, b. 9 Nov., 1695
10. iii. RICHARD TODD, b. 15 Oct. 1699; m., 3 March 1727, Mary
   Stinchcomb.
11. iv. LANCELOT TODD, b. 15 Oct., 1701; m., 11 Oct., 1727, Anna Burle.
v. ANNE TODD, b. 25 Sept. 1703.

7. JOHN TODD [3] (*Lancelot,*[2] *Thomas* [1]) inherited by the terms
of his father's will, the home plantation, and half of a

tract called Philk's Rest, the inheritance of his mother.
He lived in St. Margaret's Parish, Anne Arundel County,
and the dates here given are taken from the register of
that parish. John Todd was under 18 years old in 1690,
the date of his father's will, and he died 11 July 1733.
He married, in 1710, Katherine Smith and had issue:—

      i. ISABEL TODD,[4] b. 16 Nov. 1710.
12. ii. LANCELOT TODD, b. 16 Aug., 1713; m., 13 Nov., 1735, Rachel
        Warfield.
13. iii. JOHN TODD, b. 17 Dec. 1715; m. Ruth —.
      iv. ELIZABETH TODD, b. 15 Dec. 1720.
      v. HENRY TODD, b. 5 May, 1723.
      vi. RICHARD TODD, b. 18 Nov., 1726.
      vii. SAMUEL TODD, b. 5 Aug. 1729; m., 1 April, 1755, Ann Aldridge,
        and had a son, Thomas Todd, b. 2 June, 1756.

8. THOMAS TODD [4] (*Lancelot,*[3] *Thomas,*[2] *Thomas* [1]) was apparently the eldest son of Capt. Lancelot Todd. His wife's
name was Sophia, and their children are entered in St.
Margaret's register as follows:—

      i. ELIZABETH TODD,[5] b. 21 Oct. 1731.
      ii. LANCELOT TODD, b. 28 May, 1734.
      iii. RACHEL TODD, b. 2 June, 1736.
      iv. RUTH TODD, b. 25 Sept., 1739.
      v. THOMAS TODD, b. 17 March, 1741.
      vi. PEGGY TODD, b. 1 Nov. 1746.

9. LANCELOT TODD [4] (*Lancelot,*[3] *Thomas,*[2] *Thomas* [1]) was
born in 1716 and was living, aged 59, in 1775 (Chancery,
W. K. No. 1, 830). He married, 10 April 1744, Eleanor
Ford, according to St. Margaret's register, whence the
dates of birth of their children are also derived, and had
issue:—

      i. MARY TODD,[5] b. 15 March, 1744/5.
      ii. SARAH TODD, b. 10 July, 1747.
      iii. JOHN TODD, b. 28 April, 1750.
      iv. LANCELOT TODD, b. 2 Nov., 1754.

10. RICHARD TODD [4] (*Richard,*[3] *Thomas,*[2] *Thomas* [1]) was born
15 Oct. 1699, and married, 3 March 1727, Mary Stinch-
comb. Their marriage is recorded in St. Margaret's
register as also the births of their three children, viz:—

      i. THOMAS TODD,[5] b. 22 Dec., 1727.
      ii. RACHEL TODD, b. 9 June, 1730.
      iii. REZIN TODD, b. 26 Jan'y, 1731.

11. LANCELOT TODD [4] (*Richard,*[3] *Thomas,*[2] *Thomas* [1]) of St. Margaret's Parish, Anne Arundel County, was born 15 Oct. 1701 and married, 11 Oct. 1727, Anna (b. 20 July 1712) daughter of John Burle of Anne Arundel County. The will of John Burle dated 2 June, and proved 1 Sept. 1742 (Annapolis, xxii, 516) mentions his sons John and Stephen, who are appointed executors; his daughter Mary Boon; and his grand children Charles, Margaret, and Ann Todd. The will of Lancelot Todd is dated 12 May, and was proved 19 October, 1742 (Annapolis, xxii, 517). In it he names his son Charles; his daughter Margaret; and his youngest daughter Ann. John Burle Jr. is appointed executor. Lancelot Todd [4] and Anna (Burle) his wife had issue:—

14.   i. CHARLES TODD,[5] b. 31 March, 1729; m., 16 April, 1761, Elizabeth Page.
     ii. ELIZABETH TODD, b. 13 March, 1732.
    iii. MARGARET TODD, b. 13 Feb'y, 1734; m., 13 Aug., 1751, Joshua Merekin.
    iv. ANNA TODD, b. 25 Oct., 1737.
     v. STEPHEN TODD, b. 5 Dec., 1739.

12. LANCELOT TODD [4] (*John,*[3] *Lancelot,*[2] *Thomas* [1]) of Anne Arundel County, was born 16 Aug. 1713, and married in Queen Caroline Parish, Elk Ridge, 13 Nov. 1735, Rachel daughter of Alexander Warfield (d. 1740) and Sarah (Pierpont) his wife. Lancelot Todd [4] and Rachel (Warfield) his wife had issue:—

     i. ALEXANDER TODD,[5] b. 7 Sept., 1736; living, 1775.
     ii. LANCELOT TODD, b. 1 Sept., 1738.
    iii. RICHARD TODD, b. 20 April, 1740.
    iv. VACHEL TODD, b. 28 March, 1742.
     v. THOMAS TODD, b. 5 Oct., 1743.
    vi. SARAH TODD, b. 14 July, 1745; d. 26 Jan'y, 1748/9.
   vii. ACHSAH TODD, b. 12 Feb'y, 1746/7.
  viii. RACHEL TODD, b. 11 Jan'y, 1748/9; d. 26 Jan'y, 1748/9.
    ix. KATHERINE TODD, b. 22 Feb'y, 1749/50.
     x. RACHEL TODD, b. 17 Jan'y, 1752.
    xi. LYDIA TODD, b. 1755.
   xii. NICHOLAS TODD, b. 7 June, 1757.

13. JOHN TODD [4] (*John,*[3] *Lancelot,*[2] *Thomas* [1]) was born 17 Dec. 1715. His wife was named Ruth, and they had issue, as recorded in St. Margaret's register:—

     i. ELIZABETH TODD,[5] b. 17 Nov., 1738.
     ii. RUTH TODD, b. 4 May, 1741.
    iii. RESAN TODD, b. 24 June, 1743.
    iv. DEBORAH TODD, b. 8 Feb'y, 1744/5.
     v. ELY TODD TODD, b. 5 July, 1746.

14. CHARLES TODD [5] (*Lancelot,*[4] *Richard,*[3] *Thomas*[2]), of
Anne Arundel County, was born 31 March 1729, and mar-
ried, 16 April 1761, Elizabeth (b. 1Marhc 1739) daughter
of George and Margaret Page. The will of George Page
of Anne Arundel County is dated 24 Jan'y, and was
proved 17 March, 1768 (Annapolis, xxxvi, 304). He
names in it his daughter Mary Evitts, and his grandchildren George Pecker, Henry Todd, and Richard Todd,
all three under 16. His wife Margaret is constituted
executrix. The will of "Margaret Page, of Anne Arundel County, widow," is dated 9 Feb'y, and was proved 15
March, 1769 (Annapolis, xxxvii, 203). She mentions
her deceased husband George Page; her daughter Mary
Evitts, wife of John Evitts of Annapolis; and her grandsons George Pecker, Henry Todd, and Richard Todd.
Nathan Hammond of Annapolis, Merchant, and Mr. John
Merrikin, of Anne Arundel County, planter, are appointed
executors. According to St. Margaret's register, George
Page died 15 Feb'y 1768, and his widow Margaret 16
Feb'y 1769, while their daughter Elizabeth was born 1
March 1739. Charles Todd [5] and Elizabeth (Page) his
wife had issue:—

  i. HENRY TODD,[6] b. 31 October, 1762.
15. ii. RICHARD TODD, b. 25 Oct., 1764; d. 1790; m. Ann Merrikin.

15. RICHARD TODD [6] (*Charles,*[5] *Lancelot,*[4] *Richard*[3]) was born
25 October 1764 (St. Margaret's), and died in 1790, leav-
ing a will dated 12 Feb'y 1790, and proved 13 Jan'y 1791.
He married, 31 Jan'y 1788, Ann (b. 28 Dec. 1771) daughter of Joseph and Ann Merrikin. She married, secondly,
William Earickson of Ann Arundel County. Richard
Todd [6] and Ann (Merrikin) his wife, had an only child:—

  i. MARGARET TODD,[7] b. 1789; m. Nicholas J. Watkins of Anne
   Arundel County.

WEEMS GENEALOGY.

A contribution to the history of the Weems family is furnished in the record from a Bible originally the property of Gustavus Weems (1779-1852), of Marshes Seat, Anne Arundel County, who was a nephew of " Parson " Mason Locke Weems. The Bible was recently presented to the Enoch Pratt Free Library by Harriette Weems, a descendant of the original

468

owner. Published in 1838, by DeSilver of Philadelphia, it contains in Gustavus Weems' careful hand a full pedigree of the family from Scotch David Weems's firstborn in 1725, down to the death of his own lastborn in 1845—three generations.

Marshes Seat (Marshall Seat, Marches Seat) was the plantation of David Weems I, who in 1731, about ten years after his arrival in the colony, settled at this spot on Herring Bay. Here Mason Locke Weems, youngest of 19 children, was born in 1733. The estate passed to his brother, David Weems II, from whom it descended to Gustavus. In fact, Mrs. Emily E. Ford Skeel, in her superb *Mason Locke Weems, his works and ways,* vol. 2, page 417, cites a letter from Parson Weems to his publishers, Matthew Carey, ordering a shipment of books to be sent to " Mr. Gustavus Weems, care of Francis D. McHenry, Merch^t. County Wharf, Balt^o." This was in 1809. Mrs. Skeel, however, did not identify Gustavus, whose passion for genealogy deserves recognition.

James W. Foster.

Transcript of Family Record in Weems Bible.

No. 1.

The Ages & Death of my Wife's Children
> In the First Marriage viz.

Wm. Weems son of David Weems & Eliz^a. his Wife was born
> the 5th Day of Decr. 1725.

> Was drownded on the 18th March 1751 between Cape good
> hope & St. Helena on a four years voige East India.

John Weems 2nd Son Born March 26th 1727.

> Departed this Life the 28th Nov. 1794 aged 68 years.

David Weems 3rd Son Born Sept. 22nd 1729

> Died 12th March 1845 (sic) 1 Days Illness aged 16 years.

James Weems 4th Son Born May 22nd 1731

> Died 4th Nov. 1784 Aged 53 years.

Lock Weems 5th Son Born Feby 25th 1733

> Died 27th. May 1734 Aged 1 year

Lock Weems 6th Son Born Feby 3rd 1735

Died 16th Mar. 1753 and was burried in London in St.
Andrews Church by Capt. Luke Lane. (?)

Thomas Lane Weems 7th Son Born Feby 24th 1737 (and last)
Died 11th Feby 1779 Aged 42 years.

My Dear and Loving Wife Elizabeth Mother of the above
seven children Departed this Life on 26th June 1738 and
left six of the above Children to Bring up

David Weems 1st.

(Succeeding page)

No. 2.

The Ages and Deaths of my Second Wifes Children as follows 1z

Richd. Weems Son of David and Easter his Wife Born the 20th
Jany 1740.
Died March 10th 1780. Aged 40 years

Ann Weems 2nd Born 29th March 1742
Died June 22nd 1744

Willimina Weems 3rd Born 19th Feby 1744
Died Apl 30 1744

Susanh Weems Born 4th Mar. 1745
Died Oct. 16th 1805

David Weems 5th Do. 22 Feby 1747
Died March 4th 1747

David Weems 6th Do. 31st Mar 1748
Died March 30th 1750

David Weems 7th Do. 8th June 1750
Dead Born

David Weems 8th Do. Augst 1751
Died 22nd Jany 1820 Aged 68 5/12

Willimina Weems 9th 3rd Jany 1754
Died Nov 26th 1783 the Wife of Doct Joseph Mudd

Ester Weems 10th Born 19th Mar 1756
Died 21st Mar 1856

Wm Weems 11th Born 7 Mar. 1758
took his Life with Laudanum

Mason Lock Weems 12th Born Oc^t 1st 1759

Died in Beaufort C^t. South Carrolina May 23rd 1825 Aged 65 7/12

My Dear & Loving Wife Ester Weems Mother of the above 12 Children Died 29th Ap^l 1776, Illness 5 Days, Aged 59

David Weems Father of the above Children and those on the first page Amounting to 19 Died the 5th of May 1779 Aged 73 years

No. 3   G. W.

David Weems and Margeret Harrison

Was Married April 15th 1777

David Weems Son of David and Margeret Weems his Wife Born March 2nd 1778 had the smallpox mups H. Cof and measles, was prest by the Brittish and so often moved at last became a Brittish subject

Gustavus Weems 2nd Son Born Ap^l 2 1779

had the small pox mumps H. Coff and measles & much trouble Died 3 Octob 1852 73"6 mo

Rachel Weems 3rd Born Augst 16th 1780

Married Jesse Ewell May 24th 1804 and Died the 28th May 1817 Leaving 3 Children David Frances & Margaret & was Buried in H. Creek Church yard, Sermond preach't by J^s (?) Reed ye must be Born again 37 year

Sidney Weems 4th Born October 3^d 1782

had the small pox mumps & H cough & measles

George Weems 5th Born May 23rd 1784

had the small pox mumps H Cough & measles

Died 6 March 1853 68" 9 mo

Theodore Weems 6th Born March 9th 1786

Died in Balt^o 4th Jany 1817 Burried in H. Creek Church y^d Funeral Preach't by J^s Reed Acts 8th 9 & 11 v. For he Prayeth. 31 year

Mason Weems 7th Born Jany 20th 1789

Drownded 27th Decr. 1811 swampt Land taken up Jno Grays Landing

Entered H. Creek yd 4th Day Mar. 1811 22

Departed this Life Nov 21st 1793 in the 45 year of her life
Margaret Weems Mother of the above Children after 12
weeks Ilness under which she was supported by divine
grace & bore it with a Christian fortitude she was
resigned to Death for weeks was Looking for the happy
moment when God would take her from time to Eternity.
shee left the world in the full triump of Faith without
a groan or struggle. 23rd Nov she was Entered in H.
Creek C. yard. Sunday 1st Decr 93 Revd Ignatius Pig-
man Preach't her F^{l}. Sermond to a vast concourse of
People from the 100 Psalm 4th v. Enter into his gates
with thanksgiving & into his courts with praise be thank-
full & bless his name.

Gustavus Weems Married to M. Dorcas Gray Oct. 28th, 1806
Past happyly together about 33 years

Margaret J. Weems 1st Born 13th Decr 1807
Departed This Life Ap^{l} 6 1809. 18 Days Illness Aged
1 4/12

David G. Weems 2nd Born Oc^{t} 14 1809
Departed this life on the morning of the 29th of April 1857.
Aged 47 years.

Jane Dorcas Weems 3rd Born Oc^{t}. 27th 1812
Died in 1853

George Gray Weems 4th Born June 4th 1815
Died 16th Decr 1816 10 Days Illness Aged 18 months 12
Days

George Gray Weems 5th Born June 13th 1817
Died 27th Sep^{t} 1824 12 Days Illness aged 7 years 3 mths

Rachel Thompson Weems 6th Born Jany 14th 1821
Died March 7th 1905 at Sherwood Balt Co Md

Theo. Mason Weems 7th & Last Born Decr 21st 1822
Died 6th Ap^{l} 1845 18 Days sickness aged 23 years Enterd
in D.G.W. woods(?) Funerl Preach't By Revd Jos.(?)
Markle(?) from the 11th C. Eclesiastes 9 Verse
In pease with his God
he left this mortal Clod

My Dear & Beloved Wife Dorcas Weems mother of the above Seven Children Departed this Life Sep^t 24th 1839 after 5 months lingring sickness which was born with unflinching resignation and when ask't by the Husband if willing to Die and if in peace with God she answerd in the affirmative her Funerl sermond was Preach't by Revd J. (I. ?) O. Summers(?)/Gust Weems

Died on the 3^d October our (?) Beloved Father Gustavus Weems in his 74 —— one days sickness in hope of Life (?) without alloy D. G. Weems

(Inserted sheet)

The last respect of my ever respected and Dear Parrent to be inroled in this Bibble

On the 22nd Day of Jany 1820 Departed this Life David Weems Father of the before mentioned seven Children aged 68 5/12 years

He was confined to his room & Beed upwards of two months during which time he with perfect resignation bore the chastning hand of Affliction with intire submition sustained by Divine providence he was prepaired and resigned to his will.

In this happy state of mind he left those mondain shores of anxiety & care with a full asshureance of Blissful Eternity praising Jesus in his last expiring moments —— But a few moments before the Spirit made its escape or flight with perfect composure he called his Children to his beedside, then and there admonish't themto live peaceabilly & happily togather, this promis being made he calmly took his leave and fell asleep in the Armes of Sweet Jesus. The next day his funerl sermond was deliverd by the Rev^d Mr. Lewis Stratton in St James's Parrish (a privalage denied my Mother) to a very large and attentive audiance——from these words (Acquaint now thyself with him and be in peace thereby good shall come unto the, this text will be found in Job 22 C & 21st Verce —— after which his remains was deposited in the Churchyard to mingle with its mother Earth. Gustavus Weems.

(Verso of inserted sheet)

Rachel Harrison mother of Margaret Weems Departed this Life Jany 7th 1786. Aged 66 years was Wife to Rich[d] Harrison was the mother of 12 Children leaving ten behind her.

Dolly Chew Daughter of Rachel Harrisons and Wife to Sam[l] Loyed Chew Departed this Life Nov 6th 1791 Died happy in the Lord

Dolly Chew Daughter of Rich[d] & Rachel Harrison was born 17th Feby 1758

Margaret Weems Daughter of Rachel Harrison and Richard Harrison was Born May 17th 1753

Geo. Wallace a Scotchman came to this County the year 1774 Served his time with Weems & Morton and lived a great part of his time in our Family and Died in my House the 24th Day May 1803 Aged about 57 years. David Weems

(Succeeding Page)

Departed this Life Wm Hoopes Sep[t] 3rd 1842 about 2 years Declining until the arrow of Death Summoned him away after Seven Days Illness Died —— aged about 58 years, 33 of that he lived in my Family and has often said that Gustavus and Dorcas Weems had done more for him than all his Relations put together, when sinking was ask't if he was willing to Die as far as could be understood he assented, I pray God he was prepaired and his spirit may be at Rest, peace to his ashes —— says Gustavus Weems.

A hard working and as industrious Man ⎫ Gustavus Weems.
Cannot be found easily in all the Land ⎭

SOME OLD BIBLE RECORDS OF THE WEST FAMILY OF VIRGINIA.

FRANCIS B. CULVER.

Hidden away between the covers of old family Bibles, belonging to the descendants of ancient and distinguished families of Colonial Maryland and Virginia, are found many interesting records. Crumbling with age and fast disappearing through the lapse of time, as families move hither and thither, sometimes far from the homes of their ancestors, these old records should be systematically preserved through the coöperation of all those who are really of one common family by reason of ties of kindred and consanguinity.

It is hoped that a concerted movement may be inaugurated to preserve in a permanent and accessible form these valuable records, so precious to their possessors.

In a " Cambridge " Bible, printed by John Hayes, " printer to the University," in the year 1680, the following entries were found. On a page of this bible, and inscribed in large characters, is this entry: " Catherine West—her bible given her by Her Mother—Borne the 6th day of May, 1677." It was written so long ago that the ink has almost eaten through the page.

This valuable book is the property of Mrs. Tabitha Joynes Hance, of Baltimore, whose niece, Miss Helen Goodwyn Joynes, kindly permitted the contributor to transcribe the entries which are given hereunder.

WEST

Lt. Coll John West departed this Life the 27th day of May Anno Dom. 1703.

Mrs. Matild. West departed this Life the 3d day of Jany. Anno Dom. 1721.

SNEAD

John Snead was born 7th Jany. 1707:

Thos Snead was born 21st Decemr 1708:

Sons to Chs Snead.

Charles Snead and Catharine was married the 7th Day of January Anno Dom. 1711.

Huldah Snead was borne ye first day of March Ano Dom. 1712/13 & was Christianed ye 15th of ye same.

Huldah Snead departed this Life ye 30th day of Aprill Anno Dom. 1713.

Charles Snead was borne ye 26th of August Anno Dom. 1714.

Charles Snead departed this Life Feby. ye 18th 1720.

John Snead was borne ye 3^d day of Feby. Anno Dom. 1715 & Christianed March ye 18th.

Smith Snead was borne Jany. ye 13th, 1718.

Charles Snead ye second was borne ye 13th day of November 1723.

Charles Snead ye second departed this Life Feby. ye 23^d 1724.

Capt. Charles Snead the Elder departed this Life April the 30th 1727.

Catharine Snead departed this Life February the 19th 1750.

SNEAD

Children of Mr. John Snead, Accomac:

Charles Snead was Bornd the 26th day of December Anno Dom. 1741.

John Snead was Bornd the 10th day of March Anno Dom. 1743.

John Snead departed this Life March ye 23rd Anno Dom. 1777.

Anne Snead was Bornd 1st day of Sept. Anno Dom. 1746.

Mary Snead was Bornd ye 25th day of December Anno Dom. 1749.

Thomas Snead was Bornd ye 28th day of November Anno Dom. 1752.

Catherine Snead was Bornd ye 25th day of July Anno Dom. 1756.

Scarborough Snead was Bornd ye 23rd day of November Anno Dom. 1758.

Tully Snead was Bornd ye 10th day of July on Sunday evening Anno Dom. 1763.

Mrs. Catharine Snead departed this Life the 19th of February Anno Dom. 1750.

John Snead departed this Life the 15th day of Sept. Anno Dom. 1780.

Scarborough Snead departed this Life the 7th day of December Anno Dom. 1780.

Thomas Snead son of John departed this Life March the 20th Anno Dom. 1787.

WISE

Children to Jno. Wise:

John Wise was born 8th March 1745.

Solomon Wise was born 6th June 1748.

William Wise was born 16th Novr 1750.

Eliza Wise was born 11th Septmr 1754.

Henry Wise was born 6th Feby. 1756.

Charles Wise was born 19th June 1759.

Peggy Wise was born 11th Novr 1761.

Geo. Wise was born 8th Octor 1765.

Nancy Wise was born 17th March 1769.

Peggy Wise, mother to the aforesd children was bornd 5th day of Septem. 1726.

Nancy S. Wise, daughter of Solo Wise & Mary his wife departed this Life March 10th 1806.

Solo. Wise departed this Life the 25th Jany. 1820.

WISE

Trefania Wise was born the 11th day of April Anno 1777.

John Wise was born the 5th day of September 1780: departed this Life the 12 of October.

Peggy Wise was born July the 6th day 1786.

Nancy Selmon Wise was born July 13th 1789.

Polly Wise was born Febry the 18th 1783.

Margaret Wise departed this Life 30th November 1781.

John Wise departed this Life 8th December 1781.

SPARROW

John Sparrow was born December ye 17th 1706 about 3 o'clock in ye afternonon on a Wednesday.

Elizabeth Sparrow was borne September ye 12th 1708 about 5 o'clock in ye afternoon on a Sunday.

WINCHESTER—OWENS—OWINGS—PRICE, AND ALLIED FAMILIES.

By FERDINAND B. FOCKE.

WILLIAM WINCHESTER, maybe of the Winchester family of London and Kent, England, was born December 22, 1710. Migrated to America. Arrived at Annapolis, Maryland, March 6, 1729, in the ship *Hume*. Captain Daniel Russell, William Black (owner). He took up the occupation of Surveyor, and purchased in Frederick Co., now Carroll, about 1,000 acres, a highly cultivated farm, called " White Level." He laid out the town of Winchester on this land. Later by an act of Assembly, the name was changed to Westminster, after his home in England, as there was a Winchester (a county seat) across the line in Frederick Co., Va., which at that time joined Frederick Co., Md., Westminister is the county seat of Carroll Co., and was founded by William Winchester in 1764, incorporated in 1830, erected into a city by act of Assembly, February, 1850. William was a public spirited man and leader in all patriotic work. His name is found in the Muster Rolls. Captain Thomas Norris' Co. for 30 days, acting as Company's clerk, served in 1758 in French and Indian War.

Ref: *Maryland Historical Magazine*, Vol. 9, p. 349, Vol. 11, p. 174, Scharf's *History of Maryland*, Vol. 2, Pp. 155-174.

He served on a committee, among the number whose names are recorded are Charles Beatty, William Winchester, Basil Dorsey, John Lawrence, " of observation and carry out resolves of the American Congress and Provincial convention into execution "; the committee to raise $10,000 for the purchase of arms and ammunition, also was resolved to join with the other colonies to send relief to the poor and distressed inhabitants of Boston. He gave three sons to the Continental Army— James, George, and William. Their services to follow. He married, July 22, 1747, Lydia Richards, born August 4, 1727, died at " White Level " February 19, 1809. William died at his country seat, September 2, 1790. William and his wife are both buried in the Church-yard at Westminster, near the church which he helped to build.

Lydia, his wife, was the daughter of Edward Richards and wife Mary. One authority says, Kent Co. J, Mason Campbell says, on Choptank River. In Richards' will, September 22, 1755, he mentioned his wife Mary and daughter Lydia Winchester whose portion was one ewe and lamb. He had a large family, and left a 100 acre farm in Baltimore Co. His will is on file at Annapolis and a copy is in Baltimore City Court House.

Issue: William Winchester and wife Lydia.

(1) Catherine Winchester, born November 2, 1748, died October 6, 1815, married Edward Hotchkiss. Left Issue.

(2) William Winchester (2), born December 1, 1750, died April 24, 1812, married Mary Parks.
Issue to follow.

(3) James Winchester, born February 6, 1752, died July 27, 1826, married Susan Black.

(4) Mary Winchester, born October 17, 1755, died October 31, 1799, married ———— Roberts.

(5) George Winchester, born March 6, 1757, died July 9, 1794, not married.

(6) Richard Winchester, born April 7, 1759, died June 20, 1822, buried in Kentucky. Married Rebecca Lawrence of Baltimore Co. Md.

(7) Stephen Winchester, born May 30, 1761, died April 17, 1815, buried in Tennessee. Married Sally Howard of Baltimore Co., Md.

(8) Elizabeth Winchester, born August 19, 1763, died June 12, 1847, unmarried.

(9) Lydia Winchester, born December 27, 1766, died April 19, 1849, buried at old grave-yard, Westminster. Unmarried.

(10) David Winchester, born April 10, 1769, died January 13, 1835, unmarried. One of those appointed to receive subscriptions for the erection of the Washington Monument in Baltimore.

Ref: *Winchester Notes* by Fannie Winchester Hochkiss, p. 319.

I shall digress from the direct line to give the Revolutionary War Records of James and George, 3rd and 5th children of William Winchester. In 1776, these two boys enlisted as Privates in 3rd Maryland Regiment, Captain Nathaniel Gist, which was part of George Washington's Army. Both were promoted for bravery. James was Lieutenant in 1778, George in 1779. At the battle of Long Island, August 1776, James was wounded and taken prisoner, and confined in a British Prison ship off New York. Being exchanged, he joined the regiment of Gen. Nathaniel Green, was appointed Lieutenant, Company 8, in 1778, and Captain in 1782. He served until the close of the war. His brother George, served in the same regiment. They moved to Sumner Co., Tenn. in 1785, where they made records in Military and Civil History of Tennessee. George was killed near Knoxville, and scalped by the Indians.

James Winchester was made Brigadier-General during the war 1812. He was in command at the battle of the River Raisin; his army was defeated, and General Winchester was taken to Quebec as prisoner. After the war he returned to Tennessee. Some authorities give him credit for having named Memphis. Be that as it may, he did wield great influence in the State, being only surpassed in that score by Andrew Jackson and John Overton. James Winchester was President of the first Senate of Tennessee while his son Marcus B. was the first Mayor of Memphis. General Winchester died at " Cragfont " his family seat near Gallatin, Tennessee, in 1826.

Ref: *Tennessee Historical Magazine*, June, 1915.

William Winchester (2), son of William and Lydia, was born in Carroll Co., December 1, 1750, died in Baltimore, April 24, 1812. Interred in St. Paul burial ground. In the issue of the Baltimore *American,* April 25, 1812,—" Departed his life yesterday p. m., William Winchester, in the 62nd year of his age. His friends and acquaintances are requested to attend his funeral this afternoon at 3 p. m. from his late residence on North Howard Street. There they will walk in procession to the place of interment." William married, October 30, 1771, Mary Parks, born 1753, died at Westminster, Md., October 14, 1821, buried in Westminster Church Grave-yard. William was commissioned Justice of the Peace for Frederick Co. 1778, 1779, 1780, 1783. Signed as a member of the Association of Freeman of Frederick Co., October 1775, December 20, 1776.

Commissioned 1st Lieutenant, Captain David Moore's Co., January 10, 1777; was commissioned January 17, 1777, 1st Lieutenant in Linganore Battalion, Frederick Co. Militia. William was a leading merchant of Baltimore and a man of wealth; first President of the Union Bank of Maryland in 1804, from its organization until his decease. Also one of the original Directors in Bank of Baltimore 1795. Delegate to Assembly 1794. Elector of Senate for City 1796. In his will of March 18, 1812, mentions all his children and the five children of his son George and two of James. He gave to William and George the farm in Frederick Co. where they may reside to pay his debts to Brother David Winchester. The baptism records of five of his children are in St. Pâul Church records.

Ref: Commission Book, Maryland Historical Society, Scharf's *History of Maryland*, Vol. 2, c. 155, *Maryland Historical Magazine*, Vol. 2, p. 174, *Archives of Maryland*, Vol. 12, p. 16.

Issue: William Winchester (2) and wife Mary Parks. Possibly the daughter of Andrew Parks.

(1) James Winchester, born 1772, died 1806. Judge U. S. Circuit, at age of 28. Married Sarah Owings.
Issue: Samuel.
Ann.

(2) Lydia Winchester, born 1774, died 1821, married ———— Moore.
Issue: Maria.

(3) Mary Winchester, born 1775, died 1855, married David Armour of Tennessee.
Issue: James Armour.
Janet Armour.

(4) Sally Winchester, born 1777, died 1805.

(5) Catherine Winchester, born 1779, married ———— Wellman of Baltimore.
Issue: James.
William.
Henry.

(6) William Winchester (3), born 1781, died 1864, married May 5, 1814, Henrietta Cromwell of Pennsylvania, daughter of Thomas Cromwell.
Issue: 8 children.

(7) George Winchester, born 1783, died 1784.

(8) Rebecca Winchester, born 1785, died 1812, married James Campbell.
Issue: James Mason Campbell.
Mary Campbell, married ———— Murdoch.

(9) George Winchester, born 1787, died 1840, married Ann Owings.
Issue to follow.

(10) David Winchester, born 1789, died 1844, married Sally Forney.
    ISSUE: Sarah.
           Burrill.
           William.
           George.
(11) Charles Winchester, born 1795, died 1824, married Betsy Pannell.
    ISSUE: Lycurgus.
           Sarah.
           Mary.
(12) Lycurgus Winchester, born 1797, died 1815.

George Winchester, 9th child of William and wife Mary Parks, was born October 1, 1787, died November 2, 1840. He surveyed the Chesapeake and Ohio Canal, was one of the Presidential Electors for John Quincy Adams. He was an eminent lawyer, as told by Scharf and other historians; was the first President of the Baltimore and Susquehannah Railroad, chartered in 1828 (now the Northern Central R. R.). He had so much faith in the success of the railroad that he invested freely and lost heavily. His residence was Bolton, where the 5th Regiment Armory now stands. He gave the property called Bolton Yard to the Railroad for a depot, down Mt. Royal Ave. where the Baltimore & Ohio Railroad now stands, to Preston Street. The City of Baltimore bought from the Northern Central Railroad that portion of the property for three hundred and thirty-three thousand dollars, that George Winchester had given the Railroad. He married May 1, 1809, Ann Owings, born December, 1785, died 18—, daughter of Samuel Owings and Deborah Lynch. He married a second time, December 18, 1827, Marie Campbell Ridgely, widow of Charles Ridgely of Hampton. Marie Campbell Ridgely died November 15, 1853.

The pedigree of Ann Owings will follow.

    ISSUE: George Winchester and Ann Owings.
      (1) Mary Winchester, born 1810, married Wm. Moale of Baltimore.
      (2) William Winchester, born 1813, died 1834.
      (3) Sarah Winchester, born 1816, died 1821.
      (4) Andrew Parks Winchester, born 1817, died 1875.
      (5) Samuel Owings Winchester, born 1819, died 1820.

(6) John Marshall Winchester, born October 10, 1821, died Octo-
ber 11, 1877, married Anne G. Price of Wilmington, Del-
aware.
Record to follow.
ISSUE: George Winchester and 2nd wife, Mary Campbell Ridgely.
Louise Winchester, born 1828.
Elizabeth Campbell Winchester, born 1830, married Dr. Thomas
Murdoch.

John Marshall Winchester, 4th child of George Winchester
and wife Ann Owings, was born October 10, 1821, and died
October 11, 1877, married November 13, 1856, Ann Gordon
Price, born July 19, 1834, died July 1, 1923, daughter of
James Edward Price and wife Catharine (Sharp) Gordon.
The Price family record to follow.

John Marshall was named for Chief Justice Marshall who
was an intimate friend of his father, George Winchester. John
Marshall was a man of literary attainments, Shakespearian
Scholar, and a charm of character that made him loved by a
host of close friends. John Marshall Winchester and William
Gilmor Hoffman were partners in the stock brokerage business.
He was connected with the Chesapeake Bank, Superintendent of
the Ashland Iron Co., their property at Elm's Farm. Secretary of the Fireman's Insurance Co. at time of death.

ISSUE: John Marshall Winchester and wife Ann Gordon Price.
(1) Maria Winchester, born November 11, 1857, died March 8, 1928.
(2) James Price Winchester, born January 14, 1859.
(3) John Gordon Winchester, born September 7, 1860, died April 20,
1866.
(4) George Winchester, born February 4, 1862, died April 20, 1882.
(5) Andrew Parks Winchester, born April 17, 1865, died February 24,
1872.
(6) Sydney Winchester, born November 6, 1866.
(7) Marshall Winchester, born December 14, 1868, married Margaret
Tarleton.
Issue to follow.
(8) Lycurgus Winchester, born April 5, 1874, died August 2, 1906, married April 3, 1904, Katharine Griswold Pratt of N. Y.
ISSUE: Hope Gordon Winchester.
Katharine Lycurgus Winchester.

Marshall (1) Winchester, 7th child of John Marshall and

balance to John James and wife. Richard Owens and Wife Ann left several sons.

> Joseph who married Susanna 1690, left 4 children.
> Richard who married Rachel Beall or Bale about 1690.
> Robert, will 1678.
> William, Somerset Co., will 1690.

Richard Owens 2nd was executor of his father's Estate in 1692-1693, Trustee 1703-1705, had contention and dissensions with the other heirs, and declared his name should be no longer spelt Owens but Owings. He relinquished all claim to his father's Estate and moved with his wife Rachel to Baltimore Co. He patented lands at Elk Ridge, The Valley of Owings, Owings Adventure, the last lying on each side of Reisterstown Road, 10 miles from Baltimore extending from Pikesville to Mrs. Bell's property adjoining. Richard Owings will probated April 8, 1726.

The other Owens moved West and South and are very numerous.

Richard and Rachel gradually moved North of Patapsco River and owned many farms. They had six sons and three daughters.

1. Richard born 1692, married Sarah Scutt.
2. Rachel born 1694, married John Wilmot.
3. Henry born 1696, married Hannah ———, March 27, 1736.
4. John born 1798, married ———.
5. Robert born 1700, married Rachel. (Married Hannah, June 22, 1738.)
6. Samuel born 1702, married Urath Randall.
7. Joshua born 1704, married Mary Cockey, had daughter named Marcella.
8. Ellenor born 1706, married John Long, March 8, 1735.
9. Ruth born 1708, married Edward Ostler, March 21, 1735.

Samuel moved to his wife's property in the Green Spring Valley and Green Spring Branch, some of the buildings are now in good condition. The Owens were Quakers.

Ref: Records of the Owens family owned by Judge Albert S. J. Owens, compiled by Charles T. Cockey, History of St. Thomas Church, Baltimore Co., History of Anne Arundel Co. and Howard County by Warfield.

Samuel Owings, whose name appears on earliest records of St. Thomas' Parish, was the son of Richard and Rachel Owings. He was born April 1, 1702, in a stone house of two rooms on first and second floors, Green Spring Punch, in Green Spring Valley. The cottage was occupied from 1700 to 1870 by successive generations of Owings, being enlarged from time to time. On January 1, 1729, Samuel was married to Urath Randall, born January 1, 1713—married on her 16th birthday. She was the daughter of Thomas Randall and wife Hannah Bale, and granddaughter of Christopher Randall of Severn River who died 1684, and wife Joanna. The Randall Bible record is most complete and exact.

Samuel Owings was one of the Commissioners under the Act of the Assembly of 1741 to purchase a site for St. Thomas' Church, and received subscriptions toward the building of the same. He was one of the vestry in 1750-52-53-57, and died January 2, 1775. He was representative, Maryland Assembly 1758-1761; Justice of Peace 1744-1768. In his will (he is called Gent.), November 16, 1772, to wife Urath he gave seven negroes and life interest as long as she remained a widow, then to his children the balance of his estate. In Urath's will of November 26, 1792, she gave to Samuel his father's cane and to granddaughter, Urath Owings, she gave 12 pictures.

The first representative of the Owings family in Baltimore Co. was Samuel Owings, son of Richard and Rachel Owings, born April 1, 1702, married January 1, 1729, and died 1775 at the age of 73 years.

Ref: *History of Baltimore City and County*, by Scharf, p. 862, *Anne Arundel and Howard Co.* by Warfield.

IssuE: Samuel Owings and wife Urath Randall.

(1) Bale Owings, born May 9, 1731.
(2) Samuel Owings, born August 17, 1733, married 1765, Deborah Lynch.
(3) Thomas Owings, born October 18, 1740.
(4) Hannah Owings, born April 17, 1742, died June 2, 1745.
(5) Christopher Owings, born February 16, 1744.
(6) Richard Owings, born August 26, 1746, died September 28, 1747.
(7) Helen Owings, born 1748.

(8) Richard Owings, born July 16, 1749.

(9) Hannah, born January 27, 1751, died 1755.

(10) Rebecca Owings, born October 21, 1755.

Samuel Owings (2), son of Samuel and wife Urath, was born August 17, 1733, and died June 4, 1803, married October 6, 1765 to Deborah Lynch, daughter of William Lynch and wife Eleanor (Dorsey) Todd, widow Thomas Todd. Samuel Junior and wife Deborah went to live in a small stone and frame house, still standing in 1898. Samuel afterwards built a brick dwelling which he called " Ulm," and which stood for upper, lower and middle mills, three mills which he owned. He was suspected of leaning towards the Tories. There are 29 grants of land recorded in his name, of 13,891 acres in Anne Arundel, Baltimore, and Frederick Counties and a Shipping House in Baltimore Town. Much around Frederick. Samuel gave four acres where the Rectory of St. Thomas' now stands and sold 30 acres at $20.00 an acre for the Church. He was Vestryman 1792-1802. Represented Baltimore Co. 1771, Justice and County Commissioner 1768-1775; Lieutenant-Colonel 1777; Delegate to Legislature 1786. In his will of May 7, 1803, he mentions his wife Deborah and his 7th child Ann and her husband George Winchester. Ann was given 1,000 pounds. In the will of Deborah Owings, widow of Samuel, of November 26, 1810, she mentions Ann, wife of George Winchester to whom she gave $500, also Sarah, wife of James Winchester.

ISSUE: Samuel Owings (2) and wife Deborah Lynch.

(1) William Owings, born May 1766, married Ann Henderson.

(2) Urath Owings, born February 22, 1769, married John Cromwell.

(3) Samuel Owings, born April 3, 1770, married Ruth Cockey.

(4) Eleanor Owings, born February 7, 1772, died October 29, 1853, married Thomas Moale March 21, 1793.

(5) Sarah Owings, born December 25, 1773, married March 21, 1793, James Winchester.

(6) Rebecca, born January 12, 1776. Single.

(7) Deborah Owings, born November 12, 1777, married Peter Hoffman.

(8) Frances Owings, born September 30, 1779, married Robert North Moale, July 2, 1801.

(9) Rachel Owings, born August 27, 1781, died October 10, 1782.

(10) Mary Owings, born March 29, 1784, married Richard Cromwell.

(11) Ann Owings, born December 20, 1785, married George Winchester.

(12) Beale Owings, born November 17, 1791, married Eleanor McGruder.

Ann Owings, daughter of Samuel Owings, Jr. and wife Deborah Lynch, was born October 1st, 1787, died ———, married May 1, 1809 George Winchester of Baltimore, son of William and wife Mary Parks.

Issue, given in Winchester record.

RANDALL FAMILY.

Christopher Randall of Severn River 1675 and wife, widow Joanna Norman left two sons, Thomas and Christopher, both of whom settled in Baltimore Co. This family founded Randallstown in Baltimore Co. and were land-holders for years in that vicinity. Christopher Sr. was among the early land-holders of North Severn. He owned 3 estates, Randall's Range, Randall's Fancy, and Randall's Purchase. His will mentions his wife Joanna and Richard Owings, brother-in-law of Thomas Randall.

Thomas Randall was born in Baltimore Co. in 16—, died 1722. He married in 1707 Hannah Bale, born after 1665, will dated May 11, 1727. They were children of —— Bale, Merchant, will 1704, buried St. George Parish, Harford Co. and Urath (Carnell) 2nd husband, living in 1720. In the will of Urath Bale, she names her aunt Hannah Randall. Hannah Bale became the wife of Thomas Randall who died in 1722. In her will of 1727, she mentions her son Christopher and Urath, wife of Samuel Owings, Thomas Bale, born 1664, married Sarah Gibson, Hannah Randall, administrator Mr. Thomas Randall, October 6, 1723, he left 285 pounds. Hannah left in will February 19, 1732, to Samuel Owings in right of his wife Urath, daughter of deceased, from her father, portion of 74 pounds. In Anthony Bale, Gent, will April 16, 1720—" to my sister Hannah Randall, Plant at Patapsco, and my wife Anne Bale.

DORSEY FAMILY.

Edward Dorsey, born 1625, wife Martha, came to Maryland in 1657, was granted a tract in Anne Arundel Co. (he was a boatwright) of 400 acres, transferred in 1667 to Colonel Edward Dorsey. He came with Captain Robert Bullan in 1661. Colonel Edward was son and heir of the first Edward, the emigrant mentioned above. John and Caleb Dorsey patented a plantation called Hockley in the Hole supposed to contain 400 acres, but in 1683 it was surveyed for John Dorsey and contained 843 acres, the whole then in possession of Caleb Dorsey. Hon. John Dorsey was born in 1658, died 1714. He came in possession of Hockley in 1683. He married 1680, Pleasance Ely, and took up a tract of land at Elk Ridge, the " Isle of Ely." His widow married a 2nd time Nov. 30, 1722, Robert Wainwright. Hon. John Dorsey was Commissioned for the development of Annapolis, Anne Arundel Co., Md., 1694; Burgess 1692, 1701, 1703; member Private Council 1710, 1715; will March 22, 1714.

ISSUE: Hon. John Dorsey and wife Pleasance Ely.
  Caleb, married Eleanor Warfield.
  Edward
  Deborah, married Charles Ridgely, died 1705.

Hon. John Dorsey moved to Baltimore Co. In his will he gives to his wife Pleasance one-third of his Estate, also choice of estate at South River or dwelling on Elk Ridge. To two grandsons, Samuel and Richard of Caleb his son, the plantation called South River Quarter, it being the remainder of a tract given to his son Caleb.

Caleb Dorsey, born Nov. 11, 1685, of Hockley, married Eleanor Warfield Aug. 24, 1704, daughter of Richard Warfield and Eleanor (Browne) Dorsey. Will dated Nov. 11, 1742. He came into the possession of the whole estate.

Ref: The Dorsey Chart at Maryland Historical Society, by H. A. Browne, and Howard Co., by Warfield.

Eleanor Dorsey, daughter of Caleb and Eleanor Warfield

was born March 4, 1715, died October 16, 1760. She married
1st Thomas Todd 1730, of Todd Neck of Baltimore Co. Their
only son was Thomas 5th, who left four sons. Mrs. Todd married 2nd time William Lynch, September 6, 1740 (Born 1709-
Died 1752), son of Robuck Lynch. He moved near Pikesville.
Their daughter Deborah married Samuel Owings of Samuel
and Urath Randall. The remaining heirs of Caleb and Eleanor
will be found in Howard Co. In her father's and mother's will,
no mention of Eleanor is made, but her children are given
money.

Robuck Lynch of Baltimore County father of above mentioned William Lynch was Heir at Law of Marcus Lynch
Gallaway, Ireland. Robuck died 1716.

Richard Warfield settled near Annapolis 1639 He came
among them in 1662, located west of Crownsville, "in the
woods." His estate reached back to Round Bay on the
Severn. He owned farms "Warfield Rights," "Increase,"
"Hope" etc. He was the first vestryman of St. Thomas'
Church 1669. In 1670, he married Eleanor, heiress of Captain
John Browne. She inherited "Hope" and "Increase" in
1689. Richard signed as a militia Officer an address of allegiance to King William. He died at an advanced age in 1703-04.
In his will, he mentions his heirs, John, Richard, Alexander,
Benjamin, Rachel, Mary, and Eleanor the prospective bride of
Caleb Dorsey. Captain John Browne, father of Eleanor, with
his brother Peregrine, ran two best equipped merchant trans-
ports between Annapolis and London. Capt. Browne obtained
a warrant from Philip Calvert for 500 acres of land dated
January 16, 1659. The Browne's used upon an original will
the seal of a stork, probably, heraldic. They were closely allied
to Robert Proctor who held the port of Annapolis then known
as "Proctor's Landing."

PRICE FAMILY.

William Price was of Wales, early in the 17th Century. He settled in Kent Co., Maryland with two sons, William and Thomas. They owned a tract of land in the east side of Elk River called the " Dividings " of 600 acres, bought May 27, 1661. " Price Venture " on the west side of the Elk, also " Price Forest " and " Woodlawn Neck."

The eldest son William (2) was born 1626 and married Margaret ———. He sold " Price Forest." His oldest son William (3), a church warden of St. Stephen's Church, Cecil Co., Md., married in 1701 Mary Hyland, daughter of Colonel John Hyland from Labadeen, England, and wife Mary Dorrington. Colonel Hyland had land surveyed for him in 1677, lived at Elkton, and died January 17, 1695.

ISSUE: William (3) and Mary (Dorrington) Hyland.

> Richard.
> William (4).
> Andrew, born November 17, 1704.

Issue to follow:

> Hyland
> John
> Rebecca

Andrew Price, 3rd son of William Price and wife Mary Hyland, was born November 17, 1704, married by Rev. John Winston of St. Stephen's Church, Cecil Co., June 1725, to Elizabeth Perry.

ISSUE: Andrew Price and Elizabeth Perry.

(1) James Price, born March 31, 1727.
(2) Andrew Price, born January 20, 1729.
(3) Richard Price, born September 30, 1735.
(4) Rachel Price, born April 29, 1738.
(5) John Hyland Price, born April 22, 1744.

John Hyland Price, son of Andrew Price and wife Elizabeth Perry, was born April 22, 1744, died ———, married Rachel Benson, daughter of Benjamin Benson of Cecil Co. and Mary

Ann his wife. Benjamin was the son of Daniel Benson and wife Mary, and grandson of Daniel Benson and Mary.

ISSUE: Benson
 Hyland
 Benjamin
 Isaac
 James

Issue to follow:
 Spencer
 Elizabeth
 Sarah
 Rachel

James Price, son of John Hyland and Rachel (Benson) Price, was born in Kent Co., Md. in 1776, died in Wilmington, Del., on June 10, 1840. He married, June 12, 1802, Margaret Tatnall, born August 23, 1767, died March 21, 1841, daughter of Joseph and Elizabeth (Lea) Tatnall (Line to follow). James Price was the first President of the Union Bank of Delaware 1839, second President, Philadelphia, Wilmington and Baltimore Railway in 1837.

ISSUE: James Price and wife Margaret Tatnall.

(1) Joseph Tatnall, born May 27, 1805, died June 2, 1867, married Matilda Louisa Sanderson.
(2) John Hyland, born Jan. 11, 1804, died Dec. 25, 1866, married 1st. Margaretta Stothart, 2nd Helen Marr Gordon.
(3) James Edward, married Catharine Gordon, Nov. 25, 1833.
(4) Mary Thomas Price, born April 20, 1807, married April 20, 1826, Edmond Canby.

Issue to follow.

James Edward Price, son of James Price and wife Margaret Tatnall, was born at Harmony Mills near Wilmington, Del., Aug. 8, 1809, died July 25, 1898, married November 2, 1833, Catharine Gordon, born June 6, 1810, died July 20, 1885. Catharine was the daughter of John Gordon of Kent Co., Del. and Ann Catharine Sharp.

ISSUE: James Edward Price and wife Catharine Gordon.

(1) Ann Gordon Price, born July 19, 1834, died July 1st, 1923, married Nov. 13, 1856, John Marshall Winchester, Baltimore, Md.

(2) Margaret Tatnall Price, born April 15, 1836, died 1919, married
   April 24, 1861, Josiah Lee Johnston, Baltimore, Md.
(3) William Gordon Price, born May 2, 1838, died 1856.
(4) Mary Price, born Nov. 15, 1840, living in 1930, married Sept. 21,
   1864, Brigadier-General John Campbell, Cold Spring, New York.
(5) James Edward Price, Jr., born Feb. 15, 1842, married Nov. 25, 1865,
   Mary Pope Martin.
(6) Katharine Gordon Price, born Sept. 13, 1843, living 1930, married
   April 30, 1878, William Graham Bowdoin.
(7) Sydney Price, born Feb. 10, 1851, died 1924.

Issue of above seven children in possession of George Winchester of Wilmington, Del.

Ann Gordon Price, daughter of James Edward Price and wife Catharine Gordon was born Wilmington July 19, 1834, died July 1, 1923, married John Marshall Winchester of Baltimore.

Issue in the Winchester record.

HYLAND FAMILY.

In October 1677 " John and Mary's Highland " a tract of land of 1050 acres on west side of Elk River was surveyed for Col. John Hyland of Labadeen, England, who settled at Elk Neck, Cecil Co., Md. He also owned " Arundell," and " Triumph," a tract of 600 acres. The " Highlands " over 2,000 acres together with " John and Mary's Highland," constituted a part of St. Johns Manor, Elk River. Col. Hyland married Mary Dorrington, and died January 17, 1695, leaving two sons, John, and Nicholas, and a daughter Mary, who married William Price.

The Hylands of Elk Neck were once one of the most numerous families of Cecil County. They were descended from two brothers John and Nicholas Hyland. John was a Colonel in the British Army who had resigned because of some difficulty over his coat of arms.

Col. Hyland emigrated to Maryland during the Restoration period. Not being able to obtain his grant of land there, he went to Pennsylvania where he received 1,000 acres. He later ac-

quired property in New York State, and finally, when William
and Mary acceded to the throne was able to take up his grants
in Maryland.

His home place called "Harmony Hall" was occupied by
several generations of the Hyland family. The most important
of these occupants was Stephen Hyland who was Colonel of a
Maryland Regiment in the Revolutionary War.

Nicholas Hyland at first took up land adjoining that of his
brother, Col. John Hyland. Later he took up a large tract
along the Susquehanna where Port Deposit now stands. He
died in 1719. His Sons, Nicholas and John, according to their
Father's will were to be brought up in accordance with the
strictest rules of the Church of England.

Nicholas Hyland II was a member of the House of Delegates
1751-1766.

Robert Tatnall married, and died in England 1715. His
widow sailed from Bristol, England 1725, and settled in Darby,
Pa., with five children.

Edward Tatnall, the eldest son, was born in England about
1704, and died January 7, 1790. He settled in Wilmington,
Del., 1735, with his brother-in-law, William Shipley, and they
together were among those to incorporate the market there.
Edward was married in 1735 at London Grove Friends Meeting House, Chester Co., Pa. to Elizabeth Pennock, daughter
of Joseph and Mary (Levis) Pennock.

Joseph Tatnall, son of Edward and Elizabeth Pennock Tatnall, born 1740, and died at Brandywine Village in 1813. He
was the original owner of the flour mills at Brandywine Village
and was the most prominent miller of his time. He was first
President of National Bank of Delaware 1795. He left an
estate of $250,000.00. He was one of the town's most influ-
ential citizens. His house still standing in 1803 on Market
St., built in 1770. This house was the headquarters for
General Washington and Wayne during their stops in Wilmington. Joseph with his son-in-law, Thomas Lea, built a mill
on the north side, and several mills on the south side, which
were bought by James Price from his father-in-law.

Joseph married April 11, 1765, Elizabeth Lea, born January 15, 1744-5, daughter of James and Margaret (Marshall) Lea. On January 31, 1765, his daughter Margaret married 1st Isaac Starr of Philadelphia and had issue Isaac, and Elizabeth Tatnall Starr; married 2nd time James Price, June 12, 1802.

ISSUE: James Price, m. Margaret (Lea) Tatnall.
> John Hyland Price
> Joseph Tatnall Price
> James Edward Price
> Elizabeth Price

LEA FAMILY.

Baldwin Lea born 1550 was church worden. Dauntsey, County Wilts, England 1609. He married 1570 Elynor Dench, daughter of Thomas and Elizabeth (Knight) Dench of Longdon, County Worcester. She died in 1622.

George Lea, 1599-1640, of Christian Malford Wilts, son of Baldwyn and Elynor (Dench) Lea married February 7, 1621, at Seagry, Wilts, Sara, daughter of John and Agnes Welden. They had a son John Lea, died March 1685, at Christian Malford, married previous to 1654, Joane ————. They had a son, John Lea II, born 1661-2, baptized July 12, 1674, the American Emigrant. He had previously moved to Gloucester and had become a Quaker. Married February 1, 1697, Hannah (Hopton) Webb widow of Joseph Webb and moved to Philadelphia, died December 27, 1726. His oldest son Isaac born January 15, 1699, in Gloucester, England, resided at Darby, Pa., and moved to Concord, Chester County, Del., and married at Christ Church, Philadelphia, December 29, 1721, Sarah, daugher of Walter and Rebecca Fearne Fawcett. Walter Fawcett was representative in General Assembly Pa., beginning 1695, for several years. His daughter Sarah was born June 10, 1702, and died 1800 at the age of 98.

James Lea son of Isaac and Sarah (Fawcett) Lea was born March 26, 1723, moved to Wilmington, Del., and died of yellow fever in 1798. He married June 24, 1741, Margaret, daughter of John and Joanna (Pascall) Marshall. James was Assistant Burgess 1757-60-62, Chief Burgess 1768-69; Town Treasurer 1773-75. He was a member of Society of Friends. Will dated May 16, 1796.

His daughter, Elizabeth, married Joseph Tatnall, January 31, 1765.

For further Lea references see " The Ancestry and Posterity of John Lea of Christian Malford, Wiltshire, England, and of Pennsylvania in America," by James Henry Lea and George Henry Lea, Lea Bros. & Co. Philadelphia and New York, 1906.

PENNOCK FAMILY.

The first military Officer of England to emigrate to America, according to Pennsylvania history, was Christopher Pennock. He came to Chester Co., Pa., in 1685, where he died suddenly on June 28, 1701. He married Mary, daughter of George Collet of Clonmel, Ireland, who died in Chester Co., Pa. in 1687. Their son, Joseph Pennock was born in Clonmel, Ireland. He represented the County of Chester for twelve years, in provincial Assembly, first elected in 1716. He married Mary, daughter of Samuel and Elizabeth (Clator) Levis before two Justice's of the Peace in Court 1701. Mary was born August 9, 1685, died Jan. 2, 1741. Their daughter Elizabeth married Edward Tatnall.

LEVIS FAMILY

Mary Levis, the wife of Joseph Pennock was the daughter of Samuel Levis, born July 30, 1649 in Leicestershire, England, died 1734; came to America 1682, married March 3, 1680, Elizabeth Clator, daughter of Wm. Clator of Nottinghamshire, England. Samuel Levis was a member of the Governor's Council 1692 (Pennsylvania).

GORDON FAMILY.

James Gordon of Kent Co., Delaware, died in 1740. His son Griffith Gordon died in Kent Co. 1762. Coe Gordon, his son, died 1789.

Coe Gordon, son of James, born ———, died 1789, was second Lieutenant in Revolution. Appointed at Perth Amboy, N. J., November 14, 1776, in Flying Camp Company. He married, February 19, 1777, Sarah, daughter of Nimrod and Elizabeth (Taylor) Maxwell, born September 28, 1761.

John Gordon, son of Coe and Sarah Maxwell Gordon was born June 7, 1782, died in Wilmington July 10, 1847, married July 20, 1804, Ann Catharine Sharpe, who was only 16 years of age, died May 26, 1869. Ann was the daughter of William and Ann Catharine (Parlin) Sharpe, who was descendent from the Rudman—Tranberg—Parlin families.

ISSUE: John Gordon and wife Ann Sharpe.
  (1) Sidney—married Armand Monges.
  (2) Anne.
  (3) Charles—unmarried.
  (4) William— "
  (5) Louise— "
  (6) Sarah Matilda—unmarried.
  (7) Elizabeth—married Baker.
  (8) Catharine, born 1810, died 1885, married 1833, James E. Price.
  (9) Helen—married John Hyland Price, brother to James E. Price.
  (10) George—unmarried.

Catharine Gordon, daughter of John Gordon and wife Ann Catharine Parlin, was born 1810, died 1885, married James Edward Price, November 25, 1833, son of James Price and Margaret Tatnall.

Their daughter, Ann Gordon Price, born July 19, 1834 at Wilmington, married Dec. 13, 1856, John Marshall Winchester, born 1821, died 1877.

Refer to Winchester record.

A SECOND VISITATION OF WESTERN TALBOT [1]

EMERSON B. ROBERTS

WRIGHTSON OF "CLAY'S NECK"

Almost opposite Wade's Point, on the left of the road, a little below the village of McDaniel, and at the head of First or Harris Creek is "Clay's Neck," 100 acres, originally surveyed in the Cattaile Branch for Henry Clay. That Henry Clay is the ancestor of the great Kentuckian is surmised by no less an authority on Talbot than John Bozman Kerr.[2] The old home, demolished some years ago, was one of the oldest in Talbot. Originally the walls were of brick two feet thick, later the front and back were replaced by frame, with the brick ends standing, then years later the brick ends were torn out and the old frame part left standing with new frame ends. Through the years it served successively as a home of Clays, Wrightsons and Lowes. A brick, long treasured by Judge Slaughter, bore the date, 1610, but where the brick was burned one can only surmise.[3]

The deed from Henry Clay and his wife Elizabeth to Nicholas Lurkey, May 17, 1666, provides a name more ancient than "Clay's Neck"—therein the tract is called "Oyster Shell Poynt." Henry Clay—probably the second Henry Clay, born 5th month, 22nd day, 1655 [4]—and wife, Mary, on April 20, 1684, conveyed to James Sedgwick his plantation and lands adjoining called "Lurkey" and "Clay's Neck." By 1684 the Clays had sold the last of their Talbot property and removed to Virginia, if the surmise of John Bozman Kerr is correct.

---

[1] "A Visitation of Western Talbot," by Emerson B. Roberts, appeared in this Magazine, Vol. XLI, 235-245. (September, 1946).
[2] Oswald Tilghman, *History of Talbot County*, I, 206.
[3] Easton *Star-Democrat*, Feb. 11, 1928, tells the story and includes a photograph of the old home.
[4] Kent County Court records. *Archives of Maryland*, LIV, 38.

On the land, near the road, was the old Quaker Meeting House built by the hands of John Lowe, Robert Clark and William Worrilow. The Wrightsons, to whom the land came, to this generation respect the burying ground as sacred—plow has never turned the soil. Long since the Meeting House was pulled down but the lumber, brown with the years, was used in building two houses that yet stand across the road.

John Wrightson, the immigrant, was a Yorkshireman. Mary, his wife, had ties of kinship with several Talbot families some of which were from Yorkshire. She inherited land from Colonel Thomas Smithson, Gent., of Miles River, a member of the Provincial Council from Talbot, 1694 to 1706.[5] James Sedgwick, in his will, 1694, calls Mary and John, " couzens " and makes them his administrators.[6] " Stepney," originally surveyed for James Sedgwick, came to John Wrightson in right of his wife.[7] She had ties with Nicholas Lurkey, born in 1634, immigrant to Maryland, 1658.[8] " Lurkey," 250 acres in Talbot and Queen Anne's Counties, surveyed April 20, 1662, for Nicholas Lurkey, near the head of Harris Creek, also came to John Wrightson in right of his wife.[9] Mary Wrightson was a kinswoman of Captain James Murphy and of the Dawsons. Then there is record in the Principal Probate Registry in London of a debt to be remitted to the widow Wrightson in Talbot County.[10] With all her manifold ties it is puzzling that no combination of the records yields her maiden name.

John Wrightson's will was made March 15, 1716/17 and proven July 16, 1717.[11] He left " Lurkey " to his eldest son, John, together with " Clay's Neck" and a parcel known as " Cooper." To Francis he left " Jordin Folly ' and " Gaskin Point." To his widow he left " Reviving Springs " " at her disposing, equally among five children, Margaret, Mary, Deborah, Catherine and Thomas.'

In the period of her long widowhood, Mary was a power in

[5] Wills, Liber 13, 649, Hall of Records, and G. A. Hanson, *Old Kent*, 382.
[6] Wills, VII, 77, Hall of Records.
[7] Queen Anne's Co. Rent Roll, Maryland Historical Society.
[8] Index of Early Settlers, Land Office, Annapolis.
[9] Rent Rolls, Talbot and Queen Anne's, A 1-15, Maryland Historical Society. Wills, Liber 5, 285, and Liber 5, 77, and Testamentary Proceedings, Liber 23, 282, Hall of Records.
[10] P. C. C., 253, Greely, London. Sherwood, *American Colonists in the English Records*, 2nd Series, page 190.
[11] Wills, Liber 14, 435, Hall of Records. Baldwin, *Calendar of Maryland Wills*, IV, 121.

the community, continuing to reside on "Clay's Neck." Around that tract she consolidated the Wrightson homestead. She applied for a patent November 1, 1726, the land was resurveyed November 23, 1726, and the patent issued January 4, 1734. In her will, February 5, 1740, probated August 25, 1741, she bequeathed to her son Francis her interest in "Clay's Neck" and "Jordon's Folly." She left her grandson, James, a dwelling plantation, "Lurkey" and "Gaskins Neck." "Reviving Springs" she left to her grandsons and to her youngest son, Thomas, "should he return to claim his share." [12]

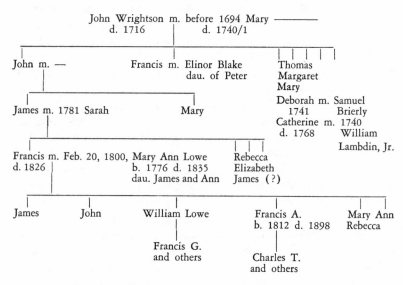

LOWE OF GRAFTON MANOR

The Manor of "Grafton," 1000 acres on the north side of Choptank and the west side of Harris Creek, has been identified with the Lowes since the days of Colonel Vincent Lowe. However, the first patent was to Colonel John Harris, merchant of London, 1659. Harris never resided in Maryland, and at his death without heirs, the patent became escheat. It was reissued, "my Lord to Vincent Lowe," in 1686. It provides "a Court Leete and Baron and all things thereunto pertaining under the Law and Custom of

[12] Wills, Liber 22, 390, Hall of Records, and Baldwin, *Calendar of Maryland Wills*, VIII, 145.

England." [13] Colonel Lowe sold portions of the manor and in his will professes the sale of other portions not recorded. " Grafton Manor " includes " Lowe's Delight," " Haddaway's Lott," " Rich Neck," " Good Luck," " Cabin Creek," " Hall's Fortune," and " Homestead," which was between the head of Grace's Creek and the Lambdin land.

The English descents of the Lowes of Derbyshire from Thomas del Lowe of Macclesfield, who died February 10, 1415, at eleven of the clock at night, are beyond the scope of this paper. [14] However, to show the relationship among the Lowe immigrants to Maryland, it is not necessary to go further back than to Vincent Lowe, born 1594, yet living in 1634, [15] one of the " Commissioners for the Better Plantation of Virginia." This Vincent Lowe married Ann Cavendish, daughter, albeit a natural daughter, of Henry Cavendish of Tutbury Priory in Staffordshire, Member of Parliament, son of Sir William Cavendish and his wife, Elizabeth Hardwick, remembered as " Building Bess of Hardwick," who, by her fourth and last marriage, became the Countess of Shrewsbury. [16] Vincent and Ann had among their ten children, Colonel Vincent Lowe of Maryland, and Jane Lowe, afterward Lady Baltimore, who came to Maryland.

Colonel Vincent Lowe, immigrant to Maryland 1672, brother-in-law of the Lord Proprietor, Member of the Council, Surveyor-General of the Province, High Sheriff of Talbot 1675/8, in 1680 and again 1685-6, one of " Ye Worshipful Commissioners and Justices of the Peace for Talbot," was one of the largest land-holders of Maryland. He married Elizabeth Foster, the widow Hawkins, daughter of Seth Foster, and through her Foster's Island or Great Choptank Island, now Tilghman's Island, came to him.

Jane Lowe, his sister, married first, Honorable Henry Sewell, of Matapany in Calvert County, Secretary of Maryland. After his death in 1665, she married in 1666 Charles Calvert, Third Lord Baltimore. [17] Jane had children by both marriages; by her

[13] *Maryland Historical Magazine*, XXXIII, 325 for references.
[14] However, these may be traced by reference to the following: Nash, *History of Worcestershire*, 1799, II, 95; *Normanorum Scriptores*, 1124; *Journal of Derbyshire*, 1881; Jewill, *Reliquary*, VIII, 113 and XII, plate 34; Wolley, *MSS in British Museum*; *Visitation of Derbyshire*, 1612; *Harl. MS* 1093; Hunter, *Familiae Minorum Gentium*, III.
[15] *Visitation of Yorkshire*.
[16] Rawson, *Building Bess of Hardwick* (London, 1910).
[17] Testamentary Proceedings, Liber I, 106, Hall of Records.

second marriage she was the ancestress of the subsequent Lords Baltimore.[18]

Two of the grandchildren, brothers, of Vincent and Ann had distinguished parts in Maryland. They were Colonel Nicholas Lowe of Talbot and Colonel Henry Lowe of Calvert County. Nicholas arrived in 1674.[19] He was a member of the Lower House 1694-5, and 1701-11. In 1711 he became Clerk of Talbot County. His Talbot Land patent, "Lowes Rambles," 1440 acres, was surveyed May 28, 1696. He married Elizabeth, widow of Major William Combes, and daughter of Edward Roe, Gent. He died October 22, 1714, in Talbot. Ebenezer Cook wrote an elegy which was printed in 1729 and is extant. The family of Colonel Nicholas Lowe does not belong to western Talbot and so is not followed here.

Henry Lowe, younger brother of Nicholas, came at the same time. He settled first in Calvert, then in St. Mary's, and like his brother, filled high office. In 1684-5 he was Collector of the Customs; 1694-7 Judge of the Provincial Court; 1698-1700 High Sheriff of St. Mary's; and, 1701-2 a Member of the Lower House. He married Susannah Maria Bennett, widow of John Darnall, and granddaughter of Governor Richard Bennett of Virginia. The Society has printed a very complete story of Colonel Henry Lowe.[20]

Two of the great-grandsons of Vincent and Ann had parts in Maryland affairs. They were the sons of John Lowe of Denby, Derbyshire, born 1642, by his second wife, Mary Stead of St. Botolph. Charles Lowe was a careful man of business and devoted to the interests of the Calverts whom he served as a secretary. The late Dr. B. C. Steiner edited some of the correspondence between Charles Lowe and Lord Baltimore.[21] There is no evidence that Charles Lowe ever resided in Maryland, but among his six sons was Stead Lowe, who came to Somerset County and married there. The other was John Lowe, great-nephew of Colonel Vincent Lowe.

Colonel Vincent Lowe died in Talbot in 1692 without issue. His landed estate totaled more than 12,000 acres in Talbot, Cecil,

---

[18] The history of Col. Vincent Lowe and of Lady Jane Baltimore are amply set forth in the records and publications of the Society.

[19] Liber XVIII, 169, and Chancery Court, PC 849, Land Office.

[20] *Maryland Historical Magazine*, II, 170, 181, 281.

[21] *Maryland Historical Magazine* III, index.

Queen Anne's, Dorchester and Baltimore counties, as well as land in Derbyshire. One of the witnesses to his will is John Lowe.[22]

John Lowe, close by ties of blood and community of property with Colonel Vincent Lowe, resided on "Grafton Manor," to which, immediately after the death of his kinsman, he took steps to confirm his title. He petitioned the Provincial Council for the assignment and the petition was granted.[23] Later he petitioned for a resurvey of "Grafton Manor" which was also granted, August 21, 1722.

John Lowe was a "convincement" of the Quakers. Thomas Taylor, William Burges, Robert Clarkson, Thomas Mears and William Durand are others who became "followers of the inner light."[24] From 1691 the name of John Lowe begins to occur in the Quaker records and in 1700 John Lowe married Mary Bartlett in Third Haven Meeting, the daughter of that steadfast old Yorkshire Quaker, Thomas Bartlett. His adherence to "the good order" no doubt did not injure his marriage suit.

John Lowe's last record in Third Haven was made 2nd month, 31st day, 1726. His will is dated 11th month, 26th day in the same year. He divided "Grafton Manor" between the two sons, he left Negroes to his two daughters and a bequest "to the Meeters at the Bayside."[25] The widow, Mary, survived.[26]

The son, John Lowe, Jr. was less a Quaker than his father. He was a large slave owner, and has left few records in the Quaker Meeting. He married twice, but all of his children were by the first wife. His will,[27] is dated 1747. The original rests in the vaults at Easton.

James Lowe, the only son, inherited most of the original "Grafton Manor," part from his father and part from his uncle Thomas, who died unmarried. He married, January 26, 1758, Ann Lambdin, a daughter of the Lambdin and Wrightson families. James Lowe's military record began in 1748 as a member of Captain Haddaway's Company of Colonial Militia.[28] The *Maryland*

[22] Wills, Liber VI, 7, Hall of Records. Baldwin, *Calendar of Maryland Wills*, II, 56.

[23] Rent Rolls, Liber I L # A, 395, and P L # 5, 402, Land Office. *Maryland Historical Magazine* XXXIII, 325 ff. *Archives of Maryland*, VIII, 448.

[24] Rufus Jones, *Quakers in the American Colonies* (1923), 329 ff.

[25] Wills, 19 141, Hall of Records.

[26] Inventory 12, 173, Hall of Records.

[27] Wills, XXV, 300, Hall of Records.

[28] *Maryland Historical Magazine*, VI, 192.

Gazette reported the arrival on Friday, May 5, 1752, of Captain James Lowe, Master of the *Elijah*, direct from the coast of Africa with " a parcel of healthy slaves, men, women and children." James Lowe is duly recorded in the Talbot Census of 1776 and in the Federal Census of 1790. Some of his transactions are in the Debt Books of 1766. In March 1756 he was one of those who befriended " the late inhabitants of Nova Scotia late set down in this Province.[29] The Council at Annapolis, Thursday, May 23, 1776, confirmed his commission in Captain Haddaway's Company of Talbot troops, 38th Regiment.[30] His sword is in the possession of the author of this article.

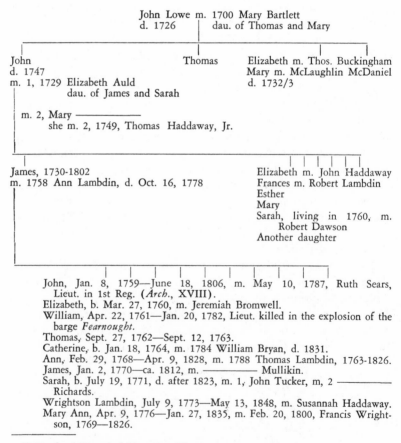

John Lowe m. 1700 Mary Bartlett
d. 1726   dau. of Thomas and Mary

John
d. 1747
m. 1, 1729 Elizabeth Auld
     dau. of James and Sarah

m. 2, Mary ————
     she m. 2, 1749, Thomas Haddaway, Jr.

Thomas

Elizabeth m. Thos. Buckingham
Mary m. McLaughlin McDaniel
d. 1732/3

James, 1730-1802
m. 1758 Ann Lambdin, d. Oct. 16, 1778

Elizabeth m. John Haddaway
Frances m. Robert Lambdin
Esther
Mary
Sarah, living in 1760, m. Robert Dawson
Another daughter

John, Jan. 8, 1759—June 18, 1806, m. May 10, 1787, Ruth Sears, Lieut. in 1st Reg. (*Arch.*, XVIII).
Elizabeth, b. Mar. 27, 1760, m. Jeremiah Bromwell.
William, Apr. 22, 1761—Jan. 20, 1782, Lieut. killed in the explosion of the barge *Fearnought*.
Thomas, Sept. 27, 1762—Sept. 12, 1763.
Catherine, b. Jan. 18, 1764, m. 1784 William Bryan, d. 1831.
Ann, Feb. 29, 1768—Apr. 9, 1828, m. 1788 Thomas Lambdin, 1763-1826.
James, Jan. 2, 1770—ca. 1812, m. ———— Mullikin.
Sarah, b. July 19, 1771, d. after 1823, m. 1, John Tucker, m, 2 ————
     Richards.
Wrightson Lambdin, July 9, 1773—May 13, 1848, m. Susannah Haddaway.
Mary Ann, Apr. 9, 1776—Jan. 27, 1835, m. Feb. 20, 1800, Francis Wrightson, 1769—1826.

---

[29] *Maryland Historical Magazine*, III, 12.
[30] *Archives of Maryland*, XI, 438.

LAMBDIN OF SUMMERTON AND WINTERTON

On Harris Creek across from "Grafton Manor" were the Lambdins. Originally of County Durham, Robert Lambdin, Gent. came to Virginia in 1638 [31] possibly with other members of the Lambdin family. With his wife, Mary, he came to Maryland, Feb. 5, 1663 [32] in the party of Captain Josiah Fendall. They purchased, November 13, in the 38th year of Cecilius, from William Killman and his wife for 6000 lbs. of tobacco "Armstrong's Folly," 200 acres, on James Island, Dorchester County. [33] This tract they sold a year later to Richard Gibbs, Merchant of Worcestershire, for 11,000 lbs. of the staple. [34] While making this profit, Robert Lambdin was dealing in Talbot land. "Rehoboth," 50 acres, on the north side of Choptank and west side of Harris Creek" was surveyed for him, May 6, 1667, and that he sold a year later to George Collison.

Robert Lambdin, like many another, came under the influence of the Bayside Quakers, but not too firmly. His name is frequent among those who signed wedding certificates, 1672-3. [35] In his will, made in 1680, when he was "aged and weak in body and dim of sight" he testifies ". . . concerning the blessed truth . . . which is the way the people of God called Quakers walk in . . . I give my testimony . . . that it is God's truth and that it is the way God appointed that man should walk . . . though I have not walked uprightly therein nor steadfastly. [36]

He left little estate, provided poorly for his widow Ann, and instructed his executors, Robert Fortune and William Jones: "Take my son from my wife she not being a woman fitting to have the education of children." William, the son, was under eighteen years of age, and from the language of the will apparently by the first wife. There seem to have been no other children except for a slight inference that may be drawn from the will of John

---

[31] Greer, *Virginia Immigrants*; see Robert, William and Martha Lambdin.
[32] Patent Records, V, 516, Land office.
[33] Old Liber I, 22 and 57 for Dorchester, Hall of Records; photostat at Cambridge.
[34] *Ibid.*, 31.
[35] Third Haven Records from 1st month, 29th day, 1668, recently rediscovered and reported in *Bulletin of Friends' Historical Society*, XXXV, 6.
[36] Original Wills, Talbot Co., Folder L, Hall of Records. The will was never accepted for probate as the court was not satisfied with the testimony of the witnesses. Testamentary Proceedings, Hall of Records.

Kersey of Talbot. Ann, the widow, became the wife of William Thomas.[37]

William Lambdin built more substantially than his father appears to have done. By patent and by purchase he built up an estate which in large part remained in the family until 1873. " Summerton," 200 acres, patented originally to Thomas Seymour, 1659, " Winterton," adjoining, surveyed June 3, 1713, and " William and Mary Addition," were patented to him.[38] By purchase from John Lowe, January 16, 1724, he secured " Rich Neck" and " Haddaway's Lott"—both parcels from " Grafton Manor." [39] He built the homes " Summerton " and " Winterton," between 1690 and 1710, the former yet standing, well treated by the years, brick, substantial and facing Harris Creek.

His will, the original of which is now at the Hall of Records, was dated November 28, 1727.[40] The final administration, June 2, 1731, reflects " all parties to be of age." [41]

William Lambdin, Jr., born 1700,[42] received " Summerton " under his father's will, but most of his father's land came back into his hands—" William and Mary Addition," at the death of his brother, John, without issue, and " Winterton," he purchased from his brother, Daniel.[43] He served in the Talbot Militia, 1732, 1748 and 1749, in Captain Haddaway's Company. His will, dated January 15, 1753, was probated September 21, 1761.[44]

A chart of the Lambdin family, so far as the present writer has traced it, follows on the next page.

---

[37] Testamentary Proceedings, 14, 77 and 79, Hall of Records, and old Rent Book 1682-1717, f. 94, Easton.

[38] Talbot Land Record, Liber III, 96, Easton.

[39] Talbot Land Record, Liber III, 153 Easton.

[40] Liber HB 2, 106, Easton. Wills, XIX, 870, Hall of Records. Baldwin, *Calendar of Maryland Wills*, VI, 144.

[41] Adm. Accts. Liber XI, 65 and Liber X, 505, Annapolis.

[42] Talbot Land Commission, 1736-45, 141, Easton.

[43] Talbot Land Record, Liber XIV, 218, Easton.

[44] Wills, 31, 439, Hall of Records, and Balance Book III, 158, Hall of Records.

Robert Lambdin m. 1, before 1671, Mary ————
d. ca. 1685
    m. 2, before 1680
Ann or Ane
she m. 2, William Thomas

William Lambdin, Sr. m. before 1694, Mary ————
d. 1727/8
m. 2, after 1721, Sarah
widow of James Auld
and dau. of Edward
Elliott [45]

Daniel Lambdin	William Lambdin, Jr.	John d. s. p.
b. ca. 1694, d. 1750	1700—1761	—George, d. May 12, 1738
m. 1, before 1717, Judith Sands,	m. 1, before 1724, Sarah	Ann, m. 1731, James Roberts
dau. of Robert Sands, Quaker	gr. dau. of Sarah Hunt of	Elizabeth, m. Nov. 12, 1731
m. 2, Jane ————	West River	Walter Nevill
m. 3, 1741, Elizabeth Haddaway	m. 2, 1740, Catherine Wright-	Sarah m. Feb. 11, 1734, John
she m. 2, before 1750 Joseph	son, d. 1768, dau of John	Rochester
Harrison	and Mary	

Daniel

Robert b. Feb. 12, 1726, d. 1775
m. Elizabeth Spry, dau. of
Thomas and Elizabeth
Mary m. William Haddaway
Elizabeth m. Apr. 20, 1750,
Francis Kersey
Sarah m. Col. William Webb
Haddaway

Robert b. Feb. 8, 1728
d. Sept. 24, 1795
Ensign in Bayside Co., Am. Rev.[46]
m. 1, Jan. 6, 1754 Frances Lowe
d. 1788, dau. of John and
Eliz.
m. 2, 1790 Mary Leeds, d. Apr.
10, 1810

Bexley John m. Eliz. Blake
George
Mary m. 1748 James Adkinson
Ann m. Robard Phillips
Elizabeth

William, d. before 1762, m. Sarah ————
John, b. Mar. 22, 1742
Daniel, "of age at father's will"
    m. 1, 1808, Eliz. Truitt
    m. 2, Eliz. Cockey
Thomas, 19 in 1753
Francis, b. 1745 m. 1, ———— Nevill
    m. 2, Margaret Haddaway, the
    widow Cooper
Wrightson, d. 1812. Mil. list of 1777
Ann, b. ca. 1735, d. Oct. 16, 1778,
    m. 1758 Capt. James Lowe of Grafton Manor
Sarah "15 in Aug. last" 1753.

[45] Liber II, 33, Easton.
[46] *American Archives*, III.

YOUNG—WOODWARD—HESSELIUS FAMILY RECORD, 1737-1820.[1]

Marriages.

Richard Young son of Col Samuel Young was married to Rebecca Holdsworth the daughter of Mr. Thomas Holdsworth June 4th 1737.

Mary Young daughter of Richard and and Rebecca Holdsworth Young was married to Henry Woodward Esq January 8th 1755.

---

[1] From Mrs. Com. Ridgely's large scrap-book. A note to Mrs. Ridgely from *Harriet Murry Evans* says: "This Record is taken from Grandma's own Bible."

Rebecca Woodward daughter of the above was married to Philip Rogers March 19 1776.

Mary Woodward 3d daughter of Henry and Mary Y. Woodward was married to James Govan May 2 1775.

Harriet Woodward daughter of Henry and Mary Young Woodward was married to Col Edmund Brice Sept. 11th 1783.

Mary Young Woodward was married to John Hesselius January 30th 1763.

Charlotte Hesselius daughter of John and Mary Young Hesselius was married to Thomas Johnson June 5 1792.

Caroline Hesselius daughter of the aforesaid John and Mary was married to Judson Claggett 5th March 1795.

Elizabeth Dulany Hesselius the youngest daughter of John and Mary Young Hesselius was married to the Revd Walter Dulany Addison 5th June 1792.

John Hesselius the only son of John and Mary Hesselius was married to Mary Wharton Williams Feb. 25th 1792.

Mary Anne Murray Johnson daughter of Thomas and Charlotte Johnson was married to Hugh Wharton Evans April 24 1815.

Births

Henrietta Maria Hesselius 1st dau of John and Mary Woodward Hesselius b. 4th March 1764.

Gustavus Hesselius son of John and Mary Woodward Hesselius b Nov 25 1765 d. Oct 2 1767.

Henrietta Hesselius 2d dau of John and Mary Woodward Hesselius b Jan 5 1768.

Charlotte Hesselius 3d dau of John and Mary Woodward Hesselius b 14 June 1770 d. Apr 27 1794.

Caroline Hesselius 4th dau of John and Mary Woodward Hesselius b June 9 1773.

Elizabeth Dulany Hesselius 5th dau of John and Mary Hesselius b Feb 2 1775.

John Hesselius 2d son of John and Mary Woodward Hesselius b 5th April 1777 d Nov. 9 1804.

[Note, in pencil: John only son of John & Mary Hesselius;
he married Mary Wharton Williams of Cecil Co.]

Mary Anne Murray Johnson dau of Thomas & Charlotte Johnson b Feb 27 1794.

Mary Anne Caroline Murray ˙dau of William and Harriet
Murray b Apr 5 1789.

William Henry Murray b Jan 7 1791.

Alexander John Murray b June 12 1793.

Edmund Brice Addison son of Walter & Elizabeth Dulany b
5th Oct 1794.

Mary Anne Young Addison dau of Walter & Elizabeth Dulany
b March 3 1797.

Lloyd Addison son of Walter & Elizabeth Dulany b Feb. 4
1799.

Augustus Addison son of Walter & Elizabeth Dulany b May 3
1805.

Deaths

Richard Young son of Col Samuel Young d Oct 4 1748 in
56 year of his age.

Henrietta Maria Hesselius dau of John and Mary Hesselius
d Sept 21 age 18 mos.

Henry Woodward d 20 Sep 1761 in 28th year.

John Hesselius Artist d Apr 9 1778 in 50th year.

Edmund Brice d Oct 5 1784 aged 32.

Elizabeth Dulany Addison dau of John & Mary Young Hesselius d July 31 1808 in 33d yr.

Caroline De Butts dau of John & M. Y. Hesselius d March 5
1817.

Rebecca Rogers dau of Henry & Mary Young Woodward d
Oct 19 1818 62 years.

Mary Young Hesselius d June 14 in 81st year.

[End of Record given by Mrs. Ridgely to A. S. D. in March
1896.]

INDEX

ADDITIONS